Ethical Standards for School Counselors*

(Adopted 1984; revised 1992, 1998, 2004 and 2010).

PREAMBLE

The American School Counselor Association (ASCA) is a professional organization whose members are school counselors certified/licensed in school counseling with unique qualifications and skills to address all students' academic, personal/social and career development needs. Members are also school counseling program directors/supervisors and counselor educators. These ethical standards are the ethical responsibility of school counselors. School counseling program directors/supervisors should know them and provide support for practitioners to uphold them. School counselor educators should know them, teach them to their students and provide support for school counseling candidates to uphold them.

Professional school counselors are advocates, leaders, collaborators and consultants who create opportunities for equity in access and success in educational opportunities by connecting their programs to the mission of schools and subscribing to the following tenets of professional responsibility:

• Each person has the right to be respected, be treated with dignity and have access to a comprehensive school counseling program that advocates for and affirms all students from diverse populations including: ethnic/racial identity, age, economic status, abilities/disabilities, language, immigration status, sexual orientation, gender, gender identity/expression, family type, religious/spiritual identity and appearance.

• Each person has the right to receive the information and support needed to move toward self-direction and self-development and affirmation within one's group identities, with special care being given to students who have historically not received adequate educational services, e.g., students of color, students living at a low socio-economic status, students with disabilities and students from non-dominant language backgrounds.

• Each person has the right to understand the full magnitude and meaning of his/her educational choices and how those choices will affect future opportunities.

• Each person has the right to privacy and thereby the right to expect the school counselor/student relationship to comply with all laws, policies and ethical standards pertaining to confidentiality in the school setting.

• Each person has the right to feel safe in school environments that school counselors help create, free from abuse, bullying, neglect, harassment or other forms of violence.

In this document, ASCA specifies the principles of ethical behavior necessary to maintain the high standards of integrity, leadership and professionalism among its members. The Ethical Standards for School Counselors were developed to clarify the nature of ethical responsibilities held in common by school counselors, supervisors/directors of school counseling programs and school counselor educators. The purposes of this document are to:

• Serve as a guide for the ethical practices of all professional school counselors, supervisors/directors of school counseling programs and school counselor educators regardless of level, area, population served or membership in this professional association;

• Provide self-appraisal and peer evaluations regarding school counselors' responsibilities to students, parents/guardians, colleagues and professional associates, schools, communities and the counseling profession; and

• Inform all stakeholders, including students, parents and guardians, teachers, administrators, community members and courts of justice, of best ethical practices, values and expected behaviors of the school counseling professional.

A.1. Responsibilities to Students

Professional school counselors:

a. Have a primary obligation to the students, who are to be treated with dignity and respect as unique individuals.

b. Are concerned with the educational, academic, career, personal and social needs and encourage the maximum development of every student.

c. Respect students' values, beliefs and cultural background and do not impose the school counselor's personal values on students or their families.

d. Are knowledgeable of laws, regulations and policies relating to students and strive to protect and inform students regarding their rights.

e. Promote the welfare of individual students and collaborate with them to develop an action plan for success.

f. Consider the involvement of support networks valued by the individual students.

g. Understand that professional distance with students is appropriate, and any sexual or romantic relationship with students whether illegal in the state of practice is considered a grievous breach of ethics and is prohibited regardless of a student's age.

h. Consider the potential for harm before entering into a relationship with former students or one of their family members.

A.2. Confidentiality

Professional school counselors:

a. Inform individual students of the purposes, goals, techniques and rules of procedure under which they may receive counseling. Disclosure includes the limits of confidentiality in a developmentally appropriate manner. Informed consent requires competence on the part of students to understand the limits of confidentiality and therefore, can be difficult to obtain from students of a certain developmental level. Professionals are aware that even though every attempt is made to obtain informed consent it is not always possible and when needed will make counseling decisions on students' behalf.

b. Explain the limits of confidentiality in ways such as classroom guidance lessons, the student handbook, school counseling brochures, school Web site or other means of student, parent and guardian communication in addition to oral notification to individual students.

c. Recognize the complicated nature of confidentiality in schools and consider each case in context. Keep information confidential unless legal requirements demand that confidential information be revealed or a breach is required to prevent serious and foreseeable harm to the student. Serious and foreseeable harm is different for each minor in schools and is defined by students' developmental and chronological age, the setting, parental rights and the nature of the harm. School counselors consult with appropriate professionals when in doubt as to the validity of an exception.

d. Recognize their primary obligation for confidentiality is to the students but balance that obligation with an understanding of parents'/guardians' legal and inherent rights to be the guiding voice in their children's lives, especially in value-laden issues. Understand the need to balance students' ethical rights to make choices, their capacity to give consent or assent and parental or familial legal rights and responsibilities to protect these students and make decisions on their behalf.

e. Promote the autonomy and independence of students to the extent possible and use the most appropriate and least intrusive method of breach. The developmental age and the circumstances requiring the breach are considered and as appropriate students are engaged in a discussion about the method and timing of the breach.

f. In absence of state legislation expressly forbidding disclosure, consider the ethical responsibility to provide information to an identified third party who, by his/her relationship with the student, is at a high risk of contracting a disease that is commonly known to be communicable and fatal. Disclosure requires satisfaction of all of the following conditions:

- Student identifies partner or the partner is highly identifiable
- School counselor recommends the student notify partner and refrain from further high-risk behavior
- Student refuses
- School counselor informs the student of the intent to notify the partner
- School counselor seeks legal consultation from the school district's legal representative in writing as to the legalities of informing the partner

g. Request of the court that disclosure not be required when the release of confidential information may potentially harm a student or the counseling relationship.

h. Protect the confidentiality of students' records and release personal data in accordance with prescribed federal and state laws and school policies including the laws within the Family Education Rights and Privacy Act (FERPA). Student information stored and transmitted electronically is treated with the same care as traditional student records. Recognize the vulnerability of confidentiality in electronic communications and only transmit sensitive information electronically in a way that is untraceable to students' identity. Critical information such as a student who has a history of suicidal ideation must be conveyed to the receiving school in a personal contact such as a phone call.

A.3. Academic, Career/College/Post-Secondary Access and Personal/Social Counseling Plans

Professional school counselors:

a. Provide students with a comprehensive school counseling program that parallels the ASCA National Model with emphasis on working jointly with all students to develop personal/social, academic and career goals.

b. Ensure equitable academic, career, post-secondary access and personal/social opportunities for all students through the use of data to help close achievement gaps and opportunity gaps.

c. Provide and advocate for individual students' career awareness, exploration and post-secondary plans supporting the students' right to choose from the wide array of options when they leave secondary education.

A.4. Dual Relationships

Professional school counselors:

a. Avoid dual relationships that might impair their objectivity and increase the risk of harm to students (e.g., counseling one's family members or the children of close friends or associates). If a dual relationship is unavoidable, the school counselor is responsible for taking action to eliminate or reduce the potential for harm to the student through use of safeguards, which might include informed consent, consultation, supervision and documentation.

b. Maintain appropriate professional distance with students at all times.

c. Avoid dual relationships with students through communication mediums such as social networking sites.

d. Avoid dual relationships with school personnel that might infringe on the integrity of the school counselor/student relationship.

A.5. Appropriate Referrals

Professional school counselors:

a. Make referrals when necessary or appropriate to outside resources for student and/or family support. Appropriate referrals may necessitate informing both parents/guardians and students of applicable resources and making proper plans for transitions with minimal interruption of services. Students retain the right to discontinue the counseling relationship at any time.

b. Help educate about and prevent personal and social concerns for all students within the school counselor's scope of education and competence and make necessary referrals when the counseling needs are beyond the individual school counselor's education and training. Every attempt is made to find appropriate specialized resources for clinical therapeutic topics that are difficult or inappropriate to address in a school setting such as eating disorders, sexual trauma, chemical dependency and other addictions needing sustained clinical duration or assistance.

c. Request a release of information signed by the student and/or parents/guardians when attempting to develop a collaborative relationship with other service providers assigned to the student.

d. Develop a reasonable method of termination of counseling when it becomes apparent that counseling assistance is no longer needed or a referral is necessary to better meet the student's needs.

A.6. Group Work

Professional school counselors:

a. Screen prospective group members and maintain an awareness of participants' needs, appropriate fit and personal goals in relation to the group's intention and focus. The school counselor takes reasonable precautions to protect members from physical and psychological harm resulting from interaction within the group.

b. Recognize that best practice is to notify the parents/guardians of children participating in small groups.

c. Establish clear expectations in the group setting, and clearly state that confidentiality in group counseling cannot be guaranteed. Given the developmental and chronological ages of minors in schools, recognize the tenuous nature of confidentiality for minors renders some topics inappropriate for group work in a school setting.

d. Provide necessary follow up with group members, and document proceedings as appropriate.

e. Develop professional competencies, and maintain appropriate education, training and supervision in group facilitation and any topics specific to the group.

f. Facilitate group work that is brief and solution-focused, working with a variety of academic, career, college and personal/social issues.

A.7. Danger to Self or Others
Professional school counselors:

a. Inform parents/guardians and/or appropriate authorities when a student poses a danger to self or others. This is to be done after careful deliberation and consultation with other counseling professionals.

b. Report risk assessments to parents when they underscore the need to act on behalf of a child at risk; never negate a risk of harm as students sometimes deceive in order to avoid further scrutiny and/or parental notification.

c. Understand the legal and ethical liability for releasing a student who is in danger to self or others without proper and necessary support for that student.

A.8. Student Records
Professional school counselors:

a. Maintain and secure records necessary for rendering professional services to the student as required by laws, regulations, institutional procedures and confidentiality guidelines.

b. Keep sole-possession records or individual student case notes separate from students' educational records in keeping with state laws.

c. Recognize the limits of sole-possession records and understand these records are a memory aid for the creator and in absence of privileged communication may be subpoenaed and may become educational records when they are shared or are accessible to others in either verbal or written form or when they include information other than professional opinion or personal observations.

d. Establish a reasonable timeline for purging sole-possession records or case notes. Suggested guidelines include shredding sole possession records when the student transitions to the next level, transfers to another school or graduates. Apply careful discretion and deliberation before destroying sole-possession records that may be needed by a court of law such as notes on child abuse, suicide, sexual harassment or violence.

e. Understand and abide by the Family Education Rights and Privacy Act (FERPA, 1974), which safeguards student's records and allows parents to have a voice in what and how information is shared with others regarding their child's educational records.

A.9. Evaluation, Assessment and Interpretation
Professional school counselors:

a. Adhere to all professional standards regarding selecting, administering and interpreting assessment measures and only utilize assessment measures that are within the scope of practice for school counselors and for which they are trained and competent.

b. Consider confidentiality issues when utilizing evaluative or assessment instruments and electronically based programs.

c. Consider the developmental age, language skills and level of competence of the student taking the assessments before assessments are given.

d. Provide interpretation of the nature, purposes, results and potential impact of assessment/evaluation measures in language the students can understand.

e. Monitor the use of assessment results and interpretations, and take reasonable steps to prevent others from misusing the information.

f. Use caution when utilizing assessment techniques, making evaluations and interpreting the performance of populations not represented in the norm group on which an instrument is standardized.

g. Assess the effectiveness of their program in having an impact on students' academic, career and personal/social development through accountability measures especially examining efforts to close achievement, opportunity and attainment gaps.

A.10. Technology
Professional school counselors:

a. Promote the benefits of and clarify the limitations of various appropriate technological applications. Professional school counselors promote technological applications (1) that are appropriate for students' individual needs, (2) that students understand how to use and (3) for which follow-up counseling assistance is provided.

b. Advocate for equal access to technology for all students, especially those historically underserved.

c. Take appropriate and reasonable measures for maintaining confidentiality of student information and educational records stored or transmitted through the use of computers, facsimile machines, telephones, voicemail, answering machines and other electronic or computer technology.

d. Understand the intent of FERPA and its impact on sharing electronic student records.

e. Consider the extent to which cyberbullying is interfering with students' educational process and base guidance curriculum and intervention programming for this pervasive and potentially dangerous problem on research-based and best practices.

A.11. Student Peer Support Program
Professional school counselors:

a. Have unique responsibilities when working with peer-helper or student-assistance programs and safeguard the welfare of students participating in peer-to-peer programs under their direction.

b. Are ultimately responsible for appropriate training and supervision for students serving as peer-support individuals in their school counseling programs.

B. RESPONSIBILITIES TO PARENTS/GUARDIANS

B.1. Parent Rights and Responsibilities

Professional school counselors:

a. Respect the rights and responsibilities of parents/guardians for their children and endeavor to establish, as appropriate, a collaborative relationship with parents/guardians to facilitate students' maximum development.

b. Adhere to laws, local guidelines and ethical standards of practice when assisting parents/guardians experiencing family difficulties interfering with the student's effectiveness and welfare.

c. Are sensitive to diversity among families and recognize that all parents/guardians, custodial and noncustodial, are vested with certain rights and responsibilities for their children's welfare by virtue of their role and according to law.

d. Inform parents of the nature of counseling services provided in the school setting.

e. Adhere to the FERPA act regarding disclosure of student information.

f. Work to establish, as appropriate, collaborative relationships with parents/guardians to best serve student.

B.2. Parents/Guardians and Confidentiality

Professional school counselors:

a. Inform parents/guardians of the school counselor's role to include the confidential nature of the counseling relationship between the counselor and student.

b. Recognize that working with minors in a school setting requires school counselors to collaborate with students' parents/guardians to the extent possible.

c. Respect the confidentiality of parents/guardians to the extent that is reasonable to protect the best interest of the student being counseled.

d. Provide parents/guardians with accurate, comprehensive and relevant information in an objective and caring manner, as is appropriate and consistent with ethical responsibilities to the student.

e. Make reasonable efforts to honor the wishes of parents/guardians concerning information regarding the student unless a court order expressly forbids the involvement of a parent(s). In cases of divorce or separation, school counselors exercise a good faith effort to keep both parents informed, maintaining focus on the student and avoiding supporting one parent over another in divorce proceedings.

C. RESPONSIBILITIES TO COLLEAGUES AND PROFESSIONAL ASSOCIATES

C.1. Professional Relationships

Professional school counselors, the school counseling program director/site supervisor and the school counselor educator:

a. Establish and maintain professional relationships with faculty, staff and administration to facilitate an optimum counseling program.

b. Treat colleagues with professional respect, courtesy and fairness.

c. Recognize that teachers, staff and administrators who are high functioning in the personal and social development skills can be powerful allies in supporting student success. School counselors work to develop relationships with all faculty and staff in order to advantage students.

d. Are aware of and utilize related professionals, organizations and other resources to whom the student may be referred.

(continued on page 633)

---

*SOURCE: The ASCA statement of Ethical Standards for School Counselors is used by permission of the American School Counselor Association.

Introduction to
SCHOOL
COUNSELING

DEMCO

Introduction to
SCHOOL
COUNSELING

Robert J. Wright

Widener University

Los Angeles | London | New Delhi
Singapore | Washington DC

Los Angeles | London | New Delhi
Singapore | Washington DC

FOR INFORMATION:

SAGE Publications, Inc.
2455 Teller Road
Thousand Oaks, California 91320
E-mail: order@sagepub.com

SAGE Publications Ltd.
1 Oliver's Yard
55 City Road
London EC1Y 1SP
United Kingdom

SAGE Publications India Pvt. Ltd.
B 1/I 1 Mohan Cooperative Industrial Area
Mathura Road, New Delhi 110 044
India

SAGE Publications Asia-Pacific Pte. Ltd.
33 Pekin Street #02-01
Far East Square
Singapore 048763

Acquisitions Editor: Kassie Graves
Associate Editor: Leah Mori
Production Editor: Astrid Virding
Copy Editor: Pam Suwinsky
Typesetter: C&M Digitals (P) Ltd.
Proofreader: Andrea Martin
Indexer: Ellen Slavitz
Cover Designer: Gail Buschman
Marketing Manager: Erica DeLuca
Permissions Editor: Adele Hutchinson

Printed in the United States of America

Library of Congress Cataloging-in-Publication Data

Wright, Robert J., 1945-

Introduction to school counseling / Robert J. Wright.

p. cm.
Includes bibliographical references and index.

ISBN 978-1-4129-7871-2 (pbk.)

1. Educational counseling. 2. Counseling in
elementary education. 3. Counseling in secondary
education. 4. Action research in education. I. Title.

LB1027.5.W75 2012 371.4—dc22 2010041061

This book is printed on acid-free paper.

11 12 13 14 15 10 9 8 7 6 5 4 3 2 1

Contents

Preface

❝ Every person has the right to be treated with dignity and have access to a comprehensive school counseling program. **❞**

ASCA / Hatch & Bowers, 2005

GOALS AND GAME PLANS ●

My goal in writing this book is to provide students with an understandable and useful guide to the critical skills and knowledge required of professional school counselors today. All too often school leaders and educational policymakers overlook the contributions that well-educated and highly motivated professional school counselors can make in schools as well as in the wider school community.

Every chapter in the text is grounded in *The ASCA National Model: A Framework for School Counseling* (American School Counselor Association/ Hatch & Bowers, 2005). In addition, the ASCA statement of *Ethical Standards for School Counselors* is reprinted with permission of the ASCA inside the front and back cover pages of this book. This statement can provide a quick reference and handy guide for school counselors as they establish their school-based practices.

In this era of austerity and accountability, school counselors need to be equipped with new skills required to meet the challenge of a new cohort of technology-dependent students. From day one of a school counselor's career, he or she must have a clear vision of the counselor's role and be ready to face the problems and tasks of the job. This includes having the flexibility to move to different school counseling venues, including counseling in a virtual school setting.

It is no longer acceptable to ignore the old problems of racism, bullying, and the intractable score gap between ethnic groups. Today school counselors must step up and provide leadership in overcoming these problems in education. This book provides both background on these issues and suggestions for counseling interventions that can result in improvement of the educational environment. This text also addresses the multifaceted role that school counselors play in advocating for and providing services to children with disabilities.

The ASCA encourages school counselors to take a leadership role in the schools in preventing problems and difficulties. This textbook employs a three-tiered approach to prevention. The narrative focuses on employing primary prevention methods as a central feature of the role for school counselors. Each chapter also presents secondary and tertiary prevention approaches that can be brought to bear as needed.

Counselors should also be prepared to provide leadership in school-based action research and with the interpretation of standardized test scores and the management of test data. Data management is more than just a teller's role; it encompasses the need for professional school counselors to have solid grounding in measurement and research and the ability to interpret, evaluate, and explain complex concepts to colleagues, students, and parents. This book addresses each of these topics with clear examples and understandable descriptions. It also provides strategies that professional school counselors can employ to ensure that every child scores at an optimal level on high-stakes tests.

This textbook goes beyond these issues and provides deep insight into the practice of effective school counseling. These descriptions and discussions of the professional practice of school counselors encompass three chapters, describing school counseling in preschools, kindergartens, and elementary schools as well as middle schools and high schools.

The textbook includes real-life examples and case descriptions that employ the major counseling techniques used in public schools today. Various chapters focus on the three levels of prevention that a school counselor can employ. For each level or prevention, various strategies and solutions are proposed. This includes numerous examples of bibliotherapy and cinema therapy as well as suggestions and approaches to use in group and individual counseling.

Multicultural techniques for counselors were drawn from both current literature and my experience growing up and later teaching in an inner-city environment. The special problem of assisting children with undocumented and language-minority parents is addressed, and ideas and examples are provided throughout the book for engaging all parents in the education and development of their children.

The book was written to address the consultative role of the school counselor. Ideas for developing a consulting practice within the school and for overcoming resistance are described in some detail.

Recognizing that no book that is a chore to read will be useful to students or faculty in a counseling program, I developed this book to be highly engaging and replete with real-world examples in each chapter.

ACKNOWLEDGMENTS ●

No project of this magnitude can be completed by one person working in isolation. This textbook would not have been possible without the encouragement, editorial assistance, intelligence and creativity, and the freely given help of my wife and partner, Jeanne.

In addition I wish to provide a word of thanks to Ms. Molly Wolf, Education Collection Librarian at Widener University's Wolfgram Memorial Library; Gloria Floyd, my secretary; and Drs. Richard and Ann St. John, my technology support team, critics, and friends.

Kudos are also due for the team at SAGE Publications, including my editor, Ms. Kassie Graves, whose belief in this project and support of my efforts have been invaluable. Also, I owe a special debt of gratitude to the editorial assistant working with this manuscript, Ms. Veronica Novak. It was Veronica who coordinated this project, bringing together the many reviews and permissions that are part of this book. I also need to express my gratitude to the editorial reviewers who worked to make this the best possible textbook. This group of faculty reviewers includes:

Victor Alvarado, The University of Texas Pan American
Theresa A. Coogan, Bridgewater State College
Joyce Pappas Finch, Texas Southern University
Delila Owens, Wayne State University

This book is affectionately dedicated to my wife, Jeanne.
It is her intellect and energy that made this project a success.
She is my tireless helper, ultimate editor, and best friend.

CHAPTER

1

School Counseling, an Evolving Profession

OBJECTIVES

By reading and studying this chapter you should acquire the competency to:

- Describe the historical development of the changing role of school counselors
- Discuss the reasons why vocational guidance was the first of the counseling specializations to develop and become part of public education
- Describe the paradigm shift in school counseling that occurred in the 1950s and 1960s
- Explain human motivation using the model developed by Abraham Maslow
- Describe the influence of Carl Rogers in the practice of school counseling
- Explain how the No Child Left Behind Act has changed the practice of school counseling
- Describe the evolution of professional associations in counseling
- Explain and describe the core principles for the ethical practice of counseling in schools

● ● ●

❝ It is not our abilities that show who we truly are, it is our choices. **❞**

Ersatz Professor Dumbledore

● INTRODUCTION AND THEMES

The history of **school counseling** parallels the development of **public education** in America. By the 19th century, public schools in America, called "common schools" (grades 1 through 8), were established in the great industrial cities and had been extended into the rural regions by the 20th century. The first public **high schools** in the 19th century were run like preparatory schools, offering only academic courses. These 19th-century high schools were revised early in the 20th century to serve a larger constituency and offer a more comprehensive curriculum. Urban high schools have served many generations of children of first-generation Americans and also have become the major education provider for minority students and for many children from impoverished homes (Tyack, 1974).

Today, school-based professional counselors play many roles and perform a myriad of duties critical to the welfare of children and the operation of schools. The American School Counselor Association (American School Counselor Association [ASCA]/Hatch & Bowers, 2005) has provided a National Model to provide a framework that when implemented places professional school counselors in the center of the education process (p. 4). However, it can also be reasonably argued that the role that a school counselor plays is one that he or she crafts.

As a school counselor, you will be provided with professional guidelines, school district job descriptions, and policy statements from the school's principal, all designed to guide your performance in the counselor's role. Yet, the work of a school counselor is defined, and given form and focus, by the individual in the job. It is the author's position that school counselors must always advocate for their profession and attempt to bend school district policies and modify school principals' requirements so as to make school policies match the ASCA National Model (see Case in Point 1.1). This may take time and careful negotiating.

CASE IN POINT 1.1

In 2006 an innovative program was launched to reduce the shockingly high **dropout rates** at many schools in Los Angeles. This program, the **Diploma Project**, involved hiring extra school counselors for 49 high schools and 31 middle schools and tasking the extra counselors to help students complete their high school educations. Counselors worked as **mentors** to students who were at risk of leaving school. Counselors helped students find solutions to problems that hindered their success. In addition to **one-on-one counseling**, this included helping these **at-risk students** pass state-mandated tests, change curriculums, or even transfer to schools more conducive to their needs. The Diploma Project was a success and had improved the dropout rate at the targeted schools from more than 50% to about 33% by 2009. It is unfortunate that Superintendent Ramon C. Cortines was forced to cut from the 2009–2010 school district budget the $10 million annual cost of the program (Blume, 2009).

Thought Question. Urban high schools can present school counselors with many seemingly intractable problems to resolve. Using your past experience and knowledge, provide a short list of priorities professional school counselors working in inner-city schools should address before others.

A BRIEF HISTORY ●

After the fall of the ancient world, in the fifth century C.E., the concept of childhood in the Western world was ignored as the population focused on subsistence farming and survival. The few boys taught by scholastic monks to read and write were the exception and were given an education only to continue the work of the monastic organization.[1] This era of little education and interest in children came to an end with the Renaissance.

At the start of the Renaissance (circa 1300 C.E.), education in Europe was hit or miss, and there were only a handful of towns where scholarship was practiced (Bologna in Italy, Cordova in Islamic Spain, Oxford and Cambridge in England). The early development of the arts and sciences during the Renaissance fostered a series of reformers and philosophers who set the model for what we now consider as the **Western view** of the world. We describe that era from about 1600 C.E. to the French Revolution (1789) as the era of the **Enlightenment**.

One of the differences between the early Renaissance and the later era of Enlightenment can be seen in the general beliefs about education. Early Renaissance scholars rediscovered classical literature and arts from ancient Greece and Rome. The implication for educators during the Renaissance was the need to emphasize instruction in the classics in their schools.

Educational Enlightenment

Beginning with philosophers and linguists including Erasmus of Rotterdam, the primacy of classicism was challenged. This challenge focused on the importance of vernacular European languages (e.g., French, Dutch, German, English). Contemporaries including John Amos Comenius along with Martin Luther advocated for publicly supported education for both boys and girls. Also, during the era of the Enlightenment, John Locke provided a model for conceptualizing the importance of experience in learning by children.

An early effort to provide **vocational guidance** occurred near the close of the Enlightenment in 1747. That year Robert Campbell wrote a guidebook for parents of young boys. That text was designed to help parents decide which skilled trade they should select for their sons. In the 18th century, the question of where to apprentice a child was of major concern for working-class parents. That guide, *The London Tradesman,* gave parents information about working conditions, wages, and what we would call today lifestyle (Inwood, 1999).

America's Schools

To understand how school counseling became part of the educational establishment, it is necessary to know about the development of high schools. At the start of the 19th century, education for adolescents from families with money was provided by private schools and **academies.** The focus of these academies was college preparation (preparatory schools), and the curriculum was generally dominated by studies of the classical languages. The first free public high schools (e.g., Latin Grammar School [1635] in Boston and Central High School [1836] in Philadelphia) were examples of that approach (Celebrate Boston, 2009; School District of Philadelphia, 2009). Mandatory education beyond the eighth grade was not a requirement for all children until after World War II (Otto, 2000). (See the description of the development of comprehensive high schools in "New High Schools" later in the chapter.)

Common schools (public elementary schools) were established in most large American cities in the 1840s and throughout America by the dawn of the 20th century (Clabaugh & Rozycki, 1990). First through eighth grade schools provided all the education that 90% of the population of 19th-century America would ever receive (U.S. National Center for Education Statistics, 2003). To prepare teachers for these schools, a new approach to higher education was started: the **normal school.** Normal schools provided a 2-year program to educate unmarried young women of good character for the education profession. College-educated men and a handful of women with bachelor's degrees were hired to teach in the new secondary schools as America moved into the 20th century (Solomon, 1985). This resulted in a two-tier system of public schools. Less-educated (normal school diploma) women taught in the elementary schools, while better-educated (bachelor's degree) and better-compensated men taught in high schools (Landman, 1992).

New High Schools

The growing population of youth in urban areas brought about a need for high schools that could do more than get students ready for college. Following the First World War, cities built **democracy's high schools,** known more generally as **comprehensive high schools** (Angus & Meril, 1999). Comprehensive high schools began offering different **curriculum tracks** for adolescents based on their mental ability and career potential scores (Reese, 2001).

Tests of mental ability were a product of the **child study movement.** Research centers, including one at Stanford University under the direction of Lewis Terman and the Vineland Training School in New Jersey under the direction of H. H. Goddard, developed and promoted the use of both ability and later **achievement tests.** These measures provided a **scientific rationale** for class and ethnic divisions that resulted within the school curriculum tracks. Recent critics have described this approach as providing a **"split-level" education** with watered-down courses for some students and a banquet of academically enriched classes for others (Angus & Meril, 1999).

American High School Curriculum

Secondary education assumed the standard 4-year design (grades 9–12) following the recommendations of the Committee on Secondary School Studies, more popularly known as the "**Committee of Ten**" in 1892–1893. Charles William Eliot, president of Harvard University, led this committee appointed by the **National Education Association (NEA)**. It established a minimum **core curriculum** of 24 high school classes, including nine curriculum areas (Ornstein & Levine, 1989). In 1906 the newly chartered **Carnegie Commission** recommended that these core courses be taught over time blocks of not less than 120 clock hours per year (Claybaugh & Rozycki, 1990).

(Continued)

(Continued)

The Carnegie Commission required that colleges participating in the Carnegie's new faculty retirement program, Teachers Insurance and Annuity Association (TIAA), enforce the 120-hour course unit rule. The Carnegie Commission would not let the faculty of colleges that did not enforce this rule on high schools participate in TIAA. Thus, by setting college admission policy, the commission was able to get its way with all of America's secondary schools. This gave birth to the 180-day school year and the 45-minute high school teaching period. The phrase **Carnegie Unit** then entered the lexicon of American education for this standard unit of instruction (Shedd, 2003).

Problems With Scientific Management of Schools

A major problem with the **tracking model** in education was the rigidity of the system. Starting in the primary grades, children were grouped for instruction by ability. Bright children were given a rich curriculum filled with challenging concepts and materials. Children who did not test as well were provided a watered-down approach to their education. After grade 8, teenagers were either sent to the adult world of work or moved into a high school curriculum track.

Once a high school student was placed on a track (college preparatory, business, vocational, and general studies), it became increasingly difficult each year for students in business, vocational, or general studies to move to a more academic track. After having spent time in a less demanding academic program, a student would need to catch up on many of the advanced courses missed previously. The whole tracking system was based on an assumption that each child's tested level of mental ability was genetically established at the moment of his or her conception and was immutable to change (Terman, 1921).

● VOCATIONAL GUIDANCE

Confusion over academic planning and selecting a vocational goal were problems for turn-of-the-century students and their families. The problem was one that every family had to solve on its own, as there were no professionals who could help high school students. The result can be read in a U.S. Census Bureau report showing that only 6% of the population of 18-year-old adolescents graduated from high school (www.census.gov/statab/hist/02HS0021.xls).

The wave of immigrant families into the cities brought tens of thousands of new high school students, many of who had poor facility with English. All of the problems we see in our inner-city high schools today existed 100 years ago, but the students were on their own to figure them out and move on.

In 1900, high schools in America were academically oriented and designed to prepare graduates for college.[2] A severe recession that began in 1897 and the low industrial skill level of American youth contributed to the expansion of the mission of the high schools of many cities. Both the industrialists and the trade unions of turn-of-the-century America championed the movement toward high schools with many tracks, not just one for college-bound students (Stephens, 1988). The first federal act to address guidance in the schools was the **Smith-Hughes National Vocational Education Act** of 1917. This law, signed by President Woodrow Wilson, provided a federal source of funding for vocational guidance programs and for the hiring of counselors. The idea behind the act was that vocational education and guidance would flourish only if protected from the academic elitism of high schools of that day.

Frank Parsons

The father of American vocational guidance and the first counselor was Frank Parsons, a polymath who graduated from Cornell University with a degree in civil engineering at the age of 18 (Glosoff & Rockwell, 1997). Later he became a lawyer, French teacher, author, college dean, and social reformer. His interests turned to vocational counseling when he began work as a counselor in a **settlement house** in Boston in 1901. In this job he assisted members of the poor and immigrant population to become employed and productive (Jones, 1994). With the assistance and cooperation of the Boston YMCA, he created a **Vocational Bureau** within the settlement house. From the director's position he helped the City Schools of Boston establish vocational counseling districtwide. By 1911 there were 100 educators in school-based vocational counseling positions in Boston (Jones, 1994). Parsons wrote the first modern textbook on vocational guidance. It was published a year following his death at the age of 54 in 1908. In that book, *Choosing a Vocation,* he presented three steps toward making a good career choice (Parsons, 1909/2006, p. 5).

Three Steps of Frank Parsons

1. The first step is to develop a clear understanding of yourself, your **aptitudes**, abilities, interests, resources, limitations, and other qualities.

2. The second step is to acquire the knowledge of all requirements and conditions of success for a vocation including the advantages and disadvantages of the vocation, compensations, opportunities, and prospects in different lines of work.

3. The final step is to apply true reasoning to reconcile the relations of these two groups of facts.

After Parsons' untimely death, a close friend, Myer Bloomfield, continued the work of the Vocational Bureau, even offering a summer course at Harvard for new teacher/vocational counselors in Boston in 1911. This became the first college-level class for vocational counselors (Thayer, Castle, De Howe, Pier, De Voto, & Morrison, 1912).

Vocational Planning

The expansion of high schools between 1900 and 1917 and their increasing list of course options were beyond the experience of many families with adolescent children. Then, as now, many parents were recent immigrants into the country who did not speak English (Williams, 1998). These two factors, along with the need of American industry for a well-trained, properly screened, and motivated workforce, made vocational guidance a necessity. These forces contributed to make vocational guidance the first specialization and cornerstone of the movement to what would become the profession of school counseling (Gysbers, 2001).

The first counselors in high schools had a single focus: vocational guidance. (See Case in Point 1.2.) There were at least two perspectives on the role and function of the first generation of vocational counselors in the school. One position was that vocational guidance should serve the need for **social efficiency** by sorting students by their various capacities and making a smooth transition for high school students into the world of work (Gysbers, 2001).[3] A second perspective was one that was encouraged by the educational philosopher John Dewey. He did not believe students should be modified to fit into industrial and clerical jobs. He wanted school counselors to work to modify industries so industry better met the needs of workers (Tang & Erford, 2004).

CASE IN POINT 1.2

Vocational guidance in public schools often involved direct teaching of vocational and occupational topics in the classroom. A national survey in 1953 found that 92,000 high school students were enrolled in a **group guidance** class and another 158,000 students were enrolled in a class on occupations (Dreese, 1957). This implies that at this high point in vocational counseling, only about 1 in 10 high school students took a vocational guidance class before graduating.

Vocational guidance classes of that era used **vocational interest tests** to help adolescent students begin to understand their own vocational interests. Topics in the typical curriculum in a vocational guidance class included learning about yourself, finding information about careers, identifying job values and prestige, job security, eventual adult lifestyle, potential economic gain, and the level of education and training needed to enter the job.

Thought Questions. Assume you are employed as a school counselor in a **middle school** in a working-class neighborhood. The school principal has scheduled you to teach one "guidance class focused on vocations and career planning." Your class meets one class period (45 minutes) one day each week for 18 weeks. The second 18 weeks of the school year you start again with another group of eighth graders. Review the list of topics used to teach vocational guidance classes 100 years ago. Which would you include and which would you not cover? What, if any, other topics would be part of your curricula for that class?

Vocational Guidance to School Counseling

Vocational planning and counseling dominated the role and job description of a **counselor** working in the new comprehensive high schools. Eventually counselors working in school settings began to assist adolescents and younger students with problems and issues in their lives. The first school counselors utilized a **mental hygiene** or medical-clinical approach that emphasized diagnosis and treatment. During the 1930s, a highly directive form of counseling in schools was developed that followed the precepts of the mental hygiene movement (Crow & Crow, 1935).

The role of school counselors had become too focused on reacting to immediate problems and serving in the role of gatekeeper by the 1980s and 1990s. The MetLife Trust along with other large philanthropies provided funding to create the **National Center for Transforming School Counseling** in 2003 (Education Trust, 2009). This organization advocated for a model for school counselors who were committed to providing equal treatment and access for all students.

In its role as a **professional association**, the ASCA also provided a framework for school counseling. In addition, ASCA provided an ethical set of canons to guide the practice of counseling in schools (see the front and back fly pages of this book). The most recent development in creating a strong professional model for school counselors was the publication of *The ASCA National Model: A Framework for School Counseling Programs* (ASCA/Hatch & Bowers, 2005).

Counseling in the Roaring 1920s

Prior to 1920, school counseling programs existed in a small number of secondary schools and school systems. The job descriptions of the earliest school counselors had a large vocational component. Yet, as soon as counselors were in place, they spontaneously expanded their roles and included areas such as the moral development and interpersonal relationships of high school students (Schmidt, 2008). The result was a drift in official job descriptions to include other missions and services for adolescents. In the 1920s the counselor's job description expanded to include helping resolve educational problems, social concerns, and the usual problems of vocational selection and preparation (Tang & Erford, 2004).

During the 1920s, states, starting with New York, established **certification requirements** for "school vocational guidance counselors." The decade of the 1920s also saw the birth of a movement for counseling in the elementary schools. These **elementary school counselors** served in many roles, including as the liaison between the school and its programs and the families of students attending the school (Burnham, 1926).

Beyond guidance tasks related to vocational preparation and selection, the model for the job of a school counselor was primarily one drawn from a medical or clinical framework. By that framework, the task of a counselor was to determine what was wrong with the client and then fix him or her. This approach fit well with the "mental hygiene" movement of the 1920s, 1930s, and 1940s. (See section following on "Mental Hygiene.")

Testing and the School Counselor

Much of the work done by those first school counselors was focused on testing and academic placement as well as providing guidance. Testing in America came into its own in the 1920s with the publication of the first group-administered measures of ability and **academic achievement** (Wright, 2008). These published tests just seemed to be fairer than other subjective methods of **assessment**, and they were widely adopted and used by counselors and other educators. Testing provided a framework for identifying students with school problems.

Early measurement devices encouraged schools to calculate an **accomplishment ratio** for everyone who took the combination of achievement and mental **ability tests**. This ratio was determined as the ratio of a student's **educational age** (EA) to his or her **mental age** (MA). This ratio linked mental age, as determined by an **IQ test,** with scores from an achievement test. The educational age in the formula is equal to the age of a group of children whose median educational achievement is the same as a particular child's level of achievement. Thus, the accomplishment ratio (AR) = *EA/MA*. By this method a child with an AR score above 1.0 would be described today as an **overachiever** because he or she is doing more than would be expected of a person with that mental ability. Likewise, an AR score below 1.0 indicated an **underachieving student** (Engle, 1945). Students with low AR scores (below 1.00) became the focus of the school counselor's efforts.

MENTAL HYGIENE ●

During the first part of the 20th century, a movement to improve the treatment and care given to mentally ill individuals was popularized following the publication in 1908 of an autobiographical account of mental illness and treatment by Clifford Whittingham Beers.[4] In educational settings this movement provided models for interpreting and diagnosing behaviors and inappropriate habits of students. The morality, sexuality, work habits, and mental ability were all fair game for well-meaning school counselors.

Framework

The mental hygiene framework held that mental illness in adulthood could have been prevented if there were appropriate intervention during childhood. **Mental hygienists** were attached to state and municipal public health offices. Graduate education in school counseling focused on training counselors to be school-based mental hygienists (Crow & Crow, 1935). These workers focused on all aspects of mental hygiene, including students in schools. A major concern of these workers was to educate parents in the "scientific approaches" to child rearing and child development.

Another factor in the growth of mental hygiene in America was the great popularity of Sigmund Freud's writings. The **psychoanalytical theory** of Freud described how early experiences of children have long-reaching impacts for the mental well-being and adjustment of adults. Therapists or mental hygienists emphasized the importance of **therapeutic intervention** in both emotional problems of young children and quotidian activities from the daily lives of children at home and school.

The mental hygiene movement influenced the early childhood curriculum framework as first approved by the National Association for Nursery Education in 1929 (forerunner of the National Association for the Education of Young Children) (Davis, Johnson, & Richardson, 1929). It was also the central organizing feature of the **emergency nursery schools** established by the **Works Progress Administration (WPA)** during the administration of President Franklin Delano Roosevelt (Wright, 2010).

Trait and Factor Theory of Counseling

> It is not enough to help counselees become what they want to become; rather it is more important to help them become what they ought to want to become.
>
> *Edmund G. Williamson*

In the late 1930s Edmund G. Williamson at the University of Minnesota developed a widely used model for counseling with students. As an administrator of the university he coined the term *in loco parentis,* describing his belief that schools and colleges have responsibility to govern the behavior of their students as though they are the students' parents (Klinkenberg & Spilman, 2002).

The **trait and factor theory** for counseling developed by Williamson provides a six-step approach based on clinical assumptions drawn from mental hygiene (Biggs & Porter, 1994). These steps include analysis of information, synthesis of what is known about the client, development of a formal diagnosis, prognosis with necessary counseling, treatment (counseling), and follow-up. The treatment phase as envisioned by Williamson was highly directive and counselor centered. Counselors were to take a position and explain to the student what he or she was to do. Williamson was philosophically opposed to the child- (client-) centered or humanistic counseling that was to dominate the field starting in the 1950s. He found the approach used by Carl Rogers and others to be **value neutral** and intellectually bankrupt (Ewing, 1975).

Beyond Mental Hygiene

Humanistic psychology originated in clinics and laboratories of Germany between the two world wars. The expulsion of Jewish scholars and other progressive thinkers by the Third Reich provided the intellectual energy needed to bring about a paradigm shift away from mental hygiene and toward a person-oriented form of **humanistic counseling** and psychology. Central to this movement were the American psychologists Abraham Maslow and Carl Rogers.

ABRAHAM H. MASLOW AND HUMANISTIC PSYCHOLOGY ●

Following World War II, millions of men and women needed to be reintroduced to their interrupted lives. To do this they had to set new goals and work toward achieving success in education, employment, socialization, and family life. These activities gave the new field of counseling a major boost (Tang & Erford, 2004).

During this post–World War II era (1945–1965), there was a major paradigm shift away from the clinical approach of mental hygiene toward a humanistic form of counseling. The returning war veterans were not ready to be told by a counselor what they should do with their lives.

Abraham Maslow (Photo 1.1) was born the same year that Clifford W. Beers (1908) published his creed about the malevolent nature of mental hospitals and therapy. Living and teaching psychology in New York during the 1930s, Maslow came to meet and be influenced by numerous European scholars who were escaping the persecutions of the Third Reich. Among these refugees were Alfred Adler, Eric Fromm, Kurt Goldstein, Karen Horney, Eric Erikson, and the Gestalt psychologist Wolfgang Köhler (Boeree, 2006).

In 1951 Abraham Maslow became chair of the psychology department at Brandeis University, where in collaboration with a member of that faculty, Kurt Goldstein, he proposed the conceptual framework for a new school of psychology and counseling known as **humanistic psychology**. Professor Goldstein was, by training, a neurologist and originator of the concept of **self-actualization** (Goldstein, 1934/1995). This new school of thought was not focused on how a counselor could fix a problem experienced by a child or other client, but rather on the capacity of individuals to become self-directing and psychologically whole. They described the task of counselors as removing the obstacles that prevented individuals from making progress toward their personal life goals.

PHOTO 1.1   Abraham Maslow

SOURCE: © Bettmann/CORBIS.

Hierarchy of Human Needs

Abraham Maslow built upon Goldstein's conceptualization and proposed a five-tier **hierarchical system of needs** that all people experience (Maslow, 1943, 1968). The model was designed to explain motivation; however, it also provides insight into the dynamics of human personality development and has clear implications for counselors. (See Figure 1.1.)

At the most basic level in Maslow's model are the **physiological needs** of the human organism. These include those of oxygen, water, appropriate foods, salt, minerals, vitamins, a regulated temperature, sleep, elimination, and so on. Without fulfillment of these physiological needs the organism will die.

A number of what Maslow described as somatic needs were not included in his list of proven physiological needs. These somatic needs included the sex drive, maternal instinctual drives, and the need for sensory stimulation and/or pleasure (Maslow, 1943).

At the next step beyond the physiological needs, Maslow proposed the needs for **safety and security**. Humans need to feel secure and have shelter where they

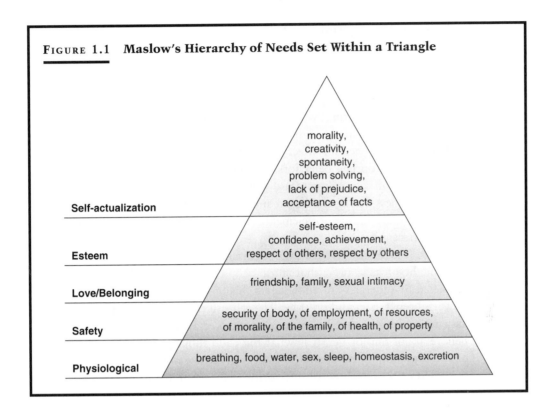

FIGURE 1.1   Maslow's Hierarchy of Needs Set Within a Triangle

are protected from malevolent factors in the environment. In advanced societies this can be seen in the need for good homes, insurance, and retirement funds (Boeree, 2006).

A child's need for safety is evident in his or her preference for some kind of undisrupted routine at home and in early education programs. Children want a predictable, orderly world. When a child perceives his or her parent's actions as being capricious and unfair, or inconsistent, he or she is likely to feel anxious and unsafe (Maslow, 1943). Likewise, Maslow posited that parents who quarrel loudly, along with those who divorce or abuse their children, promote unhealthy levels of anxiety and fear in children. Anxiety has the power to stymie the child's development at this point. This would prevent him or her from reaching step 3.

The midpoint in Maslow's hierarchy, step 3, is defined as a need for love and having a **sense of belonging**. These needs can only emerge once the physiological and safety needs have been fairly well gratified. Human beings will feel saddened by the absence of family members and friends. Maslow (1943) proposed that all people hunger for affectionate relationships with others. He made a distinction with this need with regard to sex. The affectionate needs are only sexual when they involve both giving and receiving affection and love.

This need for belonging and the affection of others extends to the need to be part of a group and to feel that one is among others who like and trust him or her. Children use scouting, Little Leagues, and other youth organizations to become part of the group, while their parents join churches, volunteer groups, and social clubs for many of the same reasons.

Thwarting this need for affection is frequently central to personal maladjustment and inappropriate behaviors. Children know the power of this need and frequently are all too willing to use social isolation as a weapon to punish their peers. Loneliness during childhood and the accompanying social anxiety it generates can be debilitating for elementary school children and caustic for adolescent adjustment.

At the fourth step in Maslow's hierarchy is the **need for esteem**. This can be thought of as a need that most people, including children, have to be respected by others. With adolescents this may take the form of a need for a powerful reputation and prestige. The **self-esteem** level of a child is developed as a reflection of what he or she interprets that others in the environment believe about him or her. It is what the child thinks others believe about his or her capabilities and talents. If esteem needs are not met, the child is likely to develop strong feelings of inferiority and discouragement and experience a loss of self-confidence.

At the highest level on the hierarchy of needs is the need for **self-actualization**. Maslow theorized that not all people reach the point at which this step is part of their life story (Maslow, 1943). Working from Goldstein's model, Maslow proposed that self-actualization refers to a need for self-fulfillment. This need can be fulfilled by becoming actualized in achieving one's potential. "This tendency might be phrased as the desire to become more and more what one is, to become everything that one is capable of becoming" (Maslow, 1943, p. 383).

Self-actualization can take many forms. It can be achieved by the teacher who wins the teacher-of-the-year prize, or the mother who is satisfied and fulfilled in the role of loving wife and caregiver in her home (Maslow, 1943). It may be the student athlete who wins an athletic scholarship, or the woman who coaches her high school team to a championship season. It may be the artist who is happy and fulfilled in his or her craft, or the airline pilot who loves to report to work each day.

Maslow noted that to reach this point a person must first have satisfied physiological, safety, love, and esteem needs. Once those steps have been achieved, a person may become fulfilled and satisfied in his or her life. When Maslow wrote this model in 1943, he also noted that such people were the exception.

CARL ROGERS AND CHILD-CENTERED COUNSELING ●

No counselor or psychologist has had a greater impact on the practice of counseling than Carl Rogers (Rogers & Russell, 2003) (Photo 1.2). Two schools of thought dominated psychology in the United States during the first 50 years of the 20th century: one was **behaviorism** and the other was **psychoanalysis**. These two models represented two completely different methods used to help individuals, but they offered little help for many students and young adults needing assistance coping with major forces in their lives.

PHOTO 1.2   Carl Rogers

SOURCE: © Roger Ressmeyer/CORBIS.

Carl Rogers proposed a humanistic approach to counseling that became a "third force" in the practice of psychology and counseling (Bugental, 1964). Rogers held several meetings with Abraham Maslow and other **phenomenologically oriented psychologists** at a state park in Michigan in the late 1950s. From these discussions emerged a new organization in 1961, the Association for Humanistic Psychology, with its own journal (Aanstoos, Serlin, & Greening, 2000). Ten years later the field was recognized by the American Psychological Association and elevated to divisional status, Division 32. This new professional organization provided five core principles for the field of humanistic psychology:

1. Human beings, as human, are more than merely the sum of their parts. They cannot be reduced to component parts or functions.

2. Human beings exist in a uniquely human context as well as in a cosmic ecology.

3. Human beings are aware and aware of being aware—that is, they are conscious. Human consciousness potentially includes an awareness of oneself in the context of other people and the cosmos.

4. Human beings have some choice, and with that, responsibility.

5. Human beings are intentional, aim at goals, are aware that they cause future events, and seek meaning, value, and creativity. (Bugental, 1964, pp. 19–25)

The approach to counseling based on the work of Carl Rogers and the other humanistic psychologists is still widely employed in educational and clinical settings today. (It is described in more detail in Chapter 6 of this book.)

● SCHOOL COUNSELING IN THE AGE OF ACCOUNTABILITY

The job of being a school counselor has become much more difficult since the passage of the 2002 and 2004 reauthorizations of the **Elementary and Secondary Education Act (ESEA)**, renamed the **No Child Left Behind Act (NCLB)** (P.L. 107–110, 2002). To understand the impact of this legislation on counselors, it is necessary to understand its impact on students, teachers, administrators, schools, and communities.

Standards-Based Accountability

During the 1990s the administration of President William J. Clinton encouraged a shift in emphasis within the schools to establish **state-level standards for learning**. These standards were written for all children, from preschool through high school graduation. These standards are sometimes abbreviated as PK–12. This move toward **standards-based education** brought with it the need for schools to test students on a statewide basis. Uniform testing made it possible to prove which schools were meeting the state's learning standards. Along with these new standards for learning came new **standards-based report card** systems, and new approaches for monitoring students needing special educational assistance, known as **response to intervention (RTI)** testing (see Chapter 7).

The administration of President George W. Bush took this concept of standards-based learning a step further and signed into law annual **mandated tests** in mathematics and reading for all students between the 3rd and 8th grades and once again in 10th or 11th grade. (Photo 1.3 shows a young student struggling with a high-stakes test.) Part of that legislation set increasingly high achievement standards that had to be met each year, leading up to the year 2014 when all (actually 97%) of the enrolled students in public and **charter schools** had to be **proficient** in reading and mathematics. The goal had to be met schoolwide and by specific groups within the schools. Each school was required to show that the schoolwide average scores for all identified groups—including students receiving special education, Native American students, non-Hispanic Black students, Hispanic students, students with one or more disabling conditions,

Anglo-White students, students from impoverished homes, and English language learners—are making **adequate yearly progress (AYP)** toward the goal of universal proficiency by 2014. The various states have each identified specific standards for student learning and have established proficiency targets for students of each grade level. Those targets or **benchmarks** are unique to each state but must be approved by the U.S. Department of Education (Wright, 2008). In addition to having good achievement levels for their students, all schools must have all enrolled students tested each year. Schools cannot have students stay at home on test day. The pressure to get all students to take the mandated state examinations has resulted in several unusual steps by school administrators. Case in Point 1.3 provides examples of this effort to be in compliance with the testing mandate.

PHOTO 1.3 Young Child Struggling With High-Stakes Kindergarten Test

SOURCE: Thinkstock Education.

CASE IN POINT 1.3

In March 2006 a local newspaper reported that a fourth grade elementary school child who had been suspended from school pending transfer to a "disciplinary school" was brought back to complete the mandated state examination. This child had been suspended for bringing a starter's pistol into his elementary school. After 5 hours of testing he was sent home to await the disciplinary school transfer (James, 2006).

In another case a boy who was hospitalized following a bicycle accident in which he crushed three vertebrae in his neck and lost the use of his right (dominant side) arm was made to take the 10th grade state assessment test in his hospital. The boy in question was most concerned with the timed essay portion of the examination. This part of the test he wrote in longhand using his left hand (DeGregory, 2005).

Thought Question. What role should a school counselor fill in tracking down missing students who must be tested under state mandates? For example, students who are suspended from school and those who are injured or ill.

A variation of the high-stakes assessment model was later incorporated into the education programs announced by President Barack Obama (U.S. Department of Education, 2010). Under his plan, "Race to the Top," schools are not punished for having problems but are encouraged and helped in meeting goals. Extra funds were awarded to states and schools for adopting a strong set of national educational achievement standards and making a number of other educational reforms. This model also maintains the high-stakes testing programs of the previous administration and keeps the pressure on educators and students.

Goals of Mandated Assessments

An important goal of the NCLB legislation was to close the gap between the achievement levels of students from different backgrounds and ethnic groups. In 2009 the NCLB Act was past the halfway mark toward its target date for having all students proficient in reading and math. Miniscule gains have been made toward reaching this universal proficiency goal, and the parallel goal of closing the **achievement gap** is not being met (Education Trust, 2010). This is not a new trend but a continuation of the pattern since the beginning of the NCLB-mandated assessments (Maxwell, 2007; Viadero, 2007). There are many reasons for this, including the quality of public schools attended by minority students. Those schools tend to enroll the greatest number of students from impoverished backgrounds, have the least experienced teachers, have the highest student absenteeism, have the greatest faculty turnover and absenteeism, and have the lowest level of parent involvement in their children's schools (Camilli & Monfils, 2004; National Assessment of Educational Progress, 2004).

Ten states have gone a step further and mandated that for a child to be promoted from third grade to fourth grade he or she must first pass the state's assessment test.[5] This has resulted in hundreds of thousands of students being made to repeat third grade. The original goal of this policy was to prevent **social promotion**. Social promotion has been described as a soft form of racism through which students were pushed along from grade to grade without regard to what they knew or what skills they had.

Additionally, 27 states have enacted laws mandating that to earn a high school diploma a student must pass the state's required high-stakes test. This gate-keeping role for proficiency tests in high school has resulted in hundreds of thousands of students who have passed all their courses and have the required graduation credits being ineligible to graduate with diplomas.[6] Once again, the burden for failing and not being awarded a high school diploma falls most heavily on African American and Hispanic students (Heubert, 2002).

Case in Point 1.4 describes the impact on students of linking grade promotion to a high-stakes test.

CASE IN POINT 1.4

In 2005–2006, 8,000 students in Florida (one of the first states to mandate promotion tests) spent a *third year as third graders*. In an attempt to prevent a build-up in the number of students stuck in third grade, Florida began to put re-repeating third grade students into fourth grade halfway through the school year. Each school district was given permission to decide how to determine whether a retained child was able to move on to fourth grade. The sad truth was that many of these students still could not be promoted at midyear because they were unable to pass the state's third grade assessment test even after 2.5 years in third grade. In 2005 one county school system in Florida gave 750 re-repeating third graders early promotion into fourth grade only to find that 84% failed the mandated examination and ended up repeating third grade yet again (Harrison, 2005). The long-range problem with all grade-retained students is that 61% of them drop out and never graduate from high school (Sparks, Johnson, & Akos, 2010).

Richard Stiggins observed that our obsession with high-stakes testing is causing major segments of our student population to be *left behind* because the mandated measures are causing many kids to give up in hopelessness (Stiggins, 2002).[7]

Thought Questions. The MetLife Foundation, along with more than a dozen other philanthropies, has funded efforts to close the gap in achievement between Anglo-White students and students of minority groups (Education Trust, 2009). One of the priorities has been to improve K to 12 school counseling among students from all ethnic groups. What aspects of the role of being a professional school counselor are related to closing the test score gap between different ethnic groups of students? In other words, what can you do to help?

Grade Retention

More students are retained in their grade for an extra year in the United States than in any other industrial nation in the world (U.S. Federal Interagency Forum on Child and Family Statistics, 2008). Yet, there is no evidence that **grade retention** has any lasting positive effect. This raises the question of who is being retained in grade? The unfortunate answer is "minority students" (Massachusetts Department of Education, 2005). Overall, approximately 3 out of 4 students retained-in-grade are members of minority groups (Florida Association of School Psychologists, 2005). African American students are the group most likely to be retained-in-grade. Two times as many African American students are retained-in-grade compared with their Anglo-White peers (U.S. Department of Education, 2006). Another group that has a disproportionately high number of students retained-in-grade is **English-language learners (ELLs)**, especially students of Hispanic heritage (Hauser, Pager, Solon, & Simmons, 2008). An analysis of Florida data by Jay Greene of the highly conservative Manhattan Institute speculated that Black and Hispanic third graders are retained-in-grade because of something related to their race, not just lower average achievement test scores (Greene & Winters, 2007).

The natural reaction of educators under this **test-induced stress** has been to identify ways to improve students' test scores. This drive for better scores has resulted in major curriculum revisions, emphasizing more time for instruction in reading and mathematics. The losers in the curriculum reshuffle have been **social studies**, the arts, and other **humanities**. Also lost are recess periods and even naptime in kindergarten (Wright, 2010).

Counselors as Test Administrators

School counselors are usually given the job of coordinating the mandated testing programs in the schools. This policy is endorsed by the ASCA and has been written into the national framework.

> School counselors should be proficient in the collection, analysis and interpretation of student achievement and related data. School counselors monitor student progress through three types of data: student-achievement data, achievement-related data, and standards and competency-related data. (ASCA/Hatch & Bowers, 2005, p. 49)

This role as the **"grand examiner"** has cost counselors their insulation from the elements of school life that is a cause of stress for teachers and that adds to the angst of students (Dollarhide & Lemberger, 2006). This has diminished the role of the counselor and made him or her suspect in the eyes of students and some teachers as being a co-conspirator in the high-stakes testing process.

The emphasis on spending more time getting ready for the test has also been problematic for counselors. Teachers are more reluctant than ever to release a student from class time to visit the school's counselor. Counselors report they

---

CARTOON 1.1 *"Modern Education"*

"SO FAR, ALL WE'RE LEARNING IS HOW TO TAKE A MATH TEST, HOW TO TAKE A SCIENCE TEST, AND HOW TO TAKE A READING TEST."

SOURCE: Cartoon by Robert Englehart. Reprinted with permission from Robert Englehart.

---

are continually struggling to prove they are important members of the school community and a valuable resource (Dollarhide & Lemberger, 2006).

TIME-EFFICIENT APPROACHES FOR SCHOOL COUNSELING ●

Today few school counselors have the luxury of following a **child-centered extended counseling** effort with an individual student. The time is just not available to spend many sessions with one student. A technique of **solution-focused brief counseling (SFBC)** has been identified and is currently being employed in school counseling offices at all grade levels (see Chapter 6 for more on SFBC).

By the 1990s the pragmatic need for an abbreviated but effective approach to counseling in the schools was clearly indicated (Littrell, Malia, Nichols,

Olson, Nesselhuf, & Crendell, 1992). This need became all the more obvious with the time constraints that mandated testing programs placed on school counseling activities.

The terms *solution-focused counseling and brief counseling* are used in the literature to describe an approach to counseling of students that can last from 1 to 10 or more sessions (Lewis & Sieber, 1997; Littrell et al., 1992; Littrell, Malia, & Vanderwood, 1995). The focus of these counseling sessions involves several steps. The first step is the identification of the problem area as the student perceives it to be. Second is the task of determining how the resolution of the problem will improve the child's life. During this step it is important to assess with the student his or her strengths and what has already been accomplished. The third step is the identification of goals (both major and smaller ones) that can be accomplished in resolving the problem. The goals make up the central feature of a plan of action for the child to follow (Charlesworth & Jackson, 2004). (See Chapter 6 for more on solution-based brief counseling in schools.)

● PROFESSIONALISM

Professional and learned societies are formed both to serve as advocates for the professional field and to provide the public with reassurance of the quality of the practice and products of its members. To become a member of a professional organization is to accept the ethical standards and precepts of that organization as one's own.

Professional Societies in Counseling

Not surprisingly, the first national association in counseling was formed by professionals engaged in vocational guidance.

National Career Development Association

The United States at the dawn of the 20th century was emerging from a severe recession and found that it could not compete with the nations of Northern Europe in the quality of industrial products. President Theodore Roosevelt and the leading industrialists of the day saw the low quality of American manufactured goods as slowing national economic progress. This led to the formation of the National Association of Manufacturers (NAM) by America's leading industrialists and entrepreneurs. It was clear to NAM from the outset that improved education for the trades was needed.

Both the National Association of Manufacturers and the American Federation of Labor looked to higher education to develop a model for the education of young people to provide the skilled source of labor needed to improve industrial output. Charles R. Richards of Teachers College, Columbia University, and James P. Haney, Director of the New York City Public School Manual Training Program, worked to develop a curriculum for secondary schools designed to meet this need and also helped form the National Society for the Promotion of Industrial Education (NSPIE) in 1906. In 1908, the NSPIE held its first convention in New York City at Cooper Union (Smith, 1999). Vocational guidance was always considered by members of NSPIE as a central part of vocational education (Stephens, 1988).

A newsletter, *Vocational Guidance News-Letter,* was distributed several times each year to vocational guidance workers by its first editor, Frederick J. Allen. This was initiated two years prior to forming an association for vocational counselors (Pope, 2008). This newsletter underwent seven name changes over the years, eventually becoming the *Career Development Quarterly* in 1986.

The National Vocational Guidance Association (NVGA) was born during the 1913 meeting of the NSPIE in Grand Rapids, Michigan (Stephens, 1988). That organization flourished and did not change its name until 1985, when it became the National Career Development Association (NCDA). That name is reflective of the evolving focus of the organization on issues less related to basic education and more directed to consulting and providing professional development in a variety of nonacademic settings.

American Counseling Association

A national association for all counselors was not founded until 1952. It was originally the American Personnel and Guidance Association (APGA). This new counselor organization was founded during a joint meeting of the four dominant organizations related to counseling, including the National Vocational Guidance Association (NVGA) [now the National Career Development Association (NCDA)], National Association of Guidance and Counselor Trainers (AGCT) [now the Association for Counselor Education and Supervision (ACES)], Student Personnel Association for Teacher Education (SPATE), and the National Association of Appointment Secretaries [now the American College Personnel Association (NCPA)] (American Counseling Association [ACA], 2009).

These organizations became the first four divisions in the larger organization. The following year a fifth division was added, the American School Counselor Association (ASCA). This growth has continued, and in 2010 there were a total of 19 divisions operating with charters from what is today the American Counseling Association (ACA). The current name was selected in 1983.

Like the NVGA, the SPATE organization has a long history. It was originally composed of the state supervisors for vocational education and vocational counseling. The organization was very influential in the 1920s, 1930s, and 1940s. This reflects the fact that the federal government, through the Smith-Hughes Act, encouraged vocational education and vocational counseling programs by funding for them through the states. This influence of the organization waned when the funds dried up in the late 1950s during the Eisenhower administration (Gysbers, 2006).

The word *trainers* in the organization's title was used for what we consider today to be **counseling education** faculty. With the growth of counselor education programs on college campuses, the organization is thriving and promoting the best practice in the education and supervision of counselors (Association for Counselor Education and Supervision, 2005).

The American College Personnel Association (ACPA) is the only original organization that has never changed its name after 1952. In 1992 it disaffiliated itself from the ACA. It was originally founded in 1924 as the National Association of Appointment Secretaries, with May L. Cheney, the director of the Office for Teacher Placement of the University of California, Berkeley, as its first president. Today its membership includes college student personnel workers from 1,500 public and private postsecondary institutions. ACPA has a total membership now exceeding 9,000 (ACPA, 2004).

Professional Training and Credentialing for School Counselors

Early vocational guidance counselors were often teachers who volunteered or were asked to "volunteer" for counseling duties. Many of these teachers were given little direction as to what the jobs involved, and most were asked to perform duties as vocational counselors in addition to their normal teaching loads (Tang & Erford, 2004). A fortunate few were given reduced teaching loads to balance their counseling responsibilities.

A movement to professionalize school counseling through state credentialing requirements began when New York established training standards and issued appropriate certification to qualified individuals (Tang & Erford,

2004). Today all 50 states plus the District of Columbia have published certification standards for the issuing of a credential to be a school counselor. Today 44 states and the District of Columbia provide a license to work as a counselor at all levels of education between kindergarten (or prekindergarten) and grade 12. The other six states provide two certificates, one for elementary school counselors and another for those who work in secondary schools.

All of these certificates require that the prospective school counselor has completed a graduate-level training program from a regionally accredited college or university. Another requirement for certification as a school counselor in most states is passing a mandatory test on either general knowledge or a specific test of knowledge about school counseling. The most commonly required test is the Praxis II: School Guidance and Counseling, mandated in 12 states and the District of Columbia. The lowest passing score on the Praxis II is required by South Carolina (550) and the highest by Oregon (610) (Educational Testing Service, 2008). Every state but West Virginia requires all new school counselors to pass a police background check to prove they are not felons or child molesters.

The ASCA provides a web page listing information on the certification requirements for school counselors in each state. This is available at www.schoolcounselor.org/content.asp?contentid=242.

The ASCA has published a framework for how school counseling programs should be organized for providing services. It also elaborates how they should be managed, and how they are best evaluated (ASCA/Hatch & Bowers, 2005). That framework, while focused on basic education, provides ideas for graduate education in school counseling and provides guidance for inservice programs for professional school counselors.

Technology Skills

One obvious area that should be added to state certification standards is technology (Morrissey & Rotunda, 2006). Up-to-date schools are fully "wired." In a wired school all records are stored electronically, and text-based communications and e-mail contacts are an ongoing activity among counselors and the teachers and other staff of the school (see Photo 1.4). Parents with students in a wired school are encouraged to hold **virtual meetings** with the school's counselor using Internet video. All standards-based report cards are electronically transmitted to the student's parents.

This standard also implies that school counselors should be able to create and maintain web pages that provide announcements and the counseling

Photo 1.4   A Wired School

SOURCE: © iStockphoto.com/take5.

activities schedule. Finally, counselors must be able to manage databases of test scores and provide leadership in conducting **school-based action research.** All these tasks require that a new set of skills be added to those counselors already are required to develop in their graduate studies. Yet, despite this need for technology proficiency, only Idaho and Nevada have technology standards written into their certification requirements for school counselors.

Proactive Versus Reactive

Critics of counselor education have pointed out that the emphasis of graduate-level preparation has been on how to be an effective helper-responder. The suggestion is that school counselors should be taught to be proactive, preventing problems, and should become leaders in their schools (House & Sears, 2002). The National Model describes quality school counseling programs as preventive in design and developmental in nature (ASCA/Hatch & Bowers, 2005, p. 28). Reese House and Susan Sears argue that counselors should be taught leadership and collaboration skills at a precertification level and also as an ongoing inservice program for counselor development. The national framework also argues for counselors to take a leadership role in the school and design preventative programs for school problems (ASCA/Hatch & Bowers, 2005, p. 24). The proactive model focuses first on tertiary prevention. This level of prevention reduces the need for secondary and primary prevention. All three levels of prevention are described as appropriate school counseling interventions throughout this textbook.

National Certifications

It is important to remember that a professional counselor is a licensed mental health worker. These counselors are graduates of nationally accredited graduate programs in counseling or counseling psychology and provide a professional service in every state but California. In 2010 an effort was under way to pass legislation in California to create a state license program for professional counselors.

There are two levels to the question of national certification as a school counselor: one addresses the counselor education program, while the other involves the state departments of education that provide the certifications needed to work in the schools.

At the first level, there are three organizations that provide colleges and universities with accreditation for their programs in teacher education and related areas. The first of these is the National Council for the Accreditation of Teacher Education (NCATE). There were 285 colleges and universities that participated in the initial year of NCATE accreditation in 1954. Since that time the number has grown to 632, with another 100 institutions in the process of applying in 2010–2011. This accrediting body coordinates its efforts with 39 of the 50 states. Thus, NCATE provides evaluations of and accrediting for the entire education programs of colleges offering teacher education in 39 states. This cuts the workload for those state departments of education.

While NCATE has standards used for evaluating many educational specializations, including administrators and **school psychologists**, it does not have specific standards for the accreditation of counselor education. For that reason, in all 50 states, the standards set by individual states are the deciding factor in whether a college gets program approval for educating school counselors.

A second national teacher education accrediting body is the Teacher Education Accrediting Council (TEAC). This organization provides broad general guidelines for college-based teacher education programs at both the graduate and undergraduate levels. In 2010 there were fewer than 70 colleges accredited by TEAC.

There are 2,467 accredited 4-year colleges and universities in the United States, approximately 1,500 of which offer certification in one or more areas of teacher education. Many of these colleges and universities provide graduate education programs in school counseling.

The only national accrediting body for counselor education is the Council for the Accrediting of Counseling and Related Educational Programs (CACREP). A list of the CACREP accredited graduate programs and contact persons is available online at www.cacrep.org/directory-2–17–09.pdf.

CACREP was chartered in 1981 as the Accreditation Board for Counselor Preparation (ABCP). This was changed to the name CACREP in 1993. The new name was selected to reflect that it services "related educational programs" and to facilitate higher education accreditation. Today CACREP is the agency used by the various state boards of professional counselors to evaluate the status of colleges preparing professional counselors.

A point of confusion for many graduate students is the difference between (1) the CACREP national certification of a college that provides graduate programs in professional counselor education and (2) the state-by-state requirements for certification as a school counselor. Accreditation by CACREP is enjoyed by 254 colleges. That accreditation provides a student with assurance that the graduate program is one that meets a national set of standards for counselors.[8] However, colleges in 45 states are accredited only by state education departments to provide certification to work as a school counselor. The state's department of education, not CACREP, must approve counseling programs if graduates are to be eligible for certification as school counselors.

Ethical Practice in School Counseling

There are several professional associations that provide guidance to school counselors about the ethical practice of school counseling. One set of ethical principles is expressed in the American Counseling Association's *Code of Ethics* (2005). This set of ethical canons can be downloaded from the ACA from their page: www.txca.org/Images/tca/Documents/ACA%20Code%20of% 20Ethics.pdf.

A statement of ethics for school counselors was first published in 1984 and updated by the American School Counselor Association in 2004. The document can be seen on the front and back fly pages of this textbook. This document can also be downloaded from www.schoolcounselor.org/files/EthicalStandards 2010.pdf. The ASCA document, *Ethical Standards for School Counselors*, addresses major ethical issues in seven sections:

1. *Responsibilities to Students.* This addresses the need to respectfully treat each child as a unique individual, maintaining confidentiality as appropriate, coordinating referrals as indicated, developing counseling plans and ethically employing assessment materials, maintaining student records, and protecting student confidentiality.[9] The counselor should also work to ensure all students and their families have access to technology needed for school success.

2. *Responsibility to Parents.* Counselors must collaborate with the child's parents and work to maintain a balance of confidential counseling with the child while respecting the rights of parents.[10]

3. *Responsibilities to Colleagues and Professional Associates.* This addresses the ethical interaction among educators and the counselor's role in providing accurate, meaningful data as needed by professionals in the best interests of the child.

4. *Responsibilities to School and Community.* These statements are in support of the child's educational program and in the child's best interests. They state that counselors know the school's mission and work to establish an educationally conducive environment, including establishing good working relationships with community agencies.

5. *Responsibilities to the Self.* This section describes how counselors strive to improve professional competence through ongoing development. The standard argues that counselors must avoid deleterious activities and anything that may be harmful to students. It also requires counselors to support diversity and monitor personal attitudes and feelings.

6. *Responsibilities to the Profession.* Counselors are required to understand and accept the ethical principles of the professional associations and become a member of ASCA. Counselors should always employ appropriate research practices when analyzing and reporting data.

7. *Maintenance of Standards.* This provides guidelines for counselors to follow in ensuring their ethical behavior.

SUMMARY

The growth of industrial centers in America and the need for educational planning with students who would enter the commercial world at the start of the 20th century was linked to the birth of vocational education and counseling. Concurrently, there was a 20th-century movement toward the humane treatment of mental illness and the parallel development of mental hygiene. Concepts of mental hygiene entered public schools and became part of ongoing counseling programs. The 1930s saw elementary school counseling start in large cities. The 1950s brought a new approach to counseling with the introduction of humanistic psychology and client-centered counseling.

In 1913 the first professional associations for counselors were formed, and the forerunner of the American Counseling Association was chartered in 1952. The following year saw the chartering of an association for school counselors. These organizations have provided counselors with a canon of ethical principles and a framework for the practice of counseling in the schools.

Standards-based education in the 1990s following the No Child Left Behind Act (2001) has placed stress on the educational system and on students. Counselors have had to find more efficient models for providing service for students in the schools.

DISCUSSION QUESTIONS

1. Use the Internet to review the curriculum of a secondary school or your state's standards for learning. Then list incidences where classicism may still be evident.

2. Interview a teacher in the upper elementary grades about the impact of mandated high-stakes testing programs. Describe how the curriculum or emphasis has changed to provide better test scores.

3. Some consider requiring test scores as a gatekeeper for promotion to be an appropriate method of preventing what has been called "social promotion." Under what circumstances is social promotion appropriate? When is the practice not appropriate? Why?

4. A number of counselors feel that value-neutral counseling and other humanistic approaches are too inefficient to be used in public schools. Under what circumstances is trait and factor theory counseling appropriate to use in public schools? Explain and elaborate on your answer.

5. Should the various states decide the requirements for becoming a school counselor, or should that be decided by national professional organizations in the field? Explain your answer in terms of professionalism and also the rights of each state's taxpayers to local control.

RELATED READINGS

American School Counselor Association/Hatch, T., & Bowers, J. (2005). *The ASCA National Model: A framework for school counseling programs* (2nd ed.). Alexandria, VA: Author.

Rogers, C. R., & Russell, D. (2003). *Carl Rogers: The quiet revolutionary.* Roseville, CA: Penmarin Books.

Sklare, G. B. (2005). *Brief counseling that works: A solution-focused approach for school counselors and administrators* (2nd ed.). Thousand Oaks, CA: Corwin.

Ungar, M. (2006). *Strengths based counseling with at-risk youth.* Thousand Oaks, CA: Corwin.

Wright, R. J. (2009). Methods for improving test scores: The good, the bad, and the ugly. *Kappa Delta Pi Record, 45*(3), 116–121.

1. Girls may have been taught to read and write at home, but there was no place in the more formal education programs for them until the 17th century in Europe and America.

2. About a third of all high school graduates, or about 28,000 young adults, went on to earn bachelor's degrees each year. This is minuscule compared to today's million and a half bachelor's degrees awarded annually.

3. The fact that many adults are not satisfied in what they do to earn a living was brought home by a 2010 Conference Report survey of American Workers. That survey found that 45% of American workers are unhappy with their jobs (Langer, 2010).

4. The book *A Mind That Found Itself* brought C. W. Beers (1908) great fame. With the help of the psychiatrist Adolf Meyer and Yale University administrator Anson P. Stokes, he was instrumental in the formation of the National Committee for Mental Hygiene in 1909.

5. These states include Delaware, Florida, Georgia, Louisiana, Maryland, Mississippi, North Carolina, South Carolina, Texas, and Wisconsin.

6. Research published in 2009 has shown that by requiring an exit examination, in California 20,000 additional students failed to graduate with a diploma than was the case before testing (Reardon, Atteberry, Arshan, & Kurlaender, 2009). Also, the greatest loss was experienced by minority students and also by girls.

7. There are three loopholes for parents to use if they want to avoid having their child retained-in-grade based on a test score. All three require that the parents move the child to another educational model. One is to remove the child and homeschool him or her. In some states this can be done with the assistance of virtual schools taught over the Internet. Another involves enrolling the child in a parochial school. The final answer is the most costly and involves enrolling the child in a private preparatory school or independent school. None of these options require the child to pass a state-mandated test.

8. Students completing a program approved by CACREP in school counseling are eligible to take the test for national accreditation by the National Board of Certified Counselors. Holding that **national license,** a school counselor would automatically qualify for state certification as a school counselor in Mississippi, Nevada, New Mexico, and North Dakota.

9. The professional associations with an interest in educational measurement have worked together to publish a combined document on testing ethics. The following are four principles drawn from that document (Joint Committee on Testing Practices, 2005).

The first of these principles for the ethical practice of testing involves communication with those taking the test. The purpose of the test and the areas to be measured should be fully understood by the test taker (or the parent or guardian) prior to the time of the test. The use of scores from the test should be explained, and the test takers should be told how long their results would be on file. The administrator should provide special **accommodations** for test takers with disabilities.

The second area involves **confidentiality**. The test administrator must ensure that the scores from individual students are disclosed only to people having a professional need for those data. The students' parents are included in the group who should have full access to the test score data. It is also critical that test materials are stored in a secure location and never released for review by others.

Third, the interpretation of scores should be carried out in a way that conforms with the guidelines provided by the test publisher. The person interpreting scores should be trained and knowledgeable of the test and its scoring system. Parents and students should be informed of the scores and their interpretation in a developmentally appropriate way. In addition, scores should be reported using understandable language that parents can follow, avoiding educational jargon. This includes **cut scores** and minimal standards for success. Scoring errors should be corrected immediately and the correction noted through all of the student's records.

A fourth issue is the use of test scores. A single score on a test should never be used to determine the placement of a student. Interpretations should always be made in conjunction with other sources of information.

A related point involves the development and selection of tests. A test or assessment should only be used for a purpose for which it was designed and standardized. The test should provide a manual documenting that the measure is valid and reliable and explaining the tasks it is designed to accomplish. Also, the measure should provide evidence that there is no consistent bias (gender, ethnic, socioeconomic status, etc.) influencing the scores. The test should provide users with clear directions for the test administration and scoring.

10. Prior to the child's 18th birthday, parents or legal guardians have the ultimate authority in matters relating to the child. Parents of dependent college students can claim their young adult as an income tax deduction until the age of 24 years (Internal Revenue Service, 2009).

2

Professional Counseling in the Schools

OBJECTIVES

By reading and studying this chapter you should acquire the competency to:

- Discuss how the role of a school counselor is similar to and different from that of a classroom teacher
- Describe the major collective bargaining units that (in most states) represent interests of school counselors and teachers
- List and explain four dimensions of the national framework
- Describe and discuss the roles of other members of the pupil service team with whom the school counselor works
- List and explain the federal laws related to the role of school counselors
- Explain the case law history that makes it possible for states to mandate graduation tests and other high-stakes tests

“Counsel woven into the fabric of real life is wisdom.**”**

Walter Benjamin (1892–1940)

● INTRODUCTION AND THEMES

Until the 1980s, school counselors were required to be former classroom teachers. The shift to having counselors who have no backgrounds in teacher education was a by-product of the shortage of certified school counselors who came from traditional backgrounds. Professional contracts for school counselors in 41 states are negotiated by one of the two major collective bargaining units that dominate education in this country, the American Federation of Teachers (the AFT of the AFL-CIO), or the National Education Association (NEA).[1] As nearly all teachers are members of the local and state teacher's unions, membership by counselors can help smooth the working relationship between school counselors and the teachers and educational specialists in the school. Survey research in one state has documented that the vast majority of school counselors are union members (Bauman, 2008).

School counselors play a number of significant roles within schools and are employed at every grade level from prekindergarten (PK) through high school. A useful taxonomy of school counseling activities is provided in the national framework for school counseling from the American School Counselor Association (ASCA). Various chapters of this text address the ASCA model.

At all levels, the school counselor works as a member of a pupil services team of specialists. This includes participation in **student assistance teams (SATs)** and multidisciplinary teams that make **entitlement decisions**. The school's counselor also has a role to play in improving and maintaining a healthy school climate for both children and teachers. It is also the school's counselor who provides research and data management leadership within the school. Counselors in the schools also need to provide secure records for individual students and guidance for parents in understanding reports and test scores from their children.

School counselors are advocates for all students, including those in need of special educational services, children of **undocumented aliens**, and children from all minority groups, including English-language learners.

Standard 1: The professional school counselor plans, organizes, and delivers the school counseling program (American School Counselor Association [ASCA]/Hatch & Bowers, 2005, p. 63).

Standard 13: The professional school counselor is a student advocate, leader, collaborator, and system change agent (ASCA/Hatch & Bowers, 2005, p. 64).

ROLE OF SCHOOL COUNSELORS   ●

There was a major paradigm shift in school counseling in the 1990s. The role of school counselors prior to that shift was to react to problems while serving as supervisors of many clerical tasks related to pupil services. The shift was described in 1996 by the Education Trust and involved a new vision for the profession and the education of professional school counselors. The new direction would ready school counselors to play leadership roles within their schools that focus on embracing educational leadership, team building and consultation, advocacy for all students, and assessment (McMahon, Mason, & Paisley, 2009).

The new vision was translated into the national framework in 2003 and 2005 by the American School Counselor Association.

The possibility of conflict and role confusion occurs in schools where the administration and some old-line counselors have not changed their focus and understanding of the job of a school counselor in this age of accountability. As was noted in Chapter 1, one key player in defining the role and job description of a school's counselor is the building principal. Modifying the counselor's role as defined by the administration may take time and careful negotiation. Research into the principal–counselor relationship has found that the principal not only plays a significant role in defining the counselor's job description but also accounts for half of the measured level of job satisfaction on the part of the school's counselor (Clemens, Milsom, & Cashwell, 2009).

The problems some counselors experience in defining their jobs and having a satisfying working relationship with their school's principal is related to the press of time and poor communication levels between them (Finkelstein, 2009).

While the core job is consistent, the role of a school counselor can change from moment to moment. At one point in the day a school counselor may be assisting a student to cope with a **personal crisis,** while at another point he or she may be teaching a classroom of students a lesson from the guidance curriculum. Later in the day, when the principal is away attending a district meeting, the counselor may be placed in the role of principal pro-tem. The counselor may handle the registration, **screening,** and placement of a new student after lunch, and after school the school counselor may be asked to present a teacher inservice education program. Later, at night the school counselor may be found leading a **parent support group** for students with disabilities. All of these tasks and many more may be involved in the role of the counselor in a school.

Typical Duties of a Middle School Counselor

All activities in this list have either explicit approbation or implied approval in *The ASCA National Model: A Framework for School Counseling Programs* (ASCA/Hatch & Bowers, 2005). Exceptions to this are the last two items in the list. These two items are frequently found in the school district contract with the teacher's union and possibly in the official job description (as approved by the school board) for the school counselor. If a counselor is not tenured, the pressure to comply with "requests" by school administrators can be overwhelming. Remember, the school's principal makes the ultimate evaluation of job performance by a counselor. This occurs annually and again when the school board is considering a permanent contract (tenure) for a school's counselor.

- Provide individual counseling (see Chapter 6) with students needing assistance coping and or adjusting

- Assist students and families who are homeless (see Chapter 9)

- Provide parent support and individual counseling for academically gifted students (see Chapter 7)

- Provide support for parents of students with special intellectual and artistic gifts

- Provide group counseling to resolve common problems among students

- Follow up with all special education students on a regular basis

- Monitor the individualized educational plans (IEPs) for special needs students

- Schedule all student assistance teams and IEP meetings and coordinate evaluation schedules

- Work with parents and provide support for special needs students

- Supervise the maintenance of all student records and ensure compliance with provisions of the Family Educational Rights and Privacy Act

- Orient new students to the school and its policies

- Teach guidance classes on matters of planning, transitions, goal setting, healthful living, bullying and peer cooperation, dangerous and inappropriate Internet use, career and vocational education, and so on

- Consult with teachers and school administrators about individual cases

- Maintain a web page that includes a counselor's schedule and notes about activities going on in school

- Initiate and maintain e-mail communications with parents and others in the school's community

- Review the publicly accessible personal web-based pages of students and others in the school's community

- Track attendance problems and work with parents and students as needed

- Observe peer interactions and student behaviors in the cafeteria, play yard, halls, bus ramp, and other public areas

- Assist administrators in constructing a master schedule for the school

- Assist individual students by adjusting their class schedules

- Supervise all schoolwide testing programs and review all test scores for possible problems and anomalies

- Review all report cards and the individual comments teachers have added to them

- Meet with parents and register all new students (the ASCA national framework labels this common practice as an inappropriate activity [p. 56])

- Serve as an emergency substitute teacher when a colleague becomes ill during the school day (the ASCA national framework labels this common practice as an inappropriate activity [p. 56])

Counselors as Educators

One hundred years ago, when counselors first became employed by high schools, they were drafted from the ranks of classroom teachers. These "selected" teachers were assigned tasks of guidance and vocational planning for students. This tradition of selecting school counselors from among certified classroom teachers was the norm until the rapid expansion of public school enrollments during the 1980s. The postwar **baby boom** of the 1950s and 1960s resulted in an expansion in the population of school-aged students that occurred at a time when state standards for certification as a school counselor became more complex. In the 1950s and 1960s it was possible for a teacher to become a school counselor without taking time off from teaching. Certification as a school counselor required only that interested teachers complete a number of inservice graduate courses during the summers and after school. The requirement for school counselors to complete a graduate degree and a supervised **internship** was not added to the standards for certification in most states until the 1970s.

The problem of finding counselors during the mini–baby boom (*boomlett* or *echo boom*) of the 1980s was evident in the problem of finding experienced teachers who wanted to begin a graduate program in school counseling. Graduate programs for counselor certification require teachers to take a semester or two off from their jobs to complete a supervised internship. In all but a handful of states, school counselors must also pass a mandatory certification examination. A result of these upgraded state certification requirements was a shortage of school counselors. Most states found it necessary to abandon the traditional requirement for counselors of first being certified as teachers. Only eight states (Iowa, Kansas, Louisiana, Nebraska, North Dakota, Oregon, Rhode Island, and Texas) and the District of Columbia continue to require that school counselors hold a valid teaching certificate and/or have teaching experience (ASCA, 2008).

Of course, having a license to be a school counselor is one thing; getting hired by a school principal is quite another. Job descriptions posted by the human resources offices of school systems are almost always purposefully vague on this question of teaching experience. Job descriptions typically require job candidates for a school counseling position to have between one and three years of **relevant experience**. This use of the term *relevant* provides the school's principal with great flexibility in making a hiring choice.[2] A principal may view only classroom teaching to be relevant, thereby excluding other highly qualified job candidates. For an example from a posted job description, see Case in Point 2.1.

CASE IN POINT 2.1

If a school board and or school district superintendent wishes to be up-front about the need for a new counselor to be a teacher, this requirement may appear in the job posting. The following is from an Internet job posting:

Position: *School Counselor*

Location: *B.A. Middle School*

Requirements: *Candidates must hold a valid North Carolina certificate as a school counselor and must be certified to teach in the state.*

The school system does not discriminate against any person on the basis of race, religion, sex, color, national origin, citizenship status, age, or handicap in its educational and employment programs.

Thought Questions. If you do not have a background as a classroom teacher, what aspects of your background would you emphasize in a job interview for a position as a school counselor with a skeptical school principal?

What steps can a nonteacher take to provide the experience base that many school administrators hope to find in job candidates for positions in school counseling?

After a person is hired as a school counselor, there is always the possibility that the school will experience an enrollment decline and need to cut the size of the professional staff. Under collective bargaining agreements, this process, **reduction in force (RIF)**, is carried out using a **seniority system**.[3] Having more than one certification (e.g., teaching and counseling) can protect a counselor's employment during the lean times.

The argument for having school counselors who have had classroom teaching experience prior to becoming counselors is usually based on "communication and credibility." This argument is made in reference to four of the five **stakeholder groups** with whom school counselors work. These groups are students, their parents, teachers, other educational specialists, and school administrators. The group for whom a counselor's background is not likely to be an issue includes people in the wider community.

Counselors' Backgrounds

Research on the question of the value of prior teaching experience is one at the heart of a bigger question of what it takes to be an effective school counselor. In a qualitative study of graduate students completing their school counseling internships, Jean Peterson and her colleagues found that interns with prior teaching experience had fewer problems in communicating, establishing their credibility, and in making presentations to classroom groups of students than was true of intern school counselors without prior teaching experience (Peterson, Goodman, Keller, & McCauley, 2004). However, Peterson et al. reported that the altered work environment of school counselors was a surprise to interns who had been teachers. Interns with teaching backgrounds were nonplused by the lack of formal structures and routines for school counselors. School counselor interns found they began to understand the school's culture for the first time. These interns were also surprised to find that they developed new attitudes toward classroom teachers and the educational process. This awareness of the existence of a culture of teachers within the school, and another of students, was not a distinction that they noticed when they were teachers themselves.

The lack of a rigid schedule and formal requirements for school counselors was not a surprise for interns who had never taught in a public school. Counseling interns who did not have teaching backgrounds found that classroom management and communication with other professionals in the school was surprisingly difficult and more complex than what they were prepared to find. Nonteaching-background interns assumed that there was a school culture, and they used their professional skills to define an appropriate role within it.

More recently, Nancy Bringman and Sang Min Lee (2008) reported that new middle school counselors with prior teaching experience had less difficulty teaching developmental lessons to classroom groups of students than was true of new counselors without prior teaching experience. However, that advantage washed out with several years of experience.

This implies that the advantage of having spent a few years as a teacher prior to becoming a counselor makes the job of a new counselor a bit easier. Yet, after a few years on the job, any advantage for counselors with prior teaching experience disappears.

Supervision of Intern Counselors

Jean S. Peterson and Connie Deuschle (2006) proposed that school counselor interns should be provided with an especially intense form of supervision to assist them in overcoming problems inherent in not having had a teaching background. Components of this intense supervisory model include information, immersion, observation, structure, and awareness. *Information* refers to providing site supervisors and school administrators with research information about trends in counseling certification and the research on the effectiveness of counselors without teaching experience. *Immersion* implies that graduate students in school counseling who have not been teachers should get early and ongoing field placement experiences in public and/or charter schools, starting with their first graduate class.[4]

The third component of **Peterson and Deuschle's model** is *observation*. This is the need for future interns to make behavioral observations of children and adolescents in school settings. They should be taught the research skills of an anthropologist and be required to study the culture of their placement school prior to starting their internship experience. Special attention should be paid to the relationship among counselors of a school, other specialists, and the school's administrators.

The need for *structure* is another component of quality supervision, including a structure for the weekly intern–supervisor meeting. Finally is the issue of *awareness*. Good teachers are aware of how children grow and how they express their **ontogenetic** and social development. Counselors, like classroom teachers, should develop classroom management and presentation skills. These two skill sets make up the concept of awareness that school counselor interns need to acquire.

Professionals in a Bargaining Unit

In 41 of 50 states, all professional school employees, including professional school counselors, are expected to become members of a collective **bargaining** unit. The National Education Association was formed during a national meeting of educators in Philadelphia in 1857. Starting with that 1857 meeting, and during the next 70 years, the faculty and administration of higher education dominated the NEA (Keck, 2009). During the 20th century, the NEA began to recruit members from basic education. This opened the door for counselors and vocational guidance workers in the schools to become members of a national association of educators.[5] In the 1960s and 1970s one state affiliate after another of the NEA organized as the representative of teachers and other educators for collective bargaining. This created America's largest employee union. The NEA also remained a professional association, setting educational policy and supporting research and writing. Today the NEA boasts membership of 3.2 million and an annual budget of more than $300 million.

The American Federation of Teachers

The domination of the NEA by college faculty made it possible for a new teacher-focused group, the American Federation of Teachers, to gain a toehold. The AFT was formed in the tradition of American trade unions, with educators' welfare as its primary focus. It began at a combined meeting of several local teacher unions in 1916, when Samuel Gompers, President of the American Federation of Labor (AFL), granted the AFT its charter (American Federation of Teachers, 2008). Today there are about 1.4 million AFT members working at all levels of education and in a number of other fields, including nursing.

Counselors and Teacher Unions

A reasonable school counselor may wonder what organizations he or she should join. Membership in the NEA or the AFT can cost a school counselor annual dues (local, state, and national) totaling $1,000 or more. This is a healthy number and one that could preclude a new school counselor from affording membership in national counseling and school counseling organizations.

It is unfortunately true that school counselors not joining the collective bargaining unit (NEA or AFT) may become ostracized by the teachers of their schools. This is especially true of a counselor who has never been a classroom teacher or works in a school with contract negotiation problems with the school board. The job of being a counselor is difficult to begin with. A decision not to be part of the bargaining unit sets the stage for the counselor being distrusted by a school's faculty. Without the cooperation of the school's faculty, the job of the counselor will be much more difficult.

Yet, it is the position of the author that professional school counselors should also join the American School Counselor Association, and if possible the American Counseling Association (ACA). These organizations are what make school counseling a profession, and they provide school counselors with cutting-edge information about the practice of school counseling. This is also endorsed by the ASCA in the national framework (ASCA/Hatch & Bowers, 2005, pp. 148–149).

> The professional school counselor: (a.) Accepts the policies and procedures for handling ethical violations as a result of maintaining membership in the American School Counselor Association.

A school counseling program based on national standards provides all the necessary elements for students to achieve success in school. This programmatic approach helps school counselors to continuously assess their students' needs, identify barriers and obstacles that may be hindering student success, and advocate programmatic efforts to eliminate these barriers.

Job Descriptions for School Counselors

The ASCA National Model: A Framework for School Counseling Program (ASCA/Hatch & Bowers, 2005) divides the role of school counselors into four core tasks: integrate school counseling into the school's academic mission, provide equitable access to counseling services and programs to all students, identify and provide students with skills and knowledge they need, and evaluate the design and delivery systems for school counseling programs.

The first component as identified by ASCA is that school counseling should be integral to the school's programs and curriculum. This is accomplished by aligning counseling services with the school's philosophy about student learning and the goals that are central to the school's curriculum. This can be done by examining the school's **curriculum map**, within the appropriate grade levels, and identifying methods for linking counseling activities to those curriculum goals.

The following URLs provide examples of school system curriculum maps.

- Grade 5 Reading, Fayette County, Kentucky

    www.kde.state.ky.us/KDE/Instructional+Resources/Curriculum+Docume
    nts+and+Resources/Teaching+Tools/Curriculum+Maps/Fayette+County+
    5th+Grade+Reading+Curriculum+Map.htm

- Grade 7, Content-Based (English as a Second Language), Mathematics, Fitchburg Schools, Massachusetts

  www.doe.mass.edu/ell/cdguide/?section=step4_cbcm

- Grade 9 World History, El Diamante High School, California

  http://visalia.k12.ca.us/teachers/cbrown01/Docs/World-History-Curriculum-Map.pdf

The ASCA national framework recommends that 80% of the available time of a school counselor be spent on direct service delivery to students. In public schools counselors are employed from prekindergarten through high school. Direct service includes individual and group counseling, consultations, and all prevention programs designed to alleviate problematic situations. Services that school counselors provide are delivered through four principle channels. These channels include **responsive counseling,** including one-on-one counseling and other individual interventions with students (see Photo 2.1). The second form of responsive counseling is through family-based interventions. The third involves assisting students plan for their futures, including the provision of traditional guidance services. The final approach involves group counseling within the school and consulting with teachers (ASCA/Hatch & Bowers, 2005).

What School Counselors Do

Various approaches to service delivery by school counselors can occur at every level, from prekindergarten through high school graduation. An integrated PK–12 approach to counseling can improve achievement and the social development of all students (Toppo, 2010). In PK–12 organizations providing counseling services there is a changing pattern or focus for the school counselor across different grade levels.

At all grade levels the school's counselor is at point for the early identification of students who may be at risk. In prekindergarten, this may take the form of spotting

PHOTO 2.1   High School Counselor and Student

SOURCE: Can Stock Photo Inc/Lisafx.

possible **child abuse** (see Chapter 9) or identifying students who may be experiencing **developmental delays.** Intake and record maintenance is another PK–12 activity for counselors, as are the tasks associated with encouraging parent engagement with the school.

The number of detained people for immigration law violations increased 45% between 2003 and 2008. This clear trend toward increased enforcement of immigration laws and the subsequent impact on young children and school students is patent (Cervantes & Lincroft, 2010). By the fall of 2010 the Department of Homeland Security had no policy recommendation in place about children that may end up in the child welfare system if their parents are deported. This issue continues to be one resolved on a case-by-case basis by federal magistrates handling the immigration cases. See Case in Point 2.2 for recent challenges of counseling children of undocumented immigrants.

CASE IN POINT 2.2

The delivery of counseling services is a special challenge for counselors working with a large population of ethnic and language minority children of undocumented immigrants. In 2009, one of every 15 students enrolled in American public schools had one or both parents who were undocumented aliens (Passel & Cohn, 2009). Only 1.5 million children are themselves undocumented, while 4 million children are American citizens by natural birthright even though they have undocumented parents. The U.S. Immigration and Customs Enforcement Service describes these families as having **mixed status**. In some states with a larger Hispanic population, the percentage of public school students with one or more undocumented parents is 1 out of 6 (Nevada) and 1 out of 7 (California) (Ferriss, 2009). These undocumented parents are the most difficult group to engage in school-based activities. Such parents have a natural, albeit unfortunate, fear of all institutions established by the government, including public schools.

School counselors should avoid placing their office in a position of being seen as an extension of federal enforcement. Yet, school counselors may not violate federal or state laws. One solution can be to employ virtual conferences with parents who are uncomfortable or afraid to enter the school building to meet with the school counselor and/or other educators. If the parents have no Internet access, this type of virtual conference can be done through computers at the community center, church, or local library. Establishing these alternative lines for communication between parents and their child's school is an important part of being a school counselor.

Thought Questions. In 2010, hardliner opponents to the natural birthright of a newborn to citizenship in the United States were called into question. Many conservative thinkers are opposed to what Senator Lindsey Graham (R) of South Carolina called "anchor babies."

The view is that children born to undocumented aliens in the United States are not U.S. citizens but citizens of their parents' homeland. Also in 2010, a state senator in Arizona, Russell Pearce (R), and state representative, John Kavanagh (R), introduced legislation requiring the birth certificates of newborn children of undocumented parents be modified to indicate their status as children of illegal aliens.

What is your position on this policy issue? How can you as a school counselor prevent your feelings from having an impact on how you approach both hardliners and those who are undocumented in your school's community? What steps can you take to assist the children of undocumented parents to have a normal school experience?

The formation of student assistance teams (SATs), sometimes called **instructional support teams (ISTs)**, is another PK–12 activity conducted to help individual students. Consulting with parents, helping in the transition between school levels, and placing students into appropriate instructional levels are other ongoing activities at all grade levels. Additional PK–12 activities involve monitoring and advocating for students with special educational needs and the maintenance of up-to-date and accurate student testing and intervention records (ASCA/Hatch & Bowers, 2005, p. 147).

Interpersonal counseling can be provided to students at every educational level. In prekindergarten and primary grades it may take the form of **structured play**. There are literally hundreds of publishers that provide elementary school counselors with the **psycho-dramatic toys** needed to provide this form of counseling intervention. The key to the successful use of these counseling approaches is preparation of the environment and the training and competence of the counselor.

As students improve in their language skills and become better able to introspect, they also become able to have one-on-one counseling sessions. These **verbal counseling** sessions can follow one of several models and approaches available for use by school counselors (see Chapter 6).

Career Education and Vocational Guidance

Another major area for school counselors is in providing leadership in **career education** programs for elementary and middle schools. These programs include teaching students how to identify various occupations that are open for them to explore and learn more about. During these activities, counselors provide students with tools needed to assess what various occupations and vocations require in terms of education and preparation. Career education is normally scheduled for about two weeks in a school and provides a time when school counselors are expected to plan and present formal classroom lessons and conduct classroom discussions. Offering students the opportunity to use computer databases to freely explore career possibilities is a central feature of this process. The logistics of this can involve the school's educational technology team, the school librarian, and the school's counselors (see Chapter 13).

Data Management and Action Research

The ASCA National Model also presents expectations for school counselors to be able to provide systematic evaluations of their counseling program (School Counselor Performance Standards Numbers 11 & 12; ASCA/Hatch & Bowers, 2005, p. 65). It also requires counselors to make policy decisions and implement programs based on careful analysis of school-based data. Educational researchers use the term **action-based research** to describe small local research efforts that provide answers to specific questions and can lead to making optimal changes in programs and procedures. (See Chapter 14 for a discussion and model for evaluation of counseling programs.)

Transcending the national framework developed by the ASCA, all state education departments require school counselors to complete graduate study in educational measurement and basic educational research. All too often these are areas of study that graduate students in school counseling tend to enjoy less than the more clinical skills-oriented classes. Yet, it is the school counselor to whom others in the school will turn for expert answers to technical questions. This skill on the part of school counselors is addressed in the ASCA national framework (ASCA/Hatch & Bowers, 2005, p. 49). Case in Point 2.3 describes a real-life example of an elementary school counselor using school data to solve a local research problem. (See Chapter 10 for a discussion of data-based research.)

CASE IN POINT 2.3

A school counselor found an anomaly in the school's test data. She conducted a small action research study to find the likely reason for the low scores on a mandatory spelling test for the middle school students. The scores on spelling were significantly lower than all the average scores on other areas of achievement being assessed. This research was done by examining the school's spelling curriculum to determine how this skill was taught in the sixth and seventh grades. The next step involved examining the test developed by the state to measure spelling skills. This research took a step frequently overlooked by school administrators. The counselor checked to ensure that all the test's modalities were familiar to all students. In this middle school, teachers taught spelling by having students memorize spelling lists.

Also, classroom teachers measured students by having them write down dictated words. However, the mandated standardized tests measured spelling achievement by having students mark all the words on a printed passage that were not spelled correctly. The students never saw this method for testing spelling achievement; therefore, they could not score well, no matter how capable they may have been at spelling. Their low scores did not indicate what they knew, only their lack of familiarity with that particular **modality of testing.**

Thought Question. Consider the data that school counselors have access to for analytical problem solving in a school setting. Make a list of all those data sources.

Advocating for Students

School counselors can easily fall into the trap of filling each day with the good, the bad, and the ugly.[6] There is always a group of students in need of individual attention and support who will spend an inordinate amount of time with the school's counselor. The counselor must find ways of ensuring that all students are provided with necessary services and that there is equitable access for all to the range of counseling services (ASCA/Hatch & Bowers, 2005, pp. 13–14).

Student Stress and Social Networking

There once was a day when schoolchildren could escape the social stressors of school when they went home. At home, in an unquestioning environment of complete acceptance, young children and adolescents could recharge and repair any psychological damage done by their peers and others during the school day. For some students, the need for their home sanctuary is acute. Many students must take the bus ride home from school in the company of a cabal of bullying peers. This experience is the cap on an otherwise miserable day of avoiding bullies and trying to keep up with their peers in class. For these highly stressed students, the safe harbor of home is desperately needed.

The advent of e-mail, Facebook, Twitter, MySpace, and a growing list of networking pages has removed this final safe harbor for students. Now they must be on stage 24/7. In 2009, research by the Nielsen Co. found that the average American teenager sends and receives 2,272 text messages each month. That is approximately 80 per day, or about 5 for every hour the student is awake (Hafner, 2009).

School counselors are caring adults who can help children and adolescents make sense of all the pressure and cope with the sources of stress. It must be assumed that all students feel the stress of growing up in a constantly changing world where there are few escapes from the constant evaluation by others.

CARTOON 2.1 "At Least Ten Texts"

SOURCE: © Zits-Zits Partnership. King Features Syndicate.

This may take the form of providing group counseling programs that focus on **coping mechanisms,** or helping a student find a teacher who can explain a homework problem, or even by finding a subsidized medical clinic for a family in need. **Advocating for students** implies a proactive and positive approach to counseling.

Counselors should get out of their offices and see the school with the eyes of a cultural anthropologist. When a counselor learns the culture of the school's students, it becomes possible to find ways to help students without their even knowing help is occurring. Suggesting seating patterns to a teacher and organizing counseling groups with a selected collection of students are such methods. Advocacy for students can also lead a school counselor to provide expert testimony in family court and before court masters (see Photo 2.2).

● COUNSELOR'S ROLE WITH MEMBERS OF THE PUPIL SERVICE TEAM

The school counselor is not alone on the school's faculty as an educator with a highly specialized job. Public schools have a number of other well-educated specialists who work to support educational programs of students. Many times it is the school counselor who is responsible to coordinate the specialists' work, collect information, and provide tracking data about individual students. Collectively these professionals make up what is called the **pupil service team** for a school.

The many tasks of the school counselor and the centrality of the role of the counselor have led to a recommendation that there be one school counselor for every 250 students in a school (ASCA, 2008). Unlike pupil-to-student ratios, parents usually do not know how many students are assigned to each counselor. For that reason the actual national average **caseload** for public school counselors is 460 (ASCA, 2009). In 2007 the state of California reported a statewide average of one school counselor for every 966 students (Rado, 2009). And in 2009 Illinois had a counselor-to-student ratio of 1,047 to 1.[7]

School Psychologist

Like school counselors, school psychologists are state-certified professionals assigned to work as part of the pupil service team. School psychologists are highly educated, with graduate education credits that total to a sum about equal to that of a person holding a doctorate. However, only a small proportion of school psychologists have gone on to earn doctoral degrees. School psychologists have responsibility to provide advanced diagnostic testing within the school and to serve as key members of all committees that could make an entitlement decision. The National Association of School Psychologists recommends that a psychologist have a caseload maximum of 1,000 students (Feinberg, Nuijens, & Canter, 2005). This goal is one rarely achieved in the real world of public schools, where caseloads are likely to be twice that recommendation.

Counseling techniques and psychotherapy are included in the graduate curriculum used to educate school psychologists. These skills can rarely be used in the fast-paced world of assessment and report writing that dominates the life of most school psychologists. In most states, the entitlement decision to change the placement or IEP of a student must be approved by a school psychologist who has been part of the student's evaluation committee.

PHOTO 2.2 School Counselor Providing Testimony in Court

SOURCE: Comstock/Courtroom Scene/Thinkstock.

School psychologists may provide **compliance testing** and periodic reevaluations of all students receiving special education services. They may also provide brief psychotherapy for students in crisis and provide faculty and staff inservice educational programs.

School Nurse

School nursing is a bachelor's degree–level (BSN) certificate requiring a valid license as a registered nurse (RN) and state certification following completion of several education classes. This rule is in place in about a third of the states. Other states require school nurses hold licenses only as registered nurses. The role of the school nurse is one that is growing and is critically important to the school. Passage of P.L. 94–142 (1975), the **Education of All Handicapped Children Act,** and the passage of P.L. 99–457 (1986), the extension of special education to younger children, changed the rules for the role of school nurses.

Today the school nurse is the school's medical professional with responsibilities for dispensing all prescription medications to students while in school, maintaining the cleanliness and sanitation of catheters and collection systems, monitoring the healing of wounds, and following up with students who are receiving powerful medications. As the school's public health officer, the nurse also maintains immunization status records and serves as the advocate for a healthy school (Wong, Hockenberry-Eaton, Wilson, Winkelstein, & Schwartz, 2001). The nurse provides screenings and cooperates in health education programs for students.

School Librarian

The school librarian's job description now also encompasses the role of media specialist for the school. As is the case with other areas of specialization, rules for certification as a school library media specialist vary from state to state. Some states require that all school librarian media specialists start their careers as classroom teachers and earn their specialist certification through postgraduate study. Other states provide a bachelor's degree–level certification option based on an undergraduate major in library media services. A few states require a master's degree in library science (MLS).

The school librarian media specialist has an important role to play in encouraging reading, helping to develop research skills, and encouraging parent involvement (Abilock, 2005). School counselors can use the knowledge of school librarian media specialists to identify appropriate literature for students in crisis. This method of using fiction to help students see possible resolutions to their personal crisis situations is known by various names, including **biblio-therapy**. The following web page provides a list of titles useful in bibliotherapy with elementary age students. This list has been arranged by problem areas: www.best-childrens-books.com/bibliotherapy.html.

School Reading Specialist

Reading specialists, also called reading teachers, are educational specialists who have original teaching certificates and have completed programs of graduate study in reading and reading remediation. As reading problems make up the vast majority of all learning problems that students experience in elementary school and beyond, reading specialists have a critical role to play in the academic life of a school. (See Photo 2.3.)

While oral language acquisition is a natural process quickly achieved by most young students (Chomsky, 2006), the acquisition of reading skills is neither intuitive nor easy, reflecting the lack of a biological imperative for reading. Five percent of all students learn to read without formal instruction, and 35% have little difficulty learning to read in school. Forty percent of all students learn to read only with considerable effort, and 20% find learning to read the most difficult task they have ever faced (Lyon, 1998; Michigan Department of Education, 2008). Severe cases of reading disability occur in about 4% of all students and can involve mirror-image (dyslexic) reading (American Psychiatric Association, 1994).

The ubiquity of reading problems makes reading specialists a major player on both student assistance teams (504 committees) and on committees when an entitlement decision may be made. School counselors can learn much about students at risk for serious learning problems by meeting and discussing educational plans with the reading specialist.

PHOTO 2.3   A Reading Specialist Helping a Student

SOURCE: © Istock Image/Monkey Business Images.

Special Educators

Special education teachers are certified by state departments of education after completing undergraduate degrees in special education and passing the states' mandated teacher assessment tests. An increasing number of certified classroom teachers in elementary education and other disciplines add state certification in special education through programs of graduate study or by having two undergraduate majors.

Teachers with special education certification teach students with mental and/or physical disabilities. Special education teachers with specializations in sensory disabilities teach students who have visual and or hearing losses. There is also state certification for students with college degrees in speech pathology who have completed either graduate or undergraduate programs in speech education. These speech teachers must also have completed internships and passed the state teacher examinations.

Students with special education needs must be evaluated before an entitlement decision can be made about their educational assistance requirements. Only following an evaluation process can the entitlement decision be made. This process involves the school counselor, who may have responsibility to call the meetings together and schedule all necessary evaluations of the child. The school counselor may also have responsibility for the ongoing monitoring of students receiving special education services and the scheduling of periodic reevaluations as prescribed on the students' education plans (IEPs). (See Chapter 7 for information about IEP development.)

Most students receive special education services in their regular classrooms. This process is referred to as **inclusion**. In large elementary schools, one or more classrooms at each grade level will be designated as **inclusion classrooms**. Teachers in the designated inclusion classroom teach a combination of students without learning problems and special education students. The teachers may or may not hold certification in special education, but all inclusion teachers are certified in elementary or early childhood education. The special education teacher spends part of each day collaborating with the inclusion teacher and doing direct instruction to small groups of students who need learning support.

At the high school level, the special education teachers work to assist students make a successful transition into their adult roles and life after high school. This is done by teaching adolescents with disabilities a special class featuring topics on self-determination, adaptive skills for independent living, and **transition planning** (Hardman, Drew, & Egan, 2008).

Contracted Specialists

School districts provide specialized help for students with special needs if those disabilities and remediation programs are spelled out on the student's IEP.

These services include, among others, physical and occupational therapists. These professionals are usually not certified by the state education departments but by the appropriate licensing boards of the states' departments of state. Each of these specialists is required to have graduate degrees in their specialization fields.

CONSULTING AND COLLABORATING ●

School counselors should contribute their specialized knowledge and skills to improve the school and its programs and assist individual students by working in partnership and collaboration with other professionals. The consultation role extends to working with and through parents of students in the school (see Chapter 11).

It has often been quipped, "A consultant is someone who comes in, borrows your watch, tells you what time it is, keeps the watch, and charges you an exorbitant fee." That is possibly true for external consultants. A school counselor should play the role of consultant while working within the school. This point about the counselor's role as a consultant is emphasized in the national framework (ASCA/Hatch & Bowers, 2005, p. 42). The counselor must always be collaborative, working in parallel to the person being assisted, while avoiding being prescriptive and directive. The counselor's immediate goal is to have the person receiving the consultation buy into the ideas being proposed. The ultimate goal is to provide help for a student or group of students (the true clients) by working with and through other people.

Counselors can be instrumental in bringing other people in the life of a student together as a team working together to effect positive change for the student. This is a systemic approach to school counseling, and it can be highly effective (White & Mullis, 1998).

It is important to recognize the value of the time contributed by teachers or parents who meet with a school counselor. Teachers have precious little free time during the school day, and parents may miss time at their jobs. For that reason it is critical for the counselor to give sincere thanks to those with whom they meet. Consultation meetings with parents should be kept positive. Tell the parents good points about the child. Encourage them to tell you about their child at home. The problem that occurs at school may not be present at home. Be gentle in probing to find the extent of the child's problem outside of school. Ask about solutions that the parent has attempted and their outcome. Then turn the discussion to other possible solutions and approaches and encourage the parents to actively participate in developing a plan of action.

Consultation meetings with teachers can start with complimentary comments about the teacher's reputation or skills, or it can get down to the business at hand. Many times teachers are drawn to the school's counselor for consultation about problematic students (Baker, Robichaud, Dietrich, Wells, & Schreck, 2009). The counselor is not normally viewed as a threatening professional as are some principals and curriculum coordinators. Many times teachers just want to talk over a problem. Counselors should make it as easy as possible for teachers to "accidentally bump into them." This can mean having unending cups of coffee in the faculty dining area at each lunch period when teachers have their lunch breaks.

Consultation with teachers or parents may meet with resistance. To reduce this likelihood it is important to first establish good rapport with the person being consulted and frame ideas in terms that are compatible with his or her value system. Resistance to change is normal in most human beings, and even accepting the idea that there is a problem to be solved may be resisted. Always reframe such setbacks and look for other approaches. (Resistance and consultation models are discussed in Chapter 11.)

Counselor Consultation for Positive School Climate

There is no better place to work than in a school with a happy faculty and engaged, hard-working students. This is the essence of a positive **school climate**. Two professional educational specialists most responsible for any school's climate are the school's counselor and principal. The school counselor is generally included as a member of the **leadership team** of the school. Frequently the counseling suite of offices is co-located near the administrative offices. At the heart of any successful school is high-quality leadership. Both building principals and the schools' counselors have enormous roles to play in creating the educational climates for successful schools (Cantwell, 2007).

From the counselor's point of view, poor school climate can result in a general feeling of malaise and a dread of going to work, while a positive climate provides a sense of being part of a close-knit professional community. This latter climate type is accompanied by feelings of professional fulfillment and pride. For school counselors, school climate is the perceived total of all interactions between all people (adults and students) with whom the counselor interacts. The role of the counselor is to work to keep these interactions productive, positive, and professional. The perception of climate by members of the school's community sets the tone for how both staff and faculty approach work and how they view their careers (Goleman, 2006). Schools with positive climates have also been found to be safe schools where acts of violence and vandalism are minimal (Hernández & Seem, 2004).

School counselors can be proactive in improving the climates of their schools. Things that work to produce good climate include clearly communicating school goals and the fair and equitable enforcement of school policies with all students. Schools where rules appear to students to be capricious or arbitrary tend to have more disruptive behaviors by students and lower levels of teacher morale (Hernández & Seem, 2004). Leadership teams in highly successful schools work to open lines of communication with students, teachers, and families. No policy is arbitrary or unevenly applied. These school leaders work to maintain a consistently high morale among faculty by being enthusiastic and optimistic about the learning potential of each student (Heck, Larson, & Marcoulides, 1990).

Counselors should always model positive behaviors for both students and faculties. Problems must never be allowed to appear intractable or go without resolution. Counselors and other members of the school's leadership should always look for solutions through cooperation and open collaboration with all stakeholders.

SCHOOL COUNSELING AND THE LAW AND CASE LAW   ●

The role of all professionals working in public education, including school counselors, is not just guided by the canons and framework of professional societies such as the ASCA but must be structured within applicable laws and regulations. There are three main sources that provide mandatory guidance for schools and their programs. These are laws passed by state and federal legislatures, opinions and regulations imposed by state and federal courts, and regulations made by state and federal departments and agencies. It is likely the least understood are the courts and the huge role they play in setting policy and requiring changes in procedures.

All state courts are subservient to federal courts on matters having to do with human rights of children and their parents. Federal courts normally use the U.S. Constitution and federal legislation to guide their decisions. The ultimate authority for both federal and state courts is the U.S. Constitution. One amendment to the constitution commonly used as the source of guidance for federal court decisions related to school matters is the 14th Amendment. This amendment has been given the sobriquet the *equal protection amendment*.

U.S. Constitution, Amendment 14, Section 1:

No State shall make or enforce any law which shall abridge the privileges or immunities of citizens of the United States; nor shall any State deprive any person of life, liberty, or property, without due process of law; nor deny any person within its jurisdiction to the equal protection of the laws. Ratified July 9, 1868.

Students With Disabilities

More than 40 years ago, the 14th Amendment provided the basis for a court decision to mandate that all students deserve a free and appropriate education.[8] Before the 1970s, public schools could, and often did, refuse to provide free public school educations for students who had significant disabilities. Students with less obvious disabilities were allowed to languish in regular education classrooms. Eventually these students dropped out of school. If parents of a child with a disability wanted to ensure that their child was appropriately educated, it was their responsibility to find a private school and pay the tuition. The public schools believed they had no role to play in the placement decision or education of students with disabilities.

Those policies changed with a federal court case known as *Parents Association for Retarded Children (PARC) v. the Commonwealth of Pennsylvania* (1971). In October 1971, Pennsylvania accepted a consent decision mandating that "all children, handicapped or otherwise, are entitled to a free and appropriate public education."

One important role a counselor should play is ensuring that the needs of special education students are never slighted or overlooked (see Chapter 7). By being proactive and advocating for special education students and their educational needs, a school counselor can reduce the potential for bitter recriminations and legal challenges. As the real Case in Point 2.4 demonstrates, if the school counselor consulted with the teacher, the counselor may have prevented the damage that occurred in the lives of students and the teacher. The Case in Point describes how the education for a student with special needs can go very wrong.

CASE IN POINT 2.4

Not all educators are prepared to teach in an inclusive classroom. The mix of students with special needs and students without disabilities in the same early childhood classroom requires great patience and a very skillful teacher.

On May 28, 2008, local news carried the story of a kindergarten teacher in Port Saint Lucie, Florida. She was frustrated by the behavior of a disabled student. She had the student stand in front of the kindergarten class and asked each class member to tell the student why they did not like him. The teacher then belittled the problematic kindergartener herself. Next she asked the other 16 kindergarteners in her class to vote on whether the offending student should be sent out of the classroom or be allowed to remain. The kindergarten class voted 14 to 2 to have the student removed.

The child's parent was not amused by this approach to behavior management. During a stormy conference with the school's principal, the child's mother revealed the boy had recently been diagnosed as having Asperger's disorder. The kindergarten teacher defended her behavior as an appropriate disciplinary approach. The administration of the Port Saint Lucie School District did not agree, and the teacher was disciplined. Meanwhile, a nationwide online petition by parents of children with Asperger's disorder collected thousands of names of people demanding action by the Saint Lucie County School District (Fox News, 2008). Later, after pressure by minority rights advocates, including the NAACP, the teacher was reinstated.

Thought Questions. What steps would you have taken in that Florida elementary school if you were the elementary school counselor in that building? Would you initiate a **tertiary prevention** program including inservice workshops for teachers? If yes, what themes would they present? If no, explain how you propose to prevent this from occurring again.

Subsequent **case law** has made it illegal to change the status of any student without providing the student and his or her family with procedural due process (*Gross et al. v. Lopez et al.,* 1975). This decision of the Supreme Court of the United States provided all schoolchildren with a guarantee of constitutionally protected rights. This also means a student cannot be expelled from school unless there has been an open hearing during which the child's parents are permitted to provide evidence and be represented by counsel. Even so, the decision of a local school board sitting as a judicial panel can be appealed to state and federal courts.[9] Additionally, all placement decisions, including whether or not special education is to be provided to a student, must make provisions for the student's parents to have input into the process.

Dangerous Counselees

In 1974 the Supreme Court of California heard the case of Tatiana Tarasoff, who was killed by her jealous former boyfriend, Prosenjit Poddar. Both students were graduate students at the University of California when Prosenjit became infatuated with Tatiana, who was not interested in him. He went to the university's counseling center for help coping with his longing for Tatiana. In counseling, Prosenjit revealed to a counselor that he fantasized the murder of Tatiana. Later he did kill her, confessed to police, and was convicted of manslaughter. The Tarasoff family sued the university, the campus police, and the counseling center and staff. The California Supreme Court decided in favor of the Tarasoff family and held that counselors and psychologists have a responsibility to provide threatened persons fair warning to avert foreseeable danger being posed by a client (Isaacs, 2003).

This ruling immediately affected school counselors. Since the California decision in 1974, the courts in 17 other states have replicated this principle of providing warning of a foreseeable danger to other people.[10] In 1986 the American School Counselor Association revised its ethical position statement to include the following: "Confidentiality must not be abridged by the counselor except when there is clear and present danger to the student and/or other persons." The American Psychological Association changed its position on confidentiality in 1981 with the following revision: "Psychologists reveal confidential information to others only with the consent of the person or the person's legal representative, except in those unusual circumstances where not to do so would result in a clear danger to the person or others" (Jacob & Hartshorne, 2003).

Counselors in elementary schools are no longer immune from this point of law and ethics. Young children today can pose a significant danger to themselves and others. A 6-year-old boy in Flint, Michigan, shot and killed a classmate in his first grade classroom (Pelley, 2000). In the spring of 2008, 11 third grade students in Waycross, Georgia, were suspended from school for plotting to murder their classroom teacher (Levine, Chambers, & Ibanga, 2008).

The *Tarasoff* case and the revised ethical statement of the American School Counselor Association provide guidance to counselors when a child brings a dangerous weapon to school, threatens violence to students and or teachers, warns of an imminent suicide, or other dangerous acts or ideations. The problems for counselors with the laws and confidentiality of students' private information extend into many domains, including students with AIDS, child abuse, family drug use, sexual abuse, and pregnancy.

Privacy and the Counseling Relationship

There are two other levels to the issue of confidentiality that a school counselor must be aware of. One is defined by federal law and deals with all school records about a child. School records, including test scores, attendance, and teacher's roll books, are legal documents that must be maintained until a student graduates or turns 18 years old. At the age of 18 years, a student achieves a measure of adult status and replaces his parents as the party having the power to decide the disposition of his school records. Parents of 18-year-old high school students may only see their children's report card or test scores with the approval of their young adult children.[11]

Before that age, school counselors must know the rights of parents in matters of school records. These rights were spelled out in 1974 in an amendment added to the Freedom of Information Act by Senator James Buckley (R-NY). The rights of students under this **Buckley Amendment** (Family Educational Rights and Privacy Act [FERPA]) are provided with two dimensions of privacy. At one level are limitations as to what type of information can be collected and maintained. The second involves limitations as to who can access that information.

FERPA provides parents with the right to access their child's educational records and to have those records presented and explained in a language they understand. This also requires that schools honor parental requests to have their children's educational records explained without confusing technical jargon. Parents have the right to add explanatory material to their child's record. At the request of a parent, schools are obligated to provide test materials and recording sheets used to collect data. That access does not require that parents be given a copy of the test booklets; they are just permitted to review the material.

Confidential Records

Counselors and other educators are not permitted to collect data on topics considered unrelated to the student's education, including parent information about sexual practices (except sexual abuse), political affiliations, mental disease or disorders, illegal and self-incriminating behavior including drug and alcohol abuse, **privileged communications** (lawyers), family or personal income, and religious practice.

FERPA also limits who can have access to a student's records. As a rule of thumb, only education personnel with a legitimate need to see the records should have access. One exception to this is the access that legitimate educational researchers can have to educational data.[12] School counselors must produce student records when they are subpoenaed or ordered by a court or when they are needed to protect the student's safety or the safety of others.[13]

As the student transitions from building to building in the school system, his or her old records should be pruned of unnecessary information. That which is beyond the current need (attendance, grades, test scores) should be thoroughly destroyed.

Related legislation, the **Grassley Amendment** of 1999, requires that parents give their permission before their children are asked to answer any survey or be part of an observational analysis or the focus of an evaluation effort. (See Exhibit 2.1 for a sample release form for parents.) This law prohibits asking any student about:

1. Sexual behavior
2. Family member's income
3. Psychological problems in the family
4. Politics or political affiliation
5. Illegal behaviors and/or demeaning behaviors by self or family members
6. Confidences shared with lawyers, clergy, or physicians
7. Appraisal or critical evaluation of family members or family friends

EXHIBIT 2.1   Sample Release Form for School Records

Request Date ____/____/_____ Date Records Sent ____/____/_____

I hereby authorize the **Granite Rock School** to immediately release the records of:

_____

Last, First, and Middle Initial

Records to be released include:

_____

_____

_____

_____

_____

_____

These records should be sent to:

_____

_____

Parent Signature _____

Date ____/____/_____

Name of Employee Sending Records _____

Initial _____

Privileged Communication

The second dimension of privacy that school counselors must understand is the concept of privileged communication. The right to have counseling considered as privileged communication can only be granted by legislation and case law. While a court can demand confidential information, privileged communications are shielded. All but a handful of states have approved license laws for professional counselors in practice. These states have also granted licensed counselors the right to "privileged communications" with their clients. Only a few states have extended this concept to include school counselors (Glosoff & Pate, 2002). The privileged communications are the right of the counselee, not the counselor. Only the counselee (or parent of the child) can waive the privilege once given.

Confidentiality is a promise made by the counselor to protect the privacy of the student and what is said during the counseling relationship. This promise must be made to each student entering into a counseling relationship, and the counselor is obligated to explain the limits of that promise prior to beginning counseling. The limits to all such promises involve court orders, parental demands, and dangers to self and others.

Thus, professional counselors working outside of schools are likely to be able to provide counselees with the assurance of privileged communications. Most school counselors can only offer student-clients a promise of confidential communications. This promise is one that may be voided by the child's parents, the *Tarasoff* ruling, and court orders.

Testing Laws

Another area where case law has had an impact on the job of school counselors is with **high-stakes tests**. Florida was among the first states to require that students pass a graduation test. In that state, before a student could be awarded a high school diploma, he or she had to pass a state literacy examination. This was challenged in 1978 when 10 African American students from Hillsborough County, Florida, failed their mandated competency tests. These students and various sponsoring organizations sued the state after the 10 low-scoring students were denied high school diplomas. The plaintiffs argued that the disproportional number of minority students who had been denied a diploma was a violation of the 14th Amendment of the U.S. Constitution.

The resolution of the case, known as *Debra P. v. Turlington*, happened in 1981. The courts ruled in favor of the state of Florida. This ruling came after the court noted the fact that Florida had aligned the test items with the curricula taught in the schools, and that all students had several opportunities to learn what was required to pass the assessment and earn a diploma. Florida awarded those students who failed the assessment **certificates of completion** that allowed them to enroll in adult education through which they could work toward their diplomas.

This same case law, *Debra P. v. Turlington,* is cited as the legal foundation in 27 states now requiring graduation tests. It also makes it legally possible for some states to prevent students who do not score well on a state achievement test from being promoted to the fourth grade.

The issue of denying a high school diploma to students with significant mental and/or physical disabilities and who cannot pass a state-mandated graduation test was resolved shortly after *Debra P. v. Turlington.* In that case from Illinois, a child with disabilities was denied a diploma after failing a graduation test. The parents sued and lost in the case known as *Brookhart v. Illinois State Board of Education* (1983). In *Brookhart* the courts expressed the opinion that school districts' desire to "ensure the value of a high school diploma" is admirable, and that the courts should avoid interfering in educational policy unless a constitutional or statutory right of the student has been clearly violated.

High-stakes tests and their aftermath take up an increasingly large proportion of school counselors' schedules. Parents and students must be carefully informed of the test outcome and consequences. All alternatives must be carefully explored and plans made for each child and adolescent with poor test scores. Teachers may need inservice training to help better understand the standardized scoring model used by the state. School principals may call on counselors to help analyze the school's scores and plan a strategy for future test score improvement.

SUMMARY

Through the 1970s, school counselors were certified classroom teachers who elected to continue their education by studying graduate level guidance and counseling. The growth of the student population and need for more school counselors occurred at a time when state standards for counselors were increased. The result has been the certification of school counselors without prior experience as classroom teachers.

The work of school counselors is multifaceted and involves a huge list of activities. In all ways, school counselors should be positive and proactive advocates for students. One facet of the counselor's job description is to serve as a member of the school's student assistance team. Another is to be ever vigilant for possible cases of child abuse. The Family Educational Rights and Privacy

Act and the Grassley Amendment define other facets of the counselor's job. These laws spell out who has access to student records and what information may be collected about each student.

Few states have extended the right of privileged communications to school counselors. For that reason, school counselors should be open with students and explain the concept of confidentiality in the counseling relationship and the limits that exist for a counselor's confidentiality.

DISCUSSION QUESTIONS

1. What should a school counselor do when he or she experiences a conflict between the wishes of the parents of a child and what the counselor feels is in the child's best interest?

2. What advantages (and disadvantages) are there for schools that hire school counselors who have not had teaching experience and who have never been certified to teach?

3. Use the Internet to determine whether your state extends the concept of privileged communication to the school counselor-to-client relationship. What advantages and disadvantages does the right of privileged communication pose for the school counselor?

4. If you live nearby, call the counselor's office of the high school you graduated from and make an appointment with the counselor. During the meeting ask to see the records the school still maintains on you. Bring your observations to class and discuss these old records about you in terms of how extensive, how accurate, and how useful they still are.

RELATED READINGS

Hardman, M. L., Drew, C. J., & Egan, M. W. (2008). *Human exceptionality: School, community, and family.* New York: Houghton Mifflin.

Hendricks, C. C. (2008). *Improving schools through action research: A comprehensive guide for educators* (2nd ed.). Upper Saddle River, NJ: Allyn & Bacon, Pearson Education.

Remley, T. P., Hermann, M. A., & Huey, W. C. (Eds.). (2003). *Ethical and legal issues in school counseling.* Alexandria, VA: American School Counselor Association.

NOTES

1. Only 9 of the 50 states have laws preventing school counselors and teachers from negotiating conditions of their jobs and compensation. These states with anti–collective bargaining laws are Alabama, Arizona, Arkansas, Colorado, Georgia, North Carolina, Texas, West Virginia, and Wyoming.

2. As is true for all professional educators, the school board, with the advice of the district superintendent, is the official body that hires schools' counselors. The role of the principal is to select the best candidate for the job, and recommend him or her to the school district's superintendent.

3. The day and hour of the school board meeting when the counselor has his or her contract signed is the starting point for the seniority clock.

4. One frequently overlooked method to gain school experience is by serving as a per diem substitute teacher. This option can also assist with the financial needs of full-time graduate students in counseling.

5. Much of the impetus to change from a higher education to basic education organization was the result of the founding of a true "teacher's union," the American Federation of Teachers.

6. My apologies to Sergio Leone for misappropriating the name given to his 1966 movie.

7. Only four states were in compliance with the standard set by the ASCA: Louisiana, New Hampshire, Vermont, and Wyoming.

8. In this law a child is defined as an individual under the age of 21 years and not having earned a high school diploma.

9. In many jurisdictions, school systems that fail to win at court are required to pay all legal fees of the parents that were the plaintiffs in the case.

10. Several states have moved away from providing the legal basis needed to sue for damages when *Tarasoff*-like circumstances occur. These states include Florida, South Carolina, Texas, and Virginia.

11. While not having legal guardianship over the 18-year-old offspring, parents of dependent college students may still claim them for income tax deduction purposes until they are age 24 (Internal Revenue Service, 2009). They may also keep them on the family health insurance plan through the student's 25th year (Thomas, 2010).

12. Since 1991 researchers collecting legitimate data within a school or with schoolchildren must have their research approved by a duly constituted **institutional review board (IRB)**.

13. The only persons from outside the child's family and school personnel who can access all school records without a court order are the recruiters of the U.S. military.

3

Counseling With Young Children, Prekindergarten to Grade 5

OBJECTIVES

By reading and studying this chapter you should acquire the competency to:

- Describe the rapidly evolving role of school counselors in preschools
- Discuss the major types of problems of affect that an elementary school counselor may see among his or her student-clients
- Describe the common stressors for students in early childhood education
- Describe interventions that can be used with young students who are experiencing problems of affect
- Describe the major types of problems with relationships an elementary school counselor is likely to see among his or her student-clients
- Explain the differences among primary, secondary, and tertiary prevention programs that can be employed by school counselors
- Establish an effective primary preventative program for bullying and cyberbullying in the elementary school
- Describe appropriate interventions for use with young students exhibiting acting-out behaviors

● ● ●

❝ If there is anything that we wish to change in the child, we should first examine it and see whether it is not something that could better be changed in ourselves. **❞**

Carl Gustav Jung (1875–1961)

● INTRODUCTION AND THEMES

School counseling is a relatively new education profession, and counseling in elementary and preschools is an even newer concept. The United States is the only Western democracy that has no national mandate for universal preschool education. In many states this gap is being filled by state government mandates for universal preschools.

Primary prevention programs for many of the problems experienced by elementary and preschool students involve identifying **stressors** in the lives of children and finding ways to remove or reduce them. The secondary and tertiary treatments for children focus on providing children with the ego strength and skills needed to resolve problems in their own lives.

Elementary and preschool counselors can establish **therapeutic communication** with young children by employing indirect methods. These indirect communication channels can involve play therapy, story-telling therapy, and other **fantasy-based methods.**

Perhaps the most troubling and pernicious problem an elementary school counselor will be asked to resolve involves bullies. In the past generation, the traditional torment that bullies could cause has been augmented by cyberbullying. At one level, all bullying is criminal behavior that can be punished in family court. At another, it implies the need for a concerted effort by the school and its counselors to prevent the behavior from occurring and to assist victims of harassment by bullies. School-based violence is not limited to the bullying of students but can also involve parents and other outsiders in a school. See Case in Point 3.1 for an example.

CASE IN POINT 3.1

In 2008 on a pleasant January morning in Cape Coral, Florida, the divorced husband of a day care teacher broke into the school where his former wife taught. The school went into lockdown, but the former husband beat down her classroom door. The teacher herded her eight 3-year-olds into the bathroom and asked them to be quiet. When she returned to face her former husband, he shot her to death in the classroom a few feet away from the terrified children huddled in the bathroom. To see press coverage of this tragedy, visit www.naplesnews.com/news/2008/jan/25/one-dead-shooting-daycare-cape-coral/.

Thought Questions. If you were a school counselor working in this school, what immediate steps would you take to help the students in this classroom? What long-range programs or interventions would you provide for these students and their families? What other programs would you initiate for students in other classrooms?

COUNSELING IN EARLY CHILDHOOD AND ELEMENTARY EDUCATION ●

To develop an integrated personality at higher and higher levels; to preserve right mental attitudes; to train in habits of healthful mental activity; to prevent mental disorder. . . . This is the teacher's great function.

William H. Burnham

In 1926 William Burnham was the first to make the case for school counselors to work in elementary schools. Burnham's textbook justified the need for counselors to perform mental health interventions that could be initiated when children were young. Even he did not foresee the possibility of organized counseling programs that begin in preschools and kindergartens and continue throughout all public school grades.

Individual Counseling Services in Early Childhood and Elementary Education

Counseling programs in the schools involve all students and are especially important for students who are at risk or who have medical and/or psychological problems. At one level, the counselor must work to prevent problems and strive to improve the school's culture and psychological climate. At another level, there is a continual stream of problems the counselor must help students resolve. Each day counselors in preschools and elementary schools are faced with numerous problematic behaviors and significant medical and psychological disorders among schoolchildren.

Problematic behaviors and disorders among school-aged children can be divided into five major groups: problems of affect (e.g., **irrational fears**), problems of relationships with others (e.g., bullying), problems of attention and focus (e.g., **attention deficit/hyperactivity disorder [AD/HD]**), problems of human development (e.g., **mental retardation**), and problems of the child's psychoneurology (e.g., **fetal alcohol syndrome**).

The problem areas can overlap, and two or more problems can occur within one child. Careful interventions by counselors during the early childhood and elementary school years can have a positive and lasting impact on young students.

Federal legislation mandates that the full spectrum of mental and physical disorders be addressed using a team approach that may include the elementary and preschool counselor. School counselors are important members of the team and often play critical roles in monitoring services provided to children as well as providing appropriate **counseling interventions**.

Counseling in Preschools

School counselors working in publicly supported preschools are a growing trend that parallels the rapid growth of tax-supported preschool education. The United States is the only industrialized democracy that does not provide universal preschool programs for all young children (Kamerman, 2005). There was a brief flirtation with universal preschool education from 1933 to 1946 (see Case in Point 3.2).

CASE IN POINT 3.2

The crash of the stock markets in October 1929 was followed during the next few years by a great economic depression. The depression resulted in the failure of banks, the closing of industrial plants, and the downsizing of governmental agencies. Another outcome was an unemployment rate of 25% in 1934. In 1932, Franklin Delano Roosevelt was elected to become the 32nd president. His party was given a majority in both houses of Congress, making it able to push recovery programs through to law. The name applied to these initiatives was the "**New Deal**." One of the initiatives of the New Deal was the Works Progress Administration (WPA). (See Photo 3.1 of a WPA nursery.)

In an effort to employ laid-off school teachers, the WPA established nursery schools throughout the country that employed thousands of otherwise out-of-work teachers (Braun & Edwards, 1972).

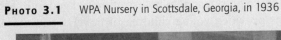

PHOTO 3.1   WPA Nursery in Scottsdale, Georgia, in 1936

These "emergency nursery schools" followed an affect-focused curriculum emphasizing the social-emotional development of children. Two other major elements in the curriculum included the health and physical growth of students. The missing component of the curriculum was the academic dimension.

After World War II, public preschools were discontinued, and parents were again responsible for the early education of their children. Many states did not mandate that school districts provide kindergarten programs for the next half-century. One state did not mandate public school kindergartens until 2007.[1]

Thought Questions. If the federal government provided the nation's families with a universal free early childhood education program, it would likely include a prescribed set of learning standards and accountability requirements. What roles would professional school counselors play in those hypothetical schools? What, if any, modifications in graduate counselor education would be needed to prepare professional school counselors to work in those environments?

Counseling in Head Start

Since being created under the presidential administration of Lyndon B. Johnson in 1965, **Head Start** has provided young children of poverty and those with special needs with high-quality preschool experiences. Prior to 1965, impoverished families had to rely on relatives, friends, home care providers, and charity-supported preschool programs for their children (Hohenshil & Brown, 1991).

Children typically enter Head Start or **Early Start** (a companion program for infants and toddlers) significantly behind their middle-class peers in cognitive and social skills and emotional strength (Zigler & Muenchow, 1992). By kindergarten these shortcomings are overcome, and Head Start graduates begin kindergarten on an even footing with all other children. Head Start programs have been shown to provide a major advantage to children who have the poorest preacademic skills when they enter public schools (Preschool Curriculum Evaluation Research Consortium, 2008; Schweinhart, 2008; Schweinhart, Montie, Xiang, Barnett, Belfield, & Nores, 2005; Zill & Sorongon, 2004).

In February 2009, President Barack Obama signed into law the **American Recovery and Reinvestment Act [ARRA]** (P.L. 111–5, 2009). That recovery act provided Head Start and Early Start a supplemental appropriation of $2 billion. These new funds were spent to expand offerings, improve staff, and hire more professionals, including counselors trained in child development (U.S. Department of Health and Human Services [HSS], 2009b).

Funding is to be used supporting staff training, child counseling, and other services, necessary to address the challenges of children from immigrant, refugee, and families taking asylum, homeless children, children in foster care, limited English proficient children, children of migrant or seasonal farmworker families, children from families in crisis, children referred to Head Start programs (including Early Head Start programs) by child welfare agencies, and children who are exposed to chronic violence or substance abuse.

SOURCE: HSS document dated April 2, 2009.

Counseling in Public Preschools

High-stakes testing programs, first mandated in 2002 under the No Child Left Behind Act [NCLB] (P.L. 107–110, 2002), have been a driving force for an expanding role of states in providing high-quality preschool education programs (Wright, 2011). This movement toward public preschool is being used to introduce academic skills to young children in an effort to improve scores on mandated high-stakes achievement tests. These achievement tests are universally required for children in public and charter schools, starting in third grade.

A number of state-supported preschool programs are focused only on meeting needs of children at risk for disabilities or learning problems. Other states are committed to providing full-time programs for all 4-year-old children. In 2006, Illinois made preschool education free to all families, income level notwithstanding (Grossman, 2006). New Jersey followed suit in 2007 with a universal free preschool program. In 2009, follow-up research in New Jersey demonstrated that the high-quality preschool programs that complemented the public schools' efforts to improve literacy and mandated reading test scores were a major success (MacInnes, 2009; Rundquist, 2009). By 2010, only a handful of states did not offer public preschool programs of any form.[2] The citizens of one state, Florida, forced a fiscally conservative state legislature and Governor Jeb Bush to initiate statewide universal preschool education by referendum. Preschool education programs conducted through public schools provide a growing area for the employment of elementary school counselors.

Another reason for progress toward universal preschool education has been the feminist movement. A call for quality preschool programs by women's rights organizations began during the second feminist movement of the 1960s and 1970s.[3]

> True equality of opportunity and freedom of choice for women requires such practical, and possible innovations as a nationwide network of child-care centers, which will make it unnecessary for women to retire completely from society until their children are grown. (National Organization for Women, 1966)

Preschool Counselor Tasks

Problems requiring direct counseling services for preschool students include many of the same ones faced by counselors working in traditional grades K–5 or 6 elementary schools. Young children can experience fears and levels of stress that are unhealthy (Paul, 2010).

They may experience delays in the normal developmental process or have cognitive/neurological disabilities. Young children can also experience overwhelming anger and lash out at others in their environments. Preschool students may experience neglect, not live in safe environments, have unhealthy diets, or not receive necessary medical and dental care. Each of these problems could involve providing service to the child while working with the child's parents and teachers.

● **COUNSELING ELEMENTARY AND
PRESCHOOL CHILDREN FOR PROBLEMS OF AFFECT**

Between 10% and 15% of all children experience **affect disorders** during the elementary and preschool years. These disorders can be mild and transient or severe and debilitating. Recent data has documented that parents are not aware of the degree to which their children exhibit symptoms of significant stress. Research by the American Psychological Association (APA) has reported that 44% of children report sleeping problems and serious disturbances, while only 13% of their parents are aware of this (Munsey, 2010). More than other topics, children report that school stress is the greatest source of anxiety and stress in their lives.

There is evidence of a genetic component to the developing personality types of children from the moment of birth onward. This genetic component provides a human **temperament type** and can be seen throughout the child's life (Kagan & Snidman, 2009). Some children avidly seek stimulation and other infants shy away from it. From these early signs comes the child's foundation for an interaction style with the world.

The plasticity of human neurology makes it possible for counselors and parents working with preschoolers to change and prevent the child from becoming overwhelmed and consumed by fear. The work of Jerome Kagan at Harvard has resulted in an estimation that 13% of American infants exhibit temperament types at birth that can lead to fearful, shy personalities by adolescence (Fox, Steinberg, Kagan, Snidman, Towsley, & Kahn, 2007).

PHOTO 3.2   Child With a Developmental Disability

SOURCE: George Doyle/Stockbyte/Thinkstock.

Another driving force behind the affect-type disorders and problems of young children is stress (Barkoukis, Reiss, & Dombeck, 2008). The stress may be a product of Kagan's temperament types interacting with the environment in ways perceived to be threatening, or the stress and **stress-induced anxiety** among children between 3 and 8 years of age may be centered on change and/or loss (Albano, Chorpita, & Barlow, 1996).

CARTOON 3.1   **Modern Childhood**

"I can't remember if it was my dad's fiancee or Mom's partner who told me how anxious and stressed I look."

SOURCE: Merv Magus.

Families on the Move

One of life's major changes for children occurs when a family moves. The impact of moving from residence to residence plays a role in poor school performance and heightened levels of anxiety (Kaase & Dulaney, 2005; National Assessment of Educational Progress [NAEP], 2004). Socioeconomic status may play a role in the achievement of children of families that move to another home. Wealthy parents move because they can; for them it is strategic and usually well planned. This is not always so for poor families, who often move because they must (Horvath, 2004). Therefore, the moves made by children of poverty may be far more traumatic than is true of children with parents who move to improve their lives. Family disruption caused by divorce combined with moving and less income has been shown to be especially problematic for elementary-aged children. Yet, many of the problems created by moving to a new school can be ameliorated by good counselors and caring teachers (Gruman, Harachi, Abbott, Catalano, & Fleming, 2008).

During the great recession of 2008–2010 (Weisberg, 2010), the number of impoverished families who had to move significantly increased, resulting in a myriad of school-related problems for students (Way, 2009). In 2009, a national report noted that more than 1.5 million children in America were homeless (National Center on Family Homelessness, 2009). This represented a 50% increase over data collected in 1999 and demonstrates the loss suffered in the great recession.

Another type of moving occurs when parents who live in impoverished communities with notoriously poor schools smuggle their children into the better suburban schools beyond their communities. This occurs frequently in suburban school systems that border large cities and is a clear sign of both the devotion of parents to their children and the desperation they feel about their home school systems (Dillon, 2007).

One group of children who move frequently and suffer little harm are the children of military personnel. The support network of other military families is one reason these children seem to thrive even though their families rarely stay at one duty assignment for more than two years (Smrekar & Owens, 2003).

Away From Home

Preschool and kindergarten represent the first time many children spend a long block of time away from their parental caregivers. Most children develop strong emotional bonds with their parents and tend to be slow to warm up to new adults in their environments. New adults and situations away from the safe harbor of the home and family can be very stress inducing for young children.

Childhood Stressors

Any change that poses a threat to the stability of the child's home or position within the family is stressful. Young children respond to stress in a number of ways. Crying and whiney complaining behavior are normal stress responses by children between 3 and 5 years of age (Applebaum, 2009). (See Case in Point 3.3 for an example of stress created by a changed home environment.)

CASE IN POINT 3.3

The ongoing wars in the Middle East have brought with them an emotional toll paid by families back home. By 2010 approximately 1 million of the troops deployed into war zones in Iraq and Afghanistan were parents (Ramirez, 2009). A quarter of them have been deployed into combat two or more times. Eleven out of every 12 of the deployed parents are the fathers of young children.

All deployments to a war zone can be disruptive and anxiety provoking to young children, but multiple deployments can be emotionally damaging on children, especially preschool children (Johns, Dimmick, Mascitelli, & Carbo, 2010). Deployments are very different than a simple change in duty station. Deployments carry the potential of going in harm's way and being injured or killed in combat. The general anxiety in a household when a parent is being deployed may increase and have an adverse impact on the child (Shaw, 2003; Thomas, 2009). School counselors have a role to play in helping the children of parents who are sent overseas on a deployment. This is especially true of schools located near large military posts and enrolling many children of service personnel (Bradshaw et al., 2009).

Army pediatricians have reported an increase in stress-related illnesses among young children on posts where many parents are being shipped out (Glod, 2008). The greatest negative impact occurs among children between 3 and 5 years of age (Chartrand, Frank, White, & Shope, 2008). These children exhibited increased levels of acting-out behaviors, including hitting, biting, and hyperactivity. The problems can continue after the deployment, when the combat-hardened soldier returns home to his or her family. As few as 50% of returning combat troopers who have clear symptoms of mental stress disorders are willing to accept help from medical or psychological personnel (Rodrigues, Renshaw, & Allen, 2010). Having one parent experiencing mental health problems can be a major source of pressure and stress for other family members (American Academy of Child and Adolescent Psychiatry, 2008).

A new *Sesame Street* video for military families depicts the Muppet character of Elmo turning to his mom and friends for support during his dad's deployment. A second video portrays a bilingual Muppet character, Rosita, being reunited with her father who returned from his deployment in a wheelchair (Jowers, 2008).

Preschool counselors on a number of military bases have begun to employ standardized measures of social-emotional development to track changes ongoing in children when a parent is going in harm's way.[4] Family counseling combined with individual **play therapy** is frequently used if the child scores low on the assessment.

Thought Question. Assume a local National Guard unit is called to active duty for a 2-year deployment and you are an elementary school counselor in a school where 15% of the families are directly affected by the call-up. The deployment is set to occur in 4 months, in July. What programs, interventions, or other steps would you take on behalf of the families and children involved?

Left untreated, a young child experiencing stress is likely to experience elevated anxiety and anxiety-related psychological and adjustment problems. These problems can manifest in poor coping skills, irrational fears, and an inability to negotiate problems of daily living (Albano, Chorpita, & Barlow, 1996). This can also be coupled with regressive behaviors and negativity among children between the ages of 6 and 8 years.

Irrational Fears

All children experience fears during childhood. These fears take many forms and can involve going to bed (lurking dangerous animals), getting on the school bus (getting injured), or simply losing sight of a parent in a store or public place (being abandoned). A recent dimension to the fear of being abandoned by one's parents involves the obsessive use of social networking by parents who ignore their children to remain in close contact with the digital world in which they are most happy (Scelfo, 2010).

Interventions are indicated whenever fears are beyond the normal range and become so debilitating as to interrupt normal activities for the child. One example of when an intervention is called for is when transient bedtime fears are replaced by major sleep interruptions accompanying **night terrors**.[5]

Need for Routine

As with changes in the home environment, young children can exhibit stress when their feelings of personal security are disrupted in the classroom. Young children like routines and are normally willing to comply with teachers and other adults. Sudden change in routines can be viewed as a loss of that stability.

One time for stress is the first day of school (Eisen & Schaefer, 2007). The moment of separation from the parent can be difficult for both young children and also for parents. At the beginning of each school year, the early childhood/elementary school counselor should spend time getting to know the new children who just started the program by visiting their classrooms. By joining in the activity of the kindergarten or prekindergarten classroom, the counselor can become a familiar and comfortable adult presence. Such visits also provide counselors with many opportunities to observe and informally interview young children. It is not just the transition from home or child care center to kindergarten that is stressful for children; all major transitions between schools and programs can be stressful.

Interventions (One-on-One)

One key to being a successful counselor with young children is in preplanning for the disruptive contingencies that can occur in a school. The goal of reducing anxiety with young children can be facilitated by reducing the sense of confusion and change experienced by young children. This includes always accompanying students who are away from their classrooms for an office visit. It also implies that other adults (e.g., speech therapists, school nurses, reading specialists, etc.) should be carefully introduced to the children they will assist.

By participating in the enrollment conferences (a.k.a. **kindergarten roundup**) during the summer months prior to the start of the school year, a counselor can get to know students and their families before the school opens. That knowledge can make it possible to plan programs and approaches specifically tailored for individual students.

Problem students should never be identified or singled out. Young students will deny they are difficult or have a problem and may withdraw if they are labeled or otherwise pointed out. Individual counseling can be handled quietly in a private office area, and the student can be assured he or she is being treated the same as other "good students."

Young children are not developmentally ready for introspective thought prior to about third grade. For that reason much of the communication between a counselor and a young child must be carried out using interactive materials. Also, young children have short attention spans, and counseling activities should be limited to 10-minute time blocks.

Play is a way for young children to experience emotional release and create a world of fantasy that they can control (O'Connor & Braverman, 1997). Free playtime is a very healing time for children. Unfortunately free playtime is often reduced to provide more time for the development of early academic skills (Appel, 2009; Thompson, 2008).

One approach to counseling with young children employs play therapy involving carefully selected puppets and dolls. This requires that the counselor maintain a collection of toys appropriate for any counseling contingency. Unlike the playground depicted in Cartoon 3.2, play therapy involves setting up the play area, free of the distraction of other children, with toys that can represent the major forces and players in the child's life (doll house, dolls, toy pets, toy car, toy bicycle, etc.). The goal is to make it possible for the child to present his or her perspective and concerns in a nonthreatening and self-healing environment. Play therapy sessions always need a block of time set aside first for free play by the child with materials while the counselor observes and

CARTOON 3.2   "My Respite"

"This place is my respite from an otherwise hectic world."

SOURCE: Merv Magus.

makes mental notes of what is being shown by the child (Landreth & Sweeney, 1997). Only after the open-ended play is it appropriate for the counselor to ask the child to use the toys to recreate a scenario where he or she experiences problems. The counselor can learn the child's perspective on the issue and help the child create a healthy resolution. (See Chapter 2.)

Some elementary school counselors keep a sand tray that is stocked with the dolls and toy components for play therapy. The use of a sand tray confines the activity area the child can use to set his or her stage for the drama being shown to the counselor.

Another approach uses books that can be read with and to the young child. These books present therapeutic stories providing the opportunity for the counselor to provide the young child with understandable approaches and resolutions to problems in a context of a fantasy. The name applied to this approach to counseling is *bibliotherapy* (Doll & Doll, 1997). The elementary school librarian is an invaluable resource whom the school counselor can use to help identify appropriate books for this purpose. The following publishers have a collection of titles for various problems facing elementary school and preschool children that may be used in bibliotherapy:

- American School Counselor Association: www.schoolcounselor.org

- Magination Press: www.maginationpress.com

- Webehave.Com: www.webehave.com/selfesteem.htm

Another related approach to providing a counseling intervention with a young child is to use one of several interactive story-telling approaches. This approach usually involves the counselor setting the stage with a story involving a cast of characters thinly disguised to represent the people in the child's environment. Some practitioners prefer to use the role of a news reporter and provide the child with an ersatz microphone and the assignment of giving a news story about something he or she feels or has experienced. Open-ended approaches to storytelling (or news reporting) give the child wide latitude to create any story. This is done with one requirement that the stories have a beginning, middle, and ending. Some ask the child to create a moral for his or her story. Another approach is to create a story line to start the child and then let the child complete the fantasy. The counselor listens and encourages the child to find solutions for problems encountered by people in the story (Kottman & Stiles, 1997; West & Dann, 1997). (See the example of an open-ended story in Case in Point 3.4.) Then the counselor provides a similar story with a different resolution designed to provide the child with an alternative solution (Gardner, 1971).

CASE IN POINT 3.4

The client is a kindergarten child showing changed and maladaptive behaviors following the divorce of his parents. The child lives with his mother and a sister who is 2 years older. The father has moved on and is forming a new family in another state. Recently the child has become withdrawn at school and is failing to keep up with others in the class. His academic development has even begun to regress. Also, he has recently shown refusal behaviors with his kindergarten teacher. The kindergarten teacher learned of the divorce during a parent conference with the child's mother. The child's mother reported to the kindergarten teacher that her son has recently experienced "severe nightmares" and bed wetting, behaviors not seen for over a year.

(Continued)

(Continued)

At the request of the kindergarten teacher, the elementary school counselor observed the child in the playground and classroom and spoke with both the child's mother and the kindergarten aide. She then elected to use a story-telling approach to assist the child to learn to cope with the stressful changes that occurred in his life. Normally she would have the child compose the stories from scratch, but to get him started on the first one she began one for him.

Counselor: *I would like you to finish this little story that I am about to tell you. It is all about a family who are going on a long vacation trip in their SUV. The mother and father are in the front and the little boy and his sister are in the back. After a long while they come to a stop on a small road in farm country with no one nearby. The father said to the family, "We ran out of gas. I will go back and buy some." When he was gone the family fell asleep and . . . [Direction to the child] You finish the story now. . . .*

Child: *They all slept a long time and a big animal with sharp teeth came and broke the car's windows. Everybody was asleep so he could get them. He jumped in the car and ate the whole family, killed them dead.*

Counselor: *I have another ending. The family was asleep when an animal approached but the boy heard it and woke up and got his mother. She chased the nasty animal away, and saved the family. My story even has a moral. It is that if you are afraid or in trouble call out for help from the grown-ups around you so they can help.*

This approach normally involves having the child create two or three new stories each session. The counselor uses the child's story as a starting point and helps him or her learn alternatives and solutions. Several sessions over the period of months may be needed to help the child learn to cope with the pain of a losing a father and living in a new arrangement.

Thought Question. Invent another story introduction for a child of similar age. This story is to help a child cope with the stress of living in a home with a dying mother (end-phase ovarian cancer), and a father distressed by the suffering of his wife. He is unable to provide much support for the young boy or the boy's older sibling.

Fourth and fifth grade students have the verbal skills needed to explain their thoughts and feelings. They also can begin to understand their own thought processes. These skills make it possible for counselors to initiate individual and small group counseling programs. It also makes it possible to provide a strengths-based approach to school counseling.

Strengths-Based School Counseling

The emphasis of **strengths-based school counseling (SBSC)** in the elementary school is the reduction of problematic dimensions by helping students build upon their own resiliency and inner strengths (Smith, 2006a, 2006b). This approach is unlike other interventions in that the counselor's job is to help the student identify his or her unique strengths and resources and develop those areas. This counseling does not cure the child in a medical sense of the word, but it makes it possible for the child to manage or avoid problems. SBSC can prevent a child who is at risk for being overwhelmed by circumstances and developing feelings of having been cut off and discouraged (Bowman, 2006). (See Chapter 6 for a fuller description of SBSC.)

Next Step

Intractable problems of anxiety and stress that pose a serious problem for the student and his or her learning and development indicate the counselor should initiate a referral for an assessment by the school's **504 committee.**[6] (See Chapter 7 for information about special education.) The difficulties experienced by kindergarteners when their stress and anxiety levels become unbearable are debilitating and related to serious illness. A Canadian study has shown that high levels of stress among kindergarteners are linked to disruptive behavior in school and pose a significantly greater chance for adolescent suicide (Brezo et al., 2008). Serious problems may also be a sign the child is experiencing an early onset mental illness that will require the intervention of the full **multidisciplinary committee** needed to make an entitlement decision. (See Chapter 7 for information on entitlement decisions.)

Interventions Through Significant Others

The idea of treating young children through working with the children's parents was an approach first described by Sigmund Freud in 1909. He presented an intervention for a child he called Hans through the boy's father (Freud, 1955/1909). In that same tradition, elementary and preschool counselors provide interventions through both the child's parents and the professionals in the school. Counseling interventions can cover a wide range of affect problems and disorders, including anxiety caused by bullies at school, marital separation and divorce, school-based fears (school phobia), irrational fears, and the need for obsessive and repetitive thoughts and/or behaviors (Barkoukis et al., 2008). (See Chapter 11 for more on consulting.)

When enlisting the help of the child's parents, counselors must be mindful of their perspectives. The cultural background of the parents may not lead them to interpret behaviors of the child in the same way as educators (Chao, Kanatsu, Stanoff, Padmawidjaja, & Aque, 2009; Paniagua, 2005). The question of context is also an issue. Background and community values and expectations can provide parents with a different view as to what constitutes appropriate child behavior (Yeh, 2004). Most school counselors have been raised to accept the values and interpret the world through the perspective of America's educated middle class (D'Andrea & Arredondo, 1999). For the most part, the values and perspective of school counselors are skewed toward those of the dominant culture and worldview. The question for a counselor to answer is whether he or she can assume an **emic** perspective in understanding and explaining a child's behavior.[7]

The Internet makes it possible for counselors to be in ongoing and open communication with parents. This level of open communication makes it possible for problems to be addressed quickly and follow-up pursued efficiently.

Elementary and preschool counselors can set up parent meetings outside of the normal school day during which time the counselor can demonstrate and explain approaches being used to help the student at school. Parents can also be shown methods they can employ at home to reinforce what is being done at school.

Parents can be shown how to observe and record incidences of behaviors and outcomes with their child. Also, during these meetings parents can be provided with observational tools and checklists to record observations of their child's behavior.

A day or two following the parent group meeting, the counselor should use the Internet, or other method, to communicate what is being done to address concerns expressed by individual parents (Bouffard, 2009).

Support Groups

Parents can also be invited to attend parent support programs outside of the normal school day. By bringing parents together with the counselor and other members of the pupil service team in an informal setting (e.g., the school library), the programs of the school can seem more understandable and approachable. Information about child development and community resources can be shared during the meetings (Thompson, 1997).

Parents of preschool-aged children should also be encouraged to attend these parent support groups. Many parents of young children can learn about their role in supporting early literacy development (Goodson, Layzer, Simon, & Dwyer, 2009). The counselor can also assist parents of preschoolers in their important decisions including summer day camp experiences and the advantages and disadvantages of **academic redshirting.** (See Case in Point 3.5 for an explanation of redshirting.)

CASE IN POINT 3.5

Parents are increasingly more likely to hold their children back from enrolling in kindergarten and first grade (Datar, 2003; Gootman, 2006; Russell & LaCoste-Caputo, 2006). This voluntary delay in starting public education is done more frequently in states where grade promotion from third grade is contingent on a test score.[8] Parents who do this want their children to be a year older and more mature than their peers entering school (Brock, 2006). This practice is so widespread that it has its own sobriquet, "academic redshirting." It is not just parents who encourage kindergarten redshirting; school administrators who are under pressure to have better test scores are holding an increasing number of children in kindergarten for a second year (Russell & LaCoste-Caputo, 2006).

There are a number of reasons why parents elect to hold their child out of school for an extra year. Generally parents see the extra year as giving their child an advantage over their younger peers. That advantage is evident in the child's size and strength, but parents also believe that the extra year in a preschool provides time for their child to become more socially competent and cognitively advanced. Additionally, parents want their child to possess more athletic skills than their peers in the same grade (Paul, 2010).

Nationally about 9% of all children are redshirted, but in some suburban neighborhoods the number is closer to 50% (Katz, 2000; Keller, 2006; West, Meek, & Hurst, 2000). The practice is more common in communities where parents are relatively affluent. Boys are more likely to be held out an extra year, as are children who were born in the fall.

Thought Questions. Under what circumstances would you as a professional school counselor support the choice of academic redshirting a child? What is the downside of academic redshirting? When would you counsel parents against the idea? Explain your position.

Parents can also offer each other self-help advice and approaches for coping with children. These group sessions provide parents with emotional support as well as information and advice. Parent groups facilitate brainstorming and problem solving by parents who have the same experiences and problems. In these meetings it is the job of the counselor to serve as the host and group facilitator.

To improve parent relations, counselors can establish a **bulletin board** for parents to use on the school's server. This bulletin board can facilitate parents asking questions of each other and receiving suggestions and tips from their peers. As it is an open posting, the counselor can monitor all traffic and postings on it.

● COUNSELING ELEMENTARY AND PRESCHOOL STUDENTS FOR RELATIONSHIP PROBLEMS

Children who experience any of a range of problems with other people around them can be taught new approaches and methods for dealing with their environments. In these cases the role of the counselor is that of a coach who is presenting the student with a new routine and set of plays to employ in life's encounters.

Bullying

The occasional sensational media story about murder or a vicious attack by one child on others has brought the attention of the public to the issue of bullying in school. These violent incidents are rare and on the decline but they are still very troubling. Recent evidence has shown that bullying behaviors may be on the decline (Finkelhor, Turner, Ormrod, & Hamby, 2010). More common are daily vicious acts of aggression and torment often rarely reported and hardly ever noticed by adults in a school. Bullies pick their time and locations well. They do not want their actions to be noticed by responsible adults (Coloroso, 2004).

Research in California has reported that 9 out of every 10 children in school have been bullied at least once, and 6 in 10 report they participated as a perpetrator in a bullying act. Others have described the problem as occurring less frequently, in the 25% range (Beaudoin & Taylor, 2009; Roberts, 2008). Yet, the problem can and all too often does lead to serious injury and occasionally a murder in retaliation. An analysis by the U.S. Secret Service (2002) reported that children who experienced significant bullying conducted 67% of all school shootings. By 2010 the notoriety that bullying has received resulted in most states passing laws making harassment and bullying in school state crimes.[9] (See Case in Point 3.6 describing an example of the outcome of bullying in school.)

CASE IN POINT 3.6

In the spring of 2009 several school districts were forced to defend themselves in civil courts after parents of elementary school suicide victims brought legal action against the districts. The cases involved elementary-aged children who were so tormented by their peers in school that they chose to end their lives. One case in Springfield, Massachusetts, involved an 11-year-old boy who hanged himself after repeatedly being called a "gay fag." There is no indication he was a homosexual, but he was a good student in school, and others did not like him getting ahead (Warner, 2009).

Another case occurred in DeKalb County, Georgia, where a fifth grader hanged himself after being taunted and harassed by bullies for being gay. Once again, there was no indication of what sexual orientation the child may have had, but his bullying peers used the homosexual epithet to taunt and isolate him (Melloy, 2009).

In both cases the parents of the dead children report that they did explain the problem to the school's administrators several times during the year, but no action was taken by the school to help the students. When educators are bystanders and close a blind eye toward bullying and harassment in school they become players in the bullying culture of the school. Research has shown that most teachers have little understanding of the bullying that is happening around them (Low, 2010). School counselors cannot allow themselves to ignore this problem and must be vigilant for potential bullying problems.

Thought Question. Assume that in the year following these tragedies, you are hired as a new school counselor in one of the schools. Outline a teacher and administrator after school inservice education program (2 hours a month for 6 months) designed to prevent this problem in the future.

Bullying behavior in school is not a recent phenomenon. In 1857, Thomas Hughes published a widely read, semi-autobiographical novel based on his school days at England's Rugby School. The book details his struggle for dignity and his battle with the penultimate bully, Harry Paget Flashman (Hughes, 2008/1857).

An early manifestation of bullying is seen in preschoolers who lash out at their peers by biting. This occurs when a young child needs to express his or her power and does not have the physical capability needed to control others or the verbal ability to control with language. The need to express control is frequently a result of frustration and/or anger.

Preschool counselors can work through the child's teachers and parents to stop the behavior. The classroom teacher should comfort the victim and ask the aggressor to help his or her target by assisting the teacher and holding ice over the injured area. New behavior patterns should be taught by reading with all the children who saw the incident a story such as Elizabeth Verdick and Marieka Heinlen's (2003) *Teeth Are Not for Biting,* or Karen Katz's (2002) *No Biting!* After reading the book the counselor should discuss what happened and how the victim felt. Finally, if it is not already posted, a classroom rule should be established: "Never hurt one another."

In the elementary grades bullying can take on either a more physically aggressive form or occur through exclusion of a child. Bullies need to feel power over others, lack empathy, and have low levels of emotional intelligence (Goleman, 1997). Good parenting involves teaching children to be empathetic toward others. Unfortunately, some adults, lacking empathy themselves, have been known to encourage exclusion and other forms of bullying. (See Case in Point 3.7 for two examples of adult complicity in bullying.)

CASE IN POINT 3.7

First:

In December of 2007 Ben Vooden, an 11-year-old boy, was found by his father after he committed suicide by hanging. During the fall of 2007 the child told his mother that he hated going to school because the other children bullied him on the school bus, and no one was his friend. Ben's mother told him to sit near the driver who could protect him from his tormenters. That idea backfired when the bus driver joined in the verbal abuse and taunting directed at the 11-year-old victim. After months of harassment, Ben snapped on the bus ride and had to be disciplined by the school's principal. (It was the same bullying bus driver that reported him to the principal.) When Ben got home his mother questioned him about why he behaved badly on the bus. He went to his room after telling his mother he was sorry. Those were his last words ever (Koster, 2007).

Second:

A student's mother, Mrs. Lawler, contacted the elementary school counselor to report that her 8-year-old daughter, Kathy, saw a girl she assumed was her friend giving out envelopes in class one day during homeroom. Kathy was told that the envelopes contained invitations to the second girl's birthday party, and that she was not invited. Mrs. Lawler called the other child's mother and was told that they placed Kathy on a "B" list, only to be invited in the event of a cancellation by a child on the "A" list.

This type of snub can become a devastating and emotionally painful moment. The mother was told by the counselor not to let her daughter attend the birthday party even if there was a cancellation. The counselor suggested that Mrs. Lawler plan a wonderful family day at the same time when the birthday party was planned.

In school the counselor met with Kathy and discussed friendships and making new friends. She also found a youth soccer league that played near where Kathy lived and provided Kathy with an invitation from the team's coach to join in the sport. A follow-up meeting was held with Mrs. Lawler at which time she was given a copy of Lawrence Shapiro and Julia Holmes's (2008) book, *Let's Be Friends: A Workbook to Help Kids Learn Social Skills and Make Great Friends.*

Thought Questions. In the first case a tragedy occurred. In the second case an effective school counselor was able to provide a solution for the parent of a child who could have been psychologically injured by the boorish behavior of others.

If you were a school counselor in Ben Vooden's school, what steps would you take to prevent the situation from escalating? How would you help Ben and his family?

One warning sign that a child is afraid of bullies at school is poor attendance. Counselors should watch the pattern of daily attendance in their school for children missing an excessive number of days. Poor attendance is linked to low achievement and low standardized test scores (Jacobson, 2008b). Chronic poor attendance can be defined several ways. In large urban areas such as New York City, it is defined as missing 10 consecutive days or 20 or more days over a 4-month term (Medina, 2008). In a suburban district, it may be locally defined as missing 10% or more of the academic year.

Cyberbullying

The advent of unlimited text messaging accounts and **social networking** web sites has resulted in making the **tween years** of the upper elementary grades the time when **cyberbullying** begins. This electronic bullying can be just as hurtful as the other forms of bullying. Public schools can face serious liability if they ignore the complaints of a child or his or her parents about being cyberbullied (Hinduja & Patchin, 2009). School districts need to have clear cyberbullying policies in place, and those policies must be enforced. The school's web page should provide cyberbullying policy information for parents and students. Part of those policies should be a statement that school officials will report all incidences of cyberbullying to law enforcement. Harassment, stalking, hacking computer use, and stealing the identity of others is against state and federal laws.

The impetus behind tougher application being made of federal laws against using telecommunications to harass others was the intense media coverage around the suicide of a 13-year-old teenaged girl in 2006. The girl lived in

Missouri, where she was in her second month as a ninth grader at Immaculate Conception School. In 2006 it was alleged she was driven to commit suicide by a neighbor, Lori Drew, the mother of another teenaged girl (Huffstutter, 2007). In 2008–2009 Mrs. Drew was prosecuted in federal court for the unauthorized use of the computer servers of MySpace. After her conviction by the jury, the trial judge threw the case out on a technicality.

School counselors can play a role in preventing cyberbullying from occurring in the first place; and, if it does occur counselors can protect the victim and stop the bully. One way to limit cyberbullying is to enlist the school's parents. Counselors should work with the school's instructional technology department to inform parents about both the academic resources of computers and the dangers represented by the technology their children use. The technology staff can explain the use of filtering devices for computers and describe how parents can monitor what their children see and show to other people. The counselor should discuss the issue of cyberbullying with parents. He or she should explain both the harm that can occur to victims and also the penalties that the bully is likely to experience.

The counselor should provide in-classroom lessons for all children on various aspects of cyber danger. School counselors are the best school professionals to lead discussions of the hurt and pain caused when a cyberbully attacks another student. One lesson should focus on what responsibilities other students who know about the cyberbullying have as members of a school community. To facilitate student help in stopping cyberbullying, the counselor should establish a web site where students and parents can anonymously describe and report incidents of cyberbullying and other forms of bullying (Emerson, 2009). Copies of all cyberbullying material seen by both victims and bystanders should be sent to that confidential web site.

Children who have been the victims of cyberbullying need to be encouraged to save copies of all bullying messages and harassing Internet contacts or messages. They should also be encouraged to create new, uncontaminated, electronic addresses and web pages and taught to use filters and blocks. The cyberbully victim needs to learn not to confront the child or other children who have been tormenting him or her. Confrontation in person can lead to public ridicule, and Internet responses can be distorted and given wide distribution. The victims need to be made aware that they are not to blame for the harassment they are receiving (Hinduja & Patchin, 2009). They also need the support of adults who can help them through the pain and loss of self-esteem that is likely to accompany being a cyberbully's victim.

Once a cyberbully is identified, he or she should be referred for disciplinary action and law enforcement informed of the inappropriate activity. The counselor can then begin an individual program to change the behavior of the cyberbully. The counselor's goal is to assist the bully in recognizing the pain a person experienced by their behavior and identify other ways of interacting.

The school administrator should request an immediate conference with the parent of the cyberbully. The school counselor can consult with the school's administrator but not interfere with the nature of punishment the offending child is given. After the punishment phase, the school counselor should meet with the parents of the offending child to discuss ways the parents can become involved in the school's effort to help their child.

Aggression and Physical Bullying

Physical bullying that begins in preschool becomes increasingly common after third grade. While not an exclusive male behavior, acts of physical aggression tend to be committed by male bullies more than by girls. Girls who are bullies tend to use relational and social forms of aggression more frequently than do boys who are bullies (Field, Kolbert, Crothers, & Hughes, 2009).

Acts of physical aggression and bullying can be directed against the person of the victim or against his or her property. Acts against personal property include damaging or stealing the victim's school materials and equipment, destroying notes and/or homework, vandalizing his or her locker, stealing lunches or money, damaging or stealing clothing including physical education uniforms and/or equipment, and vandalizing projects and other work products. Acts against property can be overt and done to taunt the victim, or conducted covertly as a way to maintain deniability while still humiliating and hurting the targeted child.

There are many victims other than just the student who is the direct target of the bully(ies). These include all other students who saw the behavior and were afraid to stop it or report it to authorities. The whole student body can become intimidated by a handful of bullies. All schools, including religious and other private schools, can have bullies (Pytel, 2007). The threat these bullies present can intimidate any student and stop him or her from reporting what is going on in the school. The victims of bullies include all students who must attend a school in which they cannot feel safe. And, bullies also hurt the school's social-emotional climate and make teaching and learning more difficult for everyone.[10]

Thefts and vandalism are violations of state laws in every state. School administrators should require the parents of bullies to make a full restitution of all loses their children cause victims. Punishment for such behavior should be part of the school's published code of conduct and part of the school district's policy documents.

In some states, school administrators have no choice about filing a police report. In Delaware all school principals are legally obligated to report to the state police, state education department, and parents of victims of all bullying attacks in the schools (Jingeleski, 1996). That state classifies bullying using terms such as Robbery II and/or Assault III. These are crimes that are classified as felonies. Delaware school administrators who attempt to cover up problems in their schools can also be arrested and prosecuted.

Primary Prevention

The role of the counselor is to prevent bullying from happening. This anti-bullying effort should include a program of primary prevention. This is a schoolwide effort involving all professionals, paraprofessionals, and technical staff who are in contact with students. The effort should be coordinated by a committee of stakeholders (including an administrator) and chaired by a counselor (Davidson & Demaray, 2006).

The first step in primary prevention is the collection of data on the amount of violent bullying being experienced by the school's students. The location and time of day when bullying incidents occur should also become part of the data collected. Bullies prefer to do their harassing of victims away from the eyes of adults and others who may report them (Graham, 2010).

The second step is the identification of goals to be met by a program. One goal must be getting student bystanders involved in stopping the bullies (O'Connell & Pepler, 1999). There are many commercially available programs that the school's anti-bullying committee can consider for adoption or adaptation. The following are examples of these curricula:

- www.urbantech.org/ylaint_confres.cfm

- www.goodcharacter.com/BCBC/PreventingConflicts.html

- http://softskillscourseware.com/pages/course.asp?id=s0606&ad=guss0606&gclid=CIvcm5-W4poCFQKenAodjEBuCg

- http://store.peaceeducation.org/?gclid=COr0-JOX4poCFQJ-xgod1kEtEA

- Olweus Bullying Prevention Program (Clemson University): www.olweus.org/public/index.page

In addition to these commercially available curriculum packages, the federal government also provides a curriculum model schools can use to create their own programs: www.ncjrs.gov/txtfiles/160935.txt.

Once a program has been developed or selected, the elementary school counselor should plan lessons and present classes throughout the school. Members of the anti-bullying committee should be called on to assist in providing inservice education programs for all teachers and school staff.

Beyond curriculum and inservice education, there are other steps that can be taken to stop school bullies. One of these is the installation of cameras and/or dummy cameras on all buses, in all classrooms, large common rooms (library, cafeteria), hallways, and all "un-owned" spaces in and around the school. Cameras should also cover the school's entrances, the playground and school's yards, bus ramp, and parking lots. By having a digital record of incidences of bullying, significant actions can be taken against the perpetrators, and the victims can be identified and helped.

Secondary Prevention

This level of prevention includes small group and individual counseling for students who may become victims of bullies. It engages potential victims in ideas, strategies, approaches to use when being bullied, and the reporting of bullies. It also includes programs for parents of both bullies and their victims (Roberts, 2008). Books, including Trudy Ludwig's *Just Kidding* (2006) and *My Secret Bully* (2005) and Jay McGraw's *Jay McGraw's Life Strategies for Dealing with Bullies* (2008), can be shared and discussed with the children.

Potential victims tend to be different from the mainstream in some dimension. This happens when children define who they are as individuals by identifying who they are not or do not want to become. The rejected model (student) all too frequently becomes the target of bullying. In that way, being perceived as somehow different creates a target that draws bullying behavior. Differences may involve androgynous or not sex-stereotyped behaviors, obesity, disabilities, stuttering, having poor motor coordination, being a language minority, wearing clothing required by the tradition of a minority religion, or just seeming to be more vulnerable. Children who have developed good coping skills including a strong sense of humor can shrug off bullies, and the bully will move on to less challenging targets.

Albert Bandura (Bandura & McDonald, 1963) developed a model for social learning that explains why some children learn to bully others. Bandura postulates that when a person in power (a bully) acts out against another and is not punished but is rewarded in some way, observers of the behavior learn to act the same way. Bullies are rarely caught, are rarely punished, and are rewarded by the respect and intimidation of their peers. To break the cycle of bullying, they must be punished so all others know bullying is not tolerated.

Tertiary Prevention

Once a student has been sanctioned by the school administrators and/or outside agencies, the school counselor can play a vital role. It is the counselor's job to find approaches and methods for teaching the student who bullies other students different methods of interacting.

Many bullies tend to see their school experience as a negative reference in their lives; other students tend to see the school experience as a positive. This **outsider** self-image is not conducive to a healthy self-concept and self-esteem. Yet, bullies can report having a great level of self-confidence. This is a reaction to the responses of other students who either are intimidated or are supplicants for the favor of the bully's attention and members of his or her "posse" (Graham, 2010). Beyond his or her obsequious band, for the bully this negative image of somehow being a misfit within the school community is a source of internalized anger and frustration (Morrison, 2002). The negative feeling that a bully holds is projected onto others who "deserve what they get." The bully is likely to not realize that by bullying others he or she is reinforcing his or her image as a misfit within the greater school community. Yet, he or she feels a need to lash out at easy targets and make others miserable. (A typical middle school bullying incident is shown in Photo 3.3.)

The counselor's role is to teach the bully how to make friends with students without using intimidation. At first this involves teaching the bully to reflect on the question of why he or she hurts other people. The counselor must get the child who bullies others to focus on the reward or what he or she got out

PHOTO 3.3   Bullying in Middle School

SOURCE: Istockphoto.com/chrisboy2004.

of being a bully. Questions such as "Did it make you feel powerful?" and "Did you plan out what you did, or was it a spur-of-the-moment idea you came up with?" Also, the bully should be made to focus on how the victim and his or her family felt about what the bully has done. To reach this point the counselor may ask pointed questions that can include, "How much (pain, damage, embarrassment) was the outcome of your bullying?" Or "Did you make your victim cry?" "Do you feel good when you hurt others?" "Do you feel other students who see you hurt a child think more highly of you for being a bully?"

Once the student gains a perspective on his or her behaviors, the next step is to teach the bully how to be popular and have friends without bullying. This may involve role playing, modeling the behaviors of socially successful children, and teaching the child to self-reward for appropriate behavior (Smith, 2002). Small-group counseling can also be employed once the bully has become capable of reflection on what his or her motives and rewards are for being a bully.

Once the student recognizes that he or she is a bully, the next phase in counseling can be initiated. Counseling with a bully involves helping the bully see the behaviors as outside of them. By compartmentalizing the behaviors, it is possible to treat the student and not constantly reference the student's "bad nature." The separation of the actor and actions that the bully committed is called **externalization**. The externalization process facilitates helping bullies identify alternative solutions and approaches for how they feel about other people (Beaudoin & Taylor, 2009).

COUNSELING STUDENTS WITH ● ACTING-OUT BEHAVIOR PROBLEMS

Refusal and Defiance

In school young children can present significant conduct problems. Refusal and defiance are two possible actions of students who are angry. Anger is a powerful secondary emotion that is triggered in all normal people following feeling a primary emotion such as frustration, fear, loss, unfairness, powerlessness, or hurt (Applebaum, 2009). This implies the counselor working with angry and defiant students should learn what the primary emotion is that triggers the anger and accompanying inappropriate behaviors.

For years schools used corporal punishment with elementary school-aged students to maintain discipline and good order. Most professional societies related to education have taken positions against the use of corporal punishment, but only 30 states have banned its practice.[11] In reality corporal punishment does not stop inappropriate behavior. By punishing a child in this way the adult educator is modeling aggression on a smaller person who is powerless to prevent it. Corporal punishment is not just counterproductive but damaging to the position of the educator. Today more than 1.5 million students are subjected to corporal punishment in school each year (National Association of School Psychologists, 2006). For the most part these children are poor, male, and from a racial minority group. Minority students are also disciplined with much harsher sanctions even when corporal punishment is not employed (Losen & Skiba, 2010). (For more on this topic, see Chapter 8.)

Acting-out behavior by children has been shown to occur more frequently when the home environment is troubled (Demaray, Malecki, & DeLong, 2006). Children who are exposed to domestic violence at home are at serious risk for conduct problems (Carrell & Hoekstra, 2008). The frustration and hurt from home can spill over in the classroom and be displaced on peers and teachers. The job of the elementary school counselor is not to stifle anger but to understand its cause and teach children to express it in more positive ways.

Counselors should watch children as they arrive at school each day. The mood a child brings to school may be seen in the last interaction between the parent driving the car and the child being dropped off. The child's mood may be seen by how peers on the school bus treat the child and how others greet the child on arrival at the school's bus ramp. Unobtrusive observation of children in the cafeteria and at recess also provides valuable sources of information for the counselor.

Primary Prevention

Elementary school counselors can work with children in classroom settings to teach **anger management skills**. This can take several class periods and involve having children describe all the things that make them angry and identify what caused that anger. Careful listening by the counselor makes it possible to develop a classroom list of anger-inciting circumstances and the likely triggering events leading to the angry feelings. Subsequent class sessions can involve actions that can be used to safely release the anger without hurting one's self or others.

When conferencing with teachers it is important for the elementary school counselor to encourage teacher colleagues to model anger management themselves and provide helpful ideas for how to approach defiant children (Mendler, 1997). This can include advice such as "Pick your fights carefully." Not every infraction must be responded to every time. Also, remind teachers to remain calm and always speak in soothing and carefully measured tones.

Secondary Prevention

Angry and defiant students should be helped first by the counselor in understanding their anger and its cause. This involves teaching the student how moods and feelings can cause confused thinking and bad acts.

The next step is to help the student find ways to make up for any damage or hurt he or she may have caused. This is more than a forced apology, but true amends for any harm that he or she caused. That is only possible when the student understands how personal actions affect others. Once this is done, the student can be introduced to ways to manage anger and rage.

Anger management involves teaching the student how to self-monitor and how to reach out for help when anger is building up within. The metaphor of a growing thunderstorm can be used to help the student know how to recognize when it is time to seek relief by talking with an adult.

Tertiary Prevention

The consequences of not providing primary and secondary prevention programs can lead some children to a serious psychological problem, **oppositional defiant disorder**, a category of the American Psychiatric Association's taxonomy of mental illnesses (1994). This disorder involves a continuity of severe defiant and oppositional behaviors that have persisted with the child for at least 6 months. The normal diagnosis of this disorder can be made when the child responds to adults with open hostility and refuses to comply with directions. These children are quick to anger and frequently exhibit rages. Also, the child with this disorder cannot accept blame and scapegoats all problems. These children are spiteful and have explosive tempers. When challenged by adults about their behaviors, oppositional and defiant children deny that they have a problem and insist that they are the victims of others. Children with oppositional defiant disorder are more often boys in elementary school. During adolescence the gender difference tends to become evened out. When a counselor feels that a student's pattern of behaviors has reached this level of severity, a referral to an individualized education plan (IEP) committee is in order. (See Chapter 7 for more about the IEP committee.)

Demanding and Inability to Delay Gratification

A core learning that should happen for all children during early childhood is to delay being satisfied in order to achieve a later goal. This is called **delay of gratification** and is a sign the child has developed good impulse control. Children who enter school expecting to get everything they want, when they want it, are doomed to disappointment and a difficult school career.

Delay of gratification has been shown to correlate with a child's later ability to develop strong interpersonal relationships, achieve well in school, and be viewed by others as a moral and empathetic individual (Bodrova & Leong, 2005; Newman, Caspi, Moffitt, & Silva, 1997). Children who can delay gratification are more able to cope with frustration well and are more resistant to **peer pressure** as they grow into adolescence (Lee, Lan, & Wang, 2008).

Below the age of 2 years, most children are ruled by their impulses. Freud hypothesized that children at this young age are dominated by their **id** (Freud, 1990/1923). He proposed that the development of a **superego** within the psyche of each child controls and directs id impulses. This development comes from parental training of the child. As parents teach their children to wait and post-pone immediate gratification in order to gain a later goal, the ability to delay gratification and control impulses develops.

Primary Prevention

Parent education efforts by the elementary school counselor can provide education on how to help students become less demanding of immediate gratification. Counselors can help parents understand the importance of being authoritative without becoming authoritarian. Capricious and authoritarian discipline at home produces children with low impulse control who do less well in school and are more easily led by their peers. Parents should teach their children that certain desired things could only be had through working and/or saving for them. This lesson is one many families learned the hard way during the Great Recession of 2008–2010 when consumer credit became tight and many families had to save money.

Counselors should work with early childhood and elementary school teachers to find approaches to instill self-control through classroom lessons. One way for all educators to teach self-control and to delay gratification is through modeling behaviors in all contacts with students and others in school (Henley, 2003). Counselors can also teach self-control and delay of gratification in the classrooms.

Secondary Prevention

Counselors can help preschool and kindergarten children learn to delay grati-fication by training them to distract themselves and talk to themselves about their later goal. These types of training improve the child's ability to self-regulate and internalize mechanisms of self-control. (See the video clip based on research at Stanford University at http://scienceblogs.com/isisthescientist/2009/09/the_marshmallow_test_and_delay.php.)

Counseling with students between 9 and 11 years can involve the use of a strengths-based counseling program. The role of the counselor becomes one of identifying the student's particular abilities and helps the client (student) see how his or her actions can be more productive and more efficacious in obtain-ing desired goals. The use of strengths-based counseling in the upper elementary grades can also be maintained through small group counseling sessions held on a regular (scheduled) basis.

Isolation and Social Withdrawal

Students who interact with their peers at a level considered to be below normal are described as being socially withdrawn or as social isolates (Rubin & Stewart, 1996). There are a few students who prefer their own company and are not all that interested in joining in with the group (Kagan, 1989). This subset of students may total 15% of the population of children in elementary school.

There is another group of students who would like to participate in social interactions with peers but have personality characteristics that interfere with joining in with others. This may include poor ego strength, making it difficult for the student to take a verbal jab. It may also be the student is socially awkward or unable to follow social rules of the school's cliques. The ritualistic aggression of social groups of students requires both ego strength and an understanding of the rules of the culture of children. Students who do not interact appropriately with their peers are quickly marginalized. Students' social groups are a harsh environment, providing no appeal process and offering no tolerance for whiners.

In a related dimension, students who lack the physical coordination and skill set may also find themselves being marginalized by their peers. This is true for both boys and girls. The counselor can easily spot this problem by watching which students are last to be selected to participate in ad hoc competitive games at recess. These students feel significant pain when their peers give them this ultimate vote of no confidence in their abilities.

By the upper elementary grades, students who exhibit this isolation may also become withdrawn and show signs of depression, poor self-perception, insecurity, and total social deference (Rubin & Stewart, 1996). To make less threatening social contacts, these students may begin to befriend children who are younger than they are. It is also likely that these students will be "culled from the herd" and attacked by the bullies at school. This extra level of torment can cause significant psychological damage.

Primary Prevention

One key to providing primary prevention is provided by the student's parents. Parents can be taught how to help their child become more forthcoming and better able to make friends. There are guidebooks that can be recommended to parents who request material they can use at home. Two examples are Elizabeth Hartley-Brewer's (2009), *Making Friends: A Guide to Understanding and Nurturing Your Child's Friendships,* and the book by Natalie M. Elman and Eileen Kennedy-Moore (2003), *The Unwritten Rules of Friendship: Simple Strategies to Help Your Child Make Friends.*

Secondary Prevention and Interventions

The elementary school counselor can play an important role in helping students who have been marginalized by their peers and become socially withdrawn. The use of group counseling methods can facilitate significant change. One approach is to create **friendship clubs** through which students who want to make new friends can meet others. During such sessions children can learn how to interact without being a "geek" or somehow "weird." Books such as the following can be read and shared on the topic of friendships:

Bradley Trevor Greive (2006), *Friends to the End for Kids: The True Value of Friendship*

Peggy Moss and Dee Dee Tardif (2007), *Our Friendship Rules*

Ashley Rice (2006), *Thanks for Being My Friend: A Special Book to Celebrate Friendship With Someone Very Important . . . You*

Another possibility is to introduce a competitive game that does not require physical coordination and strength—for example, chess. Teaching students how to play a game like chess can provide them with a chance to excel in something others cannot achieve.

SUMMARY

Today counselors work in preschools and at every grade level of the elementary school. Unlike European and Asian democracies, the United States has no national model or mandate for providing publicly supported preschool education. President Franklin Delano Roosevelt initiated free preschools under his plan for economic recovery, but they were discontinued after World War II. Head Start was started by President Lyndon Johnson's administration in 1965; it continues today and was provided with a recent boost from President Barack Obama and the American Recovery and Reinvestment Act of 2009.

Elementary and preschool counselors are in positions to help students who have a range of problem behaviors. Among these are problems of affect and of relationships. Among problems of relationships, bullying and cyberbullying are perhaps the most common and insidious. The first task of school authorities is to stop bullying from occurring and to protect its victims. Counselors have an important role to play in preventing bullying and helping students recover from the psychic damage that being a victim produces.

Problems of affect are frequently outcomes when a student experiences far too much stress in his or her life. The sources of stress are many, and the job of the counselor is to identify them and help the student learn coping methods to manage them.

DISCUSSION QUESTIONS

1. What are some reasons that the United States is the only Western industrialized democracy that has no national mandate for publicly supported preschools?

2. Explain with examples the differences and similarities among primary, secondary, and tertiary prevention programs used in school counseling.

3. What steps should a school take to stop cyberbullying of elementary school students?

4. Explain the most common causes of social isolation and withdrawal. What approaches can an elementary school counselor use to help students who have been made isolates?

5. Describe a primary prevention program to improve a child's demanding need for instant gratification.

RELATED READINGS

Drewes, A. A. (Ed.). (2009). *Blending play therapy with cognitive behavioral therapy: Evidence-based and other effective treatments and techniques.* Hoboken, NJ: Wiley.

Hanley, M. (2003). *Teaching self-control: A curriculum for responsible behavior.* Bloomington, IN: National Educational Services.

Hinduja, S., & Patchin, J. W. (2009). *Bullying beyond the school yard: Preventing and responding to cyberbullying.* Thousand Oaks, CA: Corwin.

Roberts, W. B. (2008). *Working with parents of bullies and victims.* Thousand Oaks, CA: Corwin.

Webb, N. B. (1999). *Play therapy with children in crisis* (2nd ed.). New York: Guilford.

NOTES

1. New Hampshire gave local school districts until the fall of 2007 to initiate kindergarten programs.

2. States without programs for early education in 2010 included Alaska, Idaho, Indiana, Mississippi, Montana, New Hampshire, North Dakota, Rhode Island, South Dakota, Utah, and Wyoming.

3. The first feminist movement in the United States began in New York in 1850 with the founding of an organization for women's rights. Following the Civil War many of the efforts for women's rights focused on women's property rights and ability to enter into contracts (Freedman, 2002). The appalling loss of life during the Civil War (618,000 men, or 1 of every 9 men between the ages of 15 and 40) made many young women widows. These women found state and local laws stacked against their interests. Later this first feminist movement became focused on political equality and the right to vote. This "suffrage" movement was resolved with the passage of the 19th Amendment in 1920.

4. Counselors working with children of active duty members of the armed services can never be dismissive of the real danger being faced by the parents who enter war zones. A mute testimony to these dangers can be seen in Zone 60 of Arlington National Cemetery, a section reserved for those killed in the Iraq and Afghanistan Wars.

5. Night terrors differ from nightmares in a matter of degree. Children will normally awaken during a nightmare and look for a parent to soothe them. Night terrors occur during long wave sleep, not rapid eye movement (REM) sleep cycles. They happen between 1 and 3 hours into the child's sleep cycle. Children can sleep through the experience while still crying out and thrashing in their sleep. The night terror can occur among children starting at about 40 months of age. They normally fade out over the child's elementary school years. They are thought to be stress related and can reflect a major problem in a child's life (e.g., loss of a parent). It is also possible for night terrors to awaken a child in a disoriented condition with severe sweating and a racing heart. Some children relate a terrifying story of what was experienced while they were dreaming and may be difficult to console or soothe (Carranza & Dill, 2004).

6. Section 504 of the Rehabilitation Act of 1975 requires all public schools provide the support services needed to make public education available to all children with disabilities.

7. The emic perspective facilitates understanding behaviors and events in the context of meaning shared by members of the actual culture. It implies the counselor can think and interpret as though he or she were a cultural insider.

8. These states include Delaware, Florida, Georgia, Louisiana, Maryland, Mississippi, North Carolina, South Carolina, Texas, and Wisconsin.

9. States without anti-bullying laws for schools: New York, Pennsylvania, Virginia, North Carolina, Alabama, Mississippi, New Mexico, Kansas, Nebraska, South Dakota, North Dakota, Montana, Wyoming, and Nevada.

10. Bullying can be deadly. On Monday, October 12, 2009, five middle school boys doused 15-year-old Matthew Brewer with rubbing alcohol (isopropanol) and set him on fire (Lebovich, 2009). He required a year of ongoing surgeries to regain some of his dignity; the five boys were arrested and charged with the felony, aggravated battery.

11. Corporal punishment is legal in the schools of the following states: Alabama, Arizona, Arkansas, Colorado, Florida, Georgia, Idaho, Indiana, Kansas, Kentucky, Louisiana, Mississippi, Missouri, New Mexico, North Carolina, Oklahoma, South Carolina, Tennessee, Texas, and Wyoming.

4

School Counseling in the Middle School

OBJECTIVES

By reading and studying this chapter you should acquire the competency to:

- Describe the three dimensions of brain development during pubescence and adolescence
- Describe how middle schools differ from junior high schools
- Explain the role of identity formation in the life of middle school students
- Describe and discuss major problems that can have a negative impact on identity formation
- Discuss the process and potential problems in forming a gender identity during the middle school years; discuss approaches a middle school counselor can employ to assist teens who are experiencing difficulty with establishing a gender identity
- Describe the lack of policy consistency in the juvenile justice system that many young adolescents face each year
- Describe the extent of the problem of teenage pregnancy in the United States, and describe both primary and secondary prevention programs for the middle school
- Discuss and explain counseling approaches that can be used to reduce the anxiety level of middle school students

● ● ●

❝ Youth is, after all, just a moment, but it is the moment, the spark that you always carry in your heart. **❞**

Raisa Gorbachev

● **INTRODUCTION AND THEMES**

Grown-ups and pubescent adolescents have enormous differences in how they understand the world around them. Middle school marks the era when most children enter puberty. By the age of 11 or 12 the physical growth of neurological tissues for the brain is nearing completion, but there is much more neurological work to be done before adulthood. The adolescent brain is in the process of elaborating the components that will make reasonable judgments, long-range planning, higher-order thinking, introspection, and many other aspects of adult thinking.

Junior high schools were introduced more than 100 years ago to provide a better preparation for students going on to high school than could be provided in an extended elementary school (kindergarten to grade 8). For the past 60 years, middle schools have supplanted the junior high school. Middle schools were designed to provide a **child-centered approach** for the education of early adolescent children.

One of the most challenging tasks of early adolescence is to begin the process of **identity formation**. This process continues until it results in the teenager becoming a psychologically healthy young adult. One of the tasks related to identity formation is the formation of a gender identity. Biology is the driving force that leads a child into puberty and a sexual identity, but gender identity, as opposed to sexual identity, is greatly influenced by socialization. This is a difficult process for teens who find that the gender identity best suited to their needs is not stereotypical for their biological gender.

Our society is not consistent in how to approach adolescents who have broken laws. At one level society holds a goal of reforming and redirecting youngsters who are lawbreakers, and at the other there is a desire to punish them with the same intensity as we do adults.

Another area of inconsistency is with state policies regarding teenage pregnancy. Rules for parental notification and approval for a teenaged girl to end her pregnancy vary widely, as do the limits on how helpful a school counselor can be for a pregnant girl. Related to this is the inconsistency in policy governing what schools may include in sex education programs.

CARTOON 4.1   "I Hate Puberty . . ."

"I hate puberty cause it's so unfair. Just when I want to meet girls, my face comes down with 'a terminal case' of acne."

SOURCE: Merv Magus.

Anxiety-related problems for middle schoolers can be linked to achievement stress, social anxiety, and the possibility of suffering social isolation. Middle school counselors can employ a number of approaches to reduce anxiety levels, including programs of strengths-based counseling. An example of how the technology loaded era that we live in is changing teenagers appears in Case in Point 4.1.

CASE IN POINT 4.1

My niece, at "almost" 13 years old, arrives home from school and turns on the TV and begins to text message with her Twitter account. While doing this she turns on her laptop computer and opens her Facebook account to see which of her special friends are in communication.

(Continued)

(Continued)

Many of these digital contacts are the same adolescents she just spent the day with in school. Using a free hand, she opens her backpack and pulls out homework that is soon spread over the open areas of the floor for consideration and prioritization. She lives in a completely digital world and has never "dialed a phone," wound a clock or wristwatch, listened to an LP, or even watched a black-and-white TV. She is taking virtual German language lessons over the computer and conducting library research online for her term papers.

My niece's mother worries that she must learn to slow down and focus attention to tasks that are linear in nature. Reading a textbook, listening and following the logic of the presentation of her teachers—these are skills vital to success in college and later in the real world of work.

Thought Question. Is it possible that this generation of teenagers has cognitive abilities that older generations lack? Or do these young people simply lack an ability to focus and concentrate? Make a list of the ways the role of school counselors is being changed by new technologies.

● DEVELOPMENTAL NEUROBIOLOGY OF PUBERTY

> *Plutarch (120–46 BCE) wrote that children would not listen to the good advice of their parents, listening instead to their companions who would lead them into drunken binges, licentious and dissolute behavior, sloth, and sexual escapades. (Eyben, 1993, p. 202)*

Since the dawn of civilization, adults have complained about the reckless behavior of adolescents. Today we know that there are physiological reasons for adolescent thinking patterns and their manifested behaviors. Significant anatomical differences exist between the brains of adults and those of pubescent teenagers. This fact was not lost on G. Stanley Hall (1904), author of the first textbook on adolescence published in America. Hall used literary examples to build a case that adolescence is, among other things, an era of storm and stress.[1]

The need of adolescents for recognition and the lack of an appreciation of danger, combined with the inability to exhibit good judgment, has led many a young person to attempt foolish stunts. Today the easy availability of equipment needed to make video recordings of these acts, and the instant access to Internet locations for posting the videos of the stunts, contribute to the number of dangerous, high-stakes stunts attempted by adolescents (Parker-Pope, 2010).

Human growth, including the timing and direction of growth and the elaboration of brain tissues, is established in the genetic structures of our **chromosomes** at the moment of conception. By kindergarten, between 90% and 95% of the total mass of tissues that make up the adult's brain are in place (Kagan & Herschkowitz, 2005). However, many major changes continue to occur in the organization and refinement of the brain's tissues throughout childhood and adolescence (Healey, 2004).

The changes during adolescence occur in three dimensions. First, during the tween years (10–12 years) children add considerable amounts of **gray matter** to the **prefrontal lobes** of their brains. The prefrontal lobes are just above the eye sockets and house the **executive cognitive function** center (ECF) of the brain.[2] The addition of more **neurons** (brain cells) and their connecting points, **synapses** (gray matter), along with increasingly elaborated **axons** (white matter), provides the pubescent youngster with the raw material needed to make rapid decisions, and to multitask.

Impulses of energy originate in the neurons and move through the axons into the **dendrites** and from there through the synapses, where the impulse is transferred to the next neuron. In this way impulses move through the brain and body at high speeds. What this growth during early adolescence does not provide the young person is the ability to weigh risks versus benefits, do **higher-order thinking**, make **critical judgments**, and perform **meta-cognitive thinking**, including making accurate self-evaluations. Young adolescents also experience intense emotions, variability of affect, and powerful physical attractions to members of the opposite gender (Walsh & Bennett, 2005).

The second dimension of brain growth and development in adolescence is the **myelination** of the axons of the brain cells. This process is akin to insulating electrical wires within plastic. In the same way, the developing child's brain gives each axon a coating of a fatty dielectric coating. This electrical insulation along the axon cells extends the distance and speed that **neural impulses** move throughout the brain. The process allows integration of brain regions and speeds impulses up and down the **spinal cord**. Myelination occurs from birth onward. It appears to progress fastest during the first 24 months of life and again during **puberty** (12 to 16 years). Many of the most feared neurological diseases are related to the loss of myelin in the brain.[3] (See Figure 4.1 for a representation of what a neuron looks like when magnified thousands of times.)

The third difference between the mature brain of adults and the brain of adolescents involves a process of thinning of the number of brain cells (Lopez, Schwartz, Prado, Campo, & Pantin, 2008). Synapses that are redundant or underutilized are eliminated. This is akin to the old adage "Use it or lose it." The removal of these neuron connectors produces a brain structure that is more efficient and able to function as an information processor at a faster speed. A sign of this is the greater difficulty adolescents and adults have in learning (accent-free) second languages (L-2) after the elementary school years.

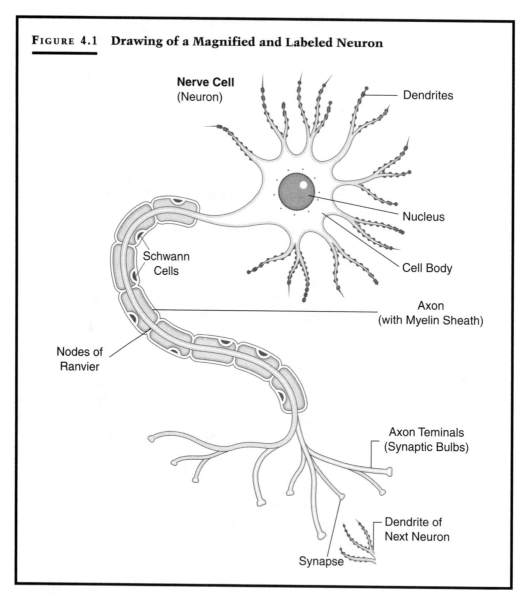

FIGURE 4.1   **Drawing of a Magnified and Labeled Neuron**

SOURCE: Adapted from Sprenger (2009), *The Developing Brain,* with permission from Corwin Press.

● AMERICAN MIDDLE SCHOOLS

In the 19th century only a small number of people went to school for more than eight grades (Margo & Finegan, 1996). Elementary schools in urban areas were designed to meet educational needs of children from first through eighth grades. Urban high schools only enrolled about a fifth of the graduates of the K–8 elementary schools (Solomon, 1975). Lewis Solomon's research also reported that rural areas offered many fewer opportunities for graduates of country schools to attend high school. In many parts of the rural South there was only one high school in a county, and it was only open to Anglo-White students (Funke, 1920).

The first **junior high school** was opened in Columbus, Ohio, in 1909. This grades 7–9 school was designed to provide a transition between the elementary schools and high schools. The goal was to better prepare students for the academic demands of high school (Ohio Historical Society, 2006). Educators believed that country schools, often just one or two rooms, could not do an adequate job of getting students ready for the demands of high school. Likewise, urban **extended elementary schools** (K–8) were not seen as up to the task of getting children ready for the difficult content they would experience with the **departmentalized teaching** done in high schools by teachers with college degrees.

Like their high school counterparts, faculties of junior high schools typically were members of subject-specific departments. Also like high schools, junior high school faculty members held college degrees in their subject areas. School districts often hired teachers into the junior high school and later "promoted" some of them to the high school. Departments in the junior high school, like those of their high school counterparts, were relatively autonomous. Junior high schools were organized and run like smaller versions of high schools. The unfortunate choice of the word *junior* foreclosed any other operational plan (Melton, 1984). The junior high school's focus was on academic rigor and the transmission of knowledge and skills, not on the student and his or her needs (Portner, 2000).

What was missing from the junior high school was any provision for the social and emotional needs of students in attendance. Students entered junior high school in seventh grade, having just left six or seven years in **self-contained classrooms**, where they were taught by one homeroom teacher. In seventh grade, they were faced with six or seven class periods a day, each taught by a different teacher.

Middle schools normally teach children who are between fifth or sixth grade and eighth grade. Instruction is carried out using **cross-disciplinary** teams. Thus a team of four or five teachers shares the same group of students all day. This makes it possible to employ collaborative instructional planning and to focus on the needs of individual students (Forte & Schurr, 1994). (See Table 4.1 for distinctions between middle schools and junior high schools.)

There are many variations on ways a school system will organize grades for instruction. By 1983, the dominant model for school system organization was the 5–3–4 plan. That calls for elementary schools to enroll children between kindergarten and grade 5, middle schools for the sixth through the eighth grades,

TABLE 4.1 Comparison of Junior High and Middle Schools

Junior High Schools	Middle Schools
• Subject centered	• Student (child) centered
• Competition of students fostered	• Teamwork and student-to-student collaboration encouraged
• Knowledge acquisition first priority	• Both affective and cognitive domains included in instructional planning
• Concepts and skills taught as separate disciplines	• Focus on creative and expressive development across the disciplines
• Subjects offered for one semester (block schedule) or one year	• Multiyear contact with a consistent team of teachers
• Structured co-curricular activity programs provided after school	• Counseling provided through and with the team of teachers
• Athletics organized around interscholastic concept	• Emphasis on intramural athletic programs
• Student schedules include study halls	• Co-curricular activities club based on interest areas
• Closed lunch periods	

SOURCE: Adapted from Forte & Schurr (2002).

and senior high school for grades 9 through 12 (Loundsbury, 2009). Many times the grade organization is selected to meet the pragmatic needs of the school district. The organization may include a middle school (grades 7 and 8), an intermediate school (grades 9 and 10), and a senior high school (grades 11 and 12). This is sometimes called a 6–2–2–2 plan. All organizations chosen by a school system may include elements of both middle and junior high schools. The great variations in organization make it impossible to have an exact number for each format used today. The best estimate by the U.S. Department of Education is that there are 15,000 public middle schools and another 1,600 junior high schools (National Center for Education Statistics [NCES], 2009). Of the total of public middle schools, only 2.5% are charter schools, and they enroll less than 2% of the population of middle school children (NCES, 2009).

Cross-disciplinary teams of four or six middle school teachers include one for each of the major content areas. The team can plan a series of **teaching units** that cover major issues and themes from the perspective of each of the various subject areas. Most of these thematic units focus on areas that have an evident link to accessible content. For example, a focus by the team on "the environment" can lead to the study of electricity in science, statistics in mathematics, the history of American conservation in social studies, and literature and writing projects in language arts class. Thematically focused and integrated content used in middle school instruction can also include themes that have an affective dimension. These themes can address the impact of smoking and drug use, bullying, career awareness and planning for life after high school, and family living.

ROLE OF THE COUNSELOR IN MIDDLE SCHOOLS　●

Problems of Adolescence

The same major themes from the elementary school years play out in the lives of students in middle schools. As is true of their younger peers, middle school students can experience significant problems of affect and relationships. In addition, a problematic dimension for adolescents is that of personal identity. A good number of these students experience learning problems and have special learning needs. (Concerns for counselors related to special education are discussed in Chapter 7.)

These possible areas of difficulty are made all the more intense by the biology of young adolescents. This developmental era is complicated by the acquisition of new **cognitive capacities** and rapidly expanding physical abilities. After the relative calm of their elementary school years, young adolescents enter middle school and find themselves engulfed in a society of pubescent peers who are in a daily struggle to wamble through layers of tense emotion and self-doubt. As a group, and individually, they are insecure in their personal identities and lack self-confidence. Yet, teens are compelled to establish themselves as individual beings, able to stand apart from their parents. Teenagers reject both parental guidance and moral direction while wanting assurance that their families are there for them to provide a safe haven and loving sanctuary.

Middle School Counseling Job Description

One-on-one and group counseling to resolve problems presented by students is a responsive task for middle school counselors. Other areas for counselors' work involve primary prevention through consultation with teachers and other educational specialists. Counselors also serve the middle school as resident research experts and local resources. This includes the ethical management of large-scale testing programs and the correct analysis and interpretation of test data for both their professional peers and their parents (American School Counselor Association [ASCA]/Hatch & Bowers, 2005, p. 49).

Another set of tasks for counselors is the provision of help for families and parents so that they can reach the goals they hold for their adolescent children. School counselors are advocates for students with special learning needs and are the source of developmentally appropriate ideas for parents of middle school students. Middle school counselors also provide a resource for the school community beyond the school and have an important leadership role to play.

In one of these roles, the counselor has a responsibility to prevent "**Momma drama.**" This flip term describes the gossip and complaints that all-too-many adults use to deride other children. The damage is done when the targeted children hear what these few vicious parents say in private. Counselors should provide a model for rectitude by discouraging parents from speaking ill of the children of others.

● COUNSELING AND ADOLESCENT IDENTITY FORMATION

Erik H. Erikson

The primary theorist of identity formation was Eric H Erikson. He saw **identity** as the fifth of the eight stages in personality development that a person experiences during the life cycle (Erikson, 1968). This development is one that occurs over a number of years, spanning the era between puberty and adulthood.

Erikson posited that human identity is forged in the crucible of adolescence. At a time when young adolescents can begin to see the tangible tasks of adulthood that lie ahead, they initiate an internal psychological revolution (Erikson, 1963). Erikson goes on to point out that adolescents search for a new continuity and sameness to replace old rules and concessions of childhood. Adolescents use cliques and crowds to help define who they are and what they believe. They attempt to define an identity by ongoing contact with their peers. Erikson described their communications as methods to project one diffuse image of themselves after another onto their friends to see what is reflected back. Adolescents are searching for the social values they will believe in and are willing to attach themselves to groups and programs that offer a resolution for their identity needs. These organizations can be positive, for example, sports teams, service clubs, various co-curricular activities, and Junior ROTC. They can also take on a negative aspect in the form of youth gangs.

School counselors frequently encourage teenage students to maintain wide groups of friends and not foreclose their friendship options by dedicating themselves to a single "best friend forever" (Stout, 2010). By having a large group of friends, the adolescent has many options for feedback and encouragement.

This attachment process can be transient and fleeting or enduring. One form of attachment during adolescence takes the form of romantic love. Love is a powerful emotion experienced with an urgency driven by physiological developments during adolescence. The danger of the adolescent era in human development is the foreclosure of the identity before it is finished being elaborated and accepted. Early marriage, gang membership, or cult membership can cause such a foreclosure and end the striving to find personal identity. The goal for adolescents must be to find a continuity of personal character and sense of personal identity while staying within the parameters of the larger culture (Erikson, 1980).

Another variation on foreclosure is formation of a **negative identity**. This is the identity of an outsider. Adolescents who are at risk for this type of identity problem develop cynical attitudes, are unable to trust adults and unable to communicate with their parents or teachers and counselors (Nowinski, 2007). The foreclosed identity can lead the teen into a **gang** of peers with similar maladaptive identities. Once in a gang, the teen finds acceptance and the protection of fellow members. Gangs are **self-reinforcing** and **self-policing**. They reward conformity with the values of the gang and punish violations of their codes. Once in a gang, it is very difficult for an adolescent to be brought back into his or her family and finish the work of developing an integrated and positive identity.

Steps to Identity

Clinical research has documented that there are four potential outcomes with identity formation (Marcia, 1980). These can be thought of as waypoints on the path to identity formation. Unfortunately a person can stall at any point and experience incomplete psychological development. We are all familiar with the perpetual adolescents among our adult acquaintances. These adults seem locked in an endless cycle of showing others who and what they are. They can't commit to a marriage or work well as a member of a team of employees.

The first of these waypoints is foreclosure that occurs when a person simply stops the process and conforms to the expectations of others without having explored many options. Becoming what others want the person to be can lead to a great deal of unhappiness in later life when the original error is realized. The second possible negative resolution is **identity diffusion**. This occurs when a person has simply given up on the task of creating a personal identity. In adulthood people with identity diffusion are "perpetual adolescents." Research with middle school children has shown that identity foreclosure and diffusion are the most common states (Allison & Schultz, 2001). One cause of foreclosure is the power of teenage love to dominate an adolescent's life, as is seen in Case in Point 4.2.

CASE IN POINT 4.2

It is very common for middle school students to experience the feelings of romantic love for the first time. Occasionally these "puppy love" affairs result in one partner becoming devoted to the other and assuming that the relationship is to be a lifelong commitment. As this period of romance occurs when youngsters are in the process of identity formation, it is possible for one or both teenagers to have an identity that becomes foreclosed. This foreclosure may become sealed if the two start a family and marry early. This issue of teen pregnancy and childbirth has been exploited by a "reality" TV show, *Teen Mom,* shown on the MTV Network in 2010. (For information about the reality TV show *Teen Mom* see http://msnbc.msn.com/id/34483616/site/todayshow/ns/today-entertainment.)

Later in life this relationship can become unraveled if one partner psychologically moves along and completes the identity formation process. This frequently occurs when homemakers return to college to complete their educations. During the educational process and related self-reflection, these adults find the need to become complete and independent people. The resolution of the **identity crisis** for one may not sit well with the partner. The resulting conflict can lead to the dissolution of the marriage.

Thought Questions. Many teenage romances come unraveled when one or both partners continue the identity formation process in a way not aligned with the other person. How much counseling in matters of romantic love should a school counselor provide adolescents? What are your personal boundaries in this area?

Diffusion can lead to a third outcome, **identity moratorium**. The military services often pitch this as a reason for a young person to join. The military is a place where individuals can take a time out from life to consider options and work on a sense of who they are. Erikson described the years that Martin Luther spent in the Catholic clergy as an identity moratorium in his life. The resolution of Luther's identity occurred when he experienced a major crisis. That crisis resolution brought with it the Protestant Reformation (Erikson, 1962).

Identity Crisis

Achieving identity often requires the young person to experience an identity crisis involving much soul searching and experimentation. It is the crisis resolution that facilitates the achievement of a sense of personal identity. The crisis may include a major revelation and/or great psychological upheaval, as in the case of Martin Luther. Or the crisis may be more inward turning with long periods spent on introspective contemplation. Once resolved, the resulting new identity provides a firm understanding of who the individual is and what he or she stands for. This dynamic entity, a personal identity, includes career and educational plans, personal values and beliefs, and a sexual orientation.

Having achieved this identity, the young adult is able to monitor and evaluate him- or herself and is free of the bug-a-bear of peer evaluations and pressures. One sign of the resolution of a personal identity is the loss of emotional responses to the young person's parents. With the resolution of the crisis, old feelings of anger or frustration toward one's parents are replaced with a new understanding of them. While still loving them, after identity formation the young adult will be able to view them as other interesting adults with whom the young adult shares a history.

Erik H. Erikson

Eric H. Erikson (1963) (shown in Photo 4.1) was the first to describe the theoretical construct of identity formation and the central role it plays in the psychological development of adolescents.

Erikson (1902–1994) lived most of his professional life in the United States, where he taught psychoanalysis at major medical colleges including Harvard. This achievement is all the more stunning when one considers the fact that he never held an earned college degree. He was born to a single mother and never knew his biological father. His mother and stepfather raised him in the Jewish faith. It has been speculated that his lifelong quest for a sense of personal identity led him to see identity formation as central to the psychology of all youth (Friedman, 2000).

After a brief attempt to study art he moved to Vienna as a private school teacher and tutor. It was there that he met and became a close friend of Anna Freud. Erikson and Anna Freud met in the 1920s when he took a job as the resident tutor to a child in the home next door to the home of the Sigmund Freud. Anna Freud provided psychoanalysis, helping Erikson achieve his identity resolution. She also introduced him to the theory and basis of psychoanalysis and helped him qualify for admission into the Vienna Psychoanalytic Institute.

PHOTO 4.1   Erik H. Erikson and Anna Freud

SOURCE: Courtesy of Harvard University Department of Psychology.

(Continued)

(Continued)

The Austrian takeover as part of Nazi Germany's *lebensraum* necessitated Erikson's hurried immigration to Boston by way of Copenhagen.

In Boston, Erikson met many of the former students of Sigmund Freud and formed his own theories of psychological development. His model for development became the basis of a new psychology based on the role the **ego**[4] plays in personality development.

Recognition of an Identity Problem

One critical skill for a school counselor is the ability to understand the culture of the school's students. Each generation of middle school students strives to create its own culture in ways that distinguish it from every generation that came before (Miller & Desberg, 2009). The culture of young adolescence can be encrypted or easily seen in their preferred media, music, lexicon and syntax, and clothing. Elements of the culture are "must-have" items for each student as he or she attempts to be part of the group. This is all normal and part of the teenager working out a personal sense of who he or she is. An **identity foreclosure** is much more than when a teen tells her parent she absolutely needs a particular sneaker or must wear a certain skirt length or style of jean. Foreclosure involves a taking over of the teenager's exploration by a group. The group literally tells him or her what to think, believe, and feel.

An example of identity foreclosure may occur when a student moves into or parallel with a clique or gang. This alignment with a group of peers may, or may not, be a bad thing. It becomes a problem when the values and beliefs of the group differ from what has been the child's norm. It also becomes a problem if the self-reinforcing and **self-punishing** power of the group overwhelms the young person's nascent sense of self.

Most organized religious groups set up programs for young people crafted to provide a resource for adolescents. These groups can help teens meet their psychological needs for belonging and friendship. An example of a negative possibility involves religious cults. These groups are built by recruiting members who are having identity problems and are willing to foreclose their options through cult membership where they must accept what they are told as absolute and beyond question.

The problem with writing about cults is that one person's cult is another person's mainstream religion or political belief system. However, for a school counselor a cult is any organization that takes over the student's effort to develop an individual identity and dictates most aspects of the student's life. Parents may be the enablers who introduced the child into their cult and are committed to raising a child who does not question their beliefs.

Schools can provide primary prevention of identity foreclosure. Programs that bring students together for co-curricular activities and/or group-based research assignments in class can help in this process. **Service learning** programs based in or near the school can also help teens with identity formation. A program of career exploration and planning can be built into the middle school curriculum. Such a program gives the counselor the opportunity to help middle school students begin to make long-range plans and focus on what they will become as adults.

There are many positive organizations in every community to serve the psychological and educational needs of young adolescents. Counselors should be very familiar with each of these organizations and make a point of learning the leaders and programs offered by each.

Partial List of Groups for a Middle School Counselor's File

- Youth Development Agencies

  Four-H: http://4-h.org/

  Masonic organizations, including DeMolay for boys and the International Order of the Rainbow for Girls:
  www.demolay.org/aboutdemolay/ and www.gorainbow.org/home/home.taf

  Scouts: Boy: www.scouting.org/ and Girl: www.girlscouts.org/

  Big Brothers and Sisters: www.bbbs.org/site/c.diJKKYPLJvH/b.1539751/k.BDB6/Home.htm

  Students Against Destructive Decisions: www.sadd.org/

  YMCA, YMHA, YWCA, etc.: www.ymca.net/

  Little League baseball and softball: http://en.wikipedia.org/wiki/Little_League

  Youth soccer leagues: www.usyouthsoccer.org/index.asp

  Youth Venture: www.youthventure.org

(Continued)

(Continued)

- Organizations Helping the Homeless

  www.ehow.com/how_2056742_volunteer-local-homeless-shelter.html

  Volunteering as an affiliate of an organization to feed the elderly and feeble: www.mowaa.org/Page.aspx?pid=183

  Volunteer coordinator at local hospitals, animal conservancy organizations

Parents can be encouraged to help their teenagers by keeping channels of communication open and flowing in both directions. Simple open-ended, nonevaluative questions designed to solicit nonemotional answers can be asked by parents, for example, "Who did you sit with on the bus today?" "What is going on with him or her?" "How's your art project coming along?" (Mullis, 2002).

Books can be shared and discussed during a parent book club run by the school's counselor. Titles such as the following can be part of that reading list:

Joe Bruzzese (2009), *Parents' Guide to the Middle School Years*

Barbara Coloroso (2002), *Kids Are Worth It: Giving Your Child the Gift of Inner Discipline*

Eileen Gallo, Jon J. Gallo, and Kevin J. Gallo (2002), *Silver Spoon Kids: How Successful Parents Raise Responsible Children*

James Holstein and Jaber F. Gubrium (1999), *The Self We Live By: Narrative Identity in a Postmodern World*

John Townsend (2006), *Boundaries With Teens: When to Say Yes, How to Say No*

Secondary Prevention

A healthy self-esteem is related to being open to personal exploration, while poor levels of self-esteem are linked to early foreclosure and/or diffusion of the identity-seeking process. The role of the school counselor is to keep the options open for young adolescents. Small-group and individual strengths-based counseling are appropriate interventions for middle school students who show signs of identity foreclosure. Strengths-based counseling for middle school students focuses on the teenager's talents, skills, and cultural and social resources. (See Chapter 6 for information about solutions-focused counseling.)

Sexual and Gender Identity

Two special concerns for identity formation are racial/ethnic identity and sexual/gender identity. (The topic of counseling with racially diverse groups of students is presented in Chapter 8.)

The development of a stable **sexual identity** is one of the central tasks of adolescence. *Sexual identity* is the term applied to the way an adolescent sees him- or herself, as either a male or female (Diamond, 2002). This inner conviction is well established in most children around the age of 30 months. Sexual identity is almost always a reflection of the physical reality of the child's body.[5] Human societies have felt a need to address the question of sexuality since the invention of written languages. (See Case in Point 4.3 for examples taken from ancient texts.)

CASE IN POINT 4.3

The first written codes of laws (Code of Hammurabi) dating to 1800 BCE prohibited incest within families but provide no approbations against homosexual behaviors beyond the immediate family. The one concern that appears in ancient law is having homosexual relations with a person who is not of an equal status, for example, with a household slave (Gerig, 2005).

Three hundred years later, the approbations about homosexuality in the Holy Bible's Book of Leviticus were written. The restrictions of the Bible only describe male homosexuality, while it occasionally condones selling daughters into sexual slavery and does not address lesbianism.

The historian John Boswell (1979) translated Plato to have said, "Homosexuality is regarded as shameful by barbarians and by those who live under despotic governments just as philosophy is regarded as shameful by them, because it is apparently not in the interest of such rulers to have great ideas engendered in their subjects, or powerful friendships or passionate love-all of which homosexuality is particularly apt to produce." Boswell's analysis of the laws of ancient Rome postulated they were written to protect children and stop rape, not to inhibit homosexuality among peers.

Move ahead in time to the Roman Empire and its senior jurist. Plutarch wrote, "No sensible person can imagine that the sexes differ in matters of love as they do in matters of clothing. The intelligent lover of beauty will be attracted to beauty in whichever gender he finds it."

Thought Question. Homophobia is a major theme used by bullies who are focused on harassing an adolescent boy. Epithets for gay students are used as "put-downs" among boys of this age. It is unusual for teenaged girls to engage in similar girl-to-girl homophobic harassment. What are the implications for these differences between the genders for school counselors working with a teenaged population?

Gender identity does not always follow the lead of the growing child's sexual identity. Gender roles are the product of the culture in which the child lives and in which he or she comes of age. It is the acceptance or rejection and/or alteration of commonly accepted gender roles that is central to forming an individual's gender identity. Teenagers can reject or modify the gender role established by the community and establish an identity at variance with what is most commonly accepted. This is a difficult step for an adolescent to take. Accepting a gender identity that includes a gender role that is different from the stereotype can cost the teenager his or her friends, draw the scorn of bullies, and disappoint parents and other relatives. The punishing power of teenage peers can lead the middle school student to closet away true feelings and foreclose that aspect of his or her true identity. The psychological and social price paid by boys that express nonstereotypical gender identities is greater than that required of adolescent girls (American Psychiatric Association [APA], 1994). One response to the problem of anti-gay bullying has been the formation of gay-straight alliances (GSAs) in more than 120 middle schools during the 2009–2010 school year (Denizet-Lewis, 2009).

During the elementary school years, a group of students may recognize that they are somehow different from their peers. This generalized feeling may be expressed in a willingness to play with opposite gender peers and enjoy opposite gender games and activities. The median age at which a child accepts a gender identity that is not stereotypical is 13 years (Sears, 1991). Acceptance of a gender identity does not require overt sexual behavior. Often it can be expressed through preferences and mannerisms and friends with whom the teen feels comfortable.

Once the adolescent has established a gender identity, that identity can be used in directing the teenager's sexual behaviors. All adolescents have a sex life (Sabatini & Reilly-Chammat, 2007). It may exist on only a fantasy level or involve abstinence, but the sexual nature of adolescence cannot be denied.

Counselor's Role in Gender Identity

The formation and acceptance of a gender role is a normal process. It is not uncommon for teenagers of both sexes to explore homosexual feelings with their most trusted peers. Approximately a third of all adolescents and young adults have had at least one homosexual contact before the age of 25 (Martinson, 2002). The majority of such encounters during adolescence are transient in nature, and less than 3% of all adults are exclusively homosexual in orientation

(McConaghy, Hadzi-Pavlovic, Stevens, Manicavasagar, Buhrich, & Vollmer-Conna, 2006).

School counselors have a critical role to play by providing all students with a safe environment and providing the full array of opportunities for participation to homosexual as well as heterosexual students (Lipkin, 2000). Too many schools are toxic for students who experience homosexual feelings. This need to provide full and equitable service and advocate for all students is built into the national framework (American School Counselor Association [ASCA]/Hatch & Bowers, 2005, p. 24).

Primary Prevention

The goal of a program of primary prevention is one that can involve great risks for the school counselor (Campbell, 1994). By one estimate, 65% of all school counselors harbor negative feelings about homosexuals (Sears, 1992). When providing faculty and staff inservice training in lesbian and gay issues and the developmental needs of students experiencing homosexual feelings, the counselor is likely to experience homophobic resistance (Uribe & Harbeck, 1992). The resistance may be passive-aggressive and involve finding ways to sabotage the counselor's efforts.

Legal Protections for Lesbian, Gay, and Bisexual Students

• Students have a legal right to form after-school clubs such as the Gay/Straight Alliance in any school that provides opportunities for other organizations to meet on campus. That includes all service clubs, Future Farmers of America, chess clubs, a debating club, Future Teachers of America, Junior Achievement, a Hispanic club, drama club, or the French Alliance.

• Students who are homosexual or bisexual must be protected from abuse and harassment and provided equal protection as all other students.

• If any students are permitted to attend school activities as a couple (e.g., dances), then homosexual couples must be admitted on an equal footing as any heterosexual couple.

• The school counselor is not the person in the school who is legally liable for ensuring that the rights of all children are protected. That person is the school's administrator (principal or director). It is the job of the counselor to advocate to the principal and other educators for the fair and equitable treatment of all students, including those who are gay, lesbian, or bisexual.

To learn more about the rights of lesbian, gay, and bisexual students, see www.aclupaorg/education/studentsrightsmanual/equalprotection/lgbtstudents.htm.

Likewise, counselors may find that parents of children who are not developing a stereotypical gender identity are unwilling to accept their child's homosexual thoughts and feelings. The counselor may even be viewed as an enemy who is poisoning their child's mind. Counselors working in middle schools should establish groups and evening programs for parents. The parents of openly gay and successful children can be asked to speak with various groups of parents. This may lead to an opportunity for the school counselor to create a parent support group for parents of adolescents who are struggling with gender identity questions. Providing parenting books that address what parents are going through in coming to accept their child's gender identity can help some of these parents. These include

Robert A. Bernstein (2003), *Straight Parents, Gay Children: Keeping Families Together*

Kevin Jennings (2002), *Always My Child: A Parent's Guide to Understanding Your Gay, Lesbian, Bisexual, Transgender, or Questioning Son or Daughter*

Bryce McDougall, Ed. (2nd ed., 2007), *My Child Is Gay: How Parents React When They Hear the News*

A third area for school counselors to provide assistance is with the gay and lesbian parents of students in the schools. There is no negative impact on the gender identity of adolescents and the orientation and identity of their parents (National Association for Research and Therapy of Homosexuals [NARTH], 2008). The counselor's goal is to fully integrate gay and lesbian families into the school community. Parent education programs can feature the award-winning hour-long documentary film *Daddy and Papa* (2002), available at www.daddyandpapa.com/order.html. A free discussion guide for this documentary film is available on the Internet: www.itvs.org/outreach/daddyand papa/. School counselors at both the middle school and high school levels can inform parents that most colleges and universities recruit gay and lesbian students and are represented at college admission fairs sponsored by gay and lesbian support groups (Schwartz, 2010a).

In addition, the middle school counselor can work with the school's librarian to ensure that books about the children of gay parents are available in the school library's young reader's section. These can include

Abigail Garner (2005), *Families Like Mine: Children of Gay Parents Tell It Like It Is*

Keith E. Greenberg and Carol Halebian (1996), *Zack's Story: Growing Up With Same-Sex Parents*

Noelle Howey and Ellen Samuels (2000), *Out of the Ordinary: Essays on Growing Up With Gay, Lesbian, and Transgender Parents*

Potential for Pathology

A tiny group of adolescents go on to develop a serious psychiatric condition described as a **gender identity disorder** (APA, 1994).[6] Teens with this disorder have intense negative reactions to all expectations, behaviors, and items related to the customary stereotype for their biological gender. As adults this group may seek gender reassignment surgery. In Western culture only about 1 male in 30,000 and 1 female in 100,000 seek this surgical solution.

MIDDLE SCHOOL COUNSELING ● FOR PROBLEMS OF RELATIONSHIPS

Mother Nature is providential. She gives us twelve years to develop a love for our children before turning them into teenagers.

William Galvin

Parent–Child Relationship

The developmental psychologist Robert J. Havighurst (1951) proposed a theory for the psychological development of individuals that included significant life tasks for each stage. One of Havighurst's central tasks for adolescence is to establish an emotional separation from parents. As parents see their child grow into adolescence, they become clear that the nature of their relationship is changing, including the rules and cultural norms of the family.

A contemporary to Havighurst, Kurt Lewin, saw adolescence as a period in development when the adolescent is changing group loyalties and membership. He described adolescents as being partly in their childhood and partly into adulthood. This type of ambiguity is reflected in how individuals are treated by adults around them. At one time we treat them as children but will not accept childish behaviors from them. Yet adolescents are barred from many freedoms and activities open to adults (Lewin, 1942).

This need for independence and the teen's quest for a sense of personal identity combine to make parenting a much more complex task than at other points in the child's life. By eighth grade, some parents and their teenagers have reached a point where lines of communication are shut down and the relationship between them is truly toxic. These same teens may find all adults to be out of touch and develop a cynical view of school and the community in which they live. At that point, young adolescents are in danger of setting themselves up with the identity of an outsider (Nowinski, 2007).

This potential is one reason parents enjoy hearing about "How to Talk to Your Teenager" during evening parent group meetings. Counselors can teach parents how to avoid power struggles with their adolescent children. Curriculum for those sessions should focus on approaches such as:

- Frequently offering the adolescent real choices among several options. When one of the options is not what the teen wants, explain the logic and rationale one time, do not debate the issue, and do not let it be brought up again.

- Listen to what the student tells about his or her school day. Use active listening, including not offering answers for problems and situations unless asked. Keep track of the names of teachers and other students so as to be able to discuss issues when invited by your teen. If you do not pay attention to your children, why expect them to pay attention to you?

- If a teen is pressured by peers to do or want to do something against parental policy, let the teenager know he or she should paint the parent as the ogre, a true offspring of Grendel. Then when the teen tells his peers that he can't comply with the group, he is off the hook. Blaming the parent can cut the adolescent free of the conflict between peers and expectations and rules of the home.

- Never set arbitrary rules and refuse to explain your position. "Because I say so" is not a reason.

- Your experience growing up is not relevant. To bring up your past experiences can make you seem to be a hypocrite, superannuated, or even quaint and ridiculous.

- Volunteering together and working for the betterment of others as a team can bring people together. This can be assisting Habitat for Humanity, reading to others and otherwise assisting in the public library, Junior Red Cross, feeding those in need, and so on. Joint experiences provide an unemotional common ground for communications between parents and their teenaged offspring.

Secondary Prevention

Middle school counselors can initiate strengths-based counseling to assist young adolescents who are unable to communicate at home and who are at risk for establishing a negative identity as an outsider. Setting the stage with the teen client can involve an acknowledgment from the counselor that the adolescent seems to be moving toward the status of an outsider. In later sessions the counselor can introduce the idea that the teen is less an outsider than a unique individual. The middle school counselor should point out the positive aspects of being an individual and work to get the teen client to embrace the same concept about him- or herself. This acceptance can then be folded into a program of strengths-based counseling.

Parents and Divorce

The number and percentage of couples getting divorced in the United States has been falling for the past 30 years ("U.S. divorce statistics," 2009). In 2005 3.6 per every 1,000 couples got a divorce. That is significantly lower than the rate of 5.3 per 1,000 in 1981. Yet it still means that there were more than 80,000 couples who were divorced in 2005. During the Great Recession of 2008–2010 the divorce rate fell again for less affluent couples and increased for couples with assets to afford the process (Center for Disease Control and Prevention, 2009; Schultz, 2008).

Altogether in the United States there are 14 million single parents who are responsible for 21 million children. About half of the single parents are divorced, a third never married, a fifth were married and their children now have stepparents, and just 1% lost their partners to death (U.S. Census Bureau, 2007a).

Problems faced by teenagers from single-parent families are made more intense if the family lives in poverty. Problems of deliberate property destruction and outright vandalism, choosing friends who get into trouble, and being cruel to others is far more common among teens from single-parent homes than when there are two parents (Ng, 2006). These problems, along with sharp mood swings, are more common among girls than boys.

The impact of a divorce on adolescents is one that will engender anxiety and guilt. Divorce frequently involves moving and/or making new living arrangements. It is likely to include shared custody and joint decision making about major issues in the teen's life. Only 16% of custodial parents are fathers. This can imply that children of divorce will have less affluent lifestyles absent the income of the father. In most states, child support payments continue until the child reaches 18 years.[7] The U.S. Census Bureau (2007b) has reported that the average award in a child custody case is under $6,000 per year per child. Less than half of the custodial parents receive their full payments. The average annual child support payment is about 65% of the court's award, or just under $4,000 per year per child.

Parents frequently do not understand the depth of the emotional longing the teenager has for stability in the family. This need to be part of a strong, close-knit nuclear family can pervade the creative products of the child and be evident in therapeutic communications (Burns, 1987).

Primary Prevention

The greatest advantage that a middle school offers for teenagers who are experiencing the dissolution of their family through divorce is consistency. Schools offer caring teachers and counselors with whom the adolescent can talk. The counselor should meet with the student's instructional team and discuss the teenager's need for security and a modicum of forbearance over small infractions. An effort should be made to recruit the team to be watchful for signs of distress and share their observations with the counselor.

School counselors should set up support groups for parents who are experiencing or who have been through a divorce. If that is not possible, outside organizations, including Parents Without Partners (www.parentswithoutpartners.org/), can be used as a referral. There are also online support networks and open forums, such as www.singleparentsnetwork.com/ and www.singleparents.org/.

Secondary Prevention

Counselors can establish support groups for children of divorce. A major focus of the group should be on learning coping strategies and sharing ideas about ways to reduce feelings of stress. The principal goal of group counseling is to assist teenaged clients in separating their lives and tasks of adolescence from their parents' struggles. Learning that others are experiencing similar emotions and feel the same sense of loss is an important lesson that the group can teach.

One approach to these support groups is to introduce a film or DVD about adolescents experiencing the divorce of their parents. A group discussion can follow the film. PG-rated films with a theme of divorce include *Fly Away Home, E.T. the Extra-Terrestrial, The Horse Whisperer, Kramer vs. Kramer,* and *Mrs. Doubtfire*. (Check in advance regarding school policy and PG-rated films.) Group counseling can also employ bibliotherapy using books such as:

Michael Bradley (2003), *Yes Your Parents Are Crazy! A Teen Survival Guide*

Lisa Schab (2nd ed., 2008), *The Divorce Workbook for Teens: Activities to Help You Move Beyond the Break Up*

Trudi Trueit (2007), *Surviving Divorce: Teens Talk About What Hurts and What Helps*

Correction does much, but encouragement does more. Encouragement after censure is as the sun after a shower.

Goethe

Juvenile Justice

One place where the question of whether a teenager is an adult or a child arises is in our court system's treatment of adolescents. Before 1825, children were tried for criminal acts in the same court system used for adults. If they were found guilty, they were punished on the same basis as adults. In 1825, New York was the first state to open a facility for housing juvenile offenders. During the next 100 years, all states followed suit, setting up separate juvenile and family court systems and devising alternatives to prisons for delinquent juveniles (Howell, 2009).

During the 1980s and 1990s, there was wide publicity of horrific crimes committed by juveniles. By 2000, 15% of all violent crime in America was committed by a person under the age of 18 (National Youth Violence Prevention Resource Center, 2007). One speculation about this increase blames it on the greater availability of firearms to children (Jeter & Davis, 2009).

A political backlash followed reports of increasing youthful violence. One outcome of the backlash was that states made it easier for prosecutors to try children under the age of 18 years as adults. There was widespread belief that strong penalties would deter delinquent acts. Today some elementary school students accused of a violent crime must face adult court. Yet, there is no consensus among states and jurisdictions as to a policy for the court's treatment of children and adolescents. Judges have considerable latitude when deciding how to try and possibly punish children. As a result, some miscreant teens face the full fury of the criminal justice system, while others are dealt with by juvenile courts. The U.S. Supreme Court has recently (2005) ruled that capital crimes committed by youth below the age of 18 years cannot result in the death penalty being imposed. That court's vote was close (5–4), and it overturned previous decisions that did permit the execution of minors convicted of committing capital crimes. The reasoning for this decision was that using the death penalty with children was a violation of Amendments 8 and 14 to the U.S. Constitution (*Roper v. Simmons*, No. 03-633[2005]).

Research has shown that when a child is adjudicated by a juvenile court he or she tends to have a lower rate of recidivism (Fagan, 1996). While sentences handed down in adult court tended to be longer for similar crimes compared with the sentences of juvenile courts, teens sentenced in juvenile court are incarcerated longer (Bishop, Frazier, Lanza-Kaduce, & Winner, 1996). This counterintuitive finding reflects the greater ease in gaining parole from an adult court. (See Case in Point 4.4 for an example of this dilemma.)

CASE IN POINT 4.4

Today, juveniles commit about 9% of all homicides in the United States. One extreme case occurred on Wednesday, November 5, 2008. On that day two men were shot to death in the small town of St. Johns, Arizona. The 8-year-old son of one of the men carried out the murders. The boy used a 22-caliber rifle he was taught to use for hunting by the father he killed. After the child shot the men he walked to a neighbor's home and told him that his father had been shot. After investigation, the Apache County Sheriff charged the boy with two counts of premeditated murder. In Arizona a child his age can be charged and tried as an adult.[8] If found guilty, the child can be incarcerated in juvenile detention until the age of 18, then be transferred to an adult prison for the rest of the sentence (25 years to life).

The boy was subjected to hours of questioning by police detectives without having a relative or lawyer present. This weakened the prosecutor's case, and a plea agreement was devised. Fifteen months later the child and his lawyer signed an agreement by which the boy pleaded guilty to one count of negligent homicide and was sentenced to an indefinite period of intensive probation and required to participate in court-assigned treatment programs.

Left unanswered by this case is the question of what age is it possible for a child to premeditate a homicide, and at what age should a child face the adult criminal justice system? To read more about this story see www.cbsnews.com/stories/2008/11/08/national/main 4586103.shtml?source=RSSattr=HOME_4586103.

Thought Question. At the opening of the chapter it was noted that the neurology of adolescence is a work in progress until the young person is out of high school. Take a position on using adult courts to try teenaged murderers and defend it to others in class. At what age should adult criminal justice take jurisdiction over children and adolescents?

Love and Sexuality

Children arrive in middle school about the same time they enter puberty. In elementary school they spent several relatively quiet years firming up a solid gender identity. Elementary school students are fierce in their dislike for anything having to do with the opposite sex. A boy in third grade may not be willing to hold a girl's hand in a classroom circle activity, but rather only touch the fabric of her sweater's sleeve. He would take it as a point of honor if his teacher scolded him for his behavior toward the girl. Teachers in the elementary grades frequently see teasing, chasing, and avoiding between gender groups (Adler & Adler, 2001). (See Photo 4.2.)

However, by sixth grade the anterior lobe of the pituitary gland in the brain of growing children changes all the rules. From that small gland come the hormones that govern the start and pace of puberty.

The drive to have sexual relations is normal and genetically programmed. The expression of that drive in sexual behaviors is governed by each society.

PHOTO 4.2   Children Holding Hands in a Circle

SOURCE: Photos.com_Education.pdf.

In the 1970s, fewer than 10% of young adolescents had experienced sexual relations prior to 10th grade (Miller & Simon, 1980). In 2005 the proportion of young adolescents who experienced heterosexual relations before age 15 increased to just over a quarter for both boys and girls. A disturbing new trend in the data about teenage sexuality is the increasing number of adolescents practicing oral sex. By 10th grade, 35% of boys report having experienced heterosexual fellatio, and 26% of all girls experienced heterosexual cunnilingus (Jayson, 2005). This trend indicates that teenagers are redefining what constitutes an intimate act. A large percentage of the girls who have participated in oral sex consider themselves to still be virgins. The psychological danger of oral sex is that one partner may feel they are being abused and made subservient to the needs of another. The resulting loss of self-esteem can be an impediment to the formation of a healthy and stable identity and impede normal relationships with peers.

In the culture of adolescent boys there is a need to have witnesses to their sexual behaviors. The result is a relative high frequency of boys describing what they have done to their peers (Miller & Simon, 1980). The likelihood of telling all the intimate details to one's peers diminishes if the boy has a high regard for the girl. However, nearly half of all first sexual encounters for adolescent boys are first- and only-time encounters. Girls, on the other hand, tend to discuss the details of their sexual encounters with a close circle of friends whether or not they plan to see the same boy again.

One reason for the increase in sexual activity by adolescents is the decreasing age for the onset of puberty. This places biological drives for reproduction into a youngster still in the process of neurological development. In 1900 the mean age at which a girl experienced her **menarche** was 17 years. In 2001, 35% of American girls experienced their menarche by age 12 (Zuckerman, 2001).

The cause of earlier onset for puberty may be related to environmental contamination by organic chemicals that metabolize into estrogen-like compounds (i.e., additives to the feeds used in agriculture). Also, the chemical bisphenol-A used in plastic bottles and containers has been linked to early onset of puberty in girls (Parker-Pope, 2009; Steingraber, 2007).

Another reason for earlier sexual activity is linked to our society. Teenagers use media, including Internet, telephony, broadcast TV, and computer games, an astounding 7.5 hours per day on average (Lewin, 2010). In many broadcast TV shows sex is depicted as an activity without risk or consequences. The more unmonitored TV that adolescents watch, the greater is their tendency to become sexually active (Collins et al., 2004). Children move into and through adolescence at different rates. There are a group of girls that achieve physical maturity before their peers. It is not uncommon for girls as young as 8 to experience early development of their breasts and auxiliary hair. There is always a possibility that an early maturing girl will feel like an outsider with her age peers. Sociological research has shown that early maturing girls are more likely to be the target of cruel jokes and labeled a "slut" or "whore" by other girls (White, 2003). Once labeled, these early maturing girls become the target of gossip, such as they have AIDS or another **sexually transmitted disease (STD)** and that they have had sex with scores of boys. This is another variation of bullying, and counselors should work to stop it and assist the girl being bullied and slandered.[9] (See a discussion of bullying in Chapter 3.)

Teen Pregnancy

The problem of teenagers becoming parents themselves prior to achieving adult status or forming a stable and positive identity is enormous. In the United States in 2002, 800,000 teenage girls became pregnant. Of them 215,000 had abortions to terminate their pregnancies (Ventura, Abma, Mosher, & Henshaw, 2006). The number of abortions may have been reduced by states that outlaw abortions for girls below the age of 18 without the permission of their parents.[10] There are a large number of teen moms in high school like the adolescent in Photo 4.3.

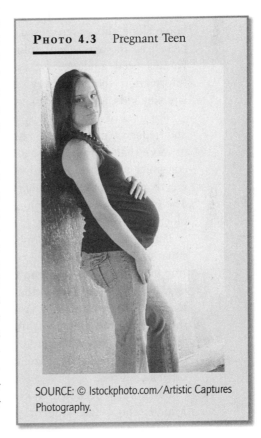

PHOTO 4.3   Pregnant Teen

SOURCE: © Istockphoto.com/Artistic Captures Photography.

The United States has a high teen pregnancy rate (Collins et al., 2004). In 2009 America was supplanted by the United Kingdom as the industrialized nation with the greatest number of teenage pregnancies (British Broadcasting Corporation, 2009; Guttmacher Institute, 2006). Yet, while prone to become pregnant, American teens experience sexual relations less frequently than their peers in other Western nations. One conclusion can be drawn about these statistics: our adolescents are less apt to employ contraceptive techniques. Even within the United States, minority girls and teens living in poverty have a far higher rate of unintended pregnancies (Finer & Henshaw, 2006).

Primary Prevention

The reduction of teenage pregnancies in a school community requires a team approach, including school counselors, school nurses, and parents. In many matters having to do with the health of children, parents prefer to hear from the school's nurse. The counselor can develop a web page with general information for parents. Announcements on the web page can include an invitation to attend a presentation by the school's nurse, or possibly a local obstetrician and the school's nurse, on the topic of teen sexuality.

Beyond the physiological issues, parents need to know that most teens become pregnant in the girl's home (Ponton, 2000). Many adolescents are **latchkey kids** who come home from school each day to an empty house. When both parents have full-time jobs, and in single-parent families, the luxury of having adult supervision after school is out of the question. In these homes, teenagers have full access to the family's liquor locker and the prescription medications stored in the parents' bathroom. They can also find and unlimber firearms stored in the home. Only 14 states have laws about children being left home alone and unsupervised. In those states, the median age of 12 has been picked as the age when children can be on their own without supervision. Parents need guidance for establishing rules about this unsupervised time. Information about latchkey children is available at www.latchkey-kids.com/latchkey-kids-age-limits.htm.

The level of sexual activity by adolescents is directly related to the intensity and frequency of parent monitoring (Huang, Murphy, & Hser, 2010). In a study of more than 5,300 adolescents, David Huang and his colleagues found that continual monitoring of adolescents beginning at the onset of puberty can greatly reduce the age at which a teenager will begin to have sexual experiences. The effect of parental monitoring is evident even when it is introduced with older adolescents.

Participation in after-school co-curricular activities is a partial solution to the situation of latchkey kids. Another solution is to have other family members stop in from time to time and visit the teen after school.

Of equal importance is the supervision children receive in homes of their friends. If the teen will be visiting in the home of a peer, parents should call the other home and verify that there is adult supervision for both teens. Similar calls should be made prior to any party or sleepover in the home of one of the teen's peers. Parents should be encouraged to watch out for each other's children.

Parents also need help in knowing about dating and setting a family policy. Middle school–aged students are generally happy to participate in sponsored social occasions with their **crowd** of male and female peers. Dating during middle school years as a couple is limited by issues of access, transportation, and cost. Each adolescent is different, and family customs and rules vary by culture; most American teens begin to date in middle school but wait until the upper grades of high school to pair up as exclusive couples.

Once parents have set a policy, it should be completely explained and then enforced. Being capricious with rules and policies is frustrating for everyone involved and can lead to resentment and rebellion. This is a theme that the counselor can develop in meetings with parent groups after school.

Secondary Prevention

Preventing teenage pregnancy has become a political issue. Many conservative politicians are opposed to teaching sex education in schools, including units on contraceptive use. They have proposed only teaching students about abstinence. President Bill Clinton signed the first abstinence-only sex education mandate into law in 1996 as part of the reauthorization of the Elementary and Secondary Education Act (Arsenault, 2001). President Barack Obama tried to cut abstinence-only sex education from the 2010 budget and replace it with a program to reduce teenage pregnancy (Crile, 2009). This approach was recommended by the Centers for Disease Control and Prevention and shown to be effective (Zehr, 2010). President Obama needed to compromise with conservative Republican members of the Senate to get funding that included money for abstinence education as well as reproductive education and pregnancy avoidance through contraceptive use (Robelen, 2010).

There is recent evidence that a values-free form of abstinence education can have a significant effect, especially among inner-city African American middle school children (Jemmott, Jemmott, & Fong, 2010). While not perfect, the compromise may eventually prove to be an effective approach to reducing teen pregnancy.

An implication of the politics of sex education is that the middle school counselor should move with caution in this area. If the school has a sex education program, the counselor can ask to participate as a guest speaker on topics such as love, responsibility, and adult commitments. If the school only offers abstinence-only programs, the counselor can advocate for a new approach.[11] In support of this advocacy is the 2009 report from the American Medical Association declaring that while abstinence should be part of sex education, it is not enough to stop teen pregnancies and STDs. Sex education should include condom use and other contraceptive methods (Elliott, 2009). One good resource for accurate information for teenaged clients is provided online by the Nemours Foundation at http://kidshealth.org/teen/index.jsp?tracking=T_Home.

Pregnant teens should be encouraged to discuss the matter with their parents. Some teens are not willing to talk with their parents and want the counselor to protect their confidentiality. School district policy or state law may determine this issue. If the counselor is obligated to inform parents, this should be told to the teenaged client up-front. The counselor can help the teenaged client in addressing her fears and concerns and offer to help the teenager discuss her pregnancy with her parents. The counselor should also attempt to work with the teen father-to-be. It is best if the consent of the girl involved is provided before contacting the male partner. His name will be well known to many other students and may even be posted on Facebook pages that are accessible to most students and school counselors.

The focus of counseling with the boy is to help him develop a plan for how he will support his offspring while working to complete his education. Boys should also be taught the important role a father can play in the development of a young child.

A school counselor cannot become the agent that arranges for a student to terminate a pregnancy. The role of the counselor is to discuss the concerns of the adolescents involved (father- and mother-to-be) and help them plan the next logical steps. In some states it is a crime known as **interfering with parental custody** for a school counselor to facilitate a teenaged client in terminating her pregnancy without parental consent. In other states parents must be notified that their adolescent daughter is having an abortion, but no consent is required.[12]

Middle school counselors can help the pregnant teen get prenatal care and proper nutritional counseling. The counselor should have a list of clinics and social agencies to which he or she can refer the teen mom-to-be. Counseling and support services are provided by community agencies such as Planned Parenthood. Their web page provides local links for service delivery: www.plannedparenthood.org/.

Tertiary Prevention

Prior to delivery of the baby, the school counselor can act as a consistent and accepting adult to whom the pregnant teen can turn for advice and emotional support. Counselors need to help the young mother understand the nature of the responsibility she is undertaking. The stress of caring for an infant all day, every day, can wear down even an adult. It can lead to resentment, anger, and possibly abuse by the teenaged mother. The resentment happens when the girl finds out that everything in her life now focuses on the infant, not on her. She must learn infant care and give up on her former social life and close clique of friends. Their lives will inevitably move on, while the teen mother's life becomes inward, turning on all about her baby.

The counselor can help the teen plan for her new life as a mother. This will include both planning for her baby and organizing another plan and schedule for the completion of her education. A key part of the counselor's work with the teenaged mother-to-be is self-reliance. The girl needs to learn that she is legally responsible for the baby and his or her care. By developing self-reliance, the soon-to-be mother can begin to organize a life plan without counting on her own mother or other relatives. Planning should involve living arrangements and a schedule for child care. Some school systems provide in-school child care for the babies of students. However, transportation of the baby and all the support materials that a baby needs must be brought to school without using school buses. A handful of school systems use the specially equipped buses designed for children with physical disabilities to transport teenagers and their babies to school. Most school systems are reluctant to assume the liability for transporting infants and babies.

Planning for the young mother's education may include computer-based instruction from home. There are **virtual schools**, some run as charter schools, available in every state. By using a virtual school it is possible for the young mother to have an appropriate educational experience while staying home with her baby. This option is one young mothers often do not want to use, as it removes them from the social environment of the public school.

Many of these issues will need the planning help and guidance that the school counselor can provide. Problems including transportation to and from the clinic, hospital, and pediatrician's office need to be addressed. Another concern for the counselor and his or her client is documentation and paperwork. The baby will need a Social Security number, and family social services should be contacted about possible public assistance. Eligibility for programs such as Women, Infants and Children can be determined by the counselor, along with arrangements for developmental screenings of the infant.

COUNSELING PROBLEMS OF AFFECT ●

Problems of affect during early adolescence generally involve mood fluctuations or significant anxiety. Mood disorders can be manifestations of mild depressions or signs of other medical problems. The most common medical problem is a viral infection, **mononucleosis** (mono). By adulthood most people show blood antibodies indicating they once had the disease.

Mononucleosis has an incubation period of up to 8 weeks when others around the youngster can become infected. Mono is transferred through body fluids, especially the saliva. The virus saps strength, produces a fever and swollen glands, and can damage major organs including the liver and spleen. Adolescents with this illness may need bed rest, and the role of the school's counselor is to set up a plan of home tutoring or virtual classrooms that keep the teen up with his or her peers. To learn more about this common infection, see http://pediatrics.about.com/od/mono/Mono.htm.

Depression can also occur among adolescents (Weller & Weller, 1991). The depression may be moderate and something that the school counselor can help with, or it can be more severe and require the expert help of medical professionals. Early adolescent depression manifests a number of possible symptoms, including weight loss, generalized **anhedonia**, changed sleep patterns, loss of energy, loss of attention and focus, feelings of hopelessness, and falling grades. Depression implies that it lasts for long periods, resulting in students appearing like the depiction in Photo 4.4.

PHOTO 4.4   Teenager in a Depressed State

SOURCE: © Istockphoto.com/aldomurillo.

Counselors can help adolescents through a period of depression by employing a cognitive therapeutic approach. (See Chapter 6 for a description of cognitive therapy.) This approach begins with identification of negative thoughts that the teenager is dwelling on. These negative thoughts can include negative views of the self, the world in general, and the future. An effective beginning step in the process is to have the adolescent client maintain a diary in which the intensity of feelings and the ongoing activity or experiences when those feelings occurred can be recorded. This can be online with Facebook or a similar system. The counselor should be given access to the student's account and be able to read the thoughts and feelings of the adolescent client. Later, after the depressive episode is over, the counselor should not access the student's account again. The therapeutic goal is to correct the cognitive distortions contained in the teen's thinking. A record of these provides insight as to what leads up to negative feelings and what context they are part of. The counselor works to replace those distorted thoughts with positive cognitions and an optimistic outlook.

Eating Disorders

One form of **hypochondriasis,** the inability to make correct interpretations related to normal body functions, is **body dysmorphic disorder (BDD).** People with BDD are unable to correctly interpret their own form and features. They tend to be preoccupied with elements of their own appearance and feel great distress over some supposed issue. Related to BDD are the serious eating disorders of **anorexia nervosa,** restrictive type, and the binge-eating-purging variation known as **bulimia** (APA, 1994). These disorders can be emaciating and life threatening. The American Psychiatric Association reports that anorexia is 9 times more likely to occur among girls than among boys. It tends to be most severe and difficult to treat if it first occurs prior to puberty. There is a far better likelihood of being able to cure the disorder if it starts after the age of 12. These eating disorders are illnesses that are part of industrialized cultures in which there is an abundance of food and are rarely seen in impoverished parts of the world. There is also a possibility that there is a genetic component to the disorder, monozygotic twins being more likely to share anorexia nervosa than are dizygotic twins of the same gender. The true eating disorder occurs in 1% of adolescent girls and must be viewed as a major medical (psychiatric) problem. The disorder is characterized by an inability to interpret body shape and size, and **amenorrhea,** with the loss of a minimum of three consecutive menstrual cycles. Treatment at an inpatient facility is often required to cure young people of anorexia nervosa.

Counselors in schools may find that up to 5% of girls exhibit subthreshold symptoms similar to the more serious eating disorders. These are described in the *DSM-IV* (APA, 1994) as having an Eating Disorder Not Otherwise Specified. In these cases the girl may exhibit many of the characteristics of a serious eating disorder but still experience her menses.

Group counseling provides an effective approach to assist these adolescents in accepting a healthier life style. One specialist that school counselors may work with in these groups is the school's nurse. Another approach is to provide adolescents with dietary information on alternate ways of eating and being healthy. The counselor can also make available support groups for young people who are considering strict vegetarian lifestyles.

Problems of Anxiety

Anxiety is one of the sources of psychic energy that propels all of us to action. At overwhelming levels it can be debilitating (Ashcraft & Kirk, 2001). High levels of anxiety can cause many physiological problems, including nausea, muscle cramps, heart palpitations, fainting, and insomnia. It can also interfere with the socialization of affected teens. Anxious teens can be described as clingy, dependent, and emotionally needy. Anxiety can also be manifested as a **panic attack** that includes a racing heart rate, rapid but shallow breathing, blotching skin coloration, and feelings of overwhelming hopelessness.

As in the case of younger children, anxiety and stress can be felt when a parent is missing from the home. For a teenager, the incarceration of a parent can be a very stressful event (Poehlmann, Dallaire, Loper, & Shear, 2010). In 2000, 1.7 million American children had a parent in prison, and another 500,000 had a parent in jail. Most caregivers for children of incarcerated parents increase the visitations to the prison once the child is in later elementary school or middle school. Research has shown that when the parental visitations are handled in a humane way by the facility, the visits can reduce the anxiety and stress felt by the teenager (Poehlmann et al., 2010).

There are various biological reasons for a teenager to develop high levels of anxiety. Additionally there are two other sources of anxiety that the school counselor can assist the teenaged client in coping with. One is high expectations by the parents. A number of middle school students have parents who are disappointed with anything less than perfection in their child. Any perceived shortcoming results in the parents withholding their affection and love. This is a powerful force driving teens to constantly feel anxious as to how they are being perceived.

The task of a school counselor in this circumstance is to work with parents to help them understand the impact they are having on their adolescent child. Parents who live their lives through the success of their children are not likely to be changed by meeting with the school counselor. After years of this approach to parenting, change will require a program of family therapy (Gormly, 2010).

The counselor should be prepared to make a referral to a mental health agency that provides family therapy. The American Association for Marriage and Family Therapy maintains a web page that provides an unscreened list of family therapists at www.aamft.org/. Counselors should always screen specialists they recommend by visiting them in their offices and discussing the therapeutic approach they use and the credentials of the therapists.

A school counselor employing cognitive therapy can assist an anxious teenaged client. Once again the first step is to help the teen client recognize when he or she is feeling anxious. Keeping an online diary of episodes of elevated anxiety and the context in which they occur can facilitate this. The counselor can employ this information to help the adolescent identify situations that trigger excessive anxiety. Coping strategies can be devised by the teenager working with the school counselor. The client can be taught to replace anxiety-increasing thoughts with reasonable approaches to problems that trigger anxiety.

Academic Stress

Even parents who do not deliberately use anxiety-provoking parenting techniques can have highly stressed teenagers. The press for good grades begins in earnest in middle school with the appearance of letter grades on report cards and the publication of honor rolls in the local news papers. High-stakes tests are mandated throughout the middle school years, and school administrators have their own careers in the balance each summer when the test scores are returned from the state's education department. Each school has a published report card showing the proficiency level of students in reading and mathematics in the school. All this builds a culture of grade and test stress that takes a toll on students and their teachers.

Middle school counselors are responsible for administering and maintaining test files for their school. This also implies that counselors have a role to play in preparing students and teachers for the tests and keeping the anxiety level to a reasonable point (see Chapter 10).

CARTOON 4.2 **Academic Pressure**

SOURCE: © Zits Partnership, King Features Syndicate.

Social Anxiety

Teens can experience difficulty in speaking before others or even answering questions in class. This type of **stage fright** can be debilitating and provoke excessive anxiety. At its core, this type of fear is an irrational fear of being laughed at and publicly humiliated. School counselors can help students experiencing **social anxiety** by using small group therapy sessions. Groups can assist the adolescent in developing the ego strength and self-assurance needed to become increasingly forthcoming. The process of the group can reinforce each participant's self-confidence, and the counselor can introduce some of the tricks of good public speakers. This can be done by having group members read and make oral reports on sections of a book about teenaged public speakers, for example, Diana Carlin and James Payne's (2001) *Public Speaking Today*.

Cliques and Isolation

A significant problem of affect is associated with social isolation. As some teens move through middle school, they become increasingly separate from their peers and families. After a day of avoiding social contacts at school they arrive home and go straight to their rooms and lock the door. They will not speak to others in the family and prefer their own company.

There are a number of reasons an adolescent may wish to be alone. However, very few American adolescents want to live the life of a reclusive ascetic. Reasons for self-imposed isolation include the possibility the teen was banished from his or her clique. Another is the potential that the teenager is experiencing symptoms of mental illness or addiction. (See Chapter 5 for a discussion of drug and alcohol abuse.)

Cliques during the school years are formed and re-formed as students move through the educational system. Membership in cliques is defined less by what and who the individual is and more by who is excluded, that is, who he or she is not. The teen may find he or she is on the outside looking in and has no wish to align with another clique with less social status than the one from which he or she lost membership. As Groucho Marx once quipped, "I don't care to belong to any club that will have a person like me as a member" (Marx, 1995).

Parents and middle school educators should watch for signs that a student is losing his or her social circle and becoming isolated. This can be easily seen at lunchtime in the middle school cafeteria when the isolated teen sits alone and avoids others. This isolation makes the teen an easy target for bullies and taunting by others. All of which reinforces the youngster's loss of self-esteem and status.

Primary Prevention

Middle school counselors can work with parents of the student to help parents open lines of communication with their child. Activities such as shopping together, volunteering together, participating together in church activities or charities, or engaging in a new sport or activity together all provide opportunity and reasons for teens to talk with their parents.

Secondary Prevention

Middle school counselors can be of help to the student using carefully selected groups. Group counseling starts with careful selection of group members, including other youngsters with similar concerns. Introducing books for discussion related to friendships and loyalty can enhance the group counseling sessions. (Books for young readers are listed in Chapter 3.) Individual counseling should focus on the adolescent's strengths and talents. (This is the basis for strengths-based counseling described in Chapter 6.)

The possibility of mental illness is more acute among socially isolated girls than boys at this age (Kwapil, 1998). **Despondency** and social isolation can become precursors to depression, **bipolar illness**, and even **schizoaffective disorder**. The worst day in the life of any parent is when they learn of the death by suicide of their child. The goal of the counselor is to prevent that from ever occurring.

SUMMARY

Parents have complained for millennia that their teenaged children do not think clearly and act impulsively. Recent neurological studies have provided a picture of why these age-old observations are correct. One effort to better prepare teenagers for the high school experience was the junior high school. Starting in the 1950s, that educational model, which focused on learning subject matter in a junior high school, was supplanted by a more child-centered approach to teaching students between ages 12 and 15. That approach is the middle school.

In addition to the problems of affect and relationships, young adolescents face a daunting personal task of identity formation. The successful completion of that task, first described by Erik H. Erikson, will provide the growing youth with a sense of who he or she is and provide a strong sense of self-esteem and **personal values system.**

It is the foundation upon which a successful adult life and marriage will eventually be based. Related to this task is the formation of a personal gender identity. Teens who do not follow the stereotype for their biological gender as established by society are likely to experience pressure from their peers and relatives. Middle school counselors can provide much assistance in this identity formation and acceptance process.

Along with physiological maturation comes the potential for teenage pregnancy. This is both a political and counseling issue. The logical primary prevention is through sex education, but state laws and local policy may limit what a counselor in the middle school can do.

The middle school years are also a time when teens experience problems of academic stress and social anxiety and experience fears of isolation. Middle school counselors can assist adolescent clients to learn to cope with and manage all of these concerns in their lives.

DISCUSSION QUESTIONS

1. Florida is the only state to outlaw gay or lesbian couples from becoming adoptive parents. Is this law appropriate? Explain and defend your position.

2. At what age should children be subjected to the adult criminal justice system? What types of crime should cause a child to be treated like an adult? Explain your reasoning.

3. With the age for the onset of puberty changing, should the age span taught in middle school also be shifted? Explain and justify your position.

4. What is an identity crisis? Explain what a successful resolution of the crisis provides for the individual. Did you experience an identity crisis in your development? If yes, describe the form that it took and when it occurred.

5. How exactly can a middle school counselor help a pregnant 12-year-old girl who insists that neither her parents nor her boyfriend should learn of her condition? What is the policy of your state for the role a counselor can legally play in such a circumstance?

6. Should middle schools publish honor rolls and provide parents with bumper stickers declaring that their child is on the honor roll? Why or why not?

RELATED READINGS

Doll, B., & Doll, C. (1997). *Bibliotherapy with young people: Librarians and mental health professionals working together.* Englewood, CO: Libraries Unlimited.

Erikson, E. H. (1968). *Identity youth and crisis.* New York: Norton.

Forte, I., & Schurr, S. (2002). *The definitive middle school guide: A handbook for success* (rev. ed.). Nashville, TN: Incentive Publications.

NOTES

1. The German term *Sturm und Drang* has been used to represent this psychological state of emotional highs and lows. Intellectual leaders first used the term in the late 18th century to express their wish to break away from the rationalism of the Enlightenment and express subjective and powerful emotions. The literary works of Schiller and Goethe and the music of Beethoven and Carl Ditters von Dittersdorf were the hallmarks of the start of this era of romanticism.

2. The executive cognitive function center has been described as the seat of "executive functioning." Executive functioning includes control and coordination of thoughts and behaviors.

3. Among these are multiple sclerosis, Alexander's disease, Canavan disease, Cockayne's syndrome, optic neuritis, Pelizaeus-Merzbacher's disease, and transverse myelitis (Swanson, 2008).

4. Sigmund Freud proposed three levels to human personality. The three are the mass of inner drives and longings, the *id*; the sense of moral righteousness and the human conscious, the *superego*; and the pattern of transactions and approaches used to

interact with the world around the individual, the *ego*. Freud's model emphasized the tension between the id and superego. Erikson's approach to psychoanalysis and his theory of development are centered on the growth and elaboration of the ego.

5. Each year a small number of children are born with the chromosomal structure of either a male or female but with apparently inappropriate genitals. This **intersexual** child may be raised by his or her parents to have the biologically wrong sexual identity. When these intersexual children reach puberty, secondary sex characteristics appear that follow the mandate of the child's chromosomes. In that way a child raised to be a girl may come to a sudden realization that she is biologically male.

6. In 1973 the membership of the American Psychiatric Association removed homosexuality from its list of mental disorders.

7. Occasionally courts require the noncustodial parent to continue child support until the minor child reaches the age of 21. This is done to help the custodial parent provide a college education for his or her child. It is occasionally ordered in the case of a child with a significant disability.

8. A decision by the U.S. Supreme Court prevents children under the age of 16 when the crime was committed from facing the death penalty (*Thompson v. Oklahoma*, 487 US 815 [1988]). This was revised to include all children below the age of 18 in the 2005 case of *Roper v. Simmons*.

9. A more dangerous and clearly illegal approach to cyberbullying known as *sexting* is described and discussed in Chapter 5.

10. The states of Alaska, California, Connecticut, Hawaii, Indiana, Illinois, Montana, New Hampshire, New Jersey, New Mexico, New York, Oregon, Vermont, and Washington all have no rules to require parental notification or consent for a girl to have an abortion.

11. A number of community-based and religiously affiliated groups have set up a system of "virginity pledges." These pledges are signed by teens while in a group setting with their program leader and are accompanied with a symbol of purity for the adolescent to wear, for example, a silver wedding ring inscribed with the word *purity*. Millions of teens have made the pledge since the movement started in 1993. Careful scientific research using a control group model of young virgin adolescents participated in a 5-year longitudinal study. The experimental group was the pledge signers, and the control group was a matched group of nonsigners. After 5 years there was no difference between the two groups in sexual behaviors; frequency of STDs; participation in vaginal, anal, and oral sex; and the age of first sexual experience. Eighty-two percent of the pledging group reported that they never signed a pledge. The pledge group was more likely to participate in risky sexual practices by being less likely to use birth control methods (Rosenbaum, 2009).

12. States requiring notification but not consent include Colorado, Delaware, Florida, Georgia, Minnesota, and West Virginia.

5

Counseling in High Schools

OBJECTIVES

By reading and studying this chapter you should acquire the competency to:

- Explain the role of high school counselors in developing the master schedule
- Describe the counselor's role in the high school's testing programs
- Explain various methods for improving test scores for students in high school
- Describe the major dialectic in college admissions philosophies
- Discuss college admission strategies that high school students can employ to enhance their chances of gaining acceptance at their first-choice colleges
- Discuss the process of identity formation in high school and explain the potential problem with identity diffusion and narcissism among high school–aged students
- Discuss the problem of date rape and other forms of violence that dating may open to a high school student
- Describe primary prevention programs for bullying in high school
- Describe the major impact that social networking plays in the lives of contemporary adolescents

66 The needs of children during adolescence are particular and acute. They need an opportunity to develop a sense of identity and to maintain the sense of security that emanates from group acceptance. **99**

Elliot W. Eisner

● **INTRODUCTION AND THEMES**

There are three primary activities that high school administrators expect school counselors to do efficiently and effectively. One is to work closely with the school's leadership in designing a master schedule and enrolling students into the courses that best meet their goals and needs within the parameters available. The second is to provide leadership in organizing, administering, and properly recording the standardized test scores for the numerous testing programs required of high school students. The third administrative expectation is that the school's counselors will provide a smooth transition for each student into a job or postsecondary education after graduation. The first of these activities is not aligned with the American School Counselor Association national framework (ASCA/Hatch & Bowers, 2005) and is an area that the counselor can work to modify. It is the position of the author that high school counselors have valuable insights regarding student interests, likes, and dislikes that should be shared with the people responsible for the master schedules.

Students' expectations of their school counselors are congruent with these administrative expectations and go on to include personal, academic, and social problem resolution. High school students want their counselors to help them resolve many of the same problems that were present in middle school. These problems of relationship and affect are ever-present issues in the lives of young people. In addition, the anxiety over testing becomes ratcheted up a notch as high school students face mandated tests required for graduation and diplomas. This is also the time in the lives of 2 million high school seniors for the dreaded College Board Examinations and/or the American College Testing (ACT) program. The task of identity formation (see Chapter 4) is ongoing, and an added dimension of vocational planning enters into the delicate calculus of the identity development process.

Parents also have their own expectations for high school counselors. Each year parents want to know how to optimize their child's chance of being admitted into a "good" college and receive the best possible tuition deal. They want the counselor to keep them informed of what is happening in the school and how their child is fitting in with the academic and co-curricular programs. They expect to be informed of any problems of attendance, interpersonal conflict, or academic slippage. About a third of the parents of high school seniors want the counselors to help their children find good jobs or vocational career paths that can begin soon after graduation.

All of these expectations make the job of being an effective high school counselor especially complex.

ADMINISTRATIVE EXPECTATIONS ●

There are nearly 16,000 high schools in America, each enrolling an average of 819 students. The mean cost of operating a high school now exceeds $1 million per month, including the salaries for two or three school counselors, two administrators, 58 other faculty, a school librarian and staff of two, school nurse, school psychologist, a custodial and janitorial staff of four, five administrative assistants, a security officer or police officer, the operation of 40 buses, and provision of a full program of athletic and other co-curricular activities (National Center for Education Statistics [NCES], 2007). Yet, for all this responsibility a high school principal earns an average of only $93,000 per year, significantly less than the senior faculty in many universities and the athletic director or head football coach of his or her high school (U.S. Bureau of Labor Statistics, 2009).[1]

Master Schedules

Counselors assigned to a senior high school should actively seek ways to be of assistance to the school's leadership team and provide a fair share of the efforts needed to operate the school (ASCA/Hatch & Bowers, 2005, p. 44). Many high school principals expect the master schedule to be designed and published by the end of the first semester of the school year. Counselors should be familiar with the enrollment trends and preferences of the high school's students and the plans and expectations parents have for their children. School counselors are likely to be the first persons to recognize the handful of students who will present complex problems of scheduling. These students include those who attend online interactive classes from outside sources as well as those enrolling in an esoteric collection of classes (Baker, 2002; Kussin, 2008). Other specialized needs include senior-year students holding part-time jobs on school time. Typically these students have completed most of their graduation credits before 12th grade. Another consideration is the scheduling of student athletes and athletic coaches who teach in the school. These teachers and students involved in interscholastic sports may require a schedule that permits early dismissals for away games or practices (Hurst, 2003). Other problem areas are providing for pullout programs—for example, programs for the gifted, English-language learner programs, the school newspaper or cable TV station, yearbook, and special education classes.

The school's leadership team must consider more than course units when building a master schedule and make allowance for instructional levels, that is, advanced placement (AP), honors, college preparatory, general or developmental, English-language learner classes, special education, and virtual classrooms and/or alternative schools. The questions of staffing and class size are administrative tasks, but the counselor is responsible for spotting potential problems with schedule drafts as they are developed and tested.

The final step in the master schedule process is scheduling all the students. This is typically done in the late winter or early spring. By starting early, the school's leadership can make arrangements for adding or transferring teachers to cover the school's instructional needs. The process may be done by hand, but most high schools use software designed to schedule students. The high school counselors must diligently monitor this process. Students can make many errors in the process of course selection that will result in their not meeting graduation requirements. Inaccurately completed computer forms and misunderstood requirements can lead to scheduling errors. The following are commercially available software systems for assisting in the scheduling process:

- A free software system is offered by Lantiv Timetabler: www.lantiv.com/en/screenshots/activities_full.gif

- Mimosa Software: www.mimosasoftware.com/mimosa.html

- TimeTabeler, a system from the United Kingdom: www.timetabler.com/faqs.html

In this era of accountability, no school counselor can afford to ignore educational measurement. As James Popham (1999) observed, all the rules changed when the local newspapers began to report test data and even rank schools based on the achievement outcome of students. Today, even the value of suburban homes is dependent in part on the ranking of a community's schools.

Manager of Test Programs

School principals assign all of the administrative tasks the school counselors are expected to complete as part of their job descriptions. The position of the American School Counselor Association (ASCA/Hatch & Bowers, 2005) notwithstanding, the tasks of school test manager are almost always assigned to the school's counselors. For that reason, high school counselors play a central role in the organization and management of large-scale testing programs in their schools.[2] This includes serving as the point of reception for all testing materials, the secure storage of test materials, the ethical administration of the tests, and the timely and secure return of all materials for scoring.[3] Many of the tasks of testing are clerical and require only the supervision of the school counselor. The tasks related to testing that require the attention of the counselor are those of interpreting score reports and helping students score as well as they can on all educational measures. Counselors are also responsible for assisting teachers, students, and parents to understand the score reports. This elaboration of tasks is built around the national framework (ASCA/Hatch & Bowers, 2005, pp. 44, 49, 51–53). (See Chapter 10 for information describing test scores and a model for interpreting them.)

There are many ongoing testing programs scheduled by state and private agencies that take place in a high school. Many of these are scheduled on Saturdays. Not all test dates for assessments such as the ACT need to be given by the same high school. The size of the high school's population of college-bound students and the interests and needs of the students may dictate which testing dates are most appropriate. High school counselors should post the new academic year's full schedule of tests and their dates on their web pages prior to August 1 each year. As the photograph of a testing environment in Photo 5.1 depicts, this is very serious business. This allows time for students to register with Educational Testing Service (ETS) for the early October administration of the Scholastic Aptitude Test (SAT) or the September administration of the ACT.

PHOTO 5.1   High School Students Being Tested

SOURCE: Digital Vision-School Days.

SAT II. In 2005 ETS did away with subtests on vocabulary and analogies and added a test of critical reading. The mathematics section of the SAT II includes 54 questions from the curriculum of algebra and geometry. A 25-minute-long essay test, critical writing, was also added.[4] This test provides **prompts** for the students to write about and scores the essays using a **rubric** of between 1 and 6 points. Professional teachers from across the country read these essays. The new test has three scores, each of which has a mean of 500 and standard deviations of 100. Thus, the aggregated mean of the SAT II is 1500 and the standard deviation is 300.[5] The new three-part examination requires 3 3/4 hours to complete. This time requirement is longer when breaks are counted into the test (see Chapter 10 for more about the SAT II).

American College Testing Program. During the 1930s one of the people whom the College Board attempted to hire was E. F. Lindquist, a professor at the University of Iowa. Lindquist elected to stay at Iowa where he developed the Iowa Every-Pupil Testing Program, which later evolved into the Iowa Tests of Basic Skills (ITBS). In 1959 he was a cofounder of the American College Testing Program, the largest competitor to ETS in the college admissions testing market (NCES, 2009).

Lindquist held a very different point of view about admissions tests. He felt that tests should not be employed to skim the cream off the top of a distribution of college applicants; rather, he believed that tests should help students plan and prepare for college (Popham, 2006). He did not have a vision of admissions testing that produced academic meritocracies on the nation's campuses; his test was designed to serve a guidance function.

Each of the subtests of the ACT has a mean score between 20 and about 21. The total is a composite, and it is approximately 21. The standard deviation is about 4.5. This means that an ACT score of 26 is the 85th percentile, while a score of 16 is about the 15th percentile. The maximum score on the ACT is 36 and the minimum is 1.

The ACT tests are measures of the skills and abilities needed by college students across four academic areas: English, mathematics, reading, and science reasoning (ACT, 1997). The ACT is taken by about as many students each year as the SAT and is the dominant college admissions test in 28 states (Midwest and South). In 2005 the ACT added an optional writing test. With this addition of a writing subtest, the ACT is nearly 5 hours long and presents an endurance challenge for test takers (Harper, 2009). (See Chapter 10 for more about the ACT.)

Merit Scholars Program. An effort by technology-dependent companies to identify and encourage America's most talented youth is the Merit Scholars

Program. The National Merit Scholarship Corporation began in 1954 as a way for businesses to contribute to the education of America's most gifted youth. The first Scholar Qualifying Test was administered in 1955 to more than 58,000 high school seniors. This test was developed by ETS for use by various scholarship-granting organizations. In 1958 the organization contracted Science Research Associates to build the National Merit Scholarship Qualifying Test (NMSQT). In 1971 the NMSQT was combined with the Preliminary Scholastic Aptitude Test (PSAT), another publication of ETS (personal communication with Gloria Davis of the National Merit Scholarship Corporation, February 3, 2005).

Today over one million students in the 9th through the 12th grades are tested as a part of this program. Of these, the 50,000 who have the highest combined scores (critical reading + math + writing skills) will qualify for recognition by the National Merit Scholars Program. Most American colleges boast the number of such students who attend their undergraduate schools. Of these students, only 8,500 will be selected to receive a one-time grant of $2,500 from the foundation.

In addition to these large-scale tests, high school counselors use online testing and paper-and-pencil tests to assist students in exploring vocational interests and aptitudes and screening for learning problems. Special education students with IEPs (individualized education plans) need to have ongoing monitoring for learning and skill development. This is also a measurement responsibility of the school counselor.

Table 5.1 provides a partial list of the testing programs in a typical senior high school for which counselors are responsible.

It's not hard to make decisions when you know what your values are.

Roy Disney

Test Preparation

It is likely that the school's principal will expect the school's counselors to provide guidance as to how the school can improve the average test scores for all students and help specific students experiencing difficulty on the tests.

Unethical and Illegal. Counselors must prevent any consideration being given to unethical or illegal practices in order to improve test scores. It is relatively easy to game the school's score profile from mandated state reports and in what is reported about test outcomes in the local press (Wright, 2009).

TABLE 5.1 **Major Testing Programs Often Managed by High School Counselors**

Testing Program	Test Takers	Time of the Year	Stipend for Counselor
Advanced Placement (AP)	10th–12th grades	3 weeks in May	No
NSMQT/PSAT	10th grade	1 Wednesday or Saturday in October	Yes
SAT	11th and 12th grades	7 Saturdays from October to June	Yes
ACT	11th and 12th grades	6 Saturdays from mid-September to mid-June	Yes*
No Child Left Behind–mandated achievement tests	10th or 11th grade	Spring term for a full week and make-up days	No
High school graduation tests (27 states)	Seniors	Periodically from January to July until student passes or is ineligible for diploma	No

*ACT provides the high school a fee of $8.00 per test that may be used any way the principal may choose.

Illegal practices include changing the students' answers on the computerized answer sheets after the test is completed and **teaching the test** to the students prior to its administration. These problems seem to erupt every spring during the mandated season for high-stakes statewide tests. These reports of educator malfeasants have the potential to erode public confidence in the integrity of education. Starting in 2005, schools in Texas, Ohio, and North Carolina have had their scores scrutinized by statistical consultants looking for cheating by educators. The states of Nevada, Louisiana, and Mississippi have hired in-house **psychometricians** to perform such reviews (Patrick & Eichel, 2006). Meanwhile, Pennsylvania, South Carolina, and Illinois include in the test developer's contract the requirement of post hoc test reviews for possible institutional cheating.

Texas hired Caveon Test Security to conduct statistical analyses of Texas test data and found that nearly 700 schools could be identified as cheating. The statistical analysis used by Caveon identified too many students marking the same pattern of answers, a similarity of patterns far beyond a statistical likelihood (Benton, 2006). Many of these anomalies occurred in the schools of Houston, where a number of administrators were subsequently demoted and teachers reprimanded or fired (Hacker & Parks, 2005). The full audit of all of Texas's schools in 2006 indicated a high probability that 1 school in 11 reported fraudulent scores on the statewide assessment. It should also be noted that many states have passed laws making it a crime for educators to cheat on these high-stakes tests. On retesting, a number of schools had average scores significantly lower than on the challenged test (Hobbs, 2009).

In 2009 the Georgia Department of Education threw out test results from the state's mandated achievement test for a number of schools. It appeared that someone in these schools erased incorrect answers and replaced them with correct answers (Badertscher, 2009).

Marginally Appropriate Approaches. There are methods for improving test scores that are legal but only marginally ethical. These include downloading old editions of the state's examinations and using them in classrooms as the principal curriculum for weeks leading up to the test date. This practice is an example of teaching to the test. Other legal but unseemly practices involve providing incentives to students to score well. These rewards have included tickets to concerts, admission to professional sporting events, and free meals at local restaurants (Belluck, 2006; Knight, 2005; Pakkala, 2006; Woods, 2007). Occasionally school administrators have even used foundation funding to present savings bonds to students who show improvement on assessments. The principal of an upper-middle-class high school that had a severe parking shortage devised a novel motivational reward. The highly coveted and very limited student parking permits were awarded on the basis of scores on the state assessment test. One school in Florida ran a cram course on nine Saturdays to get at-risk sophomores ready for the state's mandated test. They awarded perfect attendance at the Saturday *juku*[6] with a new iPod (Crouse, 2006). Other Florida high schools have provided limousine rides and prom tickets to juniors who do well on the mandated high school examinations (Bailey, 2007).

The research into the impact that these reward models have on performance has been mostly anecdotal in nature. Many of the most impoverished schools in New York City participated in a program in 2008 that paid middle school students up to $500 to improve their test scores. It worked, and those schools saw significant improvement on the average scores on the statewide assessments in 2009 (Magee & Gonen, 2009). In a statewide study in Texas, cash rewards (approximately $500 for each student) for students who score well on each AP examination and on the ATP (24 or more) or SAT II (1650 or more) resulted in significant improvement in scores from year to year (Jackson, 2008).

Schools in Florida are given a stipend of $100 for each student who scores well on the state's assessments. Some districts use those funds to reward students, while cash-strapped districts use them to buy basic supplies. Less-wealthy school districts enroll more children of poverty and tend to have lower average levels of achievement to start with. Thus, the state is rewarding some school systems for having many academically oriented, middle-class families who send high-scoring students to the schools (Keen & Brian, 2004).

Appropriate and Effective Approaches. There are effective approaches to improving the average test scores for a school and for helping individual students with low scores. One simple step a counselor can take is to keep parents informed about important dates for testing programs. Individual e-mails should be sent to parents of students involved. These e-mails supplement the general announcement on the counselor's web page. The e-mail should encourage parents to assure their teen will be well rested and will have eaten a balanced and nutritious breakfast on test days.

Time should be spent preparing all students in small groups for the format of the test and the strategy for doing well on the type of test. There are well-known and effective strategies for answering selection format questions (multiple choice) and other strategies for supply format questions (writing samples and mathematics solutions).

Students taking a college admissions test from ETS should be introduced to the support offered online, www.collegeboard.com/student/testing/sat/prep_one/prep_one.html, and for the ACT, www.actstudent.org/testprep/index.html.

Another approach is to introduce books to the students and also to their parents that teach critical test-taking skills. These offer examples and practice for the skill of being a savvy test taker. One example is Thomas Scruggs's (2000) *Teaching Test Taking Skills: Helping Students Show What They Know,* and from Learning Express's editors (2003), *10 Secrets to Mastering Any High School Test.*

As part of the high school's leadership team, the counselor can encourage the adoption of a program of curriculum development. One effective approach to improving scores from achievement tests, including the state mandated high-stakes assessments, is to carefully infuse all elements from the state's published standards into the everyday instructional program. This can be done in a workshop format with the assistance of all teachers of a subject area and the curriculum development specialist for the school system in that discipline. This approach helps the entire faculty "buy in" to the modifications. By matching each element the state mandates with instructional activities, teachers can help students be fully prepared for the test. This process of ensuring that the subject matter content and required skills are taught to every student is called "**teaching for the test**" (Crocker, 2003).

In addition to subject matter and skills, teaching for the test involves introducing students to all the test jargon they will face. For example, English teachers are apt to ask, "What is the main idea of the paragraph?" whereas the assessment will ask "What is the passage about?" or "What is the author telling the reader?" or "What is this story about?" Students need to know that all these forms are asking the same question (Greene & Melton, 2007).

In much the same way, the SAT has a language of its own, especially with regard to the 55 or 60 mathematics problems it includes (Harper, 2009). For that reason, counselors should work with principals to create places and methods for providing students help with their SAT preparation. For example, copies of software preparation for the SAT can be included in the library where students can access them during study halls, before and after school, and on weekends. Examples of these materials include two DVD-format software packages from Kaplan: Kaplan SAT ACT PSAT Platinum Edition ($34.66, 2010–2011). Another resource counselors should point out to students thinking about college is the online practice tests available from the College Board. These can be seen at www.collegeboard.com/student/testing/sat/prep_one/prep_one.html.

The provision of this type of test preparation material can help level the playing field for students whose parents do not have the money to send them to an intensive SAT preparation summer camp (e.g., www.kentsatplus.com/?gclid=CLn9g4C1y5sCFQJ2xgodk1MXnA or http://lexingtonprep.com/bizcodi/eng/pr003.php), to enroll him or her in a weekend or after-school class (e.g., www.princetonreview.com or http://huntingtonlearning.com), or to hire one of the hundreds of private tutors advertising on the Internet.

Helping Students Transition

The first school counselors hired to work in American high schools focused on the transition students made from public schools into the world of work. (Chapter 13 provides a discussion of vocational counseling with high school and vocational education students, and Chapter 1 reviews the history of the role of the first vocational counselors in senior high schools.)

High School to College

The pressure for young people to get a college education has never been greater. Today the entry-level requirement for many employers is a college degree, even if the job requires no advanced training (Whitmire, 2009). In 2008 the U.S. Department of Education released projections for 2017 indicating that there will be 3.3 million high school graduates that year. That same year there will be 2.1 million undergraduate students in college (Hussar & Bailey, 2008). This indicates that there will be more students than ever before going on to higher education.

One of the problems hidden in these projections is the 29% of all high school students who drop out prior to graduation and the 37% of all high school students who graduate from high school but lack the course preparation to begin collegiate-level studies. Of those who are college ready after 4 years of high school, 63% continue their educations in 2- or 4-year colleges (Forster, 2006).

> *The natural aristocracy I consider as the most precious gift of nature for the instruction, the trusts, and government of society. And indeed it would have been inconsistent in creation to have formed man for the social state, and not to have provided virtue and wisdom enough to manage the concerns of the society. May we not even say that that form of government is the best which provides the most effectually for a pure selection of these natural aristoi into the offices of government?*
>
> *Thomas Jefferson (1813) in a letter to John Adams*

Admissions Dialectic. Thomas Jefferson's belief in a natural aristocracy was a theme repeated by the leaders of American higher education in their admissions processes. James Bryant Conant, first board chairman of ETS, has been quoted as saying, "Each honest calling, each walk of life, has its own aristocracy based on excellence of performance."

Since the 1800s there has been enormous growth in higher education in the United States, from the 11 colleges in operation at the time of the American Revolution,[7] to the more than 2,300 4-year colleges and 1,700 2-year colleges today. In addition there are myriad trade and professional schools. These 4,000 schools and colleges represent an incredible array of institutional goals and purposes. The admission processes for those wishing to enroll in these institutions varies widely.

One type of college is concerned with enrolling the most academically talented students and weeding out less able students from the admissions pool.

This approach is one James Bryant Conant would appreciate. It is designed to create a college based on a meritocracy, where the best and brightest receive the most advanced educations. Elite colleges and universities subscribe to this approach, while most second- and third-tier colleges and universities aspire to it.

A problem for all meritocracies is ensuring that the student body is diverse and representative of the national population. There is a serious score gap that separates white and Asian students from lower-scoring African American and Hispanic students. The various reasons for this gap in test scores is beyond the scope of this text, but it is fully discussed in most texts on educational assessment and measurement (Wright, 2008, 2010). An admission problem with the score gap is that it limits the pool of high-scoring minorities from which students a college can select.

A related concern is with students who meet the criteria for admission into the highly selective colleges. These teens will have great vocabularies and be skilled at writing the standard five-paragraph essay in 25 minutes. The question that our admissions system does not address is these students' ability to think critically and have the stamina to read and understand volumes of convoluted treatises on various topics (Kirn, 2009).

Public colleges in many regions have no interest in education for only the most meritorious. These schools have an open admission policy. These "open door" colleges and community colleges admit students on the basis of academic needs and plans rather than on the basis of test scores. There are two purposes followed by most community colleges. One is to serve as the first half of a 4-year college degree. These colleges also provide a place where deficient skills can be honed and developed in support of a program of college-level studies. The other purpose is to serve as a place where students learn a skilled trade that does not require a 4-year degree.

> *At college age, you can tell who is best at taking tests and going to school, but you can't tell who the best people are. That worries the hell out of me.*
>
> *Barnaby C. Keeney*
> *President, Brown University (1955–1966)*

College Admission. The basic principle of economics that links "supply and demand" is what governs the college admissions market for the highly competitive colleges and elite universities. The number of freshman seats in the most preferred colleges is not growing, and the number of students graduating from high school is increasing. In 1993 there were 2.4 million high school graduates, and in 2008 there were 3.1 million.

To make the problem more complex for high school counselors, there is a "buzz" regarding some colleges that may reflect the rankings that are published by popular magazines such as *U.S. News & World Report*. The result is that as more students apply to a small number of colleges, those schools respond by raising their admission standards. This cycle adds to the élan of the most highly preferred colleges, and, as a result, the next year even more students apply to them. For many very bright and highly motivated high school students, the competition to get into a highly selective college has become a high-stress game that includes tutors, preparation courses, advanced placement classes, and a full schedule of athletics and/or co-curricular activities (Bowie, 2009). (See Case in Point 5.1.) This pressure can be read in the statistics of the admissions offices of the elite colleges. For the class of 2009, Harvard rejected 1,100 students who had at least one perfect SAT II score of 800 (Dillon, 2007). That same year Columbia University accepted only 8.9% of those who applied. The Great Recession of 2008–2010 did not slow the admissions pace of the elite colleges, who reported a sharp increase in applications in 2009 (Steinberg, 2009).

CASE IN POINT 5.1

The perception of a college admission crisis is expanded out of proportion in the hallways and lunchrooms of high schools when students begin to receive the dreaded "thin letters" that put them on a college's wait list. School counselors often unknowingly add to the stress and feeling of urgency by posting letters of acceptance on the bulletin boards of high schools. There once was a time, not so long ago, when the goal of going to college was to get an education. What few school counselors or parents know is that there are only about 50 colleges in the United States that send more letters of rejection than letters of acceptance (Steinberg, 2002). Parents more than their children study the details of college catalogs, attempting to ferret out the subtle differences between the top-ranked private liberal arts colleges in the Northeast (Cohen, 2006). Yet, the pressure is real and teenagers are expected to stand out and somehow appear to be stellar candidates for the college admissions office. To this end, families have been known to move to communities with less-competitive high schools. This is done to find a venue with less competition that will make it possible for the student to have a better grade point average (GPA) and higher **class rank**. Students have been known to volunteer to work with community groups and agencies, not out of a sense of duty or altruism, but to make their college applications look better (Mathews, 2005).

Thought Questions. High school counselors are provided with a range of gifts from visiting college representatives, including artistic wall posters of the college, college logo desk sets, pens, note pads, desk lamps, T-shirts, desk calendars, and desk toys. These are given in the hope they will be seen by students visiting the counselor's office. What is your position on these "presents?" How will you respond to them? Explain your position.

High school counselors have a significant role to play in making a college education available to all qualified students, especially students who would be the first in their families to attend college. In a University of Chicago study, 83% of Chicago's high school students wanted to attend college. Unfortunately, 40% of them had no idea how to apply for admission (Moore, 2008). To help make a seamless transition for graduating seniors, Chicago's schools began a program that assigned specialists in college admission to the high schools. These people help students pay for admissions tests, cover the cost of making a college application, and help collect references and edit drafts of the students' letters of application. They were able to improve the admission rate of Chicago's graduates by 15% (Samuels, 2008). Similar approaches in Baltimore and Brownsville, Texas, have also proven to be highly successful (Gewertz, 2009; Sturgeon, 2009). Much of the time of a high school counselor is spent working one-on-one with high school seniors, as depicted in Photo 5.2.

The need of some middle-class families to gain the admission of their children into elite colleges has resulted in another cottage industry. Parents can now hire private admissions counselors for their children. These "counselors" are not regulated and do not need to hold any certification or license. They often make bold promises to desperate parents. They charge as much as $15,000 for

PHOTO 5.2   College Admissions Counseling

SOURCE: © Istockphoto.com/BartCo.

their full package of services (Steinberg, 2009). These counselors advise on clothing to wear to interviews, admissions application completion, application letters, references, test tutoring, extracurricular and volunteer experiences, and even senior-year course selection.

Application Letters. Admission to college is based on a number of factors. One is the grades and quality level of the courses taken in high school. A second factor is scores on standardized tests. The third factor examined in the admission process is application letters and references. Another cottage industry has sprung up: ghost writers for application essays for some less-scrupulous students. For the most part, all admission essays are well structured and often represent a collaborative effort involving students, their parents, teachers, and high school counselors. They also tend to be bland and careful in tone (Kinzie, 2005). Most admission essays also exhibit an almost humorous tendency to bring out a latent sesquipedalian tendency among otherwise normal adolescent writers.

Admissions officers now have a new tool to identify those essays that were ghost written. These fraudulent essays can be identified by a comparison of the voice and style of the admission essay with the essay written as part of the SAT II (Lombardi, 2005). If the admission essay sounds like it was written by a middle-aged lawyer, and the SAT II essay like it was written by a 17-year-old student, fraud can be assumed.

Winning Admission Strategies. Most high school counselors are aware of several ways that a student can improve his or her chances of being admitted into

CARTOON 5.1 Plan Your P.S.V.

SOURCE: © Zits Partnership, King Features Syndicate.

a selective college. Students who apply for **early admission** tend to face a slightly less competitive admissions process. For that reason students commonly use it when applying to the very competitive colleges of the Northeast and West Coast (Pope, 2005). Early admission involves being accepted and making a financial commitment to a college in December of the senior year. There is a downside to early admission: students may change their minds about where they attend but find that their parents would lose a large deposit made to the early admission college (Marklein, 2009).

Applicants who are the children of legacy parents (alumni or alumnae) as well as those who have great athletic prowess are frequently given special consideration in the admission process (Shulman & Bowen, 2001). The advantage given to recruited athletes at selective colleges is the equivalent of 300 SAT points on the 2400-point SAT II scale. Legacy candidates for admission receive the equivalent of 240 extra points on the SAT II (Espenshade & Chung, 2005). Even the most elite of the small colleges compete in Division III of the National Collegiate Athletic Association (NCAA); this makes them open for special admissions allowances for superior athletes (Pennington, 2005).

Students with the goal of being admitted into an elite institution have adopted the strategy of applying to 15 or even 20 colleges, hoping to get into one of their top picks. This can result in a top admission prospect having 10 or more acceptances to choose among. This can turn the table on the admissions offices of even the most elite colleges as they find they must scramble to sell their colleges to the prospect. This sales effort during the spring term of the prospect's senior year can include free trips to campus and tickets to on-campus events for the student and his or her parents (Finder, 2006).

Another way to gain an admission advantage is to choose a major that is undersubscribed at a top-rated college. For example, a student who selects a popular major such as pre-law may need a combined score of 1975 on the SAT II to meet the minimum for consideration, while a student may only need an SAT II combined score of 1700 if he or she indicates secondary education as the intended major.[8]

An advantage can go to students on the basis of gender. Top liberal arts colleges—for example, Williams, Amherst, Haverford, and Swarthmore—have an excess of women who apply. For that reason, men who apply to these schools may be held to a slightly lower standard (Peck, 2003). The reverse situation holds at many top technical universities, where the shortage of women gives an admission advantage to female applicants. In the same way that colleges attempt to keep a gender balance in their undergraduate population, they also work to maintain a balance of ethnic and racial minorities at the undergraduate level.

Liberal arts colleges are aware that there are real educational advantages to students who attend colleges with an undergraduate population that is culturally diverse (Gurin, Dey, Hurtado, & Gurin, 2002).

Out-of-State Colleges. The selectivity of many "flagship" state universities is now very high and is increasing annually. This trend is likely to continue for the next few years as the number of high school graduates is increasing at a time when state legislatures are reducing university budgets (Davis, 2004; Kelderman, 2008). A number of state universities are reducing the number of in-state students who can be accepted each year in order to increase the number of out-of-state, higher-tuition-paying students who are admitted. This preference for the full-tuition-paying out-of-state student is exacerbating the admission problem for in-state students. (See Case in Point 5.2.)

CASE IN POINT 5.2

The admission problem in Texas is most acute. In an effort to open the admissions into the University of Texas and Texas A&M University for more minority students, the state adopted an admissions-by-class-standing system. Texas provides guaranteed admission and financial aid to many high-scoring (ACT, SAT II) students in the top 10% of their high school's graduating class. This has increased enrollment of students from rural Texas and significantly increased minority student representation in the student body.

On the downside of this policy, after athletes and other special cases (children of politicians and alumni legacy students) are considered, there is little space for other top students who often have very high admissions test scores and solid academic records (Barkan, 2008). As all Texas high schools do not have equal levels of academic rigor and quality, a number of superior students graduating from the better high schools but who were below the 10% cut point elected to attend out-of-state elite colleges. The result was that in 2009 the top two Texas universities were released from this requirement of enrolling all students who apply and graduate high school in the top 10%.

Thought Questions. The problem of admission for students from all backgrounds into prestigious colleges is not easily resolved. Affirmative action with set-asides for different groups is against federal case laws, and the percent solution of California, Texas, and Florida is also not working as well as hoped. The main problem with the percent solution is the uneven nature of academic rigor in different high schools and the implied assumption that voluntary segregation has occurred among high school populations.

If you were the senior admissions officer of a prestigious college, what admissions goals would you set? What policies would you have your staff follow to meet those goals?

COUNSELING STUDENTS IN HIGH SCHOOL ●

Popularity and Fitting In

The goals of most healthy high school students are to "fit in," have many friends, and do well in school. Popularity is a powerful elixir for teenagers, but it is not the same thing as likeability. The dimension of likeability describes something very different from popularity (Tugend, 2010). Likeable students are popular. Also, beautiful, powerful, and aggressive students are popular, but they are not necessarily likeable. For example, a bully may be popular but considered by most students as unlikeable. About 1 in 5 high school students is described by fellow students as highly likeable (Carey, 2008). About half of all students are of average likeability, and 30% are divided between those students who are so shy as to be unknowns, and therefore off the charts, and those who are rejected by the peer group and therefore viewed as unlikeable.

Popular students have many more opportunities to participate in sketchy behaviors. This greater opportunity along with peer pressure to remain popular is why they report experiencing sexual relations (both oral and intercourse) and experimenting with drugs and alcohol more frequently than less popular students (La Greca, Prinstein, & Fetter, 2001; Prinstein & Cillessen, 2003).

Counseling Intervention

The losers in this likeability hierarchy are those teens who are rejected and deemed to be unlikeable. These and the shy group can be helped to improve their status through group counseling and their introduction into co-curricular and after-school programs for young people. Students who are so reticent as to be off the popularity radar at school have the greatest capacity for changing their status. Those who have been rejected may find solace in a group of students with similar low peer status. The key to having positive self-esteem and being happy is for the student to feel that he or she fits in somewhere. Group sessions with these teens can teach the social graces of "breaking the ice" with others, making others feel comfortable around them by being positive, and making them feel good about themselves. Some faculty wags may deride these sessions and accuse the school's counselor of providing a charm school for the pariahs of the school.

Academic Stress and Grades

Teachers see grades in class and on report cards several ways. They see them as motivational tools as well as ways to reward and punish students for their efforts (Brookhart, 1994, 2004). One core assumption about grades is that they are unbiased; however, many students and their parents do not take that as a given. They insist on meeting with a school counselor (who has no power to influence grades), principals (who do have the power to change grades), and **central office administrators** if they feel an injustice has been done.

The real meaning of the composite grade recorded on a report card is rather murky. This grade represents many pieces of student work that have been weighted and combined into a single statement. The weighting of various achievement measures, and the addition of outside factors such as classroom behavior and perceived effort level, make report cards truly idiosyncratic products. It is not uncommon for a student who receives a grade of C to ask his or her teacher what would be necessary to get a B, only to be told to "work harder." This provides the child with virtually no guidance and reflects how report card grades have an almost ephemeral nature (Clarridge & Whitaker, 1997). At best, these grades can be viewed as a crude summary that tells nothing of the efforts and difficulties that the student experienced in learning the material. Report card grades do not demonstrate strengths, nor do they elaborate on the student's areas of weakness (Brookhart, 2004).

Yet, despite the inexact nature of grades, they are important in the lives of many high school students. In some states like California, Texas, and Florida, grades in high school can determine college admission and the financial award package a student gets for attending college. Great stress is felt by the top few students vying to give the valedictory speech at graduation. Students have been known to strategically select their courseloads so as to eke out a few hundredths of a point higher GPAs than their rivals. It is patent that to do well in high school a student must be in class. Case in Point 5.3 addresses this issue.

CASE IN POINT 5.3

A behavior of many high school students that is antithetical to good levels of academic achievement is **truancy**. School attendance is closely linked to achievement and is a sign the student is motivated to succeed (Manis, 2004; Urban-Lurain, 2000). Truancy is a major problem in urban areas where children go to school on their own, and less of a problem in the suburban and rural areas where they are bused or driven by parents from home each day. Reducing truancy is a schoolwide problem, but not the only one related to attendance. Many teenagers like to sleep in and in urban areas arrive in school several hours late (tardy). Big-city high schools have taken to scheduling homeroom period for the middle of the morning so as not to need to report late arriving students as absent.

To stop truancy, the school administration should enforce the truancy laws of the state. This will result in the parents of truant and chronically tardy students appearing in court and paying a fine. Strict enforcement of attendance laws in San Francisco resulted in a 23% reduction in truancy in 2009 (Tucker, 2009).

Thought Question. To help students get to high school on time, school counselors have been known to use school funds to buy truant and tardy students alarm clocks and teach those students how to set and use them. What other realistic steps can you think of that could help adolescents get to high school on time?

Report Card Ownership. With all report cards, the parents are the owners of the student record. It is the parents who have full responsibility for the minor children in their families. During the senior year, an exception occurs when the high school student has his or her 18th birthday. That age makes the student an adult, and the young adult owns his or her records. Parents no longer have a right to see the academic record of the 18-year-old student without written permission from the student. Public high schools need to develop release forms to distribute to students on their 18th birthdays.

Grades for Special Populations. A special problem for awarding grades in public schools is related to children at either end of the normal distribution of academic ability. Children with special needs as well as children enrolled in programs for the **gifted** need to have special care taken when crafting report cards and transcripts. One controversial approach to grading these special children is to differentially weight the classes they complete. This happens more often in high school when extra quality points for advanced placement classes are awarded to high-achieving students.

Special education students have been effectively barred from the honor rolls of their schools by the manipulation of the credit awarded for classes. This system has allowed special needs students to take home report cards reflecting their hard effort and good progress. Yet, the total number of earned credits is below the threshold for entering into the calculation of an honor roll designation. As an outcome of the **Health Insurance Portability and Accountability Act of 1996 (HIPPA)**, psychological records, including those of licensed school psychologists, are protected confidential records. This means that schools may not indicate on a special education student's permanent record or grade transcript that an entitlement decision had been made to provide the child with special education (Benitz, 2006).

There is no federal law that mandates school districts to protect the rights of gifted children. That is a matter left to the states. There are 29 states that have embraced programs for the gifted, of which only 4 provide funding and guidelines for their operation within the state's school systems.

Gifted education has always been suspect in this country. All too often it is seen as elitist and somehow un-American. Taxpayers have difficulty with the idea of spending more to educate students who have more to start with than do others. Yet, most adults have no problem having the schools offer competitive programs for elite athletes and talented young musicians. In 2005 a coalition of parent groups in suburban Montgomery County, Maryland, began a campaign to end the identification of gifted students and the termination of all special programs for gifted children (Aratani, 2005). The primary point made by this group was that programs for the gifted were not equitable and should be open to all students.

During 9th and 10th grades, students can elect honors classes, and in thousands of high schools, juniors and seniors can elect advanced placement (AP) classes and/or **International Baccalaureate (IB)** classes. Only 1 in 6 students enrolled in an AP class is in 10th grade. Both the IB and the AP programs provide the possibility of college credit for a successful performance in the advanced courses. These advanced classes have more requirements and use college-level textbooks. There is ample evidence that the AP classes require more of students and have more exacting standards (Popielarski, 1998). Research evidence has demonstrated that students completing AP classes with a final exam score of 3 or more on the 5-point ordinal scale have a significantly greater likelihood of entering college and finishing a bachelor's degree within 5 years than do other students (Dougherty, Mellor, & Shuling, 2006; Klein, 2007). It is an unfortunate fact that African American and Hispanic high school students are underrepresented in AP programs.

Minority students are enrolled in AP courses at a rate that is proportionally less than half what would be expected based on the number of minority students in high school (Wasley, 2007). In contrast, Asian American students are twice as likely to take AP courses, as their numbers would predict (Maxwell, 2007).

Most school systems give extra weight to the grades earned in advanced courses than is true for regular high school classes. Thus, students enrolled in advanced courses can give their **grade point** an upward push.

Counseling for Better Grades. At the primary intervention level are evening and Internet-based virtual programs that school counselors can provide to help parents understand the role parents play in improving their teenagers' grades.

There are three major things parents can do to increase achievement levels of their teenagers. One is to provide a quiet, distraction-free study hall at home where the student can work on homework assignments and study 6 days a week. Students who report that they do not complete their assigned homework have achievement test scores significantly below the level of students who do an hour or more of homework a day (National Assessment of Educational Progress [NAEP], 2004). Likewise, teens with parents who enforce homework rules, including no computer games or Internet socializing "during study hall," have better assessment scores (Lewin, 2010; NAEP, 2004).

Parents also need to learn about peer power and school success. Students who report that their friends ridicule others who try hard and do well in school have lower achievement than do children who do not have such friends. The influence of the choice of friends has been shown to play an important part in general academic achievement (Buoye, 2004; DeParle, 2009).

A final area in which counselors can help parents improve their adolescent's achievement and grades has to do with the use of computers. A measure of the amount of time young people play computer games and spend text messaging their peers is correlated with the scores obtained by those students on high-stakes tests (Holbrook & Wright, 2004). Parents who enforce rules limiting hours of the day that the adolescent can use all forms of media and technology have been shown to link to better school grades (Lewin, 2010).

Computer gaming can draw a teenager into an addictive relationship with its characters and story line. The incremental complexity of online computer game formats serves as a reward for teenagers. This cognitive reward makes gaming very compelling, and adolescents can spend inordinate amounts of time learning new game skills and increasing the level and complexity of play. This devotion to gaming may cause a loss of sleep, inattention, and various problems in school, including lower achievement and poor test scores. There is an online support group for parents of computer gaming–addicted children. This group is *Mothers Against Videogame Addiction and Violence* at www.mavav.org/.

Consistent increments occur in the assessment test scores of children as a function of increasing levels of parental education (Joireman & Abbott, 2004; NAEP, 2004). One of the best predictors of how well children of entire school districts will do on a statewide assessment is the average level of education of the parents of the community (Noble, Roberts, & Sawyer, 2007; Zackon, 1999). Of equal importance for the student's academic success are the goals that the parents have for his or her education. Children of parents who express the goal of eventually seeing their adolescents graduate from college achieve high scores on the NAEP.

Intervention Programs for Counseling Adolescents. Group counseling can be highly effective for helping teenagers improve their school grades. One of the best approaches to this involves teaching high school students how to set goals and plan schedules for their complex lives (Paslay, 1995). Goal setting is a method that involves setting both long-range and target goals and setting smaller goals leading to the final target. As adolescent clients achieve the goals they have set, they improve in self-confidence, feel empowered, and fulfill their need for a sense of independence. (See Chapter 9 for a description of how to teach goal setting during group counseling.)

Identity Problems in High School

As was true in middle school, the process of achieving an integrated sense of one's personal identity continues throughout the high school years. A study of high school and college age students found that about 20% had settled on an identity and felt their lives had a purpose. About half the sample was in a state of speculation and dreaming about the potential life would hold for them. These teens and young adults are **identity deferrals,** who are making progress toward finding the purpose and personal meaning of their lives. About 1 in 4 of the sample was disengaged and in a listless state (Viadero, 2008). These listless students exhibit poor levels of emotional well-being. They believe they cannot effectively cope with the range of problems encountered in daily life (Ciarrochi, Leeson, & Heaven, 2009).

The problem of identity formation is no less difficult for privileged adolescents from upper-middle-class homes (Levine, 2006). Otherwise successful teens placed under constant pressure for ever-better grades, and subjected to critical scrutiny of their appearance and body build, have been shown to experience identity diffusion, depression, and **narcissism.** Small narcissistic tendencies are normal; teenaged girls spontaneously draw pictures of idealized girls and women in their notebooks, while boys draw powerful cars and motorcycles. However, this can lead the teenager to be defensive, judgmental, and unforgiving, have frequent friendship problems, and lack an ability to commit (Novotney, 2009b).

Identity diffusion and narcissism at this stage in a teenager's life can foretell a full identity foreclosure. The possibility of foreclosure is likely to occur when the young person yields to hero worship over a celebrity or becomes addicted to a television show, especially a reality show, that builds a cult following of the participants. It can also presage both gang and cult membership.

When they don't make progress toward the formation of integrated healthy identities, adolescents lack rudders in their lives. Moral behavior patterns require that the teenager have resolved a code of personal ethics and morality. Those are elements in the formation of a positive identity. In 2008 a study of high school students found that 35% of the boys and 26% of all girls had stolen from a store within the past year (Jarc & Fox, 2008). Likewise, cheating is rampant in high schools. That same study of 30,000 high school students found 38% of students had cheated two or more times on a test during the past year.

The problem of sexual orientation and identity has the potential to cause high school students who are not able to assume the stereotypical role for their gender much difficulty. Adolescents who find that their families reject the choices they are making are likely to feel the most stress. They are also likely to experience significantly more health problems than students following the socially accepted norms for orientation and behaviors (Ryan, Huebner, Diaz, & Sanchez, 2009).

Primary Prevention

The home environment and engagement by parents is central to helping teenagers continue the process of identity development. Parents can be advised of ways to reduce the pressure and scrutiny. Counselors can emphasize the difference between success in high school and the potential of the student growing into an adult who lives a rich and full life. Parents must be shown that by focusing on the minutia of the moment they are losing sight of the big picture and may be doing long-term harm.

Parents should be advised to spend more time with their high school–aged children. This can involve service learning projects and other volunteer efforts. Parents who take time to volunteer alongside their child can build important communication bridges and help with the challenges of being a teenager today. Service-learning and other volunteer work has been shown to correlate with higher achievement levels and improve the likelihood a student will graduate (Perkins-Gough, 2009).

Counselors can employ support groups for parents of students having difficulty accommodating the sex role expectations of our mainstream culture. Methods for these groups were discussed in Chapter 4.

Secondary Prevention

Through group counseling, teenagers can learn to see how they can resolve to take charge of their own lives and move to independent places within the family. There are two films made during the 1980s that can teach some of these lessons.

Using these films must be done with caution, as they are not G-rated. The best approach is to identify several segments of the films and play them with the group, then open a discussion of how the depicted actions and behaviors relate to students' lives. The films are something of cult films, and most high school students are likely to have seen them: *Ferris Bueller's Day Off* (rebellion against a father who wants perfection in all aspects of his life, his son, his home, and his classic car), and *The Breakfast Club* (spontaneous group therapy by five high school students serving a Saturday detention).

● ADOLESCENTS AND RELATIONSHIPS

A central development in the high school years is the expansion of the circle of acquaintances that the teen will have from which to draw his or her friendship group. It is rare for high school friends to persist through the college years and into adulthood (Offill & Schappell, 2006). Most teens have scores or even hundreds of peers who follow them on Twitter or who write to them on Facebook but only a core group of close friends.

Dating

A changing pattern of boy–girl relationships also occurs in high school. Unlike middle school students, high school students have greater access to

CARTOON 5.2   **Acquaintances and Friends**

SOURCE: ©Zits Partnership, King Features Syndicate.

transportation. Dating today has been replaced by casual gatherings of teenagers who just "fool around."

An increase in the availability for "**hook-ups**" among high school students has also reduced the frequency of dating. Hooking-up implies engaging in casual sexual relationships without any expectation of an emotional commitment (Blow, 2008). Today only 1 in 4 high school seniors date frequently, while about 30% never date. See Photo 5.3 for a depiction of a high school–aged couple.

Sex

In order for fooling around to turn into sexual activity, teenagers must have time and no supervision. Latchkey students and those with excessive freedom are most likely to engage in sexual activity. Sexual activity is lowest among teenagers who live in homes with two parents and where they have super-

PHOTO 5.3   Young Love

SOURCE: Punchstock.

vision by a responsible adult (Parker-Pope, 2009). Parties at the homes of teens when the parents are out of town are a popular theme in Hollywood films. That is a scenario where sexual activity is likely.

The urge for sexual relations is never greater in the male than when he is in late adolescence. Both girls and boys feel powerful, genetically programmed urges to procreate during their adolescence. Each new generation of teenagers assumes that they invented sex and that their parents and teachers are clueless.

It is possible for girls to misinterpret the biological urge to have sexual contact with a boy as feelings of love (Weill, 2005). Our society has taught girls that sex without love is not what "good girls" would do. For that reason girls may assume they are in love and enter into sexual relations with a boy. The increase in popularity of oral sex (see Chapter 4) is possibly a way for girls to think they are protecting themselves from pregnancy and sexually transmitted diseases (STDs). Most teenagers do not know how to protect themselves and are unaware that STDs can enter the bloodstream through the mucus membranes of the mouth. It is clear that parents are not providing meaningful sex education for their adolescent age children (Brooks, 2009).

Ignorance about the use of methods to prevent STDs has resulted in a quarter of all sexually active teenagers having sexually transmitted diseases (Desmon, 2008). About half of sexually active minority teenagers have one of the STDs including the human papillomavirus (HPV). Fifteen percent of sexually active teenagers have more than one STD including Chlamydia, trichomoniasis, herpes, and HPV. Each year about 5,000 high school–aged young people become infected with the HIV virus. Unfortunately, only half of those infected know they carry the disease, and many who do know do not tell other people, including their partners (Centers for Disease Control and Prevention, 2008).

Many teenagers become sexually active because they believe their friends and the most likeable students in the school are sexually active (La Greca, Prinstein, & Fetter, 2001). High school counselors can channel the power of peer pressure to reduce the danger that sexually active teenagers expose themselves to by having unprotected sexual relations. Group counseling can focus on role playing with students both to resist having sexual relationships and to be proactive in protecting themselves.

Date Rape and Violence

The state of Rhode Island enacted a law in 2008, the Lindsay Ann Burke Act, requiring that all middle and high schools in the state teach the warning signs of being in an abusive relationship. The law is designed to provide all students between 7th and 12th grades with information as to how to get help and be empowered when being abused. These warning signs include excessive text messaging, attempts at physical control, stalking, jealousy, and separation of the teen from his or her friends and family.

Violence Against Girls. It is an affront to the beliefs that many young people have when they first feel a romantic love for a person only to find that they are being abused by that person. In many parts of the world there are few laws against hurting and abusing women and girls of one's own family (Thompson & Hickey, 2008). Despite legal protections in this country, millions of women and girls are injured by their partners each year in the United States. In 2005 national data indicated that about 1 in 8 teens are the victims of dating violence. This increases in schools located in the most impoverished communities to about 30% of all adolescent girls being abused by a friend or partner (National Institutes of Health, 2009).

Insecure high school students may try to force a student (usually a girl) into an exclusive relationship and cut her off from contacts with her friends and peers. If the girl resists she may find she is hit or otherwise abused, stalked, and harassed. The jealousy felt by the partner that results in these behaviors is a manifestation of the teen's (usually a boy's) insecurities. Many of the boys who abuse their girlfriends are the products of abusive homes and may have witnessed acts of domestic violence while growing up (Howell, 2009). When a counselor suspects that there is a problem, he or she may elect to involve the school's nurse and social worker. The nurse is in a better position to discuss injuries with the girl and her parents, and the social worker can assist with any home visit follow-ups. The school counselor can provide a solutions-focused counseling program for the girl to help her break away from her abuser.

Counselors should be aware of the laws in their states about obtaining restraining orders from a court to protect the victim from an abusive relationship. The dynamic of this problem may go beyond the school and require that the counselor help the teen and his or her family find a family therapist. Counselors should also inform the school administration and security staff of the potential danger a student may be in.

Date rape occurs when one partner goes beyond what the other partner wishes to happen in terms of sexual activity. It is possible that both date rape and an abusive relationship are something a teen may attempt to keep hidden from both parents and counselors (Olson, 2009).

Secondary Prevention. Counselors can provide class discussions with high school students in which the possibility of being forced to have unwanted sexual contacts is explored. Additionally, the ramifications of such behavior should be described. These classes can provide tips for teenagers to follow to reduce the chance of being raped by a friend or on a date.

1. Always carry a charged cell phone.

2. Trust your gut feelings; better safe than sorry.

3. Have your own money or a credit card to call a taxi as needed.

4. Be confident in yourself and in the limits you set for your behavior.

5. Try to always stay with others in a group.

6. Do not surrender control by consuming alcohol or doing drugs.

7. Never give in without screaming and shouting *"NO! Don't do that to me!"* As loud as possible, over and over.

8. Never let something you are drinking out of your possession. Date rape drugs can be added when you are not paying attention. Never accept something to drink you have not ordered and/or seen made.

If the school permits, the counselor, in consultation with the school's nurse, can also review the laws about Plan-B (morning after) contraceptive pills available to high school girls beginning at age 17 without parental consent (Gee, Shacter, Kaufman, & Long, 2008).

Bullying Harassment

Bullying in high school is just as much of a problem as it is in middle school. (See Cases in Point 5.4 and 5.5 for examples of high school bullying.) There are several differences in the process at the high school level. For one, there is a greater likelihood that the teenager who bullies others, and is caught, will be charged with a crime. These crimes can include **hazing**, a crime involving a ritualistic forced activity. A **forced activity** is any activity that is a condition of initiation or admission into an organization regardless of a student's willingness to participate in the activity (Nuwer, 2005). By 2005, 44 states outlawed hazing in schools and colleges.[9]

CASE IN POINT 5.4

A recent tool of bullies is the ability to use **sextexting** to torment victims. In 2009, 1 in 5 teenagers reported that they sent nude or seminude photos and/or digital videos of themselves to friends (Manzo, 2009). Sextexting when used by bullies can involve a boy befriending a girl, persuading her to send him a revealing digital photo of her. This private photo can be used as such or manipulated by computer software to make the girl appear to be something she is not. The photo can then be shared with hundreds or thousands of others. Even innocent photographs can be combined with pornography to make any student or teacher to appear to be something they are not. This form of harassment and bullying is considered a sex crime and can earn the bully a period of incarceration and the requirement to register as a sex offender for the rest of his or her life.

Thought Questions. To what extent should school discipline policies attempt to control the online bullying of some students by others outside of school hours or between sessions? For example, if a 14-year-old girl is the target of sextexting by a classmate during the summer break between middle school and high school, should the high school principal take disciplinary action against the perpetrator? Is online behavior a "protected" form of free speech? If you were the high school's counselor, what course of action would you recommend?

CASE IN POINT 5.5

In the fall of 2009 a 15-year-old girl, Phoebe Prince, enrolled as a freshman in a middle-class school, South Hadley High School in Massachusetts. She and her family had recently emigrated from Ireland. In the fall she had a fling with a student athlete, a behavior that enraged a clique of girls. That clique then engaged in a campaign of merciless harassment, stalking, and hounding of Phoebe. On January 14, 2010, a car full of her tormentors followed her after school, shouting insults as she walked home. That afternoon Phoebe reached her breaking point and went to her bedroom and hanged herself. Her 12-year-old sister later found her body (Cullen, 2010). Even after her death, clique members continued to use the Internet to sully Phoebe's reputation.

It took authorities several weeks to determine who the culpable students were, at which time nine students were charged by the Massachusetts grand jury with crimes including statutory rape (two boys), stalking, violation of civil rights with bodily injury, and illegal criminal harassment (four girls) and three juvenile court filings against other students too young to be prosecuted in adult court (Eckholm & Zezima, 2010). To see the press coverage of the district attorney announcing the charges in this case, see www.wwlp.com/dpp/news/local/teens-charged-in-phoebe-princes-death.

The community was outraged and the school administration, counselors, and other educators at South Hadley were excoriated in the press and at public meetings in the town. South Hadley High School did not create a task force to study the problem of bullying until March 22, 2010, a full 2 months after Phoebe's death.

Thought Questions. How can a school's counselor work to break up the malevolent power of a clique of bullies? Are the approaches the same that a school counselor would employ with a clique of malevolent girls and a clique of bullying boys? Explain why.

Other bullying at the high school level involves taunting students who are or appear to possibly be gay. Any bully caught attacking a fellow student on the basis of race, ethnic background, or sexual orientation can be sentenced to an extra measure of punishment for committing a **hate crime**. All states have provided judges in the juvenile justice system the right to enhance sentences of juvenile offenders who commit hate-inspired crimes. Even a threat to harm another person on the basis of minority status can result in the bully being punished for making a **terroristic threat**. Another form of bullying occurs when a student is made into a social outcast and is belittled and ridiculed by others in and out of school. See Photo 5.4 for an example of this form of student-to-student torment.

Photo 5.4   Teenaged Girl Being Harassed by Her Peers

SOURCE: © Istockphoto.com/Nicolesy.

Primary Prevention

The best approach to stopping bullying in the high school is to prevent it from occurring. Counselors and/or the school's administrators should set up a web page on which anyone can report bullies and bullying behaviors (Peterson, 2009). The school's handbook and the school's web page should state a strong policy regarding bullies. This should be a no-exception statement and require school officials to file a police report for every incident. School systems along with building principals can be sued by families of victims of bullying if the school fails to take immediate steps to stop bullying once it is reported. A web page reporting system provides parents and victims with a documented paper trail that requires action by school authorities. Beyond the civil authorities, schools should impose locally appropriate sanctions on the bully.

All too often school administrators have been reluctant to inform a parent that they are raising a bully. Parents do not want to hear this and are likely to become defensive. High school bullies are not new at this; they have been doing it since they were in elementary school. They know how to hide their actions or even make it appear that the victims are the root cause of the problem. Most high school bullies can convince their parents that they are innocent and that the school authorities "have it in for them."

Schools with high-tech surveillance systems can quickly prove their point to parents with digital videos of the bully in action. Once parents have been informed that their child is at risk for incarceration and possibly a lifelong sex criminal label, they tend to become more involved with supervising their high school–aged child at risk for becoming an incarcerated bully.

Secondary Prevention

Small-group or private session counseling is in order for students who report that they were bullied. The role of the assistant principal is to find out the specifics of the bullying incidents. The role of the counselor is to support and encourage the victims. Strengths-based counseling is an appropriate approach to use with these adolescents. If there are several victims of bullying, the counselor can employ group counseling methods. This approach makes it possible for members of the group to help one another identify and refine coping skills. These sessions can also focus on developing social competence and the ability to be liked by others.

Tertiary Prevention

Bullying others can become a way of life and stunt the emotional growth of the bully. Counseling sessions first must work to have the teenager accept that his or her actions are hurting others and constitute bullying. A second learning that also needs to be opened to the bullying student is that very few people like bullies, and that number gets smaller each year as we age. Once the bully has the personal insight to accept those two points, new methods for making lasting friendships and being liked by others can become part of the counseling sessions.

Social Networking

American teenagers use several forms of social networking on a daily basis. Facebook provides more than a quarter of a billion people with an access to communicate with one another using words, videos, and photographs. Users establish a free account and designate who can join their network and see all aspects of what they post on their personal pages. The user can also open parts of the page to the whole world to view. The most-liked teenagers will make their Facebook pages open to many of their peers in the hopes they will reciprocate.

Counselors can also have Facebook pages. Caution must be exercised when this is done. Students are likely to post on their Facebook pages much more than they expect the **world of adults** (parents, teachers, employers, college admissions officers, etc.) to ever learn about. The fallacy of their thinking is that these personal pages are open for others to read and, at the same time, are confidential and to be viewed only among friends (Cohen, 2009). Social networking now consumes hours of time for many adolescents, with the average American teen having sent and or received more than 2,000 social contacts a month using the various social networking sites.

As Photo 5.5 depicts, adolescents are never far from their cellular devices.

PHOTO 5.5   Teenaged Girls Texting as They Exit a School Bus

SOURCE: © Istockphoto.com /Sjlocke/Digital Planet Design.

An inappropriate time for teenagers to text message is when they are driving. Seven states and the District of Columbia have passed laws to make it illegal for a driver to text message while driving (DWT) (Britt, 2009). However, 60% of teenage drivers report that they have text messaged while behind the wheel. A total of 28 states have banned young drivers from using any form of cell phone while driving, and 7 states (California, Connecticut, Delaware, Maryland, New Jersey, New York, and Oregon) have made it illegal for a driver to use hand-held cell phones. Text messaging has been banned by state laws in 30 states. Curiously, 32 states permit school bus drivers to use their cell phones on the job (Governor's Highway Safety Association, 2010).

One place where cell phones and texting are inappropriate is in class. Case in Point 5.6 discusses that issue.

CASE IN POINT 5.6

Teens have begun to use text messaging as a method of cheating during exams and other high school tests. Texting is done during tests by teens asking for answers to questions and then sharing answers with their classmates. Adolescents have mastered the one-hand use of their texting device and can set them in silent mode so as not to call the attention of their teacher or test proctor. Another method favored by texting cheats is to buy a device that has a very high-pitch ring tone. Teenagers can hear sounds with frequencies as high as 20 kHz. The older a person becomes, the greater is the normal hearing loss in the higher frequency range. Students have spread this high-frequency ringer by using text messages.

Thought Questions. If you were a high school counselor and learned that many students were employing their communication devices to share answers during tests through a group counseling session, what would you do and how would you justify taking or not taking action? Can you violate the confidential nature of the information about academic fraud that students shared while being counseled? Or, by not making this pattern of cheating known to your school colleagues have you violated the ethical standards of the school?

Another form of social networking, Twitter first appeared in 2006. Twitter is designed as a microblogging tool that allows a user to send up to 140 characters on a message to interested followers of the user's activities and thoughts. These microblogs are called "tweets." By 2009, teenagers in America were sending and receiving an average of 75 tweets a day (Hafner, 2009). The sender of the tweets can open the message to the world or limit it to a few select friends.

The limit of 140 characters in the Twitter microblog (tweet) has resulted in wide use of abbreviations. The following are typical:

Tweet	Standard English
ASL	Age/Sex/Location
AMF	Adios mother f***er
BTW	By the way
CD9	Code 9, parents near by
FTW	For the win
GR8	Great
KPC	Keep parents clueless
IC	I see your point
IMHO	In my humble opinion
P911	Parent alert
PAW	Parents are watching
FB	Facebook
POS	Parents over shoulder
K4Y	Kiss for you
HAK	Hugs and kisses
OH	Overheard
OMG	Oh my god
TIA	Thanks in advance
TTYL	Talk to you later
TWEETSULT	Insult
TWHINER	A twitterer who only posts whiney tweets
TWITTERLOOING	Twittering from the bathroom
TWITTERHOLIC	A person addicted to twittering

SUMMARY

School administrators have several major tasks for high school counselors. One is the school's master schedule, another is the scheduling of all students, and the third is helping all eligible students into college, advanced vocational training, or good employment. A final expectation of school administrators is that the counselor will have an expertise in testing and serve as the school's test manager.

Students need their counselors to provide them with support and assistance in a number of areas. One of these is in learning to cope with the excessive pressure over grades. Another is the students' needs for the counselor to assist in overcoming bullies and developing a healthy sense of who they are and what their values are as young people approaching adulthood. Other areas are in assisting students to better resolve their identities and sexual identities. Finally, the counselor must provide help for adolescents who are being exploited or abused by their dating partners.

DISCUSSION QUESTIONS

1. What factors should be included in the decision to let a high school student enroll in an advanced placement class? How should the AP class be weighted on the high school transcript?

2. How can a high school counselor help the school's faculty ethically work for better achievement test scores?

3. What steps should a high school counselor do to help reduce teen pregnancy and the incidence of STDs among students?

4. What are creative ways a school counselor can employ text messaging?

RELATED READINGS

Kussin, S. S. (2008). *How to build the master schedule in 10 easy steps*. Thousand Oaks, CA: Corwin.

Steinberg, J. (2003). *The gatekeepers*. New York: Penguin Books.

Wright, R. J. (2009). Methods for improving test scores: The good, the bad, and the ugly. *Kappa Delta Pi Record, 45*(3), 116–121.

Zwick, R. (2002). *Fair game: The use of standardized tests in higher education.* New York: Routledge/Falmer.

NOTES

1. By 2010 that average salary for a high school counselor had reached about $75,000 per year (Schachter, 2010). Counselors are normally paid under the same guidelines adopted for teachers. The annual pay for school counselors tends to be about 6% higher than that of a teacher with the same level of education and experience, reflecting compensation for the extra 2 or 3 weeks counselors must work at the high school over the summer break.

2. The advanced placement testing program from ETS is one that the school's principal may assign to a counselor, senior department head, or assistant principal. This program requires that one person be named as the Coordinator for Advanced Placement and a second named as Alternate Advanced Placement Coordinator. They may not teach an AP class if they are coordinators. This is a huge job and requires many hours of dedicated work by the coordinator. Scheduling 20 or 30 examinations in a 2-week time, providing volunteer proctors, scheduling for conflicts—for example, students with away games or students who are ill on test days, and late test days with proctors. All this requires hundreds of hours of effort. ETS has provided a year-long timeline for the tasks of an AP coordinator at http://apcentral.collegeboard.com/apc/members/features/11858.html.

3. It is very likely that this testing responsibility will be greatly reduced for school counselors as online computer adaptive testing (CAT) replaces the standard paper-and-pencil tests of the 20th century. In the near future students will log on to computers at the high school and take the required tests. Scoring will be instantaneous and reported to the student, posted on his or her transcript or permanent record, and reported to the school's counselor. However, it will be the school's counselor who sets up the online testing system and will have the task of counseling test takers about their scores.

4. To learn more about the critical writing test or to apply to become a reader, see www.flexiblescoring-SAT.pearson.com.

5. This indicates that 34% of all student scores will fall between 1500 (50th percentile) and 1800 (84th percentile). Likewise, 34% of all scores will lie between 1200 (16th percentile) and the average of 1500.

6. *Juku* was originally a Japanese term that is now part of the American educational lexicon describing an "after-hours cram school."

7. These were Harvard (1636), William & Mary (1693), St. John's (1696), Yale (1701), Pennsylvania (1740), Moravian (1742), Delaware (1743), Princeton (1746), Columbia (1754), Brown (1764), and Rutgers (1766).

8. While undergraduate colleges provide pre-law advisors for their students, law schools do not require a specialized program of undergraduate studies. The course work required to become an English or social studies teacher is very similar to that required by pre-law majors.

9. An organization opposed to hazing provides help for victims and guidance for school officials. See www.stophazing.org/nuwer/baseball.htm.

CHAPTER

6

Models and Approaches of School Counseling

OBJECTIVES

By reading and studying this chapter you should acquire the competency to:

- Organize a plan for counseling with students experiencing different types of problems in a school setting
- Explain and describe Alfred Adler's principles of counseling as applied in schools with a preadolescent population
- Explain the principles of behaviorism as they are applied in school settings
- Explain and describe the principles of counseling as developed by Carl Rogers
- Describe the approach and explain a school application for rational emotive behavioral therapy
- Explain and describe cognitive and behavioral counseling in the schools
- Compare two models for cognitive behavioral therapy used in schools today
- Explain choice theory and describe William Glasser's model for reality therapy in the schools
- Describe the dynamics of groups and explain the principles of group therapy
- Describe the methods of solution-focused brief counseling and goal setting in the schools
- Describe the methods of strengths-based counseling in the schools
- Explain the use of technology in the delivery of virtual school counseling
- Develop a personal model for the delivery of school counseling services

● ● ●

❝ The fool tells me his reasons; the wise man persuades me with my own.**❞**

Aristotle

● INTRODUCTION AND THEMES

Standard 4: The professional school counselor provides responsive services through the effective use of individual and small-group counseling, consulting, and referral skills. (American School Counselor Association [ASCA]/ Hatch & Bowers, 2005, p. 63)

There are three major theories that have shaped how counselors provide therapeutic interventions in schools. The first of these is based on the theoretical foundation provided by psychoanalysis, first defined and elaborated by Sigmund Freud. These approaches include those that can be described as neo-Freudian and those that contain elements first identified in Freud's writings. Eric H. Erikson, Alfred Adler, and Otto Rank have built models for practice based on these approaches and theories.

The early behaviorists provided the second theory that guided approaches to therapeutic interventions. Behaviorism was first defined in psychological laboratories with carefully controlled experiments to look into how individuals learn and respond to their environments. These approaches to therapy include William Glasser's **reality therapy** and **choice theory**. Related theories describe **goal setting** and brief solutions-focused counseling, strengths-based counseling, **cognitive therapy, behavioral counseling,** and cognitive behavioral techniques. Each of these methods is based on helping clients learn new ways of thinking, processing information, and responding to their environments.

The third major theoretical basis in counseling is a uniquely American approach devised by Carl R. Rogers. His person- or child-centered (in this chapter also called "student-centered") approach is one that does away with the notion that a counselor is going to fix a problem the student is having. The approach is one that helps the student better understand his or her own thinking and find a resolution within.

School counselors have also adopted an abbreviated approach for providing student-focused interventions that are time efficient and highly effective. Central to these solutions-focused methods are strength-based school counseling and narrative therapies (Tafoya-Barraza, 2008).

The emergence of strength-based school counseling has provided school counselors with a highly effective tool for providing successful interventions in school settings. While not always appropriate for every problem, strength-based school counseling is both efficient and effective.

Dynamic interactions of a group of students working with a counselor can employ a number of approaches to therapeutic intervention. Counselors need skill and an understanding of group dynamics and theory to provide an effective program of group counseling.

A new direction for school counselors is in working within a virtual school. The online world is changing old rules about the delivery of counseling services for many students today.

People are usually more convinced by reasons they discovered themselves than by those found by others.

Blaise Pascal

Ground Rules for School Counselors

Counselors working in public schools must establish ground rules with students who begin the counseling relationship. One is that everything discussed by the student and counselor is kept in confidence by both parties.[1] Second is that there is a strict time limit to the length of each counseling session. Counselors must establish boundaries, including the fact that they are paid professional employees of the school who may never break the school's rules or policies. The counselor works in the interest of each individual student; however, as a professional, the counselor maintains a separation from students who are receiving counseling services. Finally, counselors do not play favorites, make exceptions, or do anything to discourage any student or group of students from seeking assistance.

HOW DOES A SCHOOL COUNSELOR DO THE JOB? ●

When a new school counselor begins a career, he or she must build a practice. Schools will have referral systems and children will be "sent to see the counselor"; however, an effective counselor soon develops a practice built on trust that has been earned. Students know the genuine thing when they see it, and a counselor who is trusted will have a reputation that is spread by word of mouth throughout the building and beyond into the community. This can happen only if the school counselor has the personal warmth, integrity, and skills to create a counseling environment in which students know they will be listened to by a professional adult who is nonjudgmental and who truly understands them.

The effective counselor knows counseling theories and has the ability to employ techniques that can help students.[2] Beyond that knowledge and skill base, the counselor should be an optimist who has a true belief in his or her skills and the ability of students to change and improve. To be effective, the counselor must understand students and the culture of students as well as the culture of the school. Effective counselors recognize their roles in the culture of the school. The counselor also understands and respects the society created by students but never tries to become part of that culture. This implies the counselor is with it and up to date with popular culture but does not effect airs or try to act like the students. This will be immediately detected, and the counselor will be labeled by the students a phony and subsequently lose credibility.

Central to the job is listening. This skill is one very few adults in a child's life have. The counselor must always be sensitive to all levels of communication being used by the student being counseled. Verbalizations make up one dimension; others include the student's posture and body language, facial expressions, tone of voice, and gestures. All aspects of the student-client being counseled must be mentally noted by the counselor and become part of the therapeutic dialogue.

Listening in all these dimensions leads the school counselor to be able to achieve **empathy**, the ability to sense and feel the feelings, understandings, motives, and attitude of the student being counseled as the counselor's own. The ability to understand why a student behaves in a particular way, what he or she is thinking, and what his or her motives and needs are is the essence of being a counselor. If the counselor is heard as judgmental by the student, this trusting relationship will never occur. Language by the counselor that starts with the pronoun *you* should be avoided. For example, never start a sentence with "Don't *you* think . . . ," or "*You* should/should not . . . ," or "It's really *your* doing/fault that . . . ," and so on.

Other characteristics of good, highly effective school counselors can be found in **self-reports** (Hopkins, 2005).

One is self-deprecating humor. More than 30 years ago Norman Cousins published a report demonstrating the power of humor to improve the condition of medical patients (Cousins, 1976). Counselors should make the counseling office an enjoyable, never a threatening environment. A sincere smile and pleasant greeting should go to all students in and out of the counselor's office area.

● ADLER'S THEORIES IN SCHOOL COUNSELING

Adlerian counseling holds the central belief that people are social creatures and must learn to cope effectively as members of a community of others (Adler, 1956b). Thus, the behaviors and actions of all humans are directed by social needs. From infancy onward, children work to understand the world around them and become competent within it. This inevitably leads to the child being blocked or thwarted in these efforts. One result of being blocked is a belief that one is inferior and weak. The interpretation of the world by the young child may be distorted and very wrong. This is made worse in authoritarian homes in which the child never develops the ability to express independence and competence.

Elementary school students can overcome insecurities developed earlier in their childhoods by learning to work in cooperation with others. This work is most successful if directed toward self-improvement leading to self-fulfillment. The most benefit comes to the child whose efforts add to the common good for the community (e.g., classroom). Thus, Adlerian counseling is aimed at gaining an insight into self by learning to live effectively in school and in other social settings (Daniels, 1998).

Background

Alfred Adler (shown in Photo 6.1) was a Viennese physician in general practice and psychoanalyst who was a close associate of Sigmund Freud. Adler broke with Freud in 1911 and relocated to Long Island, New York, in 1926. His debate with Freud had to do with core assumptions of psychoanalysis, including the sexual feelings of young children. Adler saw the concept of infantile sexuality more metaphorically than did Freud. Another disagreement with classical psychoanalysis was Adler's belief in the role of motivation and the child's need to move toward his or her own future. Freud's model was backward looking, attempting to learn causes of current problems through an analysis of past experiences. While Freud explored the unconscious mind for early memories, Adler tried to identify the source of the child's motivation to respond in a particular way.

During World War I, Alfred Adler was a member of the Austrian Army Medical Corp and served in a hospital for children. After the war he opened a clinic and also worked to train teachers in his psychological methods (Boeree, 2006). Today we count Alfred Adler as the first of a series of neo-Freudians that includes, among others, Erik Erikson, Abraham Maslow, and Otto Rank.

PHOTO 6.1   Alfred Adler

SOURCE: © Bettmann/CORBIS.

Adlerian Concepts

Among the firsts that Adler's writings presented was the first psychological study of **feminism** and the power dynamics between males and females. Adler argued against the cultural norm that holds boys in higher esteem than girls and where boys are encouraged to be aggressive and avoid all weakness, while girls are encouraged to be demure and shy (Rigby-Weinberg, 1986). Adler used a term **masculine protest** to describe the need of parents to raise boys to be "real men" who are brave, powerful, and stoic. The difficulty of reaching this masculine ideal can leave a little boy craving to reach it but failing and retreating into a world of power fantasies. As a young adult this can lead to vengeance, resentment, overwhelming avarice, and ambition (Daniels, 1998). Later Adler changed the term *masculine protest* to one that was more attuned to his American experience: **striving for superiority.** This became his term to describe male assertiveness and the training that boys receive to behave in "male-appropriate ways."

A second unique feature of the theory developed by Adler is that of the critical role played by feelings of **inferiority** (Adler, 1956a). Adlerian therapists believe that each infant has inborn feelings of inferiority. This inborn set of feelings is the dynamic that motivates us all to strive to overcome these feelings. All children work to become more powerful and have an increasingly superior role in their lives and to be seen by others as successful and capable. This may be the simple act of insisting on putting on one's own clothes at the age of 2 or the need to control when one goes to bed, irrespective of parental wishes.

This striving for superiority is an essential theme in all our lives. By going to graduate school and working to become school counselors, we are overcoming feelings of inferiority and striving for superiority and professional success as we overcome those negative feelings. If we fail in our attempts, and our striving is thwarted, there is a good likelihood that our feelings of inferiority will become overwhelming, and we will exhibit what Adler termed an **inferiority complex.** An inferiority complex includes an overwhelming sense of being incapable and less deserving than others. It is the essence of hopelessness and results in depression and a total loss of motivation.

A 5-year-old child will suffer any fall, and work for hours on end without complaint to develop the skill needed to ride a bicycle independently (see Photo 6.2). Adler believed this motivation was one to avoid being inferior and to establish control over that aspect of one's life.

The third major theoretical perspective provided by Adler is the important role of **birth order** in the lives of children. Many of his observations are part of the conventional wisdom of parents today. These include the likelihood that an only child will be pampered and protected by parents who are nervous about their only child.

Firstborn children have the experience of being only children and then are suddenly deprived of the spotlight and must battle to regain the attention and affection of the parents and others in the extended family. Firstborn children may become disobedient, regress to less age-appropriate behavior patterns, or become sullen and withdrawn. On the positive side, firstborn children will have experienced a richer linguistic milieu, with two parents and other adults talking and paying attention to them (Thurstone & Jenkins, 1931). Subsequent children in the family will not have that experience. Thus, firstborn children may appear precocious and assume a teacher-like role within the family.

As other children enter the family, each will see one or more of the other children as being a competitor for the affection and love of the parents. Each will accept a role within the family that provides him or her with a distinctive temperament and style of interaction. The gender of each child and the length of the time period between births become part of the Adlerian calculus of the impact of birth order (Zajonic, 1976).

PHOTO 6.2   Striving to Be the One Who Can Ride a Bicycle

SOURCE: © Istockphoto.com / Rch1.

Methods of Adlerian Counseling in Schools

Many of the methods employed by Adlerian school counselors are designed for use with preadolescent students. The central Adlerian belief is that children misbehave because they are acting out from faulty logic about how the world works. This misinterpretation occurs over time as the natural striving attempts by the child to overcome weaknesses are thwarted at every turn. The type of problem behaviors normally addressed using Adlerian approaches can be divided into four groups: attention seeking, power struggles with adults, revenge, and inadequacy (Fallon, 2004).

Changing Behaviors. The goal of counseling is to harness the child's feelings of weakness and turn them into constructive and positive behaviors (Thompson & Henderson, 2007). Most interventions are designed to teach children more productive approaches to behaving and interacting with others. Approaches discussed previously, such as play therapy and storytelling (see Chapter 3) are tools used by school counselors employing Adlerian methods. Another approach involves **role playing**. These are simulation techniques that can be used in group therapy (see section on group therapy later in the chapter).

Additionally, these methods are supplemented by a dose of **neo-behavioral** management. For example, children who need attention can be reinforced with positive attention only when behaviors occur in the appropriate context.

Power struggles are not uncommon, and teachers may need to be educated in how to avoid them. Students can present power struggles by acting in a direct and destructive way or by a more passive form of aggression. This latter form involves being forgetful, slow to respond, stubborn, and lazy. Those who insist on entering a power struggle with teachers and aides of a school can be given choices between two positive possibilities, such as, "I would like you to do either . . . or . . . Which do you want to do?" Many educators are inclined to give a choice that only hardens resistance such as, "I want you to . . . , and if you don't you will be sent to time-out."

Children are expressing a need for revenge when they exhibit behavior designed to hurt others. Little children who bite others and elementary school children who are bullies fall into this group. Adler would suggest such children are experiencing the pain of not being likeable and are possibly being abused by others. The dynamic of such behaviors is that they make the child even less likeable to others. Clear class rules about hurting others and punishment by natural consequences for inappropriate behaviors are recommended (see Chapters 3 and 4 for more on these topics). Natural consequences refer to what the Great Mikado in Gilbert and Sullivan's operetta called "making the punishment fit the crime" (Gilbert & Sullivan, 1885). Adlerians view natural consequences as what will occur if a responsible adult does not correct the child. For example, if the child forgets to bring a lunch to school, he will be hungry all afternoon, or if she does not take care of the school's equipment she will not be able to use what she broke in the future.

Children with overwhelming feelings of inadequacy sense others believe they are stupid or unable to perform at normal levels. The result is a powerful feeling of hopelessness and despair. This is a problem that can be so deeply set that a child believes all attempts to show him or her as capable are rejected and any attempts at achievement are desultory and half-hearted (Fallon, 2004). Counseling these students requires an empathetic approach in all one-to-one sessions. Counseling is best paired with positive experiences of success. This can happen by finding small jobs the student can do to "help out" in the office.

Tasks such as filing brochures or collating new pamphlets can provide many opportunities for the counselor to provide the student with positive statements about his or her work and abilities.

BEHAVIORISM   ●

A number of school counseling approaches are built upon a foundation of behaviorism. This branch of psychology dominated American university psychology departments for most of the 20th century.

The core understanding in behaviorism is that actions and behaviors of children happen as a result of experiences they had with the environment. Humans enter the world without previous learning or habits. They are equipped with certain reflexive responses that can be made to their environments but have no way to interpret and understand the world around them. John Locke has described their minds as blank slates (*tabula rasa*), ready for experience to write upon (Locke, 2004/1690).

The name *behaviorism* is derived from a belief that we can know what a child is about only through observable behaviors. Behaviorists avoid any concern with the child's inner world or the phenomenological field in which the child lives. The focus is on what the child does and how to modify those behaviors in a more productive direction.

Operant Conditioning

The association of an outcome and the antecedent behavior is the central issue for behaviorists. Children are likely to repeat an action or behavior (**operant**) that is closely followed by a pleasant outcome (**reward**) (Skinner, 1954). A key point to this system is the reward must be **contingent** on the behavior occurring first. This behavior–reward cycle will produce frequent reoccurrences of the behavior. As the child must first operate or provide a behavior, it is referred to as **operant conditioning**. A second point is the reward must be one that the child desires. If the reward is powerful and can change behavior, it is referred to as a **reinforcer**. This implies that when given, it will reinforce the occurrence of the behavior being rewarded.

If the reinforcer is viewed as a positive and desirable reward, it is described as a **positive reinforcer**. Positive reinforcers can meet a child's primary needs, for example, food, drink, and sleep. A **secondary reinforcer** makes the child feel good but is not included in his or her primary needs. These can include a star or sticker, affection, praise, or permission to partake in a favorite activity.

The use of economic rewards in education is quotidian and spreading (Wallace, 2009). From the perspective of school-aged children, the true payoffs for doing well in school are in the distant future. Students have been paid for attending after-school tutoring, scoring well on advanced placement (AP) tests, and attending Saturday and summer tutoring sessions. All of these efforts are examples of applied behaviorism in a school setting (Guernsey, 2009).

A **negative reinforcer** can also change behavior. These involve the removal of an annoying condition following the desired behavior. For example, when a parent nags a child to put away all the toys and clean up his or her room, the child may find the nagging annoying. When the child does as asked, the negative stops (no more nagging till the next time), and being left alone for a while rewards the child.

The problem for counselors and other educators using a reward system to control and change the behavior of students is knowing what is rewarding to the student. A child may crave attention and being noticed by his or her peers. This can result in the student being a constant problem for teachers. The result is that the teacher continually reprimands the student. These reprimands are a form of attention, and all the others in the room are certain to notice and respond to the student's acting out or other inappropriate behavior.

Behaviors that are never rewarded will diminish in frequency and eventually be **extinguished**. Ignoring inappropriate behavior is not an easy concept for responsible teachers or parents to understand or employ. If a child demands that he or she be given a desirable object and the responsible adult refuses, the child is likely to ratchet up the demand and become truly pestiferous. At this point the adult may make the error of giving in to the child. This adult abdication reinforces a pattern of behavior of demanding and pestering by the child. Adults who try to extinguish an inappropriate behavior, only to later cave in and give the child his or her way, produce the most resistant patterns of behavior. If a child does not know when he or she will win the contest of wills with the adult but does know that eventually the adult will give in, he or she has no reason to stop misbehaving. The frequency, intensity, and persistence of these inappropriate behaviors will increase.

● ROGERS'S PERSON- (CHILD)-CENTERED SCHOOL COUNSELING

One of the most satisfying experiences I know is just fully to appreciate an individual in the same way that I appreciate a sunset. When I look at a sunset . . . I don't find myself saying, "Soften the orange a little on the right hand corner, and put a bit more purple along the base, and use a little more pink in the cloud color. . . ." I don't try to control a sunset. I watch it with awe as it unfolds.[3]

Carl Rogers

Carl Rogers described the birth of the new form of psychological therapy occurring on December 11, 1940, during a paper presentation he made at the University of Minnesota to a meeting of the Psi Chi honor society in psychology (Kramer, 1995). Rogers followed a complex path in reaching his professional identity and developing what became known as the **third force** in therapy.

Background

Rogers was raised in a strict home with highly committed Christian parents (Rogers, 1961). His choice for higher education was the Agriculture School of the University of Wisconsin. Later he decided to do graduate work at Union Theological Seminary in New York City. That also proved to be a false start, and Carl Rogers entered Teachers College of Columbia University, where he studied child development and guidance with Leta Hollingworth[4] (Thompson & Henderson, 2007).

While working as a therapist in a child guidance clinic in Rochester, New York, he met many social workers who had been educated at the University of Pennsylvania, where they were taught by Otto Rank, an immigrant from Vienna. Otto Rank was a former acolyte of Sigmund Freud and member of Freud's close circle. In 1923 Rank broke with Freud and the traditional model of psychoanalysis and developed a different approach to therapy.

Otto Rank studied the personal struggle each person has in balancing individual **will** with the conventions and culture of society. He uses the word *will* to replace the concept of ego as developed by Erikson. To Rank, the will is a more energized form of ego that strives to provide us with independence and dominion. The best human resolution to the struggles of the human will involve acceptance of one's self and the creation of a **personal ideal** to endeavor always to achieve (Rank, 1978/1936). The term **client** entered the writings of Otto Rank to replace the medical concept of a patient. The medical concept of fixing what was wrong with a patient was replaced by the concept of helping the client own and understand what heretofore were unexplored and unacknowledged parts of the client's own inner life. Otto Rank named this therapeutic approach **relationship therapy**.

Rogers invited Rank to conduct a two-day seminar in Rochester. During those meetings Rogers refined and modified his conceptual basis for working as a therapist and began developing the new approach to individual therapy. Rogers described the significance of the impact of the Otto Rank seminars by saying, "I became infected with Rankian ideas" (Kramer, 1995). Rogers described this new approach as client-centered therapy (Rogers, 1980). Otto Rank's relationship therapy model was incorporated into the early work on child psychology and therapy by Rogers, but it was refined through Rogers's experience base of 12 years spent as a therapist working with troubled children and their families (Rogers, 1939). The new Rogerian **client-centered**[5] counseling model was the first truly American approach to psychological therapy.

Nondirective Counseling

Unlike psychoanalysis, the Rogerian approach does not dig into the **unconscious mind** or **repressed memories**. The focus is on the immediate world of the child and how the child views and understands what he or she is experiencing. This approach is described as being **phenomenological** in that it is less concerned with the scientific reality of the moment but rather is focused on how the child sees it. The key to all counseling is being an active listener: one who is totally focused on what the child is revealing and describing from his or her private phenomenological perspective (Rogers, 1977).

This requires the counselor to do anything that would help him or her enter the world of the child's subjective experiences and understandings. Included in this is the requirement that the counselor avoid interpreting what the child means, asking questions, or giving the child advice.

Congruence

The goal of counseling is to assist the child to reach a point described by Rogers as **congruence**. To reach this point of congruence, the child will need to experience a psychotherapeutic change in his or her personality structure (Rogers, 1992). The congruence that is needed is between the child's knowledge of him- or herself as a person and the ideal image he or she wishes could be achieved. This difference is **incongruence**, and it represents a source of anxiety, frustration, and maladaptive behaviors (Rogers, 1942).

Rogerian Manifesto

In his textbook on client-centered therapy, Carl Rogers laid out 19 propositions as to what a client- (child)-centered counseling intervention should assume (Rogers, 1951, pp. 483–522). The principles have been modified to fit the context of American students in the 21st century. These principles include:

1. All children and young people exist in (are born into) a continually changing world of experience (phenomenal field) of which they are at the center.

2. Children react to this phenomenological field as it is experienced and perceived. This perceptual field becomes the "reality" for each child.

3. At first, children react as an organized whole to this phenomenal field. There are no multi-taskers in the crib.

4. Children have an inborn basic tendency and striving to actualize, maintain, and enhance their base of experience as individuals. The striving is directed to increase self-regulation and autonomy and move away from being controlled by others, even loving caregivers.

5. Actions by children are purposeful and goal-directed attempts to satisfy those needs as perceived or felt by the child. Each child lives in the present and is not directed by something that occurred in the past.

6. Emotion accompanies and guides goal-directed activities and behaviors by children. The nature of the emotion is directly linked to the perceived significance to the child of its relationship to survival and the perceived enhancement it brings.

7. The best vantage point for understanding the actions and behavior of a child is from the internal frame of reference of the child.

8. A portion of the total perceptual field (phenomenological frame) gradually becomes differentiated. The sense of a unique self is developed at this time.

9. From interactions with the environment and interaction with others, the structure of the child's self is formed as a consistent conceptual pattern of perceptions of characteristics and relationships. It makes it possible for the child to think in terms of the words *I* and *me*. At this developmental point, the child is creating a rudimentary system of values.

10. Values experienced directly by the child, and in some instances those values taken over from others as if they had been experienced directly, may become distorted. Values attached to experiences are a part of the self-structure, while values introjected from others have a greater chance to become structurally changed and perceived in distorted fashion. Yet, they will seem as if they had been experienced directly and will be incorporated into what the child holds and believes.

11. As children experience life, those experiences of the world and its inhabitants may (a) be symbolized, perceived, and organized into some relation to the self, (b) become ignored because there is no perceived relationship to the self structure, or (c) simply be denied symbolization or given distorted symbolization because the experience is inconsistent with the structure of the child's self.

12. Most of the ways children behave are somehow consistent with their personal concepts of self.

13. In some instances, behavior may be brought about by experiences a child lived and that have not been symbolized. Such behavior may be inconsistent with the structure of the child's self-concept, but in such instances the behavior is not "owned" by the child. These behaviors occur as if the child were on "autopilot" and not directing the actions, as though he or she was just along for the ride.

14. Psychological adjustment exists when the concept of the self is such that all sensory and visceral experiences of the child are assimilated on a symbolic level into a consistent relationship with the concept of self.

15. Psychological maladjustment exists when the organism denies awareness of significant sensory and visceral experiences that cannot be symbolized and organized into the **gestalt** of the self-concept. When this situation exists, there is a basic or potential psychological tension (incongruence).

16. Any experience that is inconsistent with the organization of the structure of the self-concept may be perceived as a threat. The more of these perceptions there are, the more rigidly the structure of the self-concept will become organized to maintain itself and the more maladapted the child will become.

17. Under certain conditions, involving primarily complete absence of threat to the structure of the self-concept, experiences that are inconsistent with it may be perceived and examined and the structure of self-concept revised to assimilate and include such experiences.

18. When the child perceives and accepts into one consistent and integrated system all his or her sensory and visceral experiences, the child necessarily becomes more understanding of others and is more accepting of others as separate individuals.

19. As the child perceives and accepts into his or her self-concept's structure more of his or her experiences from living, the child finds that he or she

is replacing the present value system. This is especially true when values are based extensively on introjections that have been distorted and inappropriately symbolized. The goal is to reach a point when the experiences of life fit within the child's evolving valuing process.

Methods of Rogerian Counseling in Schools

Counselors employing the child-centered approach of Carl Rogers believe that children all have dignity and value and deserve respect. All children are able to make constructive change in their lives and strive to be fully actualized. Change can best occur when children are self-directed and provided opportunities to make wise choices and decisions. Children being counseled move toward improvement when the counselor is nonauthoritarian, warm and authentic, congruent, and an excellent listener; provides unconditional acceptance of the client; and views the child as competent (O'Hara, 1995). To operationalize these principles, Rogers proposed the following requirements for a counseling relationship (Rogers, 1992):

The counselor and child both recognize that they are together in a therapeutic relationship.

The child is experiencing internalized discrepancies and is psychologically incongruent.

The counselor is congruent and an integrated person. The counselor does not present a façade but is a genuine person there to provide support and assistance for the child.

The counselor provides young clients with unconditional positive regard. There is no point when it is appropriate for the counselor to chastise or point out mistakes the child has made.

The key tool of the counselor is empathy. This type of empathy requires the counselor to sense the child's private world and be able to feel as if the counselor were the child. By entering the student's world, the counselor can sense the individual's angers, fears, and confusion.

Counselors employ **open-ended questions** to help the child-clients enter into a dialogue. Open-ended prompts like "Tell me what is going on in your life this week" prevent the child from giving a one-word answer and encourage a narrative from the student. This and similar openings can begin a **therapeutic dialogue**.

A child-centered therapeutic dialogue involves **active listening,** whereby the full attention of the counselor is focused on the child and what is being expressed. The counselor must be able to recognize exactly what the child is expressing and have the ability to reflect those feelings so the child knows the counselor is "tuned in." When the counselor is reflecting the understanding he or she has developed, the counselor should use **ownership statements** for those reflective comments. Ownership is shown when the counselor starts a sentence with the word *I*. Comments such as, "I hear you saying that you feel lonely here in school," or "I think you are saying that you are angry at the limits your mom set for you."

Through these reflective statements a school counselor can also clarify the student's feelings and bring a focus to what is confusing or in conflict. Any challenge to the student's contradictions must be gentle and approached as if for clarification. The response by the counselor must always fit right into the student's mood and the content of his or her thoughts. Even the tone of the counselor's voice conveys his or her ability to sense the student's inner feelings and thoughts.

The student who is being helped by the counselor comes to recognize and accept the counselor's empathy. The school counselor is able to understand and sense the student's subjective world and still maintain a professional role apart from that of the student being helped.

Problems With Rogerian Methods in Schools

The problems for a school counselor using the child-centered approach of Carl Rogers can be divided into three areas. First is the problem of working in a school instead of a private office or clinic. On entering into a counseling relationship, students typically test the boundaries of that relationship. This may involve making vicious remarks about teachers or others in the school community. If the counselor makes a nonjudgmental reply, the student may take the counselor's empathy to imply agreement. Despite any ground rules, this supposed agreement may be reported throughout the school and cause many hard feelings. Working in a school also implies that the counselor must be careful when making an appointment to meet a student. Students must not be taken away from tests or laboratory exercises. The fact that Rogerian counseling may take many sessions and occur over several months can present a tricky scheduling problem for a school counselor. Teachers who see the same student miss time from class to meet the counselor may come to resent both the student and the counselor.

The second problem area is in documenting the value of this method. Terms used to describe the counseling process are vague and not well defined. Rogers was educated in an empirical science and made great efforts to provide operational descriptions for his work, but his model is beguiling in its apparent simplicity

(Pescitelli, 1996; Rogers, 1985). This makes it possible for poor practitioners to think they are providing child-centered therapy when they are not.

The final concern is that the model does not address developmental differences between children at different age levels. It also does not address the problem of when to use Rogerian methods with young children, children with disabilities, and those with significant mental illnesses.

ELLIS'S RATIONAL EMOTIVE ●
BEHAVIOR THERAPY IN SCHOOL COUNSELING

Everything hangs on one's thinking. A man is as unhappy as he has convinced himself he is.

Seneca

Albert Ellis began his career as a clinical psychologist in the 1940s and soon found the standard course of psychoanalysis to be too inefficient and languid.

CARTOON 6.1   Finding the Time

"I would love to meet with you, but Principal Scott insists I finish all this paperwork today."

SOURCE: Merv Magus.

Over his first decade as a therapist he developed a different, more confrontational approach to counseling. Ellis began to confront his clients with their irrational beliefs and showed them more rational beliefs and approaches to interacting with the world (Thompson & Henderson, 2007).

Ellis believed that psychological problems are the product of misperceptions and irrational cognitions (Ellis, 2001b). These irrational thought patterns are mostly the product of the clergy, educators, and our parents. In a school setting, Ellis's approach teaches students how to think about their lives in productive and qualitatively better ways. Many elementary and secondary school students are easily upset and experience inappropriate emotional feelings following interactions with others that do not happen in the desired way. These emotions lead to inappropriate and self-destructive patterns of responses. By breaking this sequence and learning different ways to interpret and understand his or her world, the student soon feels better and responds to others in more appropriate ways. This led Ellis to describe his approach to therapy as **rational emotive behavioral therapy (REBT)**. Rational thinking leads to appropriate emotions and behavior patterns.

Irrational Thinking

Ellis (2001a) has identified several descriptive terms for the type of irrational thinking that can occur, producing angst, inappropriate emotions, and self-destructive behaviors (Figure 6.1 depicts this sequence).

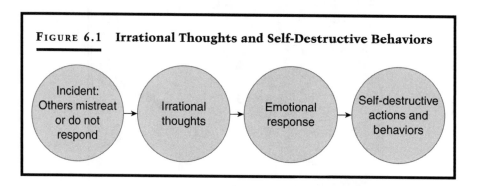

FIGURE 6.1   Irrational Thoughts and Self-Destructive Behaviors

Incident: Others mistreat or do not respond → Irrational thoughts → Emotional response → Self-destructive actions and behaviors

Irrational thinking personalizes what is not personal, magnifies the importance of what occurred, and focuses on the negative. These terms as employed by counselors are overgeneralizations of any incident in the child's life. They include:

Awfulizing: Using emotionally charged words to describe an incident in your life, such as *awful, catastrophic, crushing, life-altering,* and *disabling.*

Distortions: Creating dichotomies and categorizing everything as either clearly evil or wonderful, good or bad, absolutely disgusting or just right. Nothing exists in the space between the semantic polar opposites. For example, "If I make the second team in basketball, and am not a starter, I am a worthless athlete."

Can't-stand-it-itis: Making the emotional assumption that this is something that you can never bear or cope with, and that you have been humiliated, defeated, crushed, or somehow made impotent by this happening.

Musterbating: With highly emotionally laden statements becoming the new Savonarola,[6] making moralistic demands and telling others what they *must, ought, should, always* (or *never*) be doing. Demanding offenders must be condemned and harshly punished.

Perfectionizing: Assuming that everything about you will always be perfect. Any defeat, no matter how slight, is a major blow. Statements such as "I'm worthless, useless, disgusting, hopeless, unteachable, or stupid."

These examples of dysfunctional language and the underlying irrational thinking are normally accompanied with emotions that can lead the child to making wrong and self-destructive choices. These emotions involve anger, self-loathing, anxiety, and depression. Examples of this abound in the everyday lives of most students, as is described in Case in Point 6.1.

CASE IN POINT 6.1

A high school senior who is rejected for admission to his or her first choice college and feels like a total failure may exhibit irrational thinking and feel inappropriate emotions. If the student is able to snap back and realize that there are other good choices open for him or her, there is no problem. If the adolescent becomes depressed, is unsure of his or her ability and worth, and is totally miserable, counseling using REBT may be called for.

Likewise, an elementary school student who has experienced the death of a grandfather may be appropriately sad and grieve for the grandparent. If that normal grieving process becomes irrational, the child may lose all zest for life, believe there is nothing more to live for, and express a desire to join Granddaddy in heaven. These thoughts are aberrant and irrational and imply that the child may be helped by REBT.

Thought Question. Reflect on your own life. What major disappointments have you experienced? Write one or two down, then review all the internal conversations you had about what you did and what happened. Make a list of them and try to match them to the five overgeneralizations described by Ellis.

Methods in Rational Emotive Behavior Therapy

The first phase in REBT involves assessing the problem that is affecting the child. Getting adolescents to express their feelings and describe what they are thinking can involve Rogerian methods. Younger children who lack the ability to explain how they feel or what their thoughts are may require the counselor to employ indirect or fantasy-based methods for therapeutic communication, for example, a puppet play or storytelling (Eppler, Olsen, & Hidano, 2009). In this assessment the counselor is listening for irrational thinking that may be highlighted by the use of language patterns described previously.

Once the problem has been identified, the next task for the counselor is to find its parameters. This includes the intensity of the distress the child is experiencing, how long it has been going on, and how frequently it occurs. The issue of frequency can provide the counselor insight into what triggers the child's distress.

ABCDEs of Rational Emotive Behavior Therapy

The two linked goals of REBT are first to have the child recognize how his or her thinking is not rational and the conclusions being reached are wrong. The second is to reeducate the child in new thinking patterns and a more rational way of seeing the world around him. To do this, Ellis proposed a series of steps for the counselor to follow in helping the child (Ellis & Bernard, 1983). These steps involve:

A. Identifying the activating event

B. Identifying irrational beliefs or cognitions about step A

C. Identifying the consequences for the irrational beliefs (emotions and feelings)

D. Disputing the irrational beliefs

E. Employing effective, new, more rational thinking about the original activating incident

The following scenario is based on a problem that can happen when a student romance breaks up.

A. Girl receives a rejection from the first boy for whom she feels romantic love.

He wants to date others; she thought they were "going steady."

B. Student is crushed by the "break-up" and feels it is all her fault.

C. Student feels anger at the boy and has feelings of self-loathing and depression.

D. Counselor disputes her analysis showing that no one is at fault, and she is a worthy person who is liked by others.

E. Girl replaces irrational thinking in B with a realization that she is a competent and likeable person who can make and keep friends and that other boys are available.

Strengths of Rational Emotive Behavior Therapy

Perhaps the greatest advantage to using REBT in public school counseling programs is the fact that it can be carried out in a short time frame. The approach is one that is easy for children to latch onto and to employ when other problems arise in their futures. Thus, REBT not only helps a child experiencing a problem, but also provides a method for self-help in the future.

BECK'S COGNITIVE BEHAVIORAL ● THERAPY IN SCHOOL COUNSELING

Aaron Beck, a pioneer in **cognitive behavioral therapy (CBT)**, has modified the REBT model of Alfred Ellis by making it less confrontational and providing a strong basis in science for its techniques (Beck, 1979; Sussman, 2006). Beck has labeled the irrational thoughts described by Ellis as **automatic thoughts**. His approach to therapy is assisting the client in setting goals for interacting in the world and then reaching them by changing the distortions in cognition or automatic thoughts.

Automatic thoughts occur and run parallel to the person's ongoing interactions in the world. For example, a child sees several other children laughing and has automatic thoughts of being the butt of their humor, a person so unworthy as to be laughed at. These thoughts lead to negative emotions, loss of self-esteem, and self-defeating behaviors such as avoidance of others. The counselor's task is to teach new ways of thinking (Goode, 2000).

Methods of Cognitive Behavioral Therapy

As is true of all counseling, interventions using CBT begin with a trusting relationship between counselor and student. The first CBT counseling session is a time for the counselor to work collaboratively with the student to set goals for the counseling. Questions such as, "At the end of counseling, how would you like to be different than you are now?" These goals are then prioritized and an agenda is developed (Sussman, 2006).

Counselors begin sessions by reviewing the agenda and identifying goals for the session. It is also common to ask open-ended questions or prompts such as, "What happened this week?" or "Describe everything you do on a typical non-school day from getting up until bedtime," or "Describe what mood state you are in now."

The core of the counseling is teaching the student-client to challenge inaccurate beliefs. One technique is to teach students in therapy how to think like scientists. For example, with the case of the student who believed he or she was being laughed at, the counselor would ask the student how he or she knew that was true. "What are the chances they were laughing at a joke, or at something else?" By learning new ways of thinking through situations, the student learns a new, more positive way of approaching problems. This learned way of thinking must then be practiced between counseling sessions. This is where counselors assign **homework**. The child should write down all the incidents that came up in the time between sessions and when he or she challenged old automatic thinking with a more scientific way of understanding what happened. This may be recorded in e-mail entries that are forwarded to the school counselor between sessions. During the next counseling session, review of the homework provides information for further counseling using CBT.

Advantage of Cognitive Behavioral Therapy in Schools

The CBT approach of Aaron Beck is less labor-intensive for the counselor. The total number of sessions needed for most problems is about 10. These can occur every week at first, then become more and more separated in time as the student improves. Another advantage is the approach has been proven to work and provide an efficacious approach to counseling. The system has elaborated approaches for many different problems (depression, anxiety, personality problems, etc.) that counselors may encounter that have been tested and demonstrated to be effective (Beck, Freeman, & Davis, 2004).

● GLASSER'S REALITY THERAPY SUPPORTED BY CHOICE THEORY IN SCHOOL COUNSELING

The therapeutic model developed by William Glasser is one based on choices we make in our relationships with others. Glasser (1998) believes that inappropriate behaviors that lead a student to the counselor's office are the student's best efforts to cope with unpleasant relationship(s) and/or the failure of the student to meet his or her needs. The task of the school counselor is to help the student choose new relationship-building behaviors and to identify and use appropriate ways to meet his or her needs.

The counselor does not explore how the student may have been traumatized in the past; the focus of counseling is on the here-and-now. Part of the here-and-now is accepting consequences for inappropriate behaviors. Students will try to avoid this reality, and part of the counselor's job is to provide reality therapy. Counselors using reality therapy recognize that the only behavior each of us controls is our own. Thus, Glasser rejects the basic premise of behaviorism as mechanistic and hurting productive relationships in education; however, the word *behavior* plays an important role in the counseling process. Glasser also avoids the use of terms such as *mental illness* or *disorder*.

Glasser wants counselors to see their role as teaching students better ways to meet their needs and build more satisfying relationships. Reality therapy holds that all behavior is directed toward satisfying one or several of five universal, basic (inborn) needs: survival, love and belonging, power, freedom, and fun (Glasser, 2000). Students do not turn to counselors for help when they are in jeopardy for not surviving; that is the province of medicine. Of the remaining four needs, the need for power is central in most conflicts in school. While the five basic needs provide the motivation for all human behavior, Glasser's concept of **Quality World** describes the specific motivation for what we do. Quality World is composed of images (mental pictures) of all of the people, objects, and values that make up our vision of a good life. For each of us, our Quality World is unique; the five basic needs are universal.

Choice Theory

Glasser proposed that all people are responsible for the choices they make and that those choices can be modified by the school counselor. Choice theory is based on 10 axioms. The following statements are based on those 10 axioms.

1. The only behavior I can control is my own.

2. All anyone can give another person is information.

3. At heart, long-lasting psychological problems are problems of relationships.

4. The problem relationship is always part of our present life and linked to our behaviors.

5. Problems in our past inform what we are today, but we can only satisfy our basic needs right now and plan to continue satisfying them in the future.

6. We can only satisfy our needs by satisfying the pictures (our visualizations) in our Quality World.

7. All we do is behave.

8. All behavior is made up of four components: acting, thinking, feeling, and physiology.

9. Of these, only acting and thinking are under the individual's direct control. We can only control our feeling and physiology indirectly through how we choose to act and think.

10. All behavior is designated by verbs and named by the part that is the most recognizable.

Methods of Reality Therapy and Choice Theory in School Counseling

The goal of counselors is to improve the choices students make in their relationships. This involves replacing "deadly habits," including blaming, complaining, criticizing, nagging, punishing, threatening, and bribing with more positive approaches to interrelating with others. These positive approaches include supporting, encouraging, listening, accepting, trusting, respecting, and negotiating as equals when there are differences.

The counselor following Glasser's approach would follow the following seven steps:

1. Build a good relationship. This is the starting point for all theories and approaches to counseling.

2. Examine the current behavior. The counselor can introduce questions such as, "What are you doing?" or "How are you approaching the issue of . . . ?"

3. Evaluate whether the behavior is helpful or not. Ask questions such as, "Is what you are doing making it possible for you to get what you want?" or "So how is it working out?"

4. Develop alternative strategies with the student by brainstorming ideas and alternatives. Ask questions such as, "What other approaches could you try?"

5. Make a commitment to try selected alternatives. Ask questions such as, "Which alternative approach will you try?"

6. At a later time, examine the effectiveness of the commitment—no punishment and no excuses. Ask questions such as, "When will you do this?" or "Do you have a planned time when you will do this?"

7. Accept the logical and natural consequences of the behavior. Do not become discouraged; persevere with the student. Giving up on the student is not an option.

GROUP COUNSELING ●

School administrators often burden school counselors with large caseloads and many expectations for expert assistance. The ability to employ group counseling methods can greatly improve the efficiency of the counselor and make it possible to assist many more children.

Group Theory

Each of the major theorists in counseling has endorsed the use of groups, starting with Alfred Adler (Drinkmeyer, Pew, & Drinkmeyer, 1979). The psychotherapy model of Adler assumed that there was a social need within us all that longed for acceptance and approval from others. Students with emotional problems have generally been unable to interact with others in successful ways. **Psychoeducational groups** guided by the school counselor can teach students social skills and give them their first opportunities to be successful (Papanek, 1970). Carl Rogers (1970) wrote positively about instituting what he described as **encounter groups** in schools and other educational institutions (p. 155). Alfred Ellis supported group approaches to REBT, believing that groups can give students accurate feedback about irrational thoughts and help them try different roles and approaches to problem solving (Ellis, 1982).

Methods of Group Counseling

Counseling in the schools must match the developmental levels and needs of students (DeLucia-Waack, 2006). Before fifth grade, students have limited attention spans and are bound by a form of linear logic that emphasizes deductive reasoning and makes insight impossible (Gray, 2006; Piaget, 1953/1936, 1970). Group counseling with students at this developmental level should be focused on concrete issues that are easy to grasp and discuss. Primary-level groups should be limited to four members or fewer. Eight is the maximum for middle and high school students in a counseling group that a counselor should lead.

There are three major psychoeducational group types that a school counselor may make part of the school's counseling program (Goodnough & Lee, 2004). These are groups that encourage growth, improve school climate, and reformative groups.

Groups to Encourage Growth

There are a number of ongoing concerns students will experience as they grow and move through the grades. These groups can be focused on normal transitions that occur such as middle school to high school to college. Another focus may be on personal development, such as improving studying habits, taking

PHOTO 6.3   Group Counseling With Teenagers

SOURCE: © Istockphoto.com/JeanellNorvell.

better class notes, improving grades by using time productively, or learning to set goals and prioritizing.

Groups to Improve School Climate

These groups are established with the goal of making life better for all in a school community. The groups may be part of a program to control bullying or hazing behaviors, improve student morale, improve interracial understanding, promote tolerance, or establish support programs related to service learning experiences. (See Chapter 8 for more on counseling with diverse populations.)

Reformative Groups

These groups are established to assist students in learning to cope with difficult personal problems. Groups can address issues of individual identity, family problems (divorce, separation, grieving and bereavement), addictions, abusive families, anger management, sibling rivalry, and the host of other issues children and adolescents face growing up. These groups are also important tools for helping a school community overcome a common tragedy. Deadly violence in schools is lower today than in the 1990s, but students continue to be killed in car crashes and in other devastating accidents. Group counseling can provide immediate help for young people feeling confusion and pain.

Group Process

The use of groups by the school counselor is the most effective intervention available for most problems among adolescents (Shallcross, 2010). The key to a good psychoeducational group is a well-trained counselor who possesses sterling leadership skills. Prior to the first group session, it is best if the counselor meets individually with each student who will participate. This meeting can help the counselor and student by identifying and clarifying the student's goals in becoming part of the group. The counselor can also review rules for the group: (1) all meetings are confidential, (2) no one ever gets laughed at or teased in or outside the group, (3) each member listens very carefully to what each other member is saying, and (4) meetings start and end on time.

After ground rules are set, the first session with a new group usually needs a group activity designed to be an icebreaker and way to allow group members to get to know and trust one another. These students will know of each other as "kids" in the same school but will not know them the way members of a psychoeducational group eventually will.

Ideas for First Session Icebreakers

In several small pill cups, place four or five M&Ms in each cup and give one of these small cups of candy to each student, with instructions not to eat any yet. Next have the youngsters take turns sharing with the group something about themselves that others *do not* know. After their shared confidence, each gets to eat one M&M and then nominate another student to reveal a confidential component of his or her life and have an M&M afterward. Only when the child shares with others does he or she get to eat an M&M. If the group has more time and is into the activity, the counselor can provide yet more candy for those who wish to continue sharing.

For older students, icebreakers can be more abstract. For example, "Pretend the group was in a plane that went down on a deserted island. Each person is given the opportunity to take one item with them as they exit the plane before it catches fire. What object would you take? Why?" The counselor can have each person write down or draw their answer on a tablet, and then one at a time share their selected object and provide a reason for its selection.

The Internet offers many icebreaker ideas for counselors. One good site for these is www.icebreakers.ws.com. Another is www.icebreakers.us.com.

For each group session, the leader should have a plan of what he or she wishes to accomplish and provide exercises to facilitate reaching his or her goal. Counselors should be careful to notice and reinforce when the group is showing cohesion and support for one or more of its members. This is a good sign of the group's health. Leaders should note to themselves indications of the group developing norms. These are never expressed but always present in a working group. **Group norms** become evident when a student violates one, for example, when a student "disses" the group by putting ear buds in his or her ears and finds that others in the group are unhappy with his or her behavior.

The final group session can happen when the leader feels that the group has made all the progress possible or may have been built in as the plan for the group and spelled out in advance. Students from cohesive and well-functioning groups may feel grief and loss at its ending. The task of easing children through the transition of being in a group to not being in a group must be planned. This requires that counseling time be set aside to review the group's progress and the individual progress of its members. The final session should also have the participants complete an evaluation activity. For example, write short notes complimenting each of the other group members and telling each person what about them the author likes the most. These can be shared and included in the counselor's final group meeting.

Counselors may keep a diary of their observations following each group session. These can be reviewed prior to the next session, but not shown to or directly shared with the group. It is best to keep the existence of these notes *sub rosa*. Remember that all such notes are considered to be official school records, and can be reviewed by the parents of participants and subpoenaed by all courts.

Pragmatic Considerations

The organization, structure, and culture of most middle and high schools are not conducive to the practice of group counseling. Detailed planning and careful implementation is required to make a successful program of psychoeducational group counseling possible. For example, a group can be formed of students sharing a study hall period together.

Structural concerns are linked to the problem of scheduling. To plan a group counseling schedule, it is first necessary to introduce students and faculty to the advantages and goals of group counseling. This step is consistent with the requirement of the ASCA national framework that school counseling programs be linked to the school's mission and philosophy model (ASCA/Hatch & Bowers, 2005, p. 98).

The faculty can be approached during their regular inservice program and students met in their classes. Faculty must be assured of the importance of group counseling and also have the goals for the group counseling programs made available to them. At the end of the school year, a report to the faculty should be made by the counselors' office that provides summative statistics on the impact of group counseling during the school year.

First-year high school students will need a longer introduction to the school's group counseling program options than will students who have been introduced to group counseling in previous years. To quantify the needs for group counseling, the school counselor should design an easily understood survey of needs to be administered to all students. After the introduction, all students must sign and return the survey to the counselor at the close of the meeting. By requiring all students to return the survey, no one will be aware of which students requested services. The survey form should summarize how the group will meet weekly for the quarter (8 weeks) and last a full class period. Focus topics for the various groups being contemplated can be presented on the surveys, for example, "Kids of divorce or marital separation,"

"Effective study skills," "Coping with grief and bereavement," "Getting into and paying for college," or "Quitting smoking." The survey should ask students for other ideas for needed groups. Planning counseling programs based on empirical data also meets a mandate of the national framework (ASCA/Hatch & Bowers, 2005, pp. 53–54).

Careful administrative support, including school policies making it a requirement that teachers let students scheduled for counseling attend the session without penalty, is the bottom line (Ripley & Goodnough, 2001). This requires that the counselors agree to insist that no student can wander the halls and must report to the counseling suite on time.

Another concession is to make it possible for outside professional counselors to be used as co-therapists in the school counseling groups. Outside counselors can bring important expertise to groups in areas such as the integration of juvenile offenders, drug and alcohol addictions, family relationships, living with a sexually transmitted disease (STD), or financial management and planning, and nutritional counselors can consult on healthy living choices.

● SOLUTION-FOCUSED BRIEF COUNSELING

Time constraints on school counselors make approaches to service delivery involving only a few sessions very appealing. This need for more counseling in less time may explain the rapid expansion in the use of **solution-focused brief counseling** (SFBC) in schools (Lewis & Sieber, 1997). Some counselors have found that even single-session counseling can produce significant improvement for students receiving counseling (Littrell, Malia, Nichols, Olson, Nesselhuf, & Crandell, 1992).

The whole approach is predicated on five assumptions:

1. Concentrate on success [that which works] and change in needed areas will occur.

2. Every problem has a time when it is not present or doesn't happen. Use those times to formulate a solution.

3. Small changes in how the student behaves have a large ripple effect on others in his or her environment.

4. Students being counseled have what is needed to resolve their problems. Counselors must concentrate on those strengths and successes.

5. Always work toward positive goals. (Sklare, 2005)

Methods of Solution-Focused Brief Counseling

In using SFBC, the first session is a time for establishing good rapport and developing clear positive outcome goals between the student-client and counselor. To assist in this, the counselor may ask positive outcome questions. One of these is, "If a magic wand was waved over your head and solved your problem, what would be different?" The counselor asks follow-up questions such as, "If you were getting along better with other kids, what would you notice that you were doing differently?" The student's answer to these questions can help clarify the answer into a positive goal statement.

Goals

The best goals are behavioral and easily demonstrated and operationalized (Parsons, 2009; Paslay, 1995). Positive goals state what the student will be doing as opposed to vague goal statements such as "I want to do better on tests." The goal could provide behavioral change and be developed by the student by the counselor asking, "If you were on the road to better test grades, what would you be doing that would show that?"

Goals must never be *negative*, taking the form of either "wanting to stop doing something" or "wanting others to stop doing something." To turn these into positive goals, counselors would reply, "If you were not doing ___ (describe what the student should not be doing), then what would you be doing instead/differently/or what would you start doing?"(Sklare, 2005, p. 25).

Harmful goals involving rule breaking, illegal activities, or harming one's self or others must be avoided. Turning these into positive goal statements requires the counselor to help reframe the student's goal in a positive way to meet his or her needs. A question that can help reframe a harmful goal idea is, "What's the reason you want (don't want) to . . . ?"

Students making "I don't know" or "I have no idea" their first goal statement are expressing resistance to the process. This can be recast in positive terms by asking, "If you did know, what . . . ?" or "If you did have an idea, what . . . ?"

In setting goals, **identify exceptions**. When a student uses non-absolute terms, for example, *sometimes, almost always, usually,* or *generally*, they are indicating moments when they are successful. Focus on those positive moments and help the student clarify what is working for him or her. Also, use **mind mapping** to assist the student in identifying what he or she was doing differently when success of the identified exception was experienced. Counselors should be cheerleaders for the student by verbally rewarding these successes with praise. The final concern in goal setting is making its success measurable. This **scaling** task involves asking the student to give a numerical level to the degree he or she experiences the problem (1, lowest, to 10, highest). With each subsequent visit, the student is asked about the level of this problem. Any positive movement seen should spark praise for progress and questions of what is being done differently.

By having specific, measurable, behavioral goals and focusing on what is improving, the counselor may not need to see the student more than five or seven times after the initial session. The student is doing all the "heavy lifting." The counselor should ask the student to do a vague sort of homework between sessions. This involves writing down incidents that occurred where he or she tried out the new behavior and what happened. As with other approaches, this can be facilitated by instant communication or standard e-mail entries open to the counselor. These reports then become a focus of the subsequent sessions.

Relaxation Therapy

One brief therapeutic method that school counselors can employ with students in a group or workshop session is mind-body relaxation to reduce stress. This therapy can be effective at all grade levels, and there is anecdotal evidence that the techniques can improve scores on high-stakes tests (E. Ramirez, 2009). One relaxation method involves daily yoga exercise for 10 minutes each day in homeroom. This is done in more than 40 of the schools around the city of Chicago. Another approach is the use of deep muscle relaxation and breathing exercises. This approach is being successfully employed in the Boston area.

Both approaches need to be designed by experts in the field. Yoga instructors are certified by a national organization and must complete a 700-hour training sequence focused on anatomy, philosophy, sequencing, and alignment (see http://yoga.about.com/od/yogaenthusiast/a/teachertraining.htm). Relaxation training is part of the education of most clinical psychologists. The school's psychologist may be able to teach this program to counselors, who can then lead sessions.

> *What does not kill me makes me stronger.*
>
> *Friedrich Nietzsche*

● STRENGTHS-BASED COUNSELING IN THE SCHOOLS

Strengths-based school counseling (SBSC) is a recent approach to meeting the support needs for all students, but especially those who are at risk for psychological and educational problems (Smith, 2006a). (See Case in Point 6.2.)

As a model, it is based on building on the strength of clients to inoculate them against problems and difficulties in their lives. The strengths-based approach has been a regular part of the practice of social work for a number of decades (Saleebey, 2008). In school counseling, this is a prevention-focused approach to helping children (Galassi, Griffin, & Akos, 2008).[7] The model is truly an integrative one, incorporating a number of other approaches, including the needs model of Maslow, Rogerian counseling methods, and social work practice.

CASE IN POINT 6.2

Chris, my old tennis partner and member of our faculty, is about my age. He and I both grew up in large old East Coast cities and attended public schools. My life was well charted; I lived in an extended family of achievement-oriented strivers. His was not so clear. Chris, an African American, was raised in public housing in a city that at the time had the highest infant mortality and crime rates in the state. He never knew his father, and his mother, a laborer, raised him alone. Somehow they were able to put him through college. On graduation he became an officer in the U.S. Navy and later the Fleet Marines. After the war in Vietnam, he became a teacher; a few years later he earned a doctor of education degree and eventually became a tenured professor.

Most of the community around him when he grew up was in ruins, and most of those young people he knew as a youth have been caught up in the justice system, few graduated high school, and fewer yet went on to college. Cases such as this true story of Chris are the focus of SBSC.

Thought Question. Reflect on the people you know, including extended family members. Identify one or two and describe the special strengths they possess that made it possible for them to become fulfilled persons.

The role of the school counselor is to identify those special strengths and resilient factors in the life of a student and help him or her recognize those factors and build on them (Smith, 2006a). Students can beat the odds by confronting the world with all its problems using their strengths and resolve (Ungar, 2006; Ungar, Lee, Callaghan, & Boothroyd, 2005).

Strengths and Resiliency Factors

Strengths that contribute to a student's resilience have been organized by researchers Christopher Peterson (2006) and Martin E. P. Seligman (2004) into a list of six core strength of character factors covering a total of 24 dimensions (Haidt, 2005; Novotney, 2009b). According to Peterson (2006, pp. 142–146) these include:

1. *Strengths of wisdom and knowledge*, made up of creativity, curiosity, love of learning, open-mindedness, and having a broad perspective

2. *Strengths of courage*, composed of factors of truthfulness and authenticity, bravery and the courage to speak out when needed, persistence in the face of obstacles, and the feeling of being alive and full of zest

3. *Strengths of humanity*, including factors of kindness (helping others), being caring and loving, and having good social intelligence

4. *Strengths of justice*, involving an unbiased fairness in all matters, leadership and the ability to have others want to follow, group loyalty, and a true spirit of teamwork and team building

5. *Strengths of temperance*, comprising avoiding vengeance and being forgiving and merciful, modesty and true feelings of humility, prudence in both actions taken and words spoken, and being disciplined and self-regulated in actions and appetites

6. *Strengths of transcendence*, including an appreciation of natural beauty and excellence in the arts, spirituality and a recognition of one's place in the universe, hope and a sense of optimism, a sense of humor (without ridicule) and enjoyment of life's incongruities, and a strong sense of hope and optimism

It has been argued that four strengths can be added to this list (Smith, 2006b), including a seventh involving problem solving and analytical reasoning. This dimension includes most higher-order thinking skills. An eighth is an ability to make money and support one's self and others. The ninth includes the ability to work within the community's structures to obtain needed support and assistance. The 10th and final one includes survival strengths, including avoidance of pain and the provision of physiological and physical survival needs.

The ethnic heritage of a student can also be a resiliency factor and provide strength for developing coping mechanisms. Enrique Neblett Jr. and his colleagues have found that African American students holding an **Africentric worldview** have a protective mechanism for maintaining ego strength and coping with stress (Neblett, Hammond, Seaton, & Townsend, 2010).

Methods of Strengths-Based Counseling

As in all counseling, the first step in strengths-based school counseling is the development of a healthy therapeutic relationship with the student. Beyond the normal counseling skills, this requires a significant reservoir of optimism and a belief in the student's ability to improve (Morris & Usher, 2010).

While developing a good counseling relationship, the school counselor's second step is to begin to identify the student's strengths and special factors that make him or her resilient. This can start with having the student relate his or her life story.

The third step in SBSC is for the counselor to help the student clarify the nature of the problem that the therapy **counseling intervention** will address. A few simple questions can facilitate this step, including, "If there is one question you were hoping I would ask you, what would it be?" Another is, "Tell me your take on the problem. What is your theory about what is going on?"

Once the problem is understood and clarified, the counselor initiates therapeutic dialogues designed to instill feelings of hope and provide encouragement for the student. In this phase, praise is to be avoided, as it is a component of a contingency system that places the counselor in a judgmental role. Rather, helping the child see the possibilities for success provides encouragement. This can involve having the student retell his life story, casting himself as a survivor whose cunning and daring made it possible to survive.

Next, the school counselor works with the student to identify solutions to his or her problem. The conversation avoids discussing the problem and addresses solutions. Having ideas about solutions is a hopeful and optimistic mind-set. Finding solutions is done in much the same way as solutions-focused counselors have students explore exceptions or times when their problems do not occur. This makes it possible to identify functional answers in the search for effective strategies the student can employ. When appropriate strategies are identified, the school counselor can work to enhance the student's strengths and resilience factors. Elsie Smith (2006a) has proposed that discussing the student's ability to forgive others can reduce the anger and resentment that he or she may feel.

The various strengths that the counselor identified in the student can now be discussed. Therapy can focus on ways those strengths can be used to improve the student's competence, problem-solving ability, and resilience. By emphasizing strengths, the counselor provides the student with a sense of his or her ability to take charge of his or her own life and not be victimized. By being a survivor (one who overcomes problems) and having a survivor's mentality, the young person can feel very good about him- or herself and experience improvement in self-esteem and **self-efficacy**. Through strengths-based school counseling, a student can learn a new way to cope with life and be empowered as his or her own agent of change.

● VIRTUAL COUNSELING

The whole nature of schools and the role of school counselors are about to be changed in a dramatic way. The cause of this phenomenal educational metamorphosis is the sudden growth of technology-based distance education and the growth of **virtual schools**. Yet, most school counselor organizations have not realized what the future holds (Dahir, 2009).

The strength of this technology movement can be seen in its impact on other areas. Up until 2002, there was a clear trend toward continuing growth in **homeschooling** in the United States (Vaughn, 2003). That trend has been reversed by the growth in enrollment in virtual schools ("Home-school enrollment falters," 2005).

The National Center for Education Statistics (NCES) has been following the growth of virtual education and charted the rapid expansion taking place with both virtual elementary and secondary schools (Zanderberg, Lewis, & Greene, 2008). The federal report demonstrated that by 2005, 37% of all school districts had students attending virtual schools. The growth rate was about 60% in a 2-year span of time. Virtual schools have been able to grow this quickly by using the regulations of charter schools in many states. As a case in point, in Pennsylvania there are 11 licensed virtual charter schools enrolling nearly 20,000 students (Kurutz, 2009). In a fully staffed public school system, 40 or more school counselors would serve that number of students. Yet, in these virtual schools, there is only one school counselor providing direct service to the students. One large school system in Broward County, Florida, has created positions of virtual school counselors to assist students attending virtual classes from home (see www.bved.net/guidance.html). The Commonwealth of Virginia created a counseling program open to students attending virtual schools from Virginia. The *Virginia Handbook* for this virtual counseling system is available at www .virtualvirginia.org/educators/downloads/Counselor_Handbook_2008.pdf; the counseling program can be accessed from www.virtualvirginia.org/about/ counselors.shtml.

The reasons that these virtual schools are growing so rapidly are related to several deep-seated parental concerns. For one, parents are concerned about the "bad influences" their children will meet in public schools. Related to this is a parallel concern about bullies, the presence of drugs and alcohol on campus, and a felt need to control all aspects of their child's life (Vaughn & Wright, 2004). Another large subgroup of parents feel that public schools are far too secular and fail to teach and reinforce the religious values they teach at home. Other parents appreciate the fact that students can learn at their own pace and schedule (Slater, 2009).

Methods of Virtual Counseling

The use of online systems to provide individual and group counseling is amenable to several theoretical approaches, including solution-based counseling, cognitive behavioral therapy, and Rogerian and Adlerian counseling. The use of private chat rooms can facilitate group counseling (Anthony & Nagel, 2010).

Implications of Virtual Counseling

The implications for this trend are obvious. Counselors should become proactive and have state education departments require that counselors for virtual schools be licensed in their states. The technology for this is available, including video cameras on computers for individual counseling and the ability to use conference technology to conduct virtual psychoeducational counseling sessions.

Cyber-based virtual schools have the potential for being dangerous for students. Enrollment in a virtual school is typically done online. This can provide a back door into a seemingly child-safe environment for dangerous individuals who wish to harm young people. Students in virtual schools can contact each other either through the school's system or through social networking. The use of Facebook and other social networking can also be a problem for students, counselors, and teachers (Manning, 2010). Close monitoring is clearly needed in virtual education programs, but it is rarely provided.

Many virtual schools are for-profit and work from a business model. The following is an excerpt from a 2009 online advertisement for a counselor or advisor for a virtual charter school:

> We are creating a high-tech approach to educational support and expect our counselor to have superior customer service skills and a commitment and desire to provide the best experience possible for students and families.

The advertisement went on to list tasks including:

Be responsible for the logistics of just-in-time support and training in the form of e-blasts and electronic newsletters, and provide support for students with school set-up, first log-in, computer set-up/navigation and materials issues.

These tasks are not taught in the curriculum of any graduate counselor education program in 2010 and are not part of the professional standards for the field.

SUMMARY

A central skill for school counselors is the ability to actively listen to students and truly understand the feelings of distress and emotional responses they are experiencing. The first modern counselor advocating a child-centered form of counseling was Carl Rogers. His writings have influenced the course of psychotherapy in America and represent the "third force" in psychology. Rogers was greatly influenced by a neo-Freudian, Otto Rank. Another significant neo-Freudian of the 20th century was Alfred Adler, a therapist who included the important role played by groups and society in the structure of each individual's personality.

Neo-behavioral approaches have provided school counselors with techniques that teach students different ways to think about problems and challenges they confront in life. One of these theories, rational emotive behavioral therapy, developed by Albert Ellis, provides students with new ways to understand the world around them and also new methods to solve personal problems in the future. In a similar way, Aaron Beck's cognitive behavioral therapy teaches student-clients to challenge inappropriate thinking by using a hypothesis-testing approach stressing scientific logic. A third neo-behavioral system is the control theory and reality therapy of William Glasser. This approach emphasizes the link between the child's actions and the reality of the outcomes.

Group counseling is an effective method that can both be more time efficient for school counselors and employ peer influence in the therapeutic relationship. Time efficiency is an advantage to the counseling approach of solution-focused brief counseling. The strengths-based school counseling model is a cross-over set of methods adapted from the practice of social work. Strengths-based counselors are proactive in their efforts to build up the inner resolve and strengths of students as a way of inoculating them against potential problems.

The future of school counseling is not clear, as the nature of schools is evolving rapidly. There is a need to address the problem of providing the services of school counselors in a virtual school environment. Children exist in the real world, but many schools now exist in a cyberworld. Counseling is needed for the real-world students but must be delivered through cyberspace.

DISCUSSION QUESTIONS

1. Which of the 19 core propositions of Carl Rogers seem to hold a special meaning for you? Explain why that proposition resonates within you.

2. Review the four forms of behavior problems described in Adlerian counseling as common among preadolescents. Which do you believe to be the most difficult for a counselor to improve? How would you address that problem with an 8-year-old child?

3. Which form of reinforcement (positive or negative) works best with students? Why do you believe that? Provide several examples of each.

4. Reflect on your own "automatic thinking." What thoughts do you experience in social situations when you meet new people?

5. What advantages and disadvantages does a virtual school's counselor experience?

6 Reflect a bit on your own life and background. What are the strengths that you will bring to the profession of school counseling? What do you see as your areas for further development in working as a school counselor?

7. Reflect upon the boundaries you want to establish as a high school counselor. For example, will parents be allowed to call you by your first name? How about your student-clients? Make a list of what you see as being the boundaries you will insist on in your school counseling practice.

RELATED READINGS

Beck, A. T., Freeman, A., & Davis, D. D. (2003). *Cognitive therapy of personality disorders* (2nd ed.). New York: Guilford.

Belgrave, F. Z., & Allison, K. W. (2006). *African American psychology: From Africa to America*. Thousand Oaks, CA: Sage.

DeLucia-Waack, J. L. (2006). *Leading psychoeducational groups for children and adolescents.* Thousand Oaks, CA: Sage.

Glasser, W. (1986). *Control theory in the classroom.* New York: Harper & Row.

Rogers, C. R. (2007). *Counseling and psychotherapy: Newer concepts in practice.* New York: Houghton Mifflin.

Sklare, G. B. (2005). *Brief counseling that works: A solution-focused approach for school counselors and administrators* (2nd ed.). Thousand Oaks, CA: Corwin.

Vernon, A. (2006). *Thinking, feeling, behaving: An emotional education curriculum for children/grades 1–6* (2nd ed.). Champaign, IL: Research Press.

Vernon, A. (2006). *Thinking, feeling, behaving: An emotional education curriculum for adolescents/grades 7–12* (2nd ed.). Champaign, IL: Research Press.

NOTES

1. The exceptions are that the student cannot ask the counselor to keep illegal or threatening (toward self or others) information confidential.

2. Reading about counseling provides a general background. To actually do the work of counseling requires supervised experiences following specific training in the techniques being used.

3. Diane Albright (1994) presented this quote in an article titled, "An Unexpected Gift."

4. Leta Stetter Hollingworth completed her graduate work in psychology at Columbia University under Edward Thorndike. In 1916 she began a long career as a professor at Teachers College of Columbia University, where she founded and administered the School for Exceptional Children. She is most known for her activism in support of women's rights and her groundbreaking studies of gifted children.

5. In the early writings Rogers used the term *client-centered*, but by the 1960s he began using the term *person-centered*. This difference was made to make the term sound less formal and more focused on the individual involved. I have taken the liberty to modify this presentation using the word *student-centered* or *child-centered* as a way to distinguish counseling in the schools.

6. Girolamo Savonarola was a Dominican priest who was the leader of 15th-century Florence. He was known as being opposed to the art and literature of the Renaissance and burned many books. His strong moral code led him in opposition to the Borgia pope, Alexander VI, and what he saw as corrupt clergy. Today his name has entered the lexicon as an adjective for a person with a severe moral code and the need to enforce it on others. In view of his passion for book burning, his excommunication and execution by immolation in 1498 is a bit of an irony.

7. This preventative approach is a good fit with the ASCA national framework.

7

Counseling Children With Educational and Special Needs

OBJECTIVES

By reading and studying this chapter you should acquire the competency to:

- Describe the size of the population of special needs students attending public schools in the United States and suggest several reasons for the continuing growth in the number of children in need of special educational services
- Describe the role of school counselors with 504 committees
- Explain the steps needed to make an entitlement decision on behalf of a child with disabilities
- Describe the role of school counselors in the development and implementation of individualized educational plans (IEPs)
- Discuss the tasks of counselors in working with children and parents of children with low cognitive ability, problems of attention and focus, or life-threatening illness
- Describe autism spectrum disorders and describe how Asperger's disorder differs from the more common forms of autism
- Explain the special problems and misconceptions about children classified as being gifted, and describe the approach to school counseling with gifted and highly talented children

" Over ninety percent of the faults of children as reported by teachers are due to inattention in some form. **"**

William H. Burnham

● INTRODUCTION AND THEMES

Large urban school systems were first to address special educational needs of children with disabilities. Universal requirements for the education of all children with disabilities did not become the law of the land until 1975 with the passage of what became known as Public Law 94–142, which requires that all children be provided a free and appropriate education.

School counselors must always work in the best interest of students; however, that role can lead to ethical conflicts when providing service for students who have needs for special education programs. The huge cost of special educational services, especially in private school placements, can overwhelm a school's budget and drain programs for other students. This source of conflict is one that counselors need to address and resolve with their colleagues and administrators.

The number of students needing special educational services is huge and growing. More than any other area, problems of attention and focus are the most common reason for a student to be provided an evaluation and special services. A fast growing area for school counselors to be aware of are students with the autism spectrum disorders, including Asperger's disorder.

The role of the counselor is to provide services and advocate for all students (see Case in Point 7.1), including those who are very sick with life-threatening illnesses. School counselors need to assist the school's leadership in developing plans for how to cope with students who have life-threatening illnesses.

School counselors also have the responsibility to assist in the identification and "programming" of students who have extraordinary talents and superior levels of mental ability. Counseling with gifted students often involves dispelling myths and stereotypes held by many educators about highly intelligent students.

CASE IN POINT 7.1

A 22-year-old recent college graduate with a degree in special education found her first job in the New York City schools teaching a class of 18 high school students, each of whom had significantly impaired levels of mental capacity (IQ 35–75). Each student had an updated IEP, and each required highly individualized instruction. Rising to the challenge, the new teacher developed a series of technology-based activities (computer-based instructional activities) that matched the needs of these students. The activities included skills such as learning to tell time, using public transportation, making change, reading a menu, and taking care of personal hygiene. She also developed appropriate computer games to be played as a reward after successful work on the computerized instructional activities.

Thought Question. If you were the high school counselor working with those same students, what assistance could you provide to this class and technology-savvy teacher?

BRIEF HISTORY OF SPECIAL EDUCATION IN THE UNITED STATES

British Tradition

The foundation for providing support for people with special needs was first ensured in a law signed late in the reign of Elizabeth I of England. That law required each parish to tax the wealthy to provide basic services for the needy and mentally deficient within their communities (Horrell, Humphries, & Voth, 1999). By the 19th century these benignant policies had disappeared, and the poor and mentally deficient were herded into asylums and/or sold into indenture and transported to colonies in North America and Australia.

Colonial America

In America there were enclaves wherein humane treatment was offered to the "feebleminded" and "mentally defective," but these were the exception. Dr. Benjamin Rush, a physician in Philadelphia at the time of the American Revolution and the first surgeon general of George Washington's Army, was on the staff of Pennsylvania Hospital while teaching surgery at the University of Pennsylvania. He established the first asylum for mentally defective individuals at the hospital in 1792.

19th and 20th Centuries

The 19th century saw the dramatic increase in the United States in training schools and institutions for children with disabilities. For the most part these were residential programs located in the growing cities of the United States.

There were schools for the blind, hard of hearing, homeless and orphaned, and those with mental deficiencies. Most of these were established with private philanthropy. Boston's school committee began the first special education classes in 1838, in what it described as "schools for special instruction" (Osgood, 2008). These grew in urban areas and by 1927 a survey of 500 urban school systems identified 4,000 special education classrooms serving a population of about 78,000 students with disabilities (Osgood, 2008).

Urban Schools

The leadership role for public school-based special education was clearly carried out by the schools of the great cities. As there was no national mandate for special education until the 1970s, each state and local district set its own policies. By 1853, New York, Boston, and Philadelphia all had opened schools for "feeble-minded children." These became the first step in an elaborate set of programs found in the urban centers of 20th-century America. During the administration of President Herbert Hoover, a special White House Conference Committee on the Handicapped described the positive steps taken by both large and smaller urban areas to provide special education and the "lamentable absence" of such services in America's rural areas (Osgood, 2008). Most major city school systems began publishing newsletters describing special education programs in their cities during the 1930s. These were widely circulated among school systems.

Rural Schools

Before the 1970s, exurban and rural public schools could, and often did, refuse to provide free public school education for students with significant disabilities. Children with less obvious disabilities were allowed to attend school and languish in regular education classrooms. Eventually these students dropped out of school (Osgood, 2008). Most rural school systems simply ignored the issue of special needs students. It was not uncommon for rural school systems to expel students for not learning. If parents of children with disabilities wanted to ensure their children were appropriately educated, it was the parents' responsibility to find private schools or tutors and pay the tuition. William Gibson's play (1959) and motion picture (1962) *The Miracle Worker*, relating the true story of a tutor (Ann Mansfield Sullivan) hired to assist a multiple handicapped girl (Helen Keller[1]), caught the public's imagination but did little to improve conditions for disabled students in rural areas whose parents did not have the resources to hire private tutors. Outside of the urban centers like Philadelphia, Boston, New York, Chicago, or Pittsburgh, public school administrators believed they had no role to play in the identification, placement, or education of children with disabilities.

A National Concern

That all changed with a federal court decision from the case *Pennsylvania Association for Retarded Children (PARC) v. Commonwealth of Pennsylvania.* In October 1971, Pennsylvania accepted a consent decision mandating that "all children, handicapped or otherwise, are entitled to a free and appropriate public education." Subsequent case law by the Supreme Court of the United States (see Case in Point 7.2) made it illegal to change the status of any child without providing the child and his or her family with procedural due process (*Gross et al. v. Lopez et al.*, 1975).

CASE IN POINT 7.2

During political protests on school grounds during March 1971, scores of secondary school students in Columbus, Ohio, were suspended from school for 10 days.

In deciding this case, the Supreme Court of the United States based the decision to overturn the suspensions and clear the students' records on the 14th Amendment to the U.S. Constitution. This amendment is described as housing the "equal protection" clause (see Chapter 1 for more on this amendment as it applies in school). The court decided that schoolchildren have protected rights, including the constitutional right to "due process," along with all other rights as citizens. Thus, a student cannot be expelled from school unless there has been an open hearing when the child's parents may provide evidence and be represented by counsel. The implication goes further and also covers all special education placement decisions.

Thought Questions. Students in special education programs can and frequently do act out or bring illegal items into the school and thereby violate the school's "no tolerance policy." As a professional school counselor, what course of action would you encourage a school's principal to follow if a student in special education was found to have brought a loaded firearm into the school? Keep in mind that any other student would be expelled. Can a student in special education with an individualized education plan be sent home and required to attend a virtual school?

Parents as Advocates

All placement decisions, including whether or not special education is to be provided to a child, must make provision for the child's parents to have input into the process. The mandate for parental involvement and due process was reinforced in the 21st century by the U.S. Supreme Court (Lewin, 2009). The first steps in making a placement decision involve the school and its staff coming to an agreement with the parents as to what constitutes a **free and appropriate public education (FAPE)** for their child. The requirement for FAPE is now also stated in federal special education laws (see "Special Education and the Law" later in the chapter).

Due Process

If parents and educators of a school do not agree on a student's program, the parents are permitted to challenge the educational placement decision. Failure to reach an agreement with the school's staff of specialists and administrators means the parents' next step is to petition the board of school directors to overturn the decision made by the local school. This petition must be presented in writing and may include oral argument and expert testimony. This step is a daunting one for many parents and may be best approached with the help of expert legal counsel.

If a resolution cannot be achieved, the written decision of the school board may be appealed to an impartial due process hearing master. If the due process hearing does not support the school's decision, not only will the student's placement be changed, but the court may award parents the costs of their legal assistance and require the school system to pay all "reasonable costs" (Lewin, 2009). However, if the court finds the parental request was frivolous and without foundation, the costs incurred by the school district may be charged to the lawyer representing the parents.

The role of the school counselor is to serve as an advocate for what is best for each student. If what is best is not part of what is being proposed by the school, the counselor can advocate for what the student needs within the school. A school counselor taking a public position that opposes the school administration's action is likely to be seen by most school administrators as an act of insubordination. Naturally, a school counselor must answer all depositions and questions from court masters and judges honestly and completely.

Better Than Vouchers

One way parents have found they can provide an optimal education for their child with a disability is through the use of private special education schools. There are a number of these schools in and around metropolitan areas offering both residential and day school programs. There are specialized programs for virtually every disabling condition, and their programs are often more appealing to parents than are the special education options provided by public schools. Parents who can prove that their child is not receiving an appropriate education within the public school may request a due process hearing and present evidence that their child is not being appropriately served by the public school and request that he or she be given placement in a private school. If the impartial court master agrees with the parents, the public schools can be responsible for tuition payments and transportation costs for the disabled child to attend the private school (Lewin, 2009; Wright & Wright, 2007). (See Case in Point 7.3.)

Having a legal right and having the ability to use it are two different things. There is a gap developing between parents who are of some economic substance and who have children with disabilities and other parents who do not have large incomes and have children with disabilities. Wealthier families can afford to hire expensive legal counsel, pay for diagnostic evaluations, and pay the private special education school's $50,000 annual tuition while litigating for a year or more with the school system. Poor parents cannot afford to do that. One result is that some parents of means are gaming the system to keep their children in private schools and out of mainstream public schools. Mayor Michael Bloomberg of New York City complained that in 2008 the New York City's public schools were charged $89,000,000 for private school tuition of children with special educational needs (Lewin, 2009). This group represents only about 1% of the population of New York City children with disabilities (D'Amico, 2009).

Thought Question. The Individuals with Disabilities Education Improvement Act ([IDEIA] 2004) requires that local schools consult with private school providers when students in the private or nonpublic parochial school have special educational needs. This is spelled out as Section 612(a)(10)(A)(i)(II) and 612(a)(10)(A)(iii) through (v) of the Act. The consultation is to decide how schools can work in cooperation for the benefit of the student. It is likely that the school's counselor will play either a lead role or be a significant player in such consultations. If you, as a counselor, were asked to make a site visit in preparation for this consultation, what would you want to see? Make a list of factors and components you would include in preparation for consulting about a joint program of assistance for a student with disabilities.

SPECIAL EDUCATION AND THE LAW ●

It was once said that the moral test of government is how that government treats those who are in . . . the shadows of life, the sick, the needy and the handicapped.

Hubert H. Humphrey

First Federal Legislation

During the 1970s the federal government assumed a proactive stance regarding the education of children with disabilities. This position was fostered by the outcome of federal court challenges initiated by parents and by advocates for students with disabilities. The first federal legislation to address needs of children with disabilities was section 504 of the Rehabilitation Act of 1973. The second major piece of legislation was the Education for All Handicapped

Children Act of 1975. Its *Federal Register* identification number, P.L. 94–142, is how most people refer to the legislation. Later reauthorizations of that original bill saw it become the Individuals with Disabilities Educational Improvement Act in 2004 (Wright & Wright, 2007). These laws require that a free and appropriate public education be provided to all children with disabilities starting at birth and extending to the awarding of a high school diploma or the age of 21. The federal agency responsible for administration of special education laws and the compliance of state agencies to the parts of that law is the Office of Special Education and Rehabilitative Services (OSERS) in the U.S. Department of Education. To learn more about the work of OSERS, see www2.ed.gov/about/offices/list/osers/osep/index.html.

Instructional Materials

Another significant piece of legislation affecting children with disabilities is the Instructional Materials Accessibility Act (IMAA, 2002). This act was folded into the first reauthorization of the No Child Left Behind (NCLB) Act in 2004, where it provides guidance to educators through the publication of **National Instructional Materials Accessibility Standards**. These standards provide uniformity for books translated into Braille and other media formats. The standards also require all instructional materials including worksheets, school computers and software, and other equipment used by students with disabilities to be equally accessible and useful for them compared to what is available for students who are free of any disability. (See "Americans with Disabilities Act" later in the chapter for more on the requirements for schools enrolling students with disabilities.)

No Child Left Behind Act

More recently, the No Child Left Behind Act, first passed in 2002, has proven to be a challenge to those benignant policies expressed in the special education laws of the 1970s. The primary goal of the NCLB Act is to have all students, including those with mental deficiencies, reading and solving mathematics problems at a proficient level for their age-appropriate grade level.

One good element of the reauthorization is that it provided a requirement for educational agencies to identify and provide special services for children with disabilities beginning at birth. Another good element is that the NCLB Act forced all school systems to disaggregate achievement data and consider the success of children in each minority group. This makes the task of the school counselor much more complex, as he or she has to monitor and explain the progress of all eight identified groups (children of poverty, African American children, Anglo-White children, Hispanic children, Native American and Pacific Islander children, children with special needs, Asian American children, and English language learners) as well as data from the school as a whole. (See Case in Point 7.4.) This is over and above interpreting individual score profiles to teachers and parents. These tasks are congruent with the data management tasks described in the American School Counselor Association national framework (American School Counselor Association [ASCA]/Hatch & Bowers, 2005, pp. 49–52).

CASE IN POINT 7.4

One concern for special education students occurs in dozens of cities and seven states in which students are required to pass a high-stakes test to be promoted to the next grade. In these states students with disabilities may be retained simply on the basis of having low test scores. Yet, low test scores are one of the reasons students in special education programs were identified as being entitled to special educational services. The ironic twist is that once a student is measured on a high-stakes test as being proficient, he or she may no longer be eligible for special educational services. In other words, students receiving special educational services may be measured as being proficient and lose their learning support, or they may fail to score at a proficient level and be required to repeat the grade. It is clear that this issue needs further clarification by the states and cities where it is a policy. There is a need for the development of a transparent model for accountability with students who have special educational needs (Gaffney & Zaimi, 2003).

Thought Questions. Only 10 states (Delaware, Florida, Georgia, Louisiana, Maryland, Mississippi, North Carolina, South Carolina, Texas, and Wisconsin) will prevent a student from going on to fourth grade if he or she has low test scores. School counselors play a central role in the decision to retain a student in a grade in states and cities where it is not predicated on test scores. If you were an elementary school counselor working in one of the other 40 states, what would you suggest to the school's leadership as a policy about social promotion versus grade retention? Under what circumstances (if any) should grade retention be employed? Explain and justify your position.

Americans with Disabilities Act

A final area of federal legislation that has had an impact on the job of all school counselors is the Americans with Disabilities Act ([ADA] P.L. 101–336; 1990). This law, sponsored in the U.S. Senate by the late Edward M. Kennedy, requires that all public buildings and public areas be fully accessible by all citizens. This includes school buildings, buses and other transportation modes, museums and other off-campus locations where instruction occurs, and all playing fields and stadiums used by the school. This law requires all school facilities, including administrative centers, be retrofitted if not in compliance with the accessibility mandate.

Naturally, students with all forms of disabilities must have complete access to all school counseling services, and they must be provided those services on an equal basis with all other students. Computers in the counseling office must have accommodations for students with vision, hearing, and orthopedic disabilities. Likewise, all counseling suites must be completely wheelchair accessible (halls and doors open to a clear width of 32 or more inches and move a full 90 degrees. To reach the counseling offices, students with disabilities must not face steps or steep ramps (maximum slope function is 1:12 rise to run). (See Case in Point 7.5 for an example of a negotiation to meet this need.) Doors must have automatic opening systems and have no round, twist-type door handles. To learn more about the Americans with Disability guidelines for access to public spaces, see www.access-board.gov/adaag/html/adaag.htm.

The ADA also mandates that postsecondary education institutions make reasonable accommodations to meet the needs of individuals with disabilities in college. Enforcement of this postsecondary mandate is spotty and up for local interpretation. For that reason, high school counselors should provide careful planning assistance for both students with disabilities who are planning to go to college and their parents. Both students and parents need to be provided with information to be advocates for the college student.

CASE IN POINT 7.5

A fourth grade student suffered a spinal cord injury (C-7/T-1) in the late spring and as a result was paralyzed from her waist down. Her parents contacted her elementary school counselor to let him know the girl would return to school in the fall and needed transportation and requested a walk-through of the school with the student's occupational therapist. The counselor met with the principal before the parents and therapist arrived to discuss what accommodations were possible. The school was constructed on a hillside with three floor levels. Each level had two split-level tiers of rooms. Thus there were a total of six levels and six flights of stairs in the school. While pleasing to the eye from the outside, inside the school was a collection of hallways and staircases leading from level to level. The library was on the top level, as was the gym and other large rooms, and the school's classrooms were on the lower floors. The principal let it be known that there could be no funding for elevators. Meeting the ADA ramping requirement was out of the question, as ramps to climb a vertical 30 feet must be 360 feet in length with not less than 12 switchbacks or resting-landing areas.

The school's policy was to transfer students with this form of disability to a different, more updated school building that was in compliance with the ADA mandates. That school was several miles away and in a poorer neighborhood within the school system.

When the parents learned of this plan, they balked and threatened legal action. Their point was that their child was being singled out and given separate and inherently unequal opportunities by the school.

The counselor found a solution that cost the school just a few thousand dollars. It was his idea to purchase an electric wheelchair that climbs steps. Next, working with the grants and a funding officer (development specialist) in the district's central administration, the counselor found a grant to pay for the special use wheelchair, the iBot chair built by Johnson and Johnson, from the U.S. Department of Education, Office of Special Education and Rehabilitative Services.

Within two weeks, the girl was back in school with her old friends. Each day the driver of the special education bus assisted the girl in transferring from her home wheelchair into the school's stair-climbing chair, and off she would go for another day of school.

An American version of a stair-climbing wheelchair was introduced in 2003 and was out of production in 2009, as it was too expensive for Medicare to pay for. To learn more about the iBot chair, see www.msnbc.msn.com/id/30929301/.

For information about another stair-climbing wheelchair, see the following: www.youtube.com/watch?v=PLUTP6CXylE&feature=related.

Also see www.youtube.com/watch?v=JkfWKgtPfZl&feature=fvw.

Thought Question. Take a short tour of a high school or college campus from the perspective of a student who is wheelchair bound and has little hand or arm motion (C-5 quadriplegia). Look at all entrance doors, halls, bathrooms, water fountains, and access to common area facilities (cafeteria lines, library shelves, computer height, etc.). Make a list of any problems you encounter. Bring your list to class and discuss your findings.

ROLE OF SCHOOL COUNSELORS AS ● ADVOCATES FOR CHILDREN WITH DISABILITIES

Most parents look forward to the birth of a child with great hope and feelings of optimism. When a child is born with an easily identified disabling condition, the natural reaction of many parents is to grieve the loss of their child's future. The unfortunate truth is that this occurs many times each day among families in this country.

Epidemiology

There never has been a time when so many students with disabilities attend public schools as today, nor has the number of students in special education ever represented a larger proportion of the population of students enrolled. In 2007 there were 6,109,000 students enrolled in special education programs. The total public school population that year was 50 million. Thus, 12% of the school-aged population receives special educational services.[2] (See Table 7.1.) Counselors have an important role to play in the identification and education of these students.

Between 80% and 90% of all school-aged children with disabilities are not identified until they begin school (Barkley, 1998; Mash & Dozois, 1996). Prior to school age, parents and pediatricians normally identify major disabilities among young children. These include developmental delay, **orthopedic disabilities, genetic abnormalities,** major illnesses, and **traumatic injuries** (Raber & Frechtling, 1985). Some disabilities not normally identified until the child is of school age include attention deficit/hyperactivity disorder and learning disorders (American Psychiatric Association, 1994). The critical point is that early childhood counselors and educators

TABLE 7.1   Status of Special Education in the United States

Children Provided Special Educational Services in 2007	
Specific learning disabilities (e.g., AD/HD)	2,780,200
Speech or language impairments	1,157,200
Mental retardation (all levels)	545,500
Emotional disturbance and conduct disorders	472,400
Multiple disabilities	133,900
Autism spectrum disorder (including Asperger's disorder)	193,000
Hearing impairments	72,400
Orthopedic impairments	63,100
Major health impairments	561,000
Traumatic brain injury	23,500
Vision impairment (including blindness and low vision)	26,000
Deaf and blind	1,600
Developmental delay (incomplete data from states)	79,100
Total	6,109,600

SOURCE: U.S. Department of Education, https://www.ideadata.org/TABLES31ST/AR_2-4.htm

NOTE: Total is not summation, as many categories overlap one another.

have a central role to play in early identification of students who will need special assistance. The necessity for counselors to be vigilant about, and have sensitivity to, signs a student may need special support cannot be overstated.

Identification of Students in Need of Special Education

Teachers play the first role in the process of identifying students who may be experiencing developmental and/or learning problems. The school's counselor is the first level of the pupil services team with whom teachers will likely discuss students who may be having problems. Counselors must always be open to what teachers describe, while probing to determine if there are other nuances or instances that teachers can relate that may be part of the problem areas.

Screening

A first step in the process is to work with the teacher to have a screening conducted of the student's status. (Table 7.2 lists steps in the process of identifying students who require special services.) Prior to that screening, the counselor should talk with the child's parents to enlist their assistance and support. A screening involves a short, easily administered standardized assessment. Screening measures are not definitive and can be used as an indicator that a thorough assessment is needed for the student. The screening can be conducted by the counselor working alone or with the school's reading specialist. Well-prepared school counselors should have available and be trained to administer and interpret several screening measures.

TABLE 7.2   Steps in the Process of Identifying Students Requiring Special Services

Step	Decision to Be Made
1. Screening	Whether or not a referral for further assessment is needed
2. Assessment	What is the area of learning or developmental difficulty? Referral to student assistance team (SAT)* aka 504 committee
3. Multidisciplinary team evaluation	Eligibility (entitlement) for special services and instructional program planning conducted by the IEP committee
4. Monitoring of child	Whether the intervention is working or requires modification through the ongoing use of response to intervention probes (RTI) by the school counselor as per the child's IEP

*Various names are used for this team of educators and specialists, including instructional support team (IST) and 504 committee.

These brief measures can be useful prior to convening a student assistance team (SAT) meeting, sometimes known as an instructional support team (IST) meeting. The SATs are a normal part of the process for assisting a student experiencing a learning problem. The process is spelled out in Section 504 of the Vocational Rehabilitation Act (1973). Screening measures can also assist counselors in program planning for new students.

There are three major groups of screening measures (see Table 7.3) that the school counselor should be ready to employ. A well-stocked counseling office will have available one or more from each category, including cognitive ability, achievement and learning, and attention and focus.[3]

TABLE 7.3   Screening Measures Useful to School Counselors

Tests of Intelligence Administered One-on-One   There are five individually administered intelligence tests that are widely used in public schools. Three of the five assume that the user is qualified at a doctoral level with advanced education in educational assessment, and two tests, the Slosson Full-Range Intelligence Test (S-FRIT) and the Kaufman Brief Intelligence Test, 2nd ed. (KBIT-2), assume users are educated at a master's degree level in a field such as counseling and have advanced education in testing and score interpretation.[a]

Kaufman Brief Intelligence Test, 2nd ed. (KBIT-2)   The KBIT-2 is perhaps the most user-friendly of all the individually administered tests of intelligence. Educational specialists including school counselors and well-trained reading specialists can administer this test. The KBIT-2 requires about 30 minutes to test a student and provides intelligence scores for children as young as 4 years and as old as adults (Miller, 1995; Pearson Assessment, 2010).

Slosson Full-Range Intelligence Test (S-FRIT)   Another test that provides a quick estimate of general cognitive ability is the Slosson Full-Range Intelligence Test (S-FRIT). This measure takes about an hour to administer and score and provides an overall IQ score. Five additional subtest scores are generated by the test, including Verbal Index, Abstract Index, Quantitative Index, Memory Index, and a composite Performance Index. Qualified school counselors can administer the test. It was normed on a population of 1,500 and designed for use with children as young as 5 and as old as 21 (Algozzine, Eaves, Mann, & Vance, 1988). The upper limit of 21 may not be realistic for highly verbal undergraduate students for whom a **ceiling level** often cannot be found. The test has reasonable levels of reliability but lacks a solid grounding in cognitive theory. Likewise, it is often difficult to find a reliable **basal score** point when testing 5-year-old children with the S-FRIT (Slosson Educational Publishing, 2010).

Measures of Achievement and Learning   School counselors working in elementary and middle schools may need to make a quick estimate of a child's reading, language, and mathematics skill levels when children transfer into the school. This information can assist with developing the student's program and placement.[b]

Kaufman Test of Educational Achievement, 2nd ed., Brief form (KTEA-II Bf)   This screening test of achievement provides measures in three domains, including reading (word recognition and reading comprehension), math (computation and application problems), and written expression (written language and spelling). The KTEA-II Bf is structured to provide scores for children as young as 4.5 years through adulthood (Pearson Assessment, 2010).

Wechsler Individual Achievement Test, 2nd ed. Abbreviated (WIAT-II A)   This provides a screening assessment of achievement for children between kindergarten and college age. It requires only 25 minutes to administer and provides scores for letter and word reading, math calculations, and written spelling (Johnson, 2003). The screening test battery, WIAT-II A, is sold by Pearson Assessment (2010).

Wide Range Achievement Test–Expanded, Individual Administration (WRAT-E-IA)   The WRAT-E-IA is an individually administered screening assessment of a child's reading, mathematics, listening-comprehension, oral expression, and writing. It is standardized to provide scores for individuals between the ages of 5 and 24 years (Engelhard, Zhang, & Walker, 2005). The screening using the WRAT-E is a long measure to administer, requiring more than 2 hours to give all the subtests. It is sold by PAR Inc. (2010).

Measures of Attention and Focus   More than any other problems that students have in learning in school are the problems of attention and focus. These learning problems are not easy to measure and are normally identified by the use of observational checklists. The name attention deficit/hyperactivity disorder (AD/HD) has been adopted as the name for these learning problems.

Checklist systems can be completed by the child's teacher and parents and then reviewed by the school counselor as he or she is gathering referral data. Diagnostic guidelines provided in the *DSM* (4th ed.; APA, 1994) provide the basis for published AD/HD checklists.[c]

In reality, many children can be unable to attend and be unfocused on any particular day. For that reason the identification process requires that the problem be persistent and that observations be made over time.

Behavior Assessment System for Children, 2nd ed. (BASC-2)   BASC-2 is described as a multidimensional approach to assessing a range of childhood disorders including AD/HD. It is published by Pearson Assessment in English and in both English and Spanish (Pearson Assessment, 2010) and is used with children between 2 and 21 years of age (Reynolds & Kamphaus, 2004). It includes teacher and parent self-report questionnaires, a formal student observation system, and forms for collecting the child's developmental history. BASC-2 assesses the possibility of impairment in the child's executive cognitive function.[d] The BASC-2 was well normed and corrected for gender differences.

Brown Attention-Deficit Disorder Scales for Children and Adolescents   The Brown-ADD-Scales for Children includes a teacher questionnaire, parent questionnaire, and a semi-structured clinical interview. Administration of the questionnaire requires examiners to be trained in school counseling or special education and requires about 20 minutes to complete. Pearson Assessment sells the Brown Scales (2010). It was normed for use with a population between 3 and 12 years of age and provides comparative and diagnostic tables that extend up to age 18.

Conners Rating Scales-Revised (CRS-R)   Multi-Health Systems of Canada designed the Conners Rating Scales-Revised for use with children between 3 and 17 years of age (Conners, 1997/2000). Pearson Assessment distributes the CRS-R in the United States (2010). CRS-R provides a global index score as well as scores that align with *Diagnostic and Statistical Manual* ([*DSM*] 4th ed.; American Psychiatric Association [APA], 1994), AD/HD classification. Scoring and interpretation of the CRS-R takes about 20 minutes. There are seven subscale scores that are a part of the CRS-R: Oppositional, Cognitive Inattention and Problems, Hyperactivity, Anxious-shy, Perfectionism, Social Problems, and Psychosomatic (Hess, 2001).

(Continued)

TABLE 7.3 (Continued)

> **Scales for Diagnosing Attention-Deficit/Hyperactivity Disorder (SCALES)**   Gail Ryser and Kathleen McConnell (2002) developed an instrument that can identify children and adolescents (5 through 18 years) who exhibit AD/HD behaviors (Pro-Ed, 2010). The measure is composed of 39 Likert scale questions presented on two forms (teacher and parent). These questions yield three subscale scores aligned with *DSM* (4th ed.; APA, 1994) criteria: inattentiveness, hyperactivity, and impulsivity. The validity of the three subscale scores was well established by factor analysis (Law, 2001). This measure is a good screen for AD/HD.

[a]The three measures requiring advanced education in educational measurement are the Wechsler Intelligence Scale for Children, 4th ed.; Woodcock-Johnson, 3rd ed., NU Cognitive Test of Abilities; and the Stanford Binet Intelligence Scale, 5th ed.

[b]This brief list includes only tests widely used in public schools and appropriate for well-prepared school counselors to employ. Other measures that have not been recently updated or renormed have been excluded.

[c]Only a certified school psychologist can make the final diagnostic statement required to qualify a child for special education for all disorders, including AD/HD.

[d]The executive function is a cognitive construct describing a mental system that controls and manages other mental processes. Abilities to plan ahead and concentrate are directed by the executive function.

Differential Diagnosis of AD/HD

The American Psychiatric Association (APA) suggests that a child may be identified as AD/HD if he or she persistently exhibits an array of these behaviors in both school and home settings:

1. Inattention
    a. Fails to follow through and complete tasks
    b. Is easily distracted by the environment and others in it
    c. Finds it hard to concentrate on school work or sustain attention
    d. Does not listen when spoken to
    e. Is forgetful and tends to lose items (homework, lunch, books, etc.)

2. Hyperactivity
    a. Will climb and roam
    b. Constantly shifting from one task to another
    c. Talks excessively
    d. Is constantly on the go as if driven by a motor
    e. Is restless and cannot remain seated for a long period
    f. Does not play well with others (few friends)

3. Impulsivity
   a. Acts without thinking or planning
   b. Frequently calls out in class
   c. Frequently interrupts others and butts into conversations
   d. Cannot wait before taking a turn

4. Early Onset

There is a requirement for an early onset of the disorder. First symptoms must occur before school age, and its symptoms must persist for more than 6 months.

Student Assistance Team, 504 Committee

When a teacher and the school counselor confer after initial screening about a possible problem being experienced by a student, the first major step that can be taken on behalf of the youngster is to convene a "504 committee" to discuss the student's problem and suggest potential solutions. These committees are known by several names, including student assistance teams or instructional support team. The team is organized and brought together by the school counselor and includes the child's parent(s), classroom teacher(s), counselor, involved educational specialists (e.g., reading, art, music, and physical education teachers), the school's nurse, and the principal or designated administrator. (See the sample referral form in Exhibit 7.1.) The goals and organization of student assistance teams have been described by the New Mexico Department of Education on their web page: www.ped.state.nm.us/qab/downloads/sat/file2.pdf; information for parents is available from the Albuquerque Public Schools: www.aps.edu/aps/eldoradocluster/satp.html.

A number of school systems use brief academic probes of what students know and can be expected to do when they enter public school in first grade or kindergarten. The pattern of scores on these brief probes can provide data needed to initiate a referral and the formation of a student assistance team (504 committee). Employing response to intervention (RTI) probes every few weeks with students receiving early assistance is a way to monitor the success of the process of providing assistance (Legere & Conca, 2010).

The SAT should meet shortly after a referral is received and not wait to see "how things work out." SAT committees address educational problems students are experiencing even when the problems are not severe. The goal of the SAT process is to identify alternative solutions for students having difficulty. The school's counselor should maintain a written record of the committee's

EXHIBIT 7.1   **Sample Referral for a Student Assistance Program Team Evaluation**

Name of Student _____Gender _____ (M) _____ (F)

Date of Birth (mm/dd/yyyy) _____/_____/_____ Grade(s) Repeated _____

Number of Days Absent This Year _____ Number of Days Absent Last Year _____

Attends After-School Programs? ____(Y) ____(N) ____

   If yes, which?_____

Most Recent Test Scores:

   Date of Test _____; Test Form _____; Level of the Test _____;

Percentile Score for Most Recent Standardized Achievement Test:

     _____ Reading Total _____Reading Vocabulary _____Reading Comp.

     _____ Math Computation _____Math Problem Solving _____

     _____Writing Mechanics _____Spelling

Other Recent Tests or Evaluations _____

Synopsis of the Problem:

Related Problem Areas:

Name (Print) of Referring Teacher _____

School Building _____ Grade Level(s) _____

Phone Number _____ E-mail Address _____

work and recommendations. The written report becomes an important school record that should be referred to periodically (see Exhibit 7.2 for a sample form for this report). The counselor should also follow up on a regular basis with the teacher following a SAT committee meeting. It may be advisable to reconvene the SAT committee every 3 or 4 months during the year to tweak the program and check on the student's ongoing progress.

The Individualized Education Plan Process

When the SAT's interventions are not effective, a second, more formal referral is initiated. The 504 plan is a brief plan designed to provide a short duration

EXHIBIT 7.2   Sample Student Assistance Team Report

Student Assistance Committee Recommendations   Date _____/_____/_____

Revised Instructional Activities and Materials

Benchmark for Success

Duration of Intervention   Start Date _____   Continue Until_____

Signature of Referring Teacher _____

Signature of School Administrator _____

Signature of School Counselor _____

---

fix for a learning or behavioral problem being experienced by a student. The individualized education plan (IEP) process is more thorough and can provide a multiyear statement of educational interventions to be implemented with a student who has a disabling condition. The IEP referral includes a presentation of the initial SAT committee's materials and the 504 instructional support plan, interim reports, and recent assessment scores. The school's counselor normally has responsibility for completing the tasks related to setting up this committee. These tasks include working with the child's parents and conducting a pre-referral conference with them, collecting documents and artifacts illustrative of the problem to be addressed, coordinating schedules, and setting a meeting time and place. Other counselor tasks include reminding all parties prior to the IEP meeting and providing assistance (transportation, translator, etc., for the parents).

Individualized Education Plan Committees

The task of the IEP committee is to decide whether the student is experiencing problems that have a significant negative impact on his or her ability to learn. This is more than a diagnosis; it also includes documentation of the impact the problem is having. When this has been established through the study of data about and observations made of the student, the committee (usually chaired by a certified school psychologist or the school's counselor) makes an entitlement decision. That is, the IEP committee decides that the student is entitled to the additional services provided through special education. (See Exhibit 7.3 for a sample IEP referral form.)

Exhibit 7.3   Sample Individualized Education Plan Committee Referral Form

---

Background

Name of Student _____   Gender ___(M) ___(F)

Date of Birth (mm/dd/yyyy) _____/_____/_____   Grade(s) Repeated _____

Attends After-School Program(s) ___(Y) ___(N)

    If yes which? _____

Living Arrangements:

    (A) Parents in the home _____

    (B) Siblings in the home _____

    (C) Extended family in the home _____

Total Days Absent This Year-to-Date _____   Days Absent Last Year _____

Nature of Disciplinary Referrals (if any)

Student Assistance Program Outcome:

Describe the interventions initiated by the Instructional support team or committee.

Dates of SAT intervention: Start ___/___/_____   End ___/___/_____

Describe outcomes from the (SAT) committee.

Does the child qualify for Extended School Year services? ___(Y) ___(N)

Synopsis of the current learning problem:

Associated areas of problematic behavior:

Unmet annual goals for growth in each dimension of achievement specified in the curriculum and on the SAT report:

Goal(s)   Benchmark(s)

1.

2.

3.

4.

Academic Development

Grades for major subjects for past two years:

Year 20XX _____   Year 20XX _____

      Reading   _____   _____

      Mathematics   _____   _____

      Science   _____   _____

      Social Studies   _____   _____

Most Recent Test Scores: Date of Test ____/____/_____; Test form _____; Level _____.

Percentile Equivalents on Most Recent Standardized Achievement Test:

      _____ Reading Total _____ Reading Vocabulary _____ Reading Comp.

      _____ Arithmetic _____ Arithmetic Problem Solving

      _____ Writing Mechanics _____ Spelling

(Abv) = Above, (Pro)= Proficient, (Bgn) = Beginning, (Blw) = Below Proficient

Most recent NCLB scores: Percentile Reading _____% (Abv) _____ (Pro) _____ (Bgn) _____ (Blw) _____

      Percentile Math _____ % (Abv) _____ (Pro) _____ (Bgn) _____ (Blw) _____

      Percentile Science _____%

Other tests and scores _____

When given? _____

Name (Print) of referring teacher: _____

School building _____   Grade level(s) _____

School phone # _____   Teacher's e-mail address _____

The individualized educational plan (IEP) provides goals and approaches to be used for the student's education. It describes details about what benchmarks are to be achieved and provides a timeline for their acquisition. The degree of inclusiveness and the extent of support are described in detail in the IEP report. The IEP also provides the decision to provide **testing-accommodations** during statewide or other standardized tests, and whether the student qualifies for **extended school year (ESY) services.**[4] The IEP should also spell out standards to be used to grade and evaluate students with special needs (Jung & Guskey, 2010). It lists all educational specialists (speech therapists, hearing or vision teachers, reading specialists, physical and/or occupational therapists, etc.) and the extent they will be helping the student. All specialized materials and equipment are also detailed in the IEP. (See Table 7.4 for a list of required elements for an IEP.) Once the IEP is agreed to and signed by school administrators, the school psychologist, and the child's parents, implementation can begin. Once in place as a program for meeting the child's needs, assurance that all aspects of the IEP are being met is the responsibility of the school's counselor. For more information about IEPs, see www.ed.gov/parents/needs/speced/iepguide/index.html.

An often overlooked required part of the IEP is a specified counseling and education program for parents of children with disabilities. The U.S. Department of Education realized that educational support activities are more likely to be successful when the child's parents understand what is being done and participate in their child's support efforts (Laviano, 2009). School counselors should use this requirement as a way to have the IEP committee set out a plan for assisting parents of a child with a disability. The IEP should define who will provide the service and how and when counseling and educational support activities for the parents will occur.

TABLE 7.4 Required Elements of an Individualized Education Plan

The IEP must include the following items:

1. Child's current educational performance level across all areas of the curriculum and a description of how the disability affects the child's involvement and progress in school.

2. List of reasonable annual goals that can be accomplished during the school year.

3. Special education and related services that will be provided to the child including any modifications and program supports the child will receive.

4. Description of the extent to which the child will participate in regular classroom activities with nondisabled peers.

5. Modifications or accommodations needed for the child to take mandated standardized tests.

6. Start date when special education and related services will be provided to the child and the frequency and duration of these activities and support services.

7. Provision for the transition of the child into life after school. (This component must be in place before the child reaches the age of 14.)

8. Provision for counseling about the rights that the child will accrue upon reaching the age of 18.

9. Description of how progress toward annual goals will be measured and how the child's parents will be kept apprised of that progress.

10. A plan for the counseling and educational needs of the child's parents in support of the implementation of all elements of the IEP.

Regulations of the Office of Special Education and Rehabilitation Services, U.S. Department of Education (Individuals with Disabilities Educational Improvement Act [IDEA], 2006, P.L. 108–446 § 300.34 (8)(i))

(8)(i) *Parent counseling and training* means assisting parents in understanding the special needs of their child;

(ii) Providing parents with information about child development; and

(iii) Helping parents to acquire the necessary skills that will allow them to support the implementation of their child's IEP or IFSP.

The IEP should list any specialized equipment and materials needed for meeting the student's instructional needs. This may include headphones as part of a personalized amplification system, a study carrel, print magnification systems, wider doors, bathroom modifications, lowered work areas to wheelchair height, special personal storage areas (cubbies or lockers) appropriate for wheelchair access, and writing implements sized for a student with an orthopedic disability. The possible list of materials and equipment is immense. To prepare for the meeting of the IEP committee, the school's counselor may need to work with occupational and physical therapists to compile the list of necessary items.

Test Accommodations

Testing Environment. When a student is unable to attend and concentrate on any testing task including those created by the classroom teacher, it may be necessary to have that student tested alone in an environment free from distractions. Using a study carrel can meet this need. Naturally, someone will need to administer the test to the student. This may be done by a counselor intern, student teacher, or even a library aide. This type of an environmental modification may be needed for all children identified with AD/HD as well as students with pervasive developmental disorders (e.g., Asperger's disorder, Tourette syndrome, and many other neurological disorders). Also an environmental change may be needed for students who may be disruptive to others (e.g., Tourette syndrome), or for those who may need close supervision (e.g., oppositional defiant behavior disorder).

Time. By far the most common specific learning disability among young children in public school involves reading. Students with reading disabilities may need to be accommodated by having extra time to answer the questions on the test.

(Continued)

(Continued)

Modality. A number of students will need to be accommodated by having the test administered in Braille (e.g., students who have very low vision and blind students). Students with severe musculoskeletal spasticity and students with paresis (e.g., cerebral palsy) will need to have the test verbally administered and answered. Students with hearing disabilities may need to have headphones to facilitate hearing test directions. Students with no hearing (e.g., deaf students) may require test directions be signed.[5]

Individualized Education Plan Format

The Individuals with Disabilities Education Improvement Act (2004) requires an individualized education plan but does not prescribe a format to follow. A critical requirement for IEPs is documentation proving the student's learning is negatively affected by the identified condition or disability. Most local school systems have developed their own IEP formats. Educational software vendors now sell computerized IEP writing software. One advantage of computerized IEPs is they assure all documents are similar in quality and follow a common structure (Margolis & Free, 2001). Example software can be reviewed at the following two URLs: www.tera-sys-inc.com/ and www.iepware.com/IEPSD.html.

Response to Intervention

As is true of 504 plans, response to intervention provides a systematic method to monitor progress once an IEP has been implemented. It requires the careful charting of how a student with special needs responds to the interventions prescribed in the IEP. The school counselor may be expected to assist the special education process by periodically testing the student receiving special education and charting the student's responses to the special education interventions. RTI testing consists of a series of brief probes based on the curriculum being taught. These **curriculum-based probes** are administered every few weeks and must be carefully recorded and graphed. The special education teacher may also do this task, but the counselor should maintain a record of the probes used and a chart of outcomes.

● COUNSELOR'S ROLE WITH PARENTS OF CHILDREN WITH DISABILITIES

Generally speaking, educators and school counselors are better equipped than parents to identify children exhibiting potential learning problems. Parents lack broad experience with many children at different levels of ability and from different backgrounds. This somewhat limited viewpoint sets the parameters for what parents know about childhood behaviors, and which are within the normal range. The problem faced by a school counselor is the possible harm done by a failure to follow up and determine that a student needs special support services. Likewise, if the decision by the school counselor is to pursue a full-scale evaluation, and that effort shows there is no difficulty present, it is possible the student's parents will have been frightened for no reason. Likewise, valuable resources (staff time) will have been used without good cause.

For these reasons, it is critical for school counselors to work closely with the parents of children who may need special services. Seven of every 8 hours of the student's life are spent under the care and custody of parents; thus, parents should be seen as an invaluable resource of information about the student. Likewise, the parent's help is essential in making any individualized educational plan work effectively.

Preliminary Meetings With Parents

It is likely that parents of a child with a disability sense something is wrong before the time a school counselor makes the initial call to the parents about possibly attending a conference at school. Still, school counselors must assume that the parents may not realize that there is anything wrong at school (Lin, 2001). During such meetings, it is a good rule to let the parents describe their child and explain what they have experienced at home with their child. The counselor can provide parents with positive observations about their child before beginning to describe the nature of the child's problem area. These positive comments can involve describing the child's work habits, social interactions, and academic gains. The presentation of potential problems should be supported with the use of artifacts from the classroom and possibly digital recordings of the student struggling to learn at the pace of his or her peers. The atmosphere should always be positive and focused on solving a mutual problem. The goal is to make the parents full partners in helping alleviate difficulties experienced by their child.

The conference is an excellent time to encourage parents to keep lines of communication between home and school open. Depending on school policy, the school counselor should share his or her professional e-mail address with the child's parents and let them know the policies of the school regarding online contacts. When the counselor meets with parents, he or she should provide literature and other media resources for the parents describing the nature of the child's potential difficulty and the support programs offered beyond the school. It is also a good time to invite the parents to attend a support group sponsored by the counselor for parents of children with disabilities.

Counseling Students With Disabilities

Much of the school counselor's work on behalf of students with disabilities is carried out through primary and secondary prevention. Primary prevention activities involve the preparation of the school environment for a student with a disability. This can include physical alterations as well as the purchase of necessary assistive equipment and alternative instructional materials (e.g., Braille reference books for the library and classroom of students with visual impairments). Other activities include setting up parent support groups and providing parents of children with disabilities with resources about their child's area of disability. A final area involves following up on all aspects of the student's IEP, including setting up appointments with specialists as listed on the IEP (speech, vision, hearing, physical therapists, etc.).

Parents need to know that many of the learning problems that their child experiences do not prevent the youngster from living a full and rich life, including having a college education. No other people have the ability to encourage and advocate for children with disabilities as do parents. Research has demonstrated that parents are the key to all successful school transitions, including one from high school to college or the world of work (Kleinmann, 2001; Schiavone, 1999). (Photo 7.1 depicts a transition meeting;

PHOTO 7.1   Final Transition IEP Meeting for an 18-Year-Old Special Education Student in Grade 12

SOURCE: Istockphoto.

as an adult, the 18-year-old student is present at and participating in the IEP meeting.) The role of the school counselor is to help parents assume the role of their child's best advocate and help parents establish a plan for the future of their child beyond school.

At the secondary prevention level, school counselors should be engaged in group counseling efforts with other students in the school, assisting them in understanding the important positive role peers can play in helping students with disabilities reach their optimal levels. This may include the use of age-appropriate bibliotherapy.

Group counseling can also improve the self-esteem of students with disabilities and inoculate them against the potential corrosive effect of a bully or student who has a need to harass those with less self-assurance and *sangfroid*. One of the best secondary prevention activities that a school counselor can initiate to improve the lives of children with disabilities is to involve the whole school in a Special Olympics program (see www.specialolympics.org/).

At the tertiary level, school counselors engage in individual and group counseling programs with the student with disabilities. One of the best approaches to use in counseling students with disabilities is a strengths-based approach. Another involves the judicious use of parts of Hollywood films and DVDs. The clips from films can be drawn from some of the following:

Miracle Worker (1962), directed by Arthur Penn

Children of a Lesser God (1986), directed by Randa Haines

David's Mother (1994), directed by Robert Allen Ackerman

Forrest Gump (1994), directed by Robert Zemeckis

The Other Sister (1999), directed by Garry Marshall

Counseling Students With Moderate to Low Cognitive Ability

Within the normal population, between 2% and 3% of all children function in the low range of mental ability. The presence of Down's syndrome (chromosomal abnormality) accounts for just a fraction of these low-functioning children (Smith & Agus, 2009). Genetically directed abnormalities in the metabolism of certain proteins present in the brain account for another 10% of the cases of low cognitive functioning (Smith & Agus, 2009). Other reasons for low mental ability include both the use of legal prescription drugs (e.g., Valproate) and the abuse of legal but dangerous drugs like alcohol during pregnancy. Fetal alcohol syndrome is frequently misdiagnosed, especially if the mother lies about her alcohol use, and is identified as autism or AD/HD (Rovet, Greenbaum, & Kodituwakku, 2009).

Low-ability children are easy targets for bullies and others with a need to victimize those with less sophisticated defenses. For this reason, an important activity for school counselors is to provide primary and secondary prevention programs to thwart the harassment students with low ability could face. Support programs for parents of children with disabilities are one needed element in primary prevention. The counselor should host these meetings and arrange speakers and provide literature for parents attending the evening sessions. The counselor may need to reach out to families with children in need of special educational services in an effort to secure parental engagement and participation in parent support programs.

Another is a schoolwide program for instilling respect for all other individuals, including those with disabilities. The goal of the counselor is to stop it from being "cool" to make the student with disabilities a target. As noted previously, a schoolwide initiative such as Special Olympics is an excellent way to approach this task.

Problems students of low ability frequently face frustration at not being able to learn and respond the way his or her age-peers can (Ochoa, 2010). This frustration can have a negative impact on the student's self-esteem and spill over in the form of anger and acting-out behaviors (Mikami, 2010).

Individual and group counseling with students with disabilities must focus on the strengths and abilities that each student possesses. Examples and ideas presented during sessions should be developmentally appropriate and understandable to the student. The use of puppets and other psychodramatic materials can also assist in establishing effective communication process with students with low levels of ability.

Counseling Students With Problems of Attention and Focus AD/HD

Even though the number of diagnosed cases of AD/HD has declined since 2008, attention deficit/hyperactivity disorder is the most frequently occurring disability associated with learning problems in the public schools of the United States (Samuels, 2010). This disorder interferes with the child's neurological executive functions, including the ability to focus and attend to tasks (McLean, Worley, & Bailey, 2003). Students who cannot attend to learning tasks lack the ability to focus on classroom instruction and have great difficulty meeting the academic expectations of public schools.

One form of AD/HD was named by the American Psychiatric Association *attention-deficit/hyperactivity disorder, predominantly inattentive type* (APA, 1994).[6] As the name implies, students with this diagnosis cannot attend to learning tasks and do not have the ability to focus their efforts on a task or problem for more than a few seconds. When the child has impulsive and hyperactive behaviors, the disorder becomes *attention-deficit/hyperactivity disorder, hyperactive type*. There is also a variety of the disorder in which the child experiences both hyperactivity and an inability to focus. The American Psychiatric Association describes this as *attention-deficit/hyperactivity disorder, combined type*. AD/HD frequently occurs along with learning problems, including poor reading skills (APA, 1994). Symptoms associated with AD/HD diminish but never disappear as the individual matures. The disorder may have an adverse effect on the life of adults in college and at work (Brown, 2005).

More than 40% of all special education entitlement decisions involve AD/HD or a related learning problem (e.g., learning disability [LD]). Only 20% of children identified with AD/HD are girls (Committee on Quality Improvement, 2001). Of the children identified with AD/HD, about 2 out of 3 are also hyperactive.[7]

Parents often wonder whether there was an environmental cause for their child's AD/HD and have accused the manufacturers of childhood vaccines of being responsible for the problem. No credible biomedical research supports that likelihood; however, there is evidence for a genetic component to the problem of AD/HD (Chang, 2005). See Case in Point 7.6 for an example of a possible environmental factor in AD/HD. A point counselors should stress is that the source of the learning problem is less important than finding ways to overcome the underlying disability.

The diagnosis of AD/HD is typically compounded with anxiety, conduct disorder, and/or severe oppositional behavior (Hardman, Drew, & Egan, 2008). Attention-deficit /hyperactivity disorder is also found among students with problems in language and speech development and those with reading problems.

CASE IN POINT 7.6

Parents of children with AD/HD will frequently seek solutions for their child's condition from the Internet and many other sources. Like the family pediatrician, the school counselor is frequently asked for an opinion about these "cures."

(Continued)

(Continued)

One of the most interesting of these ersatz cures appeared in the publication of the Feingold Diet in 1974. Since that time many parents of children with AD/HD have attempted to control their children's symptoms through diet. The dietary items Feingold recommended being removed include all foods and patent medicines containing:

- Artificial (synthetic) coloring

- Artificial (synthetic) flavoring

- Aspartame, an artificial sweetener (e.g., NutraSweet)

- Artificial (synthetic) preservatives BHA, BHT, TBHQ

More than 30 years of anecdotal (nonscientific) reports have provided support for this approach to treating AD/HD (Brody, 2009; Feingold, 1974). Recently a team of medical researchers in the United Kingdom was able to scientifically document that Feingold's dietary approach inhibits the symptoms of AD/HD in young children (McCann et al., 2007). The British study used a double-blind, placebo-controlled research design. In that research, scientists could both increase the occurrence of AD/HD behaviors by increasing the amount of chemical additives in foods and significantly reduce those behaviors by the elimination of the suspect additives.

Thought Question. Open your pantry and refrigerator and make an inventory of the foods and drinks you consumed yesterday. Make a list of artificial additives included in the foods' preparation, coloration, and preservation. Could you live up to the rigor of a diet without these elements?

A common medical approach to treating children identified as having AD/HD includes the prescription of methylphenidate (dose about 0.30 mg/kg of body weight in children). The most common form of drug goes by the brand name Ritalin. Today about one million children are treated with Ritalin or similar drugs (atomoxetine and dexamfetamine).

A concern is that the use of psychotropic stimulant medication may lead to drug and alcohol addiction later in adulthood. Longitudinal research evidence has not found this to be true (Wilens, Faraone, Biederman, & Gunawardene, 2003). There are serious side effects associated with long-term use of these powerful stimulants. One is that methylphenidate can increase blood pressure, reduce appetite, cause stomach pain, increase nervousness and anxiety, and make it more difficult for the child to sleep. Many parents are reluctant to give their children this powerful medicine.

The advantage is that the drug can give the child the ability to focus attention on learning, especially in reading (Burns, 2003). It also improves the child's receptive language ability (Brown, Perwien, Faries, Kratochvil, & Vaughan, 2006). The key to the successful use of methylphenidate is careful titration of the child's serum and close monitoring by a board-certified child psychiatrist.

The role of the school counselor with students under the care of a psychiatrist for AD/HD is to monitor them and collect evidence from teachers about their progress. The resulting data should be shared with parents on a regular basis. Parents should be encouraged to share these school reports with the child's prescribing physician. Second, as these drugs are frequently abused, parents should be taught to closely monitor their presence in the home to prevent visitors or other siblings from acquiring them.[8]

One area for counselors to provide assistance for children with AD/HD is in the development of social skills (Riva & Haub, 2004). One diagnostic dimension of AD/HD is the tendency to be impulsive, a characteristic that can cost children friendships (Henderson, 2009; Mikami, 2010). The five-step approach that school counselors can introduce during simulation exercises in group therapy with AD/HD students is known as STCDT:

1. Stop.

2. Think about what you are going to do.

3. Consider what others will think about your action.

4. Devise alternative plans.

5. Take an appropriate action.

This five-step approach forces the child to reflect on what he or she is doing and how others will feel about it. Additionally, group sessions can be used to teach students how to apologize to those they hurt and how to develop friendly relationships with their peers.

School Counselors and Students With Life-Threatening Illnesses

The advent of deadly diseases in American schools is nothing new. Prior to World War II, infectious diseases including polio myelitis, influenza, rubella, tuberculosis, and scarlet fever killed and disabled tens of thousands of children each year in the United States. Entire families were quarantined in their homes or sometimes in hospital asylums until either the disease's crisis had passed or the individual(s) had succumbed to it. Entire communities closed their borders to any and all strangers during times of the spread of dangerous communicable diseases (Kraut, 1994).

Starting in the 1980s, the advent of HIV/AIDS in the schools and other highly communicable illnesses (e.g., SARS in 2003 and H1N1 swine influenza in 2010) has created another role for the school counselor. If mishandled, the presence of HIV and other devastating communicable diseases (e.g., viral and bacterial forms of meningitis) among the students of a school can be unnerving and cause a panic among both students and faculty (Gay, 2008). The primary public health officer within a school is the school nurse. The role of the counselor in assisting students with serious and life-threatening illnesses (e.g., Tay-Sachs disease, HIV/AIDS, osteosarcoma, lymphoma, Niemann-Pick disease, and sickle cell disease) can be thought of as paralleling the work of the school's nurse.

The educating of other students about the nature of illness is the task of the school's nurse. The counselor should address groups of students on the social aspects of illness (Larsen & Lubkin, 2009). Specifically, students need to learn not to fear their peers who have life-threatening illnesses but to see and treat them as they do all other students. When counseling students who have life-threatening illnesses, maintain a positive demeanor, and always allow the child all the time needed to describe how he or she feels about what is going on in his or her life. Never assume you can know how he or she may feel, but let the child tell you (Germinario, Cervalli, & Ogden, 1996).

The first step for a school counselor in a primary prevention program is to work with the school's leadership committee to establish a game plan for how the school will respond when there is an outbreak of a serious illness in the school. As part of a primary prevention program, counselors should remind teachers to maintain normal classroom procedures and maintain normal expectations from students with life-threatening illnesses. Flexibility may be needed on occasion, but the goal should be to work toward normalcy. Remind faculty of the importance of confidentiality in all matters related to the ill child and his or her family. Help faculty avoid their own prejudice and fears, and teach them to be sensitive to prejudice and fear from others around the child.

Special Cases of Autism Spectrum Disorders

Children with autism are normally identified prior to entering public schools. About 1 in 110 children are born with one of several **autism spectrum disorders** every year. These disorders involve poor verbal and nonverbal communication skills and an inability to establish friendships or feel empathy toward others. Delayed or missing speech development is another hallmark of autism, as are low levels of cognitive ability. Language (if present) is often stereotyped and repetitive of a phrase or word. Children with autism usually develop compulsive needs to use a particular sequence of activities or patterns in their lives. They are **hypervigilant** and oversensitive to environmental stimuli (Autism Society, 2006).

Asperger's disorder is one of the autism spectrum of mental disorders that involves about 1 in 160 children. There is both anecdotal proof and clinical evidence that there is a genetic vulnerability or link to Asperger's disorder and/or autism (Morrow et al., 2008). Parent advocacy groups have claimed that these disorders are caused by childhood vaccinations. Yet, to date there is no scientific evidence of255 a causal link between vaccines and this form of disability. Board-certified child psychiatrists normally diagnose Asperger's disorder through interviews with the child and his or her teachers, counselors, and parents.

Children with Asperger's disorder frequently have slightly better social skills than other autistic (Kenner's syndrome) children and have above average levels of mental ability. Young children with Asperger's disorder exhibit all the same behaviors as other bright children but do so to an extreme level or in an inappropriate format or location. Children with Asperger's disorder also tend to concentrate on a single issue or area of learning and develop a true expertise on the topic. Asperger described these children as *"kleine Professoren mit einem unglaublichen Wissen von diesem oder von diesem Thema"[9]* (Osborne, 2002). This dimension of intense learning by children with Asperger's disorder can lead these children to productive and full lives. Recent evidence points to the likelihood that Albert Einstein, Marie Curie, J. M. W. Turner, Béla Bartók, and Isaac Newton had Asperger's disorder (Ioan, 2003). Students with Asperger's disorder frequently qualify for receiving both special education support and programs for the gifted.

Parents of children with Asperger's disorder have been known to successfully sue public schools for continued special educational services for a child after high school graduation). Under the IDEIA legislation, youth below the age of 21 are eligible for special educational services.

Once again counselors working with a student diagnosed as having Asperger's disorder can work with the student in small group settings to improve his or her socialization skills. This should be paired with solution-focused behavioral counseling (SFBC; see Chapter 6) and goal setting with the child (Photo 7.2). The school counselor should maintain close contact with the student with Asperger's disorder and his or her teachers. Reports should be provided to the child's parents at regular intervals. Parents should be asked to share the school's observations and reports with the child's physician.

PHOTO 7.2   Counselor Working With a Girl Who Has Autism

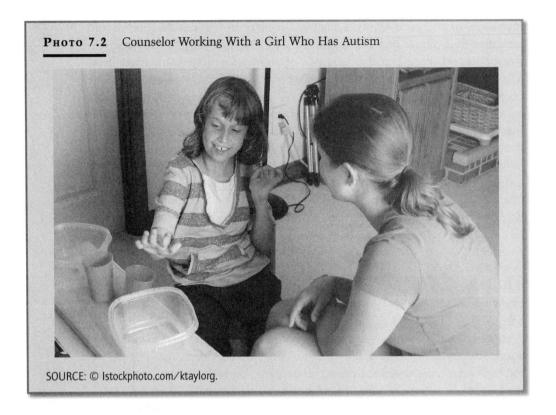

SOURCE: © Istockphoto.com/ktaylorg.

● COUNSELING GIFTED CHILDREN

Every gift contains a danger. Whatever gift we have we are compelled to express.
And if the expression of that gift is blocked, distorted, or merely allowed to languish,
then the gift turns against us, and we suffer.

Lyndon B. Johnson

Academically gifted students are a group that tests unusually well, has little difficulty learning new things, and can also experience many of the same learning and social problems as do other students. Students with academic talent have many advantages, but their ability can also be a problematic factor in their lives.

As was noted in Chapter 5, many Americans do not like the concept of providing extra services to students who have advanced skill levels to start with. One of the problems facing school leaders looking for resources to offer special programs for gifted children is that the No Child Left Behind Act drained much from the resources that once had supported extra programs for the academically talented. There is no federal law mandating that school districts provide special programs for gifted students. There are 29 states that have embraced programs for the gifted, of which only 4 provide funding and guidelines for their operation within the state's school systems.

Identification of Gifted Children

Lewis Terman initiated the original study of gifted children in America in 1927. In that longitudinal research, a child had to be nominated by his or her classroom teacher, then tested for intelligence by one of Terman's staff. To become part of the study the child had to score at an IQ level of 140 (a level reached by about 1 in 250 children). The idea of having teachers involved in the identification of gifted and talented continues today. The National Association of Gifted Children (NAGC) recommends that identification of academically gifted children involve multiple criteria, including teacher's reports, test scores, work samples, and parent recommendations (NAGC, 2008).

Each state sets the standard for defining which students are eligible for gifted education services. These definitions vary widely, but nearly all include a requirement that the gifted child have high-level cognitive functioning. This usually translates to an IQ of 130 (highest 2%) or higher. In about half of the states, making an entitlement decision for providing a child with gifted education services requires an IEP. In those states, parents can request a due process hearing to determine whether the gifted student is receiving the appropriate education. Many school systems encourage parents to avoid the due process hearing or the formality of an IEP committee and have a psychologist in private practice evaluate the child and make a recommendation as to what is the most appropriate education for the child.[10] The specific requirements by state are posted on the NAGC web page: www.nagc.org/index.aspx?id=37.

Role of the School Counselor

One role for the school counselor is to assist in the identification process for the gifted student. There is a real possibility that gifted children may be languishing and not showing their talents so as to avoid getting extra work piled on them by teachers. It is also possible that gifted children are bored with school and the endless drill for high-stakes tests and will rebel in class. There are several problems uniquely linked to highly gifted children. One is low achievement, and another is perfection seeking.

Gifted children can have attention and focus problems, making them inattentive in class, just passing time daydreaming and ignoring the teacher. These bright but inattentive students may be wallowing in ennui from lack of intellectual challenge. They may get low grades and may not turn in homework or complete other busy work. Boredom arises as gifted students need to hear about a new concept only once or possibly twice to understand and assimilate it. This fast pace for learning is a function of the greater neural efficiency in the cortex of gifted children. Average-ability students require between six and eight repetitions of new concepts to learn them, and slow children nine or more repetitions (Sousa, 2003). The repetition of what he or she already knows can be a mind-numbing experience to a gifted student. The outcome is the student escapes into his or her own private world. National data have demonstrated that the dropout rate for gifted students is not very different than the rate for regular education students (Matthews, 2008; Renzulli & Park, 2002).

Helping academically talented students can involve both group counseling with the students in question and advocating to modify the educational system for these students. One approach that has been used with academically talented students involves having them tutor others on what they already understand. Another is to give them permission to research approved topics in the library for part of the day. These topics should be within the framework of the curriculum but in an area of interest of the student. The student should be required to present the teacher with regular reports on what is being accomplished. However, no gifted student should be excused to do independent study until he or she has demonstrated that the skills being taught in the regular classroom have been mastered.

Unlike the bored and disengaged, some highly gifted children become seekers of personal perfection. These gifted children use their superior abilities to wheedle every thousandth of a grade point average point on their march to be the one selected to give the valedictory speech at graduation. They can develop compulsive behavioral patterns and close down to the ideas of others. These children look for the same perfection they seek in themselves in their friends and are likely to correct the language or try to improve others. They may speak pejoratively of others and "speak down" to their peers. It can be difficult for such students to nurture and maintain close personal friendships.

School counselors should use goal setting with these students in a counseling program employing solution-focused brief counseling. These are bright students and they are able to "get it" quickly, and they are excellent candidates for SFBC interventions. One of the goals can be to develop friendships and identify leisure activities that they can enjoy with their peers.

Counseling Parents of Gifted Children

The average salary paid to school counselors in the United States in 2010–2011 was $75,000 per year (Schachter, 2010). This was less in the urban and rural school systems and slightly higher in the wealthier suburbs. Many school counselors feel they really earn their pay whenever they work with the parents of gifted children. Yet, parents are integral to the process of gifted education (Chipego, 2004).

The school counselor should encourage parents of the gifted to provide an intellectually stimulating home environment, including many books and well-monitored computer access. Parents may need support groups in which they can interact with other parents who also are meeting the rigorous demands of a highly intelligent

---

CARTOON 7.1   "Simply S.O.P."

"It is simply S. O. P. for us to test each child and let you know if we see signs of Ivy League potential."

SOURCE: Merv Magus.

student. School counselors can assist parents in overcoming feelings of inadequacy in comparison with their student's intellectual abilities. Likewise, parents need to learn how to cope with the resentment that may be experienced by their gifted child's less intellectually endowed siblings. Information for parents of gifted children can be found on the National Association for Gifted Education, www.nagc.org/, and also at the web page of the Neag Center for Gifted Education and Talent Development at the University of Connecticut, www.gifted.uconn.edu/.

SUMMARY

The 1970s saw the federal government mandate that all school systems provide a free and appropriate education for all children, including those with disabilities. For some children with disabilities, their parents are great advocates for their needs. For many others, the school counselor must advocate for the rights and educational support of children with disabilities. One of the primary steps for school counselors working with students with disabilities is identification and initiation of learning support programs. These start with the establishment of student assistance teams (504 committees) and can move on to the convening of an individual educational plan committee. The process of identifying a student in need of special education programs involves making an entitlement decision. Counselors have an important role to play at every phase in this process including ongoing follow-up.

The most common special need experienced by students in this country involves learning support for a learning disability. Learning disabilities are usually a manifestation of AD/HD. One area where counselors can help students and parents occurs among students with significant academic ability.

DISCUSSION QUESTIONS

1. Assume a school counselor knows that a local private special education school offers a superior program to that of the public school employing the counselor. Would it be appropriate and ethical to mention the non-public option and provide information about requesting a due process hearing to the parents of the child needing specialized services provided by the private school?

   Suppose your school principal specifically told you not to mention the alternative program and the ways to apply for a due process hearing. What steps should a counselor take with that limitation?

2. What is the role of the child's parents on an IEP committee? If possible, ask a school counselor or administrator what the school's policy is regarding a student's IEP when the two parents disagree with each other about the best approach to follow with the education of their special needs student.

3. What steps should a school counselor take if a parent of a bright elementary school student reports that she has found a private psychologist who can guarantee a diagnostic report that will qualify her student for entrance into the gifted program?

4. Starting with the first informal observation by the teacher of a student's possible learning problem, list all the personnel and the amount of time each is likely to spend working on the student's behalf before the IEP is written and instituted. Then use the figure of $80 per hour[11] as the cost of these faculty and specialists (including overhead) and estimate how much it costs to reach an entitlement decision and start a program of special education assistance for one student. You may substitute the actual local average per hour cost if $80 is not appropriate in your setting.

RELATED READINGS

Hardman, M. L., Drew, C. J., & Egan, M. W. (2008). *Human exceptionality: School, community, and family.* New York: Houghton Mifflin.

Karten, T. J. (2009). *Inclusion strategies that work for adolescent learners!* Thousand Oaks, CA: Corwin.

Osgood, R. L. (2008). *The history of special education: A struggle for equality in American public schools.* Westport, CT: Praeger/Greenwood.

Sousa, D. A. (2003). *How the gifted brain learns.* Thousand Oaks, CA: Corwin.

NOTES

1. Helen A. Keller was born on a plantation in Alabama in 1880 and at the age of 19 months lost her vision and hearing to meningitis. Her parents were wealthy and able to provide the best environment for her. They consulted with Alexander Graham Bell, who led the Keller family to hire Anne Sullivan as a tutor and companion for Helen. The story of their accomplishments has been told in the literature (Herrmann, 1998) and through the Oscar-winning feature film of 1962, *The Miracle Worker*. The U.S. Treasury issued a series of state quarters in the early 2000s. The state of Alabama chose to use an image of Helen Keller as the central feature on its quarter in 2003.

2. Not all 6 million children with special needs are enrolled in public schools. Private schools for students with severe disabilities enroll about 1.5 million. The irony is that children most in need of specialized schools tend to be the most fragile and sickly. As a result many such children have poor attendance. The NCLB Act punishes schools with poor attendance, and these schools are often put into impossible positions (De Vise, 2008). On one hand they cannot change the student's placement to home-based instruction (unless that is on the IEP), and on the other, they can be excoriated for tolerating students with poor attendance.

3. If the counselor is not familiar with the screening assessments available, he or she can ask the school psychologist to provide a training session with the instrument. The publishers of the tests also provide training packages using online media. A third way to become proficient with one or more of the instruments is to attend national meetings of the counselor associations at which publishers conduct workshops for counselors demonstrating their products.

4. Special educational services can be provided during the summer break to children with special needs. To qualify a student for a summer program, the IEP committee must believe the student may lose his or her newly learned skills over summer months unless he or she is given added summer services. The IEP committee must determine the need for extra summer support services.

5. People who sign in American Sign Language (ASL) can work only for about an hour at a time. Hand fatigue requires rest breaks or two signers to spell each other during long tests. To learn more about American Sign Language, visit the University of Michigan ASL web page: http://commtechlab.msu.edu/sites/aslweb/browser.htm.

6. Prior to 1994, the designation attention deficit disorder (ADD) was generally applied to children with these symptoms. That designation has generally been replaced by the AD/HD predominantly inattentive type designation.

7. The American Psychiatric Association classification is AD/HD, predominantly inattentive type, and AD/HD, predominantly hyperactive-impulsive type. The total package is described as AD/HD, combined type.

8. Ritalin is known in the vernacular of the street as Vitamin-R and is illicitly sold for about $5.00 each for a 10-mg pill originally sold at the pharmacy window for $0.35.

9. "Little professors with an incredible knowledge of this or that topic."

10. In many expensive suburbs, there is a real push to have one's child in the gifted program at the local school. Parents see their child's abilities as confirming their own mental superiority. Among suburban parents, networks have developed identifying which local psychologist is most likely to identify a student as being gifted and which is less likely. This has created a cottage industry of gifted identification for a number of psychologists in private practice.

11. This is based on an average annual salary of about $75,000 per person for a team composed of school psychologists, school administrators, nurses, counselors, physical therapists, social workers, and reading specialists. Overhead is assumed to be about 50% of the base pay and includes health programs, Social Security, retirement, and local taxes and tariffs paid by the schools. Once a student has an IEP and is receiving services, the average cost of his or her education is approximately 1.5 times that of the student's peers who are not disabled.

8

School Counseling With a Diverse Population of Students

OBJECTIVES

By reading and studying this chapter you should acquire the competency to:

- Describe how social constructionism is a critical force in defining a personal sense of race and ethnicity
- Explain the difference in meaning between the words *race* and *ethnicity*
- Discuss the elements that compose the socioeconomic status of an individual or family
- Explain how adopting an emic perspective can assist a school counselor in working with diverse groups of students
- Describe the potential areas of psychological stress and difficulty commonly found among children of the wealthiest families
- Explain how a school counselor can assist the development of children of poverty and the homeless
- Explain the group histories and worldviews of Asian Americans, African Americans, and Hispanic Americans
- Describe effective counseling approaches to use with Asian Americans, African Americans, and Hispanic Americans

● ● ●

❝ The question is not whether we can afford to invest in every child; it is whether we can afford not to. **❞**

Marian Wright Edelman

● INTRODUCTION AND THEMES

The native people who had been living on the West Coast of Africa for thousands of years were hunted, captured, enslaved, and sold into bondage in North America beginning in 1619.[1] This evil practice continued for the next 246 years. The passage of the 13th Amendment to the U.S. Constitution in 1865 finally ended this loathsome practice in the United States.[2]

Since 1619 the issue of race and the color of one's skin has been, and continues to be, a significant issue in American life. As recently as October 16, 2009, Judge Keith Bardwell, a Republican from Tangipahoa Parish in Louisiana, refused to marry an interracial couple (White-Anglo woman and African American man) because they were not members of the same race ("Judge who refused," 2009).

In the past our laws were written to institutionalize racial groups and make it possible to enforce an American version of racial **apartheid**. Prior to a decision by the U.S. Supreme Court in 1954 (*Brown v. Board of Education*) that ended the practice of racial segregation in all public schools, and a follow-up decision (*Browder v. Gayle*) ending segregation in transportation and in all public buildings, separation of the races was the law throughout the American South.[3] Such laws, while common in many nations in the 20th century, never made sense to scientists who study the human genomic structure.[4]

Far more significant to individuals is their ethnic group membership. This membership includes issues of race and skin color but includes much more. The process of forming an identity as a member of an ethnic group involves a personal construction. This "social construction" includes the history of each family, its religion and beliefs, first language, customs, and culture. These and how others respond to us are core elements that make up the ethnic identity of each of us.[5] In some societies, including those of the United States, there is great diversity in the nature of ethnic groups that make up the culture.

The socioeconomic status of a family is composed of a number of factors, including the amount of money the family earns. Other dimensions include the family's wealth, educational capital, and the relative level of prestige of the occupations of family members. Children of wealthy families frequently exhibit a number of psychological problems in school that school counselors can address. Poverty and homelessness can have a pernicious impact on children. School counselors may play a pivotal role in bringing the help and resources of a community to the assistance of families and children in poverty.

This chapter examines the issues related to being a school counselor assisting students from the three largest ethnic minority groups in public schools today: Hispanics, African Americans, and Asian Americans. (See Case in Point 8.1.) It also examines problems related to counseling children of the wealthiest and poorest parts of the population. Each of these groups of Americans has a different history and different worldview. School counselors who are the most effective recognize and use these differences when helping students and their families. More detailed presentations of counseling with minorities and with various smaller minority groups are treated in books listed in Related Readings at the end of the chapter.

CASE IN POINT 8.1

In January 2002 the administration of President George W. Bush saw its centerpiece legislation for American education become law. That act, known as the No Child Left Behind (NCLB) Act, was a reauthorization of the original Elementary and Secondary Education Act of 1964 signed into law by President Lyndon B. Johnson. In the NCLB Act there was a provision that all public and charter schools (not parochial or private schools) had to test all students between grades 3 and 8 and again in high school for achievement. The scores had to meet minimum standards and be reported in disaggregated form by identified group, including students who are economically disadvantaged (free or reduced lunch), disabled (IEP), limited English proficient (LEP), Hispanic, White-Anglo, Native American, African American, Native Pacific Islander, and Asian American.

These categories are a collection of labels we employ to describe students and their families, but they are not orthogonal and provide much overlap. Some of these categories are racial: White-Anglo, African American, Asian American, Native American, and Native Pacific Islander. This form of classification implies that the U.S. Department of Education believes there are identifiable genetically derived **phenotypes** for these groups of students.

Impoverished students receiving a free or reduced cost lunch are a socioeconomic group and represent neither a distinct race nor an ethnic group. Likewise, the disability a child has has nothing to do with ethnicity or race. There are ethnic groups within various categories, including limited English proficient, Hispanic, Native American, African American, Asian American, and Native Pacific Islander. There is no clear ethnic group of White-Anglos, which is a possible blend of earlier immigrant populations from scores of different ethnicities.

Thought Question. What are the goals of the federal government in asking this bit of information about each student? Is it appropriate to correlate ethnicity with achievement scores? Reflect on the issue, and suggest alternative methods for organizing student achievement data for analysis and evaluation of schools and programs.

● AMERICA'S MELTING POT

Well, as in the old burning of the Temple at Corinth, by the melting and inter-mixture of silver and gold and other metals a new compound more precious than any, called Corinthian brass, was formed; so in this continent,—asylum of all nations,—the energy of Irish, Germans, Swedes, Poles, and Cossacks, and all the European tribes,—of the Africans, and of the Polynesians,—will con-struct a new race, a new religion, a new state, a new literature, which will be as vigorous as the new Europe which came out of the smelting-pot of the Dark Ages, or that which earlier emerged from the Pelasgic and Etruscan barbarism.[6]

Ralph Waldo Emerson

Assimilation

Since the 18th century there has been an effort to create a unique American culture from the amalgamation of some of the ethnic groups represented in the general population of European immigrants.[7] This process is described as one of **assimilation;** it involves groups surrendering their values and heritage and adopting the mainstream values of the larger culture (Healey, 2010). Assimilation in America has included a great deal of intermarriage and blending of families and ethnic back-grounds. The belief has been that this form of **exogamy** is the foundation of a strong and vital people.

The process of assimilation is a slow one, taking several generations before assimilation is complete. The Johnson-Reed Act of 1924 effectively ended mas-sive immigration of peoples from Central European and the Mediterranean basin nations. Research has shown that three generations are required to assimilate an ethnic group composed of white immigrants. This final wave of new Americans from Eastern and Southern Europe required more than 80 years to achieve complete assimilation or Americanization (Healey, 2010). The current wave of immigrants from the Caribbean and Central and South American nations may well require the remainder of the 21st century to reach full assimilation.

Joseph Healey (2010) describes another factor in the assimilation process, known as **ethnic succession**. As new groups of immigrants arrive in North America, they replace previous generations of immigrants in jobs and housing. This process facilitates the upward mobility of previous groups of immigrants. Thus the kitchen laborers, hotel service workers, and gardeners of yesteryear have given us today's teachers, first responders, and other members of the mid-dle classes. Children of one generation of immigrants can move upward in social class status as another new wave of immigrant workers move in to begin their **American experience.** The newly arrived Americans take the subsistence-level jobs formerly held by the previous generation of immigrants.

An amalgamation process excluded Native Americans, who were not even considered to be citizens of the land they had inhabited for 11,000 years. Native Americans were permitted to live alongside the Anglo-White population but were kept separated and denied most basic rights of American citizens. This is very different from assimilating into a culture. Assimilation occurs when intermarriages are permitted and total acceptance of one's ethnic heritage occurs. In 1924, President Calvin Coolidge finally signed the Snyder Act, making many of America's indigenous people citizens, but it was not until 1948 that voting rights were extended to Native American peoples by all states. Even equal protections spelled out by the 14th Amendment of the U.S. Constitution (1868) were carefully crafted to exclude Native Americans while granting equal rights to everyone else (Fritz, 1963).

Until very recently African Americans were also excluded from becoming fully integrated members of American culture. In 1954, in a case known as

PHOTO 8.1   Immigration Ship Arriving in New York City in 1922 Under a New Quota Law

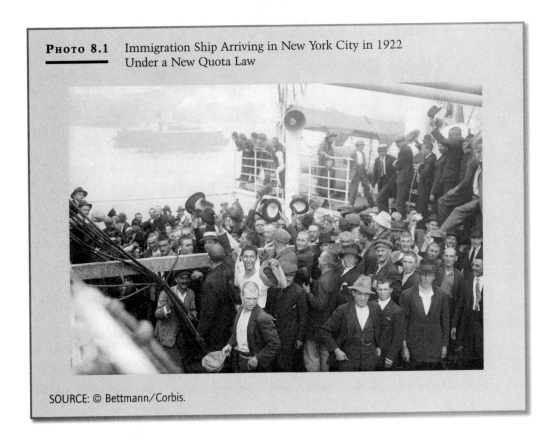

SOURCE: © Bettmann/Corbis.

Brown v. Board of Education, the concept of an American apartheid ended with the Supreme Court's overturning of the *Plessy v. Ferguson* decision of 1896. The *Brown* decision, written by the Warren Court, made huge changes in U.S. society by making it illegal for any state to maintain racial separation in public education programs. (An example of the enforcement sometimes required of this decision is shown in Photo 8.2.) Less than 2 years later, that decision was expanded by the Supreme Court to include all public transportation and public accommodations (*Browder v. Gayle,* 1956). This was done by accepting the decision made by the courts in Alabama that brought an end to the racial segregation of Montgomery's bus system.

The inclusion of African Americans into the American melting pot was further enhanced in 1967 with the end of **anti-miscegenation** laws (*Loving v. Virginia* in 1967). In this case the Warren Court cited the 14th Amendment to the U.S. Constitution, making it legal for people of different races to marry and have families, effectively ending a law in effect in Virginia and other southern states. The case came before the high court after an inter-racial

PHOTO 8.2   Photo of National Guard Escorting African American Students to School at Little Rock's (Arkansas) Central High School in 1957

SOURCE: AFP/Stringer/Getty Images.

couple were legally married in Washington, D.C., and subsequently began to live together in Virginia. They were arrested and sentenced to a year in jail with a trial judge saying:

> Almighty God created the races white, black, yellow, Malay and red, and he placed them on separate continents. And but for the interference with his arrangement there would be no cause for such marriages. The fact that he separated the races shows that he did not intend for the races to mix. (*Loving et ux v. Virginia*, 388 U.S. 1 [1967] 388 U.S.)

Assimilation in America has always included a great deal of intermarriage and blending of families and ethnic backgrounds. Bringing together two ethnic identities into one family has been the central theme of many literary comedies and films and is part of the American experience for many people. It has taken a while for the federal bureaucracy to catch up with this trend. The U.S. Census did not provide a category for mixed-race children until the year 2000. By 2008, the census estimated that there were 5.2 million Americans who reported being of mixed racial heritage and estimated the number would exceed 8 million with the 2010 census (Davis & Matthews, 2009).

Accommodation and Multiculturalism

A logical antithesis to assimilation and the American melting pot is maintaining one's heritage and culture while accommodating to the new larger society and its expectations. This concept holds that the country is strongest when the diverse talents and backgrounds of individuals and groups are respected. Social constructionists encourage counselors to facilitate individuals in organizing personal ethnic/racial identities in ways appropriate within the larger community (Lee, 2004). The implication for school counselors of **social constructionist** beliefs is that it is impossible to be expert in all ethnicities; student-clients are the true experts in their own lives and possess detailed cultural knowledge not available to the counselor (Monk, Winslade, & Sinclair, 2008). Counselors serve best if they assume a role as a learner and let the student be the guide. In a cross-cultural setting, the role of school counselor is to assist the student-client to deconstruct the complexity of his phenomenological field and strengthen his or her ability to respond to ongoing challenges.

This is not to assume that everything is relative. There are core beliefs about human behavior that are universal and transcend all races, ethnicities, and cultures. The school counselor must decide how the culture and environment of the student was shaped by community attitudes, values, and norms and whether the student is violating universal norms and expectations.

First, before attempting to perform the role of a professional school counselor in a multicultural context, one must examine one's own perspective and frame of reference and determine how to take into account or quarantine one's own perspective while assisting the student (Chinappi, 2009). Naturally, the school is also a cultural system of its own, and the counselor must find ways to provide accommodations for a student who holds culturally based values differing from the norms and rules of the school community.

● RACE IN AMERICA

Before the era of the Enlightenment (18th century) no one ever thought about the color of a person's skin or his or her race. For thousands of years slaves were the lowest level in society, and slaves could be members of any race. Two thousand years ago, Imperial Rome required 600,000 slaves to maintain its prosperity and did not care where they came from or what color they were (Scheidel, 2007). Any and all conquered people were enslaved to serve the citizens of Imperial Rome.

In America's not so distant past, state laws were enacted to arbitrarily define people as members of the various races (phenotypes). The deciding factor in defining race was frequently skin color. A problem for race-defining laws is that not all people of defined racial groups have the same color of pigment in their skin, and children in the same family can vary greatly in the tone of their coloration. Other phenotypical variations within a color group can wash out completely.

During the **antebellum** era in America, newly imported slaves were mostly from western Africa. The largest number of slaves sold and traded in the southern states in the late 18th and 19th centuries had been in the United States for many generations and was a genetic mixture of many groups, including the slaveholders. A third or more of African Americans in the United States today carry the DNA of the owners of their ancestors (Willing, 2006). The southern planters believed they were justified in keeping slaves as it had always been done, was justified in the Bible, and was even written into the U.S. Constitution (1787).[8]

End of the Concept of Race

Today the concept of various races is being supplanted. This reflects the fact that the term *race* is far too subjective and lacks any basis in science

(Wilson, 2009). Genetic science has demonstrated that different phenotypes of the species *Homo sapiens* are the evolutionary byproduct of environmental adaptation (McAuliffe, Kim, & Park, 2008). Just under 200,000 years ago modern humans evolved as a new species from the ancient **genus *Homo habilis.*** This development of a new **biped species** occurred on the savannah of Africa, near Omo in Ethiopia (Fan et al., 2002). Only 40,000 years ago, members of the new species began to move outward into several different geographical regions of the Earth (O'Neil, 2009; Tishkoff et al., 2009). As small evolutionally adaptations occurred to accommodate the new environments, these groups became recognizable as various human phenotypes (Pritchard, 2009).[9] Today there are five main phenotypes of *Homo sapiens* indigenous to Africa, but thousands of identifiable genetic groups that make up the indigenous population (Perry & Dominy, 2009). The variations within any phenotype are far greater than the variations between them. The nation of Nigeria is home to 261 identifiable genetic groups of humans but only one indigenous phenotype (West-African Man) (Willing, 2006). All of these minor phenotypical differences are tiny in comparison to the great commonality of genetics shared by all humans (Orbe & Harris, 2008).

All humans share a common set of genes (100% commonality), and all differences between groups and individuals are expressed as minor alterations of the sequencing of genetic material onto the chromosomal structures of individual humans (National Academy of Sciences, 2009). The American psychologist and theorist Robert Sternberg has discounted the whole issue of race by describing it as a social construct, not a biological one worthy of research outside of a socialization context (Sternberg, Grigorenko, & Kidd, 2005). This common heritage notwithstanding, race continues to be a very sensitive topic for most Americans. See Case in Point 8.2.

CASE IN POINT 8.2

As part of a districtwide school evaluation system, starting in 1994 all students in the 3rd through the 11th grades in Seattle's 130 public schools were surveyed each spring. In 2002 the survey was modified and questions of how students interact with other students and teachers of different races were added. It also asked if the print materials in the schools depicted "people my color." The National Education Association labeled the practice as being racist, and the American Civil Liberties Union filed suit to enjoin the district to prevent the use of the survey. The school system withdrew the measure (Galley, 2002).

(Continued)

(Continued)

Thought Questions. A significant resiliency factor for children experiencing stress in their lives is a strong sense of their heritage and knowledge that they are part of a greater community from which they can draw support. What steps can a school counselor take to help all students feel comfortable in the school counseling environment? What elements would and would not be part of the environment of your office if you were a counselor working in a multicultural school?

● SOCIOECONOMIC STATUS

There is a central factor used to separate people within our society that is neither genetic nor ethnic. Socioeconomic status in America is a function of a number of factors, including income and wealth, educational capital, and occupational prestige (Saegert, Adler, Bullock, Cauce, Liu, & Wyche, 2007).

Distribution of Income and Wealth in America

In 2009 the poverty level in the United States was set at $22,000/year income for a family of four. The U.S. Census Bureau reports that about 14% of all Americans and 1 in 5 children in this country live in poverty (2009a). Twenty-two percent of all Hispanics and a quarter of all African Americans live in poverty. The problem of poverty is more acute among families headed by a single homemaker. In the case of female-headed households, 29% of their families live in poverty. White Americans have the lowest poverty rate, fewer than 1 in 10, while 11% of Asian Americans live in poverty. Below the poverty level is a class of families attempting to survive on no income at all. These families account for about 1 in every 5 families classified as impoverished and receiving food stamps (DeParle & Gebeloff, 2010).

The distribution of wealth in the United States is badly skewed. Middle-class and lower-class families comprise 80% of the population but own only 16% of the nation's wealth.

On the other hand, the top 10% of American families by income level saw their median income rise to $139,000 a year between 2008 and 2009, and the top 5% saw their family median income reach $180,000 (Yen, 2009). By 2007 the top 1% of the American population earned a median family income of $1,100,000 per year. This top 1% own 40% of the nation's wealth

(Johnston, 2007). These most wealthy of Americans are made up of a number of ethnic groups but are predominantly Asian Americans and White Americans (U.S. Census Bureau, 2009a). The 19% of the population who make up the upper middle class and the lower part of the upper class own the remaining 44% of the nation's wealth.

Income is directly linked to the accumulation of wealth. This takes many forms, including retirement savings, home ownership, vacation home ownership, and other items of apparent value. Over time, wealth has proven to be a better indicator of socioeconomic status than has a simple measure of income (Saegert et al., 2007). Income levels of Americans fluctuate significantly over lifetimes. Wealth can be accumulated through intergenerational transfer and serve as a buffer during times when the family budget is under pressure. There is some evidence that young adults born in the 1980s and 1990s may be more concerned with lifestyle and less on the accumulation of wealth as an end in itself (Shallcross, 2009b).

CARTOON 8.1   *"The Only Portfolio That Counts"*

"The only portfolio that counts in life is a stock market portfolio, the ultimate report card of us all."

SOURCE: Merv Magus.

Educational Capital

The depth and quality of the education of individuals is a central feature in their socioeconomic status. For one, education is correlated with both personal income and the future educational attainment of children in the home. The truth is that the "education-to-income" correlation is less than perfect. We are all familiar with the student who does poorly in school and goes on to be a major success as an entrepreneur. One has to look no further than the college class-room to see highly educated but relatively low-income faculty members. There are physicians who work for charitable organizations and lawyers in the public service. However as Table 8.1 shows, there is a clear monotonic relationship between the two dimensions.

We also know that the educational attainment of students is directly influenced by expectations and goals of each child's family (National Assessment of Educational Progress [NAEP], 2004). The education level of each student's parents is highly correlated with the achievement level of each student and is a

TABLE 8.1   Income, Education, and Group Membership

Race		Overall Median	High School	Some College	College Graduate	Bachelor's Degree	Master's Degree	Doctoral Degree
Total Population	Full-time workers, ages 25–64	39,509	31,610	37,150	56,027	50,959	61,324	79,292
White Workers	Full-time workers, ages 25–64	40,422	32,427	38,481	56,903	51,543	61,441	77,906
Asian Workers	Full-time workers, ages 25–64	42,109	27,041	33,120	60,532	51,040	71,316	91,430
African American Workers	Full-time workers, ages 25–64	32,021	26,230	32,392	47,758	45,505	52,858	N/A
Hispanic Workers	Full-time workers, ages 25–64	27,266	26,461	33,120	46,594	41,831	53,880	N/A

SOURCE: U.S. Census Bureau, 2006, http://pubdb3.census.gov/macro/032006/perinc/new03_000.htm

N/A: There were fewer than the statistically required number for reporting and/or data were missing.

predictor of eventual college attendance (NAEP, 2007b). The education level of mothers of Hispanic students is lower than that of other ethnic groups and greatest for Asian American and Anglo-White mothers (Gándara, 2010). Additionally, the number of books in the home of the student is highly correlated with reading achievement (NAEP, 2007b). This leads to a cyclic system in which educated parents influence their children to obtain optimal educations and thus have higher socioeconomic status.

Occupation of Parents

One's job is a central feature in the life of adults in our society. Among other things, a job provides a continuing source of income, making it possible to sustain a style of living. A job also provides both a central feature of one's sense of identity and feelings of value as a person (Feldman, 2002). A job also provides a schedule for each of us to follow and a temporal framework for planning all of the other activities in our lives. Employment expands our social network and provides many contacts to each of us beyond our families.

Our jobs or occupations are recognized and valued to some level by those we know or meet. How one evaluates the prestige of different ways to earn a living reflects our personal values and beliefs. Some people focus on the income a job provides. An income focus would mark employment as an investment banker or trial lawyer as jobs with high prestige. A first responder like a fireman or a public employee such as a Head Start teacher's aide would be seen as having low prestige.

Other people consider the benefit to the community as a salient factor in the prestige of a job. Such people will view social workers and educators as being more prestigious than touring professional golfers or insurance company actuaries.

Another consideration in occupational or job prestige is the difficulty in learning the skill or acquiring the training needed to be qualified for the employment. This means that a job in a medical specialty such as public health, which requires a quarter-century of education to enter (12 years of public school, 4 years of college, 4 years of medical school, 4 years of a residency, and a master's degree in public health) carries more prestige than does a better paying job as a chief executive officer (CEO) of a Fortune 500 company.

Another layer of consideration in occupation prestige is the position within the occupation. Prestige is linked to ownership as opposed to working for others, to being a manager of others as opposed to having little or no supervisory responsibility, and to having access to flexible time and responsibility for setting one's own schedule as opposed to working within the constraints of a time clock (Saegert et al., 2007).

Socioeconomic Status Levels

Sociologists since the 1940s have constructed models to describe the nature of the status level of American families. Generally these are built around a combination of four dimensions: the public good done by the employment of family members, education, family income, and approximate wealth. One category system developed by the sociologists William Thompson and Joseph Hickey (2008) is built using a five-step system. There is a clear relationship between the wealth of the community in which a school is located and the ratio of school counselors to students. Wealthy schools tend to have more counselors (National Center for Education Statistics, 2009).

At the first (lowest) step of society are families referred to as the **lower class.** Depending on economic conditions, these families make up between 15% and 20% of the population. Included among this socioeconomic class are farm workers (both documented and undocumented), itinerant labors and others with seasonal employment (e.g., crossing guards), and part-time custodial and landscape workers, call center operators, and home child care operators and their assistants. These families earn near or below the poverty line, are usually poorly educated, and are frequently out of work. A small subcategory of this lower class is the **underclass.** This is composed of a relatively permanent group who are jobless, frequently homeless, and socially isolated. As a group they are at the lowest point of our society and may have given in to despair (Wilson, 1991). Many of this latter group are surviving on the streets. The number of homeless children grew rapidly during the Great Recession of 2008–2010 and is now about 2 million, or 1 of every 28 children in this country (Gewertz, 2008). In public schools, this implies that the average elementary school class has one student who is homeless.

A second step up in socioeconomic status are members of the **working class.** This group represents about 30% of the population and is composed of semi-skilled workers such as local restaurant workers, sales clerks, taxi drivers, supermarket and large discount store clerks, receptionists, warehousemen, data entry clerks, child care aides, basic construction employees (e.g., hod-carriers), barbacks (persons hired to assist bartenders), noncommissioned military officers, and medical office assistants. These people are usually educated at the high school or technical school level. They are closely supervised and normally work on a time clock. Their earnings vary from the poverty level to about $33,000/year (as of 2008). Their jobs are always at risk to the forces of the marketplace, and their health insurance coverage is a major incentive to stay employed and source of worry when a job is lost.

The third step up the ladder of socioeconomic status in America is the **lower middle class,** a group that (depending on the marketplace) accounts for about a third of all families. Thompson and Hickey (2008) have defined this group as having solid skills and educations through the bachelor's degree and earning up to about $78,000 a year. This includes most school teachers and school counselors, hotel managers, construction supervisors, local religious leaders, midlevel corporate managers, chefs and senior waiters and waitresses in fine dining restaurants, department store buyers, first responders, military officers below the field grade, and nurses and related health care employees. They have more flexibility and freedom, but their time schedule is set by their jobs.

The fourth step is populated by about 15% of the population who are members of the **upper middle class**. Most but not all families in this group earn in excess of $120,000 per year and have advanced degrees and supervisory responsibilities. Senior managers and executives, physicians and dentists, senior professors and deans, senior school district-level administrators, senior field grade and general officers below the corps commander level in the military, elected representatives, and municipal managers (e.g., chief of police in a large department), successful entrepreneurs, pastors with mega-sized congregations, and partners in large firms, including law offices employing 20 or more people.

At the top step on the stairs to socioeconomic status is the top 5% of the population making in excess of $120,000 a year. This group has a medium income of $180,000 a year. This **upper class** can be divided into a main group of 4% who make up the basic upper class and 1% at the extreme top of the top who earn in excess of $1,100,000 per year and compose an **über-class** of elite families. These millionaires have huge power and the ability to influence American institutions and politics. This über-class is a part of the upper class but has much more clout than others who are well off. The über-class controls 40% of the nation's wealth and hold dominant positions on governing boards of most industries and philanthropies. Like other members of the upper class, they are usually well educated, with many having attended the country's elite preparatory schools and prestigious colleges.

All members of the upper class have the responsibility to supervise others, create policies, and manage complex systems. These people are media managers (film and record producers and directors), administrators in research universities, members of the U.S. Senate and senior department heads appointed by the sitting president, state governors, CEOs of large companies, three- and four-star general officers in the military, well-known authors, and elite entertainers and professional athletes.

ETHNICITY ●

Each person's ethnicity can be thought of as a social construction of the individual's race, culture, and heritage. Ethnicity is also defined by the geographical location where the ethnic group was originally an indigenous people. There are literally hundreds of ethnic groups throughout the world and in countries with generous immigration policies, including the United States; most of these groups are represented in the makeup of various communities. For a list of 1,500 of the world's ethnic groups see http://en.wikipedia.org/wiki/Lists_of_ethnic_groups.

The word *ethnic* arises from two words combined in the ancient Greek lexicon meaning "heathen" and "nation." It was used to describe all who were in some way different from the people of the Hellenic world (*Oxford English Dictionary*, 2002). Today we view ethnicity as involving a conjunction of elements, including the race, customs, traditions, shared beliefs, and indigenous homeland that a group of people share. Being of the same ethnic group does not ensure that subgroups within a larger ethnic group will share the same history or values. The population of Ireland is composed of people who share a Celtic heritage but vary widely on matters of religious faith and subgroup histories. Likewise, Cuban Americans share an ethnic heritage but vary widely in phenotypical skin coloration. The hundreds of New World indigenous tribal groups share a common racial heritage but vary widely in cultures, histories, and rituals.

What holds an ethnic group together is what it shares. The core of shared historical homeland histories, personal values, rituals, customs, and beliefs comprise one's ethnicity. Most Jews in America are from the Ashkenazi ethnic group. Ashkenazi Jews share many elements of a common culture and history; yet not all Jewish families follow the same format for religious observance or are as devout as others. Some Jewish boys attend school wearing yarmulkes every day, but many do not. In a similar manner, some Muslim families have their daughters cover their hair at all times when they are in public, but many do not.

● COUNSELING IN A MULTICULTURAL SETTING

This above all: to thine own self be true,
And it must follow, as the night the day,
Thou canst not then be false to any man.

William Shakespeare (Hamlet, Act I: Scene III)

Knowing Oneself, and the Emic Approach

One implication for professional school counselors of multicultural theory is to interpret differences and behaviors as a function of the child's environment and factors of his or her socialization (Schwartzbaum & Thomas, 2008). To the extent that it is possible, counselors must learn to think from within the child's culture instead of employing a **Eurocentric** norm for determining what is and is not appropriate. There is a clear potential for the power differential between white Eurocentric school counselors and ethnic/racial minority students that can prevent effective interventions. Research has shown that more than 70% of school counselors are Anglo-White with European backgrounds (McCarthy, Kerne, Calfa, Lambert, & Guzman, 2010).

Irrespective of the school counselor's ethnicity, to be effective with all students counselors need to develop the ability to accept what the student knows about his or her culture as being beyond the counselor's experience base. To take an *emic* approach[10] to understanding what a student is expressing during counseling sessions, the counselor must suspend his or her own cultural context and see the world as the student does. Only by seeing the world as the student and his family see it is it possible for the counselor to identify strengths and assist the student-client in goal setting and planning (Sue & Sue, 2003). It is through the school counselor's increased personal cultural awareness and knowledge of his or her personal biases that the counselor can become effective in a multicultural environment (Falco, 2010).

As a group, school counselors are at the very middle of the middle class (on the cusp between lower and upper middle class). Like their teaching colleagues, most are Anglo-White, and more than a few are the first generation of college graduates in their families (McCarthy et al., 2010). To achieve their positions, school counselors must believe in the importance of education, be able to delay gratification, and recognize that personal development is possible through hard work. These are Eurocentric values common among some ethnic groups but not all.

School counselors also hold beliefs about the nature of all humans and the desire of individuals to change for the better. Beyond these, religion, ethnic heritage, and family backgrounds all are part of the makeup of each counselor's viewpoint. Recognizing these influences in one's life is central to being able to assume an emic perspective.

Changing Demographics in American Education

President Barack Obama had one White parent (mother) and a Black (African-born) father. He has elected to identify himself as an African American. President Obama is not alone, many other high-profile Americans of mixed heritage have elected to identify themselves with their minority ancestors (Kronholz, 2008).[11]

This is a major shift from the recent past in America, when being White, or being able to pass for White, carried with it many privileges in education, housing, employment, and even health care.

The blending of traditional racial groups, as noted previously, is expected to exceed 8% of the population when the 2010 census data are analyzed. The census has estimated that Anglo-White Americans will represent less than 50% of the total population by 2050. This trend will be seen first in the public schools where non-White minority students made up 44% of the population in 2007 and are growing in the share they represent by about 1% per year (U.S. Census Bureau, 2009b).

The implications for this are significant. For one, there is an urgent need to hire more school counselors with diverse backgrounds. It is also critical for schools to make every effort to recruit and hire teachers from the ethnic minorities represented in the school's population. The impact of even one good role model for minority students within a school cannot be overstated (Thomas-Lester, 2009). This need to see men of authority who share their ethnicity is even more significant for male minority students. This is one reason why the election of Barack Obama has helped improve academic motivation in the African American community (Begley, 2009).

Another implication is the need to train future school counselors to be competent in working in multicultural contexts. There is a real need to overcome racial prejudice among counseling trainees (Castillo et al., 2006; Spanierman & Soble, 2010). See Photo 8.3 for an example of successful counseling with a multi-ethnic group.

Photo 8.3 Bibliotherapy With an Ethnically Mixed Group

SOURCE: © Istockphoto.com/Track5.

Counseling Students of Wealth and Poverty

While not separate ethnic groups, students living in families of the upper class and students from the lower class can both present special problems for the school counselor.

Wealthy Children

Children of the wealthy are not immune from significant anxiety-based problems. Many of these are brought about by the indulgence of parents who have money to spend but lack the time to be effective parents. Leading Harvard psychologist Dan Kindlon has quipped about the seven deadly syndromes of rich children (Kindlon, 2001) (see box).

Kindlon's Version of the Seven Deadly Syndromes

1. *Pride*. This refers to children who are "self-centered." Unlike the pride spoken of by sixth-century Pope Gregory I, this pride can all too frequently be internalized against the student who strives to be perfect and fails. Self-harming and depressive behavior can result when a student attempts to meet a goal of perfection to win the love of an aloof parent only to fail and reinforce a cycle of self-loathing. The student's self-esteem and ability to relate with peers will suffer when this occurs.

Another variation of pride can result in too much self-esteem and lead to a demanding student who expects everyone to wait on his or her every need. School counselors can work to help children of power and wealth understand that the needs and opinions of others are as equally valid as their own. Group counseling can support this type of learning.

2. *Anger*. The open manifestation of anger can be seen in the bullying behavior of school-children and in the inward turning of the anger in the form of depression, self-destruction, and hostility. Affluent children are not alone in becoming depressed, but they often lack the amount of quality parenting time needed to defuse their concerns and heal their wounds at home. When parents are on the go, conquering the world, children can be left to fend for their own emotional development. A recent letter to the newspaper's personal advice columnist came from a nanny in the home of a very busy wealthy couple. The nanny described the emotional pain being felt by the 10-year-old child of the family who recognized that she was never an important factor in her parents' lives. See www.buffalonews.com/opinion/columns/dearabby/story/649968.html#.

3. *Envy*. Some children feel driven to the point of unhealthy obsession and cheating. These behaviors can be directed toward being the student selected to give the graduating class valedictory, or becoming the captain of the cheerleaders, or being admitted to Swarthmore College or Princeton University.

Parents who redshirt their children to give them a year advantage over their peers get the ball rolling early. Once a child realizes that the way to their parents' affection is through academic success, either they may assume the role of obsessive scholar or they may reject school, become disengaged, and develop an identity as a failure. Both are unhealthy resolutions of personal identity, and both require that a school counselor assist in goal setting and planning.

4. *Sloth*. The loss of motivation is a symptom of depression. Listlessness and disengagement are symptoms of this depressed state. Parents who hand everything to their children and never make demands on them can be the cause of this apathetic worldview and attitude (Levine, 2006). The indulgence of parents in providing money and material items but not true concern, affection, and friendship is part of this syndrome. Parent and family counseling are called for, along with behavioral therapy for the children who have tuned out and turned off.

(Continued)

(Continued)

5. *Gluttony*. Eating disorders are a major problem for American children. There are three major problems with this issue among children (see Chapter 4). One is body building and the abuse of anabolic steroids. A second is anorexia nervosa and its manifestations, including bulimia nervosa. The *Diagnostic and Statistical Manual of Mental Disorders* (4th ed. [*DSM-IV*], American Psychiatric Association, 1994) describes two psychiatric disorders for anorexia nervosa, one a restrictive type involving limiting body weight to a point at least one standard deviation below the expected range for the person's height. This body state is accomplished by extreme dieting and exercising. The other type (bulimia nervosa) involves anorexia nervosa induced through binge eating with self-induced purging, including induced vomiting, the misuse of laxatives and diuretics, and/or using enemas. Anorexia nervosa is a serious psychiatric problem and may require inpatient treatment in a mental health facility.

The abuse of anabolic steroids as a method of body building is also a serious and illegal practice. School counselors should work closely with coaches and physical educators to find ways to teach the dangers of both physical and psychological harm that result from steroid abuse. These drugs should be included on the school's drug policy statement and the consequences for their use in school detailed on the school's web page and included in the student handbook.

6. *Lust*. The point of wanting to experience all the world's sensual pleasures did not align with the asceticism of Pope Gregory I and became one of the seven deadly sins (Leyser, 2001). With the children of America's wealthy, this can be translated into the many opportunities those with money are presented. A child from the lower middle class can steal the oxycodone prescribed to his or her father for his painful back. However, children with more money can spend $200 for an "8-ball" of cocaine and develop a sustained high and possibly a major addiction.[12] More recently, wealthy young people have turned to the abuse of crystal methamphetamine, a drug that sells on the street for about $80 per gram. Like cocaine, this is an addictive illegal drug that can be snorted, smoked, or injected. It is more toxic than cocaine and causes significant facial changes with chronic users. Like cocaine, it can cause organ system failure and sudden death.

Drug and alcohol addiction can result in all children, but it is easier for children of the upper classes to acquire the illegal drugs. There is also an indication that wealthy parents are not as deeply concerned as lower class parents with drug and alcohol use by their children.

7. *Greed*. Pope Gregory I riled against the acquisitiveness of the bishops and nobility of sixth-century Europe. In modern America, there is a level of ever-expanding expectations held by the children of the wealthy. Today international travel for class trips is the norm in many suburban high schools, as are stretch limousines for high school dances. Bar or baht mitzvah receptions have been held on the *Queen Mary II*, while the gift of exotic sports cars for graduation is no longer unusual.

An eighth major source of anxiety-related problems for children of the upper middle class and upper class is the tendency of affluent parents to overschedule their children. Overscheduling is a symptom of a parenting type that attempts to micromanage by carefully structuring the life of a child. This need to micromanage, when combined with a fanatical devotion to their child and a need to be involved in every aspect of their child's day, produces the classic **helicopter parent,** ready to go on the attack to solve every problem their child has (Gibbs, 2009). These children with hovering parents are likely to have a reduced ability for developing self-reliance and creativity.

In some of our best schools, parents must actually be restrained from interfering with the instructional process. These parents will berate teachers who don't give a high grade to their child and excoriate any coach who does not feature the child's talents on the playing field. Helicopter parents will make personal contact with members of the school board to press their causes; they will fax, cell phone, and e-mail their complaints to any and all administrators. Counselors can easily be drawn into the web of these parents. Once a parent finds that a school counselor can serve his or her needs, that parent is likely to appear in the counseling suite several days each week.

These children are the most protected, programmed generation of youngsters ever (Strauss, 2006). These parents even follow their children to college and have been known to call professors to express their concerns over what is happening in the college lecture hall. Collegiate deans have been called about social snubs experienced by the progeny of upper-middle- and upper-class parents, and fraternal organizations have had their faculty sponsors called about achieving a membership rush for their child.

For many upper-class parents, any unproductive time for their child is viewed as wasted when it could be spent with the math tutor, the language coach, or the violin instructor. One outcome of overscheduling is that children and adolescents are not getting adequate time for sleep. It also damages family lives, as the family unit has less time to spend together. This product of the "millennial generation" of parents should be part of a program of parent education offered during parent meetings and support groups conducted by the school counselor. A family does not need to be wealthy to have overprotective parents, and all parents can overschedule their children. These overzealous parents need to learn to love their children without hovering over them and overseeing every detail of the lives of their sons and daughters.

School counselors can also intervene with such parents by providing a web-based parenting class for parents in the school's community.

Primary Prevention and Intervention

School-based counseling can help students learn to set goals and plan with their parents for the future. This can be best accomplished by family counseling. The use of family counseling is normally beyond the programs offered in public schools and may require a referral to a community or private psychologist or counselor. Prior to making a referral to an outside agency, therapist, or counselor, the school counselor is obligated to visit the outside office and become familiar with the competency and programs of the agency.

Children of Poverty

More children lived in poverty in 2009 than in any of the years since President Lyndon Johnson declared "War on Poverty" in 1965 (Iceland, 2006; U.S. Census Bureau, 2009a). Many of the poorest families are confined by access to social services and availability of housing to a few square miles located in the hearts of our great cities. About half of all poverty in America is rural. These rural poor families and their children are frequently overlooked. In both urban and rural cases, children of poverty have more physical illnesses, psychological disturbances, and suffer more injuries than do others living in the best neighborhoods (Klerman, 1991; McLoyd & Wilson, 1991). As a group, children of poverty see and experience more violence than do the children of wealth (Swisher, 2003). Other than assaults, the reasons children of poverty have a poorer quality of health involve nutrition, and prior to the Health Care Reform Act of 2010, lack of health insurance coverage. The undocumented poor have the most difficulty finding care for their sick or injured children. Parents must first be able to document the citizenship status of their children before they can enroll them in the national Medicaid program (Jenkins, 2006).

As was noted previously, living below the poverty line is correlated with one or more of the following: being a member of a minority, having parents with less than a high school education, living in a home headed by a single mother, and having parents who are unemployed or underemployed.

School-Based Intervention

A team effort is required to serve the best interests of children who come from impoverished backgrounds. This team should involve the school's counselors and social workers, **community resource officers**, and administration.[13] The goal is to provide the resources that are appropriate and available for impoverished students and their families.

When a counselor is first hired for a school, he or she should immediately begin to collect information about all large and small philanthropies in the school's community. This list should include agencies that help with acute and emergent problems as well as those focused on the long haul with a family. It can be as simple as the name of a grocer willing to package holiday feasts for distribution or the garden club that donates backpacks and sneakers for students at the start of the school year.

Counselors who know the families and the community around their schools can provide an informal service to unemployed parents. An evening or weekend adult class can be developed around the theme "Finding and Keeping a Good Job." By helping parents, counselors are helping students and performing primary prevention.

Schools have reporting priorities and mandates for children of the homeless (see Chapter 3). With more than 1.5 million American children (3% of the population) homeless for some part of the year in 2009, it is inevitable that most school counselors will work in schools with children who are homeless (National Center on Family Homelessness, 2009).

Beyond the required mandates for reporting, counselors should keep informal track of homeless families and be vigilant for ways to get these families into homes of their own. An important morning task for all professional school counselors involves a careful reading of the local sections of neighborhood newspapers. Items such as restraining orders, foreclosures, and arrests for domestic violence all provide important data for the counselor. In addition, job listings and housing opportunities are covered in the local paper. These items should be brought to the attention of families who may need the support but lack access to newspapers (reading disabilities, cost, low vision problems). See Case in Point 8.3 for an example of school counselors helping to find resources for families who need support.

CASE IN POINT 8.3

In a countywide school system in Florida containing 51 school buildings, including seven high schools, the school counselors worked together to create a web page on which parents in the district could place anonymous requests for the assistance of others in the district. These requests took the form of locating employment and housing. Parents were invited to learn about the system by way of the school system's newsletter. Word was also spread through the churches and community agencies in the school system. Local libraries provided computer access for parents who did not have their own systems.

(Continued)

(Continued)

In each case, the school counselor forwarded confidential responses to the requests back to the parents in need. Families in the wealthy part of the district were grateful to find willing workers who were fellow parents and lived in the community. These jobs provided both full- and part-time employment for scores of parents in need. As there were no placement costs involved, all came out ahead. Unrented apartments and duplex homes also found new tenants through this bulletin board.

Thought Questions. Assume you are a counselor in one of these high schools. How would you go about expanding the role to include finding full- and part-time employment for high school students? How would you prevent the program for students from harming the one for parents? Which should have priority? Explain your answer.

● *NO HABLO INGLÉS*: COUNSELING ENGLISH-LANGUAGE LEARNERS

Children who are ethnic Hispanics make up the largest single language minority in the United States, outnumbering all the others combined.[14] The Latino/a population is younger than other parts of the American population and has a higher birth rate than other groups (Casas, Raley, & Vasquez, 2008). This implies that even without further immigration, the proportion of Latino/a students in U.S. schools will continue to grow.

This fact has created considerable alarm among American nativists, including the former Republican presidential candidate, Patrick J. Buchanan (2002). As recently as February 2009, two members of the U.S. House of Representatives, Steve King (R-Iowa) and Bill Posey (R-Florida), proposed a constitutional amendment to make English the exclusive language of the United States.

What research has shown is that second-generation Hispanic children are normally well acculturated into the linguistic requirements of both formal and informal English. These second-generation children are likely to have lost much of their family's native language, retaining a mostly vernacular lexicon and informal syntax. By the third generation, more than 70% of all Hispanic children have lost the family's native language and are fully Americanized (Citrin, Lerman, Murakami, & Pearson, 2007). Data indicate that the pace of Hispanic assimilation into the American mainstream is faster than has been true of most earlier immigrant groups of the 20th century.

Second Language Learning

The human ability to learn more than one language is unique to our species (Mechelli et al., 2004). The age of the student learning a second language is a critical factor in the emerging literacy in the second language (L2). Typically, all students placed in an environment in which they cannot communicate with either teachers or other students will refrain from speaking. Students in an alien language environment focus on listening and attempting to create the new language from what they see and hear around them (Cook, 2008). Younger students will spend a longer period of time being mute than will their adolescent siblings. Yet, preadolescent students will have less difficulty developing fluency in the new language. This reflects the greater plasticity of their developing neurology. The language centers in the brain lose plasticity with the normal ontogenetic development during adolescence, including the normal pruning of unneeded axons and the myelination of most areas of the cortex and the corpus colostrums (see Chapter 4 for more on these neurological issues). When these neurological changes occur, learning a second language becomes much more difficult (Lenneberg, 1967). The neurology of young children is still growing and developing, giving primary grade children greater **neurological plasticity** and making learning a new language easier. Once a child reaches adolescence, that plasticity is gone and with it facility with new languages.

On average, a non-English-speaking primary grader who is immersed in a total English-speaking school environment can achieve fluency at the **Basic Interpersonal Communication Skill (BICS)** level in 1 or 2 years (Dong, 2007; Roseberry-McKibbin & Brice, 2005). However, this same student will not achieve a level of fluency in English that permits the use of context-reduced academic language known as **Cognitive Academic Language Proficiency (CALP)**. That development will normally require another 3 to 5 years (total of 5 to 7 years of immersion). During this learning process, the student will experience a period of time when he or she is **semilingual** (McLaughlin, Blanchard, & Osanai, 1995).

Semilingualism occurs when the student is not ready to speak English at the BICS level and has lost some fluency in the native language ability. Related to this is the problem that most young children who are native Spanish speakers tend to attend school in the same neighborhood. A study of schools in California found that there is a natural segregation, with most students who are English-language learners (ELLs) attending schools where the dominant population is made up of native Spanish speakers (Rumberger, Gándara, & Merino, 2006). Frequently, neighborhood schools are located in communities in which the local culture assumes a distinctively Hispanic flavor.

There are many communities in the United States where English is rarely spoken or heard. In such environments, the process of learning the English language will take longer than if the student is immersed into a total English language environment. The loss of English language skills over the summer vacation from school can be most acute for children living in communities that are Spanish language enclaves where English language skills are not reinforced or practiced.

Most kindergartens and public schools require any student who has resided in the United States for the past 12 months to complete all mandated achievement tests in English, even though English is a complex language to master as a second language (L2) (Hayden, 2008). To make the task more complex, three states (California, Arizona, and Massachusetts) have passed voter referendums into law eliminating English as a second language (ESL) programs. One result has been lower scores by English-language learners on large-scale achievement tests at the secondary school level (Zehr, 2008). The current (2010) trend is for younger L2 students to make significant progress toward reaching the mandate for proficiency in reading and mathematics in elementary and middle school (Chudowsky & Chudowsky, 2010).

School Counseling With Latino/a Students

Spanish-speaking Students can be drawn from several ethnic groups, including those from Mexico, other Central American nations, South America, and the Spanish Caribbean, including the major Antilles and the U.S. Commonwealth of Puerto Rico (Casas, Raley, & Vasquez, 2008). Because of this diversity, it is difficult to describe an archetypical child of Latino/a heritage. One common element is the concept of *personalismo,* a term describing the need felt by many Hispanics to sense they are among friends and in a comfortable environment. All school counselors should learn several greetings in Spanish. Counselors should always take time to be polite and greet parents carefully, for example, "*Buenos Dias, Senora Garcia.* Thank you for taking the time to visit with me and talk about Juan. I heard he made the baseball team, and I hope to see him and our team play next week." When greeting a Latino/a student in the office it is appropriate to begin the conversation with a pleasant greeting such as, "*Hola Jorge. ¿Como estás hoy?*" Once again, school counselors should never pretend to be something they are not. It may be better not to attempt a greeting if you are not well prepared.

Over time Hispanic families and their children will develop a sense of *confianza* with school counselors who are respectful of the child and his or her family and culture. This level of trust implies that the family assumes that you, the counselor, are working in the best interest of their child. This level of trust must be earned; it is not given as a right of advanced education or job title. As a general rule, Hispanic parents prefer to turn to trusted relatives, friends, and their clergy for assistance with their child or a problem at school (Casas, Raley, & Vasquez, 2008). A new school counselor would be well advised to take the time to meet and get to know key Hispanic social agencies in the school's community. It is also wise to include the pastor of the local parish and the principal of the parochial school of the parish. These people may well be working in parallel with the counselor's efforts with individual children in the public school.

School counselors should be especially mindful of the paramount role of the Roman Catholic Church in the Hispanic community and with individual families. From this cultural tradition comes the ideal role for women, to emulate the tranquility and purity of "Mary, the Mother of God" in a traditional (*Marianismo*) role assumed by many Latina women. The antipathy of this role is the proud, somewhat cavalier role of the Latino male (*machismo*) (Sciarra, 2004).

Hispanics frequently hold a different worldview from Anglo-White Americans. This Hispanic worldview is one that believes capricious fate and powerful forces beyond their control can influence and direct their lives. The psychological terminology applied to this belief is **external control**. Children who see themselves as the causal agents of their own successes and failures exhibit **internal control**. Also, Hispanics more frequently believe in a spiritual linkage between the human mind and the body. Because of this, counseling for change becomes more of a synergistic effort from both within and from beyond the child. This belief in an *espiritu* between the mind and body must be taken into account whenever the counselor considers requesting an individualized education plan (IEP) committee or is addressing the child's parents about problem areas.

In counseling with Latino/a students it is necessary to learn the extent to which they are steeped in the Hispanic culture and beliefs. The depth of these beliefs is influenced by the nature of the neighborhood in which the student is growing up. For example, is it a mostly Anglo-White community in which the student lives? If so, how does he feel others (Anglo-Whites) view him and his family? How many generations has the child's family been in the United States? Note well, a student who has one or more undocumented parents may not want to reveal a possible immigration problem to anyone at school. Students need to learn that immigration information is protected by the Buckley Amendment (see Chapter 2). Finally, the counselor should work to determine the degree of dissonance the student feels between the American culture of the school and the expectations from his or her home. Social construction theory would suggest the counselor has a role to play in reducing the strain a student may feel between competing expectations posed by the culture of the school and that of the home and community.

Understanding the perspective of the student makes it possible to establish an effective plan for counseling. For example, a school counselor assisting middle school Hispanic students with gender identity should build from the strengths of the *Marianismo* and *machismo* stereotypes (dedication to family) and help students see other potential dimensions within themselves (Delgado-Romero, Galván, Hunter, & Torres, 2008). Strengths-based approaches can reduce the threat level of the counseling experience and work to maintain quality communication patterns between the school counselor and student-client.

● COUNSELING AFRICAN AMERICAN STUDENTS

All populated continents on Earth have people of African descent.[15] Africans have been in North America for the past 400 years, but they have been fully enfranchised as equal partners in the American experience only for the past 50 years or so. The voting rights act of 1965 along with landmark cases decided by the Warren Court in the 1950s and 1960s brought a measure of equality before the law to African Americans. However, discrimination and **aversive racism** against African Americans continue in our current era of **transracialism** ushered in by the election of President Barack Obama (Mills, 2009).

Even though the African American community makes up slightly less than 14% of the U.S. population, more than 38% of all incarcerated people in the United States are African Americans (Bureau of Justice Statistics, 2002). In income, African American households earned a median $32,000 in 2006, while Anglo-White households had a median income of $51,000.

There are many reasons for the numerous racial disparities between sectors of our society. Among them are explanations based on blatant **racial prejudice** and the more subtle **unintentional covert racism,** sometimes called **microaggressions** (DeAngelis, 2009; Evans & George, 2008). Overt racism in our society has been greatly reduced since the era when a state governor would say, "Segregation now . . . segregation tomorrow . . . segregation forever," during an inauguration speech (Wallace, 1963). Occasionally today it can still be heard in neighborhoods and seen on the job and in schools (Cohen, 2009b; Kramer 2009). Overt racism in employment practices has been outlawed by federal legislation, that is, the Equal Pay Act (1963) and the Civil Rights Acts of 1964 and 1991. Overtly racial comments and taunting on the job are still going on today (Chernoff, 2007). These overtly racist acts constitute violations of the right of all employees to a nonhostile work environment under Title VII of the Civil Rights Act of 1964. The law prohibits use of racially derogatory speech, gestures, photographs or other depictions, and comments about skin color or ethnic characteristics in the workplace.

Unintentional covert racism includes the thousands of thoughtless or inappropriate comments made by Anglo-White people toward non-Whites. These can include both verbal and nonverbal **microinsults**. Within a racial group such behavior is described as simple rudeness and/or insensitivity. Between groups, when there has been a long history of prejudice, the rude behavior takes on a deeper meaning for the minority person on the receiving end of the comment (see Case in Point 8.4).

CASE IN POINT 8.4

On a recent transatlantic flight, long lines had formed of people checking in with their baggage. An African American family moved up and took a position in the queue for the first-class cabin. That line was much shorter than the one for coach-class passengers. The Anglo-White person ahead of the family turned and said, "Are you looking for the line for coach seats?" It can be assumed that the fellow passenger was attempting to prevent the African American family from being embarrassed at the ticket window. To the African Americans who were in the correct line, the question was seen as just another microinsult made by yet another officious White passenger.

On a national stage, Vice President Joe Biden, then a candidate for president himself, described his then-rival candidate, Barack Obama, as the country's "first mainstream African American who is articulate and bright and clean and a nice-looking guy." To see a video clip of this statement, go to www.cnn.com/video/#/video/politics/2007/01/31/snow.biden.blunder.affl.

Thought Question. Reflect a moment and then write a list of the microaggressions and unintentional covert examples of racism you have seen or experienced over the past few months.

Micro-invalidations are another form of unintentional covert racism. These are a common method of driving home the point of one's superiority over others. For example, asking a person with a Caribbean accent "What island did you come from?" carries the implication that the accented person is not really "one of us." This tells the accented person that he or she is doomed to remain a stranger in his or her adopted land. Likewise, asking a fellow employee of color "How did you get your job?" or "How did you get into that college?" implies that the minority person was incapable of achievement without some racial consideration being involved. Even compliments for a person on the quality of their "ability to speak English" can be read as a comment on how different the person is from the mainstream. Individually these comments can be ignored. Taken collectively, they become tedious and difficult to overlook.

In between the two levels of racial prejudice, overt and covert, are matters of unequal opportunity. Deirdre Royster (2003) described how African American high school graduates with the same skill set as Anglo-White graduates have less employment opportunity. This is not a function of overt prejudice but is based on the range and depth of contacts that Anglo-Whites have with people in positions to influence the hiring process. Likewise, being a legacy (having parents who attended a particular college) provides many Anglo-White high school graduates with a college admission advantage. Being a legacy can be the equivalent of adding a 10% boost to the SAT II total score when making a college application (Espenshade & Chung, 2005). In a similar way, having a close relative who is a member of a skilled trade union makes it easier for a young person who wishes to become an apprentice.

African Americans in School

There were about 8,410,000 African American students attending public schools in the United States in 2007 (U.S. Census Bureau, 2007). That same year there were 28,400,000 Anglo-White students in public schools. As a point of comparison, there were 9,600,000 Hispanic students and 2,400,000 Asian American students in public school that year.

Racial identity is part of each of us. Its development is context dependent (Noguera, 2003). Children living in diverse neighborhoods and attending racially diverse schools become aware of race at an earlier age than those children who live in homogenous communities. Children living in diverse neighborhoods have no difficulty developing friendships with children of different ethnic or racial groups. The problem becomes more complex during puberty and adolescence. The boundaries between groups take on a new meaning when the question of dating and being liked by other people who are "like me" must be addressed.

Racial Identity Formation

African American children have all the same difficulties others have in establishing personal identities. They also have the added social construction tasks of incorporating the ethnic or racial identity of a minority group into their psychological schema. Even President Barack Obama was criticized by some African American journalists for not being "Black enough" (Sarmah, 2007). This same issue is one which many African American students face each year in middle schools and high schools. To be part of a group of youngsters who share a racial identity is appealing and can lead to new patterns of friendships within schools. It can also be a point of personal pride and a resiliency factor in times of stress (Neblett et al., 2010). This may be seen in schools with diverse students, for example, when groups of African American students prefer each other's company in cafeteria seating and on the school bus. During adolescence the need to fit in and be part of a group of peers and be accepted is a powerful motivator (DeCuir-Gunby, 2009).

If the dominant culture of the African American students of a school is opposed to academic effort and success, it may be difficult for a minority student to buck the pressure that others may bring to bear on his or her striving for academic success (Noguera, 2003). Academically successful African American students run the risk of alienating their racial peers and may experience taunting for "trying to be White" (DeCuir-Gunby, 2009).

Not all African American adolescents develop an anti-academic identity. Research has shown that there are two primary identity types that account for most adolescent African American identity schema (Nasir, McLaughlin, & Jones, 2009). One of these is anti-academic and "street savvy." These students identify themselves by wearing distinctive "gangsta" clothing, speaking in **African American vernacular language (AAVL)**, and generally dismissing school as any part of their identity. This group also includes teens dabbling in low-level drug dealing and petty crime. The parent figures for this group are often overwhelmed themselves and are not engaged with their children's school.

The second group can be thought of as being "socially conscious." These students and their families are engaged with the school, connected with social structures including their church, and see themselves as being positive forces within the community. They may also use AAVL and wear popular clothing styles, but they develop identities as African Americans that are linked to a historical context (Africentric worldview) and think of themselves as part of a larger African American community. They see themselves as community leaders and change agents. One subgroup of these students includes athletes and participants in interscholastic sports.

School Rules and Policies

Policies and procedures within the school can also contribute to African American students becoming disengaged. There is evidence that African American students are more frequently punished for rule infractions in school and receive harsher punishments than do Anglo-Whites (Lewis, 2009; Losen & Skiba, 2010).

The zero-tolerance policy of public schools tends to be disproportional in its application with African American students (Hutchinson, 2000). The need for school counselors to be vigilant for this pattern by the school's disciplinarian is evident. Careful consultation by the counselor with the administrators may be needed to help bring equity and a degree of fairness to all rule enforcement in school.

In 2008, 70% of all U.S. high school students across 27 states were required to pass a test in order to earn a high school diploma. This requirement is over and above requirements of curriculum and grades. There is a persistent test score gap between African American and Hispanic students and Anglo-White and Asian American students (Wright, 2011). This disparity resulting in more African American and Hispanic test failures has been the reason many African American and Hispanic students drop out of high school. In 10 states, students must pass a test to be promoted to fourth grade. Test failures and grade retentions are far more common among African American and Hispanic students than other categories (Wright, 2008). Grade retention is an excellent predictor that a student will become disengaged from school and eventually drop out. This gap problem is also one that school counselors must work to reduce (American School Counselor Association [ASCA]/Hatch & Bowers, 2005).

The policies of communities to have totally African American–populated schools being taught by a core of mostly Anglo-White teachers and counselors are not designed for success. The evidence is that there is an increasing trend toward single-race schools (Bigg, 2009). Racially isolated, primarily minority-populated schools have been shown to have poorer levels of academic achievement and have higher counselor-to-student caseloads than other schools (National Center for Education Statistics, 2009; Viadero, 2005).

The Role of Counselors With African American Students

School counselors can provide significant data to school principals about the trends in discipline referrals by race and on the overall school climate (Matus & Winchester, 2009).

Primary Prevention

Another important role the school counselor can fulfill has to do with staff development covering topics related to the socialization of African American students.

Ideas for Inservice Topics With Faculty

1. *Time*. African American students may enter school with a tradition of "event time," not the traditional European "clock time."

2. *Rhythm*. African American culture uses recurring patterns, set in time, to give meaning to experience. It also provides internal responses to rhythms in the external world.

3. *Improvisation*. School counselors and other educators need to be able to find creative solutions to connect internal and external worlds and a method for structuring interactions among people.

4. *Orality*. Traditional African culture has a rich oral tradition. The naming of all things gives meaning to them, and the orally transmitted proverbs and sayings provide guidance in most matters.

5. *Spirituality*. Many African Americans are spiritual people believing that forces beyond themselves act in ways to affect the world of all humans. Church and pastors are important institutions in the African American community.

SOURCE: James M. Jones's TRIOS Model (2003).

School Interventions

School counselors should carefully explain their role to African American student-clients. Anglo-White counselors will be suspect until they can prove themselves as being in the student-client's corner. The process of counseling African American students requires true personal honesty and flexibility. Being genuine is essential; there can be absolutely no difference between how the school counselor feels and what is expressed to his or her client. A bogus counselor will be quickly detected and marginalized by African American students. Be willing to acknowledge that the school and other institutions in the child's life may be racist, and be empathetic to that position. Be flexible with rules about the use of AAVL and the student occasionally being late. Suggest that the student (if religious) also involve his or her pastor in helping. If invited, occasionally attend services at the local African American church.

The counseling sessions can involve group methods. Using ritualistic games and activities during group sessions to emphasize the reliance of each member of the group on one another is an effective approach. Group sessions can also examine problems of social justice and discuss ways to be proactive and a positive force within the community.

● COUNSELING ASIAN AMERICAN STUDENTS

Demography

As noted previously, Asian Americans are about 4.5% of the population of the United States. As a group, Asian Americans are younger than Anglo-Whites, and their proportion within the population is likely to increase. By the year 2050, about 10% of all Americans will be fully or in part members of an Asian ethnic group (Kim & Park, 2008). The five nations from which the largest number of Asian Americans originally emigrated are China (including Taiwan), Japan, Korea, Philippine Islands, and Vietnam.

History in America

Many Chinese were originally brought to North America to serve as laborers in the construction of infrastructure, including railroads. Racism against people of Asian heritage was one reason why many moved into ghettos of their own making in the cities of America. Recently, "Chinatowns" have taken on a more upscale and tourist aspect.

In 1924, federal legislation, the National Origins Act, signed by President Calvin Coolidge, made all Asian people "inassimilable aliens." The flow of Asians to America slowed but never stopped. The wives of thousands of U.S. Marines on the China station and the thousands of wives of soldiers from World War II and the Korean War provided a small increase in the number of Asians in America prior to the revision of the immigration laws in 1965. That act, the Immigration and Nationality Act (Hart-Celler Act, P.L. 89–236 [1965]) permitted 170,000 people to immigrate to the United States each year from the Eastern Hemisphere. That made it possible for Asian nations to become the largest source of legal immigrants into the country since the 1960s.

Perhaps the clearest example of 20th-century American racism was the signing of Executive Order No. 9066 by President Franklin Delano Roosevelt in 1942. This order created 10 concentration camps in isolated mountain areas where 112,000 Japanese American citizens were incarcerated for the crime of being of Japanese heritage. (See Photo 8.4 showing first grade children of the Weill School in San Francisco, some of Japanese heritage, pledging allegiance to the American flag just prior to the incarceration of all Japanese Americans in concentration camps in the western states.)

In August of 1988 a reparations bill passed Congress and was signed into law by President William Clinton. That law provided $1.6 billion in cash reparations paid to the surviving internees.[16]

U.S. wars during the 20th century brought other people from various Asian nations to the United States. Three groups of Asian Americans—people from the Philippines, Korea, and Vietnam—can trace their families' emigration to America as a product of war.

The Spanish-American War (April 21 to August 12, 1898) gave the United States a number of former Spanish colonies, including the semi-autonomous island archipelago of the Philippines. The U.S. Navy needed a deep-water port to support its "Asiatic Squadron" and took control of the Philippines as the ideal base for the operational support of the fleet. The indigenous leaders of the islands quickly realized that they were not being liberated from the Spanish Empire but conquered by the United States. A Philippine insurgency led by Emilio Aguinaldo followed the U.S. conquest of Spanish colonial interests. This led to the Philippine-American War from February 1899 to April 1901. The United States held the archipelago as a "territory in trust" and did not grant independence to the Philippines until 1946. The use of the Philippines as a U.S. Navy base continued for another 45 years after independence, not ending until 1991.

During those years prior to independence (1898 to 1946), Philippine nationals were encouraged to work for American companies and serve as cabin stewards on war ships of the U.S. Navy and the cruise ships of various companies. The need for farm labor in the United States resulted in many Filipino people emigrating to Hawaii and the mainland, mostly to the Southwestern states (U.S. Census Bureau, 2009a). Intermarriage was inevitable, and people of Philippine heritage became part of the American national fabric. Today people of Philippine heritage account for more than 3 million people (1%) of the population of the United States.

American missionaries of the 19th century were the first to introduce Korean immigrants into the United States. The need for inexpensive labor for agriculture in Hawaii and in the western states was related to the rapid growth of this

PHOTO 8.4 Young Students Pledging Allegiance Prior to Incarceration

SOURCE: Buyenlarge/Getty Images.

population prior to 1924. The next major influx of Korean immigration happened as a consequence of war.

War came to the Korean peninsula on June 25, 1950, when soldiers of the Communist North Korean state invaded South Korea. The war soon involved Soviet air forces flown in support of the north and ground forces of the People's Republic of China providing assistance to the regime of North Korea's Kim Il Sung. South Korea was defended by a mixed-arms corps of the United Nations. The commanders were Americans (Douglas MacArthur and Matthew Ridgway), and most of the naval, air, and ground forces were from the United States. This war stalemated and was ended by an armistice agreement in 1953. The war is still not officially over and occasionally flares up with deadly consequences ("North Korean torpedo," 2010).

The Oriental Exclusion Act of 1924 (Johnson–Reed Act, including the National Origins Act, Asian Exclusion Act [43 Statutes-at-Large 153]) closed the door to Koreans, Filipinos, and other people from Asian nations, keeping them from entering the United States. The Korean Police Action (War) in 1950–1953 saw the revision of this racist bit of legislation in 1952. Many war refugees and the Korean wives of American soldiers entered the United States after 1953. It was not until 1964 with the passage of the Immigration and Neutrality Act that the number of Koreans entering the United States began to grow rapidly. Today Korean-Americans make up about 1.5 million of the U.S. population (U.S. Census Bureau, 2009a).

Like Filipinos and Koreans, people from Viet Nam and other Indochina countries (Laos and Cambodia) also increased rapidly as a function of a war fought by the United States (1961 to 1975). Prior to 1975 there were very few people of Vietnamese heritage living in the United States. For the most part these were the spouses of American servicemen who had been stationed in Viet Nam. This war was very hard fought and resulted in the deaths of 6 million people from the region and 58,000 Americans. The people who worked for the U.S. Armed Forces in Viet Nam feared for their lives when the American forces withdrew starting in 1973. As a humanitarian step, 125,000 Vietnamese fearing for their lives were airlifted to the United States. President Ford signed an unpopular law, the Indochina Migration and Refugee Act of 1975, that provided assistance in resettling these and other war refugees in this country.

Harsh re-education programs under the new government of Viet Nam resulted in 2 million more Vietnamese, Laotians, and Cambodians escaping their country (boat people). Over a half million of these refugees ended up in the United States between 1980 and 2000. This was facilitated by the Refugee Act of 1980 (reauthorized in 1999) (Office of Refugee Resettlement, 2002). The population of Vietnamese-Americans now numbers about 1.6 million (U.S. Census, 2009a).

Asian American Culture

There is not a single Asian culture; there are many from the different nations and regions covered by the broad category *Asian*. The central features of most Asian cultures include a **conformity to the family**'s social norms and expectations, including complete and unquestioning obedience by children to their parents. Supporting and upholding the good name of the family is a paramount concern. Part of this orientation is a respect for elders and ancestors. Another related dimension of Asian culture is a strong feeling of attachment to the group or Asian community. The advancement of the group is more important than the advantage that could go to an individual.

A second set of values in Asian American culture is the individual's interpersonal harmony. This involves deference to people in authority, working toward conciliation not confrontation, demonstrating a sense of stoicism requiring the resolution of one's own psychological problems, always exhibiting a high level of self-control, placing needs and well-being of others ahead of one's own, repaying the favor or gifts from others with gifts and gestures, and exhibiting self-effacement by being truly humble and modest.

The final component of the individual's interpersonal harmony comes through hard work and educational success. Success in school or on the job also reflects well on the family and larger community and brings harmonious feelings to all involved (Kim & Park, 2008).

Asian American Students in School

As noted previously, Asian American children are not a monolith; they represent many different cultures and beliefs. Even within one culture, there are many individual differences and variations (Lewin, 2008). (See Case in Point 8.5.)

CASE IN POINT 8.5

A few years ago a graduate assistant assigned to a project I supervised came to my office. She held both bachelor's and master's degrees from universities from mainland China. She saw I was scheduled to teach a statistics class she was required to complete and wanted me to know something about her. With downcast eyes she reminded me that I know many students from China and other places in Asia who are good at science and mathematics. Before she took my class, she wanted me to know she was not one of those students, and mathematics was difficult for her.

(Continued)

(Continued)

It seems that the stereotype of mathematics whizzes coming from Asia may have been over-stated in her case and that stereotype was seen by her as threatening her place in our program. With a little tutoring by another student, she did very well that term.

Thought Question. Reflect on what you know about a minority group other than your own. Make a list of common stereotypes about the group. Next think of members of that minority who are clearly not stereotypical examples of each of the commonly held stereotypes.

Overall, Asian American students have fewer disciplinary referrals and better levels of achievement than do most other groups. These students make up less than 5% of the public school population but 10% of the places in elite and top-line universities in the United States (Lewin, 2008). Like other groups, Asian American students with college-educated parents have better levels of achievement and higher test scores than do other Asian American students. The disproportion of Asian American students in the undergraduate population caused several of the universities of California to restructure their admission policies to reduce Asian-heritage students and increase African American enrollment (Schmidt, 2007).

Asian Americans score better on the SAT and complete twice as many advanced placement classes as would be predicted by their population size (Maxwell & Emanuel, 2007). Asian American students have been reported as being more meticulous about homework and spending more hours each day studying their school-work. Parents of Asian American children structure their children's time and purchase and use educational materials to optimize what their youngsters learn (Huntsinger, Jose, Larson, Balsink Krieg, & Shaligram, 2000). TV time and the use of computer games are limited in the homes of Asian American families. One result of the lower viewing habits of TV by Asian Americans is that they are virtually invisible as characters on TV entertainment shows (Boyse, 2009).

Socialization is slowed by parents who work to ensure their Asian American girls begin to date boys at an older age than do the girls of other groups (Cheng & Landale, 2009). Asian American parents will make huge personal and financial sacrifices to provide the optimal educational experience for their children (Onishi, 2008).

School Counseling With Asian American Students

As in the case of working with other ethnic minorities, the school counselor must be very sensitive to the culture and heritage of Asian American students. One of the first problems school counselors face is that many Asian Americans prefer not to be seen needing the assistance of others outside of their family. Another is that Asian American children view the counselor as an authority figure who has the answer to the student-client's problem. The nondirective approach to personal development and understanding is an anathema to many of these students (Leong, Lee, & Chang, 2008).

Asian American students tend to be phlegmatic during counseling sessions and say the least number of words they can to convey meaning. Counselors can misinterpret this as resistance or some other problem. One of the most effective approaches with these students is solutions-focused brief counseling (SFBC). Another is to provide the student-client with homework to work on between sessions, including self-awareness exercises documented with note taking through confidential e-mail to which the counselor has private access.

Asian American parents are likely to present the counselor with a gift after their child is assisted in some way (assisted in college admission or getting into a special program). It is impolite to refuse this token, even if there is a school policy against it.

SUMMARY

America has struggled with the issue of race for more than 400 years. What we once believed to be the four or five races of the world, we now know are simply different phenotypes of the same species of mankind that evolved about 200,000 years ago and began to be elaborated with outward migration about 40,000 years ago. All humans are the sons and daughters of eastern Africa.

In the United States, we have worked to forge a single American people from diverse groups of European peoples. The inclusion of many minorities into the American mainstream has only been underway for the past 60 years or so. Prior to 1954, laws and regulations were established to enforce an American apartheid and normalize prejudice against minorities, including Native Americans, Asians, African Americans, and Hispanics. Demographic forecasts will see no one group with more than 50% of the population in American schools by 2020.

School counselors should be able to work with children from homes of great wealth and also homes devastated by grinding poverty. Children of wealth often have many psychological problems. In addition to psychological issues and problems, children of poverty have frequent health and injury problems for the schools to face. Children of each of the three major minority groups—Hispanic, African American, and Asian American—have unique histories and experiences as a people in America. This has contributed to unique worldviews that may be very different from those of school counselors. For that reason, a critical skill for counselors working in public schools is the ability to assume an etic approach when interpreting the behavior and language of minority students.

DISCUSSION QUESTIONS

1. It can be argued that the term *race* as applied to humans is archaic and obsolete. What evidence is there that it should not be used in educational and counseling policy?

2. What are the salient elements that compose a child's ethnicity? What factors are central to your personal sense of ethnicity?

3. In 1968 two African American psychiatrists published a book entitled *Black Rage* (Grier & Cobbs, 1968). From your experience and reading, is that title still one that rings true today? Explain your answer with sociopolitical and cultural examples.

4. Children of Asian heritage and Latino/a children live in closely knit families. How are the structures and dynamics of the two groups of families both different and similar to each other with respect to their beliefs about raising children?

RELATED READING

Healey, J. F. (2010). *Race, ethnicity, gender, and class: The sociology of group conflict and change*. Thousand Oaks, CA: Pine Forge.

Levine, M. (2006). *The price of privilege*. New York: Harper.

McAuliffe, G. (Ed.). (2008). *Culturally alert counseling: A comprehensive introduction*. Thousand Oaks, CA: Sage.

Pedersen, P. B., Draguns, J. G., Lonner, W. J., & Trimble, J. E. (2008). *Counseling across cultures*. Thousand Oaks, CA: Sage.

Wright, R. J. (2011). Gaposis: The use and misuse of tests. In F. W. English (Ed.), *Handbook on educational leadership* (2nd ed.). Thousand Oaks, CA: Sage.

NOTES

1. The keeping of slaves is as old as recorded history. Man has been willing to enslave anyone that could be defeated in battle or sold by a desperate parent. Even the Bible describes the practice:

"When a man strikes his male or female slave with a rod so hard that the slave dies under his hand, he shall be punished. If, however, the slave survives for a day or two, he is not to be punished, since the slave is his own property." (Exodus 21:20–21)

"Slaves, obey your earthly masters with deep respect and fear. Serve them sincerely as you would serve Christ." (Ephesians 6:5)

"When a man sells his daughter as a slave, she will not be freed at the end of six years as the men are. If she does not please the man who bought her, he may allow her to be bought back again. But he is not allowed to sell her to foreigners, since he is the one who broke the contract with her. And if the slave girl's owner arranges for her to marry his son, he may no longer treat her as a slave girl, but he must treat her as his daughter. If he himself marries her and then takes another wife, he may not reduce her food or clothing or fail to sleep with her as his wife. If he fails in any of these three ways, she may leave as a free woman without making any payment." (Exodus 21:7–11)

2. In 1981, Mauritania (western Africa) was the last nation-state on the planet to outlaw slavery. It is sad that the sex slavery of young women and girls continues today throughout the world, as does the forced labor of men and children in South America, and Africa ("World commemorates end of slavery," 2004).

3. This included Oklahoma, West Virginia, Maryland, Delaware, and the 11 states of the old Confederacy that waged a civil war against the United States from 1861 to 1865, including Texas, Louisiana, Arkansas, Alabama, Mississippi, Tennessee, Florida, North and South Carolina, Virginia, and Georgia.

4. This included laws as to who were white people, colored people, and Negros in South Africa (prior to 1994). Similar laws were in place in the southern states in the United States (prior to 1967 when the Supreme Court struck down miscegenation laws [*Loving v. Virginia*]). The most appalling consequence for laws establishing a racial group occurred in Germany under Hitler's National Socialist German Worker's Government. The "Aryan Purity Laws (1935)" defined Jews as a distinct race requiring a person with two or more Jewish grandparents to be categorized as a Jew.

5. Similar to racial differences, language minorities have also been a target for radical policies. "Then said they unto him, 'Say now Shibboleth'; and he said 'Sibboleth'; for he could not frame to pronounce it right: then they laid hold on him, and slew him at the fords of the Jordan. And there fell at that time of Ephraim two-thousand forty" (Judges 12:6).

6. Pelasgics and Etruscans were the people who populated the ancient Greek islands and peninsula about 1200 B.C.E. (Smyth, 1868).

7. Race was rarely discussed until the era of the Enlightenment when it was first described in the scientific literature. A model describing four races of humans was first proposed in 1749 in the 35-volume *Histoire naturelle, générale et particulière* describing all that was known about science in the middle of the 18th century by Georges-Louis Leclerc, Comte de Buffon.

8. The U.S. Constitution never used the word *slave* but talked around the issue. Section 2 of Article I states, "Apart from free persons 'all other persons,' are each to be counted as three-fifths of a white person for the purpose of apportioning congressional representatives on the basis of population." And Section 2, Part 3, of Article IV directs that "persons held to service or labor in one state, under the laws thereof, escaping into another will be returned to their owners."

9. The move and subsequent evolution of mankind into northern Europe resulted in people with small amounts of cutaneous melanin (pigmentation-causing material) in their skin. This genetic adaptation made it possible to produce **vitamin D$_3$** in a climate in which humans had little sun and ultraviolet ray exposure (Office of Dietary Supplements, 2009). As a result people from the cold cloudy Northern European regions evolved with very pale skin. Likewise the dark skin pigmentation of people who live under the equatorial sun reflects an adaptation designed to protect them from getting skin cancer. **Eumelanin** (dark melanin) blocks the harmful ultraviolet rays from the sun from the skin. That is why dark-skinned people who get skin cancer tend to have cancerous lesions appear on body parts with less melanin (palms, soles of the feet, and under the nail beds) (Gloster & Neil, 2006).

10. The other method for interpreting behaviors and activities of others is described as being *etic*. This approach stands outside of the student and his or her culture and defines common threads and themes that transcend the student's ethnicity and are the same in all children (Pike, 1982).

11. It is interesting to note that Queen Charlotte, wife of King George III of Great Britain, monarch at the time of the American Revolution, had an African ancestry and was part of the West African phenotype. The coronation of Queen Elizabeth II referenced her African lineage as a way to honor her great-great-great-great grandmother and show solidarity with the British Commonwealth of nations (de Valdes y Cocom, 2009).

12. An 8-ball is street vernacular for an eighth of an ounce of cocaine, approximately 3.5 grams.

13. Often overlooked is the school district's media consultant and public relations professional. Local merchants have been known to become more generous with their largess when the local press and TV news recognizes what they are contributing.

14. There are many names applied to people who have a heritage as Spanish-language speakers. The U.S. government uses the term *Hispanic* to describe all people from the Spanish-speaking Caribbean Islands, Spanish Central America, Mexico, and South America. In American vernacular it is also used in reference to Spanish- and Portuguese-speaking people from South American and European countries. The term *Latina/o* refers to the Spanish language derived from the Roman Empire's use of Latin 2,000 years ago when modern Spain was a Roman outpost. In this chapter the terms are used interchangeably.

15. People of the Transcaucases and Northern Europe began their trek out of tropical Africa about 40,000 years ago and evolved to meet environmental demands along the 30,000 years of migration from being East Africans to being White Europeans, Asians, and Native Americans. The past 2,000 years of war and commerce has resulted in many indigenous African peoples moving throughout the world and becoming part of all modern nations.

16. About a third of the population of the Hawaiian territories was of Japanese American heritage in 1942. The order did not incarcerate these 150,000 people for fear of crushing the economic life of Hawaii. Those islands saw only 1,200 Japanese visitors and a few Japanese Americans held in mainland concentration camps until the end of the war in 1945.

9

Social Problems and Emergency Counseling in the Schools

OBJECTIVES

By reading and studying this chapter you should acquire the competency to:

- Identify, evaluate, and report potential cases of child maltreatment and abuse
- Describe the problem of homelessness in the lives of America's children, and discuss the mandates counselors and schools must meet
- Explain the major reasons a student may have a pattern of poor attendance
- Describe a counseling program designed to keep a student engaged in school and attending classes
- Discuss the pros and cons regarding zero-tolerance policies
- Explain how school counselors provide testimony in juvenile courts
- Outline the developmental levels by children and adolescents in understanding death
- Explain the warning signs for and the approach to treatment of youngsters abusing drugs, alcohol, or substances
- Describe the role a counselor can play in preventing an attack against the school or its students and staff

" Live as if you were to die tomorrow, learn as if you were to live forever. **"**

Mahatma Gandhi

● INTRODUCTION AND THEMES

Of the many tasks on the school counselor's plate, one is especially critical: the task of being vigilant for students being maltreated. Child abuse is a major problem within our society that affects the lives of tens of thousands of children each year. School counselors are required by law to report suspected incidents of child abuse to state authorities. Counselors and other educators must be ever-vigilant for children suffering abuse. This problem is a major issue for education, with about 18% of all students being abused before the age of 14.

Homelessness is another overwhelming experience in the lives of an increasing number of America's children. Being forced to live in a public shelter or family car and have no permanent address or telephone cannot preclude the child from getting an education. School counselors employ a team approach to coordinate the delivery of services and assurance of the continuity of education for homeless students.

Truancy is highly correlated with dropping out of school and is a significant symptom that a student is at risk. A role of the counselor is to assist the school in developing and publicizing an attendance policy. In counseling students who are at risk, one step is to determine the reason for poor attendance. If it is disengagement, the use of individual and group counseling is needed.

Millions of children experiment with illegal drugs and alcohol each year. The school counselor has a central role to play in reducing this behavior and providing counseling programs for students who have substance abuse problems.

Juvenile justice in this country started as a method of protecting children from adult courts, prisons, and criminals. Changes to these policies have occurred recently as a reaction to an uptick in violent crime being perpetrated by juveniles. Counselors should learn how to prepare testimony and testify in court.

Children learn about grieving by watching their elders and by rehearsing the process with the backyard burials of dead birds and other found animals. The developmental phases of grieving progress sequentially until the adolescent years, at which time grief and bereavement becomes adult-like.

Violent rampages at several schools during the 1990s raised public alarm over the safety of schools and students. These attacks are rare, and they can be thwarted by schools that plan well and invest in security measures to protect students and educators. These tasks are best accomplished by employing cognitive behavioral therapy (CBT; see Chapter 6). Through this therapy, the student can learn more adaptive thinking styles and alternative behaviors for times when under emotional stress.

CHILD MALTREATMENT ●

A critical issue for all educators today is that of child abuse. Each year about 1,350 of every 100,000 children between the ages of 3 and 7 are the victims of maltreatment (U.S. Department of Health and Human Services, 2005). This social problem is also dangerous for infants and toddlers: 1,650 of every 100,000 infants are also abused and/or criminally neglected annually.

Federal data indicate that 81% of all cases of child abuse and serious neglect that result in the child's death occur to children under the age of 4. Another 12% of fatal cases occur with children between the age of 4 and 7. The number of cases of children dying at the hands of their guardians or parents is an astounding 2.03 per every 100,000 children annually (Child Welfare Information Gateway, 2006). This means that of 100,000 children born in any year, 14 will die at the hands of their caregivers before the age of 7. Related research indicates that fewer than half of all cases of child death by abuse are reported.[1] Others are covered up by well-meaning hospital staff or friendly police. In such cases, the family moves on and the child is never heard from again.

Counselors working in elementary schools and early childhood environments must be vigilant for any sign of possible **child maltreatment** and be ready to report suspicions to local authorities. The federal government does not have authority over most cases of child abuse but does provide a hotline for reporting suspected abuse cases. This hotline provides a school counselor with a referral to the appropriate local agency for child services. The hotline number is 1–800–422–4453.

In 1996, President William J. Clinton signed into law the **Child Abuse Prevention and Treatment Act (CAPTA)**, which mandates that responsible professionals, including school counselors, health care workers (including school nurses), teachers, and clergy, must report suspected cases of child maltreatment. To make these reports possible, the law also abrogates all privileges of confidentiality. The CAPTA also provides for the protection of people who file a **good faith report** of suspected child maltreatment even if on further investigation the report proves to be wrong.

There are a number of signs that school counselors should be mindful of that may indicate child maltreatment. Table 9.1 presents a checklist that

TABLE 9.1 **Checklist of Warning Signs for Child Maltreatment**

When the parent and child are present, watch for:

- Parents and children who rarely look at or touch each other
- State that they don't like each other
- Describe a negative relationship with each other

When in the presence of just the parent or primary caregiver, watch for:

- Parents with a history of abuse
- Parent who is or appears depressed and apathetic
- Is clearly drunk on a regular basis or on a drug high frequently
- Exhibits bizarre or irrational behaviors
- Offers conflicting or unconvincing explanation of a child's injury
- Blames the child for problems at home and or school
- Sees the child as a burden or as a worthless and thoroughly bad person
- Describes the child negatively or as evil and malicious
- Espouses corporal or physical punishment
- Suggests that harsh punishment be employed by teachers to control the child
- Seems nonchalant, uncaring, and uninvolved about the child's needs or personal care
- Uses the child to provide the parent with attention and satisfaction

When in the presence of just the child, watch for:

- Child who reports being injured or sexually abused by a parent, stepparent, or other caregiver or adult in the house
- Reports having night terrors (horrific nightmares) and/or bed-wetting after reaching school age
- Has a pattern of unexplained bruises, bite marks, burns, black eyes, cuts, and broken bones; radial bone fractures are very telling as they occur when a limb is twisted
- Has bad body odor and appears to be unclean and uncared for
- Has sexual knowledge far beyond his or her developmental age
- Returns to school after a school break with fading bruises and/or healing wounds
- Shrinks in the presence of adults
- Seems frightened of one or both parents and resists going home with them at the end of the school day
- Has difficulty sitting or walking especially following a visit by other adult family members
- Was not treated for a medical or physical problem brought to the parent's attention
- Reports being unsupervised at home or left in parked cars for hours
- Reports being locked in a closet for a length of time

SOURCE: Child Welfare Information Gateway (2006).

provides warning signs for school counselors to watch for with parents and students. Special vigilance by school counselors should be focused on students recently transferred from another school or program. Students should also be carefully monitored for possible maltreatment when a long-absent parent (including a parent in the military) returns home, when an incarcerated parent returns to the home, and/or when a family is in crisis or if there is a divorce in process.

Many times a child or parent can exhibit one of these signs and it is not indicative of anything but a bad day. A pattern of these signs is another matter. The best approach is for the school counselor to keep a written record of any concerns he or she may have in a dated journal. Once child maltreatment appears to be likely, then it is time to call the hotline. Having a carefully maintained written record of problems and observations will provide child protection officials with data needed to take proactive steps to protect the child. Those written comments become part of the record that is protected when a report is filed in good faith. They also may become part of an official court record and must be meticulously written and maintained.

Sexual Abuse

One especially heinous form of child abuse involves the sexual exploitation and abuse of children by pedophiles. While states vary on the age of consent of a young person for sexual relations, the diagnostic criteria of the **American Psychiatric Association (APA)** is clear. A person can be determined to be mentally ill with a diagnosis as a *pedophile* if he or she is at least 16 years old and is five years older than the child who was attacked (American Psychiatric Association [APA], 1994). Any child under the age of 13 who experiences a sexually abusive act by a pedophile is a *victim*. The actions of a pedophile can be limited to exposing himself or masturbating in front of a child or inappropriately fondling and touching the child. In the worst case it may involve sexual penetration. This abuse can also include the physical abuse of the child. Pedophilia occurs among men and women but is twice as common among males (APA, 1994). This psychiatric illness is usually considered chronic and therefore incurable.

The problem of pedophilia is made more intense with the availability of the Internet to both predators and potential victims (Wolak, Finkelhor, Mitchell, & Ybarra, 2008). Dangerous sexual predators are attracted by the explicit nature of personal profiles posted on seemingly friendly web sites. These pedophiles file-share with each other and network to locate victims near where they live and work (Wolak et al., 2008). The role of counselors is to educate parents and students to the dangers that the Internet can pose.[2]

(Continued)

(Continued)

The chronic nature of pedophilia has contributed to the passage of notification laws by the states known as **Megan's Law**. These laws are named in memory of Megan Kanka, a 7-year-old New Jersey girl who was violently raped and murdered by a recently released convicted sexual predator. A federal law resulted that requires the registration of convicted sexual offenders and that the states set up methods of keeping the public informed of the addresses of these offenders. The national web page for locating convicted sexual offenders is www.nsopw.gov/Core/OffenderSearchCriteria.aspx. In addition, most states also maintain web pages of all sex offenders registered in the state. A list of many of these is maintained by the KLAAS Kids Foundation at www.klaaskids.org/pg-legmeg.htm.[3]

Referral of Maltreatment Cases

Cases of suspected maltreatment, abuse, or neglect must be acted upon expeditiously. It is best if the counselor work in close consultation with the school's administration and other members of the school's pupil service team. However, alacrity is required. The task of investigating the problem and providing interventions will require the participation of an outside agency. The name of this agency varies by state, but it has the responsibility for the safety of children and youth. (See Exhibit 9.1 for a sample referral form.)

● COUNSELING CHILDREN OF HOMELESS FAMILIES

Dimension of the Problem

When a family is forced out of their home by foreclosure or other unplanned reason, it can be a major shock in the lives of the children involved. In 2008, the estimated number of homeless American children was more than 2% of the population (National Association for the Education of Homeless Children and Youth, 2008). In 2009 there were nearly 1,600,000 children living without a permanent home in the United States (Association for Supervision and Curriculum Development [ASCD], 2010).

Some of these children and their families are lucky and live in public and philanthropically supported shelters. Others live out of plain sight in parks, cars, and campgrounds. The resulting nomadic lifestyle prevents as many as 20% (320,000) of homeless children from attending public school (National Center on Family Homelessness, 2009). Some estimates have run as high as 550,000 children of homeless families in the United States who do not attend school (ASCD, 2010).

Exhibit 9.1 Sample Family Services Department Referral

Name of the student _____

Student's age _____

Grade level _____

Homeroom teacher's name _____

Name and address of parent or guardian _____

_____

_____

Phone number and/or cell phone number of parent or guardian _____

Case history and signs of abuse or neglect _____

_____

_____

_____

Information related to the identity of the person(s) who may be committing this child abuse and/or neglect

_____

_____

Description of student's injuries _____

_____

_____

_____

_____

_____

Extent of harm that may have been done, including physical, academic, and social-emotional _____

_____

_____

Name of Referring School Employee _____

Job title _____

E-mail address _____

School assignment or office _____

Office phone _____

Signature _____

Date _____

Homeless children have a threefold greater incidence of mental health–related problems and four times more infections and serious illnesses than do their more fortunate peers. They also live in a more violent world. By age 12, 83% of homeless children have been witnesses to acts of physical violence. Homeless girls run a five times greater risk for experiencing sexual battery or rape prior to age 18 than do girls living in home settings (Cauce et al., 2000; Snyder & Sickmund, 2006).

Speaking in Massachusetts (March 25, 2009), President Barack Obama declared that it is unacceptable for children and families to be homeless in America. To see a video clip of that speech, go to www.cbsnews.com/video/watch/?id=4890899n. President Obama provided an additional $70 million in the 2009 budget to support programs for homeless children and youth.

Homeless children and families are a major social problem faced by our country and are beyond the scope of a school system to overcome. Yet, there are ways for school counselors to help in the process.

Role of School Counselors

School counselors should strive to ensure that any school-related barriers that hinder the education of the homeless students are removed. Counselors have an obligation to ensure that every student has an optimal educational experience. This can include working with other professional specialists on the school's staff, including the school's nurse and social worker. This school-based team can coordinate service delivery, help homeless families find safe shelters, and provide needed referrals, including recommendations for free medical and dental care. Federal legislation requires that each school system establish this team approach to the problem of educating homeless students (McKinney-Vento Act, P.L. 100–77 [1987] Stat. 482, 42 U.S.C. § 11301 et seq.).

There are federal requirements for school systems to have outreach programs that assist both homeless and **unaccompanied children** in obtaining the full benefit of a public school education. These are also spelled out in the McKinney-Vento Homeless Assistance Act. That act, first signed into law by President Ronald Reagan, details what schools are required to provide to homeless and unaccompanied children. These mandated services begin with school registration (even if the child's family cannot provide educational or citizenship documents), transportation to the school of the parent's choice within the district, and tutoring and other services, including support programs that must be provided in situ. This law forces schools and school counselors to be proactive in the support of the student and his or her needs. Most school systems employ a social worker as a homeless liaison to coordinate services provided away from the school's campus. Every school counselor should have a list of quickly available social service agencies, and the name and phone number of a contact person at the agencies (see boxed list).

List of Agencies School Counselors Should Know About

- American Joint Jewish Distribution Committee: www.jdc.org/
- Catholic Charities: www.catholiccharitiesusa.org/NetCommunity/Page.aspx?pid=1174
- Harry Chapin Food Bank: www.harrychapinfoodbank.org/memberagencies.php
- The Salvation Army: www.salvationarmyusa.org/usn/www_usn_2.nsf
- Travelers Aid Society: www.travelersaid.org/tawwwdir.html
- Local independent living center (Help for children with disabilities)
- Local family guidance center
- Dental clinic on the campus of local dental college
- Eye clinic on the campus of local college of ophthalmology and/or Unite for Sight, Inc.: www.uniteforsight.org/freeclinics.php
- Free medical clinic: http://freemedicalcamps.com/
- State Office for Children Youth and Family Services
- State Department of Public Assistance
- Local office for Women, Infants and Children (Food for young children and their families): www.fns.usda.gov/wic/

TRUANCY AND SCHOOL REFUSAL ●

School administrators see truancy as a disciplinary matter. Average daily attendance in the school is the basis on which the school's budget is built. Every day a student is not in school costs the school money needed for programs and salaries. About 6.5% of all students will be chronically truant sometime during their school careers (Egger, Costello, & Angold, 2003). In San Diego, California, an accounting determined that if the 125 students of one small elementary school ($N = 367$) who were absent 10 or more days were present those days the school would have received an additional $50,000 in funding (Magee, 2010).

School counselors should view truancy as a symptom of a potentially significant problem (Klass, 2010). It can be a sign that the student is giving up and has accepted being an academic failure. This occurs when the student is frustrated with his or her difficulty learning and realizes that it is unlikely that he or she will ever be able to catch up. In general, truant students have poor relations with their teachers; many have been misplaced and are in the wrong level of class. Philadelphia-based research found that while dropouts spend several years enrolled in high school, they have missed so many days that they have few credits toward high school graduation (Neild & Farley, 2004).

There is a direct link between academic success and maintaining a pattern of good school attendance (National Assessment of Educational Progress [NAEP], 2004; Towbin, 2010). Survey research sponsored by the Bill & Melinda Gates Foundation found that 43% of high school dropouts left school because they missed too many days of class and could never catch up. They reported that each day being truant made it that much more difficult to go back to school (American Bar Association [ABA], 2006). Many students who drop out tell themselves that they will be able to get a high school equivalency through the General Educational Development (GED) test system. The unfortunate truth is that few dropouts follow through, and those who do earn a GED diploma equivalent have little economic advantage in life over other dropouts (Hetzner, 2010),

Nationwide, more than a half-million high school students drop out each year (Snyder & Sickmund, 2006). The school district of Philadelphia found that middle school students missing more than 36 days of school a year have only a 30% likelihood of ever graduating high school. The problem of the link between absenteeism and dropping out of school is made worse by local and state policies requiring students missing an excess of school days to repeat the grade or fail the class (Klass, 2010).

School Attendance Laws Vary by State

In 30 states, a student can (with parental consent) drop out of school at age 16. Another 12 states mandate school attendance until the age of 18, while the remaining 8 states require students to attend school until they are 17 years old.

In most states a student is considered to be truant and in violation of school attendance laws if that student is absent from the school in which he or she is enrolled without a valid excuse more than 4 days per month or more than 10 days per year (Lohman, 2000). Chronic or habitual truancy is defined as being out of school without a valid reason for 10% or more of the school year (20 days). Most states mandate that schools monitor the truancy of students and report cases of chronic (habitual) truancy to the superior court of the school's jurisdiction. A number of suburban school systems have reduced the problem of truancy among high school students by having their state driver's licenses revoked (Lytle, 2010). This requires a state law, but such legislation has passed in many states.

Counselor's Role With Disengaged Students

Good attendance is a powerful predictor of academic success. Fewer than 1% of students who have never been truant drop out of school (ABA, 2006). Thus there is good reason for counselors to work to prevent truancy and, by association, dropouts. Unfortunately, the number of truants and dropouts is increasing (Barton, 2006; Pascopella, 2007; Viadero, 2006). The peak year for truancy is the ninth grade, and the incidence falls as students reach the legal age to drop out of school (Heilbrunn, 2007). The primary level of prevention requires that the counselor work with the school's leadership in developing a strong, clear attendance policy. This policy, including the definition of *truancy*, should be made in writing and included in each student's handbook and posted on the school's web page. All absences by a student should be followed up with a phone call, e-mail notification, or a written letter to the child's parents (DeKalb, 2000).

Research into the problem has shown that fewer than half of high schools make any contact with parents when a student is missing from school (Gewertz, 2006). In communities where there are clear, enforced truancy policies (including prosecution of the truant's parents), the number of dropouts has been significantly reduced.

Truants tend to like company. For that reason the occurrence of one truant student can quickly escalate to include a clique of friends who frequently skip school. School counselors can turn that around and use peer pressure to help overcome the student's desire to skip out on school. Effective counseling for truancy can involve three steps. First is goal setting and academic success, the second involves group counseling, and the final phase uses choice theory with reality therapy (see Chapter 6). The school counselor's focus is on preventing the student at risk from becoming a chronic or habitual truant or being overwhelmed by the amount of learning to make up. This is one reason to

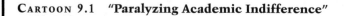

CARTOON 9.1   *"Paralyzing Academic Indifference"*

SOURCE: © Zits-Zits Partnership, King Features Syndicate

initiate interventions early, before the problem becomes severe, with many missed days.

Goal setting with small achievable goals makes the task of catching up manageable. Once it is a possibility that the student can accomplish the task, the counselor's next step is to identify resources that can be deployed to assist the student in reaching his or her subsequent goals. One may involve tutoring, another may be assistance by the school's Title I teacher or reading specialist. Group counseling can provide the youngster other role models of success and friendships to support his or her engagement with the school. The use of reality therapy can modify how students at risk for truancy and dropping out interpret the school and understand their own ability to be effective and empowered.

School Avoidance

There are two major reasons a student may not want to attend school that are not related to being academically disengaged. One of these is fear of bullies and being harassed in school and/or on the school bus. Each month 5% of all students refuse to go to school to avoid bullying or criminal behavior of their peers (Snyder & Sickmund, 2006). Bullies, harassment, and crime in school are a major problem (see Chapter 3). Occasionally school administrators make the problem worse by their actions (see Case in Point 9.1).

CASE IN POINT 9.1

In September 2009 the Corona del Mar High School in California settled a lawsuit out of court that required that all administrators complete a full-day training program on the topic of what constitutes harassment and how destructive harassment and bullying are. A number of students also had to complete a similar workshop.

The suit was filed on behalf of students who were threatened with death and being raped for appearing in the school's production of the play *Rent, School Edition*. The harassment began in January 2008, when three football players made threats against the female lead and called the male lead "gay" on a Facebook page filled with slurs and threats. Hundreds of students saw the page before it could be pulled down. This led the school administration to cancel the play. The play's cast were crestfallen at the news that their hard work was not going to be seen. Parents of the cast were not as easy to control. A federal injunction based on the 1st Amendment, guaranteeing free speech including the play *Rent,* forced the school to allow the play to go on.

The production was very well attended, and to prevent violence, the school added extra security. The administration took no action against the misogynistic and homophobic perpetrators and tried to retaliate against the girl who played the lead role of Mimi in the play (P. Cohen, 2009). That girl and her family were central figures in bringing the suit and gaining the injunction. California, like 43 other states, has a law to prevent bullying, but these laws are hard for a state to enforce, and many schools just ignore the issue. It is only when a major assault or death occurs that some schools respond (Walker, 2009).[4]

Thought Question. If you were the school counselor asked to design and conduct an inservice program as specified by the court order, what would you include in the program for the school's administration? Develop an outline (with objectives) for conducting a full-day workshop for these "educational leaders."

School avoidance can take the form of separation anxiety. This condition occurs among 2% of all children and adolescents under the age of 18 (APA, 1994; Brand & O'Connor, 2004; Egger et al., 2003).[5] It may be higher among younger children who lack the ability to verbally express their feelings and concerns (Klass, 2010). To qualify as an anxiety disorder, the condition must persist for at least 4 weeks and prevent the student from being successful at school. Most students with separation anxiety resulting in school avoidance come from small, close-knit families. Many live in single-parent homes with a parent who has received treatment for a mental health issue (Egger et al., 2003).

When forced to go to school, these students typically become inward turning, withdraw from activities, and become listless. In the morning when the student is confronted with the need to attend school, he or she may develop somatic complaints, usually involving the gastrointestinal track. Somatic complaints need to be evaluated by the child's pediatrician before any other actions are taken (Tyrrell, 2005). The child's parents may play the role of **enabler**, writing a medical excuse to the school explaining their child's need to stay at home and recover. Once at school, these students can develop powerful, albeit irrational, fears about what is happening to their loved one at home.

Symptoms tend to be worse when the student is starting a new school, experiencing a transition into first grade, or moving to middle school. By adolescence, the fear associated with separation anxiety and school avoidance can be manifested as a generalized panic attack (Albano, Chorpita, & Barlow, 1996).

Primary Prevention

School counselors can provide primary prevention programs to avoid these problems. Primary preventions include the careful introduction of students to new school environments and ongoing support for newly transferred students. This includes a home visit and inviting the child's parents to become engaged in the school and its activities. When the student realizes that there are caring adults, trusted by his or her parents, the level of anxiety about the new experiences is reduced.

Secondary Prevention

When a parent is an enabler with the student in school avoidance, he or she may provide medical excuse notes and cover for the child's absence from school (Klass, 2010). This occurs in homes where insecure parents need constant contact with their children to assure themselves of being loved. The parent in collusion with the student for poor attendance can prove to be intractable for the school. The counselor can't help people with whom he or she has no contact. The school counselor may need to enlist the help of the school's social worker to make a home visit and potentially have the school's administrator refer the problem to family court.

Tertiary Intervention

Behavioral therapies involving shaping and modeling have long been shown to be effective in reducing separation anxiety and school avoidance (Gelfand, 1978; Kennedy, 1965). This makes the use of cognitive behavioral therapy one of the most effective treatment approaches the school counselor can employ to assist a child or adolescent who is experiencing separation anxiety and school avoidance (Albano et al., 1996). Once the student-client has worked through a program of CBT, he or she is ready for an ongoing follow-up program with small group counseling focused on self-esteem and ego strength development.

JUVENILE JUSTICE SYSTEM ●

> *When the students are occupied, they're not juvenile delinquents. I believe that education is a capital investment.*
>
> *Arlen Specter*

Truancy and dropping out of school are significantly correlated with engaging in delinquent behaviors (Heilbrunn, 2007). Nearly half of all incarcerated Americans dropped out of school and do not have high school diplomas (Heilbrunn, 2007). Dropping out is normally preceded by a pattern of increasing truancy. Chronic truancy is one of the issues normally found in the life stories of many criminals.

Truancy is only a minor issue faced by family and juvenile courts today. In an average year, 2,000 children are murdered in the United States, a 44% reduction below the peak year for juvenile murder in 1993 (Snyder & Sickmund, 2006).[6] Of these murders, 75% were by firearm, and 47% of the victims were African Americans.

As noted earlier, most murders of children below the age of 6 were at the hands of their parents, while those among adolescents were committed by each other (Snyder & Sickmund, 2006). While African Americans and Anglo-White adolescents are about equally likely to be the perpetrator of a murder, the proportion of the two groups is not even.[7] One or more times each month, an average of 6% of all adolescents come to school packing firearms, while another 8% bring knives or other dangerous weapons into their schools (Forrest, Zychowski, Stuhldreher, & Ryan, 2000). (See Case in Point 9.2.)

CASE IN POINT 9.2

It was not all that long ago that members of the Boy and Girl Scouts were taught to care for and use a sharp utility knife. Even Cub Scouts were expected to learn about knives. If a scout wore a uniform to school, no one thought to check his or her book bag or backpack to see whether it

(Continued)

(Continued)

contained a "scout knife." Today, bringing this knife into school would result in the student being expelled from most public schools. More than 90% of all school systems have adopted a zero-tolerance weapons policy, and firearm possession in schools is banned by federal law (Cauchon, 1999).

This policy has even been applied to children wearing Halloween costumes that include toy guns and cap pistols or rubber swords and cardboard knives. One student who brought an antique gold pocket watch with a chain and a 1-inch gold knife attached to it for "show and tell" was expelled.

A 10-year-old in Longmont, Colorado, was expelled because her mother had put a small knife in her lunchbox to cut an apple. When the student realized the knife might violate the school's zero-tolerance policy, she turned it in to a teacher, who told her she had done the right thing. The student was subsequently expelled from school.

A student attended his prom wearing the traditional formal wear of the highland Scots (his family's heritage) including a ceremonial small knife known as a *sgian dubh* on the right leg, covered to the hilt by an argyle sock. He was expelled from school and barred from graduating.

Thought Questions. The goal of all zero-tolerance policies is the safety of everyone in the school. If you were a school counselor, what, if any, concessions to your school's strict zero-tolerance rules would you advocate changing? Explain your position.

Beyond murder, juveniles experience violent, nonfatal assaults 2.5 times more frequently than adults, at a rate of 82 per 1,000. Girls experience far more violent attacks and sexual assaults (3 girls out of every 4) than do boys, while boys experience more simple assaults than girls. About a third of all adolescents have had their personal property stolen or destroyed through acts of vandalism each year (Rainville & Smith, 2003). The violence that is apparent to parents carries over to their security expectations for their children. Case in Point 9.3 discusses this issue.

CASE IN POINT 9.3

School bus transportation is needed whenever the roads are dangerous and without sidewalks, or when the distance between a child's home and school is excessive. Yet, many suburban parents living just a block or two from their child's school have campaigned against school district plans to have the communities pave sidewalks for their children. These parents do not want their children walking to school.

There is a great deal of fear about childhood abductions and assaults by strangers. In reality, the possibility of abduction is extremely rare. While 800,000 children go missing each year, the vast majority are soon found. Fewer than 100 children are abducted and murdered in this country each year (MacPherson & McFeatters, 2000). The most dangerous child predators (previously convicted of similar crimes) are responsible for more than 60% of all such abductions and murders.[8] While these cases of abduction are rare, they have the attention of America's media and have raised the level of parental fear about safety.

Budget problems of many school systems brought about by the Great Recession (2008–2010) caused a cutback on busing. The result is that carpools abound. Also, other suburban parents living too close to their children's school for bus transportation have banded together to employ a convoy approach to moving children in safety through their communities. In these cases one parent is designated as the walker for the neighborhood's children. This parent walks along with the gaggle of local children all headed to the same school campus.

It was not that long ago that it was de rigueur for children living within a mile of their school to walk or ride bicycles to school. In 1969, 41% of schoolchildren walked or bicycled to school. By 2001, that figure fell to 13%. One likely result is greater childhood obesity, more expenses for school busing, and greater air pollution (Hoffman, 2009). Parents who resist this trend and allow their children the freedom to walk to and from school independently have described themselves as raising "free-range kids." Yet, these parents are providing children with the independence and self-confidence to compete well in the world.

Thought Question. Many school systems would prefer to buy sidewalks connecting homes to the school than maintain a fleet of school buses. As a school counselor, what proactive steps would you recommend to prepare parents who heretofore had their children bused to your building (mean distance of one-half mile) and now are about to lose that service in a community with new sidewalks and crossing guards?

Gangs and Gang-Related Violence

The level and nature of gang membership in America has changed over time. The first major era in gang membership occurred in the late 1800s, paralleling the shift of populations into the rapidly growing urban centers (Howell, 1998). Membership in gangs grew again in the 1920s in response to the continual urbanization and large immigrant populations entering the cities. In the 1960s, gangs had another resurgence related to the **baby boom** in the population, resulting in far more youth than there were employment opportunities for them. The added feature of automobiles in the United States made it possible for gangs to cover wider areas and claim more "turf" as their own. During the 1960s, spray paint in cans provided a new tool for marking territory by gangs.

In the 21st century, growth in gang membership has started to climb again. One new dimension in gangs and their development has been the appearance of gangs on the Internet (King, Walpole, & Lamon, 2007). Internet chat rooms have become virtual recruiting centers for dangerous gangs. The Internet is also used by gangs to punish victims by variations of cyberbullying known as **happy slapping**. In response, public schools are beginning to develop student rules of conduct that make using a blog or other Internet site that depicts any illegal or inappropriate behavior a violation of the conduct code (Millard, 2006).

In 2008, U.S. Attorney General Alberto Gonzales estimated that there were 20,000 gangs enrolling (full and part time) about a million youth.[9] That resurgence in gang activity and membership has been made more deadly than previous gang eras due to the easy availability of high-power, rapid-firing firearms. The use of rapid-fire guns combined with the availability of cars added a new dimension to street terror: the **drive-by shooting**. In response to this deadly gang-related behavior, states changed many aspects of laws governing the juvenile justice system (see "Juvenile Courts" later in chapter).

To be considered a gang, three or more youths must identify themselves as members and engage in overt criminal acts. The demography of a typical local gang shows they have a median membership that is between 12 and 24 years of age, and enrolls about 25 active members.[10] A typical gang is highly organized, and it polices its members to enforce the gang's rules for conduct. Almost all members are males, but gangs also have a "women's auxiliary." Girls are encouraged to participate in some gang behaviors, and if they prove themselves, they can become regular members.

Gang Dynamics

Youth gangs are clear examples of what can happen when an identity formation fails and the youth develops a negative identity (see Chapter 4). The gang provides a sense of membership and belonging and has the side advantage of providing personal security. Gangs may or not have enough resources to protect members from predators of other similar organizations, but they can pose and posture themselves to appear more dangerous than their reality (Howell, 2009). This posturing takes the form of defiance to legitimate authority, threats to do violence to others, and blustery bravado.

About 1 American child in 60 becomes a gang member. Even when a child grows up under impoverished inner-city conditions, in a neighborhood dominated by gangs, there is only a 15% chance that he or she will join a gang (Hoag, 2009). A good question is, How are gang members different from the vast majority of young people not joining gangs?

Research has demonstrated that gang members tend to have experienced abusive home environments as young children and as a consequence have significantly elevated levels of post-traumatic stress disorder (Adams, Tsytsarev, & Meller, 2009; Hoag, 2009). They also have lower **resiliency factors** related to interpersonal relationships and **self-reliance**. These factors include the ability to set goals and accomplish tasks, forge interpersonal relationships, and resolve conflict. Research on active populations of youthful gang members found that male gang members were unable to relate to their victims and were emotionally numb (Thornberry, Huizinga, & Loeber, 2003).

Gangs require several factors to form and thrive. They need a place to congregate and hang out (park, school, neighborhood mall or store); members must have time to pass with their fellow members (lack of employment or academic opportunity, dropping out of school or being fired from a job); and there must be no meaningful adult supervision or institutions (schools, churches, social services) that are effective in the lives of the young people.

On a community-wide scale, only strong community organizing efforts can control gangs. This requires grass-roots efforts by neighborhoods being led by powerful voices from community leaders. Police departments can provide support for gang deterrence by providing "community policing" programs 24 hours a day. Having police constantly patrol on foot and in the neighborhoods is a deterrent to all criminal activity, including gangs.

School Counselor's Role

The counselor can work on a case-by-case basis to make membership in a gang less appealing. By keeping the youth engaged in school and preventing truancy and dropping out, the school counselor removes a required part of gang membership. To do this, the school's counselor can employ a combination of goal setting for academic success, followed by group counseling, and finally the use of choice theory with reality therapy (see Chapter 6).

Schools designed to provide community services day and night for the entire community and that are well lit and covered with security cameras can remove a favorite meeting place for the gang. The loss of the school as a central point for the gang makes it that much more difficult to hold onto membership.

Juvenile Court

Until late in the 19th century, children ages 7 and under were considered too young to reason and therefore were incapable of committing crimes. However, any child who reached the **age of reason** (age 8) was subjected to full adult treatment for any crimes. The first court for juveniles opened in 1899 in Chicago. Many of the benignant rules and procedures established by that Chicago court are still employed throughout the country today (Mahoney & Morris, 2010; Snyder & Sickmund, 2006).

The initial focus of the juvenile court system was on the offenders, not on the offenses committed. The effort by juvenile courts was to rehabilitate the child, and confinement was always viewed as a last resort. The informal procedures followed in juvenile courts became more formal in the 1960s following decisions by the U.S. Supreme Court to require legal representation and due process for all charged juveniles.

In 1974, the United States enacted the Juvenile Justice and Delinquency Prevention Act. This act aimed to increase funding for community-based prevention programs and "deinstitutionalization" of **status offenders**. It required states to keep youth offenders protected and away from adult offenders. From the start of the juvenile justice system, courts and policymakers have recognized that children are developmentally different from adults, children are more impressionable, and they have poorer cognitive and decision-making skills (Howell, 2009).

The upturn in violent juvenile crime in the late 1980s and early 1990s resulted in both state-by-state and national backlashes against juvenile criminal behavior. In 1994 President Clinton signed into law the Gun-Free Schools Act (P.L. 103–227), mandating that a student caught entering school grounds with a weapon must be expelled for a calendar year and be referred to the juvenile justice system. This set into motion a move by school systems to broadly define weapons and establish **zero-tolerance** policies.

Recent state laws have made it much easier for prosecutors to move juveniles into adult court and have also increased the rights of victims to be heard before a judge sets the terms of a child's treatment or punishment. This has resulted in more juveniles being sent to adult lockups. Unfortunately, African American and Hispanic children are far more likely to be sent to adult courts and lockups than are their Caucasian-White peers who have committed the same crime ("Juvenile justice," 2007).

In 2007, 16% of all violent crime arrests, 47% of all arson arrests, 25% of all auto theft arrests, 26% of all arrests for crimes against property (vandalism), and 27% of all robbery arrests were of juveniles (Slowikowski, 2009). An interesting statistic is that with more than 2 million juvenile arrests each year, about 18% or 400,000 filings and incarcerations each year are for status offenses (Office of Juvenile Justice and Delinquency Prevention, 2009). (See Case in Point 9.4.) Status offenses are crimes for juveniles but not for adults. These include truancy, alcohol consumption, smoking, running away from home, and being incorrigible or unmanageable at home. With a finding that the child is delinquent, the court can send the juvenile to a camp, training school, juvenile detention center, or residential training program. Juvenile courts are often very interested in hearing from school counselors when deciding how to rule in the case of a delinquency petition.

CASE IN POINT 9.4

Pennsylvania's highest court ordered the juvenile records of thousands of young people be expunged of their delinquent complaints. It seems that two judges who ran Luzerne County's juvenile court were in the pocket of the owners of two private detention facilities for juveniles, PA Child Care and a sister company, Western PA Child Care. The judges were paid kickbacks totaling more than $2.6 million for making thousands of unwarranted incarceration decisions for children, placing them into those facilities. The state of Pennsylvania then paid the owners of the private juvenile jails $150 per child per day. The corrupt judges made certain that the 160 beds in those facilities were kept full. The two judges, Judge Mark Ciavarella and Judge Michael T. Conahan, have entered into plea deals with the federal attorney that will see them spend 7 years in federal prison and lose their state pensions and licenses to practice law (Schwartz, 2009).

Thought Questions. When adolescents are beyond the control of their parent(s) and constantly truant, is it appropriate for the justice system to intervene and place these adolescents in a secure facility for a few months of counseling and educational tutoring? Or should there be other options? Explain your position.

Counselors Providing Court Testimony

There are two types of witnesses before the courts, each with a role to play: **expert witness** and **witness of fact** (James & DeVaney, 2003). School counselors may be asked to provide testimony in either capacity. As an expert witness, the counselor's education and experience are called upon to educate the court in matters where the counselor has a documented expertise. The judge makes the ultimate determination of the qualification of the counselor to provide expert testimony. The short-term nature of the relationship between the school counselor and the student means that other mental health workers are more likely to be asked by the court to provide expert testimony.

Testimony as a witness of fact is a more common role for a school counselor to play in court. School counselors can be asked to provide testimony of facts involving a range of issues, such as suicide and violence, gang membership, child abuse and/or neglect, bullying, drug and alcohol abuse, and teen pregnancy. All testimony should be factual, jargon free, concise, unbiased, and without prejudice or opinion.

Prior to entering the court the counselor should do a bit of homework. Counselors should memorize their professional résumés and be able to list all degrees and their dates, certifications, professional memberships, licenses, continuing education, publications, and presentations. The counselor should read contemporary material about the nature of the problem being addressed by the court. Finally, the school counselor should carefully read and review his or her case notes regarding the student.

Prudent practice for a school counselor is to keep confidential case notes detailing contacts with each student. The notes should be behavioral, not gossipy, and provide actual data as to when the student visited, the nature of the problem, professional activities and strategies, consultations, referrals, and resolution (James & DeVaney, 2003). These case notes should be well organized and stored in a secure place, away from the cumulative record file about the student. Case notes can be included in the subpoena and must be taken to court, where they will become evidence. Do not take any records to court that are not described on the subpoena. Any memory aids the counselor takes into the court can be entered into the court's record as evidence and shared with attorneys for all parties. Remember that the order of a judge trumps all ethical canons about privacy and confidentiality.

Legal Counsel

If there is any possibility that the school counselor could face liability through the court's actions, he or she should seek private legal counsel. Always keep in mind the fact that the school's attorney represents the best interests of the school, not any of its employees. Court preparation, consulting an attorney, and other steps should occur only after being subpoenaed by the court. The judge in the matter has a clerk who can help the school counselor schedule when to arrive in court in order to avoid the need to wait around in the courthouse all day before being called to provide sworn testimony.

ILLEGAL DRUG AND ALCOHOL USE   ●

As noted previously, adolescents who consume alcohol are status offenders. Those who acquire and use inappropriate prescription medications are committing criminal acts. When a child or adolescent abuses a psychoactive drug or an intoxicating substance, he or she may become either **addicted** or **dependent** on its continued use. Dependency involves relying on a substance to relieve a condition or medical problem. A person with arthritis may be dependent on regular doses of opiates like oxycodone to relieve severe pain. An addiction is an aggressive and increasingly intense craving for a substance. A teen addicted to oxycodone will buy it on the street or steal it from a relative and snort or inject it into the bloodstream. Increasingly large doses will be needed, and the time interval between when the substance is craved becomes shorter over time. The withdrawal of an addictive substance may cause physiological problems for the user (Fishman, 2008).

Children and Alcohol Abuse Problems

1933 was the year the 18th Amendment was overturned with the passage of the 21st Amendment, which ended the national experiment in alcohol prohibition.[11] The outlawing of alcohol in 1920 created a new cartel of illegal producers and distributors and enriched gangs of violent dealers (Allen, 1931). After alcohol consumption was outlawed, there was a wave of defiant open lawlessness that is not too dissimilar to that of the current national policy known as the "War on Drugs."[12]

Survey data indicate alcohol use by young people increases every year starting with middle school, where 2.6% of all children report they are regular users of alcohol. By age 21, that number of drinkers rises to 67.5% (National Institute on Alcohol Abuse and Alcoholism, 2001). About 18% of all high school students use alcohol occasionally (once a month) and 11% are regular drinkers (daily use), of which 2.5% report themselves as **binge drinkers** (Substance Abuse and Mental Health Services Administration, 2002).

School Policy and Program Requirements

Alcohol abuse, like abuse of other drugs by young people, can appear as an emergency in school. Intoxication can occur for an adolescent girl after the consumption of less than two cans of beer in an hour, a single wine cooler, or a shot of

80-proof liquor. The faster metabolism and larger muscle mass of boys implies they can drink about twice the amount as can a girl before they become intoxicated. A student in school who is identified as being drunk should be transported to the local emergency room and the parents called. The juvenile division of the police department should also be called and the location of the student and his or her condition reported.[13]

It is always a good idea to conduct any evaluation of sobriety with one or more witnesses present and to make a video recording of what happened. The reason for transporting the student to a medical treatment facility is the potential for the student to sustain injury if he or she falls, becomes physically ill, or even dies of acute alcohol poisoning. The drunken student's locker and other storage areas should be emptied, secured, and sealed in a box where the contents can be examined later when the police subpoena them. This will occur if there is any likelihood that drugs were involved in the intoxication of the minor child. Child welfare workers may also want to examine the contents to determine if the parents were neglectful in making intoxicating spirits available to their child. Depending on local policy and the published code for student conduct, a student found to be in a drunken state in school might be expelled for a year and referred to the juvenile justice system.

All this may seem a bit harsh, but there is a real danger that an intoxicated student will hurt him- or herself and can present a danger to other students. This policy should be made clear in the student handbook, posted on the school's web page, and explained to parents on back-to-school nights.

Precursors

There are two main precursors related to a child becoming an abuser of alcohol or other drugs. One of these is genetic. There is clear proof that genes play a role in shaping alcoholism risk. Like diabetes and heart disease, alcoholism is considered genetically complex, involving the interaction among several different human genes (National Institute on Alcohol Abuse and Alcoholism, 2003).

The second factor is environmental and tied to the child's family life. Children with an alcoholic parent or a parent with a serious mental illness are at risk for alcoholism in part through genetics and also by what they see and learn in the home. Abusive and cold parents are more likely than those who are approachable and loving to have children who abuse all ranges of drugs, including alcohol (Mayes & Suchman, 2006).

Signs that a student is at risk for addictive behavior are falling grades and a gradual disengagement with school. This change usually includes a change in the student's close friendships with a loss of a clique of school-engaged peers. That group is replaced with a group of youngsters with poor grades, an anti-academic attitude, and occasional truancy (Zolten & Long, 1997). School counselors should make these warning signs known to parents and encourage parents to communicate any observations they have made that may imply alcohol and/or drug abuse by their child.

There have been a number of curriculum-based approaches to stop drug and alcohol abuse by students. A major funding effort to educate students to "Just Say No" was one of the latest of these, and like its predecessors it has not been successful (Eagle, 2006).

Smoking

Every day in the United States, 3,600 children and adolescents begin smoking, and 1,100 become daily smokers (G. Harris, 2009). The addiction-producing agent in tobacco is nicotine, a naturally occurring product that is also used as an insecticide. Inhaled into the lungs, it enters the blood and stimulates a release of glucose, giving an energy boost to the smoker. The pharmacology of nicotine is similar to other addictive drugs, including cocaine and heroine. Once addicted to nicotine, a person must go through a difficult withdrawal experience to become smoke-free (American Heart Association, 2009). The addiction to cigarette smoke is related to illnesses that cause the premature death of about half of addicted smokers. In all 50 states, smoking cigarettes below the age of 18 is a juvenile status offense.

The age that smokers begin their habit has been slowly increasing and is now over the age of 19 (American Lung Association, 2009). The number of teen smokers decreased by 45% during the decade from 1997 to 2007. Among the reasons for this drop in tobacco use by teens is the ban of tobacco advertising and the antismoking advertisements that have appeared in the media. Perhaps the greatest deterrent has been the cigarette tax that has made smoking very expensive for teenagers. A second reason for the reduction in teenage smoking is the total ban on smoking in most public places (Cooney, 2008). Without role models for smoking, teens are less likely to spend their money on this expensive habit.

Marijuana

The crossover between smoking and other drugs has been thought to be marijuana (Merrill, Kleber, Schwartz, Liu, & Lewis, 1999). This traditional view has been challenged and anti-marijuana laws have been modified in many states (National Organization for the Reform of Marijuana Laws [NORMAL], 2010).

Marijuana contains a natural psychoactive drug, tetrahydrocannabinol (THC), that is part of the common *cannabis sativa* plant (hemp). THC is a mild hallucinogen that interferes with short-term memory, coordination, and concentration. Medically, THC reduces nausea, stimulates appetite, and improves glaucoma by lowering intraocular eye pressure. THC has also been demonstrated to improve or even stop schizophrenia.

Much like cigarette smoking, the smoking of cannabis can lead to a range of pulmonary and other diseases. This danger of lung disease can be reduced by inhaling a vaporized form of marijuana instead of the smoke of the burning plant (Grotenhermen, 2001). There is recent evidence that the amount of THC in marijuana has increased, making the dose size a smoker experiences larger today than was true in the 1990s (Shallcross, 2009a). This increase in potency has occurred about the same time as a reduction in the amount of marijuana being used by school-aged students. There has been a shift in drug preferences since 2000 toward oxycodone-based drugs such as Vicodin and away from the hassle of carrying and using smoking materials needed to get high on THC (Reinberg, 2008).

The federal government has banned use of THC, but 14 states (as of 2010) have passed laws legalizing THC therapy under medical supervision (NORMAL, 2010). A synthetic form is manufactured and sold as the prescription medication dronabinol (U.S. Food and Drug Administration, 2009). Marijuana is not addictive but can make an adolescent dependent on it and the high that is experienced by the THC in the bloodstream.

School Policy

Smoking nicotine-containing material is not intoxicating. Many schools include tobacco-related products when they write zero-tolerance policies for drug use. If that is the school's policy, it should be well publicized, included in the students' handbook, posted on the school's web page, and explained to parents during back-to-school meetings. Smoking cigarettes is a juvenile status violation, and smoking marijuana is illegal for many adults and virtually all children. The school's policy must address the need to report the latter to juvenile authorities along with taking disciplinary steps that may include expulsion from school.

Huffing

The drug type of choice for many tweens and middle school children includes aromatic hydrocarbons. The low cost and availability of these products make it possible for teenagers to acquire them without raising the concerns of their parents. The use of common products such as model-builders' glue and cleaning solutions tops this list. Placing the hydrocarbon in a paper bag and deeply breathing the fumes into the lungs (**huffing**) produces a chemical high similar to that caused by excessive use of alcohol. The practice is extremely dangerous and causes irreparable damage to vital body organs as well as the eyes and ears. Used excessively, huffing can cause heart stoppage and death.

Commonly Huffed Inhalants

1. *Volatile hydrocarbons*: Plastic glue, carbon-tetra-chloride (cleaning solvent), gasoline, acetone (nail polish remover), methyl-ethyl-ketone (grease cleaner), and benzene (paint remover)

2. *Nitrate gases*: Nitrous oxide (dental sedative, propellant in compressed foods), amyl-nitrite and cyclohexyl-nitrite (used to relieve angina pectoris)

3. *Most propellants*: Spray paints, hair styling sprays, and other products propelled by compressed gases

---

Huffing Abuse

Students in school who are found to be high from huffing should be immediately transported to an emergency medical treatment facility and the parents notified. Emergency medical attention is called for as the student may have received a fatal dose of the inhalant that may cause a stroke or heart failure in an hour or two.

Students who have abused a chemical inhalant may be disoriented, have bloodshot eyes, a chemical odor around them and their clothing, and a bloody nose.

Prescription Pharmaceuticals

Teenagers live in homes where their siblings, parents, and grandparents may have many powerful pharmaceuticals in the family's medicine chest. These include the psychoactive stimulant methamphetamine used to treat children with AD/HD; analgesics including oxycodone and hydrocodone (i.e., Vicodin); and tranquilizers based on benzodiazepines such as Valium, Xanax, Serax, Ativan, and Librium (National Institute on Drug Abuse [NIDA], 2005). Teens who abuse these drugs usually force them into their bloodstream quickly by pulverizing the tablets and **snorting** the power into their lungs.

School Policy

The zero-tolerance policy of most schools provides for the expulsion of any student who brings any pharmaceutical product (prescription drugs and patent medicines) on campus. This has resulted in cases when the punishment does not fit the crime but is rarely questioned when a student brings and/or distributes prescription drugs in school (Seipp, 2002). Problems occur when asthma-relieving emergency medical devices and pharmacological items such as bronchial dilators are banned. These emergency items must remain with students for self-administration when the alternative is possible death or serious injury.

School Counselor's Role

Counselors have a role to play in helping formulate policy within the school. One thing school counselors can work toward is a zero-tolerance policy that provides flexibility. Girls have been expelled for bringing Midol tablets to school to help them overcome menstrual pain and discomfort; other students have been punished for having prescription eye drops with them in school to medicate against an eye infection (Kaminer, 1996). Students expelled for having over-the-counter drugs are routinely sent to a drug rehabilitation program before being reinstated in school. Ironically, such requirements reduce the value of rehabilitation programs for students who truly need the help.

In reality, overcoming an addiction requires a long-term commitment between the therapist and the client. School counselors can provide important assistance to the students with addictions by helping them and their families find appropriate community rehabilitation programs. In 2009, as few as 10% of all teenagers with serious substance addiction problems were getting appropriate treatment (Knudsen, 2009). For this reason, a number of school systems have added professional drug counselors to the noncertified staff of high schools to help addicted students ease their way back into the school's program following a period of rehabilitation. These professionals usually co-lead groups along with the certified school counselor. They may also assist with one-on-one counseling of recovering addicts.

Primary Prevention

Families are the first line of defense against drug and alcohol abuse. School counselors can make this a theme for one or more parent group sessions.

CARTOON 9.2   *"Midol Junkie"*

"Every month I become a Midol™ junkie, and they caught me at my middle school."

SOURCE: Merv Magus.

Information as well as the school's drug and alcohol policy can be posted on the school's web page.[14] The type of information parents need is twofold: they need to be taught the importance of having a loving and supportive relationship with their children, and they should be educated about the warning signs that their child may have a substance abuse problem. It is not easy for parents to realize and accept the fact that their child has a drug or alcohol problem. (See box, "Warning Signs of Drug or Alcohol Abuse.")

Another group school counselors can assist is students of parents who are addicted to alcohol or drugs and the siblings of teens with drug or alcohol addictions. These students typically have learned that they cannot count on their parents and must fend for themselves early on in life. There are a number of organizations that help students of addicted parents or those with addicted siblings. The two largest of these are AL-ANON and ALATEEN (www.al-anon.alateen.org/). Counselors should be aware that there are 11 million children and adolescents

Warning Signs of Drug or Alcohol Abuse

Parents must be willing to slow their children down when they return home from school and other activities with their peer groups and spend time speaking with them. This should include observing for possible problematic signs. The following list is a general guideline. Any teen can have an off day, but the bundling of several of these can be a serious warning sign.

- Alcohol, tobacco smoke, or pot on the breath and in the smell of his or her clothing
- Slurred speech, forgetfulness, clumsiness, and poor coordination
- Change in grades and interest in school
- Lethargy and low motivation
- Truancy
- New clique of friends
- Secrecy and excessive need for privacy
- Restlessness, rapid speech
- Chaotic affect with being quick to anger or tears
- Consistently bad (reckless) choices
- Sudden lack of money, along with petty thefts around the home

living at home with one or more alcoholic parents (National Association for Children of Alcoholics, 2005). These children and adolescents are most at risk for developing addictions.

Secondary Prevention

Counseling programs for children at risk of becoming addicted must be rooted in the empowerment of the students being counseled. This involves the use of strengths-based school counseling. Part of this process is helping children identify and build from their personal resiliency factors. This can involve both individual and group therapy.

Tertiary Prevention

Counselees abusing drugs and/or alcohol are best counseled using a combination of choice theory and reality therapy (see Chapter 6). The approach is one that will require a long-term time commitment and should be planned to last the academic year. Referral to outside drug or alcohol treatment programs may also be indicated.

SELF-DESTRUCTIVE BEHAVIORS ●

We are healed of suffering only by experiencing it in the full.

Marcel Proust

Cutting

Cutting is used to describe a compulsive need to injure and hurt oneself. Seventeen percent of all college undergraduates report that they have been **cutters** (Whitlock, Eckenrode, & Silverman, 2006). Between 75 and 90% of all cutters are girls and young women (Fox & Hawton, 2004; "Self-embedding disorder," 2008). The name *cutter* implies that they slice open their skin and draw blood using a sharp object. Others use tight rubber bands to repeatedly snap on their wrists or legs to create a painful swelling. Cutters will also burn themselves with lit smoking materials and cigarette lighters. A more recent variation of cutting involves self-embedding sharp objects into and below the skin line. The radiologists who are called upon to determine the source of an infected and painful swelling typically have been the first to identify this latter group of cutters. Infection is a major danger for all cutters, along with the possibility of a loss of the infected limb (McVey-Noble, Khemlani-Patel, & Neziroglu, 2006).

Psychology of Cutting

The act of cutting is generally viewed as an expression of internal mental anguish and the need to be punished. The acts of inflicting self-injury have been described as a "bright red scream" (Strong, 1999).

Cutting can overlap and copresent with other related disorders and be considered as symptomatic of deep-seated problems. For example, with younger children (8 to 12 years) it may be induced by the trauma of sexual abuse (McVey-Noble et al., 2006). As the student grows, cutting may occur during flashbacks brought on by **post-traumatic stress disorder (PTSD)**. Among teenagers, cutting may be part of a bipolar-type affect disorder or a borderline personality disorder (BPD) (APA, 1994). As part of the BPD, teenagers may also have difficulty sleeping and experience vivid and threatening dreams. They also may have problems regulating their mood. Their affect can be chaotic, labile one day and in a gloomy depression the next. This can be paired with a tendency to commit reckless and impulsive acts, high-risk substance abuse, and partaking in unprotected sex. About 9% of individuals with BPD eventually kill themselves.

Most school counselors do not have the skill set or therapeutic time available to help a chronic cutter. For that reason, when students with this problem are identified, the help of the parents and the immediate help of an outside organization such as the emergency division of a psychiatry department in a hospital may be needed. Once the student is out of danger of further self-destructive behaviors, psychological counseling for the student and family may be needed to help overcome the impulse to cut in the future. School counselors can support these outside agencies and may be asked by the parents to recommend the psychologist.

Cognition and Cutting

Cognitively, cutters tend to be inflexible perfectionists. This type of thinking exceeds normal achievement motivation and involves a pathological need to relentlessly pursue goals that are beyond the normal for any child. This need requires they appear, act, and perform perfectly. Naturally this leads to disappointment, a sense of failure, and feelings of being unworthy and useless (McVey-Noble et al., 2006). Cutters are unable to enjoy their achievements and see only their failure to be perfect. They defend themselves by procrastination, deliberate slowness, and by avoiding new experiences and challenges they may not be perfect in completing.

Cutting and Culture

Socially, cutters are ashamed of their behavior and try to hide it from parents and teachers. Peers of cutters may find it hard to relate to the cutter, finding the wounds repulsive and shocking. Peers are likely to help the child hide the problem but are usually uncomfortable with what they see. Cutters have a difficult time with casual friends who may see them as freaks. For that reason, cutters tend to seek each other out and cluster together at school, meet in Internet chat rooms, or tweet each other about their feelings and behaviors in real time. Self-help pages have appeared on the Internet, for example:

www.palace.net/~llama/psych/fself.html

www.essortment.com/articles/self-injury_100006.htm

www.teencutter.com/Self_Injury_Help_Support.html

Biochemistry of Cutting

There is a release of endorphins into the blood when the body senses that it is being cut. This is a natural pain reliever and provides a feeling of well-being. The result is that cutters are reinforced by the biochemistry of their brains (O'Rourke, 2009). The process starts with severe emotional pain that is relieved by physical pain, and a feeling of well-being follows.

Role of Counselors

Cutting is a behavior that the student elects to do. The process is made up of a collection of learned behaviors that reinforce the student by relieving emotional distress and pain. The job of the counselor is to teach a different approach to coping with the compulsion to self-injure when the student feels pain. It is also a task of the counselor to help the student set appropriate goals and create achievable expectations. These tasks are best accomplished by employing cognitive behavioral therapy. Through this therapy, the student can learn more adaptive thinking styles and alternative behaviors when under emotional stress. The therapy should also involve homework between sessions. The student-client should record each wave of feeling of the need to self-injure that he or she feels, when it occurred, and how it was resolved.

Suicide

One tragic thing school counselors learn is that young people will kill themselves. It is never a joke when the topic comes up with a student-client. This is not something a student "throws out to you as humor"; it is an advanced warning of what the student is thinking. There are a series of warnings a counselor can look for when identifying students at risk for self-destruction. These include:

- Being bullied by others and targeted for harassment
- Talking of reunions with dead relatives or peers

- Major stressor like the death of a loved one or a break-up in a serious relationship

- Self-destructive behaviors including drug and alcohol abuse, cutting, and recklessness

- Talking about death and dying

- Making the rounds, saying hello to old friends and liked teachers

- Giving away possessions

- Mental illness at home

- Being overweight and/or having an eating disorder

- Being "outed" as a homosexual

- Having a history of being sexually abused as a younger child

Dimension of the Problem

Each year 8 million Americans think about ending their lives, while only a half-million actually attempt suicide. Of these, 32,000 are successful (National Institute of Mental Health, 2009). Among children in the United States between ages 10 and 14, the reported rate is 13 deaths for every million children. Among adolescents between 15 and 19, the number increases to 82 deaths per million. It is estimated that there are 20 attempts for every successful suicide among young people. It is likely that police and local coroners suppress the numbers of successful suicides in an attempt to protect parents who are grieving over the loss of their child.[15]

Role of the Counselor

If a student discusses suicidal ideation, the counselor has an obligation to do everything possible to keep the student safe from him- or herself. Few children kill themselves at school; rather they do so at home, usually in the quiet of their bedrooms. Not all suicides by youth, however, are quiet and out of the way. In the fall of 2010 a freshman at Rutgers University was cyberbullied by two class-mates who "outed" him for his homosexual encounter in the dormitory. After finding the video of his encounter on the Internet, he complained to his resident assistant (RA) and later that same day leaped to his death off the George Washington Bridge (NJ-NYC) (Schwartz, 2010b).

Any attempted suicide on the school's campus must be treated as a medical emergency, and the student should be transported to an emergency trauma facility. The first priority is to ensure the physical health of the youngster. The second required step is one that parents may resist. The attending physician in the emergency room treating the student normally requires this second step. This step is a referral to the hospital's psychiatric service where he or she will be evaluated by a board-certified child psychiatrist. If the youngster is experiencing an affect disorder, a psychiatrist may be able to prescribe antidepressants or other mood-altering drugs. Depending on state laws, this move to an inpatient psychiatric unit may require the student be placed on a 3-day psychiatric hold at the hospital.

The school counselor should be aware of the possible trauma that a psychiatric placement may cause the child. The brief loss of freedom and being confined with youngsters who are experiencing major psychotic episodes may be unnerving for the student. He or she may feel heightened vigilance and mistrust of adults in the environment after release from the unit.

The counseling process with a student who has suicidal ideation or who has returned to school after recovering from an attempted suicide is the same as is done for students who inflict wounds on themselves (cutters). School-based counseling therapy may require the counselor see the student 2 or 3 times a week. During the 5 years following a suicide attempt, a previous unsuccessful attempt is the best predictor that a child will die by suicide. The goal of counseling these students is to change their way of interpreting and understanding the world and their place in it by substituting a more effective method of thinking and interpreting. Thus, the approach to counseling is one that focuses on changing the thinking of the student and identifying alternative methods to cope with emotional distress. These goals can be accomplished by employing cognitive behavioral therapy (see Chapter 6).

DEATH AND GRIEF ●

For children and adolescents, coping with the death of a loved one or friend represents a cognitive task (Maciejewski, Zhang, Block, & Prigerson, 2007). There is a developmental sequence that children go through that governs the pace of this evolution of understanding.

Emergency Counseling

Schools that experience the loss of a student through illness, in an accident, or by violence should be prepared to provide an emergency grief counseling program for all students. The developmental level of the students is an important consideration in emergency counseling; therefore, counseling models must vary by grade level. Goals for these types of counseling are to dispel rumor and false information, assure students they will be fine at school, and listen to students discuss their feelings and thoughts about what happened.

Schools can provide this emergency service following a tragic loss by using the school's social workers, school psychologists, and counselors from other buildings. The goal is to have one mental health worker in each homeroom and spend an extended period of time in group sessions within each homeroom. Children experiencing inconsolable grief should be provided private one-on-one counseling.

Teachers should be encouraged not to be too quick to remove the dead student's chair and desk from the classroom (Shallcross, 2009c). This removal can happen later when the room is being reorganized for another purpose. If a new student is transferred into the room, the dead student's desk should be removed and an obviously new one assigned to the new student.

In discussions with the class members, counselors can ask for ideas about a fitting memorial (e.g., a tree planted in the school's yard). There is a tendency for children in grief to establish makeshift memorials that may not be easily removed in the emotionally charged environment of a classroom full of grieving children.

Children's Understanding of Death

The cognitive ability to understand death follows a sequence familiar to developmental psychologists (Webb, 2002). By third grade, most children develop the understanding that death is a final and permanent state for living things. This can occur through observation of the natural world, experiencing the death of a relative, or ritual burying of small backyard animals.

Prior to school age, children do not comprehend the lack of reversibility of death and the fact that it is the end for some living organism. Much like a grandparent will disappear on an airliner one day only to reappear at the airport a few months later, a 4-year-old may see death as a temporary place visited by people. During the preschool and kindergarten years, death is simply denied. Much like getting sick, a person gets over being dead.

By first and second grades, death is understood as being a permanent state, but a condition too far away to bother worrying about. Prior to about third grade, death is compartmentalized and seen as something that happens to old and sick people (Webb, 2002).

Middle school–aged children understand the biological nature of loss of life but may need help coping with the emotional needs they feel. One concern is that teens may feel anger and frustration and act out against others, or conversely, turn against their own bodies with self-damaging and/or destructive behavior. Most children (more than 80%) at this age continue to have the belief that they are invulnerable and have little concern with death (Grohol, 2009).

Secondary school students who lose a friend or loved one may find group therapy to be a good source of comfort and support in working through grief. High school–aged adolescents at risk for addictions, or who have symptoms of depression, should be provided personalized grief counseling on a one-to-one basis.

Stages in Grieving

In 1970 Elizabeth Kübler-Ross laid out a qualitative description of the processes involved in grieving. This description also encompassed the phases people with terminal illness experience in coping with their fates. Kübler-Ross's model has been debated in the literature, but her model has been supported by empirical research (Friedman & James, 2008; Maciejewski et al., 2007). The stages overlap and are not all completed by all people. They include:

- *Shock*: The death of a loved one or friend is at first a numbing experience accompanied by a need of the adolescent to deny that it happened.

- *Pain and guilt*: The pain that a young person experiences is excruciating and may be accompanied with remorse and feelings of guilt over things left unsaid or undone with the deceased.

- *Anger*: Adolescents will feel great frustration and related aggression or anger with deep feelings of resentment related to how implacable and yet capricious the loss has been. Others around the adolescent may experience that anger firsthand if they push for early closure for the grieving process.

(Continued)

(Continued)

- *Loneliness and depression*: After 2 or 3 months the adolescent may enter a deep depression with accompanying feelings of longing for the deceased. This is a time when the youngster may want to build a shrine to the lost loved one and/or collect small artifacts of his or her life.

- *Working through*: Around 4 to 6 months following the loss, the adolescent normally begins to overcome the feelings of emptiness and despair. There are fewer periods of deep depression, and the general mood level and quality of affect are improved as the adolescent begins to formulate solutions for going on with life.

- *Acceptance*: Setting goals and moving out and into the mainstream of life marks this final stage. Acceptance is not the same as being a happy-go-lucky teenager again, but the youngster has found a way to cope with the enormity of the loss.

High school students, like their adult counterparts, experience grief over an indefinite period of time. It is not easy to work through the grieving process, but the process follows an understandable course. High school students are able to perform **meta-analytical thinking** and use self-analysis to understand the grieving process (Sanders & Wills, 2005). This makes it possible for the school counselor to employ cognitive therapy to help teenagers who have experienced a significant loss in their lives.

Grieving Children

The need for children to grieve for loved members of their families is evident. Children also grieve over the loss of friends and peers. More than 12,175 children are killed in car crashes and other accidents each year; when added to deaths by illness and other events, the total is 15,600 childhood deaths a year. This implies that a large number of children and adolescents will experience grief and bereavement over a personal loss each year (McNeil, 2008).

The process of grieving is, in part, a learned set of culturally directed practices. As much as from any source, children will take their cues about grieving the loss of a loved one from the adults around them. Grief and loss more intensely felt and expressed by adults will stimulate strong reactions among youngsters. Children of all ages need the love and support of their parents,

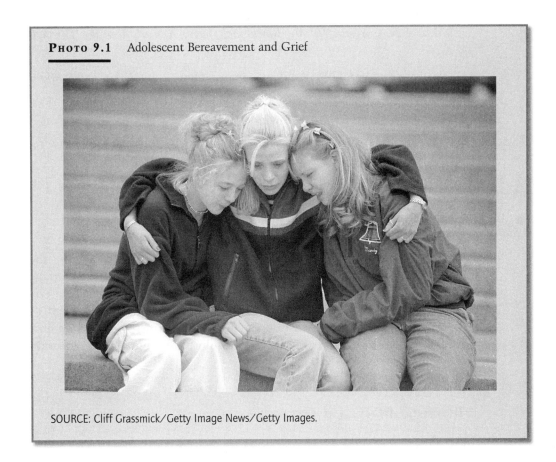

Photo 9.1   Adolescent Bereavement and Grief

SOURCE: Cliff Grassmick/Getty Image News/Getty Images.

school counselors, teachers, and peers to learn to cope with their loss and achieve a resolution of their grief.

Young children may show they are grieving by being emotionally numb, by exhibiting immature (regressive) behaviors, and/or asking questions over and over.[16] Grief may also appear as acting-out behavior in response to the anger, helplessness, or the terror being felt by the child.

Counselor's Role

Counselors can use individual therapy, including storytelling and play therapy, to assist younger children cope with their feelings of loneliness and longing for the lost loved one. Bibliotherapy can be especially effective for this task. The following books are especially helpful:

Michael A. Carestio (2010), *Black Jack Jetty: A Boy's Journey Through Grief*

Marilyn Gootman (2005), *When a Friend Dies: A Book for Teens About Grieving and Healing*

Joyce C. Mills (1993), *Gentle Willow: A Story for Children About Dying*

Michaelene Mundy (1998), *Sad Isn't Bad: A Good-Grief Guidebook for Kids Dealing With Loss*

● INTRUDERS AND SCHOOLS UNDER ATTACK

Terrorism against U.S. schools and students has happened throughout the 20th century, but it peaked in the late 1990s.[17] Terrorism and terroristic attacks involve rampages and broad attacks against many unspecified targets. They are typically focused on soft (easy to hurt) targets such as schools and children. Terrorism does not include targeted attacks against specific teachers, administrators, or the objects of unrequited affection (Langman, 2009).

Terroristic Attacks and Threats

Schools are soft and defenseless targets for anyone armed and looking to cause great suffering. Educators have recently been forced to take steps to improve the level of protection offered to students and educators (harden the schools), but few schools can ever prevent the outside world from endangering the people teaching and attending school. An exception to this general principle is described in the box, "Girard College."

Girard College

In 1831, America's richest man, Stephen Girard, died. His estate including ships, banks, farms, railroads, and coal mines had a combined worth (in 2010 dollars) of more than $100 billion. He was arguably America's richest man ever.[18] His estate was designated to create a residential school for impoverished orphans. Girard's will directed the trustees of the estate to protect children from the vagaries of the city (Philadelphia) and malevolent characters of the urban area by constructing a stone wall 20 feet high around the entire facility. Nicholas Biddle, the first chairman of trustees, sensibly had the masons sink the first 10 feet of the wall below ground. The remaining 10 feet of stone wall still surrounds the 45-acre campus in Philadelphia.

PHOTO 9.2   Girard College, Philadelphia, Pennsylvania

Today the school is home to more than 600 students (K–12); many buildings are on the National Register of Historical Places and include some of the best examples of Greek revival architecture in the country. Living at the school has been described by one of its graduates as growing up in a "stone cocoon" (DiMeo, 2000). There is little doubt that few public or private schools can offer the physical protection for students provided by Stephen Girard.[19]

Thirty-five percent of all American homes have one or more firearms (National Institute of Justice, 1997). The 200 million privately owned guns in the United States represent 31% of the world's total, while the 300 million citizens of the country represent less than 5% of the world's total population. With the huge number of privately owned firearms in the United States, the small number of terrorist attacks against schools is good news.

The easy availability of firearms does contribute to the shooting death of an average of eight children and adolescents each day in the United States. Many of these are suicides and accidental shootings (Shelleby, 2008). In addition, there are another 7,000 children and teenagers who receive nonfatal wounds from firearms each year.

In many parts of the world (Russia, Pakistan, Afghanistan), students and schools are common targets for terrorism. At the time of this writing (2011), the United States has avoided internationally based terrorist attacks against its schools and students. Yet, there have been too many terror attacks performed by deranged adults and angry young people against our schools. The death count for these attacks represents only a small portion of children killed and wounded by guns away from school. The horror of attacks like Columbine High in Colorado (April 20, 1999), where two disturbed teenagers killed themselves, a teacher, 12 other students, and wounded another 23 schoolmates, got vast media coverage and raised the fear level among families and educators alike.[20]

Prevention of Terrorism at School

As in all emergencies, the best approach is to plan for the possibility in advance. Emergency plans should include lines of responsibility during a crisis and prepare for the possibility that the person responsible for a particular task may be off campus or otherwise out of action. The plan should be drawn up by a multifaceted team including school personnel, police, EMT personnel, fire fighters, and a representative from Homeland Security. There is also a need to appoint one person to serve as the school's press contact. Without an official source of information, the media can create community-wide panic as parents hear incomplete and often misleading information.

Hardening a School Against Attacks

Making a school as safe as possible must include background checks for all school employees and contractors. The emergency planning team should survey the school building and make recommendations for hardening the school facility to the district leadership for action. This survey includes alarming garages, shops, laboratories, gymnasiums, cafeterias, auditoriums, libraries, ground-floor windows and doors and installing video cameras throughout the building and grounds. A new generation of digital video surveillance is now available that not only watches and records the actions of others but moves to the next level and analyzes and interprets what is going on (Toppo, 2006).

Lockdown emergency signals should be devised to serve as the school's "all-call" emergency notification system. Every effort should be made to provide high-quality security locks on all classroom doors, and the classroom doors should be hardened to make it difficult for an intruder to forcibly enter a locked room. Another important step in protecting schools and students from intruders involves the use of ID badges and tags for all visitors. When badges are required, faculty should receive inservice education to learn to be alert to strangers seen in the building. A high-level building security plan includes checking every few hours to see that all doors are locked and that there are no suspicious people, packages, or vehicles near the school (Poland & Poland, 2007).

To work, emergency plans must include the requirement that all possible threats are evaluated and follow-up evaluations conducted on a regular basis. Warnings can come from parents, students, and members of the school's greater community. Being vigilant and alert for students at risk for making such attacks and encouraging faculty to share creative writing and art of a violent nature with the school's counselor can provide another line of defense for the school and students (Langman, 2009).

Preventing Attacks

The best way to stop a killing rampage from occurring in a school is by knowing in advance of its possibility. The warning system that can provide counselors and other school personnel with advanced information about an imminent attack must include other students (Hernández & Seem, 2004). Among adolescent shooters there is a tendency to telegraph murderous intentions to peers and others seen as targets for the coming attacks (Viadero, 2009a). This is a signal that the teen is ready to change status within the peer group structure from being a loser to that of being a notorious antihero. As is true with gang membership, these terroristic students have been unable to take steps toward the formation of a positive and productive personal identity and are establishing a negative identity.

Group counseling and counseling classes can provide information students need to know about possible terrorism. Counselors can discuss behaviors and thoughts that are indicators of possible trouble among fellow students. The availability of confidential methods for reporting concerns and observations by students can also provide the needed "heads-up" to prevent a violent attack. School climate, including feelings of pride in a school by its students, contributes to the tendency of students to let counselors know about the potential for attacks on the school and other students (Syvertsen, Flanagan, & Stout, 2009).

Since the year 2000, there has been a downturn in the number of terroristic attacks against U.S. schools. It is possible the devastating rampage at Columbine High School in Colorado and the massacre of 32 young people at Virginia Polytechnic Institute and State University on April 16, 2007, have helped students "get it" and provide information to school authorities about potentially dangerous peers.

School counselors can also work with parent groups to help them understand warning signs that a student is depressed, suicidal, and/or at risk for hurting others. These include a discussion of isolation and loneliness, social withdrawal, and demands for excessive privacy. The importance of keeping privately owned firearms well secured in a way a teenager cannot defeat is something parents need to know.

SUMMARY

The school counselor is in a position to become aware of possible cases of child abuse and neglect. Federal and state legislation has made the reporting of suspected cases of possible abuse and neglect mandatory.

Another major problem for counselors and other educators is addressed in federal legislation under the McKinney-Vento Homeless Assistance Act. This law has set requirements for public schools for meeting educational needs of homeless students.

School achievement has been demonstrated to be tied to regular attendance, while excessive truancy has been shown to be related to delinquent behavior. A second reason that otherwise healthy students may miss an excessive number of days from school is school refusal. This may be the result of fear of bullying at school or may be a symptom of an anxiety disorder. There are methods that counselors can employ to improve school attendance and reduce truancy and school refusal.

The juvenile court system in this country was created at the end of the 19th century to protect children and teenagers from adult justice and punishments. The increase in violence during the 1990s caused many states to make it easier for courts to treat juvenile offenders as adults. Counselors must be prepared to provide testimony in a range of different cases.

One social problem schools are facing is the increase in use of alcohol and abuse of prescription medications by students. An approach to problems of drug and alcohol abuse has led to the adoption of Draconian zero-tolerance rules. Counselors can work proactively to educate parents and modify school policies to protect as many students from the dangers of drugs and alcohol as possible.

School counselors must be ready to treat students who have self-harming needs and to work with students who are self-destructive. These situations are often rooted in depression and/or a borderline personality disorder. Counseling students with suicidal ideation or those who are cutters involves changing the cognitive basis for the behavior and the use of cognitive behavioral therapy.

Each year many children lose family members, loved ones, or friends and peers to death. The ability to understand death is developmental and matures with the growth of the child. By late adolescence the grieving process experienced by young people is similar to that experienced by adults.

A major concern for many parents and educational planners is the possibility of a school invasion with a violent rampage or terroristic attack. Most schools have applied a zero-tolerance policy to bringing weapons of any type onto the campus.

Good planning and a few safety measures can reduce the likelihood a school will be targeted for acts of significant violence. Primary prevention of violent rampages involves working with the whole population of a school and raising awareness of what to watch for among students. It can also include providing methods for alerting the school's counselor and/or administration of the potential issue or concern.

DISCUSSION QUESTIONS

1. Numerous parents use corporal punishment at home every day. Corporal punishment has been described in ancient texts and is all around us.[21] How can a school counselor determine the distinction between parental use of corporal punishment and child abuse? Is there a distinction?

2. A family with two children in the elementary school where you are a counselor was foreclosed out of their home and forced to live in the family's old RV. The single mother asked you for permission to park the van overnight in the faculty parking area behind the school. She wants

the safety of the school and security provided by the regular police patrols provided for the building. She also wants easy access to outside water fountains. What would you recommend to the principal? Explain why you select that course of action. What else would you do for the family?

3. What is a status offense? How should counselors ready themselves for an appearance in family or juvenile court?

4. Do you feel school counselors should attend all funerals of students who die during the school years? Should high school counselors attend funerals of recent graduates killed during the wars in the Middle East or elsewhere? Explain your reasoning.

5. How should a policy regarding students bringing weapons, drugs, or dangerous materials into school be written? If you propose a zero-tolerance policy, how can it be effective but also evenly enforced?

6. What would you respond to a colleague who told you that if he hears the alarm indicating a dangerous intruder is in the school he will lock his office and get as far from the school as he can? What would you do in that circumstance of having a dangerous intruder in the school?

RELATED READINGS

Howell, J. C. (2009). *Preventing and reducing juvenile delinquency: A comprehensive framework* (2nd ed.). Thousand Oaks, CA: Sage.

McVey-Noble, M. E., Khemlani-Patel, S., & Neziroglu, F. (2006). *When your child is cutting: A parent's guide to helping children overcome self-injury.* Oakland, CA: New Harbinger.

Ungar, M. (2006). *Strengths-based counseling with at-risk youth.* Thousand Oaks, CA: Corwin.

NOTES

1. To put this in perspective, every year a middle school counselor with a caseload of 500 children has an even chance that 90 of those children were abused during their early years. In any one year, the number may be higher or lower, but the bottom line is that some students seeing a school counselor will have experienced one or another form of abuse at the hands of their caregivers.

2. A documentary film about the sexual abuse of boys and its aftermath was released in 2010. The film by Terri Debono and Steve Rosen is distributed by landmarkmedia.com. It has a trailer that can be viewed at www.boyhoodshadowsproject.org/boyhood-shadows-2/.

3. On October 1, 1993, then 12-year-old Polly Klaas was kidnapped at knifepoint by Richard Allen Davis during a slumber party at her mother's home. He raped and strangled her to death and buried her body in a shallow grave. He was caught, charged, and convicted of murder in 1996 and sentenced to death. As of the fall of 2010 he was still living on death row in San Quentin Prison in California.

4. States without laws to prevent bullying include Montana, Hawaii, Wisconsin, Massachusetts, North Dakota, and South Dakota. Also not included are schools of Washington, D.C. Following the brutal hazing and the hounding of a 15-year-old girl until she eventually committed suicide in South Hadley, the Massachusetts legislature passed a bill outlawing bullying in 2010.

5. An archaic term for this disorder among children is *didaskaleinophobia*, while another name once used for it is *school phobia*.

6. University of Chicago economist Steven Levitt conducted an analysis of this drop in the murder rate. He found the principal cause was the decision of the U.S. Supreme Court in 1973 to stop states from preventing women from terminating unwanted pregnancies. The decision, known as *Roe v. Wade* (1973), reduced the number of unwanted children, and Levitt's mathematical model demonstrated it was this population of unwanted children that caused the large number of juvenile murders (Levitt & Dubner, 2005).

7. This is a bit misleading, as African American students make up 16% of the student population and Caucasian-White students represent 55% of the student population.

8. The most typical victim is a randomly selected girl (3 females out of 4 victims) about age 11.

9. See report at www.usdoj.gov/ndic/pubs27/27612/estimate.htm.

10. There are gangs with national affiliations and membership in the thousands. These mega-gangs are often engaged in nationwide criminal activities such as the production, distribution, and sale of methamphetamine.

11. States that have yet to ratify the 21st Amendment to the Constitution, making it legal for adults to drink and sell alcoholic beverages, include Nebraska, Kansas, Mississippi, Oklahoma, Louisiana, North Dakota, South Dakota, and Georgia.

12. The era also gave rise to a number of high-profile law enforcement agents, including Melvin Purvis and Eliot Ness (Purvis, 2005; Ness & Fraley, 1957).

13. Field tests of sobriety are available at www.fieldsobrietytests.org/ or www .1800duilaws.com/common/field_sobtests.asp.

14. There are easily available home drug-testing kits available for parents to buy and keep at home. The purveyor of one of these suggests that parents show it to children and explain that it will be employed randomly. The idea is to make the children of the family afraid to use drugs for fear of being caught by "my dad the narc." To learn more see www.notmykid.org/resources/drug-test-info.aspx. This is not a good way to develop a relationship of mutual trust with a child.

15. In many parts of the nation there are no board-certified forensic pathologists; local funeral directors serve as the coroner and sign certificates of death.

16. The questions that young children ask most frequently relate to themselves and their world. They want to know if "anyone else is going to die." They want to know, "Why did grandmother die?" They may want to know, "Who will care for Nana's cat?"

17. In 1927 a Michigan farmer, Andrew Kehoe, carried out the first major terroristic attack against a school and its students. He had just lost his farm to foreclosure and blamed the newly constructed school for causing the tax rate increase that put him

under. He first murdered his wife, then set his farm on fire, then drove to the school and used dynamite to commit suicide and kill 38 students, the school superintendent, the town's postmaster, two teachers, and a local farmer. Another 58 people, mostly children, were wounded in the blast (Leinwand, 2001). To read about this go to www.users.on.net/~bundy23/wwom/kehoe.htm.

18. At the time of his death in 1831, Stephen Girard's fortune was larger than any American's fortune in 2010. Girard's wealth was even more than the combined wealth of Bill Gates and Warren Buffett in 2010.

19. The school, Girard College, is located in the Fairmont section of Philadelphia. The Girard College Museum in the historic Founder's Hall houses America's best collection of American-made furniture, silver, textiles, ceramics, and paintings from the federalist and early republic years: www.girardcollege.com/4398_9771410572/site/default.asp.

20. Some school systems have taken a proactive position against terror attacks. The following web page describes the steps taken by the schools of Orange County, California: www.ocps.net/op/sse/PublishingImages/Terrorism%20Guide%20OCPS.pdf.

21. Proverbs 19:18, 22:15, 23:13, 29:18.

10

School Testing Programs and the School Counselor

OBJECTIVES

By reading and studying this chapter you should acquire the competency to:

- Explain the concepts of standardized tests and standards-based testing
- Evaluate the quality of published tests and measurements used in schools
- Interpret statistical symbols for test and measurement data
- Understand the relationship of reliability to standard error
- Evaluate a test for validity and its normative group
- Describe several potential causes for the "score gap"
- Assist in the testing of students with special needs
- Establish the appropriate conditions for assessing students who are English-language learners
- Contrast the basic models of testing used by ETS with the SAT II and the ACT

● ● ●

❝ USA Today has come out with a new survey. Apparently, three out of four people make up 75% of the population. **❞**

David Letterman

● INTRODUCTION AND THEMES

The national framework for school counseling programs (American School Counselor Association [ASCA]/Hatch & Bowers, 2005) proposes that all quality school counseling is data driven and is carried out based on an appropriate analysis of data. This skill area requires that school counselors are well educated in the statistics of tests, measurement theory, and also in the evaluation and interpretation of test data.

The professional association for school counselors argues that the role of being a school's director of testing is not congruent with the job of being a school counselor (ASCA/Hatch & Bowers, 2005). Yet, it also argues that the school counselor should be the person to interpret the meaning of test scores and provide a data-driven counseling program. This incongruence is one that needs to be resolved in the future.

Beyond these professional concerns, school administrators expect that school counselors can assume the role of director of the school's testing programs and interpret test data to others (Dollarhide & Lemberger, 2006). Other things being equal, a school principal is more likely to recommend the hiring of a school counselor who has a strong knowledge base in testing and measurement (Wright & Lesisko, 2011).

School counselors have huge amounts of data at their disposal; the problem is to understand how to analyze and interpret those data.[1] The first step in the process is knowing which data provide valuable information and which are trivial.

School counselors should understand how to evaluate the quality of the tests and measurements they use. This requires an understanding of measurement concepts, including reliability, standard error, and validity. Additionally, counselors should be able to assess the appropriateness of the normative group used by published standardized tests to establish individual scores. Likewise, the school counselor should understand the concept of standards-based measurement and the establishment of cut scores for levels of proficiency.

Minority and impoverished students tend to score below their middle-class Anglo-White and Asian American peers. The reasons for this disparity are deeply rooted in U.S. society and require the efforts of both parents and school policymakers to end (Wright, 2011).

Counselors have an important role to play in testing and charting the progress of students with special educational needs. There are also thorny problems to resolve when administering high-stakes assessments with language-minority students.

Two of the most angst provoking of all tests that school counselors administer are related to college admission. The two major assessments differ in their philosophies of measurement and also their normative basis.

DATA-BASED COUNSELING DECISIONS ●

The job description established by most school boards for school counselors makes professional school counselors de facto directors of testing for their schools. The security and integrity of the testing program is the counselor's responsibility. Understanding how to gauge the quality of tests and measurements is part of being the school's resident measurement specialist. Ensuring tests are used ethically also becomes the province of the school counselor. (See Case in Point 10.1 for a discussion of the test-induced stress experienced by educators.)

CASE IN POINT 10.1

The No Child Left Behind Act has resulted in school administrators being concerned about their job security and students worried about being promoted to the next grade or earning their high school diplomas. Whole communities can experience a loss of home value when students in a local school do not score well on the mandated tests.

One major problem with statewide high-stakes testing mandates is the sanctions that can be brought to bear against schools. These punishments kick in when there is a high number of low-scoring students, resulting in an excessive amount of stress on educators.

A sad result of the stress experienced by otherwise ethical educators has been a program of educational triage. This occurs when students score low on standardized tests. Some school leaders feel they must focus their limited helping resources on students who are close to passing scores on the assessment. These students have been described as being "on the bubble" for being proficient. The ugly fact is that **bubble youngsters** get intensive help, while the lowest-scoring students at the bottom of the distribution are ignored. Students judged to be beyond the school's ability to help are provided with the educational equivalent of a palliative level of support. In other words, by as early as second grade, students are divided into three groups: those who are safe on the mandated tests; those who can be helped with extra effort; and those who are beyond the resources of the school to ever help (Booher-Jennings, 2005).

(Continued)

(Continued)

Thought Questions. Should the model described be stood on its head? That is, should schools with limited resources lavish available helping resources on the lowest-performing students and make only token efforts to assist "bubble students"? What role, if any, could a school counselor play in helping low-performing students reach the level of achievement proficiency?

School Counselors and Test Data

The array of data available to school counselors includes standardized large-scale tests of subject area achievement, state-mandated high-stakes tests, and tests for college admission. It also includes demographic data including gender, ethnicity, and primary language. Beyond that, it includes teacher observations, sophisticated psychometric assessments for the development of individualized education plans (IEPs), and the response to intervention data from monitoring students who have had a 504 committee evaluation.

The school nurse also has information on the physical and medical history of each student. Report card grades and classroom tests and measures are available for counselors to consider when designing a counseling approach for a student. Making sense of all of these forms of data and being ready to explain them to both faculty and parents is the job of the school counselor. To help counselors accomplish this, most graduate programs in school counseling include a class or two in educational statistics and measurements.

● JUDGING THE QUALITY OF TESTS AND MEASURES

A primary skill for all school counselors is to evaluate the quality of any published test by reading its test manual and accessing independent test reviews. There are hundreds of published tests for use in schools, and many of them are rubbish. Other published tests may be well designed but are still inappropriate for a particular school to use.

The first step in selecting the optimal published test for a school's use involves identifying the goals for testing. It is an axiom of measurement that the test must match the purpose and goals defined by the educators of the school. Once measurement goals have been delineated, it is then appropriate to review all possible measures that meet the identified goals for testing.

Information Sources

The largest collection of tests is the one maintained by the Educational Testing Service (ETS). That collection extends back over 100 years and includes more than 25,000 published tests. Online test descriptions can be reviewed on the ETS web page: http://ericae.net/testcol.htm#ETSTF. Independent reviews and evaluations of tests are also available from the Buros Institute of Mental Measurements on the campus of the University of Nebraska, Lincoln. A total of more than 3,500 tests are described and reviewed in this collection. Test reviewers for the Buros Institute are independent measurement specialists who are not paid for their services. These reviews and descriptions can be found on the Buros web page: http://buros.unl.edu/buros/jsp/search.jsp. In 2010, the fee for this service was $15.00 per test review. The same reviews are available online through the databases of many university library systems.

Statistical Quality Indicators

Whenever a student is evaluated, there are two unconditional requirements for the process. First, the measurement must be consistent and highly stable. This implies that similar measurement outcomes will result again when the student is reevaluated. This property is known as **reliability**.

The second required characteristic is **validity**. Valid measurements must be reliable and meet three other requirements. First, valid measurements are focused on what they are purported to assess and exhibit fidelity to the goals for the measurement. Second, they align with other measures of the student. Finally, they are developmentally appropriate, properly employed, and correctly interpreted. The first two validity issues relate to how the measurement is designed and standardized. The third factor relates to the education, ethics, and ability of the person giving the test.

Reliability

A measurement that is not reliable produces random results. Perfect reliability results in the same value or score for the student each time the measurement is administered. Thus, highly reliable scores or assessment results are stable and consistent. However, the only measures of students approaching perfect reliability are of physical characteristics: for example, height. This reflects the high degree of accuracy physical measurement tools can achieve. Other measurements may not show as much consistency when the student is retested. This type of measurement can include assessments of creativity and dimensions of the student's personality.

Reliability is reduced when a test is either too hard or too easy. Low reliability also occurs when students are distracted (e.g., a snow storm outside) or when the test's directions are not followed carefully and completely. Finally, tests administered to students who are ill or tired will also provide unreliable results.

A number of different statistical symbols are used to show the reliability of a measure (see Table 10.1). One key to understanding these reliability statistics is that any value below +0.40 is low and above +0.80 high.

No test score or any other measurement is perfectly reliable (Haertel, 2006). There is always some difference between what a perfectly accurate measurement would yield and the score we obtain from a test or some form of measurement. This small difference can place the student's **true score** above or below what was shown by a test's score. The true score is what the student knows or can do as measured in a perfect world with perfect instruments. The statistical measurement of the difference between what is obtained by an individual on a test and what his or her true score would be is called **measurement**

CARTOON 10.1   **Challenge to Test Reliability**

"These scores can't be very reliable."

SOURCE: Merv Magus.

TABLE 10.1   Reliability Coefficients and Related Statistics

Pearson Coefficient **r**   Minimum is zero, and the maximum is ±1.00; can be employed as a measure of reliability measuring stability and stability over time (**test-retest reliability**)

Spearman Coefficient ρ Greek letter *Rho*, maximum ±1.00, minimum of zero; can be employed as a measure of reliability measuring stability

Cronbach α Coefficient alpha; measure of internal consistency has a minimum of zero and maximum of +1.00

Kuder-Richardson (**K-R20**)   This measure of internal consistency has a minimum of zero and maximum of +1.00

Coefficient Kappa   Reliability measure for criterion-type measures with a minimum of zero and maximum of +1.00

Split Half Reliability $r_{\frac{1}{2}}$ Maximum ±1.00, minimum of zero; can be employed as a measure of reliability measuring stability

Spearman-Brown $r_{S\text{-}B}$ Measure of internal consistency has a minimum of zero and maximum of +1.00

Standard error of measurement   A measure of how far true score potential spreads around an obtained score; inversely linked tests of reliability

error. Publishers report a statistic called the **standard error of measurement (SEM)** in their publications. This is a statistical estimation of the average amount of *error of measurement* to be expected among a set of test scores.

Reliability Coefficients

A *reliability coefficient* can be defined as the square root of the proportion of true score differences in a set of test scores. Thus a reliability of 0.30, when squared (0.30 × 0.30), results in a value of 0.09. That value can then be changed into a percentage (0.09 × 100) that equals 9%. This value tells the counselor that only 9% of the variation among a measure's outcome scores is made of true score differences. Likewise, this tells the counselor that 91% of the variation among that test's scores is based on "measurement error." The case of a test with a reliability of 0.87 is one that has much less measurement error. The proportion of measurement error related to variations in the true scores from a test with a reliability of 0.87 is found as (0.87 × 0.87) multiplied by 100 equals 76%. That value of 76% informs the counselor that more than three-quarters of the score variations on the test are composed of true score differences. It also tells him or her that measurement error accounts for less than a quarter of the variation in outcomes.

Measurement Error

While reliability coefficients provide a good method for selecting the most stable and consistent measures, another statistic, the standard error of measurement, provides a handy guide to the meaning or value of any student's score. This published value informs the school counselor of the likelihood that any score on a measure is close to that individual's true score. Its value provides a range of possibilities. An SEM of 3 indicates that there is a 68% chance that the true score for the student is within plus or minus 3 points of what the student scored. To be more certain, if the counselor doubles the SEM to 6, the counselor can be 95% confident the true score is in the range of plus or minus 6 points (two SEM units) of what was actually scored.

As an example, the SEM for the American College Testing Program (ACT) composite score for high school seniors is 0.90 (American College Testing Program [ACT], 1997) and the composite mean (average) is 20.7. If a student achieves a composite ACT score of 23, the counselor knows, with 95% confidence, the student's true score lies between 21.2 (23 − [2 × 0.90]) and 24.8 (23 + [2 × 0.90]).

In a similar way, a graduate student in a counselor education program completed the Praxis I test required by her state education department. She earned a score of 650 the first time she took it. The national mean (average) on this test is 660, and the SEM is 25. Being knowledgeable of measurement statistics, she knows there is a 68% likelihood her true Praxis I score lies between 625 and 675. Likewise, she knows that there is a 95% chance her true Praxis I score lies between 600 and 700.

The possibility of measurement affecting any test score is evenly balanced above and below any obtained score. Thus, any score may be either inflated or suppressed by measurement error. There is also a possibility that the obtained score is on the money and is an accurate representation of the student's true score.

Validity

It is necessary for any measurement to provide consistent outcomes (i.e., be reliable) before validity is possible. One concern with the validity of a measure is that it actually measures what its users intend. Frequently there are dimensions a measurement may inadvertently be assessing instead of those targeted by the test's author. Extraneous dimensions on a test of reading may involve the student's ability to interpret teacher-read directions or the ability to use a soft lead pencil to grid-in the answer sheet. Reading ability may be the dimension that is actually central to the measurement of social studies on a test requiring students read and interpret historical or political information.

The establishment of a measure's validity can involve content and **construct validity** (Kane, 2006). **Content validity** matches a measurement's individual questions (items) with the curriculum content that is central to the goals for the measurement. Construct validity is established by demonstrating the measure provides an accurate picture of the **construct** being assessed. Constructs such as aggression, infant temperament, anxiety levels, shyness, and creativity are among the areas that can be measured by assessments. The key to construct validity is having a clear definition of exactly what is being measured and statistical proof that the test measures just that one issue and not some extraneous variables. For example, a test designed to measure Daniel Goleman's concept of **emotional intelligence (EQ)** can easily become something else, a measure of empathy (Goleman, 2004). Empathy is related to Goleman's construct, but EQ and empathy are not the same thing. To make a judgment about an EQ measure's construct validity requires the evaluator be well steeped in the theory of EQ and knowledgeable about related constructs like empathy.

All measures must also be developmentally appropriate for the student being assessed. This quality of a measure is known as **developmental validity**. To evaluate this quality, a school counselor should be familiar with the developmental status and capabilities of students who will be measured with the test. Issues such as reading skill level, neuromuscular capabilities, and emotional strength must be considered. Likewise, measures should be culturally appropriate for students being assessed. When a test is appropriate for one population of students, it may be invalid when used to measure another.[2]

Normative Groups and Test Scores

Published measures often rely on a comparison group known as the **normative group** or, more simply, **norm group**. Statistical data collected from norm groups are used to describe how any individual does compared to its members. These comparison scores may take several forms, such as percentiles, standard scores, stanines, and normal curve equivalent (NCE) scores (see Table 10.2). In addition to scores based on comparisons to a norm, scores may be reported as a simple total correct, a score known as a "raw score."

When a publisher markets a new assessment it should provide a **technical manual** describing the norm group used to provide the point of comparison for interpreting each student's outcome. The norm group should be a good representation of all students in North America today. Also, it should be large enough that when divided into subgroups by age for comparison the smaller groups still provide a representative sample of students making up the norm by age group. These norm groups should reflect all races, both genders, the various economic levels of families, and different geographic regions.

TABLE 10.2 Commonly Reported Scores

Raw Score The total number of actual items on the measure that the student answered correctly. To better understand what a raw score indicates, the test report should indicate a statement of how many questions there were in total.

Percentile A part out of 100 of equal size. A 100th part of any group or set of data or objects. If raw scores are used, they must first be arranged in an ordinal sequence from lowest (worst) to the highest (best). A percentile includes one one-hundredth of all cases. The first percentile includes the lowest one-hundredth part of the scores while the 99th percentile consists of the best one-hundredth part of the raw scores from the test.

Another method of finding a test score's percentile is by comparing that score to the scores of the norm group. This method uses the norm group to set the standard of comparison for students who take the test. If a student's score is at the center point of the norm group, it would be the 50th percentile, half of the norm group's scores above and half below. That 50th percentile also has the name **median**. If a student did better than three-quarters of the students of the norm group, his or her score would equal to the 75th percentile.

Standard Scores or Scaled Scores There are numerous formats for standard scores (SS), sometimes referred to as *scaled scores*. They all are derived mathematically from a huge normative distribution of scores. Under normal conditions, a huge distribution of test scores will follow clear mathematical laws. We know that 34% of all scores will be above and 34% below the **mean score** (arithmetic average score) by a unit of measurement called a **standard deviation**. Plus or minus one standard deviation includes the 68% of all scores closest to the mean (average).

A standard score is based on standard deviation units above (positive values) and below (negative values) the mean. To make interpretation and comparisons easier, these scores are mathematically modified to make them all positive and give them recognizable values. One commonly employed standard score is used to describe a student's IQ. Instead of values above and below the mean, IQ scores are mathematically designed to have a mean of 100. Each standard deviation is set at a value of 15. Thus an IQ of 115 is one standard deviation over the mean of 100, and an IQ of 85 is one standard deviation below the mean of 100. Because 34% of all IQ scores are between the mean (IQ = 100) and one standard deviation over the mean (IQ = 115), and the average is also the median (50th percentile), adding the two shows that an IQ of 115 is near the 85th percentile (50 + 34).

College and graduate school admission tests are also standardized scores. The SAT II is composed of three measures, each with a mean (average) of about 500 and a standard deviation of 100. Thus, half of all students score below 500 and half above. Also, an SAT II score in one area of 600 (a standard deviation over the mean) is at the 84th percentile, while a score of 400 (one standard deviation below the mean) is at the 16th percentile. The ACT has a mean of about 21 and a standard deviation of 5. Thus, the 50th percentile on the ACT is a composite score of 21. Likewise an ACT score of 11 (2 standard deviations below the mean) is in the 2nd percentile. An ACT score of 18.5 (a half standard deviation below the mean) is at the 31st percentile; and a score of 23.5 (one and a half standard deviations above the mean) is at the 93rd percentile.

Stanine   The norm group can be divided into nine parts, with the middle seven parts (stanine 2 to 8) each being one-half of a standard deviation wide. Because of the characteristic bell-shaped form of a normal distribution of scores, the central three stanines, 4,5,6, encompass 55% of all cases. Stanines 1,2,3 include the lowest 22.5% of all scores and the top 22.5% of all scores are in stanines 7,8,9. The top stanine, number 9, includes the highest 4% of scores, while the lowest stanine, number 1, includes the lowest 4% of scores.

Normal Curve Equivalent, NCE   This is a standard score that has a mean of 50. One standard deviation above the mean (84th percentile) is an NCE score of 71. An NCE score of 29 is one standard deviation below the mean, and an NCE score of 10 is the third percentile of the normative distribution of scores.

Grade Equivalent Scores   These are the most misunderstood of all scores. Most educators, without a knowledge of measurement statistics, mistakenly think that a grade equivalent score shows the grade level of work a student can do. It is true that this score should be read as a grade level expressed in years of 10-months' length. Therefore, a grade equivalent score of 4.5 indicates the fourth grade, fifth month. However most educators, and virtually all parents, mistakenly think that children who are enrolled in the fifth grade and are tested and reported to have a grade equivalent score on a reading test of 9.1 can read ninth grade books. This is absolutely wrong. What those data indicate is that the child in fifth grade did as well on the fifth grade reading test as would the average child in the ninth grade *if that ninth grader took the fifth grade test*. If the well meaning, but misinformed, fifth grade teacher assigned ninth grade material to that good little reader, the child would have great difficulty and would likely be totally lost.

Another evaluation consideration for a test is the era of the cohort of students included in the comparison sample (Kolen, 2006). Many measures base students' scores on old normative (comparison) groups. This happens when the test is not revised for 10 or 20 years. Norm group standardizations usually occur starting a year or two before the publication of new editions of the measure. Students of this day and age are very different from students of the 1980s and 1990s. Score comparisons with an old cohort are less valid than comparisons to a contemporary sample of students.

Standards-Based Assessments

State-mandated assessments employ a standards-based system for scoring and reporting student success. The process begins with a state education department establishing specific standards for what students will learn at each grade level in each subject content area. President Obama's "Race to the Top" (R2T) program in 2010–2011 provided rewards to state education departments that adopted new and more challenging educational standards devised by the U.S. Department of Education and 48 of the states. Of these, 44 states and the District of Columbia approved and adopted the new educational standards. Once new standards are in place, private educational test contractors are hired to construct tests of the learning specifications listed in the standards.

Proficiency Levels. On high-stakes tests, the **criterion-referenced** outcome for each student is reported in terms of his or her proficiency level. Proficiency levels are ordinal scores providing a qualitative general description of the student's educational attainment on the standard. Ordinal labels, such as **below proficient,**[3] proficient, and **highly proficient,** are what the student and his or her teacher see. To report these scores, the test development process involves determining a set of cut scores. Most state education departments create special committees called **Angoff committees** to decide upon cut scores (Buckendahl, Smith, Impara, & Plake, 2002).[4] Most states provide two scores for each student, a normative (percentile) score based on comparisons to others who take the state test, and criterion-referenced (proficiency) **scores** based on the established expectation set by the state. An unfortunate truth is that these cut scores are frequently manipulated to meet the political needs of policymakers in the states ("Report," 2009; Wright, 2009). This politically induced flexibility in statewide mandated tests has been described as "measuring with rubber rulers" (Jehlen, 2007; National Assessment of Educational Progress [NAEP], 2009).

In the politicized education environment of the new century, educators can no longer abstain from and hope that large-scale testing will go away. Popham (1999) observed that the rules for educators all changed when newspapers began to report test data and even rank schools based on the achievement outcome of students. Today, even the value of suburban homes is dependent in part on the ranking of a community's schools.

● SCORE GAP

Beginning with the first published standardized achievement test in 1923, America has been enamored with the idea of "scientifically" measuring what students have learned (Wright, 2008). In 2002 this movement for universal achievement testing reached its apogee with the passage of the No Child Left Behind (NCLB) Act, which mandated testing of all public school students in grades 3 through 8 and once in high school.

The losers in this era of high-stakes achievement tests are students of ethnic and language minorities and students from families of lower socioeconomic status (SES) (Matus, 2007). Starting with the first standardized tests, there has always been a clear gap between average test scores of students of different racial and ethnic heritages. Prior to the 1960s these group differences were not the focus of much interest. A pseudoscientific theory known as eugenics[5] taught that there was a genetic explanation for group differences, and there was nothing we could do to change a core-inherited trait such as the ability of a student to learn in school (Wright, 2011). That ability was believed at that time to be determined by the student's genetic inheritance of learning ability. Likewise the differences between achievement levels of students from different socioeconomic levels were explained by the migration of individuals with intellectual capital into well-paid jobs. This group tended to also be Anglo-White, thereby reinforcing group differences between SES levels and ethnic groups (Herrnstein & Murray, 1994). (See Figures 10.1 and 10.2 for examples of the "score gap.")

Schools with the lowest average scores on high-stakes tests are the schools enrolling the largest number of students from impoverished backgrounds. These schools also have teachers with less experience and who are not as well educated as their colleagues working in suburban schools (NAEP, 2009).[6] Many times these schools located in communities that are rural and urban centers of poverty have few learning resources to help teachers do their jobs effectively (see Case in Point 10.2).

CASE IN POINT 10.2

Teachers in many schools are expected to supply their own classrooms from their household budgets. This has led to the unseemly sight of teachers accepting handouts from community members in order to have enough money to put chalk on the board and paper in the hands of students. It is not surprising that this seems to occur more frequently in schools that have the largest number of students from impoverished homes. Also not surprisingly, these same schools tend to have consistently lower mean scores on high-stakes tests.

I have personally seen one local school system AstroTurf the football field the same year that it slashed the instructional support budget and removed almost all teaching materials from classrooms (Fisher, 2008). There are a number of online charities that help teachers stock their classrooms by matching donors with teachers: www.donorschoose.org.

Thought Question. During the fall term of a new counselor's first year, the school's principal will request that the counselor provide a budget for the coming year's counseling program. This is a real surprise for many first-time school counselors who must scramble to produce a workable budget. Assume you are a school counselor working alone in a small elementary school; you have one office assistant who works with you for 10 months a year. Outline all the things (expenses) you think you will need to operate a professional school counseling program for a year.

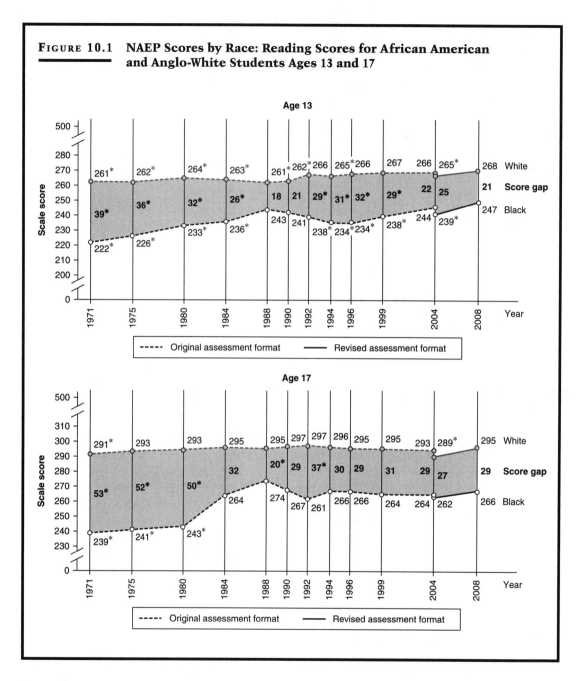

FIGURE 10.1 NAEP Scores by Race: Reading Scores for African American and Anglo-White Students Ages 13 and 17

SOURCE: http://nces.ed.gov/nationsreportcard/pdf/main2008/2009479.pdf.

FIGURE 10.2   **NAEP Scores by Race: Reading Scores of Hispanic and Anglo-White Students Ages 13 and 17**

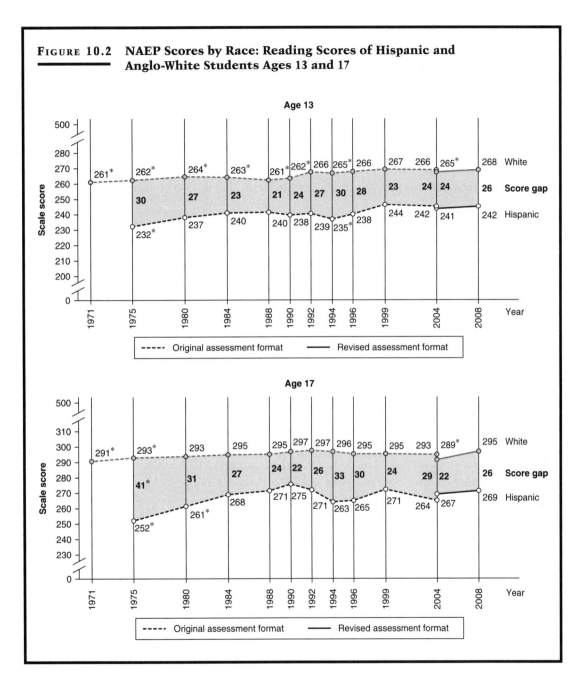

SOURCE: http://nces.ed.gov/nationsreportcard/pdf/main2008/2009479.pdf.

The first challenge to the widely believed pseudoscientific genetic explanation for group differences in levels of ability and achievement was the product of research required by the Civil Rights Act of 1964 (P.L. 88–352, § 78, Stat. 241, July 2, 1964). The great disparity between African American students and their nonminority peers on standardized measures, including achievement tests, was made obvious through the work of sociologist James Coleman. His research focused attention on the apparent failure of public schools located in the inner cities to provide effective educations for minority students living in poverty (Coleman, 1972). In addition to schools, there is also clear evidence that parenting counts and is a critical part in the academic development of children.

Family Factors

The foremost factor inhibiting academic success and good test scores for some groups of students is related to their lives at home. Recent research has shown that reading ability in middle school is significantly correlated with the amount of poverty in the community where a student lived when enrolled in first grade. This early poverty impact is one that is also present if the family subsequently moved to a better neighborhood. The poverty impact may be related to the quality of teachers or indicate a more complex sociological factor in learning (University of British Columbia, 2010).

Factors of the home that are highly correlated with school success include parents who hold high academic expectations for their children and who enforce rules regarding homework and studying at home. Typically, parents of high-achieving children are engaged in their children's school and participate in most activities sponsored by the school. These parents of high achievers work to ensure their children have excellent attendance records and participate in co-curricular activities (NAEP, 2004).

President Barack Obama called on all parents to provide academic home resources and parental encouragement for doing well in school during a speech to the NAACP in 2009 (Stolberg, 2009). He admonished some parents for being too lax and encouraged all parents to hold high expectations and require serious effort from their children. This goal of having parents take charge and accept no excuses is central to President Obama's policy and is also a key to activities a school counselor can organize to improve high-stakes test scores for all students.

School Factors

A second factor related to differences in average scores from students of various racial/ethnic groups involves American educational policy. Teachers working in schools attended by populations of students who are primarily racial minorities have less experience and are less well educated in their subjects than are teachers working in schools where most students are Anglo-White and from the middle class (Barton & Coley, 2009; Slater, 2006). Research has shown that female elementary teachers who are anxious about their own mathematics skills can pass their fears on to their students, an effect most strongly felt by the girls they teach (Kaplan, 2010). These teachers with a fear of mathematics tend to be less experienced and poorly educated in mathematics.

Within schools, African American students have been counseled into fewer advanced placement classes, and as a group enrolled in fewer advanced mathematics and science classes than their Anglo-White and Asian American peers (Ogbu, 2003). In a study of African American students from affluent homes attending suburban schools, John Ogbu concluded that as a group minority students are conflicted about peer values and expectations and are often less motivated for academic achievement than their Anglo-White and Asian American classmates. This struggle to develop an identity that includes a racial/ethnic component and is positive and academically oriented is detailed in President Barack Obama's autobiographical book, *Dreams From My Father: A Story of Race and Inheritance* (2004). High school counselors, as part of their bibliotherapy programs, can employ this book or parts of it with students struggling to resolve their ethnic and academic identities.

Psychology of Test Success and Failure

The score gap on tests has been examined by a number of authors, including Claude Steele, who presented evidence that there are extraneous factors in scores of African American and Latino/a young people. A major source of this interfering variance is produced by **stereotype threat** created by the test situation (Steele, 1997, 1999). Steele demonstrated that stereotype threat occurs when minority students are placed in a high-stakes test situation. He has shown that in those situations minority students feel the added stress of the stereotypical expectations held for them. The extra pressure caused by the fear of proving the stereotype correct correlates with lower performance.

Another problematic area is related to the linguistic aspects of the test items (Freedle & Kostin, 1997). Roy Freedle (2002) has identified differences in word utilization patterns between Anglo-White and African American adolescents. This has the potential of producing differential test item performance (Dorans & Zeller, 2004).

Another unexpected and unexplained finding is that African American high-stakes test takers perform better on the hardest test items and less well on the easiest items. This is opposite of what occurs with a population of middle-class Anglo-White students. If the harder items were to be given extra weight on the test, the score gap would be reduced by a third. Also, Freedle points out that the correction for guessing that most large-scale testing programs apply to all scores disproportionately lowers the scores of minority students, who make more errors on the easier items of the test. Freedle is also concerned with the disproportionate impact of employing a "correction for guessing" in the system of scoring. All males and African Americans tend to do more guessing on these tests than is true of other groups of students. The goal of the developers of high-stakes tests in using these "corrections to scores" is to prevent random guessing. The following formula is used by publishers of tests made with multiple-choice items, each with four answer choices. (Case in Point 10.3 explores the causes of low test validity for an individual.)

$$Total\ corrected\ raw\ score\ =\ Total\ correct\ -\ \frac{Total\ wrong}{4}$$

This presents another area where school counselors can have an impact. Schools counselors can offer group sessions focused on the topic of test-taking skills.

CASE IN POINT 10.3

A public school system in suburban New Jersey recently employed a nationally known test preparation company to use its two high schools on a series of Saturdays to offer an SAT II preparation class for a reduced price. Teenage students of the school who received a free or reduced-cost lunch had their tuition paid by a charitable foundation established by the school board. The results were positive, and the percentage of students going on to college after graduation improved.

Thought Question. Reflect on the standardized test scores you have earned over your academic career. Are your scores a good reflection of what you know and can do? If you believe the scores were too high or too low, explain what elements of your life, or of the test, caused those errors.

Gender Differences

Beginning in the 1970s and continuing through to the current decade there have been questions about the gender equity of public schools.

Laws on Gender Equity

Patent discrepancies with equipment and facilities for male athletes over those provided for female athletes came to an end in 1972 when President Richard Nixon signed into law the 1972 Education Amendment (Title IX of the Education Amendments of 1972, 20 U.S.C. § 1681 et seq.). This legislation required all gender discrimination and inequality to end and ensured that all schools and colleges provided girls and young women with the same levels of support and opportunities granted to boys and young men. One outcome of this has been expanded athletic programs and resources for girls in public schools. Another outcome has been the increase in the number of college scholarships provided to women and even the quality of transportation and accommodations afforded to women athletes for "away games" in higher education.[7]

The law was watered down in 2002 by the U.S. Education Department under Secretary Margaret Spellings. She let schools survey the interest level in sports by males and females and than set budget support funds based on the survey outcome (Lopiano, 2006). Education Secretary Arne Duncan reversed this approach in 2010, and the original meaning of the Title IX law returned to the practice of gender equity in sports and other areas of public education (Jones, 2010).

A persistent problem school administrators must address in meeting the reinstated mandates of Title IX is that as a group, boys are more eager than girls to participate in team sports (Humphrey, 2003). The expansion and diversity of scholastic intermural and personal sports and training options can assist in providing an equitable distribution of athletic opportunities. Athletic interest levels are highest among students who have parents who encourage participation in team sports, and also where schools provide encouragement and support for girl athletes (Cooky, 2009).

Role of School Counselors. Counselors can collect data and organize recommendations for the school's leadership, including the athletics director. These data can be used to respond to the evaluation mandate of both Title IX and the Women's Education Equity Act of 1974 (WEEA). (This type of counselor-initiated action research is described in Chapter 14.) Also the school counselor can provide information about the advantage of scholastic athletics to parents and students.

The Women's Education Equity Act ensured that all academic components of schools provided equal opportunity for both boys and girls. It was written to promote educational equity for girls and women, including those who suffer multiple discrimination based on gender, race, ethnicity, national origin, disability, and age; and to provide funds to help education agencies and institutions meet the requirements of Title IX of the Education Amendments of 1972.

One change facilitated under WEEA was a revision in the Preliminary Scholastic Aptitude Test (PSAT) used to select National Merit Scholarship semifinalists (students with highest scores on the PSAT). The problem with the original test was that boys tended to have much more score variability and a larger standard deviation on the PSAT than did girls. This larger standard deviation occurred because there were more extremely high and extremely low scores among the boys. When ETS scored the PSEA and identified each year's National Merit Scholar semifinalists, boys had a disproportionately large number of top scores. The fact that boys also had many more very low scores did not enter into the awarding of National Merit Scholarship semifinalist honors. By 1994, only 44% of those taking the PSAT were males, and 60% of the National Merit Scholar semifinalists were boys. This difference was statistically significant and an embarrassment to ETS and the sponsors of the annual competition for the national honors.[8] The PSAT added a writing test in 1996 to provide both a measure of writing skills for the schools to evaluate and a test in a content area that favors girls (Lawton, 1996).

Gender and Test Taking

Test-taking strategies for boys and girls differ and give boys an advantage on multiple-choice questions. Research into the pattern of responding to test items has shown that boys tend to guess more frequently than girls (Ben-Shakhar & Sinai, 1991). This more swashbuckling test-taking style of boys works best when there is no penalty for guessing, while the more reflective approach to answering test questions serves girls well when the test is not timed. Girls tend to take more time with each item and work through the question to get an answer.

We also know that the proportion of items answered by guessing is greatest toward the end of a test. This is especially true when the items are seen as very difficult and students are running short of time to complete the test (Lord, 1952). This can be seen in the fact that girls are less likely to answer all the test's questions and boys are more likely to finish all the items and even have time to go back and review some guesses made earlier.

There are small differences in the achievement test scores between boys and girls in the area of mathematics in high school. In 2008, the mean NAEP score for math for eighth grade boys was 284 and for girls 279. In high school the difference was small, with boys getting 309 and girls 303. Reading scores are also close. In grade 8, boys scored 256 and girls 264, while in high school boys had an average score of 280 and girls 291 (NAEP, 2009).

Role of School Counselors. The implication for school counselors is that test-taking strategy sessions may improve the scoring potential for all students and for both genders. Also, in the role of advocate for all students, counselors must be vigilant for occasions when school policy is not equitable for both genders.

TESTING SPECIAL POPULATIONS ●

As recently as the 1970s, students needing special educational services were frequently denied access to public schools (see Chapter 7). Most students with disabilities were educated in private specialized schools at the expense of parents. Federal legislation in the 1970s and the record of case law since that time have brought about major policy changes for our schools.

Today, the approach known as response to intervention (RTI) is widely employed with young students receiving special educational services. RTI involves having the school counselors and/or educational specialists screen all incoming students and refer those most at risk for educational problems to student assistance committees (see Chapter 7). Once a student is identified as needing special educational assistance, the counselors have a central role in their ongoing testing and monitoring.

Testing Students With Disabilities

All students with disabilities should be given an equal opportunity for success on educational measurements. Students with individualized education plans normally have testing accommodations specified in the entitlement document (IEP). (A list of possible accommodations for students with disabilities is enumerated in the box titled "Test Accommodations" in Chapter 7.)

Accommodations frequently involve providing a separate testing environment for a student with disabilities in which the needed individualization of the testing process can occur. The school counselor frequently manages this alternative testing area. In addition, the NCLB mandate provides requirements for a different form of testing to be employed with students who are at or below the lowest 3% of the population of learners in their grade (1.88 standard deviations below the mean or average, e.g., an IQ of less than about 70). This form of testing is developmentally appropriate and often requires more than one professional to individually administer to a seriously disabled student.

Students who receive special education services need regular monitoring and tracking of their progress. School counselors are often asked to assist in this process by administering, scoring, and charting results of curriculum probes for students with special needs (see Chapter 7). In a sense, RTI provides a way to assess the efficaciousness of the educational interventions directed toward individual students. By tracking these RTI scores, the school counselor can see progress and decide whether the IEP needs to be rethought.

Testing English-Language Learners

School counselors have an important role in ensuring that students in the process of learning English are not mis-tested or improperly evaluated. When an entitlement decision is to be made about the possible special education needs for a language-minority student, attention must be given to the task of providing a fair and accurate assessment. Professional education associations recommend that parents of English-language learners (ELLs) be used as a source of background information about the student before an IEP assessment is conducted (Ortiz, 2001).

In addition to assessments for student assistance efforts, ELLs should have their English language development screened on a regular basis and results shared with the student's parents (National Association for the Education of Young Children [NAEYC], 2005). School counselors who are not bilingual should use bilingual or bicultural teachers as partners in conducting assessments. Bilingual teachers who administer assessments should to be fluent in English and the student's primary language. The requirements of the Buckley Amendment require schools to be able to explain all testing and assessment outcomes in the native language of the student's parents (Jacob & Hartshorne, 2003); see Chapter 2 for information on the Buckley Amendment).

The assessor should be very familiar with the culture of the student, including social norms and appropriate behaviors. If the school system has no professional employees who are bilingual in the student's primary language, it may be necessary to look beyond the school's community for help. Assistance may be found through the family's church or on the campus of a local university or community college.

The mind that is anxious about the future is miserable.

Santana

OPTIMIZING TEST SCORES FOR ALL STUDENTS   ●

For years educational critics complained about social promotion, a policy of moving students along to the next grade so they stay with the correct age cohort group in class (Ravitch, 2000). It has been a long-standing policy of some schools to push students along through the grades irrespective of how much they learned (Thompson & Cunningham, 2000). This all ended with federal requirements for standards-based education. Part of the standards-based approach requires all students be evaluated to determine whether they have met statewide-required standards for learning. First the administration of President William J. Clinton, then the administrations of Presidents George W. Bush and Barack Obama, have relied on achievement testing to measure the degree to which each student has met the mandated standards (Anderson, 2009; Darling-Hammond, 2004).

Current federal law (NCLB Act) mandates that all schools reach annual minimum average achievement test scores for all identified groups of students. Failure to reach this point of achievement test success can cost both the school and the local community. In 2006, 23,000 schools could not meet the adequate yearly progress (AYP) mandate. Of these, 1,750 schools with 5-year histories of not meeting the required AYP criterion were either closed or disbanded and reorganized with new faculties (Feller, 2006).

Some states have begun to offer vouchers to parents of students enrolled in low-performing public schools so that these students can attend private schools. Research into this practice has not shown there to be any better achievement outcome for these private school students (Richards, 2010).

In seven states and a number of large cities, including New York, low scores (below proficient) require the student to be retained-in-grade for another year. In 2008, 30,000 students in Florida were spending a third year in third grade, having failed the state's achievement test two consecutive years (see Case in Point 10.4).

CASE IN POINT 10.4

In 2008, I saw a reorganization mandated by NCLB happen to a local high school near my home. In this school, most of the students were from working- and lower-class homes. Parents of the school's community were hard-working farm laborers, and Spanish was spoken in most homes and throughout the small businesses of the community. After 5 years of low average scores on the state's mandated achievement test, the school was ordered to close or reorganize.

(Continued)

(Continued)

The principal was forced into an early retirement, and most of its teachers (many of whom were bilingual) were summarily reassigned to other schools as far as 25 miles away or were encouraged to retire from teaching (Cox, 2007). After giving 10–20 years to the struggle to encourage learning, teachers who were being reassigned were told by district administrators *"not to take it personally."* It is no surprise that high-stakes testing in our schools is producing overwhelming pressure on everyone.

In a more Draconian move, on February 24, 2010, the Central Falls, Rhode Island, School Board followed the NCLB mandate and fired all 93 professional employees in their Coventry High School, including 74 teachers, a principal, three assistant principals, four school counselors, all reading specialists, special education teachers, four physical education teachers and coaches, the school's librarians and instructional media specialists, and the school's psychologist (Jordan, 2010).

Thought Question. It is not just teachers and administrators who may lose their jobs during a school's reorganization; also the school's counselors are at risk for being unemployed. How can the school counselor assist the school's teachers in helping every student achieve his or her optimal score on a state-mandated high-stakes assessment?

One response to this pressure has been significant modifications to what goes on in classrooms. School counselors find it increasingly difficult to take students away from exercises in which they are being drilled and otherwise prepared for the mandated state assessment. Content subject areas not emphasized on the mandated assessments have had their instructional time shortened, while core subjects on state-mandated tests—reading and mathematics—have had the amount of instructional time allocated to them increased (Jennings & Rentner, 2006). All too often this results in relentless, mind-numbing drill and countless worksheets. These extra hours can have a small positive effect on assessment scores. These gains come at high cost, as students find classroom learning to be boring and enervating.

Another group of casualties of the "drill-and-fill" approach to test preparation are gifted students (Gentry, 2006). School counselors should advocate for a rich variety of educational offerings for all students, especially the most academically talented. There is nothing inherently interesting in preparing for a test. During test preparation drills, gifted students with the knowledge and skill base to score above the proficient level will become quickly bored and frustrated by the repetitive nature of the preparation process. Meaningless repetitions of what they already understand can lead gifted students to become truant and disrespectful of the school and its teachers (see Chapter 7).

Positive Reinforcement

Schools have tried a number of marginally ethical approaches to improve student scores on high-stakes tests. Counselors have a responsibility to prevent school leaders from pushing the envelope too far in attempting to "bribe" students to do well. Throughout the country, reward programs for good or improved scores on high-stakes achievement tests are common. Students have been given gift certificates, free restaurant meals, classroom pizza parties, tickets for high-scoring students and their parents to attend sporting events, and even savings bonds and cash prizes (Elliott, 2009). Suburban high schools have awarded the premier parking spots to students with the highest scores, and improved scores have been rewarded with iPods and even tickets to a closed drawing for a new Scion automobile (Wright, 2008). In some elementary schools in Gainesville, Florida, students who performed best on the state assessment, the FCAT, got to stand in a chamber filled with swirling money for 15 seconds and grab handfuls of $1 and $5 bills (see Photo 10.1); this unusual project was cosponsored by a local bank.

Using rewards to "motivate" students to do their best work takes a toll on the morale of faculty members and may destroy the sense of the joy in learning experienced by students. These rewards also teach students a lesson that is antithetical to the goals of schools. As school counselors, we want students to become self-reliant and internally motivated learners. A more effective approach to improving academic learning with rewards is to reward the student's acquisition of skills. For example, by rewarding a third grader for the number of books he or she reads during the term, the teacher is reinforcing a skill that is central to scoring well on a high-stakes test (Aarons, 2010). By using simple rewards for academic success (test scores and grades), our schools are teaching that education is not a worthy goal by itself, not that students should perform certain educational stunts when well paid for their efforts.

PHOTO 10.1 Third, Fourth, and Fifth Graders in Florida Awarded with Money

SOURCE: Doug Finger, Photographer.

Leadership

The best option for improving scores is also one of the most ethical; and, it is a task that school counselors should play a central role in completing. This activity is the efficacious use of student data. By tracking student data on cognitive ability, attendance, and previous achievement scores, counselors identify students who are likely to have a problem passing high-stakes achievement tests. Any student who has poor attendance and low scores on either a measure of cognitive ability or academic achievement should be provided with extra help and educational assistance at least a year before taking a high-stakes examination (Wright, 2008).

In addition to data management and the early identification of students needing help, the school counselor and principal have a central role in improving student achievement levels. Analysis of more than 60 studies found that elementary school leadership style could account for positive shifts in measures of student achievement (Witziers, Bosker, & Kruger, 2003). Using data from Pennsylvania, James Cantwell (2007) identified the important role that leadership style plays in determining outcomes on a mandated statewide assessment. During his 3-year study of the highest- and lowest-scoring elementary- and middle-level schools, teachers were surveyed about school climate and their principals about personal leadership styles. In low-performing schools, Cantwell (2007) found that principals lacked awareness of their own leadership styles, and their schools had low morale levels. Moreover, educators working in successful schools were more collegial, had better communications with one another, were accepting of their colleagues, and showed sensitivity to the problems of each other. This latter type of school is one that the school counselor should work to achieve through consultation with the principal and teachers who are the social-emotional leaders of a faculty.

● COLLEGE ADMISSION TESTING

Even prior to high school, many students and their parents begin to think ahead and plan for college and college admissions (see Case in Point 10.5). For students who have parents without college experience, this planning may not start until later in the high school years. Counselors should help all students make career and life plans early in their school years (see Chapter 13). It is common for high school students to experience high stress levels brought about by the college admission process. Even students who have good grades and have always scored well on achievement tests may experience the stress of testing and college admission. College admission looms as a major source of concern for adolescents until the "fat letter" full of admission material arrives in the April mail (see Chapter 5 for more on college admission processes).

CASE IN POINT 10.5

Stanley H. Kaplan (1919–2009), the son of immigrant Jewish parents in New York City, was a superior school and college student but was rejected for admission to medical school. His frustration was directed at the privileged children of wealthy and middle-class parents who had an admission advantage.

He began doing private tutoring with high school students who were having difficulty with the newly adopted admissions test, the Scholastic Aptitude Test (now the SAT). His success with this process brought him many more students, and soon he began what became a national corporation. Anecdotal reports of gains of 200 or more points on retesting after a Kaplan course have been tempered by careful research documenting increases of about 30 points on each of the tests of the SAT. In 1984 Kaplan sold his company to the Washington Post, Inc., and retired to a rich life.

One key to Kaplan's success is the pressure that students have felt to please their parents and impress their peers with their ability to be admitted to a "good" college. Parents want "what's best" for their child and also to be able to impress others with the ability of their offspring.

Thought Questions. Reflect on a possible role change. If you ran the admissions office for a very prestigious undergraduate program in psychology and sociology, what elements would you rank as most important in selecting students from the large pool of applicants? What factors would you not consider? Justify and explain your answer.

Each honest calling, each walk of life, has its own aristocracy based on excellence of performance.

James Bryant Conant[9]

Two Goals of Admission Testing

When a school or college uses a selective admission process, the goal is to pick the most able and motivated young people. This goal can be accomplished by admitting only those who are most deserving in terms of test scores and grades. This will produce schools and colleges that are true meritocracies (Orfield, 1998). The downside of this goal can be the loss of diversity on the campuses. For example, African American and Hispanic students enroll in fewer advanced placement (AP) classes than do Anglo-White and Asian heritage students (Whiting & Ford, 2009). Yet, grades from AP classes are given greater weight in the grade point average (GPA) of high school students and are an important factor college admission officers use in reviewing an applicant's paperwork.

Admission test scores are one of only two primary predictors of college potential. The other is high school class rank derived from the GPA of students. The importance of tests like the SAT II and the ACT in the admission process is increasing because high schools have begun not reporting either GPAs or class rank (Finder, 2006). This reflects an effort by a number of suburban high schools to remove unhealthy levels of letter-grade stress on students. College admission officers have reported that half or more of their applicants' transcripts do not report the class rank or the high school GPA for the students applying for admission. The result is that SAT II and ACT scores are now more important in the admission decision than ever.

At the other end of the selectivity scale are "**open door**" colleges and community colleges. Students are admitted to these institutions on the basis of their academic needs and plans rather than on the basis of test scores. A recent survey of students who graduate from high school found that only 34% are fully prepared to begin a 4-year bachelor's-level program of college studies (Greene & Winters, 2005). Open door and community colleges provide a place where deficient skills can be honed and developed in support of a program of college level studies. For the most part, community colleges offer 2-year-long programs of study. A number of these colleges have begun to offer 4-year bachelor's degree curricula in fields of great shortage, for example, education and nursing.

SAT II

As much as anything, the SAT is the product of the Ivy League. In 1933 the new president of Harvard University, James Bryant Conant, had his admissions dean, Henry Chauncey, develop a national scholarship program for Harvard.[10] To do this Chauncey selected the SAT, a multiple-choice format test of aptitude, first developed at Princeton University and designed around the IQ test developed for recruits during World War I, the Army Alpha test. The test, then named the Scholastic Aptitude Test, became the required measure for all young men applying for the Harvard scholarships. This scholarship program made

Harvard a national university and provided an educational opportunity for young men throughout the United States.[11]

At this same time, a laid-off science teacher, Reynold Johnson, invented a machine that could read lead pencil marks on a page and sold the system to IBM (Lemann, 1999).[12] Testing using the new IBM system became greatly refined during World War II. This was done by the U.S. military that selected the College Board as the agency to test hundreds of thousands of White male American high school seniors.[13] The Army and Navy were looking for the best and the brightest young White men for officer candidacy education that was being conducted on campuses throughout the nation. This test, the Army-Navy Qualifying Test, became the true precursor of the modern SAT.

The test was not renormed until 1990, the first time in 49 years. At the time of renorming, a third section, critical writing, was added (see Chapter 5). The test name was changed to its initials and edition number, SAT II. The SAT II requires about 4 hours to administer and provides scores in critical reading, mathematics, and critical writing. In 2009, the national mean on the test of critical reading was approximately 503 with a standard deviation of 110. The mathematics test has an approximate mean of 515 with a standard deviation of 115. The critical writing test has a mean of about 495 and a standard deviation of about 110 (College Board, 2009).

ACT

E. F. Lindquist, a professor at the University of Iowa, developed the Iowa Every-Pupil Testing Program in 1931, a statewide achievement test that later evolved into the Iowa Tests of Basic Skills (ITBS) (see Chapter 5). In 1959 he was a cofounder of the American College Testing Program, the largest competitor in the college admission testing market for ETS. In 2009 1.5 million students took the SAT II while 1.6 million took the ACT (ACT, 2010).

Lindquist held a very different point of view about admission tests than was held by James Bryant Conant and Henry Chauncey of Harvard and later of ETS. He felt that tests should not be employed to skim the cream off the top of a distribution of college applicants; rather, he believed that tests should help students plan and prepare for college (Popham, 2006). He did not have a vision of admission testing producing meritocracies on the nation's campuses; his test was designed to serve a guidance function. The ACT was designed to reveal to college counselors each student's strengths and weak areas. Based on these scores individualized programs of study could be tailored for each undergraduate. Today the ACT tests are measures of the skills and abilities needed by college students across several academic areas: English, mathematics, reading, writing, and science reasoning (ACT, 1997). The ACT is taken by about as many students each year as the SAT and is the dominant college admission test in 28 states (Midwest and South). (See Figure 10.3 for a map showing the distribution of ACT and SAT II.)

Strategic Test Choices

School counselors in high schools in the Northeast, upper Midwest, and on the West Coast have often suggested that students take the ACT along with the SAT II. Until recently the rate of minority students taking the ACT instead of the SAT has been below what the population statistics of college bound students would predict. This trend began to turn around in 2005 and had improved significantly by 2010 (ACT, 2010). This East Coast, West Coast, and Great Lakes tendency for high school counselors to prefer students take the ACT in addition to the SAT II reflects a belief by counselors that the normative comparison group used by the SAT is more competitive than the norm group used by the ACT. This

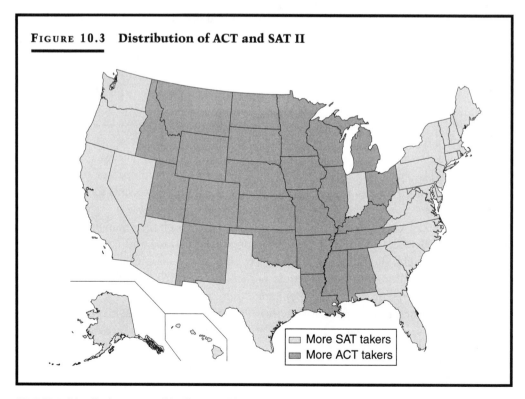

FIGURE 10.3 Distribution of ACT and SAT II

More SAT takers
More ACT takers

SOURCE: Wikipedia: http://en.wikipedia.org/wiki/ACT.

opinion is based on the higher average scores on the NAEP from states in the Northeast, upper Midwest, and West Coast and lower scores in states from the South, Southwest, and central Midwest (NAEP, 2010). Most colleges accept either test in the admission decision process, and students can elect to have their best-looking test score forwarded to the college admission office.

Both testing systems are working toward the day when all testing will occur online. This change is already in place with the graduate admissions tests of ETS, including the online version of the Graduate Record Exam (GRE).

Role of School Counselors

The two admission tests are highly reliable measuring devices. This results in a small standard error of measurement. A small standard error provides little room for test improvement to occur between retesting experiences. (See Case in Point 10.5.) With focused instruction such as that offered by commercial test preparation programs the maximum amount of improvement for a typical student is likely to be less than a half standard deviation (50 points on any SAT II subtest or 150 overall).

School counselors can encourage students to begin the test preparation activities early for the SAT II and the ACT. Unfortunately that call for early preparation often falls on the deaf ears of teenagers. One approach to sparking freshman and sophomore interest in working to improve their skills is to have a college-bound senior or college freshman who is a high school alumnus or alumna meet with small groups of high school students and the school counselor.

The counselor should ensure that a variety of test preparation materials are available where all students can have free access to them, for example, in the school's library or open computer laboratory. Parent groups can also be focused on the things they can do to help their children qualify for admission to a wide choice of colleges. Many parents will be interested in evening workshops focused on financial aid. By linking the two topics—financial aid and the admission process and preparation—school counselors may be able to reach a larger audience of interested parents.

SUMMARY

A central task for school counselors is to serve as resident experts on educational measurement and assessment. In this role counselors should be knowledgeable of basic measurement statistics as they relate to the quality and appropriateness of published tests or measurements.

Not all ethnic groups score equally on standardized tests. The differences are linked to three principal factors: the expectations, goals, and effectiveness of the student's family in providing a quality academic background, the quality of the educational environment within the student's school, and the socialization of the student into a society of peers.

Socialization differences have resulted in a small achievement gap between boys and girls in terms of mathematics (favoring boys) and reading (favoring girls). Title IX addressed inequality in educational opportunities and interscholastic activities in 1972. That legislation notwithstanding, there is still work to do to provide parity for girls and women in academic settings.

School counselors have responsibility to ensure that testing and assessment requirements of each student with an IEP are fulfilled and appropriate records maintained. Likewise, school counselors should create the appropriate linguistic environment for testing students who are English-language learners.

Some of the most stressful testing experiences for high school juniors and seniors are the college admission tests and the weeks between administration and score report. Getting students ready to take these tests is a job that, if possible, should be begun before the testing year is well under way.

DISCUSSION QUESTIONS

1. Case in Point 10.1 presents a clear ethical problem. What should a school counselor recommend to a school's leadership to prevent educational triage from occurring when resources are limited?

2. Is there a cognitive elite (see note 6) and is its membership influenced by family genetics? What level of ability to learn in school would you expect your own children to have, assuming your marriage partner is similar in ability and background to you? Explain your positions on these questions with examples.

3. Examine your own test-taking style. What testing format works best for you to show your true level of learning? What new test-taking skills would improve your scores on standardized tests?

4. Review the major tests you have taken (e.g., SAT II, GRE, ACT, Praxis, etc.). Which of them made an accurate measurement in your case, and which did not? Next evaluate the validity of the measures that are off the mark. Did they over- or underestimate your abilities and skills? What proof can you provide for those conclusions?

5. Propose an appropriate and fair model for testing students who are in the process of learning the English language. Include considerations of the students' ages, years in the United States, and home backgrounds in your testing model. Then compare it with the federal guidelines: http://www2.ed.gov/policy/elsec/guid/lepguidance.doc.

RELATED READINGS

Gargiulo, R. M. (2008). *Special education in contemporary society: An introduction to exceptionality* (3rd ed.).Thousand Oaks, CA: Sage.

Obama, B. (2004). *Dreams from my father: A story of race and inheritance.* New York: Three Rivers Press/Random House.

Wright, R. J. (2008). *Educational assessment: Tests and measurement in the age of accountability.* Thousand Oaks, CA: Sage.

Wright, R. J. (2009). Methods for improving test scores: The good, the bad, and the ugly. *Kappa Delta Pi Record, 45*(3), 116–121.

NOTES

1. *Data* is a plural word in English. The singular form for one point from a set of data is a *datum*.

2. When test scores are returned to the school counselor from the testing agency, a detailed examination looking for potentially invalid scores should be made before scores are posted on the student's records. If a determination is made that a score is not valid, the school counselor may enter a note on the student's permanent record so indicating and providing an abbreviated reason for that decision.

3. Students who score below proficient on the mandated statewide assessments can be the reason that a public school gets a failing report card and can be in danger of being reorganized or closed.

4. An Angoff committee consists of between 50 and 100 educators and testing experts brought together by a state education department who study the questions available to measure each learning standard. The committee may also write questions as needed for the high-stakes test being standardized. The committee decides how many items must be passed to reach the various criterion levels (cut scores).

A parallel method uses a similar committee to review potential test items arranged from easiest to most difficult. This sequence is developed by pilot testing the possible test questions with a group of students. Each evaluator independently places book-markers in the stack of sequenced test items indicating the cut score levels. Next the committee works to reach a consensus on the most appropriate location of the book-marks (cut scores). Naturally, this method is known as the **bookmarking method**.

5. The eugenics movement was a grass-roots effort by Anglo-White people to improve the White race by using the principles of racial hygiene and working to pass

legislation against miscegenation. The movement was supported by test data supposedly documenting the inferiority of some racial groups and superiority of Anglo-Whites. Racial hygiene led to passage of laws enforcing the sterilization of people who scored low on the tests of mental ability. Thousands of Americans were sterilized against their will during the 1920s and 1930s.

6. University of California at Berkeley psychologist Arthur R. Jensen proposed that 70% of each person's mental ability is inherited from their biological parents. He postulated there are two distinct types of mental ability. Type I involves traditional associative learning and retention of input and rote memorization of simple facts and skills. Jensen proposed this basic form of mental ability is equally distributed to all populations. Type II intelligence is an analytical and language ability type in which Caucasian/Whites and many Asian Americans score well (Jensen, 1969, 1972a, 1972b, 1981). Jensen believes African Americans and many Hispanics are deficient in the inheritance of Type II intelligence.

Jensen's position was endorsed in 1994 with the publication of Richard J. Herrnstein and Charles Murray's *The Bell Curve*. In that book the authors proposed the test score gap that existed between ethnic and racial subgroups was also seen in a score gap between identifiable socioeconomic groups within subpopulations. Gaps were explained as the product of differential group inheritance of mental ability. Herrnstein and Murray proposed the existence of a "cognitive elite" that had migrated into the professions and corporate leadership and was skewed toward well-educated upper- and upper-middle-class families.

7. In 2007 almost all American colleges were unable to fully comply with the requirements of gender equality required by Title IX. That year 56% of all undergraduates were women and only 42% of the athletics department budget was spent for women's programs (Cheslock, 2007).

8. The National Merit Scholarship Corporation began in 1954 as a way for businesses to contribute to the education of America's most gifted youth. The first Scholar Qualifying Test was administered in 1955 to more than 58,000 high school seniors. This test was developed by ETS for use by various scholarship-granting organizations. In 1958 the organization contracted Science Research Associates to build the National Merit Scholarship Qualifying Test (NMSQT). In 1971 the NMSQT was combined with the Preliminary Scholastic Aptitude Test (PSAT), another publication of ETS (personal communication with Gloria Davis of the National Merit Scholarship Corporation, February 3, 2005). Today more than 1 million students in the 9th through the 12th grades are tested as a part of this program. Of these, the 50,000 (top 3%) who have the highest combined scores (critical reading + math + writing skills) will qualify for recognition by the National Merit Scholars Program.

9. President, Harvard University (1933 to 1953).

10. In 1948 the Educational Testing Service was chartered with Henry Chauncey as its first president and James Bryant Conant as its first board chairman.

11. Harvard University became a coeducational institution in 1943 when some women from Radcliffe College were allowed to attend classes at Harvard College.

12. Johnson went on to become an employee of IBM. Later he was the inventor of the magnetic disk drive and video tape. He was awarded the National Medal of Technology by President Ronald Reagan in 1986.

13. The U.S. military was not desegregated until President Harry S Truman's Executive Order No. 9981 on July 26, 1948.

11

Professional School Counselors as Consultants

OBJECTIVES

By reading and studying this chapter you should acquire the competency to:

- Explain the advantages of using consultation as part of the services offered by professional school counselors
- Describe four different modes or approaches professional school counselors use when providing consultations in their schools
- Discuss the steps used to train teachers for employing a behavioral approach to shaping student behavior
- Explain why the school's principal should receive a consultation visit by the school's counselor
- Discuss the legal and ethical issues raised when a professional school counselor provides consulting services to a teacher
- Describe the sources of and methods for overcoming resistance to counselor consultation by both educators and parents

● ● ●

❝ The best way to escape from a problem is to solve it. **❞**

Robert Anthony

● **INTRODUCTION AND THEMES**

Professional school counselors are provided with the opportunity to learn many skills by their graduate programs. One of these skill areas is the art of consultation. Consulting skills are among the most useful capabilities a school counselor has for making a change in the lives of troubled students (Gibson, 2004). In the past, as much as half of a professional school counselor's day was spent coping with the minutia and bureaucratic needs of the counseling office (Partin, 1993). The national framework as devised by the American School Counselor Association (ASCA) (American School Counselor Association [ASCA]/Hatch & Bowers, 2005) has recommended that these activities be reduced to about 15% of the school counselor's time (p. 55). One method of finding more opportunities to assist students and provide responsive services is through consulting (Watson, Butler, Weaver, & Foster, 2004). Heretofore, school counselors have rarely if ever been considered when policymakers formulate plans to improve schools or close the achievement and testing gaps among groups of students (Center on Educational Policy, 2010). Yet, school counselors who have good consultation skills can play a vital role in helping a school community improve.

The constituents of school counselor consultation include three major groups: school administrators, teachers and paraprofessional staff assistants, and the parents of students being served. Counselors occasionally pursue a fourth possible consultation on behalf of students that involves social and family service agencies not directly affiliated with the school. When consulting with these agencies, it is necessary to have the written permission of the legal guardian or parent of the child. No information can be exchanged between the agency and the school's counselor without prior approval.

DeWayne Kurpius (1978) proposed that there are four major models for school counselors to employ in delivering consulting services. In all models for consultation, the counselor is ultimately assisting students.

The vast majority of consultations involve changing or somehow improving behaviors and work habits of one or more students. For that reason, **direct behavioral consultation (DBC)** is the most common approach used by school counselors (Watson et al., 2004). DBC is most widely used for behavioral disturbances and improving teachers' classroom management skills. The approach has proven to be one that can change both instructional practices of classroom teachers and the behavioral outcomes for students. An additional approach the counselor may elect to use in consultation provides educators and/or parents with solution-focused brief consulting techniques that may be used with problematic students (Kahn, 2000).

Standard 4: The professional school counselor provides responsive services through the effective use of individual and small-group counseling, consulting, and referral skills (ASCA/Hatch & Bowers, 2005, p. 63).

CONSULTATION BY PROFESSIONAL ● COUNSELORS WITHIN THE SCHOOLS

The professional school counselor who is providing services is one of three legs of the consultation model. The other two legs are the consultee (educator) who must implement the ideas of the consulting counselor, and the ultimate client, the student being helped (Baker, Robichaud, Dietrich, Wells, & Schreck, 2009).

ASCA Statement on the Consulting Role of Professional School Counselors

The new framework for professional school counselors emphasizes preventative approaches for service delivery. These preventative approaches are comprehensive in scope, and developmental in nature. The ASCA (ASCA/Hatch & Bowers, 2005) statement describes the consulting process as being a responsive service on par with individual and group counseling interventions conducted in the school (Baker et al., 2009).

The ASCA National Framework on the Nature and Delivery of "Responsive Services"

Counselors consult with parents or guardians, teachers, other educators, and community agencies regarding strategies to help students and their families. (ASCA/Hatch & Bowers, 2005, p. 42).

Through consultation, partnering, collaborating, and learning, school counselors provide important contributions to the school system. Counselors must consult with teachers, staff members, and parents or guardians regularly in order to provide information, to support the school community, and receive feedback on the emerging needs of students (ASCA/Hatch & Bowers, 2005, p. 43).

Advantage of Consulting

One reasonable question that any school counselor may ask is, "Why must I learn to consult when I can simply cope with children's problems independently?" One answer to that question is quickly learned when a new professional school counselor realizes that the same students with the same problem keep returning to the counselor's office. These recidivists can be helped through interventions of the counselor, but until the counselor employs a holistic and systemic approach to the problem, progress will be slow, with many incidences of backsliding (White & Mullis, 1998).

Improving Efficiency in School Counseling

The holistic approach assumes that children live and grow within a complex environment that includes many significant adults. Among these significant adults are teachers and other specialists of the child's school. Children are helpless to effect changes in the school or with their parents. For that reason, individual and group counseling, especially with young children, has a limited range of possibilities for improving a child's circumstances. Consultations between the school's counselors and faculty can result in highly productive and efficient solutions to problems students experience and bring about real change (White, Mullis, Earley, & Brigman, 1995).

The work of a professional school counselor with an active consulting practice within the school can significantly reduce the number of referrals to the counselor's office (Clemens, 2007). Teachers are occasionally too quick to refer a troublesome student to the counselor with the expectation that the school counselor will somehow immediately make the pestiferous or uncooperative child better.

By initiating a consultation with the teacher, it is possible to work to improve the student's pattern of behaviors in the future. Consultation involves several steps (see "Steps in Providing Consultation in a School" following) and can provide the teacher with the knowledge and insight to prevent many behavioral problems in the future (Watson et al., 2004). The net result of consulting with teachers is that office referrals for one student may be reduced or even eliminated.

Consultation and Staff Relations

By using consultation to work through teachers, a professional school counselor can have more time to do a professional and competent job. If the normal pattern prior to consultation had been for a particular student to be referred to the office once a month, the elimination of that student's problematic behaviors could provide 20 or more hours during the year for the counselor to help others.

Beyond the efficiency of the school counselor's efforts, parents who are provided with consultation focused on their children will have reduced concern and experience less angst over questions related to how their children are coping in school. Teachers also benefit by being better able to teach without the disruption a problem student creates. Finally, the student gains by having improved his or her attitude and finding more satisfying and productive methods for dealing with life as a student.

Professional bonds of mutual trust and cooperation can develop when professional school counselors provide consultation for education professionals working in their schools (Kurpius, 1978). This positive and trusting climate is an essential component of an effective professional school counseling program (Sexton, Starr, & Fawcett, 2005).

The Art of Being a Consultant

Professional teachers often know when they are having problems but lack the means to determine specifically what is wrong. With a little special help, they can define the nature of the problem and resolve the difficulty (Kurpius, 1978). School counselors are in a perfect position to provide that special help.

Perhaps the best way for a professional school counselor to advertise his or her service as a consultant is by using a simple prop: a coffee cup. Every school has one or more places where teachers gather over coffee, relax, and "let their hair down." These places may be near the cafeteria, a designated faculty lounge, or a conference room that was commandeered by the school's teachers years before.[1] By taking the coffee cup along, the professional school counselor will appear to be just another educator needing a cup of the potent brew that most faculty rooms offer. Visiting these "teacher-only" areas on a regular basis will expose the professional counselor to all manner of topics discussed, including discourses about troublesome students and the families of those students. An important skill for the counselor is not to be drawn into this conversation too fast; a second skill is not to lose track of the fact that much of what is heard is either hearsay or is from only one teacher's perspective. Teachers, like all people, can become frustrated and need to vent feelings of anger and hurt. By listening and collecting background data, the school's counselor can develop a large reservoir of information that may be employed in consultation or in another mode of service delivery. The key is not to offer unsolicited advice. The first step is to learn the background information needed to provide reasonable help by listening.

The art and skills of consulting as a professional school counselor are made easier by the observation that administrators and educators will gravitate toward a school counselor perceived to be competent, who keeps confidences, and is generally viewed as a solid and well-grounded professional (Clemens, 2007).

Steps in Providing Consultation in a School

In 1978, DeWayne Kurpius published a model for the steps normally followed in providing consulting services by a school's counselor. This statement of a model was modified in 1993 to expand it into a more generalized approach for mental health consultation (Kurpius & Fuqua, 1993). Since that time the model has been adopted and modified by other counselor educators (Baker & Gerler, 2004; Cobia & Henderson, 2007).

In this chapter the Kurpius and Fuqua (1993) model is presented reflecting the contemporary consulting role of professional school counselors. By this model, counselors consulting with educators and administrators of their schools may employ one of the following approaches. In each of these approaches the teacher (educator) is the consultee and the ultimate clients are students receiving the indirect services of the professional school counselor who is providing consultation.

Provision of Immediate Direct Services

There are times in a school when the relationship between a teacher and one or more students is rapidly becoming toxic. In such a case the teacher may appeal directly to the professional school counselor for a "quick fix." This request may also come to the counselor from the principal (or assistant principal), or the teacher's department head or team leader. Administrators realize that the teacher turnover rate in schools with school climate problems is significantly higher than in schools where the faculties are comfortable in their role and feel successful and appreciated (Ahmed, 2009). Perceived poor student discipline and deportment also subtract from the morale of any school's classroom teachers. As a result, schools with poor student discipline and poor student behavior have much higher teacher turnover than schools without such problems (Ingersoll, 2004).

At the heart of any successful school is high-quality leadership working in partnership with a well-run office of professional school counselors. Both professional school counselors and the school's leadership have enormous roles to play in creating the educational climate for successful and happy schools (Wright, 2009). Good school counselors are engaged in what is going on in the school and are ready to work with teachers to make every classroom a power-ful center for learning.

During times when a "quick fix" is needed, consultation by a school coun-selor is less likely to build a model for long-term action and more likely to describe, demonstrate, and model immediately available ideas. This approach has been termed the "tell, show, do" model of consultation (White, Mullis, Earley, & Brigman, 1995). When teachers have behavioral and classroom man-agement problems, a competent school counselor will not hesitate to go into classrooms and work with teachers to identify solutions and try alternative approaches. (See Case in Point 11.1 for a successful example.)

CASE IN POINT 11.1

I was once one of two middle school counselors in a building with a student population of 950 students between the sixth and eighth grades. In the late fall, a well-thought-of teacher of science in the eighth grade became pregnant. She was required by her physician to get bed rest starting then, in her fourth month of gestation. Understandably, she went on immediate leave of absence for health reasons. I, a former science teacher, was asked to fill in until a new science teacher was found.[2] Fortunately, that task only took two school days. Her replacement was a former officer of the U.S. Navy who had a 20-year record of service in the surface fleet as a deck officer. He had a solid background in engineering sciences and had led many men and women under his commands.

A week later he was in my office begging for me to help him manage several of the five classes he was assigned to teach each day. He told the principal our students were unteach-able and disrespectful and that he would quit that very day unless he got immediate help. As I knew the subject area, and the students, I was asked by the principal to help this novice teacher. The teacher was so frustrated that he immediately accepted my help as a consultant.

I observed his first and second classes the next morning and saw significant acting-out behav-ior by a number of the boys, all to the appreciative giggles of many of the girls. The new science teacher did not know the names of all of the students, and when he spotted acting-out behav-ior he would shout, "You there, sit down and pay attention." The usual result was a loud rejoin-der, "Who me? I didn't do nothun." This went on for both classes. His next period was a break for preparation. This provided a time when I could meet with the teacher and his team leader. The team leader was a highly experienced teacher who was aware of the difficulties any new teacher faced in the middle of the year. After describing what I saw, she and I discussed a plan of action with the novice. Step 1 was for him to use the seating chart and immediately learn the names of his students and then to use the "name-describe-explain" approach to classroom man-agement. The team leader agreed with this idea, and during the fourth period that day I taught the first third of the class (15 minutes) while the new teacher and the team leader watched.

(Continued)

(Continued)

At the first inappropriate behavior I averred, using my "outdoor voice," "Phillip [name], stop bothering with Suzanne's backpack [describe], you can't afford to miss this material, so pay attention to what is going on [explain]." The novice took over and taught the remainder of his class using this approach, and he did well. The next class the team leader taught the first 15 or 20 minutes and the novice watched her teach his students. I covered the team leader's regular class so she could be there with the new teacher. By the end of one day, the problem seemed on the way to a resolution, the new teacher had his confidence back, and students were learning science again.

Thought Question. Assume the same circumstance described above, and you are the professional school counselor. In this new case the novice teacher was concerned with rude and vulgar language being used by some students to each other and to the teacher. What immediate fix would you provide to help the teacher survive long enough to establish him- or herself?

One pitfall counselors must avoid when using this form of consultation is letting teachers transfer ownership of the problem. By asking for help, the teacher must understand that the counselor has not assumed responsibility for it (Kurpius, 1978, p. 336). One way to ensure that the teacher continues to work on the skill set needed to resolve classroom problems involves doing follow-ups with the teacher and providing continuing consulting.

When both appropriate and agreed to by all parties, the counselor and consultee may elect to engage another professional in the process. In most states, team leaders and department heads do not have supervisory authority and are less threatening partners for participating in a consultation. On the other hand, school administrators (principals and instructional supervisors) do have supervisory and evaluation authority within a school and may be viewed by some teachers as a threat to their job security if they become engaged in problems a teacher is having in the classroom.

Arbitration, Mediation, and Resolution

In much the same way as providing direct consultation, the professional school counselor may be called upon by any of a number of stakeholders to provide immediate help in resolving an interpersonal problem through arbitration and/or mediation. Students, administrators, teachers, or even parents may request this service. Two things are needed for this form of counseling to be initiated: one is a seemingly intractable problem between two parties, and the other, two or more antagonists willing for the school's counselor to facilitate a solution. For the most part these mediations are between students, and they may have been started at the request of a teacher or administrator who became aware of the bad feelings between two or more students.

There are several steps to being a successful facilitator/arbitrator. The first is to set ground rules, for example, each party listens without interruption to the position of the other person. No one is permitted to walk out or to shut down and play being comatose. Next, the counselor must be confident that he or she has heard and fully appreciates both positions and all relevant background material related to the problem. The third involves the counselor restating (for clarity) both sides of the dispute. Next comes brainstorming for potential compromises that can resolve the impasse. Finally, when both parties are ready, draw up in writing an agreement spelling out the resolution and have all stakeholders sign the document (Runde & Flanagan, 2007).

A large-scale variation on this approach to conflict resolution takes the form of a primary intervention program introduced through the guidance curriculum developed and offered by the professional school counselor. This program involves training "peer mediators" in the skills of conflict resolution. There are published curricula for these programs, or the school's counselor may design one for local use. The ASCA national framework encourages these programs as appropriate responsive services designed for prevention: "Many counselors train students as peer mediators, conflict mediators, conflict managers, tutors and mentors" (ASCA/Hatch & Bowers, 2005, p. 42).

There are a number of media-supported conflict resolution curricula sold for use in the schools. These include:

- The *Life Skills Curriculum* from the National Urban Technology Center

  www.urbantech.org/ylaint_vp_confres.cfm

- The *Conflict Resolution Curriculum* from the North Central Regional Educational Laboratory

  www.ncrel.org/sdrs/areas/issues/envrnmnt/drugfree/sa2conre.htm

- *Conflict Resolution: Steps for Handling Interpersonal Dynamics* from Bonner Curriculum

  www.bonner.org/resources/modules/modules_pdf/BonCurConflict Resolution.pdf

- *Managing Student Behavior in Today's Schools* from the College of Education of the University of Florida

  http://education.ufl.edu/web/?pid=299

Counselor-Initiated Consultation to Assist the Consultee

Within an informal setting (e.g., coffee klatch), a school counselor may learn of a significant problem a teacher is having working with one or more students. After doing background research, the counselor can be ready to offer the teacher consultation to help resolve the problem. The necessary background research involves reviewing the student's cumulative records, observing the student in other settings, and through informal conversations with other teachers and with the school's disciplinarian (assistant principal). The teacher should be approached only with an offer to collaborate and consult when the professional school counselor believes he or she has something to contribute (Baker et al., 2009). As in the case of any individual counseling, the consultee must be carefully listened to and drawn into the process of self-learning and clarifying. Counselors should only offer ideas as needed and focus on helping the teacher-consultee see new approaches and ways to interact with the student through the guided insight provided in consultation. The effort by the counselor is to be collaborative, collegial, and helpful to the teacher while never being pedantic and telling.

In this approach and also the next one, background research is essential. If the counselor feels unprepared to provide the needed help, no consultation should be initiated. A misguided effort can do great damage to the reputation of the school counselor.

In both formats for providing consultation, counselor initiated and consultee initiated, the ultimate client is the student or students who are affected by the change in instructional behavior by the teacher.

Consultee-Initiated Consultation

The consultation process may be teacher initiated and come in the form of a request for ongoing assistance working with a student who is experiencing problems learning or with his or her behavior. In this case the consultee is asking for more than a brief intervention or a prescription for curing the problem. There is solid evidence demonstrating that some teachers achieve superior classroom outcomes while others do not (Taylor & Olsen, 2010). It is the task of a school's leadership team, including counselors, to assist each teacher to reach his or her optimal level of efficacy.

Background research and reconnaissance needs to be carefully completed prior to collaborating in developing a plan with the consultee. The goal of the collaboration is a prescriptive plan for action by the consultee to carry out during the school year. The plan should be developed jointly, and the consultee should provide the commitment to follow it as designed and initiate all steps of the plan as agreed upon. Perhaps the best model for this type of consultation is the DBC approach discussed in the next section.

The plan for action should also provide a method for evaluating its degree of success. This combination of problem identification, consultation, and outcome analysis can make the consultation an action research effort.

Direct Behavioral Consultation

Student behavior and attitudes are the focus of most referrals that teachers send to school's offices (Robinson & Ricord Griesemer, 2006). These concerns may be best resolved not just by intervention with the student but through a consultation with the teacher. In such a case, the consultation would involve teaching the educators basic techniques from **learning theory** that can modify inappropriate or maladaptive student behavior. The behavioral approach is based on the idea that maladaptive behaviors by students have been learned by the student as a way to cope with his or her environment. As **learned behaviors,** they can be extinguished and replaced with appropriate, adaptive behaviors.

School counselors can be highly effective in changing the classroom behavioral management practices of consultees (teachers) when a direct behavioral consultation (DBC) model is followed (Sterling-Turner, Watson, & Moore, 2002). This approach involves having the school's counselor teach the theory and skills of behavioral intervention with problematic students to the teachers.[3] The process involves not just verbal instruction but practice sessions, including a hands-on experience when the teacher can modify and improve his or her techniques with the guidance of the school counselor (Watson et al., 2004). Survey research with school psychologists has shown that about three-quarters of school administrators and two-thirds of classroom teachers support the employment of direct behavioral consultation (Wilczynski, Mandal, & Fusilier, 2000).

Steps in Direct Behavioral Consultation. The *first step* in the process involves helping teachers develop the skills to identify the problem and define its parameters. As in all counseling and consultation, the first step begins with the counselor actively listening to the teacher describe the problem. Probing questions can follow, such as these three:

1. What immediately precedes the student acting this way?

2. What are the other students doing while this is ongoing?

3. What is your way of responding to those actions?

These three questions can provide the professional school counselor with information needed to identify the cycle of cues and rewards associated with the undesirable behavior.

The first question, "What proceeded the behavior?," may identify the environmental trigger that initiates inappropriate behavior or activity. The second and third questions provide cues to the possible rewards that the student receives for inappropriate behavior (Bowen, Jenson, & Clark, 2004).

To verify the description of the student and the problem, the counselor should schedule time to observe the student in a less restrictive environment (e.g., lunch recess, the bus ramp, or during a club period). With this observational step, the counselor can gain insight into how the teacher processes and reacts to the student's behaviors. Direct observations by the counselor also provide data to help develop a baseline of behaviors that will be targeted for change through the consultation.

During the *second step*, the analytic step, the professional school counselor organizes the information gained through background research, teacher reports, and direct observation. From these data, the counselor develops a model explaining how and why the inappropriate behavior occurs. Along with the model for understanding the genesis of problematic behaviors with the student, the counselor presents a plan of action for the teacher-consultee to follow.

The third step in DBC is to provide the opportunity for the teacher to practice the behavior while in ongoing consultation with the counselor. One highly effective method to impart these skills to the teacher is for the counselor to model the classroom management actions to be taken and have the teacher repeat the process. The counselor may accomplish this instructional task with the consultee by observing in the teacher's classroom and providing ongoing coaching. This is not a subtle process, and care must be taken to protect the dignity and authority of the teacher. One way this can be done is through a planned co-teaching experience with both the teacher and counselor in the same classroom teaching a topic that intersects the school's counseling goals and is also a topic appropriate for subject area content. For example:

Mathematics Class: The math of test scores SAT II, ACT, or NCLB

English Class: How to score well on the mandated writing skills test

Social Studies Class: Bullying in school and throughout history

Science Class: The neurobiology of addiction

A *fourth step* has the counselor follow up by observing the teacher several more times and occasionally modeling the behavioral control system as a refresher for the teacher. During this phase, the counselor may find other teachers are interested in learning and having individualized consultations. One method involves the provision of an inservice program for teachers who volunteer to learn more about direct behavioral consultation.

The *last step* is to conduct a follow-up evaluation of the behavioral consultation. The optimal outcome is that the consultee has acquired a new skill set that serves him or her well and improves the teacher's classroom management and confidence in the role of educator.

Resistance to Consultation by Some Educators

There is a perceived power difference between school counselors who can come and go as they need and who have private offices and administrative assistants, and classroom teachers who are tightly scheduled and often cannot even use the faculty toilet without first finding someone to "watch my class for me please." Counselors do not have extra duties that teachers do. They do not monitor the student cafeteria, supervise the playground, or manage the loading and offloading of students from the school's buses. Because of graduate-level education and working extra days in the summer, most school counselors also make a little more money than teachers.

The reality is that counselors are not administrators and cannot hire or fire anyone. Yet, the perceived gulf can contribute to the sense of distance between teachers and counselors and make teachers reluctant to seek or accept consulting from a school's counselor.

Fear of Failure

Young teachers who have not yet earned tenure in their jobs may be very slow to accept any ideas or advice that implies they are in some way incapable of doing their jobs. No one, especially an untenured teacher, wants to be blamed for causing a problem.

Teachers know that they are captains of a small ship each time they close the doors to their classrooms and begin to teach. The room full of students is a small isolated world in which the teacher operates independently. The reality is that teaching can be a lonely and isolating profession (Schlichte, Yssel, & Merbler, 2005). This also contributes to the belief of some teachers that they can tough it out alone, without help from a school counselor.

Fear of Change

More experienced teachers may view the counselor as too young to know what he or she is talking about (see Case in Point 11.2 about my own experience) or may be set in their ways and resist any and all change. This is seen in statements such as, "I taught her mother and she was just as bad . . . ," or "I've done it this way for almost 30 years, and I see no good reason to change now . . . ," or "There is nothing that can be done; he's just 'dumb-as-a-post' and will never graduate anyway . . . ," or "All he needs is the 'board of education' applied to his backside."

Albert Ellis (2002) suggested that resistance to change may be linked to anxiety on the part of the teacher. Change and the introduction of new behaviors is anxiety provoking in many people, and change is what the school counselor is proposing. Even though the old tried-and-true techniques are not working, the teacher resists making any modification or attempting any alternative approaches (p. 28).

Resistance should never lead the counselor into a power struggle with the teacher; rather, resistance should be viewed as important information that can be used to strike an eventual compromise (Brigman, Mullis, Webb, & White, 2005; White et al., 1995).

CASE IN POINT 11.2

There were several unexpected resignations at a high school in the district where I was a middle school science teacher. The school system was located in a working-class neighborhood, and I was unexpectedly appointed to fill the position of high school counselor and assigned a caseload of 400 11th and 12th grade students. I was 24 years old at the time and had a master's degree earned on a part-time basis. When I began as the high school counselor, the ink was not yet dry on my state certificate permitting me to hold the job.

With few exceptions, the high school faculty were a quarter-century older and more experienced in education than I was. I soon realized that being called the "kid in the counseling office" was not contributing to my role as a professional. It was well into the spring of my first year as a school counselor before I was trusted enough to be asked to consult by a teacher having problems with several male students in her English class. After learning about her students and observing them in and outside of the classroom, I was ready to meet with her. I let her know that the boys were all baseball team members and were anxious to get out of her last period class to go to team practice. We collaborated on a plan that had me move the disruptive team members out of that class and into one of her sections of English taught earlier in the day. Those earlier classes became oversubscribed, but her last period class became smaller, and happier. The team members who were switched were given last period study halls from which the team coach could have them released to the practice field.

The flexibility I was willing to provide in helping solve this problem boosted my reputation, first with the English Department, then with other teachers in the school. By the end of the year I was able to work as a consultant with most of the faculty.

Thought Question. While being a young professional school counselor can be problematic, it also has a number of advantages. What advantages do young school counselors have compared with older counselors?

Fear of Success

There is another reason that some experienced teachers may resist consultation that can be described as "fear of success" (Ellis, 1985). There are schools in which teachers who have a reputation for being successful with troubled students are then assigned students whom no one else can handle. The last thing such a strategic teacher wants to do is star in the remake of the film *The Dirty Dozen*[4] (White & Mullis, 1998).

Overcoming Teacher Resistance

To overcome resistance, the school counselor should determine whether resistance is based on fear or whether the consultee does not approve of the course of action being proposed. For example, some teachers believe that all students should be treated exactly the same. For a teacher holding that value, the counselor's idea for a change in the teacher's behaviors toward a single student may be anathema. It is important to assure the teacher-consultee that his or her knowledge of this student, and students in general, is highly regarded by the counselor. Also, the consultee should know that the counselor finds the teacher's expertise vital to the success of the consultation process.

The whole consultation process should be positive and upbeat. A professional school counselor should find areas of agreement and identify values held in common with the consultee and use them as the starting points in building rapport. To move the process along, the counselor must show true empathy for the concerns, fears, and values of the consultee. This also means that the consultee may be important in setting the pace of the process.

Consulting With School Administrators

Standard 6: The professional school counselor discusses the counseling department management system and program action plans with the school administrator. (ASCA/Hatch & Bowers, 2005, p. 64)

The first consultation for a new professional school counselor should be with the school's principal. Even an experienced counselor should set an early meeting when a new principal is assigned to his or her school. During this consultation, the school counselor should learn what the principal's primary goals are and discuss ways the school's counseling staff can contribute to meeting them. The first consultation should also discuss the goals and objectives of the school's counseling office for the year. During this meeting, the school's counselor should also describe how consultation can be employed in the school to improve overall school climate and student outcomes (Brigman et al., 2005).

Counselor Ethics in Consulting

Three may keep a secret if two are dead.

Benjamin Franklin

Consultation in the schools implies that three parties (teacher, counselor, and sometimes the student) are involved and their efforts are confidential. Franklin's quip notwithstanding, professional school counselors have an obligation to offer ethically sound consulting services (Parsons & Kahn, 2005).

Ethical Practice

One cornerstone of ethical consultation is having the **informed consent** of the consultee. This requires that the counselor (consultant) help the consultee understand the nature of a consulting relationship, including an awareness of the potential for problems to develop. The role of the consultant and the tasks of the consultee should be clear and fully understood.

A second requirement for ethical practice is the need for confidentiality. All counseling activities of a professional school counselor must provide a safe, confidential, and trustworthy experience for the client. This does not change when the consultee is the agent receiving the counselor's services. The problem of maintaining confidentiality is magnified when services are being provided through one or more consultees. Richard Parsons and Wallace Kahn (2005) proposed several things a school counselor can do to maintain the trust of clients and consultees and protect their confidentiality while working within an organizational context involving many people. A modified list of these includes:

1. Engage all of the school's faculties and paraprofessionals in respecting the confidentiality of others, including students. This should be a central part of the culture of the school (post it on the school counseling office's web page).

2. Establish limits for information distribution for each participant in the consultation activity. This is done on a situational basis (in other efforts the rules may change).

3. Provide information to consultees on a need-to-know basis. As information is shared, a final reminder should be given about the need for confidentiality.

Legal Context

The U.S. Constitution does not provide a direct statement about the privacy rights of individuals. Some of the various states do provide statuary protections for the contacts between the professional school counselor and individual students. This form of protection is called *privileged communication*. These communications are never entirely protected, as a counselor has an obligation to break confidence when there is a potential that the client (student) will hurt him- or herself or someone else.

By sharing with the teacher (consultee) confidential records and some of the privileged communications the counselor has had with the student, the counselor has opened several legal issues to examination (McCarthy & Sorenson, 1993). One federal law, the Family Education Rights and Privacy Act (FERPA) of 1974 (discussed in Chapter 2) protects student records from many individuals.[5] When consulting with a teacher, the confidential student records may be read and discussed in the process of providing assistance for the student. The same rule holds true for consulting with the parents of a student who has not reached the age of 18 (age of adulthood).

Consultees who are teachers or parents may also examine official counseling records. Private counseling notes kept by and for use by the school counselor may not be shared. Once someone other than the counselor sees those notes, the status of the notes changes from private, highly confidential information into official school records.

Wrap-Up

Consultations by a professional school counselor are goal directed and focused on finding a resolution to a problem. When the point is reached that the consultation is brought to a conclusion, the last step is to evaluate the process. This is much like the evaluation phase in action research (see Chapter 14). One method of collecting evaluation data about the process is to employ a questionnaire like that shown in Exhibit 11.1 with the consultees (teachers).

EXHIBIT 11.1   **Sample Evaluation Questionnaire**

To what extent do you agree with the statements on this questionnaire?

1. The counselor listened and understood my point of view.
   a. Total and complete agreement
   b. Partial agreement
   c. Total disagreement
   d. I just cannot be sure and make that judgment

2. I felt the counselor was a trustworthy partner in the consultation.
   a. Total and complete agreement
   b. Partial agreement
   c. Total disagreement
   d. I just cannot be sure and make that judgment

3. The counselor providing the consultation had the interests of the students I teach as the focus of the process.
   a. Total and complete agreement
   b. Partial agreement
   c. Total disagreement
   d. I just cannot be sure and make that judgment

4. My job as a teacher was made easier by the help of the consultation.
   a. Total and complete agreement
   b. Partial agreement
   c. Total disagreement
   d. I just cannot be sure and make that judgment

5. One or more students have been helped through the changes I made as a result of the consultation.
   a. Total and complete agreement
   b. Partial agreement
   c. Total disagreement
   d. I just cannot be sure and make that judgment

Other data sources for the wrap-up evaluation may be found in the cumulative records of the affected students, overall test data, attendance records, disciplinary referrals, and the work products of students. Other data sources are observations and opinions of parents. The school administration may also contribute information to the wrap-up process, as may paraprofessional employees affected by the consultation activities.

CONSULTATION WITH PARENTS BY ● PROFESSIONAL SCHOOL COUNSELORS

We must always act on the assumption that the parents are not respon-
sible for all the bad qualities the child shows.... Parents should never be
reproached, even when there are just grounds. We can achieve much
more when we succeed in establishing a sort of a pact, when we per-
suade the parents to change their attitude and work with us according
to our methods.

Alfred Adler

Children develop their values and beliefs about others and themselves from people around them in their families (Adler, 1931). For that reason, school counselors need to view the student within the context of his or her family. Professional school counselors are not trained to provide therapeutic interventions to families, but they can consult with family members or even conduct small group sessions for the parents of students receiving interventions within the school. Consultations with parents and other family members can be highly effective because of the high degree of interdependency among family members (Mullis & Edwards, 2001).

Family Dynamics

To be better able to provide effective direct service for a troubled student, the school counselor should explore and understand the dynamic forces at play within the student's family. In addition to making interventions more effective, such understanding may also help teachers become more receptive to consultations about students for whom the family context is in havoc.

Boundaries

There is a need for clear boundaries and defined roles within families. Intact families that are healthy environments for children are structured with some form of hierarchy. In that hierarchy parents hold most power and resources, and children follow the lead of the parents (Minuchin, Lee, & Simon, 2006). In many cultures the family is not considered complete without including a number of extended members, for example, grandparents, uncles, and others. In this country, extended families are frequently established to support the structure of a parent-centered family organization by providing additional child care and support. Problems arise when there is dissention and clear boundaries are blurred, with adults disagreeing on child-rearing policies and procedures.

Life Cycle of the Family

One aspect of family dynamics is a function of the normal life cycle of modern American families. The loss of a parent through separation, divorce (see Case in Point 11.3), war deployment, or a combination of these can bring great stress to the lives of all concerned. This is especially true for younger children in the family. The impact is greater at younger ages, as little children do not have the ego strength or developed coping mechanisms to be resilient in times of great stress. Other life cycle factors are the birth of a new baby, the addition of grandparent(s) into the home on a long-term basis, death of a loved one, the incarceration of a family member, or having a sibling move away from home (military, college, marriage, etc.). Moving to a new home and changing schools, or having a house fire or other natural disaster disrupt the home, are also sources of great stress on children.[6]

CASE IN POINT 11.3

In November 2009 a disturbing letter was sent to a newspaper columnist that related the story of a girl who at the age of 15 was thrust into the center of a nasty divorce. A mother desperate to win at all costs accused her husband of serious abusive crimes. To "protect the girl" the court removed her from the parental custody of both parents while the charges and counterclaims were investigated. The letter writer explained that this was a traumatic experience for her, and it left her an emotional cripple filled with anger and resentment for the next 10 years of her life. By the age of 25 she reported being over that terrible place in her life. In the letter she never mentions receiving any mental health support from a school counselor or other mental-health professional.

Thought Questions. What could a professional school counselor have done when the girl was a teenager to reduce the negative impact and emotional pain she experienced? Many times a parent will subpoena the school's counselor to provide evidence during a deposition related to a custody decision. Beyond providing clear and honest testimony, what role can a school's counselor play in the life of a student caught up in a contested divorce case?

Stress on families and their children are acute in times of economic downturn. When a parent loses a job, and/or the family's home is in foreclosure, the stress levels can be excessive. The impact of poor economic conditions, such as the Great Recession of 2008–2010, can be felt by families who are not in economic difficulty but are compelled to take in relatives who have lost their homes.

When the family's problems seem intractable and beyond the capacity of the school counselor to resolve, referral to community agencies and mental health systems is appropriate. Remember the dictum of the ASCA national framework: "School counselors do not provide therapy" (ASCA/Hatch & Bowers, 2005, p. 42). Therapeutic interventions are provided by other school and community agencies, including community mental health clinics, school psychologists, family and social service agencies, hospitals, and charitable agencies with community outreach programs such as the following:

- Salvation Army: www.salvationarmyusa.org/usn/www_usn_2.nsf/vw-local/Programs

- Mental Health America: www.nmha.org

- Catholic Charities: www.catholiccharitiesusa.org/NetCommunity/Page.aspx?pid=1174

- Association of Jewish Family and Children's Agencies: www.ajfca.org

Cultural Sensitivity

Parents often find themselves caught between the demands and values of current society and those of significant members of the extended family. Other family members are often very ready to provide discipline ideas and all manner of other child-rearing advice. This need to criticize or kibitz in the raising of children of others is one of the most popular of indoor sports.[7] Being sensitive to this family conflict may involve asking a question such as, "What do other family members think of your . . . [describe an issue] . . . with your child?" "How do you handle differences of opinion around the dinner table when your child-raising practices are discussed?"

When consulting with parents, two goals for the school counselor are to help parents have confidence in their approach to parenting and to understand the abilities and strengths of their child. Counselors can also provide parents with the ego strength to avoid making dramatic changes each time relatives suggest they know "just what the child needs." This goal of empowerment may be opposed by strong forces at home. Frequently child-rearing and discipline ideas have deep cultural links and are part of the family's ethnic identity (Mullis & Edwards, 2001). The task of the counselor is to get parents to articulate what practices are being followed, then asking probing questions about those practices, such as, "What do you think is the best approach?," or "Is there something else you thought of trying?"

Since the Y generation[8] has begun to have children of its own, the suburbs have seen the growth of an overly protective type of parent. These parents have been described as helicopter parents, willing to hover over their child and always ready to swoop in to solve any problem or difficulty their child encounters (see Chapter 8 for more about these parents). The counselor consulting with such parents may need to help them see the true inner strengths and resiliency of their children and help them provide the "space" their children need to grow. A movement of some parents away from the highly protective and structured approach to child rearing have used the term **"free range children"** to describe the parenting model of providing children with the freedom to solve problems, set the pace for their own development, and select their own interests and activities (Gibbs, 2009).

Special Case of the Noncustodial Parent

In every school there are noncustodial parents attending activities their children participate in and discussing their children with counselors and teachers. Noncustodial parents are one possible outcome of a divorce and represent a large group of individuals. The ASCA has recognized the needs and opportunities that noncustodial parents represent.

> The school counselor is sensitive to changes in the family and recognizes that all parents, custodial and noncustodial, are vested with certain rights and responsibilities for the welfare of their children by virtue of their position and according to the law. (ASCA, 2004, B1-d)

There are times when the courts will order a noncustodial parent to avoid all contact with the child and the child's family. The custodial parent normally provides the school with this type of information. Such information can be verified by the school's social worker or by reviewing court documents at the local courthouse. Once again, this is a reason why most professional school counselors read the court records that are regularly published in the local newspaper. A question about the potential danger posed by the noncustodial parent may be answered by reviewing the national hotline of convicted sexual offenders at www.nsopw.gov/Core/Conditions.aspx (see Chapter 9 on this issue).

It must be remembered that noncustodial parents are still parents and as such deserve to be treated with dignity and included in the school's outreach to parents (Wilcoxon & Magnuson, 1999). One obvious necessity for a school counselor is to learn the state's laws governing access to student records for noncustodial parents. Another proactive step is to learn what both the custodial and noncustodial parents wish in terms of access to records. The school counselor should be familiar with the terms of the divorce as they relate to the child and the child's records. For example, questions of whether either parent may pick up the child after school or after a late activity must be known and shared with all teachers and paraprofessionals (e.g., bus drivers) involved. The counselor should find a way to keep the lines of communication open to both parents while staying abreast of all changes in the divorce decree or court orders as related to the child and parental rights.

A second proactive action the school's counselor can initiate is to educate the faculty and paraprofessionals of the need to provide two letters, and two e-mail blasts, one to each home, when school information is being sent out. Unless prohibited, the school should be viewed as being evenhanded and equitable with both parents.

One gaping pitfall to avoid is scheduling both parents in a way that could lead them into conflict. Also, avoid being drawn into providing postdivorce therapy to one or both of the child's parents (Wilcoxon & Magnuson, 1999).

Finally, remember that students are the ultimate focus of the school counselor. Children long for stability and often fantasize about the parents and family being reunited. The younger the children involved, the stronger that wish may be.

Consultation Process With Parents

As in the case of consultations with teachers, the first step in the process is a review of all known information about the family and its members. This includes other children who may be enrolled in other schools of the school system. Another step can include a quick review of the police blotter and local court records as posted in local newspapers. If the family has significant problems, they may have already come to the attention of local authorities.

Parental consultation may be counselor initiated, or the child's parent may initiate the request. In either case, the first step is to establish rapport and listen with intensity (active listening) to what the parent has to say. This active listening combined with empathy and encouragement can forge a good working relationship (Reed, 1985). As an icebreaker, counselors can employ small talk, for example, discussing the success of the high school's athletic program or talking about previous school contacts to establish rapport. School counselors should work to make parents feel comfortable talking with someone on the school's mental health team about their child. **Mimesis**, which means to imitate, describes how a school counselor can use the family's communication style (e.g., formal versus informal) to bridge the gap between home and school (Minuchin, 1974).

Counselors should always be professional, but the level of language used can be adjusted to align with what is most comfortable for the parents.

Counselor-initiated consultations with parents are normally part of a plan for helping a troubled student-client. The consultation plan may involve enlisting the parent both as a source of background information and as a resource for implementing change in the child's life. To reduce the potential for resistance, the change in approach or behavior being asked of the parent can be a small matter or task. For example, the counselor can ask the parent to make a small change in his or behavior, such as the regular devotion of 15 or 20 minutes to playing with or enjoying the company of the child each day. Just this little change can have a stunning impact on the child. A behavioral explanation of this change is that it serves as a signal for the start of the time when the adult changes from being mentally at work into the casual mode of being at home. This small modification can have a powerful ripple effect on the child and be seen in attitude and school behavior (Hirschland, 2008).

Sometimes parents need only to be reassured that they can "take charge" and provide the needed structure, set limits, and establish boundaries for their children. Children thrive in homes that have clear rules, a known organization, and structure (Coopersmith, 1967).

Family rituals have an important bonding role in the lives of both children and parents and serve to reduce the overall stress level within the family. Rituals such as those at bedtime and storytelling or reading together have enormous power to change a troubled child and also provide a sense of purpose and meaning for the parent.

The consultation may include having the parent look over the child's daily homework or provide a quiet place, without electronic gadgets, where the child can read and outline assignments for class. The consultation could work to get the parent to take the child to the public library every two weeks, where both parent and child can select books to be read for pleasure.

The counselor may help the parent understand the principles of reinforcement and shaping new behaviors on the part of the child. Teaching a parent how to extinguish inappropriate behaviors is difficult, but the rewards to the parent who is successful in stopping bad behavior can be huge (Ducharme, 2007).

Resistance

Parents may also resist the need to make any changes and may not even believe there is a problem. One technique that has been successful with parents who refuse to acknowledge the presence of a problem is to provide digital video proof. Classroom cameras should never be hidden, and questions about their presence should be answered directly, for example, "The camera is to observe how I am teaching and you are learning in my classes." Children are very comfortable being around electronic devices and should habituate to a small video camera recording the class onto a digital file. Witnessing such documented problems the student is having can make it easier for parents to accept the need to work with the professional school counselor. The use of video should be considered only in the case of total refusal by parents to cooperate, and after other avenues have been tried and have not been successful.

Reasons for Parental Resistance

Parents who had bad experiences years ago when they were students may feel uncomfortable around educators. For such parents, even entering a school building can be a stress-provoking experience. The family may be under stress over an illness, divorce, or job loss and be unable to focus on problems their children are having in school. Some parents have taken a fatalistic attitude and see the child as "damaged goods" that cannot be repaired. Statements such as "He's just like his old man, dumb-as-a-post and lazy to boot," or "She's as shifty and nasty as her mother, a worthless druggie who made my life miserable."

Resistance may reflect parents' lack of sophistication and fear they will have nothing worthwhile to contribute (Brigman et al., 2005). Other parents have "heard it all before" and do not wish to be blamed again for their child's problems.

Overcoming Resistance

When meeting with parents, a school counselor should avoid appearing judgmental or in any way disrespectful. A good opening is to get parents to describe the normal morning routine around their home. This introductory line of questions also provides an opening for the counselor to express empathy for the complexity of getting everyone cleaned, dressed, fed, and off to school and work (Mullis & Edwards, 2001).

It is less important to know the source of the resistance being expressed by the parents than it is to find ways to defeat it. One method involves **normalizing** the child's problems. By normalizing, the counselor helps parents see how their child is responding within the margins of what is normal. If the consultation was initiated by the counselor to engage the parents in getting the child to do homework, statements such as the following can help the parents realize the problem is not all that difficult to resolve: "A lot of families have this problem with their teenaged children," or "This is fairly common among children in the middle school."

Another method that can be used to engage parents is by reframing the problem from a major negative issue into something more manageable and quotidian. A family may have initiated the consulting request because "Our daughter is sneaking out of the house at night when we are in bed. Lord only knows what she is up to gallivanting around in the middle of the night." Just as a politician's press aide can spin a serious political problem into something else, the professional school counselor should develop the ability to reframe problems: "Rebellion among adolescents is fairly commonplace. It is likely she is showing you she wants a bit more control over her life and choices." Then, "Perhaps we can find ways she can have a bit more freedom and input with the decisions about her activities" (Mullis & Edwards, 2001).

SUMMARY

Consultation by professional school counselors is normally conducted with fellow educators and school administrators and with parents of a school's students. The American School Counselor Association has included consultation as a basic skill of professional school counselors. In addition to being an efficient method for a school's counselor to deliver needed services, consultation can also strengthen the professional bonds among a school's counselor and the instructional staff and faculties.

Resolutions a counselor may achieve through consultation include immediate problems a teacher may have with some students or a problem a student is having that is best resolved indirectly by working through a teacher. Counselors can also be called upon to arbitrate and mediate interpersonal problems among students. A more efficient approach to working case by case with conflict resolution is to make it part of the guidance curriculum. By teaching conflict resolution in the classroom, the counselor can "deputize" a coterie of students to help reduce student-to-student problems in the school. Not all teachers are open to having the school's counselor provide them with consulting services. This reluctance may be related to fear of looking bad, or fear of doing well and being assigned many more problematic students.

School counselors consult with the building administrators to develop a good working relationship and provide support for the administration's efforts and goal attainment. Professional school counselors consult with parents to assist the family's children in school. Parents can provide the counselor with critical insights into the dynamic factors within the family impinging on the child and affecting his or her behaviors in school.

School counselors can refer complex cases to outside agencies and also consult with those agencies as the need arises. The ethics of outside consultation require both the counselor and agency to have prior approval of the parents to share confidential information about the child.

Perhaps the most commonly adopted method for counselors to employ when providing consultation regarding classroom management is direct behavioral consulting. This five-step process makes it possible for teachers to reduce inappropriate behaviors by students and replace them with productive and appropriate behaviors.

DISCUSSION QUESTIONS

1. What are some reasons the ASCA included skills as a consultant as a component of what a professional school counselor should be competent to do?

2. Some critics have pointed out that behavioral techniques are degrading and dehumanizing to students. What are the arguments on both sides of having a counselor employ direct behavioral counseling?

3. Each professional school counselor has an individual background and unique skills that he or she brings to the job. Many of these can be employed in establishing and carrying out a consulting relationship within the school. Take a moment to take stock of yourself. Make a list of these personal qualities, and describe how they could be helpful when consulting in a school.

4. List several issues in consultation that are likely to be positively or negatively affected by issues of ethnic diversity and differences between counselors and consultees.

5. Suppose your first job offer was to return as a counselor to the high school from which you graduated. What potential professional and practical problems and advantages would you foresee if you accepted the position?

RELATED READINGS

Brigman, G., Mullis, F., Webb, L., & White, J. (2005). *School counselor consultation: Developing skills for working effectively with parents, teachers, and other school personnel.* Hoboken, NJ: Wiley.

Christensen, O. C., & Schramski, T. G. (Eds.). (1983). *Adlerian family counseling: A manual for counselor, educator, and psychotherapist.* Minneapolis, MN: Educational Media.

Mendler, A. N. (1997). *Power struggles: Successful techniques for educators.* Rochester, NY: Discipline Associates.

Parsons, R. D., & Kahn, W. J. (2005). *The school counselor as consultant: An integrated model for school-based consultation.* Belmont, CA: Brooks/Cole, Thomson.

Worden, M. (1994). *Family therapy basics.* Pacific Grove, CA: Brooks/Cole.

NOTES

1. A number of school counselors prefer to remain aloof from the schools' faculties and eschew the "faculty room." This creates a barrier between the faculties and the counselors. Such barriers inhibit the development of mutual trust and impede cooperation.

2. The use of a counselor as a substitute is not appropriate under the national framework (ASCA/Hatch & Bowers, 2005), but this case occurred long before the new guidelines. In reality today, each school counselor must decide for him- or herself whether to step up and help a school principal during a brief personnel crisis. The school's principal plays a significant role in defining a school counselor's career, making a refusal to help out a difficult decision.

3. There are a number of behavioral techniques that can be used to modify behaviors of students. These include establishing performance contracts, setting up token economies, and using behavioral analysis and contingency reinforcement.

4. The 1967 movie set in the European theater of World War II starred Lee Marvin, Ernest Borgnine, Telly Savalas, Charles Bronson, and James Brown. The film was written by E. M. Nathanson and directed by Robert Aldrich. The story line has a good field-grade officer (played by Lee Marvin) lead a band of 12 soldiers convicted of capital crimes on a mission behind enemy lines.

5. This law, also known as the Buckley Amendment, allows educators with a legitimate educational need to have access to the records. In addition, parents, military recruiters, and federal agents auditing educational programs have access to confidential student records.

6. The Children's Health Fund estimated that of the 600,000 people displaced for more than a month by the damage caused by Hurricane Katrina in 2005, 160,000 were children. Of these, 20,000 children from the poorest families had no permanent home 3 years later. Of all the children, about 50,000 have shown signs of diminished academic ability, poorer health, and/or problems of mental health (Redlener, 2009).

7. In 2010 the Amazon book list contained a total of more than 64,000 titles on raising children.

8. The Y generation are the grandchildren of the first wave of baby boomers. Members of the Y generation were born after 1980.

CHAPTER

12

Professional School Counselors With Parents and the Greater Community

OBJECTIVES

By reading and studying this chapter you should acquire the competency to:

- Explain the impact of parents in the development of a student's academic socialization
- List the various components of public school education for which families are expected to pay and describe several strategies for paying for them
- Prepare for a counselor–parent meeting
- Develop programs to improve parental engagement and involvement at the elementary, middle, and high school levels
- Provide leadership in engaging language-minority parents in the school and its programs
- Describe the contemporary history of school reform in the United States
- Describe how a professional school counselor can facilitate school program reform committees

❝ I'm not a teacher: only a fellow traveler of whom you asked the way.
I pointed ahead—ahead of myself as well as you. **❞**

George Bernard Shaw

● INTRODUCTION AND THEMES

About 89% of a child's life is spent in the care and custody of parents. This length of time makes the influence of parents very significant in the academic socialization of children. Parental poverty makes the socialization task even more difficult; an extra barrier to this process occurs when parents have a limited proficiency in English and are unfamiliar with North American culture. School counselors can find ways to prevent children who are from poverty and diverse cultural backgrounds from missing out on any co-curricular or academic advantage.

Counselors can support all parents to be engaged in their children's school. Counselors can also coach parents to help them develop skills that will enable parents to be involved in their child's academic development at home. Parents who are English-language learners (ELLs) present special problems for the counselor who is finding ways to encourage their engagement. The professional school counselor can use various methods, including language outreach efforts, to overcome these problems.

Education in the United States was sharply critiqued in the 1980s in a widely read report from the office of Secretary of Education, Terrell Bell. One outcome of the critical voices of that era has been the standards-based education movement and high-stakes testing mandates. Reform of public schools is ongoing and often is carried out at the local level. Professional school counselors have important skills that can assist in facilitating reform committees working in schools.

● SCHOOL COUNSELOR'S ROLE IN PARENTAL ENGAGEMENT

Parental Impact

Students enrolled in primary grades experience about 1,000 hours of classroom instruction each school year. This represents about 11% of a child's life. The other 89% of the time children are in the custody and care of their parents.

The important role of parents in the education and academic development of their children cannot be overstated. School success becomes possible when parents establish a climate that nurtures and supports their child's academic growth. Laurence Steinberg (1996) has argued that the goal of every parent should be to raise children who are truly engaged in learning. Pundits providing parental advice have come and gone, but the importance of the parental role in each child's academic development remains unquestioned (El Nokali, Bachman, & Votruba-Drzal, 2010).[1]

The importance of the parental role was written into federal legislation in 2002. Part of the No Child Left Behind Act (NCLB) required that all schools have a parent involvement policy designed to engage students' parents in school (Jacobson, 2008a). The law also mandated that parents have an opportunity to serve in leadership and advisory roles with parent–school committees (Epstein & Sheldon, 2006). In many schools it is the role of the school's counselor to form these parent advisory boards and provide them with ongoing support and guidance. (See Case in Point 12.1.)

CASE IN POINT 12.1

In the fall of 2009 a Wayne County, North Carolina, middle school adopted a plan proposed by the school's parent advisory board to have teachers improve the grades of students who donated money to the committee's efforts. The parent advisory board wanted funds for the purchase of new technology for the school. Under the advisory board's plan, which was approved by Susie Shepard, the school's principal, a donation of $20 bought a student the right to have 10 points added to any two tests of his or her choosing. A $60 donation bought the student the right to raise his or her grade on two tests by 20 points and admission for two people to a fifth period dance and private pizza party. When challenged, the school's principal stated that "a 10 point addition to two tests was unlikely to change a student's final grade" (Veltri, 2009).

Thought Questions. What the press reports did not describe was the role of the school's counselor in this program. If you were the middle school counselor, what steps would you have taken with the parent advisory board? To what extent can a parents group be directed by school personnel such as the counselor?

Moderating Effect of Poverty

Every child is born with numerous abilities and areas of potential development. The grinding and pernicious impact of poverty in the United States takes a large toll in loss of human potential and human abilities going undeveloped. Poverty plays a major role in developmental delay and disabilities in children. Approximately 1 in 5 American children lives in poverty, of which more than half live in rural communities (see Chapter 8). Of the 50 counties in the United States with the greatest percentage of families living in poverty, 48 are in rural communities (Save the Children, 2009). More recent research has documented the negative role that living in a poor neighborhood can have on the development of reading skills (University of British Columbia, 2010).

The impact of poverty is additive over the years in both academic loss, and the tendency for maladjustment (Evans & English, 2002). By the time young people are high school seniors, the effect of impoverished living, especially in single-parent families, is even more pronounced. High school students from intact families have far better school attendance and better grades and measured achievement than do children of divorce (Ham, 2003). It seems that the negative impact on children and youth of living in a single-parent family is greater on boys (lacking a consistent father figure) than it is on girls (Palosan & Aro, 1994).

The ability of a school's educational programs to have a positive impact on children from impoverished backgrounds is inversely related to the proportion of students living below the poverty line who are attending the school (Levitt & Dubner, 2005). When a school draws its student population from a cluster of impoverished homes, it is more likely to be underfunded, have less well-prepared faculties, and have an administration stretched to the limit to develop and implement an effective curriculum.[2] Schools in impoverished communities tend to have the highest faculty turnover and employ the least experienced teachers and counselors (Hanushek & Rivkin, 2006).[3]

Antecedents of Children Living in Poverty. Poverty in the United States is directly related to the likelihood a young child will experience a traumatic injury or develop a chronic illness, including asthma and HIV/AIDS, during childhood and can even lead to an early death (Bassuk & Friedman, 2005; Klerman, 1991). Both malnutrition and the potential for experiencing a traumatic injury are quintupled among the children of homeless families (Bassuk, Konnath, & Volk, 2006).

Most children living in poverty are being raised in single-parent families (U.S. Department of Health and Human Services, 2009a). The single-parent status may be the choice of a parent who either divorced or never cared to marry his or her partner, or it may have occurred with the death of a partner. It is the single-parent head of household who is often the most harassed and busy of people. These single parents often are most in need of assistance by the school's counselor. (See Case in Point 12.2.) Unmarried women below the age of 30 deliver almost half (44%) of all children born in the United States (Barton & Coley, 2007). Thirty percent of all students in public schools live in single-parent families; and 40% of those students from single-parent homes live in poverty (U.S. Census Bureau, 2007a). (See Figure 12.1.)

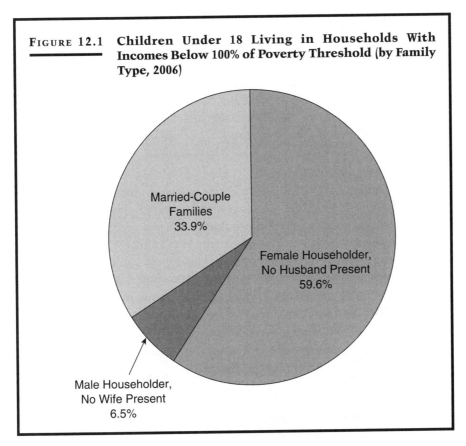

FIGURE 12.1　**Children Under 18 Living in Households With Incomes Below 100% of Poverty Threshold (by Family Type, 2006)**

SOURCE: U.S. Census Bureau, Current Population Survey (2007a).

NOTE: The U.S. Census Bureau poverty threshold for a family of four was $20,614 in 2006.

CASE IN POINT 12.2

Anna Freud (the youngest child of Sigmund Freud) published the first psychological study of children separated from their fathers by war. She collected data from children enrolled in the Hampstead Wartime Nursery for Homeless Children, a residential school she established in wartime London. Her World War II findings about the deleterious impact of separating children from their families have influenced social policy since that era. Our reticence to remove children from their homes and place them in institutions is one example of her influence. She was a powerful advocate for supporting troubled children within their families (Yorke, 1996).

(Continued)

(Continued)

Thought Questions. When a child is separated from a loved parent through incarceration following the parent's conviction for a serious crime, there is likely to be stress-induced repercussions seen in the child.[4] What role can a professional school counselor play to alleviate these likely problems with elementary, middle school, and adolescent students? In what ways should counseling be similar and different for these age groups?

Nuclear families have been the foundation upon which civilization has been built (see Case in Point 12.3). Children living in nuclear families that include both a father and mother have better achievement and are more successful in school than children who live in single-parent families (Dawson, 1991). A longitudinal study of elementary school students in Canada found significantly better achievement among children of two-parent families compared with children living with one parent (Adams & Ryan, 2000). This finding was more intense for families that were less wealthy.

CASE IN POINT 12.3

Archaeological research in central Europe has unearthed proof that nuclear families are a long-standing feature of Western civilization (Haak et al., 2008). The discovery from Saxony-Anhalt, Germany, has been dated by isotopic analysis as being from 2700 B.C.E.[5] Archaeologists found several well-preserved ancient graves. The graves tell the story of a family that was attacked by others with arrows and the resulting violent death of several children and an adult male and female. All were ritualistically buried, adult male and female facing each other with the children aligned between them. The bodies were covered and the heads were aligned to point toward the Southern Hemisphere. DNA analysis confirmed the unfortunate family was a nuclear family of two adults and their two preadolescent children. One point from this field study is that the nuclear family predates recorded history and may be as old as our species.

Thought Question. There are authors today making the case that the construct of an ideal nuclear family is now dé classé. One proposal is to describe modern families as "postmodern" (Hareven, 1987). The term **postmodern family** encompasses singles living alone, homosexual couples with or without children, single parents, and extended families with one or more grandparents playing pivotal roles. Is there such a thing as a postmodern child? Describe various impacts different postmodern families are likely to have on the children they raise.

Professional School Counselors and Children in Poverty. Although the school counselor is not prepared to provide social work or family therapy, he or she can work to find ways to keep parents of families living in poverty connected to their children's education. The counselor should provide a way that parents can attend parent–teacher conferences. This may require working with the school's instructional technology professional to provide parents who cannot come to the school with "virtual conferences."[6] Another task is working to ensure that there are no language barriers for parents, especially parents without documentation and language-minority parents living in poverty (see Chapter 8). School counseling programs that employ multiple strategies to support students and their parents have been proven to improve both student achievement and social skills (Boxx, Petrie, Walsh, & Orecchia, 2010).

Problem of Money. In a similar way, the school counselor should work to ensure that all children, especially children in poverty, have a complete kit of school supplies and ensure they are never charged for field trips or special events. These steps must be taken in a way that preserves the dignity of both the parents and children. Likewise, high school counselors should find funds to make it possible for all students who are able and interested in taking advanced placement (AP) classes to have the cost of the Educational Testing Service (ETS) examination covered. The cost of AP examinations in 2010 was $86.00 each. ETS provides a partial scholarship for students in poverty (as certified by the counselor or designated test coordinator) of $22.00. This lowers the test's cost to $56.00 each for impoverished students (College Board, 2010). As motivated and bright students may take two or three AP classes in their junior and senior years, that represents a cost burden that many families cannot sustain. For some families, it could literally be a choice between putting food on the table and paying the ETS bill.

Cost of College Application Process. The fact that some students from impoverished backgrounds wish to apply to college should be celebrated and made hassle free for the students. In 2010–2011 the SAT II with one advanced test cost $47.00 and $21.00 for each additional advanced test. That same year the ACT, including the advanced writing test, cost $48.00. As most students take both tests two times, this can place a burden of more than $200.00 on an impoverished family.

High school counselors can work to find sponsors for all specialized education related costs, for example, co-curricular activities, tests, and field trips, faced by students from impoverished backgrounds. Community service clubs such as the English Speaking Union, Kiwanis, Rotary, Lions Clubs, Elks, Moose, Independent Order of Odd Fellows, and the Junior Chamber of Commerce may all be willing to help sponsor needy students with good academic potential and high motivation. Addresses of the meetings for these clubs are normally posted in local newspapers and listed on outdoor advertising in the community. The counselor can locate the local branch leadership through the national web pages for these service organizations. The cost to the school counselor for getting the support of a service club is often to provide one or more luncheon speeches to the local membership.

Pay to Play. Another area where a school's counselor may be able to help a student from an impoverished home is by encouraging athletic participation. Athletic participation along with other co-curricular activities has been shown to improve student achievement and grades, and improve the student's appeal to college admissions officers. Both average grades and the number of classes passed are positively related to participation in after-school sports (Benson, 1994).

In middle school and high school there are frequently costs involved for student athletes. Some schools require that a fee be paid for participating. Students may be required to purchase personal equipment such as spikes, running shoes, tennis racquets, protective equipment including mouth guards, and baseball gloves. It can easily cost a family more than $100 to have a child participate in a low-cost athletic program. One study of scholastic ice hockey found that participation on the team cost students' parents thousands of dollars a year (M. Harris, 2009). About 65% of children from upper-middle-class families participate in team sports, while only 44% of working-class families have children participating.

Professional school counselors can work with team coaches to ensure that no student is "cost out" of participating. In the role of advocate for students, the professional school counselor should work to have fees for participating in co-curricular activities waived for students who receive a free or reduced-cost lunch (children of poverty). A major source of external funding that the school's counselor may approach to solicit funds for student athletes is the sports booster club in the high school. This group of parents and interested alumni raises funds and supports various activities related to schools' athletic programs. (See Table 12.1 for a sampling of the costs of sports team participation.)

Nutritional Support. Students who may qualify for a free or reduced-cost lunch or a free breakfast should have these provided (see Table 12.2 for more of the qualifications for a free or reduced cost lunch). The school counselor can make certain all qualified students are provided with the benefits of these nutrition programs. Beyond the school's campus, the school's counselor can work in cooperation with the school's social worker to ensure that impoverished families of the school community are receiving all appropriate assistance, including food baskets and holiday gifts for children, from charitable organizations. (Some of the many community resources were listed in Chapter 9.)

TABLE 12.1   Ancillary Costs for Participating in a School-Sponsored Team Sport

Required physical by physician	$50–$100
Athletic support underwear, male	$10–$75
Athletic underwear	$30–$100
Baseball or softball glove	$100–$400
Running shoes	$150–$300
Ice skates	$75–$350
Tennis racquets	$75–$500
Mouth guard	$10–$50
Tennis/basketball shoes	$100–$160
Track spikes, football cleats, baseball spikes	$75–$150
Golf clubs (starter set)	$175–$500

TABLE 12.2   Income Eligibility Guidelines for a Free or Reduced-Cost Lunch (2009–2010)

Household Size	Maximum Household Income		
	Poverty Line	**Reduced-Cost Lunch**	**Free Lunch**
2	$14,570	$26,955	$18,941
3	18,310	33,874	23,803
4	22,050	40,793	28,665
5	25,790	47,712	33,527
6	29,530	54,631	38,389
7	33,270	61,550	43,251
8	37,010	68,469	48,113

SOURCE: U.S. Department of Agriculture (2009).

NOTE: The price for a reduced-cost lunch is $.50 per day.

Home Environment

An academically conducive home environment is one in which parents monitor how their child's time is spent. For example, in homes with high-achieving students, the amount of time the youngster spends playing computer games is limited, as is the amount and type of television shows the child views. About 15% of the variation in students' standardized test scores is the product of these two variables: time spent watching TV and time spent playing computer games (Holbrook & Wright, 2004). See Case in Point 12.4 for more on the dangers of addiction to computer games.

CASE IN POINT 12.4

Video games become more lifelike and sophisticated each year. Online games are updated on a regular basis, even while a player is engaged in the virtual world of the game. The games require a high degree of attention and concentration and pay off the player with new and cognitively greater challenges at each level of success. Many games pit the player against a field of other players in this country and around the world. Cognitive rewards provide a powerful reinforcement for many young people. Gamers engaged competitively with others tend to be males, while girls prefer solo-person computer games ("AP-AOL games," 2006). The result is the youngster is pulled into an extremely alluring world in which some children can escape from reality and be heroes who do awe-inspiring deeds and become conquering victors. The result can be a child who develops a pathological addiction to the games. Richard Bartle (1996) developed a matrix of personality types associated with game behaviors and devised a 30-question measurement to assess these personality types: www.mud.co.uk/richard/hcds.htm.

Survey research by the Harris Poll and the National Institute on Media and the Family suggests that 8.5%, or about 2 in 23 students, between the ages of 8 and 18 years have an addiction to computer games. This addiction is similar in its pathology to gambling addiction (Gentile, 2009). Typically, addicted gamers are male, experience falling grades, loss of friends, avoidance of home life and interaction, and are compelled to get back to the game when away from a computer. While playing, they lose themselves in the computer action and thereby have no sense of time or even their biological needs. The introduction of cell phone gaming, and also the super-game platform Wii, has made it easier for a gamer to develop a true pathological addiction. The fact that computers are ubiquitous in our world today means there is no way to avoid being near one.

There is an online support group for parents of computer-gaming addicted children. This group is Mothers Against Videogame Addiction and Violence: www.mavav.org. There is also an online, homemade documentary depicting Internet game addiction. This Armature Studio production may be over the top, but it does show the intractable nature of Internet game addiction: http://video.google.com/videoplay?docid=1641116117087180693#.

Thought Questions. If a school has an open computer laboratory that students can access during lunch hour and study halls, what policy would you encourage the principal to establish for its use? What recommendation would you make to the principal for use of Internet connected–handheld devices by students while they are in school?

The best thing a parent can do for a child's academic development is to provide a positive academic role model. It is not the parents' possession of high school diplomas and college degrees that is the causal factor in the achievement of school-aged children; it is the parental attitude toward education and expectations held for their child. Children of parents who express lofty goals for education achieve better scores on the National Assessment of Educational Progress (NAEP) examinations than do children who have indifferent parents (Halpern, 2006).

Counselors' Role in Students' Home Life

Themes of home organization for academic success and educational expectations are topics that professional school counselors should take into the community through parenting seminars, public presentations, local newspaper guest editorials, and the counseling office web page. If the parent advisory board publishes a newsletter, the school's counselor can serve as its editor and add important ideas and suggestions in the paper for all parents. There will be cases when coaching parents in a group session will not be effective. In such cases an individualized session or two may be indicated. This consultation can be scheduled with parents in the form of a simple parent conference.

Special Problem of Language-Minority Families in Poverty. The relationship among parental practices, school engagement, and educational outcomes has been well documented over the years (Sternberg, Dornbusch, & Brown, 1992). When parents are engaged with the child's school to assist with class activities, chaperone events and trips, and also work cooperatively to resolve learning problems, the student learns to value school and adopt academic goals. By seeing his or her parents working along with his or her counselor and teachers, the young student learns that education is important and valued by his or her parents. There is also evidence students are given more attention by their school counselors and teachers when parents are engaged with the school (Pomerantz, Moorman, & Litwack, 2007). The positive impact of parental engagement can be measured across all ethnicities and income levels (Glanville & Wildhagen, 2007).

Living in a low-income household and not being familiar with the language or culture of the community is a double burden carried by many recent immigrant families in the United States. These factors make engagement with the school difficult for parents (Carreón, Drake, & Barton, 2005; Sohn, 2007). The key for a school counselor to engaging parents from different cultures is respect. Personal respect and learning basic phrases in the parent's primary language can go a long way to make parents feel comfortable in an American school setting (see Chapter 8). A school can also show respect by hiring as many professionals and paraprofessionals as possible who are bilingual and bicultural. These personnel can provide a bridge to the parents of the community. Outreach to the various ethnic and language minority communities is essential to improving engagement.

> *The only reason I always try to meet and know the parents better is because it helps me to forgive their children.*
>
> M. Louis Johannot
> Head Master of Ecole Le Rosey
> Canton Du Vaud, Switzerland

Meetings Between School Counselors and Parents. The first priority during a parent conference is to put the parents at ease and prevent any feelings of confrontation (Mendler, 2006). This may be achieved by starting the conference by encouraging parents to discuss their observations and raise any questions they may have. After parents have made their comments, it is then appropriate for school counselors to ask general questions of parents about their children at home.

Getting a feel for the student's schedule and activities away from school can provide professional school counselors with important insights to the student and his or her behaviors. These questions can be directed to gain an approximation of the time spent by the child playing computer games and watching TV, reading for pleasure, doing homework, and participating in sports. The child's schedule, including the amount of time he or she sleeps at night, is also an important piece of information to gain.

School counselors should be positive when describing the student at school in domains such as work habits, social interactions, and academic development. Problem areas for the student should be posed in terms of how the school and parents can work as a team to improve the current status (see Chapter 11 for more on consulting with parents).

Conferences also provide an excellent opportunity to remind parents to keep lines of communication open between home and school. The counselor should show parents how to access the school's web page and contact the school's various offices. Depending on school policy, the school's counselor can share his or her e-mail address with parents and let them know policies of the school regarding online contacts.

A new direction in parent conferences with school counselors involves the use of video-conferencing technology. Modern home computer systems are frequently equipped with video cameras, making the two-way meeting easy to accomplish. This application of technology is actually a videophone system connecting the school computer equipped with a video camera with a similar unit at the home or office of the parent. One advantage to this approach is that it makes conferences possible with parents who cannot take time off from work to attend.

When a counselor has made the decision to meet with a student's parents, he or she needs to do a lot of preparatory work. The school's counselor should review the following data sources in preparing to meet with a student's parents:

1. All teachers with whom the student has regular instructional contact

2. Coaches and co-curricular activity directors who have contact with the student

3. All disciplinary and attendance records

4. At the elementary level, all relevant student portfolios

5. The student's health file

6. Standardized test scores for past 2 years

7. Observations of paraprofessionals including recess aides, library assistants, cafeteria aides, and bus route drivers

8. Other educational specialists (school psychologist, reading specialist, speech teacher, professional librarian, school nurse, and principal or vice principal) who have had contact with the student

It is usually a good idea for a school counselor to summarize data that is amassed prior to meeting with parents into a few points that can be written in précis form on a small note card. It is off-putting for parents to watch while page upon page of notes by the counselor are reviewed in front of them.

In addition to this student-focused research, the professional school counselor may need to review clinical research related to the student's circumstance.

If bibliotherapy is indicated for the parents, appropriate titles should be selected and available.

> *If public education does not take into consideration the circumstances of family life, and everything else that bears on a man's general education, it can only lead to an artificial and methodical dwarfing of humanity.*
>
> *Johann Pestalozzi*

● OPTIMIZING PARENTAL ENGAGEMENT AND INVOLVEMENT

When parents are engaged and involved with their child's school, the probability that the child will have better grades, higher achievement, and better adjustment to the expectations and demands of the school's environment is enhanced significantly (NAEP, 2004). Engagement includes belonging to the parents association, volunteering to assist on field trips and outings, and having regular meetings with the child's teacher. Survey data demonstrate that only 56% of all parents attend scheduled teacher conferences, and only 40% review their child's homework (Markow & Martin, 2005). A statistical analysis of longitudinal data by the economist Steven Levitt confirms the role of both parent engagement and parent involvement in the success of students in school (Levitt & Dubner, 2005).

Involvement occurs mostly at home and is composed of parent support activities focused on improving learning in school. For example, reading to young children is a starting point in the process. At each developmental level, parental involvement plays a supportive role facilitating children's learning (Gold, Simon, & Brown, 2005).

Helping Parents Get Ready for a Teacher Conference

The attendance rate for parents at teacher conferences is directly related to the wealth and income of the parents (Scott, 2009). It is critical to improve the level of engagement of all parents, especially parents living in the poorest conditions. Counselors can provide leadership in developing parent-to-school cooperation and parental engagement.

Most elementary schools provide time in the fall when all parents are encouraged to have individual conferences with their children's classroom teachers. Frequently parents will feel inadequate and not able to ask questions during parent–teacher conferences. This along with scheduling and baby-sitting problems will inhibit parental attendance. These and other barriers for parents to overcome in order to attend a parent–teacher conference are issues the school's counselor can address.

Counselors can provide virtual conferences as needed. The use of virtual conferences can eliminate the problem of scheduling for working parents and make it possible for the parents and teacher to virtually meet at any time convenient for both parties. The problem parents have with finding baby-sitting so they can attend the conference can be resolved by hiring paraprofessionals to provide a drop-in child care option in the school's cafeteria. High school students earning service learning credits and volunteers from service clubs can supplement this group of caregivers. As each parent conference requires less than an hour, this in-school child care program will have a high turnover rate.

CARTOON 12.1 **"Parent Involvement"**

"Sometimes I wish our school did not try quite so hard to get parent involvement."

SOURCE: Merv Magus.

Professional school counselors should help parents get ready to meet with their child's teacher. This can be done by publishing ideas for questions that parents may want to have teachers answer during the conference. This same list should also be shared with the school's faculties and administration. The following is a list of possible items for parents to ask:

1. Ask your child what you should ask the teacher. Then ask the teacher the child's questions and others you may have.

2. How are grades determined when report cards are expressed in standards?

3. How does my child get along with his or her peers?

4. What is my child's apparent attention span?

5. Does my child pay attention and follow directions?

6. What are my child's greatest strengths?

7. Is my child a disciplinary problem?

8. What dimensions of my child are least advanced?

9. What can I do to support what is going on in school?

Engagement and Elementary School Parents

The education critic Chester Finn once averred, "What's most important for all parents is to share responsibility with the schools for how well their children learn" (Finn, 1991, p. 271). This parent engagement effect is a consistent that works no matter how wealthy or poor a family may be (Gonzalez & Wolters, 2006). Table 12.3 presents a short list of factors that indicate the level and quality of home–school communication and cooperation.

TABLE 12.3   National Standards for Parent–Family Involvement

Communicating   Communication between home and school is regular, two-way, and meaningful.
Parenting   Parenting skills are promoted and supported.
Student learning   Parents play an integral role in assisting student learning.
Volunteering   Parents are welcome in the school, and their support and assistance are sought.
School decision making and advocacy   Parents are full partners in decisions that affect children and families.

SOURCE: Adapted from Epstein, Coates, Salinas, Sanders, and Simon (1997).

School Counseling for Fully Engaged Parents

Professional school counselors can provide the structure for contacts that draw parents into activities of the school. All contacts between the school and parents must be designed to foster a trusting and mutually respectful approach and encourage ongoing parent participation.

For example, all schools hold open houses. This tried-and-true technique can be off-putting for many parents who see schools as intimidating and foreboding places (Hill & Tyson, 2009). As was noted in Chapter 11, this parental attitude may reflect the parents' school problems from years ago, or it can be the product of being poorly treated during an earlier school contact. These background differences contribute to the difference in impact that parental engagement has across different ethnic groups (Musu, Chang, Werner, & Karabenick, 2008). To break this cycle, Joyce Levy Epstein and her colleagues at Johns Hopkins University suggest an approach that stresses informal contacts with parents prior to the time of formal conferences (Epstein, Sanders, Salinas, Jansorn, & Voorhis, 2002). That model is now part of the National Network of Partnership Schools (NNPS) (Dessoff, 2008). Epstein's model includes several types of involvement that school counselors can employ to establish good levels of engagement with parents.

Among ways parents can be drawn into the school's programs are assemblies that give parents a participatory role. Epstein suggests creating informal channels through which educators and parents can meet. Informal channels may include holding a picnic or barbecue during the week prior to the school's opening. Working with other school professionals, school counselors can coordinate a family story-reading day when parents and other family members are invited into the classroom to read stories to small groups of children. When these days are scheduled several times during the school year, with different parents reading to children each time, many children and parents can feel the pride of being part of a school's instructional activity.

Activity Planning

To plan ways to optimize parental engagement, the school's counselor can survey parents to learn what things they wish to see the school provide for both students and the larger school community. This survey of preferred activities can be done over the Internet or during a back-to-school night. The goal is to provide a way for parents to have input on the type of informal and structured (formal) activities they would like to see the school develop and the programs it can offer.

The Public Broadcast System, PBS, provides more than 90 online classes for educators. These classes can be used to earn graduate credit at a number of colleges. One class titled "Connecting Family, Community, and Schools" runs 30 hours and can carry 2 credits. To learn more about this offering, see www.pbs.org/teacherline/catalog/courses/INST320/.

Once plans for the year have been organized and placed on the school's master calendar by the counselor, he or she should publicize that list. This can include publishing brochures for advertising plans and use of local shopping outlets and community churches to distribute information to parents and other members of a community. Direct mail and Internet advertisements are other approaches for school counselors to use to get the word out about school activities. If appropriate, all brochures (advertisements) and the school's web page should be bilingual.

Informal activities for improving parent engagement should be listed along with the more formal activities. Informal activities include opening school resources (e.g., swimming pools, libraries, computer centers, vocational counseling and employment information, and topical education programs) to the community. Other activities school counselors can develop include setting up interactive (Internet or telephonic) homework assistance, holding monthly student recognition awards assemblies, and engaging families in charitable drives to help feed the truly indigent in the community.

One special group of parents for school counselors to get to know and include in school programs are members of the U.S. military. Even though these families must always be ready to pick up and move to another location, the local schools should work to include them in the life of the school.

Sometimes a parent may be a member of the National Guard or active reserves, and even their neighbors may not know that the parent is an active member of the reserves (Cromartie, 2010). This can make the job of the counselor more complicated if or when the parent receives an unexpected notification of a call to active duty. Not being aware of parents who are reservists in the military can make it difficult for a counselor to provide interventions and assistance for their children. This is an excellent reason for school counselors to spend time reviewing student enrollment data. If the question of military status is not asked, the counselor should work with the school's leadership in revising the enrollment form.

Special Case of Adolescents

The last thing in the world a teenager is likely to want is to have his or her mother serve as a chaperone on a class field trip (Hill & Chao, 2009).

Research by Nancy Hill has verified observations of experienced professional school counselors about the changing dynamic between parents and teenagers. This change is most evident as teenagers transition first into middle school and beyond to high school. Starting in elementary grades, parents' engagement in their child's school programs has a positive impact on achievement (Englund, Luckner, Whaley, & Egeland, 2004). At the elementary level, participation by parents in school functions and activities is important for a child's success, but it needs to be supplemented by another type of involvement at home: acting as positive role models, reading with children, and checking homework.

The 3 years that teenagers spend in middle school can be a time when students develop new discipline problems, experience loss of self-esteem, and have less engagement with school and their personal academic development (Hill, Tyson, & Bromell, 2009). This is known as a loss in **academic socialization**. Loss in the level of academic socialization is not inevitable. Middle school teens who perceive their parents as being both involved with school while they are at home and involved *in situ* at the school itself experience greater academic success than their peers (Eccles & Harold, 1996). *Involved at home* refers to parents who (1) check and verify homework, (2) provide a quiet work and study area and enforce a study hall each evening in their home, and (3) encourage reading and verify that assigned chapters are read each day. Home-based school involvement when paired with involvement in the actual school's activities makes a powerfully motivating force for positive academic socialization (Dubner & Levitt, 2005). Teachers posting daily assignments on the school's web page facilitate these parental engagement activities. Once the posting of homework and project dates is a policy, the school's counselors can work to keep parents informed of how to access this source of information.

While the involvement of parents in activities of the high school wanes with the student's age, parental engagement through home-based efforts can continue to have a positive impact on achievement. Good academic work habits developed during middle school can carry over through high school and college and beyond. This is true for both minority and Anglo-White students (Jeynes, 2007). These work habits are learned through the continuing support of the teenager's academic socialization (Viadero, 2009b).

Transition Into Secondary Education

Better-educated parents have less trouble relating to academic challenges their adolescent children face. Better-educated parents understand how to select courses that lead into a career path, and they are primed to start early getting their offspring ready for each new grade level and challenge. This capacity for better-educated parents to have an impact on the motivation and academic achievement of their middle school and high school students takes the form of the usual heightened engagement with school along with involvement by providing instructional support at home (Hill & Taylor, 2004).

Teenaged children of less well-educated parents and parents living in poverty may find direct parental pressure for academic success is not very effective in modifying adolescent behavior or in improving levels of achievement. These parents frequently experience pushback by their teenaged children, reflecting many factors linked to academic socialization. Many less well-educated parents do not know how to go about pressuring and encouraging their children to be academically successful. In some cases, it is the parents' own history with school that shapes how they provide for the academic socialization of their children. Parents who are uncomfortable in school settings, or not at ease when around teachers, may be indifferent to the education process but feel obligated "to say something" to their teenagers (Hill & Taylor, 2004).

School Counselors Coaching Parents. One area in which the school's counselor can provide a critical intervention with parents involves teaching them to encourage academic development of their children. This is critical for those parents who are least prepared to encourage academic development and socialization of their teenagers.

One approach that a professional school counselor can use to help parents is by providing after-school or online coaching in parenting. Through coaching, the counselor works to shape parenting skills so as to improve student outcomes. It is always better to start this effort when the student first enters school, but any transition point, such as the start of middle school, is an excellent time to provide parents with coaching.

Coaching is always a positive and encouraging effort. Parents do not need a lecture or criticism but are usually open to positively framed suggestions. Coaching examples are provided in the box "Sample Coaching for Parenting."

Sample Coaching for Parenting

Interactions between parents and children shape much of children's behavior. The pattern of interactions between parents and their children is part of each family's culture and reflects both expressed and hidden family rules (Goldenberg & Goldenberg, 1996). It is only by interrupting old communication patterns that change will occur. For example, parents can be coached as to how to encourage their child into developing a healthy self-concept and sense of empowerment.

These feelings have a lot to do with academic success. Feelings of empowerment are sometimes described as the child's **locus of control**. The academic socialization of a child requires that the student see him- or herself as the ultimate cause of various successes and problems at school. This view of oneself as the origin of personal success and failure is described as having an **internal locus of control** (Keith, Pottebaum, & Eberhart, 1986).

Its opposite involves scapegoating and blaming others for failures, while believing success is only a matter of favoritism or simple good luck. Two dimensions of personality, self-esteem and locus of control, are both central to each student's academic success and are both heavily influenced by parents (young years) and peers (adolescence) (Chubb & Fertman, 1997).

Self-esteem refers to an individual's perceived assurance of personal worth (Chow, Thompson, Wood, Beauchamp, & Lebrun, 2002). *Locus of control* refers to a person's beliefs about control over life events. When parents encourage their children and value the opinions and efforts of their children, the youngsters will see themselves as worthwhile and capable.

One skill a counselor can coach a parent to develop is the ability to ask questions as to why the young person thinks or feels in a particular way. Counselors are professional listeners; it is that same skill of truly listening to a child that can be a great bridge builder between the parent and child (Sears, Sears, & Pantley, 2002).

Coaching goal: To have parent show positive regard to his or her child

Counselor to parents: "We all really need to have others appreciate us. This can be especially true for our children. By saying, and meaning things like, 'I am so happy you are my son or daughter,' or 'I can't think of a thing I would rather do than share my time with you,' you are letting your child know that he or she is appreciated."

Coaching goal: Respect and appreciate the child's opinions

Counselor to parents: "We enjoy having others appreciate and listen to our opinions; children also enjoy having opinions that are accepted by others. You can make a big difference by saying things like, 'Should Mommy wear her hair up or down tonight?' or 'What brand of breakfast cereal should I buy at the store today?' or 'Why don't you pick the next DVD we order from Netflix?'"

Coaching goal: Improve the internal locus of control of the child and reduce scapegoating

Locus of control can be enhanced by parents who say things such as, "I like what you picked to wear to school" or "It is a shame you did not make the team this year. If you would like I will work out with you this year and you can try out again next fall."

Another important coaching lesson for the school's counselor to provide to parents is the need to avoid put-downs. Parents should be taught to avoid witty and sarcastic cuts that are too easy for adults to make. Many times well-meaning parents are not aware of just how frequently they put their child down.

One method to use when coaching this issue is to make a digital recording of a parent and child engaged in a task. Asking a parent–child pair to solve a puzzle or similar cognitive task together as a team can provide the opportunity to observe and record their interactions. Personal experience has shown parents will be shocked to see just how many times they were dismissive of their child's efforts. Below the adolescent years, children lack the verbal facility to make quick rejoinders back to their parents who have made one or more sarcastic comments; however, during adolescence when young people have the needed verbal fluency, parents may decide to change the rules and label such comments as "rude." This capricious change is likely to be seen by teenagers as unfair and an abuse of parental authority. The shift to a new rule structure provides another reason for him or her to ignore what the parents have to say.

This anti-put-down policy should be extended to include older siblings toward younger children, visiting relatives, and even grandparents. The world provides many disappointments and put-downs for children; the home should be a place of comfort and support.

Coaching for Academic Socialization. Academic socialization is a process that should begin during early childhood years and continue into adulthood. It starts with reading at home. Home reading involves reading both to children and with children; it also includes regular visits to public libraries and bookstores. Parents who show a general interest in school and what goes on in their child's classes each day impress upon their youngsters that school is to be highly valued.

When coaching parents who have middle school grade-level children, the counselor should demonstrate how to encourage their teenagers to think about a personal career path. As career ideas are discussed, parents will need the counselor-coach's help in guiding the process of setting goals that will lead toward the desired career (see Chapter 13 for information on vocational and career counseling).

During this process, counselors can coach parents to communicate high expectations and personal academic values to their teenaged children. Parents with little or no advanced education can be provided with the needed guidance information and skills to help their children. Good coaching should have the goal of placing less extensively educated parents on an equal footing with parents who have had more formal educational experience. Thus, parent coaching should provide the "equipment" needed to be successful in this effort. Part of that equipment includes helping parents understand and feel comfortable with the high school offerings through which their child must navigate. It also includes a realistic picture of expectations of colleges. Costs and options open to students for gaining college admission and paying for an advanced education should be shared with parents beginning in their child's middle school years.

As with all good coaching, school counselors should provide practice sessions during which parents can hone their new skills. This can be done individually or, more efficiently, in after-school parent support groups. Another good approach with busy parents and school counselors is to set up virtual group sessions for parents over the Internet.

Secondary school students can also become academic coaches and mentors for younger children. This process has great credibility with elementary school students who look up to high school students with awe. See Case in Point 12.5 for an example of this approach.

CASE IN POINT 12.5

Teenagers can be recruited to work to improve the academic socialization of younger children. High schools that require students to earn a service learning credit are in a good position to initiate this approach to academic development through the use of teen academic coaches. For example, one professional school counselor employed in an urban elementary school worked through the school district's high school coaches to recruit African American and Hispanic high school varsity athletes. The elementary school served a high-poverty community, and 90% of the students enrolled in it were members of minority groups. After careful training by both the school's counselor and the reading specialist, the high school athletes went into regular classrooms where they read stories from standard children's literature to children in kindergarten and first grades. This activity provided student athletes with a service learning experience while it provided primary grade students with powerful role models for learning to read.

On the second or third return visit to the elementary school, a number of student athletes brought their parents and/or older siblings along to see them "teach." The high school students took great pride in working with and being role models for young students. Participating student athletes also gained a great deal from the experience. They grew in their abilities as oral readers and improved their own academic self-concepts during their year as "teachers."

Thought Question. As tween age students (10 to 12 years old) enter adolescence, they may become less easily impressed by the role models of their childhood. As a middle school counselor, what ideas can you provide to use role models to improve the academic socialization of students between the fifth and eighth grades?

Engagement and Language-Minority Parents

The problem of finding ways to increase the engagement of Hispanic and other language minority parents is one that has an extra degree of complexity. Both Hispanic and Creole-speaking parents frequently find they face daunting barriers when they try to become involved with the education of their children (Carreón, Drake, & Barton, 2005). Barriers are more than just language; they include cultural expectations, familiarity with cultural norms established for education in the United States, and in some cases fear of possible consequences for being undocumented (Arias & Morillo-Campbell, 2008). The problem that Latino/a parents face must be made a primary concern for education policymakers because Hispanic students represent the fastest-growing minority group in our schools.

Parents from Asia, Haiti, and many Hispanic cultures are unfamiliar with the role taken by American educators. (See Case in Point 12.6.) The partnership between home and school is not one they are familiar seeing. From their experience, someone so authoritative (a school counselor or teacher) never consults the working poor about the education and socialization of their children (Sohn & Wang, 2006). For this reason they are frequently unprepared and embarrassed to be invited to become engaged with the school.

CASE IN POINT 12.6

Hispanic students are not the only language-minority group populating our public schools. Another significant language minority in the schools consists of students from Asian American families. These students are often overlooked in making specialized plans because children of Asian ancestry tend to do so well on standardized tests and earn superior grades in the classroom.

A suburban New York school system found that many of its best students came from the 30% of the school's population representing an Asian heritage (primarily Chinese, Korean, and Vietnamese). These Asian cultures emphasize family values that are "Confucian based," including the veneration of older people, filial piety, and age stratification (Chao, Kanatsu, Stanoff, Padmawidjaja, & Aque, 2009). While they were superior students, their parents were rarely seen in the school or during school activities. The Asian community has great respect for educators in general and does not wish to bother teachers and counselors. While they lavish school counselors with Christmas gifts, they avoid attending information programs about college aid and admissions and often refuse to join parent organizations (Hu, 2008). Asian parents prefer to consult with family members about these matters.

In New York, the district's administration and professional school counselors developed a federal grant that paid for classes for adult learners of English and the customs of North American society. This activity was one that was well received and made a difference in improving the level of engagement of members of the Asian American community with the school system.

Thought Question. What is another method that a school's counselor can employ to improve the engagement of Asian American parents with their children's school?

There are several ways school counselors can build bridges to reach parents of students who are English-language learners. A first step is through inservice education of teachers and members of the support staff with the culture and history of the ELL students in the school. Another is to encourage the hiring of as many qualified bilingual teachers and staff members as possible.

Finally, school counselors can help establish nontraditional involvement activities that are reciprocal among the school, parents, and the wider community (Arias & Morillo-Campbell, 2008). A reciprocal program is one that develops parents as volunteers in the school so that they give back while gaining something for themselves through their efforts. This makes it possible for parents to feel a sense of *orgullo* (personal pride). Research has shown that schools that reach out and invite parents to volunteer and assist in school programs can be very successful. When Hispanic parents were asked why they became school volunteers, they answered that schools were respectful of them and provided for their needs. Small gestures by the school can be important in making volunteering parents feel at home. Little courtesies such as a separate room (lounge) for volunteers to use in the school can be powerful motivators. Language is another motivator. Hispanic parents appreciate school staff and administrators who try to speak some Spanish (Quintanar & Warren, 2008).

Role of School Counselors in Team Planning and School Improvement

As noted previously, there is an ongoing effort to bring parents into the schools and have their concerns heard. This is one aspect of current school reform efforts and mandated in federal legislation. There are a number of different aspects to reform efforts being made.

History of Contemporary Education Reform Efforts

The enterprise of public education is labor intensive, and by the 1970s that labor force of professional educators was well organized and sophisticated in the tactics of legislative influence and lobbying. By organizing into professional unions, educators, including school counselors, were able to improve both their standard of living and the school environment where they taught.[7] The perspective of the major unions for educators is that teaching is a profession, and as a profession, curriculum and standards for learning are the province of educators. Until recently, educators saw the role of elected school boards as just providing the needed resources for the teaching and learning activities of the schools.

When states took back control and empowered school boards, the game changed dramatically. This new perspective brought discord, and several states saw statewide job actions for better pay and reasonable classroom support (e.g., March 4, 1968, in Pennsylvania) (Pennsylvania State Education Association, 2010).

Unions representing educators aligned most of their political support behind progressive candidates and conservatives began to see unions as opponents.

The power of teachers to control their work environment took a big hit during the last quarter of the 20th century with the publication of a number of reports and reviews highly critical of education in the United States. These included the First and Second International Math Study (FIMS & SIMS) and the Third International Math and Science Study, TIMSS (National Center for Education Statistics [NCES], 2004), as well as the widely read report, *A Nation at Risk: The Imperative for Educational Reform* (National Commission on Excellence in Education, 1983). The media coverage and political fallout from these and other reviews of American education created an added impetus for statewide educational reform programs.

> International comparisons of student achievement completed a decade ago reveal that on 19 academic tests American students were never first or second and, in comparison with other industrialized nations, were last seven times.[8] (National Commission on Excellence in Education, 1983, p. 8)

These critics failed to take into account flaws in the research design and sampling inadequacies of the international comparative studies. In the United States, students who are just learning English as a second language and students in special education are included in standardized testing programs.[9] This is not the case elsewhere. Another sampling error involves the fact that virtually all

U.S. students attend comprehensive high schools. This also isn't the case in all industrialized countries, where attending an academic high school requires that adolescent students applying for admission have high assessment test scores (Berliner & Biddle, 1995).

The reality is that many states within the United States have school systems that would compare very well with the top tier of nations in the international studies. Those states that invest less in the education of their children tend to skew our national average downward. An analysis by David C. Berliner (1997) has suggested that the removal of five states (Louisiana, Alabama, Florida, Georgia, and Mississippi) would raise the United States into the upper quartile of nations. Berliner (2004) also posited that the American public schools are providing an exceptionally high quality of education for middle-class communities where financial support for education and community interest in schools are high.

Problems with the sampling used in other nations and other measurement errors have been pointed out, but the general public has never gotten over the belief that American education is somehow deficient and that it is the fault of educators. Calls for reform went so far as to propose the disbanding of all public schools and school systems. A number of these reformers felt that once all school administrators were dismissed, the schools would be reopened as private companies owned and operated by educators and parent cooperatives (Bennett, 1992; Chubb & Moe, 1992; Evers & Walberg, 2004; Finn, 1991; Ravitch, 2000).

In answer to challenges posed by education reformers of the 1980s and 1990s, schools moved to standards-based education that specified exactly what a student will learn in every subject area each school year (Rose, 2009). The annual measurement of the achievement of these standards for learning was mandated in 2002 with the passage of the No Child Left Behind Act. President Barack Obama continued the testing mandate along with providing a call for more uniformity in the evaluation of the achievement of learning standards from state to state (Jackson, 2009).

School-Based Reform and the Counselor

Since 2002, most public schools have initiated reform efforts to improve the instructional process with the goal of better achievement of educational standards by students. Most of these are local and are carried out within individual schools (Aladjen & Borman, 2006). These local efforts normally employ a comprehensive plan for the reform effort. A total of 29 evidence-based models for school reform have been identified in the literature (Borman, Hewes, Overman, & Brown, 2002).

Dimensions of School Reform. There are three major dimensions that reform efforts follow. One is instructional and involves modifying how and what is being taught (Project Appleseed, 2008). This could involve a new language arts curriculum or a new approach to the teaching of middle school math. Ideas for these reforms originate beyond the schools. They are often the product of learned and professional societies. Implementation of such reforms normally involves the work of school-based committees.

The second dimension relates to those hired to teach in our schools. The NCLB Act mandated that all secondary school teachers have subject matter majors in the areas they teach. That regulation was impossible to reach without greatly enhancing the pay base for many teachers in fields such as mathematics, science, modern languages, and computer science. This reflects the fact that corporate America also wants these people and has the money to hire them. The teacher certification rules were relaxed, and "alternative channels" were provided to ensure that there would be people to teach in the schools.

Counselor's Role in School Reform. An important task of the school's counselors is to provide data and other unbiased information that reform committees will need as they work. It is likely that the school's counselors will need to provide this service to several reform committees established to address different curriculum concerns within the school.

A third dimension for reform to follow is administrative in nature and involves procedures and leadership issues. At one level this may include the implementation of the ASCA's national framework by the school's counseling office (American School Counselor Association [ASCA]/Hatch & Bowers, 2005). It can also involve parent advisory boards and communities of friends and supporters of the school. Administrative tasks such as scheduling and team or department structuring are frequently addressed by these reform efforts.

Coaching of School Reform Committees. All change and reform can trigger defensive behaviors and increase the anxiety level of professionals working in the school. It is in this regard that the professional school counselor can play an important facilitative role (Higgins, Young, Weiner, & Wlodarczyk, 2009).

The school counselor should seek opportunities to coach local school reform committees. One special set of skills of school counselors is the ability to solve problems in **interpersonal process** (Reinberg, 2008). This can include working to resolve interpersonal conflicts and tensions among committee members and reinforcing prosocial behaviors by committee members.

As attractive as this approach seems, it is time consuming and not efficient, and it can even be counterproductive. It has been argued that it is far better for school counselors to focus their efforts on the committee's **task-oriented processes** (Higgins et al., 2009). These include building a sense of commitment to the reform project, helping the committee identify members with useful talents to solve problems of the project, and assisting the committee to establish an effective strategy for completing assigned tasks.

SCHOOL COUNSELORS AND ●
THE COMMUNITY BEYOND THE CAMPUS

Professional school counselors have the ability to extend their influence for school enhancement and student development into the broader community. This can improve the school's public relations and community acceptance. It can also provide support to projects and programs of the school counselor's office.

Advisory Councils

These councils are required under a mandate of the 2002 No Child Left Behind Act, and if carefully managed by the school's counselor can improve levels of trust, community–school cohesion, and morale (Boult, 2006).

School councils can play a leading role in improving the literacy level of students and their families. For example, the parent advisory council can develop a book club for parents. It can also sponsor a book exchange program run from a booth during fund-raising activities at school. These book exchanges can provide slightly used children's books to members of a younger audience who need things to read. It can also help parents find interesting literature to nurture their own reading.

One thing a school's counselor can do is to provide secretarial support for the council. Minutes can be kept and filed by the counselor, and the counselor can ensure that an agenda is prepared and distributed prior to meetings. The school's counselor should also work with the council's leadership to develop a statement of bylaws or operating principles for parent groups and advisory councils. Prior to publication, that document should be approved both by the school's principal and at the school district level.

Once approved, the operating statement (bylaws) can be used to expand the representation of community members on the council, including representatives of major houses of worship, service clubs, social service organizations, and local businesses. The addition of community agencies and businesses provide the council with greater fund-raising and outreach capacities.

Business Contacts

School counselors can develop community contacts with local businesses. These contacts can be of reciprocal benefit. Businesses and service organizations can provide volunteers and guest speakers, in-kind contributions, part-time employment for high school students, material and equipment assistance, and cash grants. Schools can provide community agencies with student volunteer helpers who are earning service learning credits. Businesses and agencies can have information about them distributed with the new student welcome packages that the counselor provides to parents of all students transferring to the school. Similar information can also be disseminated from a booth during activities and programs in the school.

School counselors can also provide a seminar every few years to introduce real estate agents to the school and all of its strengths. This can help realtors sell local homes. Seminars also make good friends of the real estate agents and brokers of a community who can help the school in the future with securing a place to live for new teachers and staff.

SUMMARY

Schools see students for only a small portion of their lives. Most of the time children are in the care and custody of their parents. This contributes to the great impact that parents have on the academic socialization and development of their children. Poverty exerts a negative effect on the potential good that parents can do in providing a positive socialization experience for their children.

Counselors can provide the means to ensure that students from poor home environments are not excluded from any school activity or advantage because they lack funds to pay for it. School counselors need to work to make it possible for all parents to attend school conferences, even language-minority parents. This can include preparing parents for teacher conferences. There is a natural developmental shift in the optimal parenting model with regard to engagement and involvement with school at different grade levels.

Contemporary school reform efforts have been initiated to assuage concerns of members of the public about the skill level of American students. Many earlier international comparisons were not positive about the outcome of education in this country. Local educational reform efforts can be facilitated by the application of the skills of the professional school counselor.

DISCUSSION QUESTIONS

1. If you attend a college graduation you will see several major financial donors to the institution receive doctorates in *honoris causa* such as a doctorate of legal letters (L.L.D.), a doctorate of arts in humanities (D.A.), or a doctorate of science (D. Sci.).[10] The question is, How can the awarding of an advanced degree (in *honoris causa*) be all that different than what went on in Principal Shepard's middle school when grades were improved for a cash donation?

2. Many secondary schools allow the public to access the school's open computer area after school hours and on weekends. What rules for access and use would you encourage the school's administration to establish for its use?

3. As a professional school counselor for a middle school in your community, what materials would you include in the gift package that goes to all parents with students transferring into your school?

RELATED READINGS

Boult, B. (2006). *176 ways to involve parents: Practical strategies for partnering with families* (2nd ed.). Thousand Oaks, CA: Corwin.

Epstein, J. L., Sanders, M. G., Sheldon, S. B., Salinas, K. C., Jansorn, N. R., Van Voorhis, F. L., Martin, C. S., Thomas, B. G., Greenfield, M. D., Hutchins, D. J., & Williams, K. J. (1996). *Partnership-schools manual: Improving school, family, and community connections*. Thousand Oaks, CA: Sage.

NOTES

1. Parents are referred to throughout the chapter. It must be recognized that this includes the persons who care for and nurture the child. Such people may be parents, grandparents, legal guardians, and foster parents.

2. It takes about 2 years to acclimate new teachers or counselors to a school and its programs. When a school principal must replace a third of the faculty every year, he or she has no time to implement plans for improvement. Copious amounts of time must be spent helping develop new professionals instead of on school improvement.

3. One of the reasons for this is the contract that teachers' unions have negotiated in most communities (NB: Texas and a few other states have outlawed teacher negotiations). Those contracts provide the opportunity for teachers and counselors to transfer to other schools within the district on the basis of their seniority (Frankenberg, 2006).

4. In 2008, 1 in every 31 American adults was in prison or on probation. Of these, 1 in 11 African American adults was a prisoner or parolee, as was 1 of every 27 Hispanic adults (Pew Center on the States, 2008). Projections now show that by 2030 the population in prison or probation will total 15% of all Americans.

5. C.E. is an abbreviation for the "Common Era" and is the scientific (i.e., nonreligious) numeration for what was once referred to as *Anno Domini* or A.D. The Latin translates as "Year of our Lord." Likewise, scientific literature refers to B.C.E. for Before the Common Era instead of B.C., which is an abbreviation for time before Christ.

6. Sixty-two percent of American households had access to the Internet in 2009. Access was related to age and income. Younger people and those with money had more access (Edwards, 2009).

To close the gap, many school systems now lend laptop computers to students to take home and use during the school year. This policy is growing and supported by the 2009 Recovery Act (P.L. 111–5) (e.g., http://sp.parkston.k12.sd.us/Students% 20Documents/Laptop%20Policy.pdf and www.absolute.com/resource_center/casestudies/ Dysart_USD). Parents who do not have computers may access them in public libraries, their local parishes or churches, or in community agencies.

7. This brief history did not occur in several southern states, including Texas, where it was made illegal for educators to negotiate and participate in collective bargaining.

8. Unfortunately, the National Commission on Excellence in Education never identified the tests or the samples that were tested. They did not even reveal which industrialized countries took part in the comparisons.

9. In 2005 there were 11 states that met the NCLB testing requirement in the student's native language. The International Educational Agency (IEA) makes no such accommodations in the international studies it sponsors.

10. *Honoris causa* is a Latin term meaning for "the sake of honor." It is used when a university confers an honorary degree upon a person. Honorary degrees are frequently awarded for great achievements, such as the honorary L.L.D. awarded by Notre Dame University to President Barack Obama on May 17, 2009.

The first American to earn an honorary doctorate in science was Benjamin Franklin, who was awarded two, one by the University of St. Andrews (1759) and one by the University of Oxford in 1762. Honorary degrees are also very commonly given to those who have made a major donation to a school such as the honorary doctorate of science (D. Sci.) awarded to William C. Carey, a real estate and financial mogul in New York City who donated $50 million to Arizona State University to help fund a business school named for him.

13

Counselor's Role in Career Development and Planning

OBJECTIVES

By reading and studying this chapter you should acquire the competency to:

- Discuss the requirements for school counseling programs for career counseling activities as described by the American School Counselor Association and the National Career Development Association
- Explain and contrast the career developmental theories of John Holland and Donald Super
- Explain what goes into a career portfolio and how it is used
- Describe how legislation limits the type of career assessments that a professional counselor may employ in a school setting
- Explain the three levels of training used to define the ethical use of psychological measures, including career assessments
- List two major sources of unbiased test evaluation information
- Compare and contrast three major systems for providing career information and exploration for students from elementary school through high school graduation

● ● ●

❝Public education is the key civil rights issue of the 21st century. Our nation's knowledge-based economy demands that we provide young people from all backgrounds and circumstances with the education and skills necessary to become knowledge workers. If we don't, we run the risk of creating an even larger gap between the middle class and the poor. This gap threatens our democracy, our society and the economic future of America.**❞**

Eli Broad

● INTRODUCTION AND THEMES

High school students today must expect that they will change careers throughout their lives. To be prepared for this new world of work, students need skills that enable them to explore careers, develop career plans, and monitor their personal career paths for life. Professional school counselors have a major role to play in this effort.

Four major theories about the process of developing career goals and making well-informed decisions based on one's individual personality have emerged and are reviewed in this chapter. These theories have provided theoretical frameworks for a number of published career development systems. Career development begins during the preschool years and follows a developmental course throughout school and adult years. Counselors can assist students to understand many roles they will be called upon to play in life, including the role of worker.

Standard 3: The professional school counselor implements the individual planning component by guiding individuals and groups of students and their parents or guardians through the development of educational and career plans.

● WORLD OF WORK IN THE 21ST CENTURY

Anyone who has participated in a carpool to work knows that all workers do not view their employment in the same way. The work that we do may be seen simply as a means of survival and something to be tolerated until the weekend or next holiday; or, it may be seen as a way to meet certain psychological needs and provide a sense of fulfillment. To some professionals in the field, the job of a school counselor may be viewed only as an emotionally exhausting and draining job. Other professional school counselors will feel the same emotional fatigue but also experience powerful feelings of fulfillment and satisfaction knowing they are making a positive difference in the lives of students.

The U.S. Bureau of Labor Statistics (2009) reports that the average person will change jobs approximately 11 times prior to age 50. These changes will be accompanied by an average of five periods of unemployment that extend several months. Major career changes occur for the average worker three times over a lifetime. A career change implies a major redirection and the acquisition of a new skill set. The job of the professional school counselor is to help students be prepared for this new flexible era of employment. Gone forever are the days of graduating from high school and being employed by one manufacturing industry for life (Burns, 2006). A corporation that once provided stability with guaranteed employment in exchange for being organizationally focused and loyal has been forced to change into a lean and streamlined smaller version of its old self. The globalization of manufacturing and international competition has made this a necessity. We have gone from lifetime employment to perpetual job searching and ongoing career planning.

The National Career Development Guidelines from the National Career Development Association ([NCDA], 2007) have as a goal for all young people the creation and management of a career plan. The key is teaching young people to manage changing goals and to monitor their career paths as they go through the years beyond school and college. Each student's career plan in high school should meet that individual's personal goals for life both within and beyond school and have checkpoints and mechanisms for restructuring later.

This teaching process should provide the student-client with a range of beneficial and interesting activities in which to participate. Every volunteer activity and part-time job has something to teach the student about what he or she may want to learn and which skills he or she should develop.

One approach to providing both academic motivation and career education involves building adult-like employment activities into the school program. This may involve having an engineer spend a few days working alongside the physics teacher discussing how what is being taught in that class relates to the job requirements of an engineer. A writer or professional editor can perform a similar service for high school English teachers and their students. The goal is to make education relevant and linked to career planning (Allen & Allen, 2010). (See Case in Point 13.1.)

When conducting career education, John Krumboltz (2009) suggests that the counselor inquire about an unplanned (unexpected) happening in the student's life that influenced his or her goals and current plans. Krumboltz argues that **happenstance** often guides individuals into certain pathways. Counselors can use unusual occurrences to help student-clients learn about their goals and understand their choices.

> ## CASE IN POINT 13.1
>
> In 2009, a 14-year-old girl wrote to a newspaper advice column asking for help with her jealousy toward her peers who had so much more than she and her family could afford. She resented the fact that others had concert tickets, fashionable clothing and accessories, and other trappings of affluence that she could not afford.
>
> The columnist pointed out that at every income level there are people who have more; thereby, comparing oneself to others is a self-defeating exercise. The advice columnist suggested the girl consider all of her qualities that make her unique and special as a person.
>
> To see the newspaper column, go to www.uexpress.com/dearabby/?uc_full_date=20090328.
>
> *Thought Questions.* The columnist never suggested that the girl begin making money herself. High school students can look for part-time jobs such as baby-sitting and helping neighbors do lawn care, shovel snow, rake leaves, and so on. In many ways part-time jobs help develop work values and attitudes.
>
> If this girl came to you as her school counselor, what goals for counseling her would you set? Would you refer her to ways of earning her own income? Explain your answer and give examples from your own experiences.

A career should never be something that simply happens to a person. For that reason the American School Counselor Association (ASCA) has made career planning and development a priority for professional school counselors. (See Table 13.1.)

TABLE 13.1   Relationship Between ASCA Standards and NCDA Guidelines

Goals	ASCA National Standards	NCDA Guidelines
Investigate Careers	Standard 4: Students will acquire the skills to investigate the world of work in relation to knowledge of self and to make informed career decisions.	Competency 9: Understanding of how to make decisions Competency 10: Awareness of the interrelationship of life roles
Career Success	Standard 5: Students will employ strategies to achieve future career success and satisfaction.	Competency 11: Awareness of different occupations and changing male/female roles
Relationship Between School and Work	Standard 6: Students will understand the relationship between personal qualities, education and training, and the world of work.	Competency 12: Awareness of the career planning process

SOURCE: American School Counselor Association/Hatch & Bowers (2005), p. 33.

The history of professional school counseling is tied to the need that high school students had for vocational guidance and planning a hundred or more years ago (see Chapter 1). Yet, because of so many other priorities this component of the contemporary school counselor's job can be overlooked. (See Case in Point 13.2.)

CASE IN POINT 13.2

The Bill & Melinda Gates Foundation funded a national survey of young adults on the topic of the quality of help and advice they received in high school from their school counselors. The focus of the research was on career and educational planning. The report published by Public Agenda reported that 60% of the high school graduates saw their school's counselors as being feckless and of little value (Johnson, Rochkind, Ott, & DuPont, 2010).

In March 2010, the ASCA responded saying the report from Public Agenda proves the organization's point that there are not enough school counselors to effectively help each student with individual planning and college admission counseling (ASCA, 2010). The point was made that the national average caseload for a school counselor of 460 students is 84% greater than the recommended caseload of 250. The ASCA also pointed out that too much time of school counselors is used in solving administrative problems—for example, scheduling errors—within the school.

Thought Questions. How can a high school counselor become engaged in career and educational planning with a large population of young people preparing for college and career entry? How much of the counselor's time should be devoted to the tasks related to this issue?

The process of helping students develop personal career paths involves developmental learning and explorative tasks that begin in the elementary school. In middle school the career planning process takes on new meaning as students begin to align career goals and high school course selections. The high school counselor has the responsibility to refine the career path the student developed in middle school and organize appropriate courses and experiences to prepare the student for the transition into postsecondary education, military experience, or career placement.

What complicates this process is the changing nature of modern employment and the changing expectations of those who hire the next generation of youth. We are well along the road in the United States to a postindustrialized society that employs people in knowledge-related forms of work (Thompson & Hickey, 2008). (See Case in Point 13.3.) Our business organizations are flatter today than the top-down frameworks of the 19th and 20th centuries. This makes the 21st-century business organization not just lean but always poised to move quickly, adopting and making optimal use of new technologies (May, 2009). This organizational change implies that new employees must have flexible skill sets and the ability and desire to learn new approaches and rapidly adapt to change.

The global economy has created a glut of unemployed young workers, many of whom are well educated (Herr, 2009). These facts make the career interventions and educational programs of professional school counselors all the more important.

CASE IN POINT 13.3

I grew up in a large city during the 1950s. As a child I walked to a neighborhood school each day; during my walk I saw many jobs and occupations that have since disappeared. I watched two men deliver large blocks of ice each morning to neighborhood restaurants, and I saw coal handlers carry huge bags of coal on their backs to deposit into home coal bins.

I rode in elevators operated by professional operators. My grandfather was a "fireman" on engines of the Norfolk and Western Railroad, and my future mother-in-law worked as a stenographer and typist.

Thought Question. Make a list of current jobs and occupations that you believe will disappear over the next 50 years. Compare your list with those developed by others.

At the start of the 20th century, employers wanted production employees with a limited range of skills that were highly focused for the efficient completion of required production tasks. The acknowledged father of the vocational counseling movement in the public schools was Frank Parsons, who wrote the following description of the skills needed to be a journeyman in the mechanical trades:

1. Knowledge of the trade

2. Skill of hand and eye

3. Ability to work from drawings and to draw

4. Care and accuracy

5. Quickness

6. Loyalty

7. Hearty obedience to orders (Parsons, 1909, p. 51)

● CAREER THEORIES

All too often a school system's career development program is not created systematically and represents a hodge-podge of school counselors' input from different grade levels. Thus the career-vocational education and counseling programs in one school of a district may not match those going on in another, and the elementary, middle, and high school programs have little in common. What these school counseling programs lack is a unifying theme and the guidance provided by a consistent framework for understanding the career development of children and young people (Niles & Trusty, 2004).

Well-designed career interventions and educational programs offered by professional school counselors must address three issues. One is the developmental aspect of how career awareness and vocational preferences arise in children and young people. The second is the personality development associated with career development; the final consideration is the pattern of abilities and aptitudes of the individual student.

Career development begins in the preschool years with the acquisition of early work fantasies and the first job aspirations (Stoltz, 2010). These are informed by adults in the growing child's environment as well as by the juvenile literature and mass media to which the child is exposed (Feldman, 2002). The fantasy life of the young child is filled with images of what he or she will do for a living as an adult. Many of these are stereotyped and heroic in nature.

By elementary school, the perspective of the child's peers as to the nature of the "world of work" becomes a major factor in shaping the individual child's occupational personality and career understanding.

Part-time jobs and a wider range of peers in middle school further expand the teenager's understanding of career options (Krumboltz, 2009; Roney & Wolfe, 2000). Students who hold part-time employment may achieve a level of cognitive reality that the daydreams of being an employed grown-up cannot reach. The career musings of middle school students become increasingly more perspicuous whether or not they are employed. How teenagers see their future has a major influence on career attitudes, work habits, and how they grow into adulthood (Asakawa, Hektner, & Schmidt, 2000).

One essential element in achieving a well-adjusted adult personality is achieving an integrated personal identity. The process of identity development may carry over from high school into college and the young adult's life. Part of the process of resolving a personal identity is the young person's growing career awareness and preferences (Erikson, 1968).

> The inner sense of ego identity, then, is the accrued confidence that the inner sameness and continuity prepared in the past are matched by the sameness and continuity of one's meaning for others, as evidenced in the tangible promise of a "career." (Erikson, 1963, p. 262)

Career development is also linked to specific aspects of personality development for each individual (Feldman, 2002). **Personality traits** are relatively permanent features of the individual and are rooted in earliest years of child-hood and molded by experiences throughout childhood. Traits such as agree-ableness, openness to experience, and conscientiousness have a lot to do with a person's career and the degree of success an individual experiences when working (Hogan, Hogan, & Roberts, 1996).

A third aspect of career development and planning is the individual's ability and talents. Many of us once aspired to be professional athletes, but without what Howard Gardner would label "bodily-kinesthetic intelligence" we grew into more prosaic roles and careers (Gardner, 1999).

Professional counselors have many resources available to assist students in focusing on the possibilities that life holds and planning how to reach their per-sonal goals. A number of published career guidance materials include measures of aptitude and ability with measures of career preference and career-personality type. These career guidance materials are built on a theoretical foundation of career development (see "Career Assessment Measures" later in chapter for descriptions of some of these tests).

Social Construction and Career Planning

Career planning is intertwined with each student's sense of personal identity. Growing up and developing a personal identity has an extra layer of complex-ity in the cases of African American, Hispanic, and other minority students. The Protestant work ethic that is a central force to career planning involves a world-view that is not universally shared across all groups. The idea of delayed grati-fication, strong individualism, and competition with everyone else is not part of all cultures (Johnson, 2006). The personal values and sense of who one is within the family and ethnic culture are central to each young person, especially for the youth of ethnic minorities. School counselors must always be respectful of the values and beliefs of the student and his or her family. The goal of the counselor is to assist the student to negotiate the larger context of the dominant culture while making it possible for the student-client to keep a sense of fidelity to the ethnic group and family. One approach to these tasks is through consultations with the family and student (Young & Valach, 2004).

Another reference group that helps shape the relationship of students to school is the students' peers. Minority peers can exercise great control over students who are attempting to form identities as both students and members of the minority group (Radziwon, 2003; Stinson, 2006). This peer influence is in the form of group norms, beliefs, and values that each student will be mea-sured against by his or her peers. Susceptibility to peer pressure is highest at early adolescence, when the need to belong is at its zenith. Coincidentally, this is the same developmental era when the student is starting to refine career goals and formulate academic plans.

Theory of Frank Parsons

In Chapter 1 the important role of Frank Parsons was noted as the modern founder of professional counseling services in public schools. He was a pioneer in vocational counseling and developed a **state-trait model** for understanding career counseling activities. Parsons (1909) posited that there are three broad factors in making an appropriate vocational choice. These include:

1. Self-understanding, including aptitudes, abilities, interests, ambitions, resources, and limitations (and their causes)

2. Understanding of careers and jobs, including requirements and conditions of success, advantages and disadvantages, compensation, opportunities, and prospects in different lines of work

3. Careful reasoning to align the two areas (p. 5)

Parsons elaborated on the third item by saying that the young person needs the careful and systematic help of a vocational counselor to make the greatest decision of his or her life. His approach-assisted students match their traits with various conditions (states) that a work environment would impose.

Theory of Anne Roe

Professor Anne Roe was the first American psychologist to construct a classification system for occupations (Wrenn, 1985). This taxonomy started with the organizational system created by the U.S. Census Bureau and grouped occupations by the nature of interpersonal relationships required of the jobs (Roe, 1956). Her taxonomy included eight broad classes of occupations and six levels of complexity of tasks required for the various jobs. The eight categories were Service Occupations, Business Contact, Organization Focused, Technology, Outdoor, Science, General Cultural, and Arts and Entertainment. Later, after collaboration with Donald Super, the original eight categories of Anne Roe were reduced to six.

The second dimension of occupational and career choice Roe explored had to do with motivation (Simpson, 1980). For this dimension she adapted the

Maslow Hierarchy of Needs to explain why individuals are motivated to enter certain occupations (see Figure 1.1 in Chapter 1). Roe's approach saw specific elements of jobs as satisfying the needs of both career professionals and corporate employees. This combination of an individual's traits or abilities and the various vocational states categorized her approach as a state-trait approach to understanding career development.

Theory of John Holland

Holland asserted that an individual's vocational and career interests are personality dimensions (Bradley, Brief, & George, 2002). To explain his theory, Holland created a six-factor model for human occupational personality types (Holland, 1997). (See Figure 13.1.) While his **personality types** classify all people as one-dimensional, the model assumes that people with other employment personality types are also appreciated by each of us. Thus we can have friends, vocations, and pastimes drawn from other areas than the one that is central to us (McDaniels & Gysbers, 1992). Holland's career assessment

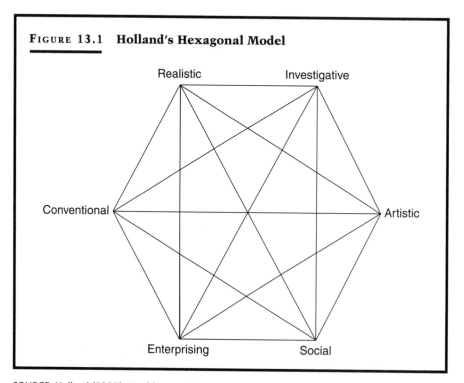

FIGURE 13.1 Holland's Hexagonal Model

SOURCE: Holland (1985). Used by permission.

instrument, the Self-Directed Search (now out of print), defines occupational preferences in terms of six primary personality types: Realistic (R), Investigative (I), Artistic (A), Social (S), Enterprising (E), and Conventional (C) (Holland, 1997). The Holland model arranged the six personality types in a hexagon, with each type having a closely regarded type next to it; each personality type is located across from its opposite personality type. Holland's RIASEC model is a core part of a modern career decision instrument, the Harrington-O'Shea Career Decision-Making System-Revised (described later in the chapter).

Evidence has been reported implying that preferences found by measures of Holland's model do not provide highly accurate predictors for later job satisfaction (Nauta, 2010). One implication for counseling is that individuals in the real world frequently do not have the luxury of pursuing an occupation congruent with their interests.

Theory of Donald Super

Donald Super viewed career development as a lifelong task that was constantly being refined and modified (Super & Haddad, 1943). The path of an individual's career follows a developmental sequence of life stages that Super labeled (1) growth and the development of a self-concept; (2) exploration and tentative steps to career planning; (3) establishment and mid-career; (4) maintenance and renewal; and (5) decline (Super, Sverko, & Super, 1995). His theory suggested that vocational development might be viewed as ongoing, with the implication of a changing self-concept and the continual striving for self-actualization (Gies, 1990).

Donald Super realized that an individual does not move through life in a vacuum but rather interacts with others and defines a life coordinated with others and continually changing over time. The elaboration of that concept was presented in a "rainbow graphic" (Super, 1980). The graphic makes it possible to visualize the many concurrent roles each of us plays at various points in the life span (see Figure 13.2).

The actual process of selecting one or another career path is linked to each person's work values (Super, 1970). Our values, as opposed to our interests, are the essence of what we are. Interests are viewed as more ethereal and changing as the environment changes. For a school counselor to understand a student's needs and guide him or her in making a career path selection, it is necessary to focus on the central work values of the young person. This concept of Donald Super has been operationalized in the Kuder Career Planning System (see later in chapter).

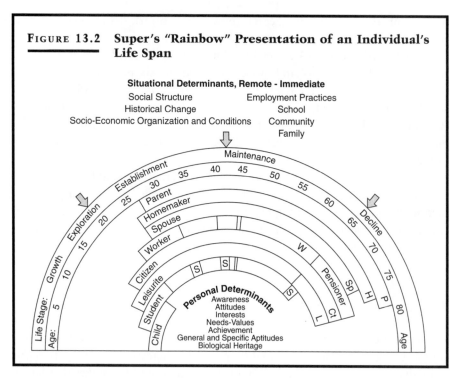

FIGURE 13.2   Super's "Rainbow" Presentation of an Individual's Life Span

SOURCE: Super (1980).

● PROFESSIONAL SCHOOL COUNSELING AND CAREER DEVELOPMENT

Career development and educational planning by the professional school counselor is inexorably linked to child and adolescent development (Hobson & Phillips, 2004). As such, counseling interventions to enhance career development and planning with students should be developmentally appropriate and instituted on a K–12 basis.

To eventually make a serious commitment to a vocation the individual experiences growth in four dimensions. The first of these is the inexorable cognitive development and an ever-expanding awareness of the world. This growth leads to increasing amounts self-directed exploration into future jobs and career paths. It may take the form of fantasy play and role play. The third part of the normal developmental process for developing a career focus is **circumscription**. This process involves the rejection of ideas not seen by the individual as a good match or as uncomfortable within his or her social context. This discarding of possibilities can be seen in the sex-stereotyped behaviors of young children.

The circle of choice possibilities becomes smaller as the youngster examines possibilities viewed as appropriate to his or her social circle. Counselors can help student-clients by assisting them in making an inventory of their skills and interests and developing a conceptualization about their future lives as adults. The resolution of a career goal requires that the individual reach an accommodation with the possible and personal desires and wishes (compromise) (Gottfredson & Lapan, 1997; Henderson, Hesketh, & Tuffin, 1988).

Career Development Interventions in Elementary School

A major focus of career interventions with elementary school students is delivered through consultation with parents. Unfortunately, most parents have little knowledge about career development (Niles & Trusty, 2004). Parents need to be taught to find teachable moments with their children, for example, when the media portray a gender role stereotype, or when the child peruses the toy catalogs that come into the home. Once a teachable moment arises, parents need to be ready to share their values, aspirations, and beliefs with their child.

Parents have great influence in helping young children develop work-related values and being open to explore many options. Parents can also encourage this exploration process through the child's play behavior and fantasies. Young children look up to and admire their parents, making the parental influence most salient. Counselors can also introduce career topics to parents over the counseling office's web page and even through personal communication systems like Twitter and Facebook.

Career Development Interventions in Middle School

Middle school students need to begin career planning and linking their career goals with their educational options. This requires that school counselors help middle schoolers acquire work-related skills that will optimize each student's choices. These skills include self-understanding, a positive self-concept, and the ability to interact well with others (Collison, 1991).

Another of the tasks for professional school counselors to address with middle schoolers involves establishing the link between what is learned in school and the world of work. Adolescents should acquire skills to search career options and explore various occupational possibilities (Niles & Trusty, 2004). (See Case in Point 13.4.)

CASE IN POINT 13.4

One of the counseling activities traditionally part of every elementary and middle school is the "Career Fair." School principals tend to like these annual career days, as they provide good public relations for the school. By making contacts with local business and professionals, the school counselor gains important new community contacts and resources.

On the down side, this annual event requires many hours of the professional school counselor's time to line up adult speakers who can represent various occupations and jobs. This can prove to be a major problem, as many skilled workers are paid by the hour and cannot leave work. One solution for this is to ask the local trade unions to send representatives to talk about their craft or skill areas. Many professions such as real estate agents have flexible time and are more than glad to speak to youngsters. Recruiting specialists from the armed forces are also very willing to meet with students, as are local politicians holding elected offices.

Then comes the job for the counselor of publishing a schedule and thumbnail description of each presentation for all students. Next each student must be surveyed for their top choices, registered, and given a schedule to follow for the career fair. A problem with registering students to attend several of the various speakers' presentations is trying to ensure that each speaker has an adequate number of students attending his or her presentations. Some professions, such as veterinarian and law enforcement professional, will draw too many interested students, while others, like machine tool maker, will be ignored.

Getting speakers vetted by law enforcement so they can be legally in a school (background checks) is another concern. On the big day the task becomes one of deploying teachers to host speakers and getting everyone into correct classrooms and other meeting spaces.

Thought Questions. What positive outcomes can result from having a career fair? What alternative methods could be used to achieve the positive effect of the traditional career fair? Make a list of friends and others you feel comfortable in calling upon to provide a presentation to school students.

Finally, students should be taught to reflect on various options and make realistic decisions. Counselors must assist students in setting personal career goals and planning how to progress along the path to reach them. These efforts are best organized into a **career-planning portfolio**. This portfolio can be expanded on a regular basis as students explore their options and research ideas. Beyond occupational explorations, the portfolio should include ideas about the life of the student 10 and 20 years out of school. Questions of where and how the student plans to live should be addressed in the portfolio, including the student's thoughts about eventually being part of his or her own new family.

From the 1920s to today, psychologists have been creating and standardizing career exploration and development systems. A number of these, now in their fourth generation, are Internet based and interactive. While nothing can replace the career intervention provided by a professional school counselor, these systems can make it possible for more students to be assisted in the career development process. Each of the published career development systems is designed to interface with the school counselor.

Career Development Interventions in High School

High school is the time when students have the task of bringing into sharp focus their personal career goals and charting the paths to get there. Tentative career ideas from middle school years need to be crystallized and organized into a plan to transition from high school into the next phase of life (Niles & Trusty, 2004).

One approach to helping students prepare for this transition is through the use of group guidance starting in the freshman or sophomore year of high school. These group sessions can focus on the outcome of career interest and/or work value scales data.[1] At this stage the school counselor does not need to push to have students commit to one specific job or career; rather it is better to explore the range of possibilities that align to the occupational cluster area shown to be of interest and value to the student on the career assessment measure. One way to make the groups efficient is to bring students together who share a common occupational preference cluster of scores, for example, Holland's Career Personality Type.

Another approach to accomplishing this is by introducing the concept of **"possible self"** to secondary school students (Chalk, Meara, Day, & Davis, 2005; Perry & Vance, 2010). This process can involve several questionnaires that ask students to picture themselves in the future (10 years out) as adults holding each of a short list of occupations. The occupations are selected to cover a range of prestige levels and sex-role stereotype possibilities. Next the counselor asks the students to judge these possible future occupations as ones they will avoid or have an interest in learning about. Later the counselor can work with students individually or in small groups to discuss their hopes and fears related to their rankings.

A less structured approach to employing a "possible self" approach in middle school and high school counseling begins with a direction to the student-client:

When most kids think about the future, they often focus on what they may become. Sometimes kids experience fear of what they could be like as people and how others will view them. Some just think about all the new experiences that they will have while others hold wishes about what they could do as an adult. Our future wishes may be a fantasy like winning the lottery or finding buried treasure, others very basic like starting a family and being a good parent.

On the page below please list *all* hoped-for possible selves that may be in your future. Place a check next to those that you think will actually come true in the future.

Next make a list of possible selves that you fear may happen and that you want to avoid. (Knox, Funk, Elliott, & Bush, 2000, p. 304)

These answers can be employed by the school's counselor to assist the student in understanding how his or her aspirations are organized. The sensitive counselor can also use these to spot possible conflicts that are expressed as adolescent fears. Many of these may be related to family and/or peer expectations and norms.

Students With Special Needs and Transition Planning

Having all students grow and reach their full potential is a national goal and is incorporated into the mandates of federal law as part of the Individuals with Disabilities Educational Improvement Act (IDEA). By the end of middle school, the individualized education plans (IEPs) of students with disabilities must contain a **transition plan** detailing each student's vocational or career goals. In addition to the career plan, the transition plan should include high school classes, experiential programs, postsecondary education planning, and a life plan for living arrangements and possible employment after school. It must also have been developed with the student and his or her parents fully involved (Clark & Davis, 2000). The law also specifies that by the student's 17th birthday he or she must have been notified that the student will assume all parental rights, including the responsibility to sign off on his or her own IEP, when he or she reaches majority at age 18. (See Chapter 7 for a discussion of this issue.)

The IEP committee, including the student and his or her parents, usually carries out the transition planning. An expert from the larger community who has knowledge of community resources may augment this group. Frequently this person is a professional vocational counselor from the state's department of vocational rehabilitation (Sax & Thoma, 2002).

Other specialists who may be asked to participate in the transition include community advocates for people with disabilities, a physical therapist, an expert in adult education, a state employment service specialist, an occupational therapist, a representative of assistive technologies enterprises, a counselor from an independent living center, and a specialist in recreation and leisure. Many times it is the responsibility of the professional school counselor to organize this expanded IEP-transition planning meeting and to follow up on all recommendations and required elements in the student's IEP for transition.

CAREER ASSESSMENT MEASURES FOR SCHOOL COUNSELING ●

The number of instruments available for school counselors to use is enormous. There are hundreds of assessments related to career development and vocational assessment. However, there are four major constraints on the use of these measures.

Limitations

Limitations to career assessments start with federal law. The Family Educational Rights and Privacy Act (FERPA) of 1974, as amended in 2008, presents the first obstacle. This act imposes a restraint spelled out in the U.S. Code of Laws (20 U.S.C. § 1232g; 34 CFR Part 99). Under provisions of FERPA, school counselors should inform parents prior to collecting data of a psychological, personality, or interest type. Parents must be given the right to inspect instruments and surveys prior to their use (Gerstein & Gerstein, 2004) (for more about FERPA see Chapter 2).

Also, the Individuals with Disabilities Education Act of 2002 has a more stringent guideline, requiring explicit informed consent prior to administering any measurement that could be considered to be a personality assessment (Jacob & Hartshorne, 2003). This act requires parental participation in all assessments of a "psychological nature."

The second limitation is that of the level of education a professional school counselor should have before ethically administering and interpreting any standardized personality measure. Publishers include a statement in advertising information about their assessments stating the needed level of training.

The American Psychological Association (APA) established the level of training needed for administering different assessments. APA provides a three-level classification of qualifications for test administrators. The APA qualification statement was a part of the association's first ethical statement published in 1950. Even though other statements on qualifications and ethics have superseded it, the original three-level model continues to be widely used today by publishing houses to limit sale of their product line to educators and clinicians capable of correctly using testing materials.[2]

Level A: Qualification requires that the individual has an ethical need to use these measures. No specialized education in testing and assessment is required. This level of qualification includes most classroom teachers. The types of measures appropriate at this level include **curriculum-based probes** and standardized group-administered achievement tests, including high-stakes state-mandated achievement assessments.

(Continued)

(Continued)

Level B: An educator qualified to use Level B tests and assessments must have earned a master's degree in an appropriate field of education, counseling, or psychology (or related field) and have specific training in measurement including measurement statistics. Teachers with collegiate education in child development and early childhood assessment may also qualify at Level B without a master's degree. Members of professional organizations that require that their members be well qualified in test administration and interpretation also qualify at Level B. These organizations include, among others, the American Counseling Association, the International Reading Association, and the American Speech-Language-Hearing Association. Level B includes most group-administered tests of intelligence, aptitude, attention deficit disorder scales, and occupational preference measures.

Level C: These measures require the individual to be highly educated and have had advanced training in educational and psychological measurements. Typically these people hold doctorates in educational, school, or counseling psychology, or have a Ph.D. in a related clinical field in psychology. They hold advanced licensure from a state agency and are members of professional associations such as the American Psychological Association (Divisions: 12 Clinical, 16 School, 17 Counseling, or 29 Psychotherapy), the American Counseling Association, or the National Association of School Psychologists. These professional associations require adherence to an ethical canon related to education and training of those using Level C tests. These measures include most individually administered tests of intelligence and personality.

The third limiting factor involves local policies. Most school districts have established policies and procedures for using psychological evaluation instruments that are not part of a formal entitlement evaluation. The following written policy of Oregon's Helix School District illustrates the point:

> Psychological evaluations will be made only after informed and written consent is obtained from the child's parent or surrogate, unless the student is of legal age to give his/her informed and written consent. Psychological data will be only one of several criteria used for determining any change in a student's educational program. Psychological data older than three years will not be used as the basis for prescriptive teaching or placement. (Helix School District, 1997)

The fourth obstacle inhibiting professional school counselors from using interest and integrated interest-aptitude measures in the practice of school counseling is the cost involved. The Armed Services Vocational Aptitude Battery (ASVAB) does not charge the school system for its use, but the private companies that publish all other measures are not so generous.

Evaluating a Career Planning Measurement

Because school counselors decide how to spend school system money for counseling materials, including career counseling systems, it is imperative that the counselor make the best possible choice. As a starting place, professional school counselors can read test manuals that are a required part of a specimen set of test materials from a publisher. Look for the measure's goals and philosophical foundation in the manual. The goal statements should match those of the school's counseling program.

Next, examine the normative groups used to set the scoring system. Is the normative sample appropriate to contemporary students? Is it representative of minorities? Is there evidence that males and females are appropriately assessed, or is there a scoring bias?

Check the reliability of the various subtests. Reliability quotients (consistency measures) of 0.80 and above are generally viewed as large enough to base a counseling intervention on those data (Nunnally & Bernstein, 1994). Stability coefficients (test-retest reliability) above 0.75 are also considered to be highly stable and appropriate to serve as the basis of an intervention. Interest test scores tend to be stable over time and can be reliable over 25 years (Lawler, 1993; Strong, 1955).

CARTOON 13.1   Misinterpretation of Career Decision Measure

"Your career test lists: Architect, Astronomer, Aero Space, and Archeology. You must have got an 'A' on it."

SOURCE: Merv Magus.

Validity measures tend to run lower, and measures of predictive validity in the 0.50 to 0.70 are considered good (Nunnally, 1972). It is not always possible to provide a numeric (correlation) value to a vocational assessment's validity. It has been suggested that test publishers **bootstrap** validity evidence by combining numerous examples, correlations with other measures, the general consensus of users, and the concordance of the measure to the theoretical model it is built to assess (Kane, 2006).

Test manuals provided by publishers must always be viewed as sales documents. You may assume the technical information presented in manuals is likely to be "spun" to put the best possible light on the instrument.

Unbiased Reviews

There are two major sources of unbiased evaluations used for vocational and career planning. One is *A Counselor's Guide to Career Assessment Instruments* (Whitfield, Feller, & Wood, 2009). This edited book provides a compendium of 71 different test reviews written by university faculty and practitioners. The second is the *Mental Measurements Yearbooks* published by the Buros Institute of Mental Measurements of the University of Nebraska. The Buros system provides independent online reviews of more than 500 instruments designed for career and vocational planning and assessment. In addition to those measures, Buros lists another 250 assessment instruments for career and vocational counseling that it did not review.

Career preference and exploration systems are moving rapidly to online formats. The online system can simultaneously assess a student's interest levels for career possibilities while measuring abilities, aptitudes, and work values. Once testing is completed, the online systems then provide students with career profiles, possible job types, job vignettes, and can lead them on online career explorations (Herr, 2009).

The following evaluations are frequently seen in regular use in the counseling offices of public schools (Giordano & Schwiebert, 1997). Several have two or three individual tests that are part of the system for career development. These measurement batteries cover a range of different dimensions of career and vocational measurement.[3]

Armed Services Vocational Aptitude Battery

About half of the high schools in the United States offer the ASVAP as a free service for interested students. This test has three versions. One is a longer paper-and-pencil version, and one is a computer-adaptive version. The latter form is shorter and is designed for use on-site in military recruiting centers.

The ASVAB is given in high schools, free of charge by Department of Defense (DoD) personnel. It was last normed in 1980 with a national population of young men and women ($N = 12,686$) who were part of the National Longitudinal Study of the United States sponsored by the U.S. Department of Labor. It provides 10 subtests and a combined score known as the Armed Forces Qualifying Test (AFQT). In addition there are five other combined scales reported based on the subscales of the ASVAB (Weitzman, 1985). There are a great number of what the military describe as **line scores,** which combine various subtests and composite scores to define cut scores for certain training programs.

Reliability studies carried out in the personnel research centers of the Department of Defense have shown the various versions of the ASVAB (Forms 8 through 11) are highly reliable; all subtests are also very stable. The median reliability coefficient for subscale consistency is $r \approx 0.80$ (Palmer, Hartke, Ree, Welsh, & Valentine, 1988). The subscales are General Science (GS), Arithmetic Reasoning (AR), Word Knowledge (WK), Paragraph Comprehension (PC), Numerical Operations (NO), Coding Speed (CS), Auto Shop Information (AS), Mathematics Knowledge (MK), Mechanical (ML), and Electronics Information (EI). The combined scales include Armed Forces Qualification Test (WK + PC + AR + 1/2NO), Verbal (WK + PC), Mechanical (2AS + GS + ML), Administrative (NO + CS + WK + PC), General (WK + PC + AR), and Electronics (AR + MK + EI + General).

Validity studies with hundreds of thousands of recruits have provided a database used to define cut scores required for recruits to enter into training programs for hundreds of different military job specializations. All together there are 23 major career divisions of the U.S. military. For example, the cut score to enter training as a Satellite Communication Systems Operator-Maintainer is 120 correct out of a possible 155 questions on the Electronics Composite score (the Department of Defense line score). In comparison, to become an infantryman requires a score of 90 correct on a Combat Composite composed of 164 items, half of which are part of a timed coding task.

After less than 2 hours of testing, students receive a good picture of their aptitude and whether they meet the military's requirements to be trained in particular career-oriented skills. While the instrument provides no empirical evidence of the validity of subtest and composite scores, it does have high levels of reliability.

The Department of Defense claims that there is an 80% concordance between careers open in the civilian marketplace and skill sets that members of America's armed services have when they leave the service (U.S. Department of Defense, Recruitment Command, 2009). The DoD does not provide statistical validity statistics for scores needed for various job titles.

Career Interest Inventory

The Career Interest Inventory (CII) is a career interest survey designed for use with high school students. It provides information to assist students to explore educational and occupational alternatives, learn about careers, and set goals for their futures (Psychological Corporation, 1990). The instrument consists of a series of five-point rating scales through which the student shows the degree of interest in a list of possible work activities (e.g., run a printing press or draw illustrations for books). There are two levels for the CII, Level 1 for junior high school use (grades 7–9), and Level 2 for high school and beyond (grades 10–12). Level 1 has 152 items plus a student workbook designed to start students thinking about their career paths (Zedeck, 1998). Level 2 uses 170 job activity statements to provide high school students with their profiles.

The instrument was empirically constructed using factor analysis to provide scores for 15 possible fields for employment as defined by the *Dictionary of Occupational Titles* (now out of print). This relationship with the system developed by the U.S. Department of Labor once made it easy for the counselor to key student scores to guidance material prepared by the federal government. The 16 occupational fields are Agriculture, Health Services, Management, Clerical Services, Customer Services, Sales, Fine Arts, Mathematics, Science, Educational Services, Social Science, Legal Services, Benchwork, Building Trades, Machine Operation, and Transportation.

Level 1 also provides a list of 16 high school subjects and another 16 co-curricular activities keyed to the junior high school student's pattern of career interests. That is refined to a list of 20 college majors and entry-level positions keyed to the Level 2 interest scores.

The CII was normed concurrently with the Differential Aptitude Tests (described later in chapter below) using an overly large sample of possible items. This **oversampling** was corrected by removing items not empirically aligned with one of the 16 career fields (Schafer, 1998). The CII is highly reliable and analytically structured to have content validity with the *Dictionary of Occupational Titles*. The reliability assessment was based on internal consistency (reliability) coefficients in the high range ($r = 0.90$). They were based on a sample of 34,000 subjects selected as a nationally representative normative group. Scores provide separate norms for males and females, and categories exhibit significant divisions.

The CII is now out of date and does not provide information about 21st-century emerging vocational trends. Students' responses to the CII tend to skew toward glamour areas for employment, such as medical, management, and scientific

(Schafer, 1998). A better approach would be to renorm the CII and structure it to align with the new Standard Occupational Classifications known as O*NET. Pearson Assessment offers counselors (Level B training) the opportunity to buy an Examination Kit for $27.50 (2010).

Career Orientation Placement and Evaluation Survey, Career Abilities Placement Survey, and Career Occupational Preference Survey

In the 1960s Robert Knapp published research describing a method to divide areas or clusters of occupational preferences and various levels of occupational possibilities within those areas of interest. His early work was based on the theoretical foundation in the model for understanding the psychology of occupational choices provided by Anne Roe in 1956. At first the 1966 General Aptitude Test Battery (GATB; discussed further later in chapter) was paired in validity research with the new interest survey developed by Robert Knapp (Knapp & Knapp, 1976; Knapp, Knapp, Strnad, & Michael, 1978).

Interest Inventory

The modern COPSystem Career Guidance Program (COPS) incorporates an occupational preference survey with a battery of eight ability measures, the Career Ability Placement Survey (CAPS), and a measure of vocational values, the Career Orientation Placement Evaluation Survey (COPES) (Knapp-Lee, Knapp, & Knapp, 2007). The COPS Interest Inventory consists of 168 items, measuring job interest related to the 16 COPSystem Career Clusters. Each career cluster is keyed to high school and college curriculum as well as to occupational information. COPS also provides interpretive material to facilitate career exploration, featuring career and educational planning worksheets along with a listing of suggested activities to guide students to ways of gaining experience. The model for this system is also described in a circular graphic form (see Figure 13.3).

The COPS Intermediate Inventory (COPS II) provides a measure of interests based on knowledge of school subjects and activities common to students in the fourth grade through high school. The publisher of this system is Educational and Industrial Testing Service (EdITS) of San Diego. They also offer a Canadian-normed version and a Spanish language version of the COPSystem Interest Inventory.

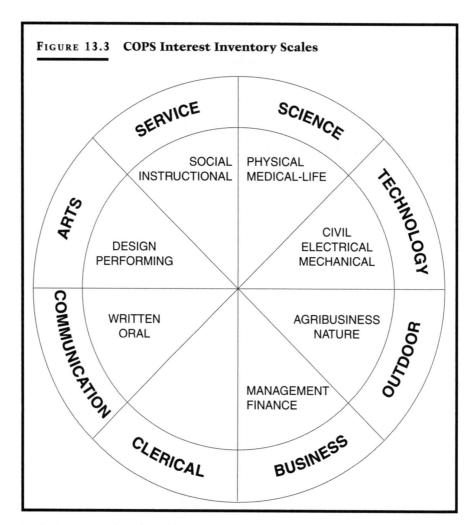

FIGURE 13.3 COPS Interest Inventory Scales

SOURCE: Knapp-Lee (2000). Used by permission.

The COPSystem was normed in 1999 using 2,056 male and 1,241 female students in the 11th grade through college from across the United States. Separate normative scoring systems have been developed by gender. Internal consistency of the 14 cluster scores is good (median r = 0.89) (Knapp-Lee, 2000). Stability after one year is also good, with the median value of r = 0.71. Predictive validity is also good, with 71% of college undergraduates' election majors aligned with their measured interest scores from the COPS. Concurrent validity between the CIOS Interest Inventory scores and other career interest surveys has been low (Best & Knapp-Lee, 1982).

Career Ability Placement Survey

This assessment is a multidimensional battery designed to assess various abilities related to job success. As can be seen on Figure 13.3, CAPS keys each of its eight subtests to entry requirements for the 16 occupation clusters identified by the COPSystem. CAPS scores are interpreted on a normative basis by grade level and reported as percentile scores. No interpretations are done on a gender-specific basis. These eight scores are described by the publisher as:

1. MR: Mechanical Reasoning measures how well a person can understand mechanical principles and devices and the laws of physics.

2. SR: Spatial Relations measures how well a person can visualize or think in three dimensions and can mentally picture the position of objects from a diagram or picture.

3. VR: Verbal Reasoning measures how well a person can reason with words and the facility for understanding and using concepts expressed verbally.

4. NA: Numerical Ability measures how well a person can reason with and use numbers and work with quantitative materials and ideas.

5. LU: Language Usage measures how well a person can recognize and use correct grammar, punctuation, and capitalization.

6. WK: Word Knowledge measures how well a person can understand the meaning and precise use of words.

7. PSA: Perceptual Speed and Accuracy measures how well a person can perceive small details rapidly and accurately within a mass of letters, numbers, and symbols.

8. MSD: Manual Speed and Dexterity measures how well a person can make rapid and accurate movements with his or her hands.

Test-retest reliability (2-week interval) is in the good range (median $r = 0.83$) (Bullock & Madson, 2009). The CAPS authors used concurrent validation to document the concordance of CAPS scores with equivalent scores from the Differential Aptitude Test (DAT) and the General Aptitude Test Battery (median $r = 0.68$) (Knapp, Knapp, & Michael, 1977). Correlations were also used to document that conceptually similar areas of the CAPS and the DAT are moderately linked (median $r = 0.70$). The COPSystem also has employed factor analysis to confirm that the eight CAPS ability scores have appropriate factor loadings (correlations) on the components of the COPS.

Career Orientation Placement Evaluation Survey

The third measure of this system is designed to measure a student's vocational values. It consists of 160 questions expressed as dichotomous alternatives such as:

I value activities or jobs in which I
    (A) team up with others.
    (B) work on my own.

The scores from the COPES are reported for the eight subtest scales in the form of work-value dichotomies, including Investigative versus Accepting, Practical versus Carefree, Independence versus Conformity, Leadership versus Supportive, Orderliness versus Flexibility, Recognition versus Privacy, Aesthetic versus Realistic, Social versus Reserved.

The reported internal consistency reliability of the COPES scores is in the moderate range (median $r = 0.76$). The COPES employed factor analysis to confirm that the 16 cluster scores from the COPS Interest Inventory aligned appropriately with the eight dichotomous work values scores.

In general, the COPSystem is a coordinated group of measures that interlock to provide assessments of students' vocational interests, abilities, and values. It provides the raw material to provide middle school students with career education and interventions. It provides needed elements to develop career plans for students and help chart courses that high school students should complete to meet their career goals.

The COPSystem is published and sold by EdITS. The cost of the three specimen kits are COPS $37.50, CAPS $37.50, and the COPES $9.00. A good alternative is the Counselor's Pack that includes all three for $20.00.

Chronicle Career Quest

The Chronicle Career Quest (CCQ) is a group-administered measure designed and normed for high school students to use. It provides three scores for three sections: an interest inventory, a self-scoring interpretation guide, and a career paths occupational profile (Chronicle Guidance Publications, 1993). The Chronicle Career Quest Interest Inventory (CCQII) is constructed around 12 broad areas of occupational interest. The 12 domains represent occupational areas identified by the U.S. Department of Labor: Artistic, Scientific, Plants and Animals, Protective, Mechanical, Industrial, Business Detail, Selling, Accommodating, Humanitarian, Leading Influencing, Physical

Performing. On the short form, items present a job or career activity (e.g., caring for plants) and ask students to respond using a "like versus dislike" (dichotomous) format answer. That format is expanded to three levels on the long form: Uninteresting, Interesting, and Very Interesting.

The test publisher provides two versions of the measure: a short form with nine items per occupational dimension, and a long form with 12 items for each of the 12 dimensions (144 total items). The advantage of this approach to measurement is that it provides the client's individual evaluation of each of 144 different occupation types.

After completing the Chronicle Career Quest Interest Inventory, the student is provided with his or her profile of score totals in the 12 domains. These are then explored by the students in the Interpretation Guide describing different occupations in each of the domains. In the final step, the student uses the Career Paths Occupational Guide to explore in depth one or more careers, including tasks and duties to be performed, opportunities for advancement, education and training requirements, and hours and expectations of management.

In general, the CCQII has good internal consistency and reliability, with quotients averaging $r \approx 0.80$ (Daniel, 1995). It used factor analysis to select items that matched each one of the 12 domains and resulted in a 12-factor solution. This provided the CCQII with a tacit form of validation evidence. The long form of the CCQII has significantly better reliability than the short version. This reflects the longer list of items measuring each domain and the use of a 3-point scale in lieu of the dichotomy-type scoring system employed on the short form.

This measure is published by Chronicle Guidance Publications. They sell a starter kit including 25 long-form tests for $107.00. These tests can be scored by hand and do not have a requirement for advanced education for their administration.

It can be concluded that the Chronicle Career Quest system is an appropriate, less expensive method to employ with high school students as part of a larger career education and counseling effort (Thompson, 1995).

Differential Aptitude Tests-Fifth Edition

As the United States geared itself up to enter World War II, an industrial psychologist, George Kettner Bennett, and his colleagues were devising measures that could be useful in the selection and placement of people into new positions where their utility for the war effort would be optimized. One of his early tests (circa 1940), the Bennett Mechanical Comprehension Test, survived to become part of the Mechanical Reasoning Subtest of the Differential Aptitude Test (DAT). The first edition of the eight-test battery of the DAT was published in 1947 (Kelley, 2009).

There are two levels to the DAT-5th ed., one for grades 7–9 and one for grades 10–12 (Bennett, Seashore, & Wesman, 1992). This two-level system is matched to the companion scores that come from an administration of the Career Interest Inventory. Both levels of the DAT use eight subtests to provide measurement of the following three domains of aptitude:

1. *General Cognitive Abilities:* Contains verbal reasoning and numerical ability. These tests measure the ability to learn in an occupational or training setting, specifically the ability to learn from books and manuals, self-instruction, trainers, teachers, or mentors.

2. *Perceptual Abilities:* Abstract reasoning, mechanical reasoning, and space relations. Measures the ability critical to dealing with things, rather than people or words.

3. *Clerical and Language Skills*: Spelling, language usage, and clerical speed and accuracy.

When the DAT-5th ed. was normed in the late 1980s there was clear evidence of a gender difference in scores across subtests. That bias resulted in lower scores for girls on the Mechanical Reasoning and Space Relations subtests and higher scores than boys on measures of Spelling, Language Usage, and Clerical Speed and Accuracy. As the norms are now older than the people taking the DAT-5th ed., it is difficult to make a good interpretation of their meaning.

The DAT-5th ed. can be a grueling experience for younger students, as it requires more than 2.5 hours of actual test time. As much as another hour may be needed to give instructions, distribute and collect back materials, and provide time for students to take short breaks. If the DAT-5th ed. is paired with the Career Interest Inventory, which requires another 30 to 45 minutes to complete, an entire school day may be lost to testing. Most school counselors plan to have the DAT-5th ed. and CII administered over several days to avoid the possible fatigue factor that might reduce the test's validity.[4]

The DAT-5th ed. was normed on a national sample of 84,000 young people in the late 1980s. Statistical analysis of those data found high levels of internal consistency (reliability) with a median of $r = 0.88$ and alternative form reliability with a slightly lower median of $r = 0.83$ (Hattrup, 1995). The only subtests with low reliability are the Perceptual Abilities measure, with reliabilities in the 0.50 range.

Concurrent validity of the DAT-5th ed. is evident in its predictive (correlational) relationship with both cognitive measures and tests of student achievement (Wang, 1993). The measure's General Cognitive Abilities Subtest correlates well with SAT scores (both verbal $r = 0.68$, and math $r = 0.77$), as well as with the ACT total composite score ($r = 0.76$) (Schmitt, 1995).

The test is published by Pearson Assessment and does not provide a Spanish version. A counselor's Examination Kit that includes the DAT-5th ed. manuals and the CII cost professionals (minimum of Level B training) $53.00 to purchase.

Overall, the DAT-5th ed. has been used by schools and employers since 1947 and has helped school counselors provide career planning to American students for many years. The greatest concern with the DAT-5th ed. is that the modern cohort of young people is very different from adolescents of their parents' and grandparents' generations. New norms are clearly needed, along with consideration of the new reality of employment and careers in the 21st century.

Harrington-O'Shea Career Decision-Making System-Revised

The Career Decision-Making System-Revised (CDM-R) provides a method of career planning that aligns career interests with job choices and school subjects for middle and senior high school students (Harrington & O'Shea, 2005). Thomas Harrington and Arthur O'Shea based their system on Holland's (1997) model of occupational personality types. Like the theory of John Holland, the CDM-R provides six interest area scores. Students completing the CDM-R are provided with comprehensive Job Charts listing typical jobs associated with each of the six areas along with the educational requirements for those jobs. The CDM-R has two forms, one for middle schools and one for use in senior high schools. The system requires 25 minutes to administer Level 1 to a classroom of middle school children (and older students with reading disabilities), and 45 minutes to administer Level 2 to senior high school students.

Level 1 (middle school version) provides an introduction to career planning (Campbell & Raiff, 2009). At the middle school level it also describes school subjects that should be completed in high school for particular job titles. The comprehensive Job Chart discusses work values, career trends, and abilities needed to work in the field of choice (Kelly, 2005). Level 1 (middle school version) uses 96 interest survey items that produce scores on the six dimensions theorized by Holland and then iterates them with Holland's work environment scores to produce 18 clusters of possible occupations. These six dimensions are given labels more aligned with the planning needs of high school students (see Table 13.2).

The high school CDM-R (Level 2) is designed for high school and college age students. Unlike the middle school version, students are first asked about their abilities, future plans, work values, favorite school subjects, and career choice before they complete the 120-item occupational interest measure. Items of the interest measure have been statistically tested and found to be gender and culture neutral. The current version (2010) projects occupations out to the year 2014, and includes a number of emerging fields in science, technology, engineering, and mathematics, the so-called **STEM** jobs (Kelly, 2005). Scores from this measure combine the six occupational dimensions with scores from Holland's list of RIASEC work environment dimensions. The result is 18 separate career clusters, each consisting of occupations with similar RIASEC codes to those preferred by the student on the first phase of testing with the CDM-R. See Table 13.3 for an example of the 18 cluster names associated with the renamed RIASEC codes.

Pearson Assessment offers this career interest assessment system at a (2010) cost of $450.00 per classroom. This includes enough forms for 25 students,

TABLE 13.2 New and Original Names for the Six Original Holland Personality Types

CDM-R	RIASEC
Crafts	R-Realistic
Scientific	I-Investigative
The Arts	A-Artistic
Social	S-Social
Business	E-Enterprising
Office Operations	C-Conventional

SOURCE: The Harrington-O'Shea Career Decision-Making System-Revised (CDM-R). Copyright © 1992, 1994, 1996, 1998, 2000, 2003, 2005, 2008 Career Planning Associates, Inc. Reproduced with permission of the publisher NCS Pearson, Inc. All rights reserved.

"The Harrington-O'Shea Career Decision-Making" and "CDM" are trademarks of Career Planning Associates, Inc.

TABLE 13.3   Eighteen Clusters of Occupation Types from the CDM-R

CDM-R Career Clusters Organized by CDM-R Career Interest Area					
Crafts	**Scientific**	**The Arts**	**Social**	**Business**	**Office Operations**
Manual	Math-Science	Literary	Customer Service	Sales	Office Operations
Skilled Crafts	Medical-Dental	Art	Personal Service	Management	Data Analysis
Technical		Music	Social Service	Legal	
		Entertainment	Education		

SOURCE: The Harrington-O'Shea Career Decision-Making System-Revised (CDM-R). Copyright © 1992, 1994, 1996, 1998, 2000, 2003, 2005, 2008 Career Planning Associates, Inc. Reproduced with permission of the publisher NCS Pearson, Inc. All rights reserved.

"The Harrington-O'Shea Career Decision-Making" and "CDM" are trademarks of Career Planning Associates, Inc.

seven interest-to-career videos, and a manual for the test administration and interpretation of the measurement's results. Undefined discounts are available for large-scale purchases from Pearson. The paper-and-pencil version is available in both Spanish and English. The Level 2 (high school) CDM-R is also available online in English from Pearson Assessment. Its cost is set on a sliding scale by the size of the order. Pearson charges (2010) $5.95 per online student use if the counselor orders more than 250 uses in a year for his or her school. For more information see http://psychcorp.pearsonassessments .com/HAIWEB/Cultures/en-us/Productdetail.htm?Pid=Pa_CDM-Internet& Mode=summary.

The Harrington-O'Shea system provides a series of short videos depicting how interest areas identified by the CDM-R relate to job clusters, college majors, and training programs. The videos depict enthusiastic people engaged in real-world experiences who provide students with insider views of more than 100 careers. Running time is 7 minutes per video.

The CDM-R is a stable measure with test-retest reliabilities over $r = 0.80$ and in the $r = 0.90$ range for alternate form reliability and internal consistency (Pope, 2005). Studies of concurrent validity indicate that the CDM-R (high school) is well correlated with the vocational aspirations of postsecondary technical school students (Kelly, 2005).

The CDM-R is a reliable system for both career preference identification and exploration. As the Harrington-O'Shea system can be used with students in middle school as well as with high school students, it can be integrated into a long-term career-vocational education program.

Kuder Career Planning System

The Kuder system for career planning is a fourth-generation measurement and a direct legacy of the Kuder Interest Inventory of 1939 (Thompson, 1995). It has been estimated that more than 100 million people throughout the English- and Spanish-speaking worlds have completed one of the Kuder assessments (Schenck, 2009).

The Kuder system provides three levels of career planning and exploration. One level is the Kuder Galaxy system, designed for use with preschool through grade 5 students. It engages students in exploring the world of possibilities through a series of developmentally appropriate interactive explorations. The Kuder Galaxy, like all fourth-generation measures, is an online system. Kuder's Galaxy also provides easy-to-interpret counselor printouts and related printouts for parents to see that demonstrate the interests of their child.

Middle school students use the Kuder Navigator system to examine the various occupational areas open for their consideration. The Navigator also links high school curricula to the various career paths being examined. To help career planning it provides an online timeline for career planning. Like the Galaxy program, the Navigator provides printouts for students, parents, and counselors (Harrington, 2007).

High school students can participate in the Kuder Journey system. This career exploration system provides an in-depth personal analysis of career possibilities. It provides a focus on emerging and high-demand jobs. The counselor's printout is designed to help career goal setting and career planning. Kuder's system also provides information students need to select courses in high school aligned with their career plans. It also provides ideas for college majors and postsecondary curricula to consider.

There is little description in any of the materials published by Kuder as to the ethnicity of persons in the normative groups or how they were sampled from the population. Also, there is no statistical evidence about a possible gender bias in the scores from the various assessments of the Kuder system.

An important theoretical base for the Kuder Career Planning System is provided by the incorporation of Strong's Work Values Inventory as part of Kuder's measuring process. It is unfortunate that the Strong Inventory, like other elements of the Kuder system, has a problem caused by poor definition of its normative population. The Strong Work Values Inventory provides different patterns of scores for males and females and for different ethnic groups. For those reasons, school counselors must use caution when providing vocational planning and counseling services with minority students using the Kuder Career Planning System.

Instruments of the Kuder system have good internal consistency (see statistics following) and provide user-friendly information for students, parents, and counselors. The system employs a state-of-the-art interactive approach providing superior career planning information. Kuder provides school systems with tools needed to initiate PK–12 career and occupational development and planning. The online cost for an individual student to be assessed using the system (2010) is $39.00 per student. Kuder does provide discounts for large-scale users of the system.

Kuder Skills Assessment

This measure is used with middle school through high school students and is part of the data set for the Navigator and Journey systems from Kuder. The Kuder Skills Assessment (KSA) is a measure of occupational self-efficacy. It is designed to identify career components a student is confident in being able to master and those the student feels may be beyond what he or she can do or learn. Authors of the skills assessment argue that ability is a critical factor in being successfully employed. They go on to argue that standard measures of cognitive ability or IQ do relate to school and college success but not to success in the world of work. For that reason they have developed this self-report of abilities. Psychometric evidence does support their contention (Zytowski, D'Achiardi, & Rottinghaus, 2009).

The short version of the KSA consists of 90 items that report scores for six career clusters: Business Operations, Sales/Management, Outdoor/Mechanical, Arts/Communication, Science/Technical, Social/Personal Services. A longer version, 170 items, provides these six career cluster scores and also scores for the 16 occupational clusters identified by the U.S. Department of Labor and Department of Education (U.S. Department of Labor and Department of Education, 2009).

The KSA short form was normed using a national sample of 668 males and females between the 9th grade and college age. The longer version used a different national sample of 2,001 people between age 13 and college age. The measure has superior internal consistency (reliability) for all six occupational cluster scores (median $r = 0.89$) as well as in the format with 16 scales (median $r = 0.91$) (Zytowski et al., 2009). The KSA does not address its stability (reliability over time) or the validity of the instrument. The authors defend this position, arguing that the instrument is organic and changing with the individual: "Skill levels assessed by the KSA, like other skill assessments, should not be considered fixed attributes. They may be attributed in part to opportunity and experiences" (Zytowski et al., 2009, p. 19).

Kuder Career Search With Person-Match

The Kuder Career Search (KCS) With Person-Match consists of three components: Preference Record, Kuder Career Clusters, and Person-Match. It provides traditional paper-and-pencil versions, but the online system provides better career exploration options through interactive presentations of occupational possibilities as seen through the eyes of employees in more than 2,500 jobs. The KCS is available in both English- and Spanish-language versions.

This version of the Preference Record employs a forced choice format wherein the subject is asked to rank order, in terms of personal preference, three different activities. A total of 60 different triads are included in the measure, making a total of 180 individual activities being ranked within groups of three. None of the activities of the scale name a job title or field of study. On the KCS, only work-related activities are ranked on a "most- to least-preferred" scale. The activities are presented with a transitive verb and an object. The list of activity statements are related by the use of similar transitive verbs while the object is flexible, such as in the following triad:

Collect the signatures of famous people

Collect butterflies

Collect coins

Scores from the KCS are reported in terms of the six career clusters noted previously for score reports from the Kuder Skills Assessment. They can also be presented following the 16-career clusters of the U.S. Department of Labor.

Person-Match is a method for providing students with job sketches from workers with whom they share similar preferences for activities. As noted, the Kuder database of job sketches includes 2,500 examples. It also provides information to aid students in exploring in-depth career possibilities by referring them to federal job data information in the O*NET (http://online.onetcenter.org/) that matches their pattern of interests.

The KCS was built by using 48 of the original items of the earlier editions of the Kuder Preference Record. Its standardization of the cluster scores has a normative base in a poorly defined sample of 8,791 males and females from middle school to adult (Zytowski, 2009). Two small sample stability (reliability) studies show the KCS to have good reliability, with median coefficients of $r = 0.87$ and $r = 0.78$ (Ihle-Helledy, Zytowski, & Fouad, 2004; Kelly, 2002). The pattern of correlations found in a study of 197 "career-confused" freshman college students by Kevin Kelly (2002) did not find evidence of the concurrent validity for the KCS scores. In a similar manner, Kristen Ihle-Helledy and her colleagues could not find support for the concurrent validity of the KCS with scores from the Career Search Self-Efficacy Scale (Ihle-Helledy et al., 2004; Solberg et al., 1994). The author of the new edition of the Kuder Career Search has taken the position that the KCS and Person-Matching system is not a measurement that lends itself to studies of concurrent validation (Zytowski, 2009).

This instrument provides a highly creative approach to assisting students to explore their options and plan for their vocational futures. Matching work and activity interests of students to people rather than to occupational titles humanizes and provides a context that is missing elsewhere (Schenck, 2009). The KCS also exhibits a persistent problem of documentation with quantitative information. The measure does not provide data describing its normative base and providing evidence of its utility.

Super's Work Values Inventory-Revised

Donald Super (1910–1994), a contemporary of Frederick Kuder (1903–2000), also had an interest in the psychology of vocational choice. His focus was on the formation of personal work-related values. Super's position was that the work-related values of an individual are closely linked to the career choices of the person (Super, 1970). Super developed and standardized research instruments in the 1950s. These early versions led to the commercial publication of a measure, the Super Work Values Inventory, which employed three questionnaire items to measure each of 15 values, for a total of 45 questionnaire items. Each questionnaire item was answered using a 5-point Likert-type scale, ranging from "Not important at all" to "Crucial." The center point in the 5-point scale is "Important," and it is defined as "I would like it but other things are more important." For example,

In terms of job satisfaction how important are the following factors of your employment?

1. Being told when I've done a good job

   A. Crucial for me
   B. Moderately important for me
   C. An important concern, but other things are more important
   D. Less important
   E. Not important at all

The 1970 version of Super's measure was revised into a 12-value scale (6 items per scale, total 72 items) when it was adopted as part of the Kuder Career Planning System. The 12 work-related values are

1. *Achievement*: Know by my results when I've done a good job

2. *Challenge*: Can test the limits of my abilities

3. *Coworker relations*: Work with people I like

4. *Creativity*: Need to come up with new ways to do things

5. *Income*: Am paid enough to live really well

6. *Independence*: Decide how to get my tasks done

7. *Lifestyle*: Employment that lets me lead the life I want

8. *Prestige*: Feel like my work is very important to society

9. *Security*: Will never get laid off

10. *Supervision*: Have a boss who recognizes my value

11. *Variety*: Don't do the same thing all the time

12. *Workplace*: Work in comfortable conditions (Zytowski, 2004, p. 13)

The norming of the 12 scales involved a poorly defined national sample of 8,785 men and women who were at least 14 years old. There is evidence that there are differences in the pattern of responses between secondary school boys and girls. Donald Zytowski (2004), and Patrick Rottinghaus and Donald Zytowski (2006), reported that boys rate Supervision, Achievement, Variety, and Workplace as more important than do girls, who rate Creativity as more important than do males.

Validity evidence for the SWVI-R was provided in a factor analytic study of the responses of 426 undergraduate freshmen students at Ohio State (Robinson & Betz, 2008). While this was not an ideal sample to represent a diverse population of American secondary school students, the researchers did find that there are four underlying scales (latent factors) within the SWVI-R. These include:

1. Environment (Coworkers, Lifestyle, Security, Supervision, and Work Environment)

2. Esteem (Achievement, Mental Challenge, and Prestige)

3. Excitement (Creativity, Independence, Mental Challenge, and Variety)

4. Safety (Income, Independence, and Security)

Carrie Robinson and Nancy Betz (2008) also found significant differences in the pattern of answers from Anglo-White, African American, and Asian American undergraduates. This raises questions regarding the interpretation of scores for minority students.

Myers-Briggs Type Indicator

The Myers-Briggs Type Indicator, Step II (MBTI) is a self-report instrument designed to assess an individual's psychological type preference (Briggs et al., 2001). Originally designed during World War II to help match employee "types" to occupations best suited to them, it has found many uses in individual counseling, career counseling, and in high school counseling offices.

MBTI Step II has a theoretical basis in the psychology of Carl Gustav Jung, founder of personality archetypes and analytical psychology (Edinger, 1992). The instrument resists defining personality traits but does provide four bipolar dimensions of an individual's personality, Extraversion-Introversion (E-I), Sensing-Intuiting (S-N), Thinking-Feeling (T-F), and Judging-Perceiving (J-P). When these are combined to provide a personal profile, the result is 16 different possible types. For example, the personality type of a friend of mine on the faculty is an ISTJ Type, or Introversion (I), Sensing (S), Thinking (T), and Judging (J). Each of the 16 types is further elaborated with five facets composed of between 5 and 9 items. The 20 facets and four dimensions provide an integrated topology of the client or student's personality type.

The MBTI Step II was normed using a national sample of 1,380 adults of varying ages. One problem with using this instrument with high school students is that the median age of the normative sample was 50 years. The sample also is skewed toward Anglo-White people and has an excess of women in the normative database.

Technically, the MBTI Step II reports reasonable reliability, with a median reliability coefficient for all dimension and facet scores of $r = 0.77$. The validity of the instrument can be found in its 60-year history of success as an instrument used by thousands of professional counselors (Hess & Lanning, 2003).

The MBTI Step II is best employed by counselors with Level B training and supervised experience in Myers-Briggs administration and interpretation. However, the publisher also provides a self-administering and scoring form available online for a fee ($29.00 in 2010). Consulting Psychologists Press sells the paper-and-pencil version for $29.41 (in 2010) per student administration.

Strong Interest Inventory and the Skills Confidence Inventory

Vocational counselors and professional school counselors have employed various forms of the Strong Interest Inventory (SII) since the Strong Vocational Interest Blank was published in 1927. The original version was designed to assist the vocational counseling of military personnel reentering civilian life. The placement of military veterans into appropriate civilian careers is still a major task for professional counselors today, and the SII is often part of that intervention (Shallcross, 2010).

Strong Interest Inventory

Today the SII is primarily employed to help students understand their career interests in terms of the demands of various jobs and their personal preferences for work-related activities and tasks (Jenkins, 2009). The Strong measures underwent a major revision 60 years after the first edition when the publisher tested more than 55,000 employees from a range of enterprises. These employees were happy in their jobs and had at least 3 years of work experience (Kelly & Sheehan, 2003). Data from those 55,000 subjects provide the profile of people working in 244 different occupations, including emerging employment areas. The SII uses those data to interpret the interest profiles of students today and indicate what careers are close matches for the students' interests.

The rights to the Strong Interest Inventory were sold by Stanford University to Consulting Psychologists Press (CPP) in 2004. One of the developments with the test that year was the publication of a new edition and normative base for the SII (Strong, 2005). Occupations and profiles identified on the 1994 edition were updated to keep current with contemporary employment trends.

The SII questionnaire is designed for use with students from the ninth grade through college. It uses 291 questionnaire items, starting with a description of a job activity responded to by students using a 5-level Likert-type scale: (5) Strongly Like, (4) Like, (3) Indifference, (2) Dislike, (1) Strongly Dislike.

Recent editions, including the current version of the SII, have adopted the theoretical basis provided by John Holland and his theory of occupational personality types. The six-factor approach exemplified in Holland's hexagon is reported on the SII as six General Occupational Themes (GOTs). The individual score profile for a student provides these six GOT scores. These scores follow Holland's nomenclature: Realistic (R), Investigative (I), Artistic (A), Social (S), Enterprising (E), and Conventional (C).

Next, the student profile provides 30 Basic Interest Scales (BIS) arranged to show the student his or her level of interest in various broad occupational categories, for example, athletics, science, electronics, and performing arts. On each of the BIS scales, the individual profile presents a list of occupations (Occupational Scales [OS]) that fit the student's interests. These possible 244 potential occupations are reduced to a list of the 10 most likely for the student. A list of the five occupations least similar to the student's profile is also provided. (To see a sample of the 21-page high school profile from one student's SII, visit www.cpp.com/Pdfs/smp284210.pdf.)

The SII is available in Spanish, Korean, and Portuguese in addition to American English. There is also an Anglicized version for use in British Commonwealth nations.[5] The 2004/2005 edition of the SII has OS scores based on the score profiles of 55,000 normative subjects from the late 1980s, first published in 1994. The six GOT scores and 30 BIS scores are based on a 2003 sample of 2,250 employed men and women selected by a stratified random sampling from a population of 20,000 individuals who used an online job search. The reliability of all three sets of scores is high and runs in the 0.80 to 0.95 range (Jenkins, 2009). Validity studies are described in the literature for the SII that employed confirmatory factor analysis. Other validity evidence showing the concordance between SII scores and college majors is described by Jenkins (2009). Another approach to validity involving the correlation of OS scores with appropriate GOT scores has also shown the SII to be valid (Gasser, Borgen, & Larson, 2007). The SII has been shown to have small differences in score patterns for males and females. Reliability values are provided separately for both males and females. Few differences have been found on the scores of the SII as a function of ethnic group membership, and minorities are proportionately represented in the sample of 2,250 subjects.

Overall, the SII is a technically sound method of collecting, organizing, and presenting information to students to assist career planning. When completed with the Skills Confidence Inventory (SCI; see following section), the SII provides a school counselor with the data needed to assist students to set their own goals and establish career plans.

The SII requires about 30 minutes to complete online and about 40 minutes to complete the paper-and-pencil version. The online system is being adopted by a number of school systems for their high schools as well as by career service offices of universities (Yarnall, 2007). The online version is sold for $49.00 per student. It can be seen at www.skillsone.com. Large-scale purchases can bring the price to the $10.00 range. Counselors can acquire a set of manuals and forms, the Strong Practitioner Library Set, from CPP, Inc., for the 2010 price of $119.00.

Skills Confidence Inventory

This measure was developed and published in 1996 to provide a measure of personal self-efficacy for the job activities of the six career types as developed by John Holland (Harmon, Borgen, Berreth, King, Schauer, & Ward, 1996). The SCI is scored along six General Confidence Theme (GCT) scores keyed to Holland's six occupational personality types.

The six GCT scales were normed on a 1993 sample of 1,147 working adults and 706 college students. It was not updated when the new edition of the SII was published in 2004. Internal consistency scores are high for the GCT scales, ranging in the mid-0.80s. The GCT scores have been empirically shown to differentiate between students for 21 of 24 BIS scores from the SII. The 1994 edition of the SII had only 24 BIS scales as opposed to the 2004/2005 edition's 30 scores.

The SCI requires about 25 minutes of testing time and is available online. It has both French Canadian and American English versions. The six GCT scores have clear practice implications for school counselors working with secondary school students. Counselors can purchase a manual for the SCI for $38.50 (2010) from CPP, Inc.

While the SCI is a valid predictor of the Holland categories, and a reliable instrument, it is based on a dated normative group that was not a nationally representative sample of all regions, socioeconomic status levels, and ethnic groups. For those reasons it should be used with caution.

Occupational Information Network

The U.S. Department of Labor/Employment and Training Administration has begun to provide an online service of career information that can be used by students and others to begin the occupation search and planning process. The system maintains a file of 965 careers and occupations and is updated periodically. These occupational descriptions, including education and training requirements, are collected from practitioners in the actual fields of work (www.onetcenter.org/overview.html). Thus, it is a good source of information about emerging jobs in the STEM fields as well as jobs in the "green economy." Job descriptions and related information is organized along the taxonomy of

23 clusters identified by the U.S. Standard Occupational Classification System (U.S. Bureau of Labor Statistics, 2010). This system also provides online assessments to help individuals gauge the suitability of their backgrounds with the needs of various occupations. It can be used and accessed without a fee. At the time of this book's publication (2011) the O*NET was usable and a valuable tool, but still being constructed and elaborated.

SUMMARY

In the 21st century it is expected that people will be changing careers and jobs more frequently than in the past. One role for the professional school counselor to play is to facilitate the acquisition of skills needed by high school students to develop career plans and the capacity to modify them over their lifetimes.

Theories about how we go about selecting a career began with a state-trait model proposed in 1909 by Frank Parsons. The work of Anne Roe provided the first attempt to link eight factors of the psychology of individuals to the jobs people select. John Holland provided a six-factor model for understanding the personality work types or occupational career types of individuals. Donald Super moved away from the measurement of interests and devised a way to interpret job selection based on personal work values.

These theories are used as the basis of a number of career development assessments. These include COPESystem (Anne Roe); CDM-R and SII (Holland); and the KCPSystem (Super). The measures of aptitude and potential for learning, the ASVAB and the DAT, are both empirically derived based on the cognitive skills a person needs to succeed. The Myers-Briggs is based on the psychological theory of personality types first proposed by Carl Gustav Jung, a neo-Freudian psychoanalyst.

DISCUSSION QUESTIONS

1. After reading the short list of skills Frank Parson believed a journeyman mechanic working in the mechanical trades needed to have in 1909, develop and refine a list of skills needed by a 21st-century employee of a mechanical trade, for example, a tool and dye fabricator, auto transmission repair mechanic, or jetliner mechanic (i.e., F.A.A. license as an Airframe & Powerplant Maintenance Specialist).

2. Use the copies of Buros Mental Measurements Yearbooks on your university library database and select one measure of career preference or vocational choice not covered in this chapter. Read about the test and decide whether the measure is one that a school counselor could justify spending school district funds on.

3. Visit the university's counseling center and speak with a counselor about the career assessment measures used by that office. What instruments are used? How are they employed in counseling interventions, and how were they selected? As an alternative, visit a local middle school or high school (or even your alma mater) and ask the same questions.

RELATED READINGS

Csikszentmihalyi, M., & Schneider, B. (Eds.). (2001). *Becoming adult: How teenagers prepare for the world of work.* New York: Basic Books.

Holland, J. L. (1997). *Making vocational choices: A theory of vocational personalities and work environment* (3rd ed.). Lutz, FL: Psychological Assessment Resources.

Whitfield, E. A., Feller, R. W., & Wood, C. (2009). *A counselor's guide to career assessment instruments* (5th ed.). Broken Arrow, OK: National Career Development Association.

NOTES

1. Specific data from aptitude tests should not be openly shared.

2. Pearson Education, Inc., the country's largest test publisher, uses a similar system for qualifying people to use its products. The Pearson system has four levels. Level 1 is similar to Level A, Pearson's Level 2 to Level B, and Level 3 to Level C. Pearson added another level, M, for users who are licensed medical practitioners.

3. They are organized in alphabetical order so as to avoid the appearance of a ranking system.

4. It can be difficult for professional school counselors to justify the loss of instructional time to classroom teachers who have the responsibility of helping all students reach a level of proficiency on state mandated high-stakes tests.

5. George Bernard Shaw may have been correct when he quipped, "England and America are two nations separated by a common language."

14

Data Management, Action Research, and the Evaluation of School Counseling Programs

OBJECTIVES

By reading and studying this chapter you should acquire the competency to:

- Describe appropriate indicators of quality for professional school counselors and their programs
- Design school counselor program surveys for use in programmatic evaluations
- Develop action plans based on data from school counselor–initiated surveys of the three major stakeholder groups
- List and describe the seven steps for conducting a systematic evaluation of a school counseling program
- Discuss the various applications for information gathered in the form of a systematic evaluation of a school's counseling program
- Organize a systematic evaluation for a school counseling program
- Plan and execute school-based action research from the position of a school counselor

“ Not everything that counts can be counted, and not everything that can be counted, counts. ”

Albert Einstein

● INTRODUCTION AND THEMES

The American School Counselor Association ([ASCA]/Hatch & Bowers, 2005) has made a clear statement in *The National Model: A Framework for School Counseling Programs* that school counselors should be equipped and able to serve in the role of researcher/evaluator. These are outlined in the box, "Data Management and Research Standards for Professional School Counselors."

Data Management and Research Standards for Professional School Counselors

Use of Data—A comprehensive school counseling program is data driven. The use of data to effect change within the school system is integral to ensuring every student receives the benefits of the school counseling program. School counselors must show that each activity implemented as part of the program was developed from a careful analysis of students' needs, achievement, and/or related data.

Action Plans—For every desired competency and result, there must be a plan outlining how the desired result will be achieved. Each plan contains:

1. competencies addressed

2. description of the activity

3. data driving the decision to address the competency

4. timeline in which the activity is to be completed

5. who is responsible for delivery

6. means of evaluating student success

7. expected results for students

SOURCE: Executive Summary of the ASCA National Model: www.schoolcounselor.org/files/Natl%20Model%20Exec%20Summary_final.pdf.

In addition, the ASCA also calls for school counselors to have the knowledge and skills to perform regular programmatic evaluations, listed in the box, "Research Standards for Professional School Counselors."

Research Standards for Professional School Counselors

School Counselor Performance Standards—The school counselor's performance evaluation contains basic standards of practice expected of school counselors implementing a school counseling program. These performance standards should serve as both a basis for counselor evaluation and a means for counselor self-evaluation.

    Program Audit—The primary purpose of collecting information is to guide future action within the program and to improve future results for students.

SOURCE: Executive Summary of the ASCA National Model: www.schoolcounselor.org/files/Natl%20Model %20Exec%20Summary_final.pdf.

This chapter introduces methods and techniques that can be employed to help school counselors make data-based decisions. It also introduces methods to evaluate school counselors and their counseling programs.

The primary approach to systematic evaluations used in schools today involves the Context, Input, Process, and Product (CIPP) evaluation model of Daniel L. Stufflebeam (2003). The CIPP model provides valid and reliable methods for assessing the extent to which goals and objectives held by the school's counseling program's stakeholders have been met. This requires the systematic collection and analysis of formative and summative data, thoughtful analyses, and careful report writing.

The ASCA has also called for a program audit each year. The annual audit is similar to the CIPP model for systematic program evaluation employed by grant-funding agencies, including the U.S. Department of Education and most private philanthropies. The audit is conducted to determine the extent to which a school's counseling program is in compliance with the 13 performance standards of the ASCA. There is considerable overlap between the two, and data collected for one can be applied to the other.

Standard 8: The professional school counselor collects and analyzes data to guide program direction and emphasis.

Standard 11: The professional school counselor develops a results evaluation for the program.

Standard 12: The professional school counselor conducts a yearly program audit. (ASCA/Hatch & Bowers, 2005, p. 64)

In addition to program evaluations and annual audits, school counselors are expected to participate in and possibly lead action research efforts in the school. Action research is a pragmatic approach to addressing local problems in an educational setting. The role of a professional school counselor offers many opportunities for counselors to take a leadership role in the use of carefully designed action research to improve practice and the quality of the school's environment and educational outcomes. The model for conducting action research, with and without collaboration with others, was developed by Kurt Lewin in the 1940s.

● QUALITY INDICATORS (VARIABLES) FOR SCHOOL COUNSELING PROGRAMS

In a research context, all indicators of the degree of quality of a school's counseling program are called *variables*. There are dozens of possible quality indicators for a school's counseling program. As an example, one quality indicator is the counselor-to-student ratio. The recommended ratio for a high school is one counselor for every 250 students. This ratio may be considered as the dependent variable in a study that simply compares schools on the basis of this ratio. A dependent variable is the measured outcome for a research study. In this simplistic example, the number of counselors various schools have employed can be considered the dependent variable.

The same ratio of counselor to students can be an independent variable in a study measuring the impact of school counselors on another variable, such as the number of students scoring below proficient in reading on the state-mandated assessment. In that case, the number of low-scoring (below proficient) students is the dependent variable being influenced by the independent variable, the student-to-counselor ratio.

As noted, the number of possible variables used for the evaluation of counseling programs is very large. Goals selected for study and the objectives set for the counseling program should determine what quality indicators (dependent variables) are used to assess the school's counseling program (Morkides, 2009). Goal setting and the development of annual objectives require input from representatives of all groups who are stakeholders in the programs of the school's counseling office.

School Counseling Program Advisory Board

The school counseling program advisory board (SCPAB) is made up of stakeholders in a school counseling program and may include members of the student services committee of the school district's governing board, administrators, the school's faculty, paraprofessional and support staff, students, parents, and members of the broader community. This SCPAB should advise the school's counselors on establishing a school counseling philosophy for the program and also provide guidance in setting annual objectives and priorities for the program. The goals, objectives, and priorities become the plan of action for the school's counselors and also provide an objective basis for a systematic evaluation of the counseling program. A partial list of variables that may be used in the evaluation of the success of the school's counseling program is presented in the following box.

Variables That Can Be Used as Quality Indicators for a School's Counseling Program

- Number of disciplinary referrals to the principal's staff

- Percentage of recidivists with additional disciplinary referrals after counseling

- The method used to recruit the school counseling program advisory board (SCPAB)

- Frequency of SCPAB meetings

- SCPAB organization model

- Year-to-year change in the number of students making the honor roll

- Dimension of gap among various ethnic groups of students in terms of honors and advanced placement enrollment

- Year-to-year change in the number of students failing to be promoted or failing individual classes

- Year-to-year change in the number of students scoring below proficient on mandated state assessment tests

- Year-to-year reduction in the achievement test score gap among identifiable groups of students

- Number and representativeness of the group of parents attending after-school conferences

- Efforts (number and frequency) being made to increase parental involvement

- Efforts to welcome parents who are English-language learners to participate in counseling program activities

- Resources offered by the school's counseling program for non-English speakers

- Number of successful transition plans developed with, and approved by, parents of children with special needs

(Continued)

(Continued)

- Number of teacher–counselor consultations during the year

- Teacher evaluations of the effectiveness of teacher–counselor consultations (e.g., anonymous questionnaire)

- Readability and completeness of the school counselor's web page

- Number of "hits" on the school counselor's web page

- Publication of school counselor's calendar on the school's web page

- Number of students expelled for violating the school's "zero-tolerance policy"

- Extent of parent volunteerism in the school and related activities (e.g., chaperones)

- Year-to-year change in the school's dropout versus graduation ratio

- Evidence of career placement or college admission for high school's graduates within 6 months of graduation

- Year-to-year change in the number of student pregnancies and births

- Survey evaluation data (anonymous) from stakeholders as to the perceived effectiveness of the school's counselor(s) by groups of stakeholders, including teachers, educational specialists in the school, parents, and students

- Student–counselor contact hours disaggregated to show one-to-one, group sessions, and classroom intervention programs

- Evidence that all groups of students are receiving an equitable distribution of counseling services

- Successful versus unsuccessful 504 committees or student assistance teams (success indicates a resolution of the problem without an individualized education plan [IEP] committee)

- Year-to-year change in the attendance rate of students

- Number and quality of extramural community visits with local employers, parents of students, community leaders including local clergy, and community organizations

- Number of appearances in family and/or juvenile court and a summation of the outcomes from such appearances

- Number of speaking engagements made to local organizations

- Number of sessions and participation level in parent groups sponsored by the school's counselors

- Evidence of ongoing and systematic programs for primary prevention

- Documentation of efforts to assess the dimensions of need within the school for counselors to address

- Number of children receiving in-classroom primary and secondary prevention programs (success of programs in terms of measurable outcomes, e.g., disciplinary referrals)[1]
- Implementation of an organized guidance curriculum aligned with the counseling office action plan
- Accessibility of counseling office for students with disabilities
- Privacy offered to student-clients when visiting the counselor's office

Stakeholder Survey of Potential Goals for the School's Counseling Program

The best school counseling programs are designed to meet needs identified by the school's primary groups of stakeholders. Exhibits 14.1, 14.2, and 14.3 present three sample surveys, one for each level of public education. Separate surveys can be made for stakeholder groups, including faculty members, parents, and students. Exhibit 14.1 is a sample elementary survey for parents, Exhibit 14.2 a middle school teacher survey, and Exhibit 14.3 a high school student survey.

EXHIBIT 14.1   Sample Survey for Parents of Elementary School Students

---

Shirley Hufstedler Elementary School
Igneous Rock School District

1. Your relationship to Hufstedler School

    _____ I am a parent of or guardian for one or more students

    _____ Other, please elaborate: _____

    Please indicate how you perceive the following factors about school life.

2. My child (children) feels safe in school.

    _____(A) Full Agreement

    _____(B) Mostly Agree

    _____(C) Mostly Disagree

    _____(D) Completely Disagree

    _____(E) I Cannot Be Certain

(Continued)

Exhibit 14.1 (Continued)

3. My child (children) dreads going up against the bullies at school.

____(A) Full Agreement

____(B) Mostly Agree

____(C) Mostly Disagree

____(D) Completely Disagree

____(E) I Cannot Be Certain

4. My child (children) reports that there are many fights at school.

____(A) Full Agreement

____(B) Mostly Agree

____(C) Mostly Disagree

____(D) Completely Disagree

____(E) I Cannot Be Certain

5. I am worried about my child needing special education.

____(A) Full Agreement

____(B) Mostly Agree

____(C) Mostly Disagree

____(D) Completely Disagree

____(E) I Cannot Be Certain

6. My child (children) looks forward to going to school each day.

____(A) Full Agreement

____(B) Mostly Agree

____(C) Mostly Disagree

____(D) Completely Disagree

____(E) I Cannot Be Certain

7. My contacts have shown that teachers and others in the school treat me with respect.

____(A) Full Agreement

____(B) Mostly Agree

____(C) Mostly Disagree

____(D) Completely Disagree

____(E) I Cannot Be Certain

8. My child (children) has **not** had personal items or lunch money taken from him or her.

____(A) Full Agreement

____(B) Mostly Agree

____(C) Mostly Disagree

____(D) Completely Disagree

____(E) I Cannot Be Certain

9. The school library is helpful and my child (children) brings home books to read for pleasure.

____(A) Full Agreement

____(B) Mostly Agree

____(C) Mostly Disagree

____(D) Completely Disagree

____(E) I Cannot Be Certain

10. My child (children) feels left-out of social activities because of our socioeconomic status level.

____(A) Full Agreement

____(B) Mostly Agree

____(C) Mostly Disagree

____(D) Completely Disagree

____(E) I Cannot Be Certain

11. My child's (children's) teachers seem fair and equally concerned for all children.

____(A) Full Agreement

____(B) Mostly Agree

____(C) Mostly Disagree

____(D) Completely Disagree

____(E) I Cannot Be Certain

12. I understand the grades and reports that are sent home about my child (children).

____(A) Full Agreement

____(B) Mostly Agree

____(C) Mostly Disagree

____(D) Completely Disagree

____(E) I Cannot Be Certain

13. There is a hidden drug and/or alcohol problem among the children at this school.

____(A) Full Agreement

____(B) Mostly Agree

____(C) Mostly Disagree

____(D) Completely Disagree

____(E) I Cannot Be Certain

(Continued)

EXHIBIT 14.1 (Continued)

14. I wish I could transfer my child (children) and could afford the tuition costs of sending (him/her) to a good private school.

____(A) Full Agreement

____(B) Mostly Agree

____(C) Mostly Disagree

____(D) Completely Disagree

____(E) I Cannot Be Certain

15. Students seem prematurely concerned with sexuality and reproduction.

____(A) Full Agreement

____(B) Mostly Agree

____(C) Mostly Disagree

____(D) Completely Disagree

____(E) I Cannot Be Certain

16. My child (children) seems lonely and spends a lot of time in solitary activity.

____(A) Full Agreement

____(B) Mostly Agree

____(C) Mostly Disagree

____(D) Completely Disagree

____(E) I Cannot Be Certain

17. Some children carry hidden guns and knives to school.

____(A) Full Agreement

____(B) Mostly Agree

____(C) Mostly Disagree

____(D) Completely Disagree

____(E) I Cannot Be Certain

18. My child (children) seems to be responsible and caring.

____(A) Full Agreement

____(B) Mostly Agree

____(C) Mostly Disagree

____(D) Completely Disagree

____(E) I Cannot Be Certain

19. I am having an increasingly difficult time keeping lines of communication open with my child (children).

____(A) Full Agreement

____(B) Mostly Agree

____(C) Mostly Disagree

____(D) Completely Disagree

____(E) I Cannot Be Certain

20. I would like the school counselors to conduct evening or weekend group meetings focused on the following topics. (Check all you are interested in attending)

____Using the school's web pages

____Opportunities for parents to volunteer in school

____Keeping lines of communication open with my child

____Preventing my child from smoking

____Preventing my child from alcohol/drug abuse

____Having a popular child

____Planning fun and also educational family vacations

____Looking forward to high school

____Surviving my child's puberty

____Dating

____Sexuality and the tween years

____Telecommunications and American children

____Improving motivation and academic drive

____Interpretation and understanding report cards

____Parent support group for special education

____Parental support group for eating problems

Other _____

EXHIBIT 14.2   Sample Survey for Middle School Teachers

Donald Super Middle School

Sedentary Cliffs School District

Your relationship to Donald Super School

___I am a full-time teacher or educational specialist in Donald Super School (Yes) (No)

___I am a part-time teacher or educational specialist in Donald Super School (Yes) (No)

___Other. Please elaborate: _____

Which department or team are you a member of this year? _____

What topics would you like the school's leadership to provide as seminars for teachers?

Topic_____

Do you have a presenter in mind? (Yes) (No)

Name of presenter: _____

(Continued)

Exhibit 14.2 (Continued)

Please indicate how you perceive the following factors about school life and your job here at Donald Super School.

1. I could use assistance with difficult conduct cases in my classroom.

   (Yes) _____ (Occasionally) _____ (Not an issue) _____

2. I would like the school counselor to teach students better study skills.

   (Yes) _____ (No, not an issue) _____

3. I would like to integrate career education into my curriculum.

   (Yes) _____ (Ask me later) _____ (Not interested) _____

4. I am worried about the amount of alcohol and drug abuse in this school.

   (True) _____ (Not an issue) _____

5. I wish to improve my teacher-to-parent communication skills.

   (True) _____ (Not a problem) _____

6. I would like to improve my student conferencing skills.

   (True) _____ (Not a problem) _____

7. I need information to use to help improve my students' college admission test scores.

   (True) _____ (Not a problem) _____

8. I need to know ways to improve my students' test scores on the high-stakes tests.

   (True) _____ (Not a problem) _____

9. I need to learn how to mediate arguments before students become violent.

   (True) _____ (Not a problem) _____

10. I need training on how best to work with students with disabilities.

    (True) _____ (Not a problem) _____

What are the strengths of the school counseling program at this school?

_____

_____

What are things that could be improved with this school's counseling program?

_____

_____

Exhibit 14.3   Sample Survey for High School Students

J. Bruce Ismay Senior High School
Granite Cobblestones School District

What is your grade level? _____ Your gender (Male) _____ (Female) _____

Did you attend middle school in the Granite Cobblestones School District?

(Yes) _____ (No) _____

Have you used the school counselor's web page?

(Yes, frequently) _____ (Occasionally) _____ (Never) _____

If never, please explain why._____

Please indicate how you perceive school life in Ismay Senior High School.

1. The homework requires too much time to complete.
   (True for me) _____ (Sometimes) _____ (Not at all) _____

2. I am worried about weapons I have seen brought into the school.
   (True to me) _____ (Sometimes) _____ (Not at all)) _____

3. I wish I were not being bullied over the Internet e-mail and through social networks.
   (True for me) _____ (Not at all) _____

4. Drugs and alcohol are a real problem in this school.
   (True) _____ (Some days) _____ (Never happens) _____

5. I need more information about sex and my personal sexuality.
   (True for me) _____ (Not at this time) _____

6. This high school is too easy and I wish it offered interesting but harder classes.
   (True for me) _____ (Sometimes) _____ (Never) _____

7. I would like to learn more about career planning.
   (True for me) _____ (Not yet) _____

8. I need ideas about how I can make and keep more friends.
   (True for me) _____ (Occasional problem) _____ (Never an issue) _____

9. The school is run by bullies and unfriendly cliques.
   (True for me) _____ (Occasional problem) _____ (Never an issue) _____

(Continued)

Exhibit 14.3 (Continued)

10. Students from different ethnic groups avoid each other in this school.

    (True) _____ (Usually the case) _____ (Not the case) _____

11. My parents are good listeners and help me all the time.

    (True for me) ___ (Occasionally true) _____ (Not true) _____

12. I wish I could talk over a problem with a counselor.

    (True for me) _____ (Not just now) _____ (Never) _____

13. I need information about colleges and financial aid.

    (True for me) _____ (Not just now) _____

14. I am unhappy about what is going on in my family.

    (True for me) _____ (Sometimes) _____ (Not a problem) _____

15. My study habits need improvement.

    (True) _____ (Occasionally) _____ (Not a problem) _____

16. I am very concerned because I have homosexual thoughts.

    (True for me) _____ (Occasionally) _____ (Never) _____

17. I find myself lonely and depressed increasingly often.

    (True for me) _____ (Occasionally) _____ (Never) _____

18. I am secretly cutting or hurting myself.

    (Frequently) _____ (Occasionally) _____ (Never) _____

19. I have many friends whose company I enjoy.

    (True for me) _____ (Sometimes true for me) _____ (Not at all) _____

20. I have thoughts of suicide.

    (Frequently) _____ (Occasionally) _____ (Never) _____

● FORMAL EVALUATION OF SCHOOL COUNSELING PROGRAMS

> *The most important purpose of evaluation is not to prove but to improve.*
>
> *Egon Guba, quoted by Daniel L. Stufflebeam (2008)*

The systematic and ongoing evaluation of school counseling programs is a recent phenomenon that has gained deep roots with the requirements of the ASCA national framework (ASCA/Hatch & Bowers, 2005). In addition to requirements of the professional guidelines of the ASCD, whenever state and school district funds are involved there is a need for accountability, and an

CARTOON 14.1 **"What the Children Think"**

"I am surveying what the children think about the job the school's counselor is doing."

SOURCE: Merv Magus.

evaluation is required to justify the program. To ensure that a school counseling program is well funded and staffed, it is critical that it be able to "prove" its merits through systematic and scientific evaluations (Whiston, 2002).

In 1965 a requirement for educational evaluation was made an integral requirement for *all* education programs receiving external funding by the federal government. Under these regulations, any federal money used to support any aspect of a school's counseling program requires an evaluation. For example, if Title I funds are used to support an elementary school's counseling program, an evaluation of that program must be included as part of the overall evaluation of the school's Title I activities. The source of guidance provided by the U.S. Department of Education for these evaluations is the document *Education General Administrative Guidelines* (EDGAR). Information about the mandates of the EDGAR is available at www.ed.gov/policy/fund/reg/edgarReg/edgar.html.

Evaluation Professionals

This need for schools and their programs to be held to account spurred the development of the field of educational evaluation. In 1985 a new professional society, the American Evaluation Association (AEA), was formed. Today this association of 4,000 educational evaluators publishes several journals and holds annual meetings at which new developments in the science of school and program evaluation are presented. This association has defined an *evaluation* as activities required for "assessing the strengths and weaknesses of programs, policies, personnel, products, and organizations" (American Evaluation Association [AEA], 2005).

Educational evaluation includes the knowledge base of educational measurement used to design and select appropriate measures. It also draws from the educational research literature for the establishment of data collection methods and from educational statistics for data management and analysis. Finally, a systematic educational evaluation will also draw from the techniques of **qualitative research** methods such as **ethnography** and participant observation, **hermeneutics,** and connoisseurship (Patton, 1987).

Context Input Process and Product Model for Systematic Evaluation

All educational programs are highly complex enterprises. This is especially true for programs in school counseling. As such, a complete evaluation of counseling programs is also a highly complex endeavor. Not only are the systematic evaluations of counseling programs complex, but they are also difficult to do well (Eisner, 1985). The difficulty lies in the fact that services and programs must be provided to meet a multitude of student and community variables, such as socioeconomic level, cognitive ability, educational expectations, community resources, family's primary language, and parental academic motivation and interests. These and many more considerations moderate how the counseling program of each individual school is organized to serve its stakeholders.

Another source of complexity for educational evaluators of school counseling is the fact that one counseling methodology is not universally employed within a school. Unlike teaching mathematics, where there is a basic curriculum and sequence of instruction to follow, counselors live and work in an environment that is continually changing. Also, two school counselors using the same approach to their work can get very different results for their efforts. This reflects the fact that school counseling is not a routinized production task but is a very personal art form (Lowenstein, 1999). In addition to the goal of having a school counseling program that is aligned with ASCA's national framework, high schools that have **regional accreditation** also are called upon to conduct regular evaluations of all aspects of their programs. Earning accreditation includes writing a detailed self-study and having an external evaluation team provide *in situ* confirmation of how the school and each of its divisions, including the school counseling program, has met the standards of the accrediting body (Middle States Association, 2009).

Standards for Evaluation Quality

Evaluation methodologies range from the appropriate to the inane. In 1981 a set of standards for evaluating how high-quality evaluations are conducted was published (Stufflebeam, 1981). These standards for evaluation were updated again in 1994 by the American National Standards Institute. These standards are presented in four broad areas:

1. *Utility*: Describes the evaluator's credibility and capability to carry out all aspects of the evaluation and related analyses, including the careful identification and engagement of appropriate stakeholders, writing clear and precise interim and final reports, and designing and using appropriate survey instruments for data collection

2. *Feasibility*: Addresses questions of a practical nature such as cost, time commitments for essential personnel, and the local politics steering the evaluation of the school's counseling program

3. *Propriety*: Concerns human relations among those who are party to the evaluation, including subject rights and anonymity, data confidentiality, integrity of all outcome statements regarding individuals, and related responsibilities for evaluation management

4. *Accuracy*: Involves the quality of all formative and summative data, the accuracy of all analysis and statistical presentations in the report, and the scientific justifiability of conclusions

More is available on these standards for evaluations at www.ericdigests .org/1996–1/the.htm.

● STEPS IN A SYSTEMATIC EVALUATION

In the process of evaluating an educational program such as a school's counseling activities, there are seven basic steps. These start with (1) the identification of stakeholders, then (2) the setting of goals for the evaluation. Next comes (3) the establishment of evaluation objectives and (4) the development of a management plan to achieve those goals. The next steps include (5) collection and analysis of appropriate data and (6) using those analyses to write a final report. The final step (7) is the dissemination of the results of the evaluation.

Steps 1 and 2: Stakeholder Identification and Goal Setting

The use of stakeholders helps the whole school community "buy into" the school's counseling efforts and improves working relationships among all concerned (Greene, 1987). Goal-setting tasks should be conducted with representatives from each of the stakeholders groups (e.g., building representative to the district's collective bargaining unit, parent leader of the school's parent advisory board, student council president, and an administrator). This step is part of the Utility standard for quality evaluations (Joint Committee on Standards for Educational Evaluation, 2008).

The goal-setting process sets the focus of the school's counseling program for the coming year. It also provides the means for evaluating the success of the efforts of the counselors.

School counselors must be mindful of the private agendas that some stakeholders may bring to the process of evaluating the program. (See Case in Point 14.1.) As each stakeholder or group of stakeholders becomes involved with the process, it is important for the counselor to determine what, if any, special interest the stakeholder may represent. The counselor responsible for the evaluation has the job of understanding and keeping all hidden agendas in check.

CASE IN POINT 14.1

Many states require local school systems to develop a strategic or long-range plan following a cycle, usually 5 years. Much work, often including a self-study, goes into these plans. The self-study is conducted following an evaluation model. It is unfortunate that, once completed and filed in the state education department office, these evaluations are rarely looked at again and are not examined until the next cycle for mandated planning comes around.

In one school system that was working to devise a plan to evaluate the high school counseling program, the director of pupil services for the school system had an agenda of his own. He had volunteered to supervise the development and writing of the strategic plan and the accompanying evaluation for the whole high school. In a sense he became both the evaluator and the primary stakeholder. It seems that he was applying to replace the high school's retiring principal. He used the evaluation component of the strategic plan to provide evidence of the quality of his performance. Most of the evaluation became skewed toward his areas of responsibility and away from other areas of the high school.

Thought Question. Test scores of the school's students influence the pay of some educators in a number of school districts. This process is known as merit pay. If your school was to implement a merit pay system, what indicators would you want to serve as a basis for your pay as a school counselor?

It is also necessary to identify concerns stakeholders may have with the program evaluation process (Fleischman & Williams, 1996). For the most part, educators view themselves as being overworked, underpaid, burdened with great responsibility, and given no real authority. It is easy for educators to become skeptical of an evaluation process and view it as just another waste of their time.

To avoid resistance from teachers, the school counselor should work with the advisory committee of stakeholders during the late spring or early fall to design a set of specific goals for the coming year. The stakeholders' committee also has the responsibility to write an evaluation management plan, including the actual questions to be answered during the year to assess the counselors and their efforts.

Step 3: Setting the Objectives

The step immediately following goal setting involves developing evaluation objectives aligned with each of the goals. The advisory committee of stakeholders has the task of reviewing and approving objectives for counseling program goals and evaluation. Of special note is the fact that school counseling program evaluations should always include teachers in the loop (Wolf, 1990).

During the year the person designated as the evaluator of the counseling program should keep lines of communication open by holding occasional virtual meetings and through the use of e-mail.[2] An interim formative report should be prepared about halfway during the academic year. This report provides counselors with a tentative analysis of how goals are being met. A formative report from the evaluation is likely to result in tweaking ongoing counseling activities.

Step 4: Developing a Management Plan

Once the goals are set, and each of the objectives for the evaluation identified, it is then possible to devise an evaluation management plan. The Feasibility standard for evaluations can be addressed by developing a comprehensive, practical, and frugal evaluation plan to assess the effectiveness of the school's counseling program.

A specific data collection strategy needs to be devised for assessing each objective. This process starts by listing all evaluation tasks that will be designed and completed for the evaluation. Evaluation tasks and activities are formative in nature and collected as the school year goes along.

The two most critical questions to be asked when designing a management plan are (1) when each part of the evaluation should be conducted, and (2) who should have the responsibility for doing the various data collection tasks. This is best expressed graphically as a two-axis **Gantt chart**. This chart is essentially a timeline for what will occur and when it will happen. The abscissa of this type of chart is a timeline extending throughout the school's year. The ordinate of the Gantt chart presents a list of tasks required for the school counseling program's evaluation (Clark, Polakov, & Trabold, 2010). Bars on the chart provide a visual reference for the timing and sequence of evaluation activities. If several people are responsible for collecting data for the evaluation, the name of the person tasked with each component can be imposed on the Gantt chart's timelines.

The management plan should also specify data collection procedures to be used with the evaluation of the various dimensions of the school's counseling program. This information can be added to the structure of the Gantt chart (see Table 14.1).

The plan should address the organization and storage of all evaluation data. This includes all data and artifacts brought together in the evaluation process.

Evaluating a school counseling program raises special problems related to the nature of the evaluation data. Data collection must occur in legal and ethical ways that provide safeguards for the rights and welfare of students, educators, and others. This is part of the Propriety standard for evaluations conducted in educational settings. The plan should specify who has access to the evaluation data and what security measures are appropriate for the evaluation's files.

TABLE 14.1   Gantt Chart of High School Counseling Program Evaluation Based on Student Input Sample From 2 of 12 Goals That Were Addressed

Goal: Provide Career Guidance		Evaluation Indicator of Success
1. Expand general library holdings in career education	(Counselor A) **************	1. Count of new career software and new career focused books for young readers
2. Provide career choice tests during career education classes	(All Counselors) ***********	2. Total number of tests administered and follow-up counseling sessions
3. Workshops on interviewing and job applications	(Counselor C) *************	3. Number of workshops, and total hours of student attendance
4. Contact regional employers for possible beginner jobs	(Counselor C) *************	4. Number of contacts made, number of job openings identified
5. Job placement for non-college bound students	(All Counselors) **********	5. Year-to-year change in % of graduates employed 20 or more hours per week

Goal: Reduce Bullying Behaviors		
1. Follow up on anonymous postings on counselor web page	(All Counselors) ************************************	1. Reduction in number of referrals for harassing and bulling behavior
2. Victim group counseling sessions	(All Counselors) ********* *********	2. Survey of students for outcome of counseling program
3. Parent support group for the families of bullying victims	(Counselor B) ***** *****	3. Parent attendance count and survey of parental perception of session effectiveness
4. Behavioral counseling with bullies	(Counselor B) *********************************	4. Reduction in rate of recidivism for counseled bullies

| When task should be completed | S----O----N----D----J----F----M----A----M----J----J | |

Step 5: Data Collection and Analysis

There are numerous factors in any school environment that can cause students to exhibit changes. The effectiveness of the school's counselor is one such factor, but there are alternative explanations for changes that may occur in any school environment. These factors confound what is found during the evaluation and reduce the **internal validity** of the evaluation. The goal for the evaluator is to establish a data collection plan that optimizes the likelihood that all evaluated outcomes are a function of the school counseling program's efforts and are not brought about by extraneous factors.

Potential factors that can invalidate the findings of an evaluation of a school's counseling program were first organized into a taxonomy by Donald T. Campbell and Julian C. Stanley (Campbell & Stanley, 1963). This taxonomy was published in the first edition of the *Handbook of Research on Teaching* (Gage, 1967). Variations on this model for organizing the threats to the validity of educational research have appeared over the years in all educational research and evaluation textbooks. The approach discussed here is a compilation of these efforts and a reorganization of them to address contemporary school counseling programs. New dimensions of potential invalidity are also included.

As described in Table 14.2, there are three major areas of school life that can contaminate the evaluation data from any effort to assess the quality of a school's counseling program. These areas include (1) time-related factors, (2) measurement-related factors, and (3) design-related factors. (See Case in Point 14.2 for a situation involving possible research errors.)

CASE IN POINT 14.2

The three school counselors of a middle school decided to provide a series of group sessions for small groups of seventh grade students who had been harassed during the previous year (their sixth grade) by bullies in the school. Each counselor scheduled a series of group sessions with between 6 and 8 of the seventh graders. Counseling was provided in a series of four group sessions, each with three weekly meetings. The first group meetings started in October, the next in January, one was provided in March, and the last session occurred in late April and early May. These seventh graders were taught strategies for overcoming the impact of bullying behavior. At the program's start in October, and again at the conclusion of the sessions in the spring, students answered a questionnaire as to how problematic the bullying behavior was for them that year. The counselors were delighted to see that virtually every student found that harassment was no longer a problem for them.

Thought Question. What errors in research design may have served as a possible explanation for this outcome? (*Hint*: See Maturation and History in Table 14.2.)

TABLE 14.2   Factors of School Life Related to Reducing Internal Validity of a School-Based Evaluation of a Counseling Program

Time-Related Factors

Each of these factors is linked to the length of time the evaluation requires to complete. Most evaluations of counseling programs are longitudinal studies that run throughout the school year. The potential for a loss of validity in an evaluation as a function of time can be divided into three areas of concern.

1. *Maturation*. As time passes, students age and mature. This simple fact of life can produce differential outcomes at different ages and stages of human development. The issue of maturation can have a powerful effect when the counseling of second and third grade children is evaluated. This developmental stage (7–9 years old) is one of rapid cognitive and conceptual development. Development and improved social understanding will occur whether the child meets with a counselor or not. Throughout every lifetime there are identifiable points in time when each child is optimally sensitive and ready for cognitive reorganization and accepting of a new level of understanding. For example, during the middle school years, children begin to wrestle with the tasks of identity formation and learning a new level of interpersonal skills.

2. *History*. This term is better thought of as "current events." This factor describes how ongoing ecology and human interactions can have a nonrandom effect on the outcome of a counseling program. If a school counselor made the mistake of attempting to collect meaningful data on October 31 or November 1 of any school year he or she would quickly realize a powerful effect known as Halloween. There are a dozen or so days throughout the school year when the collection of meaningful data in a public school is impossible (e.g., field day, pep rally days, field trip days, etc.). Other issues can be more prosaic. For northern schools there are snow days. I know from personal experience that no one, including school counselors, is "on task" in a school once a heavy snowfall has begun. In southern states there are tropical storm days. The antics of the school custodian on a riding lawn mower outside the classroom of children being tested has also been shown to interfere with data collection (Page, 1975). Even the disruptive impact of one child acting out can distort evaluation outcome data and have an adverse impact on an ongoing counseling activity (Peckham, Glass, & Hopkins, 1969).

3. *Mortality or Mobility*. Families move into and out of communities every day. This simple fact can play a major role in the outcome of a school counselor's work. The loss of even a single child can change the dynamic and *einstellung* of a counseling group. The addition of students into school can also have a profound impact on the operation of the counseling program. Once the school year is underway, an additional student will take extra time and effort by the school's counselor to conduct screenings, provide the student and his or her parents with an orientation, and identify an appropriate placement or roster of classes to follow. Time must also be spent in helping teachers understand the new student's needs and background. That time can only come from the time that would have been spent on others needing the counselor's attention. Thus, the addition of new students has the effect of diluting counseling effectiveness. Some schools experience extraordinarily high rates of turnover. In urban areas it is not unusual for a third or more of all students to move to different schools each year (Coulton, Theodos, & Turner, 2009). This implies that there could be several new students for the school counselor to register every week.

(Continued)

Table 14.2 (Continued)

Major disruptions (e.g., school renovation and reconstruction, or a violent gang disturbance) in the school can also profoundly affect both counseling programs and their evaluation (Lesisko & Wright, 2010). Smaller disturbances to the ongoing activities can occur frequently in schools by administrators who love to use the school's public address system throughout the school day.

Measurement-Related Factors

Each of the next three factors is linked to the sequence and type of testing that an evaluator uses. This issue works at several levels. For one, all stakeholders responding to the counselor's survey may not perceive measurements as having the same amount of *gravitas*. Administrators have much more faith in the value of measures of all types than do classroom teachers. Thus the selection or development of a measure is an important consideration in any evaluation study (Guskey, 2007). Once a measure is selected, the problem becomes one of how and when it is employed.

1. *Instrumentation.* This term is used as shorthand to represent changes occurring with the measuring technique and instruments over time. This can involve the subtle changes that occur with interviewers, observers, and raters. This change is a normal process reflecting the experience people gain over time as an evaluator. It also describes changes that may occur with test materials that are reused. Any items handled by children in group sessions will deteriorate with time and use. Even the practice subjects receive in the use of computerized testing software can change the outcome of data collection.

2. *Testing.* If a pretest is used to evaluate a counseling program's effectiveness its presence may alert the student-clients to issues in the program deemed to be important. There is also a normal tendency for most scores on any measure to improve slightly on a second testing. When a test or measure (pretest) causes direct or indirect changes in subsequent measurement (posttest) outcomes, that pretest is referred to as being a **reactive measure.** The closer together in time two sequential measures occur, the greater the potential for the first to be a reactive measure and interfere with the other. This effect has been demonstrated in a number of personality and intellectual areas with children, even with studies of cognition (Roediger & Karpicke, 2006).

3. *Regression Toward the Mean.* What Sir Frances Galton (1886) originally referred to as "regression toward mediocrity" is known today as regression toward the mean. This statistical principle provides a mathematical model explaining why unusually high scores on any measure tend to move lower on retesting. The movement is in the direction of the mean (average) on retesting. Likewise, low scores tend to improve on retesting to scores slightly closer to the mean (average) score. In an evaluation of the impact of a counseling intervention, an initial low score on a measure of a dependent variable such as self-esteem may improve later on retesting as a function of regression toward the mean.

Design

The design features of the evaluation can have an impact on the outcome of the study. There are ways to organize data collection for systematic educational evaluations to avoid some of these validity problems (Suter, 2006). For example, to avoid pre- and posttesting a random sample of students can experience the pretest and a second **random sample** take the posttest. Assuming all students receive the intervention, an expression of its effectiveness will be seen by comparing the pretest and posttest data. The two groups (experimental and control) can be compared only when the two groups were truly randomly selected.

1. *Selection.* The issue of selection (random versus **sample of convenience**) is easily linked to comparisons that may be made when evaluating a school's counseling program. For example, if state assessment scores for students who were given a workshop on test-taking skills are compared (as part of the evaluation of the counseling program) with scores from students of a neighboring school that did not provide its students with the test-taking program, then selection may pose a problem. The problem is that students in the two schools may be very different. This practice of comparing samples of convenience is very common in evaluation and is fraught with the potential for error. Fortunately, systematic evaluations of school counseling programs are usually self-contained. Most comparisons are made over time with the same subjects.

2. *Interpersonal.* The nature of human beings poses significant problems for the evaluator. Within this category are two related problems of **envy** and the **spread of effect**. When some students are selected (**experimental group**) to take part in a "special counseling program," it is natural for those not included (**control group**) to feel envious. This may result in subtle aggression against the program and its participants by those left out. To keep the peace, peer counselors not providing the special program are likely to share it with others, making any comparison between the two groups of students meaningless. Finally, there is another potential problem with nonselected students showing an unusual level of competitiveness. Some children in the control group will show their envy and resentment by working to ensure that they produce a better outcome than the new counseling program under study. Conversely, it is also possible for other students to see being in the control group as confirmation that they are not respected, and they may become increasingly disengaged from the school.

3. *Change and Growth.* There is a natural tendency for the evaluator of a school counseling program to draw conclusions from what appears to be the change in scores from pre- to posttests. These before-and-after comparisons present a special statistical problem of loss of reliability. The subtraction of pretest scores from the posttest scores for students provides what are known as **subtraction residuals**. These residuals have very low reliability and are, for the most part, composed of measurement error (Wright, 2008). For that reason they are neither reliable nor valid for use in an evaluation.*

4. *Novelty.* Most classroom teachers are familiar with the feature-length movie *The Dead Poet's Society*, starring Robin Williams as an iconoclastic teacher (Haft, Witt, & Thomas, 1989). In order to break the mindset of a classroom of preparatory school students, the teacher did several absurd stunts such as standing on his desk to teach. Naturally such behaviors caught the attention of the otherwise uninspired students. While the act is interesting and novel today, the logical question is, "What is the next act?" Students can be excited and interested in a novel approach or technique, but when the luster of this *dernier cri* has worn off, so will the motivation and interest in the program. Educational evaluators must be mindful of this tendency for the novelty of a new program to bring about a temporary change of its own accord. For example, being invited to participate in a group by the counselor may be a novel experience that will stir interest, but after a few sessions, when the novelty wears off, the counselor will need to introduce new dimensions and activities for the group. There is a need for children of the 21st century to need ever more stimulation to remain engaged (Thomas, 2009).

*The appropriate method to use in comparing pre- and posttesting scores is through the use of regression residuals. This is a basic statistical process that requires a knowledge of linear correlation (Kremelberg, 2010).

Part of Step 5 involves careful record keeping. The Accuracy standard for the evaluation of a school's counseling program requires careful program documentation. The documentation includes all meeting notes, attendance sheets, surveys and questionnaires, tests, disciplinary records, and so forth. For that reason one critical role that must be assigned to someone on the evaluation team is that of secretary/librarian. There will be an incredible amount of paperwork generated during an evaluation. These raw documents must be collected, organized, and stored. This is best done by using a scanner and setting up a number of computer files. Remember, all files should be both secured and backed up. Also, the evaluator should keep a detailed journal documenting every step in the process including any departure from the protocol provided in the management plan. The fact that the systematic evaluation is a part of an accountability demonstration makes it subject to accounting oversight. Documented activities in a journal are an artifact that an outside accrediting body may wish to examine.

Another part of Step 5 includes the collection of evaluation data. As the evaluation is likely to be conducted throughout the school year, it may include observational data, meeting notes, test grades, counseling records, and various products of student learning. Other data sources may require the development of questionnaires and survey research. Careful selection of published assessment instruments and their appropriate and ethical use may also provide sources of evaluation data. The key to using any published measure successfully is knowing the instrument well and being scrupulous in following the published directions for both administering and scoring of the measure (see Chapter 10 for information on assessing the quality of a measure).

Accurate and careful data analysis is also part of the fifth step. This is directly related to the Accuracy standard for educational evaluations. Analysis follows data collection and is integral to the evaluation. Data analyses require the qualitative assessment of observational data as well as the statistical analysis of test scores and other quantitative data. Together these two forms of data are combined into a final report for the counseling program.

Step 6: Evaluation Report Writing

This sixth step also addresses the Utility issues in the standards for program evaluations. The Utility standard requires the final report to provide a clear description of the school's counseling program. It should provide an accurate statement of the findings and provide clear and unbiased interpretation of all data.

As all data were collected to answer specific questions based on goals and objectives for the counseling program's year, the final report should also address each goal and objective. The final report should present all relevant evidence collected and analyzed for each objective. A conclusion statement should be made regarding each of the objectives. Conclusions may include both kudos and problem areas. The final summary statement should list all successes and problem areas and point ahead to the goals for the next year.

At its core, the final report reflects the considered judgment of its author, the evaluator. It is unlikely that the school will be able to afford to hire an

CARTOON 14.2   "Figure 1 and Figure 2"

"Figure 1 shows our school's recent test scores and Figure 2 shows how our school's counselors were able to reanalyze the data."

SOURCE: Merv Magus.

independent evaluator to provide an unbiased professional evaluation.[3] For that reason, one of the school's counselors is likely to serve in the role of evaluator.

To reduce the possibility of impropriety in the evaluation of the counseling program, the school's administration may assign a senior faculty member (e.g., department head or team leader) to serve as a coevaluator or elect to have an assistant principal or school psychologist serve as the lead evaluator or as a coevaluator. Another possibility is to involve a counselor from another school in the district to evaluate the school's counseling program. All of these approaches can improve the credibility of the evaluation, but each has its own potential problems. Many of these problems are interpersonal and should be fully and frankly discussed prior to any plan being finalized.

Step 7: Publication

The seventh step in an evaluation is the publication of the final report and the wider dissemination of the results. All too often the final report from a systematic evaluation of the school's counseling program ends up forgotten and filed in a school's archives. The best result that can occur from the final evaluation report is that its analysis and recommendations become incorporated into the plans for the coming school year and adopted as part of the new year's evaluation and school counseling plan of action.

Prior to dissemination of the final report, the evaluator should discuss the report with stakeholders who participated in the process. One focus of these discussions should be ways to carry out the recommendations and ideas from the evaluation (Erford, McKechnie, & Moore-Thomas, 2004).

The final report can be used as a basis for publishing a brochure about the school's counseling program. Most office computers provide software that can be used to publish a simple bi-fold statement. Cut and paste some photos or logos, and use a color printer, and the brochure can become an effective advertisement about the activities of the school's counseling program. This work makes a good summer activity for the school counseling office personnel.

The report can also be modified and used to produce a PowerPoint presentation. The PowerPoint can be used with school groups such as parent organizations and the local school board.

In an edited form, the final report can be uploaded onto the counseling office's web page. Another option is to write a column for a community newspaper. Local community newspapers are frequently platforms for local advertising, and editors are often desperate for interesting content for their publications.

An article about the successes and activities of the local school counseling program is one that would be a good fit to the needs of many community newspaper editors.

Other venues for dissemination include the **"rubber chicken circuit."** This odd sobriquet describes the numerous lunch and dinner meetings the counselor can attend as the "guest speaker." Payment for providing one of these community service presentations is usually a free lunch or dinner. During these luncheons or dinners, the visiting school counselor is expected to make a speech or some form of presentation about the counseling activity at the school. This presents the counselor with the opportunity to make a pitch for support for different projects and funds to meet student needs at the school. Either a brochure or a PowerPoint presentation can become the basis for making the after-dinner remarks. Service clubs and community booster clubs have regular meetings and are always on the lookout for someone who can speak for 15 or 20 minutes on a topic of community interest. Local newspapers normally list these clubs and their meeting locations. The organization's program chair is the contact person for speakers being scheduled.

School Counseling Program Audit

The American School Counselors Association developed and published a worksheet useful for auditing the extent to which a school counseling program is meeting the specifications and mandates of The ASCA *National Model: A Framework for School Counseling Programs*. That audit form is found at www.ascanationalmodel.org/files/Program%20audit.pdf. The form is an 11-page checklist that can guide a school's counseling program and help it align its programs and activities with the national framework.

SCHOOL-BASED ACTION RESEARCH   ●

An increasingly important role for the professional school counselor to play is as the resident authority for conducting research in the school (Bradbury, Mirvis, Neilson, & Pasmore, 2007). To qualify for a state license, school administrators, educational specialists (e.g., reading specialists), and school counselors are all required to complete graduate work in educational statistics, research methods, and testing and measurement. Counselors are in the best position to hone these skills and develop an important research expertise

(Portman, 2004). Research skills represent an element school counselors can employ to meet the challenge of the national framework of the ASCA for school counselors to become leaders in the school setting (Hatch, 2004).

The first step in developing impressive research skills involves reading the scientific literature for the school counseling profession (Akos, 2004). An ongoing reading plan should allow time each week to read and reflect upon journal articles. One problem with the profession of school counseling is that few counselors have developed the scientific mindset that can appreciate and value research being done in the field (Bauman, 2004; Rowell, 2006). In this era of accountability, a lack of appreciation for scientifically derived evidence of the effectiveness of counseling programs can put the entire profession at risk (Whiston, 2002). By becoming familiar with trends and directions of the research in the field, the professional school counselor can better advocate for important roles the school's counseling community can play in the betterment of a school's academic, social, and professional lives.

> *Statistics: The only science that enables different experts using the same figures to draw different conclusions.*
>
> *Evan Esar*

There are a number of different approaches to research that can be conducted in the varied fields of education. Qualitative research tends to be field based and draws research methods from the anthropological study of cultures. Other methods are empirical and employ structured research designs and analytical methods from the physical sciences. These empirical methods employ both correlational and experimental techniques. Both of these approaches, qualitative and empirical, may require the school counselor to have a coach from a local university to assist in research design and analyses of data.

Action research is a third method. The concept of conducting action research, a school-based, highly pragmatic approach to problem solving, was the original idea of Kurt Lewin, a founding father of phenomenological psychology and field theory.[4] Lewin's model as applied to school-based action research includes the following steps: (1) identification of a potential problem needing resolution, (2) reconnaissance of data and examples that are potentially related to the problem, (3) analysis of the data from the reconnaissance, (4) formulating an action plan to change the problematic situation, (5) carrying out the actual ideas in the action plan, (6) collecting and analyzing outcome data keyed to the action plan, and (7) if needed, amending what was done and developing a new action plan.

Action Research Cycle

Lewin proposed a model for action research that was very different from the empirical approach employed throughout American psychology during the 20th century. He believed that research should be focused on solving real-world problems and not employed as a method to answer a simple research question. Lewin recognized that problems could require more than one attempt to resolve. The Lewin model provides for replanning and iterating modified plans until the problem is resolved (Ferrance, 2000). To demonstrate this concept, Lewin used a spiral with seven steps. The cycle described here is a modification of the original model, designed around the tasks of conducting research in a public school environment. This model also has been expanded to eight steps, including the development of a revised plan. (See Figure 14.1.) By focusing the research on solving a real problem, Lewin invented a system of action research that closes the gap between research and practice (Rowell, 2006).

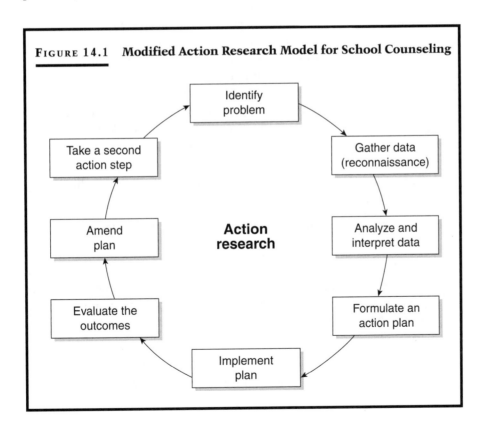

FIGURE 14.1   Modified Action Research Model for School Counseling

A single professional school counselor working alone can carry out action research, or action research can be done in collaboration with other professionals in the school (Rowell, 2006). The advantages of working in collaboration with colleagues are many, and the downsides are few.[5] Collaboration may involve internal personnel, including administrators, school psychologists, and other educational specialists, or it may involve extramural experts, including counselor educators and their graduate students, drug counselors, and family counselors from the community.

Step 1: Problem Identification

The first step in solving any problem is defining it in clear terms so that others can recognize and understand the problem. The problem may be documented in the goal statement that the school counseling program has adopted for the year, and the outcome of the action research effort may be used to provide information and guidance for the program's evaluation.

Problems that may be addressed by action research should be practical, with a goal of improving current counseling practice, the climate of the school, or the educational outcomes for the school's students. This form of research does not address broad theoretical questions, nor does it provide the wherewithal to change national educational policy. It is local, timely, and on-target for meeting the needs of a school, or occasionally a school district.

As problems addressed are quotidian and local, they may include all the issues faced by an active school counselor. These may include solving school counseling research problems such as the following sample of five questions:

1. Can parent education programs after school hours improve school attendance by students with high levels of absenteeism?

2. Can nutrition-focused counseling groups reduce the incidence of students with eating disorders?

3. Can the use of infant simulator dolls (e.g., Baby Think it Over®) with all nulliparous seventh and eighth grade girls reduce the incidence of teenage pregnancy? What is the optimal length of such a program? Should it include boys? What family life education program works best with simulator dolls?

4. What elements are most effective in a test preparation program designed to help students prepare for high-stakes tests mandated by the "Race to the Top" program?

5. Can financial aid information programs geared to both parents and their high school children improve the number of seniors applying to attend college after high school?

Step 2: Gathering Data (Reconnaissance)

Once a problem has been identified there is a need to document the current status of the problem area. This two-phase process starts with reconnaissance of the field or setting involved as the focus of the study (Lewin, 1948). The purpose is to verify that all ancillary research questions and issues are identified and included in the action research.

In question 3, about using an infant simulator, ancillary issues involve whether to include boys, how long the middle school children should be burdened with artificial infants, and what follow-up or small group activities should be included.

The second phase is to identify data that support the need to resolve the problem. These data may be drawn from the data collected to plan for the goals and objectives for the school counseling program's evaluation. Or, these data may be drawn from ongoing records and referrals to the counseling program during previous years.

Step 3: Analyzing and Interpreting the Data

At this preliminary phase, data gathering may occur rapidly as the action research planning process moves quickly along to the planning phase.

Background data on the current status of any of the issues addressed can be collected and summarized. For example, by collecting information on the proportion of seniors applying to college over a period of a few years, the counselor has the local data needed to compare his or her school with published regional and national trend data. This preliminary step can identify how critical this problem is. Likewise, information on the number of students with eating disorders in high school may be collected and compared with other local, regional, or national data to identify whether there is a significant problem among the students of the counselor's school.

Step 4: Formulating an Action Plan

Having collected well-documented information about the nature of the problem, the school counselor should discuss the problem with the advisory board and the school's administration. Input from these groups can help refine the scope and direction of the action research. Only after aligning interested parties can the school counselor initiate the next step, development of an action plan. The action plan may use the information from the reconnaissance and data-gathering phase as a **base line** when proposing intervention programs. The advisory committee and school administration should also vet the final plan. Once approved, the action plan is ready to be initiated by the school counselor. The ultimate goal is always to modify the current state of affairs in the school by taking proactive action. The action plan spells out the independent variable (treatment) and describes how the level of success for the effort will be assessed (dependent variable).

Part of all action plans is a statement of how outcomes will be assessed. A project to reduce absenteeism may begin to see results within a week following the first parent session. Other studies may require a longer, **longitudinal data** collection. The key to all data collection is precision in collecting information and the organization of data for analysis. Data must always be collected using methods that both protect the need for the study to identify individuals over time (longitudinal research) and provide for the confidentiality of all identifying information. Likewise, data must be summarized and stored in ways to ensure the anonymity of individuals involved.

Step 5: Initiating the Action Plan

Care in carrying out each step described in the action plan and the careful documentation of all procedures is needed when any local research plan is initiated. The documentation may be in the form of a research journal or diary. These forms of documentation are needed to provide a trail of evidence that can stand up to any external scrutiny. The project's record should document all action research activities along with any anomalies and creative modifications that transpired. Much of the same information may appear in other locations, including the school counseling program's evaluation or in the attendance logs and meeting notes from groups and parent training sessions. Yet, it is necessary to have a single repository of what happened during the full action research project. Later, these notes, along with background information and outcome data, could become part of a presentation before a state or national professional association.

Step 6: Analyzing Data and Evaluating the Outcomes

One of the canons of the scientific model is that research cannot prove anything beyond the possible chance of ever being wrong. There is always a small level of chance of being wrong in making a statement about what any research effort found. These levels of chance about being wrong in making a conclusion from data are shown on research presentation tables as a less-than sign and level of probability (e.g., $p < 0.05$). This presents what research scholars describe as the "05" level of significance. The "01" level of significance is shown as ($p < 0.01$). The "05" value can be interpreted as documenting that if this study were independently repeated 100 times, there would be only 5 chances in the 100 repetitions that the findings would lead to a different conclusion. Likewise, the researcher may report the "01" level ($p < 0.01$). This is an indication there is only 1 chance in being wrong with this conclusion in 100 attempts at the research. The "01" level implies that we can have confidence in the finding happening 99 times out of 100 (Salkind, 2004). (Establishing these levels is a topic taught in classes involving inferential educational statistics and is beyond the scope of this text.)

Most action research avoids these calculations and focuses on a simple presentation of what happened when the action research plan was implemented. Most presentations employ a graphic display such as a **pie graph, bar graph,** or **histogram** to describe what occurred.

A pie graph can be employed to depict any proportional form of data. It can show areas of expense in the budget of the counseling office or the proportion of students achieving below proficient, proficient, and above proficient on a statewide assessment. A reader will be readily able to understand the impact of a test-taking program if one pie chart is used to depict proportions of proficiency scores prior to when counselors began a program of testing skill development, and a second pie chart is used following the intervention (see Figure 14.2).

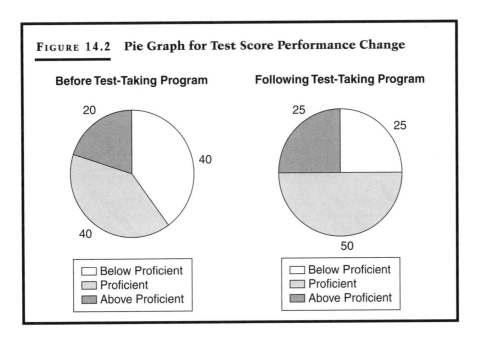

FIGURE 14.2   Pie Graph for Test Score Performance Change

Before Test-Taking Program

Following Test-Taking Program

A bar graph is another example of an easily understood data presentation method. Bar graphs are used to show any of a wide range of data types. The format of a bar graph presentation includes vertical bars, the height of which depicts the frequency of occurrence of some particular dimension. Bars normally start on the abscissa at a point with a value of zero on the ordinate. The taller the bar, the larger the value, as seen on the ordinate for the data set in Figure 14.3.

A histogram can be used to depict the number of unexcused absences by students. In Figure 14.4, the ordinate is the number of disciplinary referrals, and abscissa are months of the school year. Months of a year follow a specific sequence or order. This fact implies the use of a histogram requiring that one

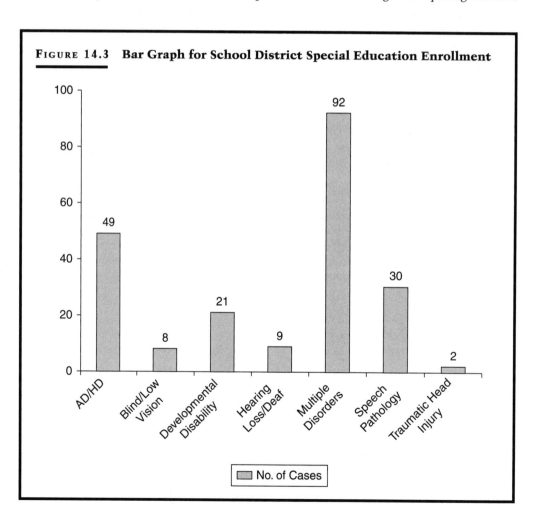

FIGURE 14.3   **Bar Graph for School District Special Education Enrollment**

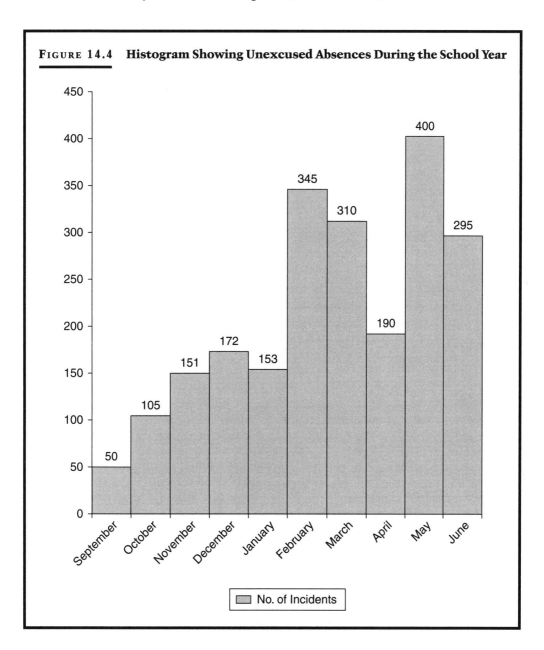

FIGURE 14.4   **Histogram Showing Unexcused Absences During the School Year**

of the two variables being depicted is an ordered sequence. Bar graphs and pie graphs have no such requirement. The format of a histogram, unlike a bar graph, has each column in contact with the ones next to it. This demonstrates the invariant sequence in the ordered variable.

Step 7: If Indicated, Amend the Action Plan and Repeat the Process

With the analysis of the outcome report based on information and data from the action research effort, a decision can be made as to whether or not the original problem has been solved with the intervention studied by employing action research. If the problem is resolved only one more step needs to be made with the action research project. That is to write up the outcomes and make the report available to other professional school counselors. This can be done by posting the effort on the state web page for professional school counselors or presenting findings during a state or national meeting of professional counselors.

If the conclusion of those reviewing the report is that there is still more work to be done, then the action research effort can be revised and prepared for another round. Data from the project just completed can serve as the new baseline for the next phase of action research.

The genius of the model for action research developed by Kurt Lewin is that it turns around and begins anew until the problem is resolved. Some problems are seemingly intractable—for example, closing the achievement gap between students from different ethnic groups[6]—while others, like improving parent engagement with the counselor's web page, can be easier to achieve.

SUMMARY

In the early 21st century, professional school counselors must have the technical skills needed to conduct a systematic evaluation of a school's counseling program. The evaluation process requires the involvement of an advisory committee of stakeholders to set goals and develop objectives for the school's counseling program to reach during the year. The best evaluations are conducted following recommendations of professional societies in educational evaluations and the guidelines of the U.S. Department of Education (EDGAR).

There are a number of factors within a school that can interfere with the collection of meaningful data. Each of these must be taken into account whenever a school's counselor devises an evaluation plan or action research project.

Annual audits of the school counseling program are another requirement of the ASCA (ASCA/Hatch & Bowers, 2005) and are described in Standard 12. These audits are completed using an 11-page questionnaire.

The profession of school counseling has adopted a model for data-driven service delivery. One implication is that school counselors can organize and present data in understandable formats. Another is that school counselors can develop plans of action research for implementing interventions and new approaches to solving problems. These skills are empowering to the counselor and should be developed and honed by all professional school counselors.

DISCUSSION QUESTIONS

1. Visit the government web page for the Education General Administrative Regulations: www.ed.gov/policy/fund/reg/edgarReg/edgar.html. Review two sections, part 98 and part 99. Make a brief list of new issues related to student records that you learned from this experience. Share your findings with others in your class.

2. Visit a local high school (only if accredited by your regional accreditation organization, e.g., Southern States Association of Colleges and Schools) and ask to read that high school's accreditation report as it relates to the high school's counseling services. Take notes on the self-study portion and of any unusual or idiosyncratic issues in the document. Also, note any sections or items you are surprised to find were not included. Without revealing the name of the school or faculty involved, share your observations with others in the class.

   As an alternative, visit your university's library and read the Student Services section from the last regional accrediting report. Focus on student counseling services and answer the same questions posed above.

3. What are the potential problems associated with having a school psychologist or the school's assistant principal serve as the evaluator of the school's counseling program?

4. From your observation and experience, what is a reasonable research problem that a school's counselor can use action research to address?

RELATED READINGS

Kapp, S. A., & Anderson, G. R. (2009). *Agency-based program evaluation: Lessons from practice.* Thousand Oaks, CA: Sage.

Marshall, C., & Rossman, G. B. (2010). *Designing qualitative research* (5th ed.). Thousand Oaks, CA: Sage.

Salkind, N. J. (2004). *Statistics for people who think they hate statistics* (2nd ed.). Thousand Oaks, CA: Sage.

Samaras, A. (2010). *Self-study teacher research: Improving your practice through collaborative inquiry.* Thousand Oaks, CA: Sage.

NOTES

1. Data on the quality of school-based prevention programs have shown that they are usually poorly implemented and carried out (Gottfredson & Gottfredson, 2002).

2. Care should be taken to ensure that information shared with stakeholders is not of a confidential nature.

3. Evaluators are normally compensated on the basis of the complexity of the program. This may be done as a percentage (e.g., 5%) of the total departmental budget including salaries. Local universities with graduate programs in educational evaluation may provide a supervised graduate student evaluator at a lower price.

4. Kurt Lewin (1948) proposed that "it is a type of action-research, a comparative research on the conditions and effects of various forms of social action, and research leading to social action. Research that produces nothing but books will not suffice" (p. 202).

5. Graduate students in research-intensive programs are rarely permitted to employ action research as part of their master's degree theses or doctoral dissertation projects. Collaboration is not congruent with the goals of graduate programs focused on developing independent scholars and researchers (Dolbec & Savoie-Zajc, 1995). The organic nature of action research also violates assumptions of a faculty research committee that the scholarship being completed by the student is exactly what the committee originally approved.

6. One of the standards, 8.4, of the ASCA performance standards requires all school counselors to design programs to close the achievement gap between ethnic groups and analyze data to monitor progress toward that goal.

Glossary

ability tests Measures designed to assess one or more area(s) of human ability including cognitive ability.

academic achievement A measurable quantity of academic learning that has occurred.

academic redshirting When parents of a young child elect not to enroll that child in school until he or she is a year older than the normal cohort of kindergarten students. This is done to provide the child with a developmental advantage over his or her peers.

academic socialization The process of instilling academic values and goals for achievement among students.

academies Private schools first established in colonial times that taught a classical curriculum to boys and teenaged youth.

accommodations Modifications in the testing or evaluation environment that are made to compensate for a student's disabling condition, which make the test more fair and inferences made on the basis of its scores more accurate.

accomplishment ratio A quantitative system for determining how efficacious the learning process is for a student. It is a statement combining the student's cognitive ability and achievement level into a single score. High scores show efficient learning, and low scores are indicative of underachievement.

accountability Being held to account for both the expenditure of educational funds and the achievement outcomes for students.

achievement gap Mean (average) group differences between identifiable subgroups of the population on standardized achievement test scores.

achievement tests Tests measuring an individual's knowledge of specific facts and his or her proficiency in completing cognitive processes such as problem solving.

action-based research School-based research first described by Kurt Lewin. The focus is on solving an immediate problem that is usually not theory based but is pragmatic in nature.

active listening Listening focused totally on what another is saying, including the underlying feelings and emotions being expressed.

addicted Compulsion to use increasing amounts of a habit forming material (e.g., alcohol or drugs) to meet physiological needs linked back to the habit-forming material.

adequate yearly progress (AYP) The proportion of a school's students who achieve at a proficient or better level each year, as well as the attendance rates for the mandated tests, and the eventual graduation rates for the schools.

advanced placement (AP) College-level instruction and curriculum taught in any of 37 different high school courses under contract with ETS.

advocating for children A proactive and positive approach to school counseling that reduces problems by stopping them before they happen.

affect disorders Any of a number of mental disorders characterized by extreme and rapid changes of mood and feelings (e.g., bipolar disorder).

African American Vernacular Language (AAVL) American English dialect commonly found among populations of people living in the southern states of America and also common among African Americans in most regions of the United States.

Africentric worldview Personal perspective emphasizing the central role of African people cultures and history. The worldview includes a reaction to hundreds of years of racism and subjugation by the Proto-Indo-European peoples of the Western world.

age of reason 18th- and 19th-century concept that children reach an adult-like level of reasoning ability at the age of 7 or 8 years.

alternative schools School (public or private) employing curricula and methods that are nontraditional. Many of these schools serve special needs populations.

amenorrhea Abnormal suppression or absence of menstruation.

American Counseling Association (ACA) Organization of professional counselors founded in 1952 as the American Personnel and Guidance Association.

American experience History of experiences of a family from the day they arrive as immigrants into the United States.

American Psychiatric Association (APA) Professional organization of psychiatrists dating from 1844, when it was founded as the Association of Medical Superintendents of American Institutions for the Insane. It is the publisher of the *Diagnostic and Statistical Manual,* 5th ed., providing criteria for making diagnostic statements about mental status.

American Recovery and Reinvestment Act (ARRA) Act signed into law on February 13, 2009, spending $787 billion to stimulate the U.S. economy. It is generally credited as being partially responsible for bringing an end to the Great Recession of 2008–2010.

American School Counselor Association (ASCA) Professional organization of school counselors and school counselor educators, founded in 1952; now one of the 19 divisions of the American Counseling Association.

anger management skills Skills needed for a person to avoid uncontrollable angry outbursts. Skills make it possible to reduce triggering incidents and overwhelming feelings of frustration and rage.

Angoff committees Committees of experts brought together to set the minimum level for cut-off scores on a high-stakes test. Named for William H. Angoff of ETS.

anhedonia Psychological condition characterized by inability to experience pleasure in normally pleasurable acts.

anorexia nervosa Psychologically induced eating disorder involving a grossly distorted body image. More common among early teenaged girls and young women.

antebellum Of or related to the era in American history following independence and proceeding the American Civil War.

anti-miscegenation Laws and cultural vituperations against the intermarriage and/or sexual relations between members of different racial groups.

apartheid Official policy of racial segregation usually carried out in combination with economic and political discrimination.

aptitudes One's ability or skills to do or learn useful operations including school-based academic learning.

Asperger's disorder A mental disorder that appears during early childhood characterized by severe impairment in social interaction skills and the development of repetitive actions and behavioral patterns.

assessment The measurement of one or more variables related to the current condition, ability, status, or knowledge of an individual.

assimilation The surrender of one's personal ethnic group heritage and culture and adopting a broader set of beliefs and the culture of the larger community or society.

at-risk students Children endangered by environmental, congenital, or health-related problems for developmental and/or educational problems.

attention deficit/hyperactivity disorder (AD/HD) Disorder of a child's ability to attend to and focus on learning that may appear prior to school age and be manifested by impulsivity, high, randomly directed activity; and inattention to tasks and directions.

autism spectrum disorders (ASD) Related group of pervasive developmental disorders including early infantile autism, autism, childhood autism, Kanner's disorder, and Asperger's disorder.

automatic thoughts Aaron Beck's concept of inappropriate thoughts that interfere with rational thinking. Their correction is central to cognitive behavioral therapy.

aversive racism Overt acts of racial disparity against an ethnic or racial group.

axons Usually long, single nerve cells that serve as the white matter of the human brain and are the source of all meaningful neurological activity.

baby boom Era associated with persons born between the years 1946 and 1964 producing a upturn in the population.

bar graph Linear graphic data presentation for nominal data where one axis shows classifications and the other frequency of occurrence.

bargaining unit Organization of educators working collectively to negotiate wages and working conditions. Often part of national unions, AFT, or the NEA.

basal score Score on a standardized test with items arranged in ascending order of difficulty below which an individual makes no errors.

base line Rate of a behavioral occurrence prior to intervention or a treatment.

Basic Interpersonal Communication Skill (BICS) The everyday level of language used in social settings. The language used by students on the playground and in the lunchroom or in sports.

behavioral counseling Approach to counseling focused on changing patterns of behavior by teaching new methods for interacting with the environment.

behaviorism A school of psychology that takes the objective evidence of behavior (as measured responses to stimuli) as the only concern of its research and basis for theory development.

below proficient Score on an achievement test that falls below the minimum score (set by an Angoff committee) required to have met a prescribed standard for learning.

benchmarks Points of reference based on a standard for learning, including illustrative examples of successful completion or achievement.

bibliotherapy The use of reading materials for help in solving personal problems or for psychiatric therapy.

binge drinkers People who periodically consume excessive amounts of alcohol beverages to the point of intoxication.

biped species Animals that have evolved to stand and walk about on hind legs. Humans are included in this group.

bipolar illness Mental disorder in which the individual experiences abrupt but nonetheless huge mood swings from euphoria (mania) to periods of deep depression.

birth order The ordinal sequence that children are born into a family.

body dysmorphic disorder (BDD) A mental disorder providing those affected with distorted self-images leading to excessive concern regarding physical appearance.

bookmarking method Method for establishing cut scores for proficiency tests. Testing experts working from a compilation of test items arranged from easy to difficult use markers to show where they believe cut scores should be established.

bootstrap Bringing together many validity estimates from studies and estimating the true validity as lying within an estimated confidence band of possible validity values.

bubble youngsters Students who scored just slightly below the level of proficient on a high-stakes test. These students are most likely to receive the most support and help from the school.

Buckley Amendment The Family Education Rights and Privacy Act, often known by the name of the senator who was instrumental in its passage, James L. Buckley. This law provides rules for educational record keeping, psychological testing, and parental rights.

bulimia Form of eating disorder based on body dysmorphic disorder and anorexia nervosa involving binge eating or drinking followed by purging.

bulletin board Internet page hosted on a school's computer server that makes it possible for a community of users to post items or requests and be answered by other members of the community.

bullying Treating abusively, intimidating, or harassing another person (usually less powerful and vulnerable).

career education Organized educational program designed to help students identify their career goals and learn the needed educational steps to achieve those goals.

career-planning portfolio A file (electronic or paper) into which a student can collect ideas about career and lifestyle goals to which he or she can refer when making a career plan. Normally part of a career education program.

Carnegie Commission Commission of senior educators that in 1906 called for the standardization of high school curricula and schedules.

Carnegie unit A unit of instruction that requires 120 clock hours to present. This time may occur in units of 45 minutes for 180 school days. Block schedules can provide a Carnegie unit of instruction in time blocks of 90 minutes for 90 days.

case law Decisions made in response to a suit of law by a federal or state court establishing new procedures or social policy, and having the full enforcement power of a law.

caseload The number of cases handled (as by a school counselor) during a particular period.

ceiling level Item on a test (arranged with increasing levels of difficulty) above which it is assumed the student will not answer any questions correctly.

central office administrators Licensed professionals working as part of the school district's leadership with the school system's superintendent.

certificate of completion A document indicating a student attended 4 years of high school but did not earn a high school diploma.

certification requirements Mandates of a state education department as to what educational and *in situ* experiences are needed to earn the required certification to work in public and charter schools in a particular capacity (e.g., school counselor).

charter schools Semi-autonomist schools established with state/school district approval to offer a more experimental curriculum and approach to public education.

child abuse Maltreatment or significant neglect of a child resulting in death, injury, or emotional harm, and/or the sexual exploitation of a child by adults.

Child Abuse Prevention and Treatment Act (CAPTA) Federal law requiring the states to set penalties for any adult who abuses a child and any adult(s) who knew of the abuse and took no steps to stop it. School counselors and other educators must report cases of child abuse and significant neglect.

child-centered approach Educational approach supportive of the developmental needs of students and less focused on the details of the curriculum. The approach most frequently seen in middle school organization and philosophy.

child-centered extended counseling A program of child-centered reflective counseling (e.g., Rogerian) that normally requires several sessions a week and lasts for an academic year or more.

child maltreatment One of several terms describing child abuse.

child study movement Era beginning in the 19th century when the methods associated with modern science were applied to the systematic study of human infancy and childhood.

choice theory   Theory of William Glasser that posits that the only person's behavior we can control is ours. The choices each person makes are based on perceived needs and can be modified through reality therapy.

chromosomes   Threadlike strand of DNA located in cell nuclei carrying genes. Each human has 23 chromosomes in each living cell.

CIPP   Four parts to a standard evaluation of an educational program including Context, Input, Process, and Product.

circumscription   Part of developing a "career focus" involving the rejection of less appropriate ideas and tentative plans while focusing on a few appropriate possibilities.

class rank   The absolute position, or rank, of a student compared to his or her peers in terms of total grade point average.

client   Term first used by Carl Rogers to replace the term *patient* that was in common use by mental hygienists at the time.

client-centered   Rogerian therapy providing clients with active listening, unconditional positive regard, and empathetic reflection.

Cognitive Academic Language Proficiency (CALP)   The level of language required for formal academic learning in content-based subject fields.

cognitive behavioral therapy (CBT)   Short-term therapeutic approach based on the concept that our thoughts about issues and things affect our emotional responses, communications, and behaviors. It uses a here-and-now focus.

cognitive capacities   Levels of the various cognitive (mental) capabilities of an individual. Most theories provide for between three and eight different areas of these mental abilities.

cognitive therapy   See **cognitive behavioral therapy**.

Committee of Ten   NEA committee of scholars in 1892–1893 that formulated a curriculum for high schools to follow. Later, the Carnegie Commission required that colleges only accept students from high schools following the NEA Committee of Ten model.

common schools   Name given by Horace Mann to what are now known as public schools. Supplanted in the American lexicon by *public school* around 1900.

community resource officers   Police officers trained to work with the public. In schools they provide a first point of contact for students and educators with the criminal justice system.

compliance testing   Periodic revaluations and testing of students as required in the student's **individualized education plan** or **504 plan**.

comprehensive high schools   High schools offering a range of programs beyond just college preparatory.

confianza   Spanish word for trust and confidence.

confidential records   All academic and other records held and collected in a school must be held in strict confidence and only shared with parents and educators with a need to see them. The original NCLB Act (2002) also makes all school records open to U.S. military recruiters.

confidentiality Disclosure of information about a student only to those with a legal right to know, e.g., parents, and educators working with the student. Also keeping testing material stored so that it is not viewed by anyone until it is administered, and then returned to secure storage.

conformity to the family Adherence to the values, traditions, and expectations of the family and its background ethnic culture.

congruence Ultimate goal of client-centered counseling when the client's ideal self and self-perception are in harmony, or congruent.

construct Organization constructed in the mind and shared by many others as providing meaning and structure, e.g., depth perception, human creativity, beauty, and intelligence.

construct validity A validation technique used with variables of hypothetical traits or abilities lacking an operational (observable) definition. This involves demonstrating both the legitimacy of the variable and the measure of it.

content validity The fidelity of the test items to the topic taught and/or the goals of the curriculum area being measured.

contingent Presentation of a reward contingent on a behavior that was first exhibited.

contracted specialists Paid licensed specialists brought into schools to work with certain students with needs beyond the scope of education of the school's personnel, including psychiatrists, physical and occupational therapists, audiologists, and dental hygienists.

control group One of two or more randomly assigned groups in an experiment. The control group does not receive the experimental treatment and provides a point of comparison for the other groups.

coping mechanisms Mental mechanisms that enhance an individual's ego strength and make the person mentally stronger and better able to withstand peer pressure or harassment, e.g., the teachings of one's cultural heritage, a sense of humor, and compensation.

core curriculum The high school curriculum recommended by the Committee of Ten, including a distribution of courses that involve both classical and modern languages, mathematics, sciences, geography, government, and history.

counseling education Preservice programs of graduate studies and experiences to prepare professionals for the field. Inservice programs designed to assist working counselors learn new methods and improve old skills.

counseling interventions Individual and group approaches to helping young people improve their lives, educational attainment, mental status, and lifelong career plan.

counselor Originally a teacher who helped students plan for careers. Now, it is a professional position assisting all students with personal, educational, and career planning needs.

counselor's schedule Posted (web page and hallway bulletin board) schedule of a school counselor's daily, weekly, and monthly office hours, group sessions, after-school activities, special programs, and important dates to remember (e.g., test filing dates for college admissions and financial aid).

covariance   The amount of common variance shared by two different measures. It is reported as a coefficient of correlation.

criterion-referenced scores   Scores presented in terms of reaching or failing to reach an absolute standard for correctness on the measure.

critical judgments   Rational and well-balanced decisions made by adults and young adults after the maturation of the individual's neurology.

cross-disciplinary   Instructional organization with teachers of math, language arts, social studies, and science all sharing the same set of students throughout each school day.

crowd   The large group of peers that a student strives to be part of during adolescence. Crowd members share a common value set and are loosely defined within the larger population of the age cohort.

curriculum-based probes   Brief tests (5 to 10 minutes) that are administered on a regular basis and are part of a curriculum-based measurement.

curriculum map   A publicly available document that captures the scope and sequence (the school's master plan) of the learning objectives, activities, and assessments in each subject and in each grade.

curriculum tracks   High school curriculum structures organized to focus a student's learning toward a career goal or higher education.

cut scores   The raw scores on a standards-based test that denote a break between two ordinal levels of success (e.g., proficient vs. highly proficient).

cutters   Young people, usually girls, who mutilate their bodies to relieve deep feelings of anguish and pain. Often associated with post-traumatic stress disorder.

cyberbullying   Use of the Internet and/or various social networks to harass, humiliate, intimidate, or otherwise make life miserable for another person.

date rape   A sexual assault that occurs between two people who know each other and who may be dating.

deferral   Psychological postponement of the tasks involved in **identity formation** and adulthood, resulting in a prolongation of the time of adolescence.

delay of gratification   The ability of an individual to plan ahead and delay being rewarded or satisfied in the present recognizing that bigger rewards will come in the future if one delays being gratified now.

democracy's high schools   Sobriquet used to describe the first comprehensive high schools. The name relates to the educational opportunities afforded to the students not planning to attend college.

dendrites   Tiny arm-like projections from neurons that are covered with synapses. The synapses are used to transmit impulses from neuron to neuron by an electrochemical process.

departmentalized teaching   Administrative division of a secondary school's faculties so that all teachers of a similar subject meet and plan together, e.g., English department or science faculty.

dependent   Human condition when an individual depends on a particular drug or elixir to improve his or her condition or difficulty.

Not an addiction, which is an ever-increasing craving and physiological necessity.

dependent variable Variable that is expected to change or otherwise be modified by the introduction of some environmental change (independent variable).

depression Mental state including a loss of all joy in life and inability to take pleasure in that which once was pleasurable. Low self-esteem and a loss of motivation often accompanied by excessive use of alcohol and long periods of sleep are common.

despondency Precursor for depression, involving listless behavior with dejection and feelings of sadness.

developmental delays Significant departures from the normal pattern of growth and development in terms of cognitive and or physical growth.

developmental validity An expression of the age and status appropriateness of the measurement tasks included on a test.

Diploma Project A program in the schools of Los Angeles (2006–2009) involving hiring extra school counselors for low-performing schools to help students as mentors and improve completion rates. It was very successful, but when the city ran out of money it was cut.

direct behavioral consultation (DBC) Counselor consultation with teachers involving the direct teaching of ways to change student behavior using problem solving and behavioral analysis techniques.

drive-by shooting Using a firearm from the window of a moving vehicle. The technique is used to intimidate, but it often leads to bystanders being hurt.

dropout rate Proportion of students who leave school without ever completing their high school diploma.

early admission College admission process begun early in the senior year and providing a decision by early December. The decision is binding and a student may not change his or her mind if accepted under early admission.

Early Start Downward extension of Head Start to include infants and toddlers at risk for a disability.

EDGAR Education Department Guidelines and Regulations provides regulations for conducting evaluations in federally funded (e.g., ESEA) educational settings

Education of All Handicapped Children Act P.L. 94–147, mandating that all public school students, irrespective of disability status, be provided a thorough and efficient education through the high school diploma or age 21.

educational age Ratio score created by division of achievement by mental ability (IQ).

ego Hypothetical construct first proposed by Sigmund Freud to represent the organized and realistic part of the developing human psyche.

Elementary and Secondary Education Act (ESEA) The Elementary and Secondary Education Act, passed in 1965 (P.L. 89–10 [1965]). The law became the central education initiative of the administration of President Lyndon Johnson.

elementary school counselors Professional counselors with special training in child development and counseling techniques for young children.

emergency nursery schools During the Great Depression, child care centers created by the Works Progress Administration under the administration of President Franklin Delano Roosevelt set up to provide free universal child care.

emic Understanding the perspective and deep meaning of the behavior of others by being able to assume their point of view.

emotional intelligence (EQ) Ability to accurately understand and interpret one's own emotions and feelings, as well as able to understand and accurately interpret the emotions felt by others and problem solve with these emotion data.

empathy Being able to experience emotions that match those being experienced other people.

enabler One who makes it possible for another person to continue inappropriate or self-destructive behavior.

encounter groups Groups of clients brought together to explore their self-understanding and communication ability with others. These groups usually follow a Rogerian approach in their operation.

English-language learners (ELLs) Students for whom English is not the native language and who are in the process of learning to achieve English at a cognitive academic level of proficiency.

Enlightenment Era in Western civilization beginning at the conclusion of the renaissance and the English restoration and extending to the Romantic era (1688–1820). The American Revolution was greatly influenced by the liberal values and philosophy of the Enlightenment.

entitlement decisions Decisions involving the provision of services or other assistance needed to "level the playing field" for students who have special needs.

envy Motivational factor that a control group may feel once learning that the experimental group is getting more and better treatment.

equal protection Statement included in the 14th Amendment to the U.S. Constitution that has been used to argue for the inclusion of special education students in all aspects of public school programs.

espiritu Belief in a spiritual linkage between the human mind and the body.

ethical practice Following the set of ethical principles as expressed in the American Counseling Association's *Code of Ethics* (2005).

ethnic succession As new groups of immigrants arrive in North America they replace previous generations of immigrants in their jobs and housing. This process facilitates the upward mobility of previous groups of immigrants.

ethnography A qualitative research method that collects data by the direct, real-time observation of subjects in their natural setting. The researcher may or may not participate as a member of the group being observed.

eumelanin Dark melanin that blocks the harmful ultraviolet rays from the sun from the skin protecting equatorial humans from skin cancers.

Eurocentric Worldview and perspective of Western Europe and North America in terms of values, beliefs, and culture.

executive cognitive function Cognitive process that controls and manages other mental processes and operations.

exogamy Interbreeding across different ethnic or racial groups.

experimental group Subjects selected at random to participate in an experiment in which they are provided a special (experimental) treatment.

expert witness A person providing testimony in court or in a deposition based on his or her documented expertise on the subject at hand.

extended elementary schools Elementary schools providing educational programs for students through the 8th grade (K to 8).

extended school year services (ESY) A student in special education can be provided with an academic summer program if it is written into his or her IEP.

external control Worldview that one is but a pawn in an environment filled with powerful forces acting capriciously and controlling one's fate.

externalization Helping a client compartmentalize his or her inappropriate actions while working on finding and developing appropriate methods for interpersonal contacts in the future.

extinguish The termination of a habitual or highly learned response pattern.

Family Educational Rights and Privacy Act (FERPA) Federal legislation passed in August of 1974 as P.L. 93-380, § 513. The legislation provides for the absolute right of parents to both the privacy of their children's educational records and full access to those records.

fantasy-based methods Related methods that can be used to assist young children to to express their concerns and fears through the fantasies they create.

feminism Political ideal that women and girls should share equal educational, social, and economic opportunities and protections as afforded to men and boys.

fetal alcohol syndrome Abnormal dimensions of development in cognitive, neurological, and physical aspects of a child whose mother drank alcohol during her pregnancy.

504 committee Educational support committee established to identify and implement school based programs to assist students with learning and or behavior problems. Mandated by provisions of the Rehabilitation Act [34 C.F.R. §104.3(k)(2)].

forced activity Hazing and other unwanted behaviors required by powerful others of a student as part of a ritual of membership or right of passage.

free and appropriate public education (FAPE) Requirement of P.L. 94–142 (Education of All Handicapped Children Act) for the education of *all* students by the public schools.

free range children Humorous sobriquet describing children given freedom by their parents to experience a less structured and controlled childhood.

friendship clubs Groups established by a school counselor through which students wanting to make new friends can meet others. During such sessions students can learn how to interact without being "geeks" or somehow "weird."

gang A semi-structured group of adolescents working together on antisocial and often illegal activities.

Gantt chart Two-axis chart simultaneously depicting the timeline for a project and the tasks to be completed along the timeline. This chart can also identify the key personnel responsible for each of the tasks. Named for an American engineer, Henry Lawrence Gantt.

gender identity Incorporation of gender role into one's personal identity. If gender identity is aligned with the expectations of the greater society, the process will be relatively easy; however, if not congruent with society's expectations the process of incorporation will be difficult for the young person.

gender identity disorder Rare mental disorder involving rejection of all facets and symbols of one's biological gender. In adults this disorder can lead to surgical reassignment of the individuals' gender.

genetic abnormalities Any of hundreds of variations from the normal human genome resulting in a birth defect (e.g., spina-bifida).

genus *Homo habilis* Humanoid creature that first appeared during the Pleistocene period; a precursor of *Homo sapiens* that first appeared 1.5 million years later.

gestalt German term in psychology describing how a pattern of elements does not account for the whole entity, which is always more than the sum of its parts. The sum of perceptions and experiences will never account for the complexity of the gestalts of the world devised by each individual.

gifted Educators consider gifted students to have special talents and high levels of academic aptitude (e.g., IQ ≥ 130).

goal setting Setting realistic, positive, and measurable goals to help clients improve areas of difficulty in their lives.

good faith report A report to appropriate authorities about a potential case of child maltreatment, made without malice and in the best interest of the child. The reporting person is granted immunity for all penalties if the report was later found to have been made in error.

grade point An ordinal number replacing a letter grade, usually from 4 = A to 0 = F. The points awarded can also be weighted to account for the level of difficulty of the course.

grade retention Occurs when a student is required to remain in the same grade for another school year while his or her peers move ahead to the next grade level.

grand examiner Fanciful role students may assign to a counselor too closely aligned to the testing programs of a school.

Grassley Amendment 1999 amendment that expanded the Buckley Amendment to require parental permission before any systematic evaluation of a student, or even the completion of a questionnaire by a student.

gray matter Mass of axons and other neurological components making up the working part of the brain in cognition.

group guidance Group instruction by a school counselor on topics of interest to clients.

group norms Rules and group expectations imposed on all individual members.

happenstance Random occurrence in the life of an individual that can result in a major decision or life altering change (e.g., career path change after a summer job).

happy slapping Brief violent attack against a random target typically recorded and replayed on social networks.

hate crime Legal term describing any crime against an individual (or individual's property) that was carried out because of the target's minority status or gender role.

hazing Uncomfortable or noxious behavior forced by senior members of a group on younger students as part of a ritual or right of passage.

Head Start Program started by President Lyndon Johnson in 1965. It was originally a summer program for children of poverty. It is now part of the Department of Health and Human Services and provides educational, nutritional, and developmental assistance to 925,000 preschool children from impoverished families a year.

Health Insurance Portability and Accountability Act of 1996 (HIPPA) Federal law that includes a privacy rule mandating the confidentiality of health (including mental health) reports for children and other persons.

helicopter parent Parent who tightly monitors his or her child and directs his or her life. He or she swoops down on any educator or coach who dares to cause the child not to feel appreciated and revered.

hermeneutics Analytical interpretation of verbal and written communications for their deeper meaning.

hierarchical system of needs Organization of human needs from the most immediate and basic to the most advanced and self-actualizing.

high schools Secondary schools typically organized to teach students in the 9th or 10th grade through the 12th grade.

higher-order thinking Thinking skills including critical analysis, evaluation, and problem solving.

highly proficient Standards-based score on an achievement test indicating a student achieved significantly more than was required.

high-stakes tests Tests for which failing scores carry serious consequences and sanctions for students and/or educators.

histogram A representation of a frequency distribution having rectangular bars of different lengths. The height of each bar represents the score frequency on an ordinal variable.

home schooling Parental instruction of children at home, frequently with the assistance of homeschool cooperatives and Internet-based instructional support.

homework Academic tasks assigned by teachers to be completed by students at home.

Homo sapiens Species of all human beings on Earth. *Homo sapiens* emerged about 200,000 years ago in equatorial East Africa.

hook-up Vernacular term used by youth to describe brief meaningless sexual relations.

huffing Vernacular term used by youth to describe inhaling aromatic hydrocarbons to the point of becoming intoxicated.

humanistic counseling Client-centered approach whereby the counselor neither imposes solutions nor analyzes past experiences. The focus is on the client in the present.

humanistic psychology An existential approach to understanding human behaviors employing a holistic focus on the perceptions and interpretations of the world made by the client.

humanities Academic disciplines including the arts, literature, philosophy, and history.

hypervigilant A heightened sensory level accompanied by exaggerated (hyper) behaviors designed to detect trouble and fend it off.

hypochondriasis Excessive preoccupation about possible medical problems and conditions accompanied by a constant somatic focus and self-diagnosis.

id Hypothetical construct of Sigmund Freud to explain part of the human psyche. Id is an uncoordinated set of instinctual needs and deep desires. Much of this structure is present from birth.

identify exceptions A step in goal setting during solution-focused brief counseling when the counselor helps the student-client realize that the problem does not *always* exist, and there are exceptions when other outcomes occur.

identity Identity formation is the principal task of adolescence and early adulthood. It encompasses all a person feels he or she is and longs to become. It defines the life course a person will follow and makes a happy and successful life possible.

identity crisis A developmental phase marked by intensive analysis and exploration of different ways of looking at oneself with the final goal of establishing one's personal identity.

identity diffusion Occurs when an individual is unable to establish an identity and experiences problems with issues such as gender identity, moral ambiguity, general feeling of being a phony and hollow, and inability to make emotional commitments including a lack of real commitment to a life plan.

identity foreclosure Youthful individual unable or unready to achieve identity formation may commit to others to serve as his or her source of identity. This leads to letting others dictate choices and goals (e.g., peers and or cults).

identity formation Process that may be proceeded by an identity crisis resulting in establishing a sense of who and what one is all about. It includes a sense of commitment to a full life through family and careers.

identity moratorium Individual uses powerful organizations or tasks to hold the identity formation crisis off for a period of time (e.g., living at college, joining the armed forces, or joining a religious order).

in loco parentis Concept from English common law meaning that educators can discipline students with similar rights to those of parents.

inclusion Heterogeneous mixing of students with special education needs with fully able students.

inclusion classrooms Classrooms populated with a mix of students receiving special education with others who have a normal pattern of learning. Frequently co-taught by a special education and regular classroom teacher.

incongruence One cause of stress and unhappiness is the lack of congruence between the perceived self (self-concept) and the ideal self that an individual strives to become.

independent variable Factor that is used to cause change in a dependent variable.

individualized education plan (IEP)   Plan required by law (IDEIA) for all disabled students that includes goals, services, accommodations, and description of how progress toward the goals will be measured. Required for every disabled student attending public school.

inferiority   Alfred Adler proposed that all human infants realize their inferior status among older family members and will normally strive for superiority. This striving is innate and serves as a major source of human motivation and drive throughout life.

inferiority complex   The acute sense of being inferior to others and unable to become their equal. May manifest as shyness and timidity in social settings.

informed consent   Legal requirement that a client (student's parent) is fully informed of an intervention's good and possible harmful outcomes prior to initiating it.

institutional review board (IRB)   College board of faculty and other stakeholders who review research and thesis proposals to protect the rights of participants or animal subjects.

instructional support team (IST)   A committee made up of the student's parents and all school personnel responsible for the student being referred for intervention. Formed in order to share information and address educational problems the student is having, in order to map out strategies for the teacher and parent (also called **student assistance team** [SAT])

interfering with parental custody   Taking a minor child without informed consent to provide a service or program that the parents are not likely to approve (e.g., taking a pregnant girl to an abortion clinic).

internal control   Same as **internal locus of control.**

internal locus of control   A locus of control whereby the individual sees him- or herself as the source of any failure or success.

internal validity   The linkage of the research question being asked and the research methods employed to answer the question. High internal validity implies that there are no viable alternative explanations for the outcome when the research methods are used.

International Baccalaureate (IB)   Challenging 2-year academic program covering the last 2 years of high school and preparing students to enter college with several advanced course credits.

internship   *In situ* experience in a school setting under the mentorship of an experienced school counselor, now part of the state certification standards for the various state education departments.

interpersonal counseling   A brief form of one-to-one counseling commonly done at all grade levels in public schools.

interpersonal harmony   A goal of many children of Asian American heritage to have all generations of a family living in harmony and peace by following the traditional approaches to childhood defined by that culture.

interpersonal process   Use of small group counseling to study communication among group members with the goal of improving the human relations and communication skills of participants.

intersexual Human with mixed gender organs representing both sexes brought about by a chromosomal or morphological anomaly.

interventions Organized efforts by a professional school counselor to improve the circumstance or condition of one or more students through the appropriate practices of counseling.

IQ test A measure of cognitive capacity along a range of dimensions needed for success in public schools.

irrational fears An intense fear of a person, object, animal, or condition that has little if any likelihood of ever being a problem, a phobia.

juku A private school (Japan and America) open after school and weekends specializing in direct instruction and test preparation.

junior high school School organization with grades 7 to 9 together where they are taught by subject area content specialists. First offered to provide a more substantial curriculum in preparation for high school.

kindergarten roundup The process of bringing together and enrolling students in a public school kindergarten program.

latchkey kids Children who return from school each day to a home where there is no parental or other adult supervision.

leadership team School-based team that may include the principal and assistant principals, athletic director, area department heads or team leaders, school counselors, school nurse, and senior librarian.

learned behaviors Responses, or pattern of responses, reinforced until well learned by an individual.

learning theory Model explaining highly complex processes done by individuals learning new material, concepts, and skills.

line scores Cut scores (for tests established by the military training command) required to begin training for various specializations.

locus of control Personality factor involving a core belief as to an individual's ability to control his or her own fate, success and failures, and events affecting him or her.

longitudinal data Data collected from a group of subjects over a long time frame. Multiple tests or observations are made on the same group of subjects and analyzed for trends.

lower class The 30% of the population with low paying semi-skilled jobs.

lower middle class The 30% to 35% of the population with solid educations and skills and good annual incomes ($35,000 to $80,000 a year). Group includes teachers, school counselors, nurses, and many similar positions.

machismo Stereotypical masculine behaviors in Hispanic folk culture involving exhibition of excessive behaviors including chauvinism, vanity, and assertiveness.

mandated tests Tests required by state regulation or law.

Marianismo Stereotypical female role in Hispanic folk cultures based on the purity and reverence of the Virgin Mary.

masculine protest Construct proposed by Alfred Adler to describe the rejection of the stereotypical feminine role by some women and girls.

mean score Score point that corresponds to the arithmetic center of a set of data.

measurement error A standard (normal curve) distribution of differences expected to occur above and below an observed test score on retesting the same student using the same measurement device.

median The score equal to the center of a rank ordered data set. The 50th percentile.

Megan's Law Federal legislation (P.L. 104–145) designed to be implemented by the states in an effort to protect children and others in the United States from sexual predators.

menarche The point in a girl's puberty when she experiences her first menstrual bleeding.

mental age A measure of the difficulty level of problems that a person can solve, expressed as a comparison to a reference sample of subjects of a particular age.

mental hygiene Movement to free all people of mental disorders by applying a cause-and-effect approach involving (1) diagnose the patient, (2) provide a treatment, (3) evaluate the patient's outcome.

mental hygienists Mental health workers providing care following a mental hygiene model for service.

mental retardation Déclassé terminology for a person that scores significantly below the mean on measures of mental ability.

mentor One who assumes responsibility for the education and training of one or more protégées.

meritocracy The organization of a system where rewards are provided to those shown through competition to be deserving of merit. Meritocracies are designed to reward talent, competence, and effort, not connections and social standing.

meta-analytical thinking The ability to contemplate one's own thinking processes and employ self-analysis to work through personal problems. (See **meta-cognitive thinking.**)

meta-cognitive thinking The process of thinking and analyzing one's own thoughts and mental processes, similar to meta-analytical thinking, but focused to one's own problem solving methods.

microaggressions Small but damaging aggressions against members of minority groups, e.g., the display of the Confederate battle flag or Nazi swastikas, providing better, more efficient service to people of one group at the expense of people of a minority.

microinsults Rude and insensitive comments inadvertently made that cause an emotional hurt on the part of the person to whom it was directed.

micro-invalidations Rude and insensitive comments made inadvertently that reduce the value of accomplishment of another person.

middle school School organized to serve needs of early adolescent students using a child centered curriculum. Normal grades include grade 5 or 6 through grade 8.

mimesis The art of being able to employ a linguistic style familiar and comfortable to a client-student during counseling.

mind mapping Two dimensional, nonlinear notation system for organizing information and finding creative linkages and cause-effect sequences.

mixed status Children who are born in the United States and thereby have natural citizenship. even though one or both of the child's parents are undocumented.

modality of testing   Format employed to construct questions and problems used on tests.

Momma drama   Description of emotional responses to the ongoing problems of being a parent. It includes belittling other children to make one's own appear better.

mononucleosis   A highly communicable fatigue producing viral infection, frequently occurring among adolescents and young adults.

multidisciplinary committee   Team of educators, specialists, and a child's parents working to design appropriate educational activities and instructional approaches to help the student learn.

myelination   An insulating sheath that wraps around the axon of nerve cells in a process that is completed in adolescence. Myelin insulation improves the speed and precision of movement of electrical stimuli in the brain.

narcissism   Psychological term describing excessive thoughts about and a preoccupation with one's personal needs and appearance. Vanity and conceit are related constructs.

National Assessment for Educational Progress (NAEP)   The only nationally representative test given continually since 1969.

National Center for Transforming School Counseling   A national commission funded by MetLife and others to improve and professionalize the role of school counselors and make school counselors more central in tasks related to school improvement.

National Education Association (NEA)   Organization formed as a professional association in 1857. It has developed into a 3.5 million member association dedicated to the welfare of educators and improvement of educational outcomes for all students.

National Instructional Materials Accessibility Standards   Federal standards included in the 2004 version of the No Child Left Behind Act requiring all instructional materials be accessible to students with disabilities, including Braille versions of books and references.

national license   National certification as a school counselor by the National Board of Certified Counselors, a division of the American Counseling Association.

national model   *The ASCA National Model: A Framework for School Counseling Programs.*

National Vocational Guidance Association   Professional organization for vocational counselors begun in 1913 that became a division of the American Counseling Association.

need for esteem   Fourth step in Abraham Maslow's five-step hierarchy of needs describing the human longing for respect and friendship of others.

negative identity   Those identifications and fragments of inconsolable rage against social norms and standards can coalesce into an identity; the result is negative, unhealthy, and the identity of an outsider.

negative reinforcer   A form of punishment. It may include the loss of a privilege or desired object, or it may be the application of an undesirable (painful) stimuli.

neo-behavioral Not strictly adhering to the tenets of classical conditioning and pure behaviorism. The approach incorporates cognitive mediation and observational learning.

neural impulses Small electrical charges that move through the neurons of the brain and central nervous system to initiate actions and/or cognition.

neurological plasticity The human brain's capacity to be remapped or configured to meet physiological challenges by adding, rerouting, or trimming neurons and cortical ganglia.

neurons Living cells of the brain and central nervous system designed to facilitate the movement of electrical impulses for signaling, initiating movement, or cognitive processing.

New Deal Economic recovery program initiated by President Franklin Delano Roosevelt between March 1933 and the start of World War II.

night terrors Known as *Pavor Nocturnus,* a condition of extreme terror occurring while sleeping during which the subject may not be able to regain a clearly conscious mind. Usually accompanied by somnambulism followed by a return to sleep.

No Child Left Behind (NCLB) Act A revamping of the Elementary and Secondary Education Act in 2002 (P.L. 107–100). The goal of the law was to "close the achievement gap with accountability, flexibility, and choice, so that no child is left behind."

norm group Sample of subjects selected to represent the range of typical performances on a measure.

normal school 19th- and early 20th-century providers of postsecondary education designed to prepare young people (mostly unmarried women) to become elementary school teachers following a 2-year curriculum of study.

normalizing Helping teachers and others see a student's behaviors in context as a variation of normal behaviors for the age and developmental level.

normative group A distribution of measurement scores from a group of subjects with known characteristics (age, sex, grade in school, etc.) with whom a person's performance may be compared.

one-on-one counseling The counseling process carried out by one counselor working with a single client-student.

online testing Administration of tests using the computer and a central server providing questions and receiving and processing answers. It includes Computer Adaptive Testing (CAT).

ontogenetic Referring to the normal sequence and pattern of growth of young organisms following the genetic code within them from conception to adulthood.

open door College admission policy designed to accept students based on their plan for furthering their education not their test scores or high school class standing.

open-ended questions Questions for which there are no clear right or wrong answers, designed to help the client open up and feel comfortable in a counseling relationship.

operant Voluntary learned behavior whereby the subject operates on his or her environment to gain a desired outcome (reward).

operant conditioning   Carefully structuring the client's environment to teach him or her desired operants. This involves shaping the natural state of behaviors of the client.

oppositional defiant disorder   Mental disorder characterized by frequent temper tantrums, active and open defiance of adult rules and policies, revenge seeking, and spiteful behaviors.

orthopedic disabilities   Disabling conditions related to musculoskeletal systems and connective tissues needed for normal mobility.

outsider   Child with a negative self-image and poor self-esteem. Not part of the normal social organization of a school or community.

overachiever   Student who achieves significantly better than that which tests of ability predict.

oversampling   Selecting larger subpopulations than would be normal than when strict proportional sampling is employed. Used to make accurate statements about small minority groups.

ownership statements   Comments used by counselors to provide reflective statements to clients without making them feel threatened or challenged by the comment or observation.

panic attack   Sudden onset of overwhelming fear and anxiety following spontaneous release of a large amount of adrenaline into the bloodstream. Hyperventilation and tunnel vision often accompany the attack.

parent support groups   Any of a variety of groups of parents that meet after school hours to share information and provide ideas and assistance to one another. Group may be led by a school counselor and focused on particular common problems such as raising children with special needs.

peer pressure   Pressure to comply with group norms and values exerted by one's peer group of friends and acquaintances.

personal crisis   A point in time when an individual is overwhelmed by complexities and expectations in his or her life and can no longer cope with life's problems.

personal ideal   The personal image held by an individual of what he or she wishes to be.

personal values system   An individual's ego structures related to character, ethos, and guiding beliefs.

personalismo   Hispanic culture in the United States stresses the importance of personal relationships and working with agencies and resources that are known and trusted.

personality traits   A core fixture of a person's personality based on early interactions during infancy and built upon throughout childhood.

personality types   Distinct organizations of feelings, attitudes, temperament, and beliefs into an individual's system to interact with the world.

Peterson and Deuschle's model   Approach used by counselor educators to provide supervision and training for school counselors who have never worked as teachers and have little knowledge of schools and school cultures.

phenomenological   Related to the subjective way individuals experience the world around them. Individuals interpret and incorporate new experiences into a framework unique to them as they perceive the world.

phenomenologically oriented psychologists Psychologists employing a wider perspective as to what clients experience compared to the narrow limits of behavioral psychology and positivistic research.

phenotypes Traits of an organism that are an expression of its genes, that may be modified in expression by environmental interactions or circumstances.

physiological needs Core needs of an organism required for the maintenance of life.

pie graph A circle drawing where the interior 360° are divided proportionally to present a nominal distribution of data.

play therapy Therapeutic communication method for use with children for whom verbal representations are not yet developmentally available.

positive reinforcer Any object or environmental change that causes a desired behavior by an individual to reoccur.

possible self The individual's ideas about the various aspects of what he or she could become along with fears of what he or she may become.

postmodern family A non-nuclear family in which configurations can include single parents, homosexual couples as parents, and other nontraditional forms.

post-traumatic stress disorder (PTSD) Anxiety-based mental disorder of reoccurring incidence following the experience of, or witnessing, a terrifying and traumatic event.

prefrontal lobe Anterior part of the frontal lobes of the brain where much of higher-order thinking, judgment, and problem solving take place. It is one of the last regions of the brain to reach full maturity.

primary prevention programs Intervention aimed at avoiding a problem before it has a chance to occur.

privileged communication Confidential information and/or communications between one person and a member of a protected profession that cannot be broken without the person's approval.

professional association Organizations of professionals in a field to set the standards for practice, support research, and communicate with the public and profession.

proficient A level of academic achievement equivalent to the minimum requirement set in the state's standards for learning.

prompts Written conceptual expressions provided to students taking a test of writing skills. They serve to guide students and provide the theme for their essay writing.

psychoanalysis Method employed to analyze psychic disorders through various approaches to "talk therapy."

psychoanalytical theory Original theory was developed by Sigmund Freud and modified by a number of his students. It is based on a belief of the importance of past experiences influencing current behaviors.

psycho-dramatic toys Use of play materials (toys) to facilitate therapeutic communication with children too young to verbally express deep emotions and feelings.

psychoeducational groups Counseling groups focused on any of various tasks. The groups usually employ a maximum of client-led discussion. One goal of these groups can be improving clients' interpersonal skills. The process involves role playing and teaching better methods for interacting with others.

psychometrician Person with advanced education in the statistical principles of measurement, test development, and score interpretation.

puberty Period in human development when hormones of the pituitary gland begin to direct rapid growth and sexual maturation of the child.

public education Educational programs, usually schools, open to all children of a community established and managed with the use of money raised by the community through the levy of taxes and fees.

pupil service team Various educational professionals, including the school counselor, who have responsibilities for aspects of the education, health, and safety of students in a school setting.

qualitative research Research method assuming multiple dynamic realities that can only be understood in context.

Quality World Component needed (according to William Glasser) to make choices. Individuals construct it from all admired objects and ideas in their lives and compare new experiences to it to make a choice.

racial prejudice An insidious hatred, holding preconceived opinions and fears about members of other groups. Intolerance of individuals of different racial backgrounds.

random sample Selection of members or elements to be included in a sample in such a way that each element of the original population has an equal chance of inclusion.

rational emotive behavioral therapy (REBT) Neo-behavioral therapy system developed by Alfred Ellis involving teaching the client better ways to interpret interactions with the environment without resorting to self-defeating patterns learned in the past.

reactive measure A pretest or post-test that can interact with the test taker to change the impact of an intervention or therapy in an artificial way.

reality therapy Counseling method developed by William Glasser that focuses on the here-and-now and choices that individuals make and the consequences of those choices.

reduction in force (RIF) Downsizing an organization by laying off or firing employees.

regional accreditation The six regions of the United States each having an independent board tasked to evaluate, and when appropriate, accredit higher education units (and some secondary schools) as meeting the approved standards of the regional board.

reinforcer Any object, activity, or event that serves to increase the occurrence of a desired behavior when administered following the exhibition of that behavior by a subject. A reward.

relationship therapy Name given by Otto Rank to describe the new form of client-centered psychotherapy.

relevant experience A loosely defined term that appears on many job descriptions to afford the administrator wide latitude in hiring personnel.

reliability A statement of the stability and/or consistency of the test scores from the administration of a measure.

repressed memories Specific memories (frequently traumatic) that have been actively expunged and are not available for recall.

resiliency factors Factors in a child's life or part of his or her psyche that can provide protection from environmental factors and forces that may be harmful.

response to intervention (RTI) Approach to assisting students with learning problems, including provision of needed, research-based instructional assistance and the close monitoring of the intervention's success and problems.

responsive counseling School counseling intervention (one-to-one or group) initiated in response to a problem or need of one or more individuals.

reward A reinforcer used to shape and control an individual's behavior.

role playing Simulations created by counselors to allow clients to experience and practice new approaches to various interpersonal interactions.

rubber chicken circuit Lunch meetings held by local chapters of service organizations. School counselors frequently serve as the after-luncheon/dinner speaker on the circuit.

rubric An ordinal sequence of qualitative ranks with definitions and examples for each level that can be used to evaluate performance assessments.

safety and security The second level of five on Maslow's hierarchy of human needs, involving security, employment and income, family, and health.

sample of convenience A nonstatistical sample drawn from subjects available to the researcher and not representative of a larger population.

scaling In counseling, the establishment of an ordinal scale with a client that can be used to report the progress he or she feels is being made during the course of the intervention.

schizoaffective disorder Disorder of affect and mood that may include hallucinations, chaotic thinking, antisocial behaviors, and depression.

school avoidance Formerly "school phobia." Anxiety disorder that prevents a child from being away from home to attend school.

school-based action research Method of systematic educational inquiry based on Kurt Lewin's model. It is grounded in the practical needs of a school and its programs, not in theoretical models, making it a bottom-up system of research.

school climate Perceptions of educators and students of the environment of a school, emphasizing issues of safety, collegiality, cooperation, mutual support, and respect.

school counseling One of a number of professional specialists employed by schools to assist students. Professional school counselors focus upon individual student's academic, personal, social, and career planning needs.

school counseling program advisory board (SCPAB)   Board of local stakeholders in the quality of a school's counseling program.

school psychologists   Educational professionals certified by state education departments to provide for the mental health of school students.

scientific management   Imposition of the industrial management system of Frederick Taylor in schools as a method of improving outcomes (test scores) while reducing costs and enhancing efficiency.

scientific rationale   Test scores providing a "scientific" basis for dividing and tracking students for instruction according to their "ability levels."

screening   Brief measure of an aspect of a child's ability, skills, or achievement.

secondary prevention   Intervention programs involving screening or making an early determination of possible problems and initiating interventions before they become major problems.

secondary reinforcer   Reward or reinforcer that has no immediate value but is an icon for primary rewards for which it can later be redeemed.

selection format questions   Objective test questions that require the test taker to respond to a prompt (question or stem) by selecting which of several answers is correct (e.g., true-false format, multiple choice, and matching).

self-actualization   Highest need on Maslow's hierarchy describing the human longing to achieve a state of fulfillment and satisfaction with a life being well led.

self-contained classrooms   Classrooms that have students representing a full range of abilities and taught by one teacher.

self-efficacy   The extent to which a person believes he or she can be successful and effective in his or her efforts.

self-esteem   The evaluation made by an individual of his or her self-concept.

self-policing   In sociology, group behavior focused on enforcing rules and norms of the group.

self-punishing   In sociology, group behavior of providing punishments to violators of the group's rules and norms.

self-reinforcing   A goal for learning. The ability to measure one's success and provide one's own rewards without needing primary or secondary reinforcers.

self-reliance   A personal confidence that one is able to meet the challenges of life and is capable of resolving life's problems. (See **self-efficacy**.)

self-report   Any of a number of reflective descriptions, including diaries, written by a person about him- or herself.

semilingual   Point in learning a new language when the learner is partially literate in both languages but is losing elements of the primary language.

seniority system   Any system that provides advantages to those employees who have the longest employment history with the organization.

sense of belonging   Level three of five on Maslow's hierarchy of needs, encompassing the need to be associated and have affectionate relations with others.

service learning Program of providing academic credit (required as part of the curriculum) for providing a service (*pro bono publico*) for the improvement of the greater community.

settlement house Center where private philanthropy supports a range of social services for those in need.

sextexting Sending sexually explicit photographs or videos of oneself over social networking or standard telephony to friends and others. Can be a form of child pornography.

sexual identity Recognizing and inculcating one's biologically given gender into one's overall personal identity.

sexually transmitted disease (STD) Any of various bacterial or viral infections transferred between humans by an interchange of bodily fluids, usually during sexual contact.

Smith-Hughes National Vocational Education Act Federal law passed in 1917 that provided vocational education and vocational counseling for America's high schools.

snorting Inhaling psychoactive drugs that have been pulverized into a powder. (See **huffing.**)

social anxiety Common anxiety felt by many individuals who must address an audience or group of others; stage fright.

social constructionist Counselors and others who endeavor to learn how individuals and groups organize and perceive their social reality.

social efficiency Early goal for school-based vocational counselors to provide an efficient transition of students from secondary education into postgraduation employment.

social networking Personal communication system of texting and videos using telecommunications to keep a cadre of friends and acquaintances informed.

social promotion Decision to promote a student to the next grade level even though he or she is not achieving up the standard for entering the next grade.

social studies School curriculum area including history, anthropology, economics, political science, sociology, and psychology.

solution-focused brief counseling (SFBC) A systematic approach to counseling that focuses the client on solutions not problems. Solutions are proposed by the client and provide pragmatic solutions to possible problems.

special education Educational programs designed to meet specific learning needs of students with disabilities. Programs are mandated under the Individuals with Disabilities Educational Improvement Act of 2004 (P.L. 108–446).

special needs children Children who have been identified as having a specific disability in one or more of the following areas: cognitive, physical, or sensory.

spinal cord Part of the body's central nervous system along the midline of the back. It carries impulses up from peripheral nerve sensors to the brain and impulses down from the brain to the distal tissues of the body with action instructions.

split-level education Tracked education providing curriculum of different levels of complexity and expectation to students according to scores they achieve on standardized tests.

spread of effect Sharing of a treatment by the group receiving it to other groups and individuals in the population.

stage fright See **social anxiety.**

stakeholder groups People within an organization who perceive themselves as possibly being affected by a study or evaluation of that organization.

standard deviation The square root of variance. The square root of the sum of the squared individual variations of scores from the mean score.

standard error of measurement (SEM) A statistic used to estimate the probable range within which a person's true score on a test falls. The standard deviation of scores obtained around an individual's true score.

standards-based education Educational system with a curriculum designed in terms of specified learnings and skills in all subjects and grade levels.

standards-based report card Report card describing a student's academic progress in terms of the achievement of enumerated standards for learning and the rubric for making grading decisions.

state-level standards for learning Statewide, approved, and highly specified goals for student learning in every grade and for all subject areas.

state-trait model A stable factor in the psyche (e.g., anxiety) that varies little in intensity. It develops over a lifetime and changes little after childhood. The state of any factor is a temporary adaptation and may change dramatically from occurrence to occurrence. A state can be modified through learning and therapy.

status offenders Children who violate laws by committing acts that are not illegal for adults, e.g., consuming alcohol.

STEM Acronym for science, technology, engineering, and mathematics.

stereotype threat The extra stress felt by minority students facing high-stakes standardized tests. This stress is related to dominant stereotypical expectations held for those students by the larger society.

strengths-based counseling Counseling system that builds on what is going well in a client's life now and in the past; helps the client find ways to repeat those successes to resolve current problems.

stress-induced anxiety One of the psychological responses to experiencing one or more stressors in one's life.

stressors Perceived threats to one's status or well-being by outside forces, resulting in increased and potentially debilitating anxiety. Stressors can cause harmful physiological responses and damage to body systems, including the immune system.

striving for superiority Concept proposed by Alfred Adler to describe one of the core human motivations from infancy onward. Perceived failure to obtain it can result in overwhelming feelings of inferiority.

structured play A format for play therapy involving the counselor setting the stage with toys and materials selected to evoke conditions and issues in a child's life.

student assistance teams (SATs) Teams of educators including the school counselor brought together to create plans that can help a student learn and respond better to his or her school experience. It may be formed as a **504 committee**. (See **instructional support team [ISP]**.)

subtraction residuals That which remains when two numbers are subtracted. If the two are correlated tests on one group of students, the residuals will have low reliability.

superego A hypothetical construct for a part of the human psyche that mediates and regulates our actions and thoughts by imposing guilt and anxiety for failure to follow well-learned rules and moral precepts from our early childhood years.

supply format questions Test questions requiring the test taker to provide the answer to a question (e.g., completion questions, fill-in questions, and essay [extended-response format] questions).

synapses Points of closest contact between adjacent neurons where a biochemical reaction will occur as needed, permitting an electrical impulse to move from one neuron to the next.

systemic interventions Various primary, secondary, and tertiary programs for improving the academic and social condition of students and school communities.

targeted attacks An assault directed at a specific individual.

task-oriented processes Processes that facilitate the smooth operation of a committee or group that has a specific goal to achieve.

teaching for the test Teaching the knowledge base and cognitive skills that make up the state's learning standards.

teaching the test The direct instruction of students in preparation for a high-stakes test by teaching specific items from released test files.

teaching units Organized programs of instruction covering a logical and coordinated block of material for the teaching-learning process.

technical manual Manual of information provided to users by the publishers of tests and assessments providing detailed psychometric information about the measure and its development.

temperament type An inborn trait of all individuals that sets the pace for each individual's interactions with the environment; e.g., some people are reflective and slow to make decisions, while others are impulsive and are uncomfortable in slowly working through problems.

terroristic threat A threat to commit a violent crime in a way that terrorizes a person or creates a general panic among a group.

tertiary prevention Providing counseling services to a client(s) once there is a clearly defined problem requiring immediate attention.

test-induced stress Anxiety-related problem occurring when a student is being tested or otherwise evaluated. Known as test anxiety, it can debilitate a student to the point of being unable to take the test and/or have somatic symptoms including projectile nausea as a result of the testing situation.

test-retest reliability The correlation between the scores from two sequential administrations of a test to one group of subjects providing an estimation of test stability.

testing-accommodations Providing non-standard testing conditions for students with disabilities as a way to provide them with a level playing field.

therapeutic communication The way counselors talk with clients to assist them in resolving problems and improving their lives. The method of communication varies with the developmental level of the client and his or her interest in the counseling process.

therapeutic dialogue In school counseling, the various approaches used when improving communications and engaging clients to partake in a meaningful counseling relationship.

therapeutic intervention Action of a professional counselor to modify or otherwise change a student-client's life and psyche to facilitate well-being and provide the student with a sense of his or her own efficacy.

third force Name applied to client-centered, phenomenological approaches to psychotherapy and counseling. The first two forces are behaviorism and psychoanalysis. Term is applied to the model first delineated by Carl Rogers.

time-efficient approaches Theoretically based, efficient approaches to counseling in a short period of time, usually fewer than 10 sessions.

tracking model System for grouping students for instruction based on scores on standardized tests. (See **scientific rationale**.)

trait and factor theory The model used for many occupational exploration systems. These are based on measuring traits (abilities and skills) of individuals and matching them to the job factors of various possible occupations. Formerly used to explain how counselors should learn the patient's traits and then devise a therapeutic intervention that was the best fit to the diagnosed needs.

transition plan Individualized education plan that is designed to assist the student with special needs transition into life after leaving public school.

transracialism Era in time when issues of one's race are of little consequence and concern. First suggested as occurring with the election of President Barack Obama in 2008.

traumatic injuries Any injury to the organism that involves deep and severe destruction with ripping, penetration, immolation, electrical or chemical burns, or crushing of the individual. Injuries may or may not be fatal but they are severe.

truancy Unexcused and illegal absence from school.

true score An observed score plus or minus some amount of error.

tween years Childhood era between the age of about 9 or 10 years and the age of 13 or 14 when children are entering puberty and reaching the apex of their growth spurts.

über-class Top 1% of the population of America with a mean family income (2010) of $1.1 million annually.

unaccompanied children Children who are both homeless and have no parents or guardians.

unconscious mind   Construct of Sigmund Freud describing a large segment of the human psyche that cannot be accessed by normal cognitive processes but that exerts influence on our thoughts, emotions, and actions.

underachieving student   Student exhibiting a pattern of achievement below that which is expected based on ability test scores and/or previous work.

underclass   Small subgroup of the lower class of Americans living far below the poverty line. They are often homeless and unemployed and living on the street. There were in 2010 2,000,000 children living without permanent homes and part of this American underclass.

undocumented aliens   Individuals who entered the United States without going through the standard legal immigration process or who have entered with a legal visa that has expired.

unintentional covert racism   Thoughtless racism characterized by unrecognized (by the perpetrator) microaggressions against members of minority groups. Usually these microaggressions are in the form of verbal statements or gossip.

upper class   The highly educated top 5% of Americans of the leadership and advanced professional class earning a mean family income (2010) of $180,000 or more per year.

upper middle class   Well-educated professional and supervisory class making up about 15% of the population, with family incomes between about $80,000 and $120,000 per year in 2010.

validity   A statement of both the appropriateness of the test and its components and of the veracity of the test scores and their interpretations.

value neutral   Criticism of client-centered counseling as not providing direct instruction in "appropriate values."

variables   Factors, conceptual entities, characteristics, or attributes likely to vary between individuals and/or within individuals over time.

verbal counseling   Any of various approaches open for use by school counselors once a student is developmentally ready to reflect on his or her actions and feelings and profit from verbal interaction with a school counselor.

virtual meetings   Meetings between two or more people facilitated by computer technology and telephony.

virtual schools   Schools conducted online where students telecommute to their classes. Some are established as charter schools. All states provide at least one virtual school option.

vitamin D3   Vitamin necessary for human life that is manufactured in the lower layer of the skin in reaction to exposure to the ultraviolet rays of the sun.

Vocational Bureau   Office within a private not-for-profit agency dedicated to providing vocational guidance and vocational education.

vocational guidance   Program of activities and instruction designed to help young people learn about different career possibilities and opportunities open to them, and to help find career opportunities most aligned with their interests, talents, and personalities.

vocational interest tests   Measurement devices designed to help students identify clusters of possible career choices that are the best match to their interests.

wait list   Not an outright rejection but placement on a list of college applicants who have not been granted admission but are being held for possible later consideration.

Western view   Philosophic conception of the world and humans based on an assumption of rationalism and built on logic and the scientific method, pragmatism, and materialism.

will   In the theory of Otto Rank, an expression of the individual's choices and responsibility for personal morality and actions.

wired   A school or other facility ready for the optimal amount of instructional and communication technology needed to facilitate learning.

witness of fact   A subject called to testify in court or be deposed so he or she can describe what was witnessed or provide other facts known to the subject.

working class   Class of Americans making up about 30% of the population, including semi-skilled and modestly educated workers with a mean income (2010) between $19,000 and $35,000 per year.

Works Progress Administration (WPA)   President Franklin Delano Roosevelt's Depression-era program to put Americans back to work by hiring them to construct public projects and provide services to people. In 2010 dollars, the WPA spent $110 billion and employed more than 3,000,000 individuals or about 4% of the adult population of that era.

world of adults   Wide population of adults committed to careers, families, and communities where they are responsible for their actions, health, and welfare.

zero-tolerance   The automatic imposition of severe punishments and the criminalization of students for bringing into school any of a long list of prohibited items.

References

Aanstoos, C. S., Serlin, I., & Greening, T. (2000). History of Division 32 (Humanistic Psychology) of the American Psychological Association. In D. Sewsbury (Ed.), *Unification through division: Histories of the divisions of the American Psychological Association, 5*. Washington, DC: American Psychological Association.

Aarons, D. L. (2010, April 21). Rewards for students spawn mixed results, four-city finds. *Education Week, 29*(29), 13.

Abilock, D. (2005, October). We're here! Great digital teacher-librarians. *Knowledge Quest, 34*(1). Retrieved June 19, 2009, from staging.ala.org/ala/mgrps/divs/aasl/aaslpubsandjournals/kqweb/kqarchives/volume34/34–1_homepage.pdf

ACT. (2010). *The condition of college and career readiness.* Quadrennial Report. Retrieved October 8, 2010, from www.act.org/research/policymakers/cccr10/pdf/ConditionofCollegeand CareerReadiness2010.pdf

Adams, G. R., & Ryan, B. A. (2000, June). *A longitudinal analysis of family relationships and children's school achievement in one and two parent families.* Québec City, Montreal, Canada: Human Resources Development. Retrieved December 5, 2009, from www.hrsdc.gc.ca/eng/cs/sp/sdc/pkrf/publications/research/2000–000180/page08.shtml

Adams, N. L., Tsytsarev, S. V., & Meller, P. J. (2009, Spring). The relationship between childhood traumatic experiences and gang-involved delinquent behavior in adolescent boys. *Journal of the American Academy of Special Education Professionals.* Retrieved September 22, 2009, from aasep.org/aasep-publications/journal-of-the-american-academy-of-special-education-professionals-jaasep/jaasep-spring-2009/the-relationship-between-childhood-traumatic-experiences-and-gang-involved-delinquent-behavior-in-adolescent-boys/index.html

Adler, A. (1931). *What life should mean to you.* Boston: Little, Brown.

Adler, A. (1956a). Masculine protest and critique of Freud. In H. L. Ansbacher & R. R. Ansbacher (Eds.), *The individual psychology of Alfred Adler* (pp. 44–68). New York: Basic Books.

Adler, A. (1956b). Personality theory and its development. In H. L. Ansbacher & R. R. Ansbacher (Eds.), *The individual psychology of Alfred Adler* (pp. 21–43). New York: Basic Books.

Adler, A. (1978/1930). *The education of children.* Washington, DC: Regnery.

Adler, P. A., & Adler, P. (2001). *Peer power: Preadolescent culture and identity.* New Brunswick, NJ: Rutgers University Press.

Ahmed, A. (2009, June 29). Teacher turnover plagues Chicago public schools. *Chicago Tribune*. Retrieved November 27, 2009, from archives.chicagotribune.com/2009/jun/29/local/chi-chicago-public-schools-studyjun29

Akos, P. (2004). Outcomes research on school counseling. In B. T. Erford (Ed.), *Professional school counseling: A handbook of theories, programs, and practices* (pp. 35–42). Austin, TX: CAPS Press, an imprint of PRO-ED.

Aladjen, D. K., & Borman, K. M. (2006). An introduction to comprehensive school reform. In D. K. Aladjen & K. M. Barmen (Eds.), *Examining comprehensive school reform* (pp. 1–10). Washington, DC: Urban Institute Press.

Albano, A. M., Chorpita, B. F., & Barlow, D. H. (1996). Childhood anxiety disorders. In E. J. Mash and R. A. Barkley (Eds.), *Child psychopathology* (pp. 196–241). New York: Guilford.

Albright, D. E. (1994). An unexpected gift. *Journal of Humanistic Education & Development, 32*(4), 188–189.

Allen, F. L. (1931). *Only yesterday: An informal history of the nineteen-twenties.* New York: Harper & Row.

Allen, J. P., & Allen, C. W. (2010). The big wait. *Educational Leadership, 68*(1), 22–26.

Allison, B. N., & Schultz, J. B. (2001). Interpersonal identity formation during early adolescence. *Adolescence, 36*(143), 509–523.

American Bar Association (ABA). (2006). *Truancy/dropouts: The relationship between truancy and dropping out of high school.* Washington, DC: Commission on Youth at Risk, American Bar Association. Retrieved September 16, 2009, from www.abanet.org/youthatrisk/factsheets/truancy dropouts.shtml

American College Personnel Association (ACPA). (2004). *About us.* Retrieved March 31, 2009, from www.myacpa.org/au/au_index.cfm

American College Testing Program (ACT). (1997). *ACT assessment: Technical manual.* Iowa City, IA: ACT.

American Counseling Association (ACA). (2005). *Code of ethics.* Alexandria, VA: American Counseling Association. Retrieved June 19, 2009, from www.counseling.org/Resources/Code OfEthics/TP/Home/CT2.aspx

American Counseling Association (ACA). (2009). *Our history.* Alexandria, VA: American Counseling Association. Retrieved March 31, 2009, from www.counseling.org/AboutUs/OurHistory/TP/Milestones/CT2.aspx

American Evaluation Association (AEA). (2005). *About us.* Retrieved August 22, 2005, from www.eval.org/News/news.htm

American Federation of Teachers (AFT). (2008). *History.* Retrieved April 14, 2009, from www.aft.org/about/history/

American Heart Association (2009). *Nicotine addiction.* Washington, DC: American Heart Association. Retrieved September 26, 2009, from www.americanheart.org/presenter.jhtml?identifier=4753

American Lung Association. (2009). *Smoking and teens fact sheet.* Washington, DC: American Lung Association. Retrieved September 26, 2009, from www.lungusa.org/site/c.dvLUK900E/b.39871/

American National Standards Institute. (1994/1995). *The program evaluation standards.* Washington, DC: ERIC Clearing House on Assessment and Evaluation. (ERIC Document No. ED385612.)

American Psychiatric Association (APA). (1994). *Diagnostic and statistical manual of mental disorders* (4th ed.). Washington, DC: American Psychiatric Association.

American School Counselor Association (ASCA). (2004). *Ethical standards.* Alexandria, VA: American School Counselor Association.

American School Counselor Association (ASCA). (2008). *Student to counselor ratios.* Retrieved May 30, 2009, from www.schoolcounselor.org/content.asp?contentid=460

American School Counselor Association (ASCA). (2009). *2007–2008 Student to school ratios.* Washington, DC: American School Counselor Association. Retrieved January 18, 2010, from www.schoolcounselor.org/files/Ratios2007–2008.pdf

American School Counselor Association (ASCA). (2010, March 4). *Response to Public Agenda report.* Retrieved April 17, 2010, from asca2.timberlakepublishing.com/content.asp?contentid=599

American School Counselor Association (ASCA)/Hatch, T., & Bowers, J. (2005). *The ASCA National Model: A framework for school counseling programs* (2nd ed.). Alexandria, VA: American School Counselor Association.

Anderson, N. (2009, September 25). Unions criticize Obama's school proposals as Bush III. *Washington Post.* Retrieved November 5, 2009, from www.washingtonpost.com/wp-dyn/content/article/2009/09/24/AR2009092403197.html

Angus, D., & Meril, J. E. (1999). *The failed promise of the American high school, 1890–1995.* New York: Teachers College Press.

AP-AOL games poll reveals surprising profile of gamers; urbanites outplay suburbanites online, men more likely to form ongoing friendships with other online players, solo-play reigns supreme among women. (2006, May 8). *Business Wire.* Retrieved April 26, 2010, from http://findarticles.com/p/articles/mi_m0EIN/is_2006_May_8/ai_n16347960/

Appel, A. (2009, March 10). Loss of recess time decried. *New Haven Independent.* Retrieved June 17, 2009, from http://newhavenindependent.org/archives/2009/03/let_them_play.php

Applebaum, M. (2009). *How to handle hard-to-handle preschoolers.* Thousand Oaks, CA: Corwin.

Aratani, L. (2005, August 25). Group seeks to end gifted designation: Label unfair to kids, members say. *Washington Post.* Retrieved July 17, 2009, from www.washingtonpost.com

Arias, M. B., & Morillo-Campbell, M. (2008). *Promoting ELL parental involvement: Challenges in contested times.* Tempe: Arizona State University, Education Policy Research Unit. Retrieved June 18, 2009, from http://epslasu.edu/epru/documents/EPSL-0801–250-EPRU.pdf

Arsenault, S. (2001). Values and virtue: The politics of abstinence-only sex education. *American Review of Public Administration, 31*(4), 436–454.

Asakawa, K., Hektner, J., & Schmidt, J. (2000). Envisioning the future. In M. Csikszentmihalyi & B. Schneider (Eds.), *Becoming adult: How teenagers prepare for the world of work* (pp. 39–64). New York: Basic Books.

Ashcraft, M. H., & Kirk, E. P. (2001). The relationships among working memory, math anxiety, and performance. *Journal of Experimental Psychology: General, 130*(2), 224–237.

Association for Counselor Education and Supervision (ACES). (2005). *About ACES.* Retrieved March 31, 2009, from www.acesonline.net/about.asp

Association for Supervision and Curriculum Development (ASCD). (2010). Create a welcoming classroom for homeless students. *Education Update, 52*(6), 1, 6–7.

Autism Society. (2006). *Facts and statistics.* Bethesda, MD: Autism Society. Retrieved September 11, 2009, from www.autism-society.org/site/PageServer?pagename=about_whatis_factsstats

Badertscher, N. (2009, July 8). CRCT scores thrown out at four Georgia schools. *Atlanta Journal Constitution.* Retrieved July 10, 2009, from www.ajc.com/hotjobs/content/metro/stories/2009/07/08/cheating_schools_CRCT.html

Bailey, P. (2007). Students get prizes for taking science test. *Miami Herald.* Retrieved January 29, 2007, from www.miami.com/mld/miamiherald/

Baker, D. R. (2002). *Teacher perceptions of the educational outcomes for direct instruction in a compressed video classroom environment within remote classrooms at the secondary school level.* Doctoral dissertation, Widener University (ProQuest No. 3056384).

Baker, S. B., & Gerler, E. R. Jr. (2004). *School counseling for the twenty-first century* (4th ed.). Upper Saddle River, NJ: Pearson.

Baker, S. B., Robichaud, T. A., Dietrich, V. C. W., Wells, S. C., & Schreck, R. E. (2009). School counselor consultation: A pathway to advocacy, collaboration, and leadership. *Professional School Counseling, 12*(3), 193–199.

Bandura, A., & McDonald, F. J. (1963). The influence of social reinforcement and the behavior of models in shaping children's moral judgments. *Journal of Abnormal and Social Psychology, 67,* 274–281.

Barkan, J. (2008, Spring). Alive and not well: Affirmative action on campus. *Dissent.* Retrieved July 10, 2009, from www.dissentmagazine.org/article/?article=1162#

Barkley, R. A. (1998). Attention-deficit/hyperactivity disorder. In E. J. Mash & R. A. Barkley (Eds.), *Attention-deficit hyperactivity disorder: A handbook for diagnosis and treatment* (2nd ed., pp. 63–112). New York: Guilford.

Barkoukis, A., Reiss, N. S., & Dombeck, M. (2008). Forms and causes of childhood disorders. *Mental Health Net.* Retrieved May 26, 2009, from www.mentalhelp.net/poc/view_doc.php?type=doc&id=14487&cn=37

Bartle, R. A. (1996). *Hearts, clubs, diamonds, spades: Players who suit MUDS.* Retrieved April 26, 2010, from www.mud.co.uk/richard/hcds.htm

Barton, P. E. (2006). The dropout problem: Losing ground. *Educational Leadership, 63*(5), 14–18.

Barton, P. E., & Coley, R. J. (2007). *The family: America's smallest school.* Princeton, NJ: Educational Testing Service.

Barton, P. E., & Coley, R. J. (2009). *Parsing the achievement gap.* Princeton, NJ: Educational Testing Service. Retrieved September 9, 2009, from www.ets.org/Media/Research/pdf/PICPARSINGII.pdf

Bassuk, E. L., & Friedman, S. M. (2005). *Facts on trauma and homeless children.* Newton Center, MA: National Child Traumatic Stress Network. Retrieved January 7, 2009, from www.NCTSNet.org

Bassuk, E. L., Konnath, K., & Volk, K. T. (2006). *Understanding traumatic stress in children.* Research report. Newton Center, MA: National Center on Family Homelessness. Retrieved January 8, 2009, from www.familyhomelessness.org/pdf/Characteristics_Needs_Homeless_Families.pdf

Bauman, S. (2004). School counselors and research revisited. *Professional School Counseling, 7*(3), 141–151.

Bauman, S. (2008). To join or not to join: School counselors as a case study in professional membership. *Journal of Counseling & Development, 86*(2), 164–177.

Beaudoin, M., & Taylor, M. (2009). *Responding to the culture of bullying and disrespect* (2nd ed.). Thousand Oaks, CA: Corwin.

Beck, A. T. (1979). *Cognitive therapy and emotional disorders.* New York: Plume/Penguin.

Beck, A. T., Freeman, A., & Davis, D. D. (2004). *Cognitive therapy of personality disorders* (2nd ed.). New York: Guilford.

Beers, C. W. (1908). *A mind that found itself: An autobiography.* London: Longman, Green.

Begley, S. (2009, January 23). An "Obama effect" on Blacks' test scores? *Newsweek.* Retrieved October 23, 2009, from http://blog.newsweek.com/blogs/labnotes/archive/2009/01/23/an-obama-effect-on-blacks-test-scores.aspx

Belluck, P. (2006, February 5). And for perfect attendance, Johnny gets . . . a car. *New York Times.* Retrieved September 15, 2007, from www.nytimes.com

Benitz, C. (2006). *The relationship of HIPAA to special education.* Logan, UT: Mountain Plains Regional Resource Center. (ERIC Document No. ED498479).

Bennett, G. K., Seashore, H. G., & Wesman, A. G. (1992). *Differential Aptitude Test* (5th ed.). San Antonio, TX: Pearson Assessment.

Bennett, W. L. (1992). *The devaluing of America: The fight for our culture and our children.* New York: Summit Books.

Ben-Shakhar, G., & Sinai, Y. (1991). Gender differences in multiple-choice tests: The role of differential guessing tendencies. *Journal of Educational Measurement, 28*(1), 23–35.

Benson, M. T. (1994). *Cohort trends in college academic performances of 1984–1988 freshman student-athletes.* Report No. NCAA-93–01. Overland Park, KS: National Collegiate Athletic Association. (ERIC Document No. ED381045)

Benton, J. (2006, September 2). Cheating: It's in the numbers. *Dallas Morning News.* Retrieved September 7, 2006, from www.dallasnews.com/cgi-bin/bi/gold_print.cgi

Berliner, D. C. (1997, February). *Manufacturing a crisis in education.* Keynote address. Eastern Educational Research Association, Hilton Head Island, SC.

Berliner, D. C. (2004, March/April). *If the underlying premise for No Child Left Behind is false, how can that act solve our problems?* Occasional research paper no. 6. Iowa Academy of Education. Retrieved June 23, 2005, from www.finefoundation.org/Welcome.html

Berliner, D. C., & Biddle, B. J. (1995). *The manufactured crisis: Myths, fraud, and the attack on America's public schools.* Cambridge, MA: Perseus.

Bernstein, R. A. (2003). *Straight parents, gay children: Keeping families together.* New York: Da Capo.

Best, S., & Knapp-Lee, L. (1982). Relationship of interest measurement derived from the COPSystem Interest Survey and the Kuder General Interest Survey: Construct validation of two measures of occupational activity preferences. *Educational and Psychological Measurement, 42*(4), 1289–1293.

Bigg, M. (2009, January 14). *U.S. school segregation is on the rise: Report.* Reuters. Retrieved January 16, 2009, from www.reuters.com/articlePrint?articleId=USTRE50D7CY20090114

Biggs, D. A., & Porter, G. (1994). *Dictionary of counseling.* Santa Barbara, CA: Greenwood Press.

Bishop, D. M., Frazier, C. E., Lanza-Kaduce, L., & Winner, L. (1996). The transfer of juveniles to criminal court: Does it make a difference? *Crime and Delinquency, 42*(2), 171–192.

Blow, C. M. (2008, December 13). The demise of dating. *New York Times,* p. A17.

Blume, H. (2009, March 23). L.A. District to end high-profile dropout-prevention program. *Los Angeles Times.* Retrieved March 24, 2009, from www.latimes.com/news/education/la-me-dropout24–2009mar24,0,5116617,print.story

Bodrova, E., & Leong, D. (2005). Self-regulation: A foundation for early learning. *Principal, 85*(1), 30–35.

Boeree, C. G. (2006). *Abraham Maslow: A biography.* Unpublished manuscript. Shippensburg University, Psychology Department. Retrieved June 19, 2009, from http://webspace.ship.edu/cgboer/maslow.html

Booher-Jennings, J. (2005). "Below the bubble": Educational triage and the Texas accountability system. *American Educational Research Journal, 42*(2), 231–268.

Borman, G. D., Hewes, G. M., Overman, L. T., & Brown, S. (2002). *Comprehensive school reform and student achievement: A meta-analysis.* Report no. 59. Baltimore, MD: Center for Research on the Education of Students Placed At Risk. Retrieved December 12, 2009, from www.csos.jhu.edu/CRESPAR/techReports/Report59.pdf

Boswell, J. (1979, August 31–September 3). *The church and the homosexual: An historical perspective.* Keynote address to the Fourth Biennial Dignity International Convention, San Diego, CA. Retrieved June 29, 2009, from www.fordham.edu/halsall/pwh/1979boswell.html

Bouffard, S. M. (2009). Tapping into technology: Using the Internet to promote family–school communication. In N. E. Hill & R. K. Chao (Eds.), *Families, schools, and the adolescent: Connecting research, policy, and practice* (pp. 147–161). New York: Teachers College Press.

Boult, B. (2006). *176 ways to involve parents: Practical strategies for partnering with families* (2nd ed.). Thousand Oaks, CA: Corwin.

Bowen, J. M., Jenson, W. R., & Clark, E. (2004). *School based intervention for students with behavior problems.* New York: Kluwer Academic/ Plenum.

Bowers, J., & Hatch, T. (2001). The brain storm. *ASCA School Counselor, 39*(1), 16–19.

Bowie, L. (2009, April 12). Teens under stress in top college competition: Straight-A's, perfect SATs sometimes won't cut it. *Baltimore Sun.* Retrieved April 13, 2009, from www.baltimoresun.com/news/education/bal-md.achieve12apr12,0,4616458.story

Bowman, P. J. (2006). Role strain and adaptation issues in the strength-based model: Diversity, multilevel, and life-span considerations. *Counseling Psychologist, 34*(1), 118–133.

Boxx, S. M., Petrie, J. T., Walsh, M. E., & Orecchia, A. C. (2010, August 12). *"City Connects" and student families.* Poster session presented during the annual meeting of the American Psychological Association, San Diego, CA.

Boyse, K. (2009). *Television: What do I need to know about children and TV?* Ann Arbor: University of Michigan Health Science Center. Retrieved October 28, 2009, from www.med .umich.edu/yourchild/topics/tv.htm

Bradbury, H., Mirvis, P., Neilson, E., & Pasmore, W. (2007). Action research at work: Creating the future following the path from Lewin. In P. Reason & H. Bradbury (Eds.), *The SAGE handbook of action research: Participative inquiry and practice* (pp. 77–92). Thousand Oaks, CA: Sage.

Bradley, J. C., Brief, A. P., & George, J. M. (2002). More than the big five personality and careers. In D. C. Feldman (Ed.), *Work careers: A developmental perspective* (pp. 27–62). San Francisco: Jossey-Bass.

Bradley, M. J. (2003). *Yes your parents are crazy! A teen survival guide.* Gig Harbor, WA: Harbor Press.

Bradshaw, A., Watts, K., Holt, B., Davis, M., Clark, T., Alexander, S., & Brown, F. F. (2009). Children of war: Working with children of deployed military personnel. *NC Perspectives: A Journal of the North Carolina Counseling Association, 2*(1), 3–16.

Brand, C., & O'Connor, L. (2004). School refusal: It takes a team. *Children & Schools, 26*(1), 54–64.

Braun, E. P., & Edwards, S. J. (1972). *History and theory of early childhood education.* Worthing, OH: C. A. Jones Publishing.

Brezo, J., Barker, E. D., Paris, J., Hébert, M., Vitaro, F., Tremblay, R. E., & Turecki, G. (2008). Childhood trajectories of anxiousness and disruptiveness as predictors of suicide attempts. *Archives of Pediatrics & Adolescent Medicine, 162*(11), 1015–1021.

Briggs, K. C., Myers, I. M., Quenk, N. L., Kummerow, J., Hammer, A., & Majors, M. S. (2001). *Myers-Briggs type indicator, Step II* (Form Q). Palo Alto, CA: Consulting Psychologists Press.

Brigman, G., Mullis, F., Webb, L., & White, J. (2005). *School counselor consultation: Developing skills for working effectively with parents, teachers, and other school personnel.* Hoboken, NJ: Wiley.

Bringman, N., & Lee, S. M. (2008). Middle school counselor's competence in conducting developmental classroom lessons: Is teaching experience necessary? *Professional School Counseling, 11*(6), 380–385.

Britt, R. R. (2009, May 21). 60 percent of teens text while driving. *Live Science.* Retrieved July 15, 2009, from www.livescience.com/health/090521-dwt.html

Brock, K. C. (2006, March 14). Are they ready to go? Some experts believe starting school late can give kids an edge. *Southern Illinoisan.* Retrieved July 18, 2009, from www.southernillinoisan .com/articles/2006/03/16/life/doc441687574ba81571918947.txt

Brody, J. E. (2009, January 20). Trying anything and everything for autism. *New York Times,* p. D7.

Brookhart, S. M. (1994). Teacher's grading: Practice and theory. *Applied Measurement, 7,* 279–301.

Brookhart, S. M. (2004). *Grading.* New York: Pearson Education.

Brooks, M. (2009, December 7). *Half of teenage girls have STIs by 2 years of first sex.* Reuters. Retrieved September 28, 2010, from www.reuters.com/article/idUSTRE5B646K20091207

Brown, R. T., Perwien, A., Faries, D. E., Kratochvil, C. J., & Vaughn, B. S. (2006). Atomoxetine in the management of children with ADHD: Effects on quality of life and school functioning. *Clinical Pediatrics, 45*(9), 819–827.

Brown, T. E. (2005). *Attention deficit disorder: The unfocused mind in children and adults.* New Haven, CT: Yale University Press.

Bruzzese, J. (2009). *Parents' guide to the middle school years.* New York: Celestial Arts/ Random House.

Buchanan, P. J. (2002). *The death of the west: How dying populations and immigrant invasions imperil our country and civilization*. New York: St. Martin Griffin.

Buckendahl, C. W., Smith, R. W., Impara, J. C., & Plake, B. S. (2002). A comparison of Angoff and bookmark standard setting methods. *Journal of Educational Measurement, 39*(3), 253–263.

Bugental, J.F.T. (1964). The third force in psychology. *Journal of Humanistic Psychology, 4*(1), 19–25.

Bullock, E. E., & Madson, M. B. (2009). Review of the COPS career guidance program: Career occupational preference system interest inventory (COPS), Career ability placement service (CAPS), Career orientation placement and evaluation survey. In E. A. Whitfield, R. W. Feller, & C. Wood (Eds.), *A counselor's guide to career assessment instruments* (5th ed., pp. 119–126). Broken Arrow, OK: National Career Development Association.

Buoye, A. J. (2004). *Capitalizing on the extra curriculum: Participation, peer influence, and academic achievement*. Unpublished doctoral dissertation, Notre Dame University.

Bureau of Justice Statistics, U.S. Department of Justice. (2002). *Demographic trends in correctional populations by race*. Retrieved October 27, 2009, from www.ojp.gov/bjs/glance/tables/cpracetab.htm

Bureau of Labor Statistics. (2009). *Occupational Outlook Handbook, 2008–2009*. Washington, DC: U.S. Department of Labor, Bureau of Labor Statistics. Retrieved July 6, 2009, from www.bls.gov/oco/ocos251.htm

Burgess, J. S. (2004). *The tradition of the Trojan War in Homer and the epic cycle*. Baltimore: Johns Hopkins University Press.

Burnham, W. H. (1926). *Great teachers and mental health*. New York: D. Appleton.

Burns, K. (2006). *The new paradigm in recruiting*. MRI Network for Global Recruiting. Retrieved December 21, 2009, from www.mrinetwork.com

Burns, M. E. (2003). *A comparison of reading comprehension in children with attention deficit hyperactivity disorder, with and without the effects of stimulant medication*. Unpublished doctoral dissertation, Widener University. (ProQuest No. AAT 3114590).

Burns, R. C. (1987). *Kinetic-house-tree-person drawings (K-H-T-P): An interpretative manual*. New York: Brunner/Mazel.

Camilli, G., & Monfils, L. F. (2004). Test scores and equity. In W. A. Firestone, R. Y. Schorr, & L. F. Monfils (Eds.), *The ambiguity of teaching to the test: Standards, assessment, and educational reform* (pp. 143–157). Mahwah, NJ: Lawrence Erlbaum.

Campbell, D. T., & Stanley, J. C. (1963). Experimental and quasi-experimental designs for research on teaching. In N. L. Gage (Ed.), *Handbook of research on teaching* (pp. 171–246). Chicago: Rand McNally.

Campbell, G. (1994). Coming out of the cloakroom. In K. Jennings (Ed.), *One teacher in 10* (pp. 131–136). Los Angeles: Alyson Books.

Campbell, V. L., & Raiff, G. W. (2009). Review of the Harrington-O'Shea Career Decision-Making System-Revised. In E. A. Whitfield, R. W. Feller, & C. Wood (Eds.), *A counselor's guide to career assessment instruments* (5th ed., pp. 262–267). Broken Arrow, OK: National Career Development Association.

Cantwell, J. G. (2007, February). *The principal's role in statewide testing: A national, state, and local school district perspective*. Paper presented at the annual meeting of the Eastern Educational Research Association, Clearwater, FL.

Capuzzi, D. (1994). *Suicide prevention in the schools: Guidelines for middle and high school settings*. Alexandria, VA: American Counseling Association.

Carestio, M. A. (2010). *Black Jack Jetty: A boy's journey through grief*. Washington, DC: Magination Press, American Psychological Association.

Carey, B. (2008). Spot on popularity scale speaks to the future; middle has its rewards. *New York Times*, p. D5.

Carlin, D., & Payne, J. (2001). *Public speaking today*. Lincolnwood, IL: National Textbook.

Carranza, C. R., & Dill, J. R. (2004). *Banishing night terrors and nightmares: A breakthrough program to heal the traumas that shatter peaceful sleep.* New York: Kensington.

Carrell, M. E., & Hoekstra, M. L. (2008). *Externalities in the classroom: How children exposed to domestic violence affect everyone's kids.* Social Science Electronic Publishing. Retrieved May 27, 2009, from http://papers.ssrn.com/s013/papers.cfm?abstract_id=1231694#

Carreón, G. P., Drake, C., & Barton, A. C. (2005). The importance of presence: Immigrant parents' school engagement experiences. *American Educational Research Journal, 42*(3), 465–498.

Casas, J. M., Raley, J. D., & Vasquez, M. J. T. (2008). Adelante! Counseling the Latina/o from guiding theory to practice. In P. B. Pedersen, J. G. Draguns, W. J. Lonner, & J. E. Trimble (Eds.), *Counseling across cultures* (6th ed., pp. 129–146). Thousand Oaks, CA: Sage.

Cauce, A. M., Paradise, M., Ginzler, J. A., Embry, L., Morgan, C. J., Lohr, Y., & Theofelis, J. (2000). The characteristics and mental health of homeless adolescents: Age and gender differences. *Journal of Emotional and Behavioral Disorders, 8*(4), 230–239.

Cauchon, D. (1999). Zero-tolerance policies lack flexibility. *USA Today.* Retrieved September 18, 2009, from www.usatoday.com/educate/ednews3.htm

Celebrate Boston. (2009). *Site of the first public school.* Celebrate Boston.com. Retrieved September 24, 2010, from www.celebrateboston.com/sites/latin-school.htm

Centers on Educational Policy. (2010, April 13). *Improving low performing schools: Summary of a forum.* Retrieved April 17, 2010, from www.cep-dc.org/index.cfm?fuseaction=document_ext.show DocumentByID&nodeID=1&DocumentID=306

Centers for Disease Control and Prevention, U.S. Department of Health and Human Services. (2008, August). *HIV/AIDS among youth.* Retrieved July 15, 2009, from www.cdc.gov/hiv/resources/ Factsheets/youth.htm

Centers for Disease Control and Prevention, U.S. Department of Health and Human Services, National Center for Health Statistics. (2009). *Marriage and divorce.* Retrieved September 17, 2010, from www.cdc.gov/nchs/fastats/divorce.htm

Cervantes, W., & Lincroft, Y. (2010). Caught between systems: The intersection of immigration and child welfare policies. *First Focus.* Retrieved September 8, 2010, from www.firstfocus.net/ library/reports/the-impact-of-immigration-enforcement-on-child-welfare

Chalk, L. M., Meara, M. N., Day, J. D., & Davis, K. L. (2005). Occupational possible selves: Fears and aspirations of college women. *Journal of Career Assessment, 13*(2), 188–203.

Chandra, A., Lara-Cinisomo, S., Jaycox, L. H., Tanielian, T., Burns, R. M., Ruder, T., & Han, B. (2010). Children on the homefront: The experience of children from military families. *Pediatrics, 125*(1), 16–25.

Chang, K. D. (2005, June 20). Attention-deficit/hyperactivity disorder. *E-Medicine.* Retrieved June 30, 2005, from www.emedicine.com/med/topic3103.htm

Chao, R. K., Kanatsu, A., Stanoff, N., Padmawidjaja, I., & Aque, C. (2009). Diversities in meaning and practice. In N. E. Hill & R. K. Chao (Eds.), *Families, schools, and the adolescent: Connecting research, policy, and practice* (pp. 110–125). New York: Teachers College Press.

Charlesworth, J. R., & Jackson, C. M. (2004). Solution-focused brief counseling: An approach for professional school counselors. In B. T. Erfort (Ed.), *Professional school counseling: A handbook of theories, programs, and practices* (pp. 139–148). Austin, TX: CAPS Press, an imprint of PRO-ED.

Chartrand, M. M., Frank, D. A., White, L. F., & Shope, T. R. (2008). Effect of parents' wartime deployments on the behavior of young children in military families. *Archives of Pediatrics & Adolescent Medicine, 162*(11), 1009–1014.

Cheng, Y. A., & Landale, N. S. (2009, March). *Adolescent precursors of early union formation among Asian American and Whites.* Working paper, Max Planck Institute for Demographic Research. Retrieved October 28, 2009, from www.demogr.mpg.de/papers/working/wp-2009–020.pdf

Chernoff, A. (2007, January 5). Employees find noose hanging at work. *CNN U.S. News*. Retrieved October 28, 2009, from www.cnn.com/2007/US/01/05/chernoff.noose/index.html

Cheslock, J. (2007). *Who's playing college sports?* East Meadow, NY: Women's Sports Foundation. Retrieved November 3, 2009, from http://wsf-staging.mediapolis.com/binary-data/reportcard/fullreport.pdf

Child Welfare Information Gateway. (2006). *Recognizing child abuse and neglect: Signs and symptoms.* Retrieved February 19, 2008, from www.childwelfare.gov/pubs/factsheets/signs.cfm

Chinappi, J. (2009). Multicultural counseling: Etic vs. emic. *BrightHub*. Retrieved October 5, 2009, from www.brighthub.com/education/languages/articles/5286.aspx

Chipego, A. D. (2004). *Factors associated with the attitudes of elementary level classroom teachers toward gifted education.* Unpublished doctoral dissertation, Widener University. (ProQuest No. AAT 3120729).

Chomsky, N. (2006). *Language and the mind* (3rd ed.). New York: Cambridge University Press.

Chow, P., Thompson, I. S., Wood, W., Beauchamp, M., & Lebrun, R. (2002). Comparing the personal development of college students, high school students with prison inmates. *Education, 123*(1), 619–641.

Chronicle Guidance Publications. (1993). *Chronicle career quest.* Moravia, NY: Chronicle Guidance Publications.

Chubb, J. E., & Moe, T. M. (1992). Educational choice: Why it is needed and how it will work? In Chester E. Finn Jr. & Theodore Rebarer (Eds.), *Education reform in the 90's* (pp. 36–52). New York: Macmillan.

Chubb, N. H., & Fertman, C. I. (1997). Adolescent self-esteem and locus of control: A longitudinal study of gender differences. *Adolescence, 32*(125), 113–130.

Chudowsky, N., & Chudowsky, V. (2010, April 7). *State test score trends through 2007–2008, Part 6: Has progress been made in raising achievement for English language learners?* Washington, DC: Center on Educational Policy. Retrieved April 17, 2010, from www.cep-dc.org/document/docWindow.cfm?fuseaction=document.viewDocument&documentid=305&documentFormatId=4630

Ciarrochi, J., Leeson, P., & Heaven, P. C. L. (2009). A longitudinal study into the interplay between problem orientation and adolescent well-being. *Journal of Counseling Psychology, 56*(3), 441–449.

Citrin, J., Lerman, A., Murakami, M., & Pearson, K. (2007). Testing Huntington: Is Hispanic immigration a threat to American identity? *Perspectives on Politics, 5*(1), 31–48.

Clabaugh, G. K., & Rozycki, E. G. (1990). *Understanding schools: The foundations of education.* New York: Harper & Row.

Clark, H. B., & Davis, M. (2000). *Transition to adulthood: A resource for assisting young people with emotional or behavioral difficulties.* Baltimore, MD: Paul H. Brookes.

Clark, W., Polakov, W. N., & Trabold, F. W. (2010). *The Gantt chart: A working tool of management.* Ithaca, NY: Cornell University Library/Nabu Press.

Clarridge, P. B., & Whitaker, E. M. (1997). *Rolling the elephant over: How to effect large-scale change in the reporting process.* Portsmouth, NH: Heinemann.

Clemens, E. (2007). Developmental counseling and therapy as a model for school consultation with teachers. *Professional School Counseling, 10*(4), 352–359.

Clemens, E. V., Milsom, A., & Cashwell, C. S. (2009). *Professional School Counseling, 13*(2), 75–85.

Cobia, D. C., & Henderson, D. C. (2007). *Developing an effective and accountable school counseling program* (2nd ed.). Upper Saddle River, NJ: Pearson.

Cohen, K. (2006, July 7). Why colleges should thank private admissions counselors. *Chronicle of Higher Education*, p. B20.

Cohen, P. (2009, September 11). School district settles lawsuit over "Rent." *New York Times*, p. C5.

Cohen, R. (2009a, July 12). A Facebook teaching moment. The Ethicist. *New York Times Magazine*, p. 17.

Cohen, R. (2009b, August 2). Problem hires. The Ethicist. *New York Times Magazine,* p. 14.

Coleman, J. S. (1972). The evaluation of equality of educational opportunity. In F. Mosteller & D. P. Moynihan (Eds.), *On equality of educational opportunity* (pp. 146–167). New York: Random House.

College Board. (2009). *SAT® percentile ranks: Critical reading, mathematics, critical writing.* Retrieved November 5, 2009, from http://professionals.collegeboard.com/profdownload/sat_percentile_ranks_2008.pdf

College Board. (2010). *SAT II® fees.* Retrieved January 4, 2010, from www.collegeboard.com/student/testing/sat/calenfees/fees.html

Collins, R. L., Elliott, M. N., Berry, S. H., Kanouse, D. E., Kunkel, D., Hunter, S. B., & Miu, A. (2004). Watching sex on television predicts adolescent initiation of sexual behavior. *Pediatrics, 114*(3), 280–289.

Collison, B. B. (1991, June). Knowing the music for the dance: The national career development guidelines and national priorities. In J. Miller, J. Goodman, & B. Collison (Eds.), *The national career development guidelines: Progress and possibilities* (pp. 37–58). NOICC Occasional Papers. (ERIC Document No. 339869).

Coloroso, B. (2002). *Kids are worth it! Giving your child the gift of inner discipline.* New York: Collins Living/Harper Collins.

Coloroso, B. (2004). *The bully, the bullied, and the bystander: From preschool to high school: How parents and teachers can help break the cycle of violence.* New York: Collins Living/Harper Collins.

Committee on Quality Improvement and Subcommittee on Attention-Deficit/Hyperactivity Disorder. (2001). Clinical practice guideline: Treatment of the school-aged child with attention-deficit/hyperactivity disorder. *Pediatrics, 108*(4), 1033–1044.

Conners, K. (1997/2000). *Conners' rating scales–Revised.* Toronto, Ontario, Canada: Multi-Health Systems.

Cook, V. (2008). *Second language learning and teaching.* New York: Oxford University Press.

Cooky, C. (2009). "Girls just aren't interested": The social construction of interest in girl's sport. *Sociological Perspectives, 52*(2), 259–284.

Cooney, E. (2008, May 6). Eateries' smoking ban is dissuading teens. *Boston Globe.* Retrieved September 26, 2009, from www.boston.com/news/local/articles/2008/05/06/eateries_smoking_ban_is_dissuading_teens?mode=PF

Coulton, C., Theodos, B., & Turner, M. A. (2009). *Family mobility and neighborhood change: New evidence and implications for community initiatives.* Washington, DC: Urban Institute. Retrieved November 15, 2009, from www.urban.org/UploadedPDF/411973_family_mobility.pdf

Cousins, N. (1976). Anatomy of an illness (as perceived by the patient). *New England Journal of Medicine, 295*(26), 1458–1463.

Cox, J. (2007, February 16). Two schools face overhaul after failing standards for five years. *Naples Daily News.* Retrieved November 4, 2009, from www.naplesnews.com/news/2007/feb/16/two_schools_face_overhaul_after_failing_standards_/

Crile, S. (2009, June 7). Obama ends abstinence–only funding in his budget. *Huffington Post.* Retrieved July 2, 2009, from www.huffingtonpost.com/2009/05/07/obama-eliminates-abstinen_n_199205.html

Crocker, L. (2003). Teaching for the test: Validity, fairness, and moral action. 2003 NCME presidential address. *Educational Measurement: Issues and Practice, 22*(3), 5–11.

Cromartie, J. (2010, Fall). On guard: Identifying military families in your school can be tricky. *Florida School Counselor,* 10.

Crouse, J. (2006, March 27). Students rewarded for sacrificing Saturdays for FCAT training. *Lakland Ledger.* Retrieved July 17, 2009, from www.theledger.com/article/20060327/NEWS/603270345

Crow, L. D., & Crow, D. A. (1935). *Mental hygiene in school and home life for teachers, supervisors, and parents,* New York: McGraw-Hill.

Cullen, K. (2010, January 24). The untouchable mean girls. *Boston Globe.* Retrieved April 17, 2010, from www.boston.com/news/local/massachusetts/articles/2010/01/24/the_untouchable_mean_girls/

Dahir, C. A. (2009). School counseling in the 21st century: Where lies the future? *Journal of Counseling & Development, 87*(1), 3–5.

D'Amico, D. (2009, June 24). Few in N.J. affected by special education tuition ruling. *Atlantic City Press.* Retrieved August 31, 2009, from www.pressofatlanticcity.com/education/press/article_922f4abd-0e07–57af-a415–4679bc64b96f.html?mode=print

D'Andrea, M., & Arredondo, P. (1999). Promoting human dignity and development through diversity. *Counseling Today, 41*(10), 16, 22.

Daniel, L. G. (1995). Review of the Chronicle Career Quest®. In J. C. Conoley & J. C. Impara (Eds.), *The 12th mental measurements yearbook* (pp. 193–197). Lincoln, NE: Buros Institute of Mental Measurements.

Daniels, V. (1998). *Alfred Adler's "Individual Psychology."* Unpublished manuscript. Sonoma State University, Department of Psychology. Retrieved July 25, 2009, from www.sonoma.edu/users/daniels/Adler.html

Darling-Hammond, L. (2004). From "separate but equal" to "No Child Left Behind": The collision of new standards and old inequalities. In D. Meier & G. Wood (Eds.), *Many children left behind: How the No Child Left Behind Act is damaging our children and our schools.* Boston: Beacon Press.

Datar, A. (2003). *The impact of changes in kindergarten entrance age policies on children's academic achievement and the child care needs of families.* Report RGSD-177, 2003. Santa Monica, CA: Rand Corporation, Pardee Rand Graduate School.

Davidson, L., & Demaray, M. K. (2006). *Best practices in bullying prevention and intervention programs.* Report adapted from National Association of School Psychologists. Retrieved May 28, 2009, from www.guidancechannel.com/default.aspx?M=a&index=1933&cat=17

Davis, G. (2004, July 2). Today, even B students getting squeezed out. *Chronicle of Higher Education.* Retrieved April 21, 2005, from http:chronicle.com/weekly/v50/i43b02001.htm

Davis, K., & Matthews, C. M. (2009, July 10). Mixed-race in U.S. struggle to form political, personal identities. *News 21.* College Park, MD: University of Maryland. Retrieved October 4, 2009, from http://thenewvoters.news21.com/mixedrace/mixed-race-us-struggle-form-political-personal-identities#

Davis, M. D., Johnson, J., & Richardson, A. E. (1929). *Minimum essentials for nursery school education.* Washington, DC: National Committee on Nursery Schools, Standards Subcommittee.

Dawson, D. A. (1991). Family structure and children's health and well-being: Data from the National Health Interview Survey on Child Health. *Journal of Marriage and the Family, 53,* 573–584.

DeAngelis, T. (2009). Unmasking "racial microaggressions." *Monitor on Psychology, 40*(2), 42–45.

DeCuir-Gunby, J. T. (2009). A review of the racial identity development of African-American adolescents: The role of education. *Review of Educational Research, 79*(1), 103–124.

DeGregory, L. (2005, February 10). For sick kids, FCAT's just one more exam. *St. Petersburg Times.* Retrieved March 20, 2006, from www.sptimes.com

DeKalb, J. (2000). *Student truancy.* ERIC Clearing House, Digest 125. (ERIC Document No. ED429334).

Delgado-Romero, E. A., Galván, N., Hunter, M. R., & Torres, V. (2008). Latino/a Americans. In G. McAuliffe (Ed.), *Culturally alert counseling: A comprehensive introduction* (pp. 323–352). Thousand Oaks, CA: Sage.

DeLucia-Waack, J. L. (2006). *Leading psychoeducational groups for children and adolescents.* Thousand Oaks, CA: Sage.

Demaray, M. K., Malecki, C. K., & DeLong, L. K. (2006). Support in the lives of aggressive students, their victims, and their peers. In S. R. Jimerson & M. J. Furlong (Eds.), *Handbook of school violence and school safety: From research to practice* (pp. 21–30). Mahwah, NJ: Lawrence Erlbaum.

Denizet-Lewis, B. (2009, September 27). Coming out in middle school. *New York Times Magazine,* pp. 36–41. Retrieved January 23, 2010, from www.nytimes.com/2009/09/27/magazine/27Out-t.html

DeParle, J. (2009, April 19). Struggling to rise in suburbs where failing means fitting in. *New York Times,* pp. A1, A20.

DeParle, J., & Gebeloff, R. M. (2010, January 3). Living on nothing but food stamps. *New York Times,* pp. A1, A18.

Desmon, S. (2008, March 12). 1 in 4 teen girls has an STD. *Boston Globe.* Retrieved July 15, 2009, from www.boston.com/news/nation/articles/2008/03/12/study_1_in_4_teen_girls_has_an_std?mode=PF

Dessoff, A. (2008). Action teams. *District Administration, 43*(6), 41–44.

De Valdes y Cocom, M. (2009). *The blurred racial lines of famous families, Queen Charlotte.* Boston: WGBH Education Foundation. Retrieved October 21, 2009, from www.pbs.org/wgbh/pages/frontline/shows/secret/famous/royalfamily.html

De Vise, D. (2008, October 14). School attendance law "gone awry." *Washington Post,* p. A1.

Diamond, M. (2002). Sex and gender different: Sexual identity and gender identity are different. *Clinical Child Psychology and Psychiatry, 7*(3), 320–334.

Dillon, A. (2004, May 26). *Education in Plato's Republic.* Paper presented at the Santa Clara University, Markkula Center for Applied Ethics. Retrieved December 21, 2007, from www.scu.edu/ethics/publications/submitted/dillon/education_plato_republic.html

Dillon, S. (2007, April 4). A great year for Ivy League schools, but not so good for applications to them. *New York Times.* Retrieved April 22, 2009, from www.nytimes.com/2007/04/04/education/04colleges.html

DiMeo, M. R. (2000). *The stone cocoon.* Bloomington, IN: AuthorHouse.

Dolbec, A., & Savoie-Zajc, L. (1995, April 13). *Problems emerging from the practicing of action research in graduate programs in education.* Paper presented at the International Conference on Teacher Research, University of California, Davis. Retrieved November 19, 2009, from www.eric.ed.gov/ERICDocs/data/ericdocs2sql/content_storage_01/0000019b/80/13/e8/01.pdf

Doll, B., & Doll, C. (1997). *Bibliotherapy with young people: Librarians and mental health professionals working together.* Englewood, CO: Libraries Unlimited.

Dollarhide, C. T., & Lemberger, M. E. (2006). "No Child Left Behind": Implications for school counselors. *Professional School Counseling, 9*(4), 295–304.

Dong, Y. R. (2007, Summer). Learning to think in English. *Educational Leadership, 64,* 22–26.

Dorans, N. J., & Zeller, K. (2004). *Using score equity assessment to evaluate the equitability of the hardest half of a test to the total test.* Retrieved September 4, 2009, from http://ftp.ets.org/pub/res/researcher/RR-04-43.pdf

Dougherty, A. M., Dougherty, L. P., & Purcell, D. (1991). The sources of management resistance to consultation. *School Counselor, 38*(3), 178–186.

Dougherty, C., Mellor, L., & Shuling, J. (2006). *The relationship between advanced placement and college graduation.* Austin: University of Texas, National Center for Educational Accountability.

Dreese, M. (1957). Group guidance and group therapy. *Review of Educational Research, 27,* 219–220.

Drinkmeyer, D. C., Pew, W. L., & Drinkmeyer, D. C. Jr. (1979). *Adlerian counseling and psychotherapy.* Monterey, CA: Brooks/Cole.

Dubner, S. J., & Levitt, S. D. (2005, May 4). Do parents matter? *USA Today.* Retrieved December 7, 2009, from www.usatoday.com/news/opinion/editorials/2005-05-03-parents-edit_x.htm

Ducharme, J. M. (2007). Tailoring the Incredible Years parent programs according to children's developmental needs and family risk factors. In J. M. Briesmeister & C. E. Schaefer (Eds.),

Handbook of parent training: Helping parents prevent and solve problem behaviors (pp. 305–344). Hoboken, NJ: Wiley.

Eagle, S. (2006). *Drug education: A study.* Unpublished meta-analysis, University of Michigan. Retrieved September 25, 2009, from sitemaker.umich.edu/eagle.356/dare

Eccles, J., & Harold, R. (1996). Family involvement in children's and adolescents' schooling. In A. Booth & J. Dunn (Eds.), *Family-school links: How do they affect educational outcomes?* (pp. 3–34). Mahwah, NJ: Lawrence Erlbaum.

Eckholm, E., & Zezima, K. (2010, March 29). Six teenagers are charged after classmate's suicide. *New York Times.* Retrieved September 25, 2010, from www.nytimes.com/2010/03/30/us/30bully.html

Edinger, E. (1992). *Ego and archetype.* Boston: Shambhala.

Education Commission of the States. (2008). *Collective bargaining agreements.* Retrieved January 8, 2009, from http://mb2.ecs.org/reports/Report.aspx?id=173

Education Trust. (2009). *About Education Trust.* Retrieved January 6, 2010, from www.edtrust .org/dc/tsc

Education Trust. (2010). *Gauging the gaps: A deeper look at student achievement.* Retrieved January 17, 2010, from www.edtrust.org/sites/edtrust.org/files/publications/files/NAEP%20Gap.pdf

Educational Testing Service. (2008). *Praxis™ technical manual.* Princeton, NJ: ETS. Retrieved October 29, 2009, from www1.ets.org/Media/Tests/PRAXIS/pdf/PraxisTechnicalManual.pdf

Edwards, T. (2009, June 3). *Internet use triples in decade, Census Bureau reports.* Press release. Washington, DC: U.S. Census Bureau, U.S. Department of Commerce.

Egger, H. L., Costello, J. E., & Angold, A. (2003). School refusal and psychiatric disorders: A community study. *Journal of the American Academy of Child and Adolescent Psychiatry, 42*(7), 797–807.

Eisen, A. R., & Schaefer, C. E. (2007). *Separation anxiety in children and adolescents: An individualized approach to assessment and treatment.* New York: Guilford Press.

Eisner, E. W. (1985). *The art of educational evaluation.* London: Falmer Press of Taylor & Francis.

El Nokali, N. E., Bachman, H. J., & Votruba-Drzal, E. (2010). Parent involvement and children's academic and social development in elementary school. *Child Development, 81*(3), 988–1005.

Elliott, V. S. (2009, June 29). AMA meeting: Comprehensive sex ed said to have most impact. *Amednews.com.* Retrieved July 3, 2009, from www.ama-assn.org/amednews/2009/06/29/prsh0629.htm

Ellis, A. (1982). Rational-emotive family therapy. In G. M. Gazda (Ed.), *Basic approaches to group psychotherapy and group counseling* (pp. 381–412). Springfield, IL: Charles C Thomas.

Ellis, A. (1985). *Overcoming resistance: Rational-emotive therapy with difficult clients.* New York: Springer.

Ellis, A. (2001a). *Feeling better, getting better, staying better: Profound self-help for your emotions.* Atascadero, CA: Impact Publishing.

Ellis, A. (2001b). *Overcoming destructive beliefs, feelings, and behaviors.* New York: Prometheus.

Ellis, A. (2002). *Overcoming resistance: A rational emotive behavior therapy integrated approach* (2nd ed.). New York: Springer.

Ellis, A., & Bernard, E. M. (1983). An overview of rational-emotive approaches to the problems of childhood. In A. Ellis & M. E. Bernard (Eds.), *Rational-emotive approaches to the problems of childhood* (pp. 1–43). New York: Plenum.

Elman, N. M., & Kennedy-Moore, E. (2003). *The unwritten rules of friendship: Simple strategies to help your child make friends.* London: Little, Brown.

Emerson, A. (2009, June 10). Officials hope anonymous online reports will reduce bullying. *Tampa Tribune.* Retrieved June 15, 2009, from www2.tbo.com/content/2009/jun/10/100022/na-school-board-confronts-bullying/

Engelhard, G., Jr., Zhang, B., & Walker, C. M. (2005). Review of the Wide Range Achievement Test-Expanded ed. Individually Administered. From R. A. Spies & B. S. Plake (Eds.), *The 16th mental measurements yearbook*. Retrieved July 2, 2005, from www.unl.edu/buros/

Engle, T. L. (1945). *Psychology: Principles and applications.* Yonkers-on-Hudson, NY: World Book.

Englund, M. M., Luckner, A. E., Whaley, G. J. L., & Egeland, B. (2004). Children's achievement in early elementary school: Longitudinal effects of parental involvement, expectations, and quality of assistance. *Journal of Educational Psychology, 96*(4), 723–730.

Eppler, C., Olsen, J. A., & Hidano, L. (2009, June). Using stories in elementary counseling: Brief, narrative techniques. *Professional School Counseling.* Retrieved July 10, 2010, from http://findarticles.com/p/articles/mi_m0KOC/is_5_12/ai_n32149153

Epstein, J. L., Coates, L., Salinas, K. C., Sanders, M. G., & Simon, B. S. (1997). *School, family, and community partnerships: Your handbook for action.* Thousand Oaks, CA: Corwin.

Epstein, J. L., Sanders, M. G., Salinas, C., Jansorn, N. R., & Voorhis, F. L. (2002). *School, family, and community partnerships: Your handbook for action* (2nd ed.). Thousand Oaks, CA: Corwin.

Epstein, J. L., & Sheldon, S. B. (2006). Moving forward: Ideas for research on school, family, and community partnerships. In C. F. Conrad & R. Stein (Eds.), *SAGE handbook for research in education: Engaging ideas and enriching inquiry* (pp. 117–138). Thousand Oaks, CA: Sage.

Erford, B. T., McKechnie, J. A., & Moore-Thomas, C. (2004). Program assessment and evaluation. In B. T. Erford (Ed.), *Professional school counseling: A handbook of theories, programs, and practices* (pp. 303–309). Austin, TX: CAPS Press, an imprint of PRO-ED.

Erikson, E. H. (1962). *Young man Luther: A study in psychoanalysis and history.* New York: W. W. Norton.

Erikson, E. H. (1963). *Childhood and society* (2nd ed.). New York: W. W. Norton.

Erikson, E. H. (1968). *Identity: Youth and crisis.* New York: W. W. Norton.

Erikson, E. H. (1980). *Identity and the life cycle.* New York: W. W. Norton.

Espenshade, T. J., & Chung, C. Y. (2005). The opportunity cost of admission preferences at elite universities. *Social Science Quarterly, 86*(2), 293–305.

Evans, G. W., & English, K. (2002). The environment of poverty: Multiple stressors exposure, psychophysiological stress, and socioemotional adjustment. *Child Development, 73*(4), 1238–1248.

Evans, K. M., & George, R. (2008). African Americans. In G. McAuliffe (Ed.), *Culturally alert counseling: A comprehensive introduction* (pp. 146–187). Thousand Oaks, CA: Sage.

Evers, W. M., & Walberg, H. J. (Eds.). (2004). *Testing student learning: Evaluating teaching effectiveness.* Palo Alto, CA: Hoover Institution Press.

Ewing, D. B. (1975). Direct from Minnesota—E. G. Williamson. *Personnel and Guidance Journal, 54*(2), 77–87.

Eyben, E. (1993). *Restless youth in ancient Rome* (2nd ed.). New York: Routledge.

Fagan, J. (1996). The comparative advantage of juvenile versus criminal court sanctions on recidivism among adolescent felony offenders. *Law and Policy, 18*(1 & 2), 77–115.

Falco, L. D. (2010). Multicultural issues in counseling. *Counseling Today, 52*(9), 20–21.

Fallon, M. K. (2004). Adlerian therapeutic techniques for professional school counselors. In B. T. Erford (Ed.), *Professional school counseling: A handbook of theories, programs, and practices* (pp. 113–122). Austin, TX: CAPS Press, an imprint of PRO-ED.

Fan, J., Gehl, D., Hsie, L., Shen, N., Lindblad-Toc, K., Laviolette, J., et al. (2002). Assessing DNA sequence variations in human ESTs in a phylogenetic context using high-density oligonucleotide arrays. *Genomics, 80*(3), 351–360.

Feinberg, T., Nuijens, K. L., & Canter, A. (2005). *Workload vs. caseload: There's more to school psychology than numbers.* NASP Communiqué Vol. 33, no. 6. Retrieved April 16, 2009, from www.nasponline.org/publications/cq/cq336workload.aspx

Feingold, B. (1974). *Why your child is hyperactive.* New York: Random House.

Feldman, D. C. (2002). Stability in the midst of change: A developmental perspective on the study of careers. In D. C. Feldman (Ed.), *Work careers: A developmental perspective* (pp. 3–26). San Francisco: Jossey-Bass.

Feller, B. (2006, May 9). Rising number of schools face penalties. *Boston Globe*. Retrieved May 11, 2006, from www.boston.com

Ferrance, E. (2000). Action research. *Themes in Education*. Providence, RI: LAB, of the Education Alliance at Brown University. Retrieved November 19, 2009, from www.alliance.brown.edu/pubs/themes_ed/act_research.pdf

Ferriss, S. (2009, April 15). New report on California's illegal immigrants finds population of young families. *Sacramento Bee*. Retrieved June 19, 2009, from www.sacbee.com/capitolandcalifornia/story/1781007.html

Field, J. E., Kolbert, J. B., Crothers, L. M., & Hughes, T. L. (2009). *Understanding girl bullying and what to do about it: Strategies to help heal the divide*. Thousand Oaks, CA: Corwin.

Finder, A. (2006, March 5). Schools avoid class ranking, vexing colleges. *New York Times*. Retrieved March 5, 2006, from www.nytimes.com

Finder, A. (2006, May 20). Admissions officials lament practice of signing on with more than one college. *New York Times*. Retrieved September 27, 2010, from www.nytimes.com/2006/05/20/us/20deposit.html

Finer, L. B., & Henshaw, S. K. (2006). Disparities in rates of unintended pregnancy in the United States, 1994 and 2001. *Perspectives on Sexual and Reproductive Health, 38*(2), 90–96.

Finkelhor, D., Turner, H., Ormrod, R., & Hamby, S. L. (2010). Trends in childhood violence and abuse exposure: Evidence from two national surveys. *Archives of Pediatrics and Adolescent Medicine, 164*(3), 238–242.

Finkelstein, D. (2009, May). *A closer look at the principal-counselor relationship: A survey of principals and counselors*. Retrieved September 8, 2010, from http://professionals.collegeboard.com/profdownload/a-closer-look.pdf

Finn, C. E., Jr. (1991). *We must take charge: Our schools and our future*. New York: Free Press.

Fisher, A. (2008). New football fields: Replacing grass with artificial turf to cost Collier schools over $6M. *Naples Daily News*. Retrieved November 8, 2009, from www.naplesnews.com/news/2008/aug/09/new-football-fields-replacing-grass-artificial-tur/

Fishman, S. (2008). *Addiction v. dependence on pain medications*. Newsletter, Pain Management Center. Retrieved September 26, 2009, from http://health.discovery.com/centers/pain/medicine/med_addict.html

Fleischman, H. L., & Williams, L. (1996). *An introduction to program evaluation for classroom teachers*. Arlington, VA: Development Associates. Retrieved November 16, 2009, from http://teacherpathfinder.org/School/Assess/assessmt.html

Florida Association of School Psychologists. (2005). *Position statement on Florida's third grade retention mandate*. Tallahassee, FL: Author.

Florida teacher allegedly lets kindergarteners kick autistic boy out of class in *Survivor*-like vote. (2008, May 28). *Fox News*. Retrieved June 19, 2009, from www.foxnews.com/story/0,2933,358956,00.html

Forrest, K. Y., Zychowski, A. K., Stuhldreher, W. L., & Ryan, W. J. (2000). Weapon-carrying in school: Prevalence and association with other violent behaviors. *American Journal of Health Studies, 16*(3), 133–141.

Forster, G. (2006, March 10). The embarrassing good news on college access. Opinion. *Chronicle of Higher Education*. Retrieved July 10, 2009, from http//chronicle.com/free/v52/i27/27b05001.htm

Forte, I., & Schurr, S. (1994). *Interdisciplinary units and projects for thematic instruction*. Nashville: Incentive Publications.

Forte, I., & Schurr, S. (2002). *The definitive middle school guide: A handbook for success* (rev. ed.). Nashville: Incentive Publications.

Fox, C., & Hawton, K. (2004). *Deliberate self-harm in adolescence.* Philadelphia: Jessica Kingsley.

Fox, N. A., Steinberg, L., Kagan, J., Snidman, N., Towsley, S., & Kahn, V. (2007). *Preservation of two infant temperaments into adolescence.* Monographs of the Society of Child Development. Hoboken, NJ: Wiley-Blackwell.

Frankenberg, E. (2006). *The segregation of American teachers.* Cambridge, MA: Harvard University, The Civil Rights Project.

Freedle, R. O. (2002). Correcting the SAT's ethnic and social-class bias: A method for reestimating SAT scores. *Harvard Educational Review, 72*(3), 1–43. Retrieved June 21, 2005, from http://gseweb.harvard.edu/hepg/freedle.html

Freedle, R. O., & Kostin, I. (1997). Predicting Black and White differential functioning in verbal analogy performance. *Intelligence, 24,* 417–444.

Freedman, E. B. (2002). *No turning back: The history of feminism and the future of women.* New York: Ballantine Books, a division of Random House.

Freud, S. (1955). Analysis of a phobia in a five-year-old. J. Strachy, trans. In A. Freud (Ed.), *Standard edition of the complete works of Sigmund Freud* (Vol. 10, pp. 1–150). London: Hogarth Press. (Original work published 1909)

Freud, S. (1990) *The ego and the id.* J. Riviere, trans. New York: W. W. Norton. (Original work published 1923)

Friedman, L. J. (2000). *Identity's architect: A biography of Erik H. Erikson.* Cambridge, MA: Harvard University Press.

Friedman, R., & James, J. W. (2008). The myth of the stages of dying, death and grief. *Skeptic, 14*(2), 37–41.

Friesen, G. (Producer), & Hughes, J. (Director). (1985). *The breakfast club.* Motion picture. U.S. distributor: Universal Pictures.

Fritz, H. E. (1963). *The movement for Indian assimilation, 1860–1890.* Philadelphia: University of Pennsylvania Press.

Funke, L. (1920). The Negro in education. *Journal of Negro History, 5*(1), 3–15.

Gaffney, J. S., & Zaimi, E. (2003, November 14). *Grade retention and special education: A call for a transparent system of accountability.* Paper presented at the Conference of the Teacher Education Division, Biloxi, MS. Retrieved May 27, 2008, from http://faculty.ed.uiuc.edu/gaffneyj/RetentionSpecialEd.pdf

Gage, N. L. (Ed.). (1967). *Handbook of research on teaching. A project of the American Educational Research Association.* Chicago: Rand McNally.

Galassi, J. P., Griffin, D., & Akos, P. (2008). Strengths-based school counseling and the ASCA National Model. *Professional School Counseling, 12,* 176–182.

Galley, M. (2002, May 22). Seattle student survey's race questions stir controversy. *Education Week, 21*(34), p. 3.

Gallo, E., Gallo, J. J., & Gallo, K. J. (2002). *Silver spoon kids: How successful parents raise responsible children.* Columbus, OH: McGraw-Hill.

Galton, F. (1886). Regression toward mediocrity in hereditary stature. *Journal of the Royal Anthropological Institute of Great Britain and Ireland, 15,* 246–263. Retrieved November 17, 2009, from www.jestor.org/pss/2841583

Gándara, P. (2010). The Latino education crisis. *Educational Leadership, 67*(5), 24–30.

Gardner, H. (1999). *Intelligence reframed: Multiple intelligence for the 21st century.* New York: Basic Books.

Gardner, R. A. (1971). *Therapeutic communication with children: The mutual storytelling technique.* New York: Science House.

Garner, A. (2005). *Families like mine: Children of gay parents tell it like it is.* New York: Harper Paperbacks.

Gasser, C. E., Borgen, F. H., & Larson, L. M. (2007). Concurrent validity of the 2005 Strong Interest Inventory: An examination of gender and major field of study. *Journal of Career Assessment, 15*(1), 1–21.

Gay, M. (2008, November 9). H.I.V. scare unnerves a St. Louis high school. *New York Times.* Retrieved November 11, 2008, from www.nytimes.com/2008/11/09/us/09hiv.html

Gee, R. E., Shacter, H. E., Kaufman, E. J., & Long, J. A. (2008). Behind-the-counter status and availability of emergency contraception. *American Journal of Obstetrics & Gynecology, 199*(5), 478.

Gelfand, D. M. (1978). Social withdrawal and negative emotional states: Behavior therapy. In B. B. Wolman (Ed.), *Handbook of treatment of mental disorders in childhood and adolescence* (pp. 330–353). Englewood Cliffs, NJ: Prentice Hall.

Gentile, D. (2009). Pathological video-game use among youth ages 8 to 18: A national study. *Psychological Science, 20*(5), 594–602.

Gentry, M. (2006). No Child Left Behind: Gifted children and school counselors. *Professional School Counseling, 10*(1), 73–81.

Gerig, B. L. (2005). Homosexuality in the ancient near east, beyond Egypt. *Education Week, 28*(33), 10–12. Retrieved June 29, 2009, from http://epistle.us/hbarticles/neareast.html

Germinario, V., Cervalli, J., & Ogden, E. H. (1996). *All children successful: Real answers for helping at-risk elementary students.* Lanham, MD: Scarecrow/Rowman & Littlefield Education.

Gerstein, R. M., & Gerstein, L. (2004). *Education law: An essential guide for attorneys, teachers, administrators, parents and student advocates.* Tucson: Lawyers & Judges Publishing.

Gewertz, C. (2006, March 8). H. S. dropouts say lack of motivation top reason to quit. *Education Week, 25*(26), 1, 14.

Gewertz, C. (2008, November 5). Districts see rising numbers of homeless students. *Education Week, 28*(1), 7.

Gewertz, C. (2009, June 10). Building a culture aimed at college: Urban high schools take on a complex mission. *Education Week.* Retrieved September 25, 2009, from www.edweek.org/ew/articles/2009/06/11/34college.h28.html

Gibbs, N. (2009). Can these parents be saved? *Time, 174*(21), 50–57.

Gibson, D. M. (2004). Consulting with parents and teachers: The role of the professional school counselor. In B. T. Erford (Ed.), *Professional school counseling: A handbook of theories, programs, and practices* (pp. 349–355). Austin, TX: CAPS Press, an imprint of PRO-ED.

Gies, V. (1990). Developing a personal career counseling theory: An overview of the theories of Donald Super and David Tiedman. *Guidance and Counseling, 6*(1), 54–61.

Gilbert, W. S., & Sullivan, A. S. (Knight Commander, Order of Bath). (1885). *The Mikado.* Libretto W. S. Gilbert, Music by Sir A. Sullivan. Retrieved July 27, 2009, from www.imagi-nation.com/moonstruck/albm64.html

Giordano, F. G., & Schwiebert, V. L. (1997). School counselors' perceptions of the usefulness of standardized tests, frequency of their use, and assessment training needs. *School Counselor, 44*(3), 198–205.

Glanville, J. L., & Wildhagen, T. (2007). The measurement of school engagement: Assessing dimensionality and measurement invariance across race and ethnicity. *Educational and Psychological Measurement, 67*(6), 1019–1041.

Glasser, W. (1998). *Choice theory: A new psychology of personal freedom.* New York: Harper Collins.

Glasser, W. (2000). *Counseling with choice theory: The new reality therapy.* New York: Harper Collins.

Glod, M. (2008, July 17). Coping with their parent's war: Multiple deployments compound strain for children. *Washington Post.* Retrieved July 18, 2008, from www.washingtonpost.com/wp-dyn/content/article/2008/07/16/AR2008071602878_pf.html

Glosoff, H. L., & Pate, R. H. Jr. (2002). Privacy and confidentiality in school counseling. Special issue: Legal issues in school counseling. *Professional School Counseling, 6*(1), 20–28.

Glosoff, H. L., & Rockwell, P. J. Jr. (1997). The counseling profession: A historical perspective. In D. Capuzzi & D. R. Gross (Eds.), *Introduction to the counseling profession* (2nd ed., pp. 3–47). Needham Heights, MA: Allyn & Bacon.

Gloster, H. M., & Neil, K. (2006). Skin cancer in skin of color. *Journal of the American Academy of Dermatology, 55*(5), 741–760.

Gold, E., Simon, E., & Brown, C. (2005). A new conception of parent engagement: Community organizing for school reform. In F. W. English (Ed.), *The SAGE handbook of educational leadership* (pp. 237–268). Thousand Oaks, CA: Sage.

Goldenberg, I., & Goldenberg, H. (1996). *Family therapy: An overview* (4th ed.). Pacific Grove, CA: Brooks/Cole.

Goldstein, E. B. (2009). *Encyclopedia of perception.* Thousand Oaks, CA: Sage.

Goldstein, K. (1934/1995). *The organism.* Cambridge, MA: Zone Books, an imprint of MIT Press.

Goleman, D. (1997). *Emotional intelligence: Why it can matter more than IQ.* New York: Bantam Books, an imprint of Random House.

Goleman, D. (2004). *Emotional intelligence, working with EQ.* New York: Bloomsbury.

Goleman, D. (2006, September). The socially intelligent leader. *Educational Leadership, 64*(1), 76–81.

Gonzalez, A., & Wolters, C. A. (2006, December). The relation between perceived parenting practices and achievement motivation in mathematics. *Journal of Research in Childhood Education, 21,* 203–217.

Goode, E. (2000, January 11). A pragmatic man and his no-nonsense therapy. *New York Times.* Retrieved July 29, 2009, from www.schematherapy.com/cognitive/CTNYT2000.htm

Goodnough, G. E., & Lee, V. V. (2004). Group counseling in schools. In B. T. Erford (Ed.), *Professional school counseling: A handbook of theories, programs, and practices* (pp. 173–182). Austin, TX: CAPS Press, an imprint of PRO-ED.

Gootman, E. (2006, October 19). Those preschoolers are looking older. *New York Times,* p. A24.

Gootman, M. (2005). *When a friend dies: A book for teens about grieving and healing.* Minneapolis: Free Spirit Press.

Gormly, K. B. (2010, January 18). Can parents take advocating for kids too far? *Pittsburgh Tribune Review.* Retrieved September 17, 2010, from www.pittsburghlive.com/x/pittsburghtrib/lifestyles/family/s_662804.html

Gottfredson, D. C., & Gottfredson, G. D. (2002). Quality of school-based prevention programs: Results from a national survey. *Journal of Research on Crime and Delinquency, 39*(1), 3–35.

Gottfredson, L., & Lapan, R. T. (1997). Assessing gender based circumscription of occupational aspirations. *Journal of Career Assessment, 5*(4), 419–441.

Governor's Highway Safety Association. (2010). *Cell phone and texting laws, September 2010.* Retrieved September 28, 2010, from www.ghsa.org/html/stateinfo/laws/cellphone_laws.html

Gray, P. O. (2006). *Psychology* (5th ed.). New York: Worth Publications.

Greenberg, K. E., & Halebian, C. (1996). *Zack's story: Growing up with same-sex parents.* Minneapolis: Lerner Publishing Group.

Greene, A. H., & Melton, G. D. (2007, August 16). Teaching with the test, not to the test. *Education Week, 26*(45), 30.

Greene, J. C. (1987). Stakeholder participation in evaluation design: Is it worth the effort? *Evaluation and Program Planning, 10*(4), 379–394.

Greene, J. P., & Winters, M. A. (2005, February). *Public high school graduation and college-readiness rates: 1991–2002.* Education working paper no. 8. New York: Manhattan Institute for Policy Research. Retrieved November 5, 2009, from www.manhattan-institute.org/html/ewp_08.htm

Greene, J., & Winters, M. A. (2007). Revisiting grade retention: An evaluation of Florida's test-based promotion policy. *Education Finance and Policy, 2*(4), 319–340.

Greive, B. T. (2006). *Friends to the end for kids: The true value of friendship.* Riverside, NJ: Andrews McMeel.

Grier, W. H., & Cobbs, P. M. (1968). *Black rage.* New York: Basic Books.

Grohol, J. M. (2009, June 29). 1 in 7 teens think they'll die young. *Psych Central News.* Retrieved September 24, 2009, from http://psychcentral.com/news/2009/06/29/1-in-7-teens-think-theyll-die-young/6804.html

Grossman, K. N. (2006, July 26). Law opens free preschool to middleclass. *Chicago Sun-Times.* Retrieved July 28, 2006, from wwwsuntimes.com

Grotenhermen, F. (2001). Harm reduction associated with inhalation and oral administration of cannabis and THC. *Journal of Cannabis Therapeutics, 1*(3 & 4), 133–152.

Gruman, D. H., Harachi, T. W., Abbott, R. D., Catalano, R. F., & Fleming, C. B. (2008). Longitudinal effects of student mobility on three dimensions of elementary school engagement. *Child Development, 79*(6), 1833–1852.

Guernsey, L. (2009, March 3). Rewards for students under a microscope. *New York Times.* Retrieved July 30, 2009, from www.nytimes.com/2009/03/03/health/03rewa.html

Gurin, P., Dey, E. L., Hurtado, S., & Gurin, G. (2002). Diversity and higher education: Theory and impact on educational outcomes. *Harvard Educational Review, 72*(3). Retrieved April 22, 2005, from http://gseweb.harvard.edu/~hepg/gurin.html

Guskey, T. R. (2007). Multiple sources of evidence: An analysis of stakeholders' perceptions of various indicators of student learning. *Educational Measurement: Issues and Practice, 26*(1), 19–27.

Guttmacher Institute. (2006). *U.S. teenage pregnancy statistics, national and state trends, and trends by race and ethnicity.* Retrieved January 19, 2010, from www.guttmacher.org/pubs/2006/09/12/USTPstats.pdf

Gysbers, N. C. (2001). School guidance and counseling in the 21st century: Remember the past into the future. *Professional School Counseling, 5*(2), 96–105.

Gysbers, N. C. (2006, February). Improving school guidance and counseling practices through effective and sustained state leadership: A response to Miller. *Professional School Counseling.* Retrieved March 31, 2009, from http://findarticles.com/p/articles/mi_m0KOC/is_3_9/ai_n26777962

Haak, W., Brandt, G., de Jong, H. N., Meyer, C., Ganslmeier, R., Heyd, V., et al. (2008, November 17). Ancient DNA, strontiym isotopes, and osteological analysis shed light on social and kinship organization of the later Stone Age. *Proceedings of the National Academy of Sciences of the United States of America, 105*(47), 18,226–18,231.

Hacker, H. K., & Parks, S. (2005, February 16). Some states getting tough on cheating. *Dallas Morning News.* Retrieved February 16, 2005, from www.dallasnews.com

Haertel, E. H. (2006). Reliability. In R. L. Brennan (Ed.), *Educational measurement* (4th ed., pp. 65–110). Westport, CT: American Council on Education/Praeger.

Hafner, K. (2009, May 26). Texting may be taking a toll on teenagers. *New York Times,* pp. 1, 6.

Haft, S., Witt, P. J., Thomas, T. (Producers), & Weir, P. (Director). (1989). *Dead Poets Society.* Motion picture. U.S. distributor: Buena Vista Picture Distribution.

Haidt, J. (2005). *The happiness hypothesis: Finding modern truth in ancient wisdom.* New York: Basic Books.

Hall, G. S. (1904). *Adolescence: Its psychology and its relations to physiology, anthropology, sociology, sex, crime, religion, and education.* New York: D. Appleton.

Halpern, D. F. (2006). Assessing gender gaps in learning and academic achievement. In P. A. Alexander & P. H. Winne (Eds.), *Handbook of educational psychology* (pp. 635–654). London: Taylor & Francis Group, Routledge.

Ham, B. D. (2003). The effects of divorce on the academic achievement of high school seniors. *Journal of Divorce & Remarriage, 38*(3), 167–185.

Hanushek, E. A., & Rivkin, S. G. (2006, October). *School quality and the Black-White achievement gap.* NBER working paper no. W12651. Palo Alto, CA: Stanford University, Hoover Institution. Retrieved February 24, 2007, from http://ssrn.com/abstract=940600

Hardman, M. L., Drew, C. J., & Egan, M. W. (2008). *Human exceptionality: School community, and family.* New York: Houghton Mifflin.

Hareven, T. K. (1987). Historical analysis of the family. In M. B. Sussman & S. K. Steinmetz (Eds.), *Handbook of marriage and the family* (pp. 37–55). New York: Plenum.

Harmon, L. W., Borgen, F. H., Berreth, J. M., King, J. C., Schauer, D., & Ward, C. C. (1996). The skills confidence inventory: A measure of self-efficacy. *Journal of Career Assessment, 4*(4), 457–477.

Harper, C. (2009, June 12). Two professors retake the SAT: Is it a good test? Commentary. *Chronicle of Higher Education,* pp. A30, A31.

Harrington, P. (2007). *The Kuder® career planning system.* Adel, IA: Kuder. Retrieved December 29, 2009, from www.kuder.com/contact-us.html

Harrington, T. F., & O'Shea, A. J. (2005). *The Harrington-O'Shea career decision-making system-revised.* San Antonio, TX: Pearson Assessment.

Harris, G. (2009, September 23). Eye on youths, U.S. bans flavored cigarettes. *New York Times,* pp. A1, A4.

Harris, M. (2009, September 9). Kids sidelined from sports by price to pay: Study. *The Gazette* (Montreal, Québec, Canada). Retrieved December 5, 2009, from www.montrealgazette.com/story_print.html?id=2000813&sponsor

Harrison, S. (2005, June 28). Midyear promotions: Half flunk FCAT again. *Miami Herald.* Retrieved June 29, 2005, from www.miami.com/mld/miamiherald/news/local/

Hartley-Brewer, E. (2009). *Making friends: A guide to understanding and nurturing your child's friendships.* Cambridge, MA: Da Capo Lifelong Books.

Hatch, T. (2004). *The ASCA national model: A framework for school counseling programs,* one vision, one voice for the profession. In B. T. Erford (Ed.), *Professional school counseling: A handbook of theories, programs, and practices* (pp. 235–256). Austin, TX: CAPS Press, an imprint of PRO-ED.

Hattrup, K. (1995). Review of the Differential Aptitude Test, 5th ed. In J. C. Conoley & J. C. Impara (Eds.), *The 12th mental measurements yearbook* (pp. 301–305). Lincoln, NE: Buros Institute of Mental Measurements.

Hauser, R. M., Pager, D. I., Solon, J., & Simmons, S. J. (2008). *Race-ethnicity, social background and grade retention.* CDE working paper 2000–08. Madison: University of Wisconsin, Center for Demography and Ecology.

Havighurst, R. J. (1951). *Developmental tasks and education.* New York: Longmans, Green.

Hayden, S. (2008, October 16). Why is learning English so difficult? *Suite 101.* Retrieved May 20, 2009, from http://esllanguageschools.suite101.com/article.cfm/why_is_learning_english_so_difficult

Healey, J. F. (2010). *Race, ethnicity, gender, and class: The sociology of group conflict and change* (5th ed.). Thousand Oaks, CA: Pine Forge.

Healey, J. M. (2004). *Your child's growing mind: Brain development and learning from birth to adolescence.* New York: Broadway.

Heck, R. H., Larson, T. J., & Marcoulides, G. A. (1990). Instructional leadership and school achievement: Validation of a causal model. *Education Administration Quarterly, 26*(2), 94–125.

Heilbrunn, J. Z. (2007). *Pieces of the truancy jigsaw: A literature review*. Denver: National Center for School Engagement. Retrieved April 20, 2010, from www.schoolengagement.org/TruancypreventionRegistry/Admin/Resources/Resources/PiecesoftheTruancyJigsawALiteratureReview.pdf

Helix School District, R-1. (1997). *Psychological testing of students* (rev. 2000). Retrieved December 21, 2009, from http://policy.osba.org/helix/J/JHDA%20D1.PDF

Henderson, N. (2009). *ADHD—a guide for families*. Washington, DC: American Association of Child and Adolescent Psychiatrists. Retrieved September 9, 2009, from www.aacap.org/cs/adhd_a_guide_for_families/resources

Henderson, S., Hesketh, B., & Tuffin, K. (1988). A test of Guttfredson's theory of circumscription. *Journal of Vocational Behavior, 32*(1), 37–48.

Henley, M. (2003). *Teaching self-control: A curriculum for responsible behavior*. Bloomington, IN: National Educational Services.

Hernández, T., & Seem, S. R. (2004). A safe school climate: A systematic approach and the school counselor. *Professional School Counseling, 7*(4), 256–262.

Herr, E. L. (2009). Career assessment: Perspectives on trends and issues. In E. A. Whitfield, R. W. Feller, & C. Wood (Eds.), *A counselor's guide to career assessment instruments* (5th ed., pp. 13–26). Broken Arrow, OK: National Career Development Association.

Herrmann, D. (1998). *Helen Keller: A life*. Chicago: University of Chicago Press.

Herrnstein, R. J., & Murray, C. (1994). *The bell curve: Intelligence and class structure in American life*. New York: Free Press.

Hess, A. K. (2001). Review of the Conners' Rating Scales, Revised. In B. S. Plake & J. C. Impara (Eds.), *The 14th mental measurements yearbook* (pp. 331–337). Lincoln, NE: Buros Institute of Mental Measurements.

Hess, A. K., & Lanning, K. (2003). Review of Myers-Briggs Type Indicator® Step II, Form Q. In B. S. Plake, J. C. Impara, & R. A. Spies (Eds.), *The 15th mental measurements yearbook* (pp. 611–616). Lincoln, NE: Buros Institute of Mental Measurements.

Hetzner, A. (2010, June 20). Report reveals GED recipients fare little better than dropouts. *Journal Sentinel*. Retrieved June 25, 2010, from www.jsonline.com/news/education/96769349.html

Heubert, J. P. (2002). *High-stakes testing: Opportunities and risks for students of color, English-Language Learners, and students with disabilities*. Wakefield, MA: National Center on Accessing the General Curriculum. Retrieved January 6, 2010, from www.cast.org/publications/ncac/ncac_highstakes.html

Higgins, M., Young, L., Weiner, J., & Wlodarczyk, S. (2009). Leading teams of leaders: What helps team member learning? *Phi Delta Kappan, 91*(4), 41–45.

Hill, N. B., & Chao, R. K. (Eds.). (2009). *Families, schools, and the adolescent: Connecting research, policy, and practice*. New York: Teachers College Press.

Hill, N. B., & Taylor, L. C. (2004). Parental school involvement and children's academic achievement. *Current Directions in Psychological Sciences, 13*(4), 161–164.

Hill, N. B., & Tyson, D. F. (2009). Parental involvement in middle school: A meta-analytic assessment of the strategies that promote achievement. *Developmental Psychology, 45*(3), 740–763.

Hill, N. B., Tyson, D. F., & Bromell, L. (2009). Developmentally appropriate strategies across ethnic and socioeconomic status: Parental involvement during middle school. In N. E. Hill & R. K. Chao (Eds.), *Families, schools, and the adolescent: Connecting research, policy, and practice* (pp. 53–72). New York: Teachers College Press.

Hinduja, S., & Patchin, J. W. (2009). *Bullying beyond the school yard: Preventing and responding to cyberbullying*. Thousand Oaks, CA: Corwin.

Hirschland, D. (2008). *Collaborative intervention in early childhood: Consulting with parents and teachers of 3- to 7-year-olds.* New York: Oxford University Press.

Hoag, C. (2009, August 2). LA tries test to find kids likely to join gangs. *San Francisco Chronicle.* Retrieved August 3, 2009, from www.sfgate.com/cgi-bin/article.cgi?f=/n/a/2009/08/02/national/a114714D26.DTL

Hobbs, T. D. (2009, July 22). Math scores plunge in TASK retest at Lang Middle School in Dallas ISD. *Dallas Morning News.* Retrieved July 23, 2009, from www.dallasnews.com/sharedcontent/dws/news/localnews/stories/DN-DISDbond_11met.ART.State.Edition2.4629e56.html

Hobson, S. M., & Phillips, C. A. (2004). Educational planning: Helping students build lives by choice, not chance. In B. T. Erford (Ed.), *Professional school counseling: A handbook of theories, programs, and practices* (pp. 325–339). Austin, TX: CAPS Press, an imprint of PRO-ED.

Hoffman, J. (2009, September 13). Why can't she walk to school? *New York Times,* pp. ST1, ST14.

Hogan, R., Hogan, J., & Roberts, B. W. (1996). Personality measurement and employment decisions. *American Psychologist, 51*(5), 469–477.

Hohenshil, T. H., & Brown, M. B. (1991). Public school counseling services for prekindergarten children. *Elementary School Guidance and Counseling, 26*(1), 4–11.

Holbrook, R. G., & Wright, R. J. (2004, February). *Non-curricular factors related to success on high-stakes tests.* Paper presented at the annual meeting of the Eastern Educational Research Association, Clearwater, FL.

Holland, J. L. (1985). *Making vocational choices: A theory of vocational personalities and work environments* (2nd ed.). Upper Saddle River, NJ: Allyn & Bacon.

Holland, J. L. (1997). *Making vocational choices: A theory of vocational personalities and work environment* (3rd ed.). Lutz, FL: Psychological Assessment Resources.

Holland, J. L., Shears, M., & Adrian, H. B. (2001). *Self-directed search* (2nd Australian ed.). Camberwell, Melbourne, Australia: Australian Council for Educational Research.

Holstein, J. A., & Gubrium, J. F. (1999). *The self we live by: Narrative identity in a postmodern world.* New York: Oxford University Press.

Home-school enrollment falters; 20 years of growth halts; impact of virtual schools felt. (2005, August 1). *Milwaukee Journal Sentinel.* Retrieved July 31, 2009, from www.redorbit.com/news/education/193546/homeschool_enrollment_falters_20_years_of_growth_halts_impact_of/index.html

Hopkins, G. (2005). School counselors reflect on what makes them effective. *Education World.* Retrieved July 27, 2009, from www.education-world.com/a_curr/curr198.shtml

Horrell, S., Humphries, J., & Voth, H. (1999, June). *Destined for deprivation: Human capital formation and intergenerational poverty in nineteenth-century England.* Barcelona, Spain: Universitat Pompeu Fabre, Faculty of Economic and Business Sciences, Centre for Economic Policy Research. Retrieved August 31, 2009, from http://papers.ssrn.com/s013/papers.cfm?abstract_id=254329

Horvath, W. J. (2004). *Selected factors related to the success of transfer students into a rural school district from grades six through twelve.* Unpublished dissertation, Widener University.

House, R. M., & Sears, S. J. (2002). Preparing school counselors to be leaders and advocates: A critical need in the new millennium. *Theory Into Practice, 41*(3), 154–162.

Howell, J. C. (1998). *Youth gangs: An overview.* Washington, DC: U.S. Department of Justice, Office of Juvenile Justice and Delinquency Prevention. Retrieved September 22, 2009, from www.ncjrs.gov/pdffiles/167249.pdf

Howell, J. C. (2009). *Preventing and reducing juvenile delinquency: A comprehensive framework* (2nd ed.). Thousand Oaks, CA: Sage.

Howey, N., & Samuels, E. (2000). *Out of the ordinary: Essays on growing up with gay, lesbian, and transgender parents.* New York: St. Martin's/Stonewall Inn Editions.

Hu, W. (2008, November 12). School district tries to lure Asian parents. *New York Times*. Retrieved December 11, 2009, from www.nytimes.com/2008/11/12/education/12parents.html

Huang, D.Y.C., Murphy, D. A., & Hser, Y. (2010, August 12). Poster presented during the Annual Meeting of the American Psychological Association, San Diego, CA.

Huffstutter, P. J. (2007, November 26). Girl's suicide after online chats leaves a town in shock. *Boston Globe*. Retrieved May 29, 2009, from www.wired.com/threatlevel/2009/05/defense-government-made-lori-drew-symbol-of-cyberbullying/

Hughes, J. (Producer & Director). (1986). *Ferris Bueller's day off*. Motion picture. U.S. distributor: Paramount Pictures.

Hughes, T. (2008/1857). *Tom Brown's school days* (reissue ed.). New York: Oxford University Press.

Humphrey, J. (2003). *Child development through sports*. New York: Routledge.

Huntsinger, C. S., Jose, P. E., Larson, S. L., Balsink Krieg, D., & Shaligram, C. (2000). Mathematics, vocabulary, and reading development in Chinese American and European American children over the primary school years. *Journal of Educational Psychology, 92*(4), 745–760.

Hurst, T. A. (2003). *High school administrators', teachers, coaches', and activity sponsors' perceptions of school calendars*. Doctoral dissertation, Loyola University, Chicago. (ProQuest No. AAT 3084727).

Hussar, W. J., & Bailey, T. M. (2008). *Projections of education statistics to 2017*. NCES 2008–078. Washington, DC: National Center for Education Statistics.

Hutchinson, E. O. (2000, October 24). Zero tolerance: Fueled by behavior or racism? *Los Angeles Times*. Retrieved October 28, 2009, from www.commondreams.org/views/102400–102.htm

Iceland, J. (2006). *Poverty in America: A handbook* (2nd ed.). Berkeley, CA: University of California Press.

Ihle-Helledy, K., Zytowski, D. G., & Fouad, N. A. (2004). Kuder Career Search: Test-retest reliability and consequential validity. *Journal of Career Assessment, 12*(3), 285–297.

Ingersoll, R. (2004). Revolving doors and leaky buckets. In C. Glickman (Ed.), *Letters to the next presidents: What we can do about the real crisis in public education* (pp. 141–147). New York: Teachers College Press.

Internal Revenue Service. (2009). *Child and dependent care expenses*. Publication 503. Washington, DC: Department of the Treasury. Retrieved January 6, 2010, from www.irs.gov/pub/irs-pdf/p503.pdf

Inwood, R. (1999). *A history of London*. New York: Carroll & Graf Publishers, an imprint of Avalon & Co.

Ioan, J. (2003). Singular scientists. *Journal of the Royal Society of Medicine, 96*(1), 36–39. Retrieved September 10, 2009, from www.pubmedcentral.nih.gov/articlerender.fcgi?artid=539373

Isaacs, M. L. (2003). The duty to warn and protect: Tarasoff and the elementary school teacher. In T. P. Rimley Jr., M. A. Herman, & W. C. Huey (Eds.), *Ethical and legal issues in school counseling* (2nd ed., pp. 111–129). Alexandria, VA: American School Counselor Association.

Jackson, C. K. (2008). Cash for test scores. *Education Next, 8*(4). Retrieved July 9, 2009, from www.hoover.org/publications/ednext/27020009.html

Jackson, D. (2009, March 9). Obama urges education reform. *USA Today*. Retrieved December 12, 2009, from www.usatoday.com/news/washington/2009-03-10-obamaeducation_N.htm

Jacob, S., & Hartshorne, T. S. (2003). *Ethics and law for school psychologists* (4th ed.). Hoboken, NJ: Wiley.

Jacobson, L. (2008a, April 30). Parent's role in schools earns fresh respect. *Education Week, 27*(35), 16.

Jacobson, L. (2008b, October 1). Absences in early grades tied to learning lags. *Education Week, 28*(6), 1, 12.

James, D. D. (2006, March 14). 4th-grader suspended for carrying starter pistol receives amnesty to take FCAT. *South Florida Sun-Sentinel.* Retrieved March 27, 2009, from www.sun-sentinel.com

James, S. H., & DeVaney, S. B. (2003). Preparing to testify: The school counselor as court witness. In T. P. Remley Jr., M. A. Hermann, & W. C. Huey (Eds.), *Ethical and legal issues in school counseling* (2nd ed., pp. 309–319). Alexandria, VA: American School Counselor Association.

Jarc, R., & Fox, V. (2008, November 30). *Josephson Institute's report card on American youth: There's a hole in our moral ozone and it's getting bigger.* Retrieved July 14, 2009, from http://charactercounts.org/programs/reportcard

Jayson, S. (2005, October 18). Teens define sex in new ways. *USA Today.* Retrieved July 2, 2009, from www.usatoday.com/news/health/2005-10-18-teens-sex_x.htm

Jehlen, A. (2007, April). Testing: How the sausage is made. *NEA Today.* Retrieved April 15, 2007, from www.nea.org/neatoday/0704/coverstory1.html

Jemmott, J. B. III, Jemmott, L. S., & Fong, G. T. (2010). Efficacy of a theory-based abstinence-only intervention over 24 months: A randomized controlled trial with young adolescents. *Archives of Pediatrics and Adolescent Medicine, 164*(2), 152–159.

Jenkins, C. L. (2006, October 8). Rules deter poor children from enrolling in Medicaid. *Washington Post.* Retrieved October 26, 2009, from www.washingtonpost.com/wp-dyn/content/article/2006/10/07/AR2006100700843_pf.html

Jenkins, J. A. (2009). Review of the Strong Interest Inventory Assessment Tool. In E. A. Whitfield, R. W. Feller, & C. Wood (Eds.), *A counselor's guide to career assessment instruments* (5th ed., pp. 309–319). Broken Arrow, OK: National Career Development Association.

Jennings, J., & Rentner, D. S. (2006). *Ten big effects of the No Child Left Behind Act on public schools.* Washington, DC: Center on Educational Policy. Retrieved November 9, 2006, from www.cep-dc.org

Jennings, K. (2002). *Always my child: A parent's guide to understanding your gay, lesbian, bisexual, transgender or questioning son or daughter.* New York: Fireside, an imprint of Simon and Schuster.

Jensen, A. R. (1969). How much can we boost IQ and scholastic achievement? *Harvard Educational Review, 39,* 1–123.

Jensen, A. R. (1972a). *Genetics and education.* New York: Harper & Row.

Jensen, A. R. (1972b). Interpretation of heritability. *American Psychologist, 27*(10), 973–975.

Jensen, A. R. (1981). *Straight talk about mental tests.* New York: Free Press.

Jeter, A., & Davis, K. (2009, May 10). Armed and dangerous: The new reality of teen crime. *Virginia-Pilot.* Retrieved July 2, 2009, from hamptonroads.com/2009/05/armed-and-dangerous-new-reality-teen-crime?page=1

Jeynes, W. H. (2007). The relationship between parental involvement and urban secondary school student academic achievement: A meta-analysis. *Urban Education, 42*(1), 82–110.

Jingeleski, J. S. (1996). *The perceived impacts of House Bill 85 on school violence in Delaware public junior and senior high schools.* Unpublished doctoral dissertation, Widener University.

Johnson, D. P. (2006). Historical trends and their impact on the social construction of self among Hispanics and its impact on self-efficacious behaviors in training and careers. *Journal of Hispanic Higher Education, 5*(1), 68–84.

Johnson, J., Rochkind, J., Ott, A. N., & DuPont, S. (2010). *With their whole lives ahead of them: Myths and realities about why so many students fail to finish college.* A Public Agenda report for the Bill & Melinda Gates Foundation. Retrieved April 17, 2010, from www.publicagenda.org/files/pdf/theirwholelivesaheadofthem.pdf

Johnson, K. M. (2003). Review of the Wechsler Individual Achievement Test, 2nd ed. Abbreviated. From B. S. Plake & J. C. Impara (Eds.), *The 15th mental measurements yearbook [Electronic Version]*. Retrieved September 1, 2009, from www.unl.edu/buros

Johnston, D. C. (2007, March 29). Income gap is widening, data shows. *New York Times*. Retrieved October 20, 2009, from www.nytimes.com/2007/03/29/business/29tax.html

Joint Committee on Standards for Educational Evaluation. (2008). *The program evaluation standards* (2nd ed.). Iowa City, IA: Center for Evaluation and Assessment, University of Iowa. Retrieved November 16, 2009, from www.wmich.edu/evalctr/jc/

Joint Committee on Testing Practices. (2005). Code of fair testing practices in education. *Educational Measurement: Issues and Practice, 24*(1), 23–27.

Joireman, J., & Abbott, M. (2004). *Structural equation models assessing relationships among student activities, ethnicity, poverty, parent's education, and academic achievement*. Technical Report No. 6. Seattle: Washington School Research Center. Retrieved August 21, 2005, from www.spu.edu/wsrc/Ethnicity,%20parents%foreward.htm

Jones, J. (2010, April 21). Biden, Duncan, tout Title IX policy change. *Diverse Issues in Higher Education*. Retrieved April 23, 2010, from http://diverseeducation.com/article/13722/biden-duncan-tout-title-ix-policy-change.html

Jones, J. M. (2003). TRIOS: A psychological theory of the African legacy in American culture. *Journal of Social Issues, 59*(1), 217–242.

Jones, L. K. (1994). Frank Parson's contribution to career counseling. *Journal of Career Development, 20*(4), 287–294.

Jordan, J. D. (2010, February 24). Every Central Falls teacher fired, labor outraged. *Providence Journal*. Retrieved April 24, 2010, from www.projo.com/news/content/central_falls_trustees_vote_02–24–10_EOHI83C_v59.3c21342.html

Jowers, K. (2008, June 27). Elmo and friends to visit children at bases. *Navy Times*. Retrieved July 22, 2008, from www.navytimes.com/news/2008/06/military_sesamestreet_tour_062608w/

Judge who refused to marry interracial couple asked to resign. (2009, October 16). *Fox News*. Retrieved October 19, 2009, from www.foxnews.com/printer_friendly_story/0,3566,567842,00.html

Jung, L. A., & Guskey, T. R. (2010). Grading exceptional learners. *Educational Leadership, 67*(5), 31–35.

Juvenile justice in America. (2007, June 12). *New York Times*. Retrieved September 19, 2009, from www.nytimes.com/2007/07/12/opinion/12iht-edjuvenile.1.6629602.html

Kaase, K., & Dulaney, C. (2005, May). The impact of mobility on educational achievement: A review of the literature. E & R Report No. 4.39. *Research Watch*. Wake County Public Schools, NC. Retrieved November 29, 2006, from www.wcpss.net/evaluation-research/reports/2005/0439mobility_review.pdf

Kagan, J. (1989). Temperamental contributions to social behavior. *American Psychologist, 44*(4), 668–674.

Kagan, J., & Herschkowitz, N. (2005). *A young mind in a growing brain*. Mahwah, NJ: Lawrence Erlbaum.

Kagan, J., & Snidman, N. (2009). *The long shadow of temperament*. Cambridge, MA: Bilknap Press/Harvard University Press.

Kahn, B. B. (2000). A model of solution-focused consultation for school counselors. *Professional School Counseling, 3*(4), 248–254.

Kamerman, S. B. (2005). Early childhood education and care in advanced industrial countries: Current policy and program trends. *Phi Delta Kappan, 87*(3), 193–195.

Kaminer, W. (1996). Teen-age Midol junkies. *Slate*. Retrieved October 5, 2009, from www.slate.com/id/2400/

Kane, M. T. (2006). Validation. In R. L. Brennan (Ed.), *Educational measurement* (4th ed., pp. 17–64). Westport, CT: American Council on Education/Praeger.

Kaplan, K. (2010, January 26). Female teachers may pass on math anxiety to girls, study finds. *Los Angeles Times.* Retrieved January 29, 2010, from www.latimes.com/features/health/la-sci-math 26–2010jan26,0,1152085.story?track=rss

Katz, K. (2002). *No biting!* New York: Grosset & Dunlap.

Katz, L. G. (2000). *Academic redshirting and young children.* Champaign, IL: ERIC Clearinghouse on Elementary and Early Childhood Education. Retrieved September 7, 2006, from www.kidsource .com/education/red.shirting.html

Keck, D. J. (2009). *NEA and academe through the years: The higher education roots of NEA, 1857-present.* Washington, DC: National Education Association. Retrieved April 18, 2009, from www2.nea.org/he/roots.html

Keen, C., & Brian, K. (2004, August 12). School test rewards produce growing disparity between rich, poor. *University of Florida News.* Retrieved July 9, 2009, from http://news.ufl.edu/ 2004/08/12/schooltests/

Keith, T. Z., Pottebaum, S. M., & Eberhart, S. (1986). Effects of self-concept and locus of control on academic achievement: A large-sample path analysis. *Journal of Psychological Assessment, 4*(1), 61–72.

Kelderman, E. (2008, October 14). Fresh round of state budget cuts hits higher education. *Chronicle of Higher Education.* Retrieved July 10, 2010, from http://chronicle.com/daily/2008/10/5085n .htm?utm_source=at&utm_medium=en

Keller, M. (2006, July 5). Academic redshirting is getting a mixed report card. *Los Angeles Times,* p. B3.

Kelley, K. N. (2009). Review of the Career Interest Inventory (CII). In E. A. Whitfield, R. W. Feller, & C. Wood (Eds.), *A counselor's guide to career assessment instruments* (5th ed., pp. 127–136). Broken Arrow, OK: National Career Development Association.

Kelly, K. R. (2002). Concurrent validity of the Kuder Career Search Preference Activity scales and career clusters. *Journal of Career Assessment, 10*(1), 127–144.

Kelly, K. R. (2005). Review of the Harrington-O'Shea Career Decision-Making System-Revised. In R. A. Spies & B. S. Plake (Eds.), *The sixteenth mental measurements yearbook* (pp. 434–440). Lincoln, NE: Buros Institute on Mental Measurements.

Kelly, K. R., & Sheehan, E. P. (2003). Review of the Strong Interest Inventory. In B. S. Plake, J. C. Impara, & R. A. Spies (Eds.), *The fifteenth mental measurements yearbook* (pp. 893–899). Lincoln, NE: Buros Institute of Mental Measurements.

Kennedy, W. A. (1965, August). School phobia: Rapid treatment of fifty cases. *Journal of Abnormal Psychology, 70,* 285–289.

Kim, B. S. K., & Park, Y. S. (2008). East and Southeast Asian Americans. In G. McAuliffe (Ed.), *Culturally alert counseling: A comprehensive introduction* (pp. 188–219). Thousand Oaks, CA: Sage.

Kindlon, D. (2001). *Too much of a good thing: Raising children of character in an indulgent age.* New York: Miramax Books.

King, J. E., Walpole, C. E., & Lamon, K. (2007). Surf and turf wars on line: Growing implications of Internet gang violence. *Journal of Adolescent Health, 41*(6: Suppl. 1). Retrieved January 25, 2010, from linkinghub.elsevier.com/retrieve/pii/S1054139X07003667

Kinzie, S. (2005, December 30). Writing your way into college. *Los Angeles Times.* Retrieved January 3, 2006, from www.latimes.com

Kirn, W. (2009). Life, liberty and the pursuit of aptitude. *New York Times Magazine, 158*(54,727), pp. 11–12.

Klass, P. (2010, September 14). When a doctor's note for a student doesn't help. *New York Times*, p. D5.

Klein, A. (2007, February 5). Researchers see college benefits for students who took AP courses. *Education Week, 26*(22), 7.

Kleinmann, E. L. (2001). *A longitudinal analysis of the NELS:88 data: Selected factors predictive of job satisfaction of students with mild orthopedic and learning disabilities.* Unpublished doctoral dissertation, Widener University. (ProQuest No. AAT 3003353).

Klerman, L. V. (1991). The health of poor children: Problems and progress. In A. C. Huston (Ed.), *Children in poverty* (pp. 136–157). New York: Oxford University Press.

Klinkenberg, K., & Spilman, K. (2002). *Edmund G. Williamson papers.* Twin Cities: University of Minnesota, Twin Cities, University Libraries.

Knapp, L., & Knapp, R. R. (1976). *Career ability placement survey.* San Diego, CA: Educational and Industrial Test Service.

Knapp, R. R., Knapp, L., & Michael, W. B. (1977). Stability and concurrent validity of the Career Ability Placement Survey (CAPS) against the DAT and the GATB. *Educational and Psychological Measurement, 37*(4), 1,081–1,085.

Knapp, L., Knapp, R. R., Strnad, L., & Michael, W. B. (1978). Comparative validity of the Career Ability Placement Survey (CAPS) and the General Aptitude Test Battery (GATB) for predicting high school course marks. *Educational and Psychological Measurement, 38*(4), 1,053–1,056.

Knapp-Lee, L. (2000). *COPS-P Examiner's manual.* San Diego, CA: Educational and Industrial Training Service.

Knapp-Lee, L., Knapp, R. R., & Knapp, L. F. (2007). *COPS career guidance program: Career occupational preference system interest inventory (COPS), Career ability placement service (CAPS), Career orientation placement and evaluation survey (COPES).* San Diego, CA: Educational and Industrial Testing Service.

Knight, H. (2005, December 12). Offering incentives boosts attendance and test scores. *San Francisco Chronicle.* Retrieved December 12, 2005, from www.sfgate.com

Knox, M. E., Funk, J., Elliott, R., & Bush, E. G. (2000). Gender differences in adolescents' possible selves. *Youth and Society, 31*(3), 287–309.

Knudsen, H. K. (2009). Adolescent-only substance abuse treatment: Availability and adoption of components of quality. *Journal of Substance Abuse Treatment, 36*(2), 195–204.

Kolen, M. J. (2006). Scaling and norming. In R. L. Brennan (Ed.), *Educational measurement* (4th ed., pp. 155–186). Westport, CT: American Council on Education and Praeger.

Koster, O. (2007, April 20). Found hanged, the bullied 11-year-old boy who even the bus driver called names. *Daily Mail.* Retrieved May 29, 2009, from www.dailymail.co.uk/news/article-449548/Found-hanged-The-bullied-11-year-old-boy-bus-driver-called-names.html

Kottman, T., & Stiles, K. (1997). The mutual storytelling technique: An Adlerian application in child therapy. In J. Carlson & K. S. Slavik (Eds.), *Techniques in Adlerian psychology* (pp. 338–346). London: Taylor & Francis Group.

Kramer, D. (2009, September 7). Fairview Park Black family finds noose, hate note in their yard. *Cleveland.com.* Retrieved October 27, 2009, from ww.blog.cleveland.com/metro//print.html

Kramer, R. (1995). The birth of client-centered therapy: Carl Rogers, Otto Rank, and "the beyond." *Journal of Humanistic Psychology, 35*(4), 54–110.

Kraut, A. M. (1994). *Silent travelers: Germs, genes, and the "immigrant menace."* New York: Basic Books.

Kremelberg, D. (2010). *Practical statistics: A quick and easy guide to SPSS, STATA and other statistical software.* Thousand Oaks, CA: Sage.

Kronholz, J. (2008, June 12). The definition of whiteness continues to shift. *Wall Street Journal,* p. A10.

Krumboltz, J. D. (2009). The happenstance learning theory. *Journal of Career Assessment, 17*(2), 135–154.

Kübler-Ross, E. (1970). *On death and dying.* New York: Macmillan.

Kuder, Inc. (2003). *Kuder® Career Search (KCS), Test Manual.* Adel, IA: Kuder.

Kuder, Inc. (2007). *Kuder Skills Assessment, Manual.* Adel, IA: Kuder.

Kurpius, D. J. (1978). Consultation theory and process: An integrated model. *Personnel and Guidance Journal, 56*(6), 335–338.

Kurpius, D. J., & Fuqua, D. R. (1993). Fundamental issues in defining consultation. *Journal of Counseling and Development, 71*(6), 598–600.

Kurutz, D. R. (2009, January 12). Hard times cut state cyber school enrollments. *Pittsburgh Tribune-Review.* Retrieved July 31, 2009, from www.pittsburghlive.com/x/pittsburghtrib/print_606700.html

Kussin, S. S. (2008). *How to build the master schedule in 10 easy steps.* Thousand Oaks, CA: Corwin.

Kwapil, T. R. (1998). Social anhedonia as a predictor of the development of schizophrenia-spectrum disorders. *Journal of Abnormal Psychology, 107*(4), 558–565.

La Greca, A. M., Prinstein, M. J., & Fetter, M. D. (2001). Adolescent peer crowd affiliation: Linkages with health-risk behaviors and close friendships. *Journal of Pediatric Psychology, 26*(3), 131–143.

Landman, R. (1992). *From normal schools to state colleges: A political, social, and economic history of normal schools in Massachusetts.* Unpublished dissertation, Boston College. (ProQuest No. AAT 19217455). Retrieved January 4, 2010, from http://proquest.umi.com/pqdlink?Ver=1&Exp=01–03–2015&FMT=7&DID=745938621&RQT=309&attempt=1&cfc=1

Landreth, G. L., & Sweeney, D. S. (1997). Child centered play therapy. In K. J. O'Connor & L. D. Braverman (Eds.), *Play therapy theory and practice: A comparative presentation* (pp. 17–45). New York: Wiley.

Langer, G. (2010, January 5). A run at the latest data from ABC's poobah of polling. *Evening News Report,* ABC Television. Retrieved January 6, 2010, from http://blogs.abcnews.com/thenumbers/

Langman, P. (2009). *Why kids kill: Inside the minds of school shooters.* New York: Palgrave Macmillan.

Larsen, P. D., & Lubkin, I. M. (2009). *Chronic illness: Impact and intervention* (7th ed.). Sudbury, MA: Jones & Bartlett.

Laviano, J. (2009). Raising children with special needs is tough: Parent training counseling under the IDEA. *Special Ed Justice* Online journal. Retrieved September 4, 2009, from www.connecticut specialeducationlawyer.com/tips-for-parents/raising-children-with-special-needs-is-tough-parent-training-and-counseling-under-the-idea/

Law, J. G. Jr. (2001). Test review of the Scales for Diagnosing Attention-Deficit-Hyperactivity Disorder. From B. S. Plake & J. C. Impara (Eds.), *The 15th mental measurements yearbook.* Electronic version. Retrieved September 1, 2009, from the Buros Institute's *Test Reviews Online* Web site: www.unl.edu/buros

Lawler, P. (1993). A longitudinal study of women's career choices: 25 years later. Pre-convention workshop from the annual meeting of the American Association of University Women. *Gender issues in the classroom and on campus: Focus on the twenty-first century* (pp. 187–192). Washington, D.C.: American Association of University Women.

Lawton, M. (1996). PSAT to add writing test to settle bias case. *Education Week*, p. 9. Retrieved November 3, 2009, from http://192.192.169.250/edu_message/data_image/DG/1996/0025E.PDF

Learning Express (Ed.). (2003). *10 secrets to mastering any high school test*. New York: LearningExpress.

Lebovich, J. (2009, October 18). Burned teen's agony is heard on 911 tapes. *Miami Herald*, pp. 1A, 9A.

Lee, P., Lan, W., & Wang, C. (2008). Helping young children to delay gratification. *Early Childhood Education Journal, 35*(6), 557–564.

Lee, T. (2004, April 15). *Social-constructivism, self-categorization, and racial identity*. Paper presented at the annual meeting of the Midwest Political Science Association, Chicago, IL. Retrieved January 25, 2010, from www.allacademic.com/meta/p82361_Index.html

Legere, E. J., & Conca, L. M. (2010). Response to intervention by a child with a severe reading disability: A case study. *Teaching Exceptional Children, 43*(1), 32–39.

Leinwand, G. (2001). *1927: High tide of the 1920's*. New York: Basic Books.

Lemann, N. (1999). *The big test*. New York: Farrar, Straus & Giroux.

Lenneberg, E. H. (1967). *Biological foundations of language*. New York: Wiley.

Leong, F. T. L., Lee, S., & Chang, D. (2008). Counseling Asian Americans: Client and therapist variables. In P. B. Pedersen, J. G. Draguns, W. J. Lonner, & J. E. Trimble (Eds.), *Counseling across cultures* (6th ed., pp. 113–128). Thousand Oaks, CA: Sage.

Lesisko, L. J., & Wright, R. J. (2010, April 30–May 4). *Stress and the administrator of rural schools being rebuilt*. Paper presented at the annual meeting of the American Educational Research Association, Denver, CO.

Levine, A., Chambers, A., & Ibanga, I. (2008, April 7). Third grader at center of teacher attack plot speaks: Tmanni Adams said she was too frightened to tell administrators about plot. *New York, ABC World News*. Retrieved April 21, 2009, from http://abcnews.go.com/print?id=4602938.

Levine, M. (2006). *The price of privilege: How parental pressure and material advantage are creating a generation of disconnected and unhappy kids*. New York: HarperCollins.

Levitt, S. D., & Dubner, J. S. (2005). *Freakonomics: A rogue economist explores the hidden side of everything*. New York: Harper Perennial.

Lewin, K. (1942). Field theory and learning. In N. B. Henry (Ed.), *The psychology of learning. The 41st yearbook of the National Society for the Study of Education, Part II* (pp. 215–242). New York: National Society for the Study of Education.

Lewin, K. (1948). *Resolving social conflicts: Selected papers on group dynamics* [G. W. Lewin, Ed.]. New York: Harper & Row.

Lewin, T. (2008, June 10). Report takes aim at "model minority" stereotype of Asian-American students. *New York Times*. Retrieved June 12, 2008, from www.nytimes.com/2008/06/10/education/10asians.html

Lewin, T. (2009, June 23). Court affirms reimbursement for special education. *New York Times*. Retrieved August 31, 2009, from www.nytimes.com/2009/06/23/education/23special.html?_r=1&pagewanted=print

Lewin, T. (2010, January 20). Children awake? Then they're probably online. *New York Times*, pp. A1, A3.

Lewis, R. E., & Sieber, C. (1997). Individual counseling: Brief approaches. In D. Capuzzi & D. R. Gross (Eds.), *Introduction to the counseling profession* (2nd ed., pp. 141–165). Needham Heights, MA: Allyn & Bacon.

Lewis, S. D. (2009, June 24). Michigan study: African-American students disciplined disproportionately. *Detroit News*. Retrieved October 28, 2009, from www.truthout.org/062409EDA

Leyser, C. D. (2001). *Anxiety and asceticism from Augustine to Gregory the Great.* New York: Oxford University Press.

Lin, W. V. (2001). *Parenting beliefs regarding young children perceived as having or not having inattention and/or hyperactivity-impulsivity behaviors.* Unpublished doctoral dissertation, University of South Dakota. (ProQuest No. AAT 3007070).

Lipkin, A. (2000). *Understanding homosexuality, changing schools.* Boulder, CO: Westview Press.

Littrell, J. M., Malia, J. A., Nichols, R., Olson, J., Nesselhuf, D., & Crandell, P. (1992). Brief counseling: Helping counselors adopt an innovative counseling approach. *School Counselor, 39*(3), 171–175.

Littrell, J. M., Malia, J. A., & Vanderwood, M. (1995). Single-session brief counseling in a high school. *Journal of Counseling and Development, 73*(4), 451–458.

Locke, J. (2004/1690). *An essay concerning humane understanding* (2nd ed.). Retrieved July 28, 2009, from www.gutenberg.org/etext/10616

Lohman, J. (2000). *Truancy laws.* Report 2000-R-095. OLR Research Report. Retrieved September 16, 2009, from www.cga.ct.gov/2000/rpt/olr/htm/2000-r-0957.htm

Lombardi, K. S. (2005, November 2). Detecting tutor's hand in applicant's essay. *New York Times.* Retrieved November 3, 2005, from www.nytimes.com/2005/11/02/nyregion/02essay.html

Lopez, B., Schwartz, S. J., Prado, G., Campo, A. E., & Pantin, H. (2008). Adolescent neurological development and its implications for adolescent substance use prevention. *Journal of Primary Prevention, 29*(1), 5–35.

Lopiano, D. (2006). Save Title IX: A call to action. *Woman's Sports Foundation.* Retrieved April 23, 2010, from www2.ed.gov/news/pressreleases/2006/10/10242006.html

Lord, F. M. (1952). The relationship of the reliability of multiple-choice to the distribution of item difficulties. *Psychometrika, 17*(2), 181–194.

Losen, D. J., & Skiba, R. (2010). *Suspended education: Urban middle schools in crisis.* White paper. Montgomery, AL: Southern Poverty Law Center. Retrieved August 9, 2010, from www.splcenter .org/sites/default/files/downloads/publication/Suspended_Education.pdf

Loundsbury, J. H. (2009). Deferred but not deterred: A middle school manifesto. *Middle School Journal, 40*(5), 31–36.

Lowenstein, L. (1999). *Creative interventions for troubled children and youth.* Toronto, Ontario, Canada: Champion Press.

Ludwig, T. (2005). *My secret bully.* Berkeley, CA: Tricycle Press, an imprint of 10 Speed Press.

Ludwig, T. (2006). *Just kidding.* Berkeley, CA: Tricycle Press, an imprint of 10 Speed Press.

Lyon, R. L. (1998, April 28). *Overview of reading and literacy initiatives of the Child Development and Behavior branch of the National Institute of Child Health and Human Development, National Institutes of Health.* Report to the House of Representatives, Committee on Labor and Human Resources. Washington, DC. Retrieved July 1, 2005, from www.readbygrade3.com/lyon.htm

Lytle, J. (2010, June 20). School attendance policy. *Naples Daily News,* p. B3.

Maciejewski, P. K., Zhang, B., Block, S. D., & Prigerson, H. G. (2007). An empirical examination of the stages of grief. *Journal of the American Medical Association, 297*(7), 716–723.

MacInnes, G. (2009, May 20). Preschool and early reading: How Obama can learn from New Jersey's expensive effort to narrow the achievement gap. *Education Week, 28*(32), 22–23.

MacPherson, K., & McFeatters, A. (2000, October 1). Child abduction-murders: Why? *Pittsburgh Post Gazette.* Retrieved September 15, 2009, from www.post-gazette.com/headlines/ 20001001killings3.asp

Magee, K., & Gonen, Y. (2009, June 8). Learn-N-Earn plan pays off. *New York Post.* Retrieved July 9, 2009, from www.nypost.com/php/pfriendly/print.php?url=http%3A%2F%2Fwww.nypost.com %2Fseven%2F06082009%2Fnews%2Fregionalnews%2Flearn__earn_plan_pays_off_173099.htm

Magee, M. (2010, August 28). School absenteeism has its costs. *Sign On San Diego*. Retrieved September 3, 2010, from www.signonsandiego.com/news/2010/aug/28/school-absenteeism-has-financial-social-costs/

Mahoney, E. B., & Morris, R. J. (2010, August 12). *Defining and assessing juvenile competency to stand trial: A state by state comparison.* Poster session during the annual meeting of the American Psychological Association, San Diego, CA.

Manis, C. (2004). *Do attendence rates of students correlate to the Standard of Learning Math Test scores in grades 5 and 8?* Research paper. Virginia Commonwealth University. Retrieved July 15, 2009, from www.math.vcu.edu/NSF_Grad_Teaching_Fellows/FinalPapers/CManisFINAL.pdf

Manzo, K. K. (2009, June 17). Administrators confront student "sexting." *Education Week, 28*(35), 8.

Marcia, J. E. (1980). Identity in adolescence. In J. Adelson (Ed.), *Handbook of adolescent psychology.* New York: Wiley.

Margo, R. A., & Finegan, A. (1996). Compulsory schooling legislation and school attendance in turn-of-the-century America: A "natural experiment" approach. *Economics Letters, 3*(1), 103–110.

Margolis, H., & Free, J. (2001). The consultant's corner: Computerized IEP programs: A guide for educational consultants. *Journal of Educational and Psychological Consultation, 12*(2), 171–178.

Marklein, M. B. (2009). Many who get early admission to college regret choice. *USA Today.* Retrieved July 17, 2009, from www.usatoday.com/news/education/2009–02–12-early-admissions_N.htm

Markow, D., & Martin, S. (2005). *The MetLife survey of the American teacher: Transitions and the role of supportive relationships.* New York: Harris Interactive.

Martinson, F. M. (2002). *The quality of adolescent sexual experiences.* St. Peter, MN: Books Reborn. (First published in 1974). Retrieved June 26, 2009, from www.ipce.info/booksreborn/martinson/adolescent/Adolescent.pdf

Marx, G. (1995). *Groucho and me.* New York: Da Capo Press. (Originally published in 1959)

Mash, E. J., & Dozois, D.J.A. (1996). Child psychopathology: A developmental systems perspective. In E. J. Mash & R. A. Barkley (Eds.), *Child psychopathology* (pp. 3–62). New York: Guilford.

Maslow, A. H. (1943). A theory of human motivation. *Psychological Review, 50,* 370–396.

Maslow, A. (1968). *Toward a psychology of being* (2nd ed.). New York: D. Van Nostrand.

Massachusetts Department of Education. (2005, April). *Grade retention in Massachusetts public schools: 2003–2004.* Malden, MA: Massachusetts Department of Education.

Mathews, J. (2005, June 14). Where some give credit, others say it's not due. *Washington Post,* p. A14.

Matthews, M. S. (2008). What about gifted students who drop out? *Duke Gifted Letter, 8*(2). Retrieved September 10. 2009, from www.dukegiftedletter.com/articles/v018n02_ee.html

Matus, R. (2007, June 3). FCAT tests us; So what? *St. Petersburg Times.* Retrieved June 2, 2008, from www.sptimes.com

Matus, R., & Winchester, D. (2009, March 13). Disrespect can pass as racism in class. *Tampa Bay Times.* Retrieved March 17, 2009, from www.tampabay.com/news/article983906.ece

Maxwell, L. A. (2007, February 14). The other gap. *Education Week, 26*(23), 25, 27–29.

Maxwell, L. A., & Emanuel, H. (2007, February 14). The other "gap." Perspective. *Chronicle of Higher Education, 26*(23), pp. 25, 27–29.

May, K. E. (2009). *Work in the 21st century: Career development.* Washington, DC: Society for Industrial and Organizational Psychology. Retrieved January 4, 2010, from www.siop.org/tip/backissues/tipapr97/may.aspx

Mayes, L. C., & Suchman, N. E. (2006). Developmental pathways to substance abuse. In D. Cicchetti & D. J. Cohen (Eds.), *Developmental psychopathology: Vol. 3, Risk, disorder, and adaptation* (pp. 599–619). New York: Wiley.

McAuliffe, G., Kim, B. S. K., & Park, Y. S. (2008). Ethnicity. In G. McAuliffe (Ed.), *Culturally alert counseling: A comprehensive introduction* (pp. 84–104). Thousand Oaks, CA: Sage.

McCann, D., Barrett, A., Cooper, A., Crumpler, D., Dalen, L., Grimshaw, K., et al. (2007, November). Food additives and hyperactive behaviour in 3-year-old and 8/9 year-old children in the community: A randomized, double-blind, placebo-controlled trial. *Lancet, 3*, 1560–1567. Retrieved September 7, 2009, from www.ncbi.nlm.nih.gov/pubmed/17825405

McCarthy, C., Kerne, V., Calfa, N. A., Lambert, R. G., & Guzman, M. (2010). An exploration of school counselor's demands and resources: Relationships to stress, biographic and caseload characteristics. *Professional School Counseling, 13*(3), 146–158.

McCarthy, M. M., & Sorenson, G. P. (1993). School counselors and consultants: Legal duties and liabilities. *Journal of Counseling & Development, 72*(2), 159–167.

McConaghy, N., Hadzi-Pavlovic, D., Stevens, C., Manicavasagar, V., Buhrich, N., & Vollmer-Conna, U. (2006). Fraternal birth order and ratio of heterosexual/homosexual feelings in women and men. *Journal of Homosexuality, 51*(4), 161–174.

McDaniels, C., & Gysbers, N. C. (1992). *Counseling for career development: Theories, resources, and practice.* San Francisco: Jossey-Bass.

McDougall, B. (2007). *My child is gay: How parents react when they hear the news* (2nd ed.). Bel Air, CA: Allen & Unwin.

McGraw, J. (2008). *Jay McGraw's life strategies for dealing with bullies.* New York: Aladdin, an imprint of Simon & Schuster.

McLaughlin, B., Blanchard, A. G., & Osanai, Y. (1995). *Assessing language development in bilingual preschool children.* Program Information Guide Series, No. 22. Washington, DC: George Washington University, School of Education and Human Development, National Clearinghouse for Bilingual Education.

McLean, M., Worley, M., & Bailey, D. B. (2003). *Assessing infants and preschoolers with special needs* (3rd ed.). Upper Saddle River, NJ: Prentice Hall.

McLoyd, V. C., & Wilson, L. (1991). The strain of living poor: Parenting, social support, and mental health. In A. C. Huston (Ed.), *Children in poverty* (pp. 105–135). New York: Oxford University Press.

McMahon, H. G., Mason, E. C. M., & Paisley, P. O. (2009). School counselor educators as educational leaders promoting systemic change. *Professional School Counseling, 13*(2), 116–124.

McNeil, D. G. Jr. (2008, December 10). Report sounds alarm on child accidents. *New York Times,* p. A8.

McVey-Noble, M., Khemlani-Patel, S., & Neziroglu, F. A. (2006). *When your child is cutting: A parents' guide to helping children overcome self-injury.* Oakland, CA: New Harbinger.

Mechelli, A., Crinion, J. T., Noppeney, U., O'Doherty, J., Ashburner, J., Frackowiak, R. S., & Price, C. J. (2004, October 14). Neurolinguistics: Structural plasticity in the bilingual brain. *Nature, 431*(7010), 757.

Medina, J. (2008, October 21). Report cites chronic absenteeism in city schools. *New York Times.* Retrieved October 23, 2008, from www.nytimes.com/2008/10/21/nyregion/21attend.html

Melloy, K. (2009, April). Another 11-year-old commits suicide: Anti-gay taunts cited. *EDGE, Boston.* Retrieved May 28, 2009, from www.edgeboston.com/index.php?ch=news&sc=&sc2=news&sc3=&id=90214

Melton, G. E. (1984). The junior high school: Successes and failures. In J. H. Lounsbury (Ed.), *Perspectives: Middle school education, 1964–1984* (pp. 5–13). Columbus, OH: National Middle School.

Mendler, A. N. (1997). *Power struggles: Successful techniques for educators.* Rochester, NY: Discipline Associates.

Mendler, A. N. (2006). *Handling difficult parents: Successful strategies for educators.* Rochester, NY: Discipline Associates.

Merrill, J. C., Kleber, H. D., Schwartz, M., Liu, H., & Lewis, S. R. (1999). Cigarettes, alcohol, marijuana, and other risk behaviors. *Drug and Alcohol Dependence, 56*(3), 205–212.

Michigan Department of Education. (2008). *Helping children learn to read.* Retrieved August 4, 2008, from www.michigan.gov/printerFriendly/0,1687,7-140-5233-23207—,00.html

Middle States Association. (2009). *Candidacy for accreditation, Policy statement.* Philadelphia, PA: Middle States Association of Colleges and Schools. Retrieved April 28, 2010, from www.css-msa.org/pdfs/policies/Candidacy.pdf

Mikami, A. Y. (2010, September). *Social context influences on children's peer relationships.* Psychological Science Agenda. Washington, DC: American Psychological Association. Retrieved September 23, 2010, from www.apa.org/science/about/psa/2010/09/social-context.aspx

Millard, E. (2006). Up for debate. *District Administrator, 42*(9), 60–61.

Miller, D. (1995). Review of the Kaufman Brief Intelligence Test. In J. C. Conoley & J. C. Impara (Eds.), *The 12th mental measurements yearbook* (pp. 533–536). Lincoln, NE: Buros Institute of Mental Measurements.

Miller, J., & Desberg, P. (2009). *Understanding and engaging adolescents.* Thousand Oaks, CA: Corwin.

Miller, P. Y., & Simon, W. (1980). The development of sexuality in adolescence. In J. Adelson (Ed.), *Handbook of adolescent psychology* (pp. 383–407). New York: Wiley.

Mills, J. C. (1993). *Gentle Willow: A story for children about dying.* Washington, DC: Magination Press/American Psychological Association.

Mills, K. I. (2009). Race relations in a new age. *Monitor on Psychology, 40*(4), 28–30.

Minuchin, S. (1974). *Families and family therapy.* Cambridge, MA: Harvard University Press.

Minuchin, S., Lee, W., & Simon, G. N. (2006). *Mastering family therapy: Journeys of growth and transformation.* Hoboken, NJ: Wiley.

Monk, G., Winslade, J., & Sinclair, S. (2008). *New horizons in multicultural counseling.* Thousand Oaks, CA: Sage.

Moore, R. (2008, May 21). The maze to the college doorstep. *Teacher.* Retrieved July 10, 2009, from www.teachermagazine.org/login.html?source=www.teachermagazine.org/tm/articles/2008/05/21/34tln_moore.h19.html&destination=www.teachermagazine.org/tm/articles/2008/05/21/34tln_moore.h19.html&levelId=1000

Morkides, C. (2009). Measuring counselor success. *Counseling Today, 52*(1), 38–41.

Morrison, B. (2002). *Bullying and victimization in schools: A restorative justice approach.* Trends and Issues in Crime and Criminal Justice Series, no. 219. Canberra, Australia: Australian Institute of Criminology. Retrieved June 3, 2009, from www.aic.gov.au/publications/tandi/ti219.pdf

Morrissey, D., & Rotunda, R. (2006). *School counselor certification in New York State: Answering the questions of the day.* Report of the Ad Hoc Committee on Certification and Preparation of the New York State School Counselor Association's Governing Board. Retrieved April 1, 2009, from www.nyssca.org/Linked%20Documents/School%20Counselor%20Certification%20in%20NYS-answering%20the%20Questions%20of%20the%20Day.pdf

Morrow, E. M., Yoo, S. Y., Flavell, S. W., Kim, T. K., Lin, Y., Hill, R. S., et al. (2008). Identifying autism loci and genes by tracing recent shared ancestry. *Science, 321*(5,886), 218–223.

Moss, P., Tardif, D. D., & Gels, A. I. (2007). *Our friendship rules*. Gardiner, ME: Tilbury House.

Mullis, F. (2002). How was your day? Using questions about the family's daily routine. In R. E. Watts (Ed.), *Techniques in marriage and family counseling Vol. 2* (pp. 133–138). Alexandria, VA: American Counseling Association.

Mullis, F., & Edwards, D. (2001). Counseling with parents: Applying family systems concepts and techniques. *Professional School Counseling, 5*(2), 116–124.

Mundy, M. (1998). *Sad isn't bad: A good-grief guidebook for kids dealing with loss*. St. Meinrad, IN: Abbey Press.

Munsey, C. (2010). The kids aren't all right. *Monitor on Psychology, 41*(1), 23–25.

Musu, L. E., Chang, P., Werner, S., & Karabenick, S. A. (2008, March 23–27). *Family involvement and student motivation: The role of student perceptions, gender, and racial differences*. Paper presented at the annual meeting of the American Educational Research Association, New York.

Nasir, N. S., McLaughlin, M. W., & Jones, A. (2009). What does it mean to be African American? Constructions of race and academic identity in an urban public high school. *American Educational Research Journal, 46*(1), 73–114.

National Academy of Sciences. (2009). *Tracing similarities and differences in our DNA*. Retrieved October 19, 2009, from www.koshland-science-museum.org/exhibitdna/intr003.jsp

National Assessment of Educational Progress (NAEP). (2004). *The nation's report card*. Washington, DC: National Center for Education Statistics. Retrieved July 7, 2005, from http://nces.ed.gov/nationsreportcard

National Assessment of Educational Progress (NAEP). (2007a). *Mapping 2005 state proficiency standards onto the NAEP scales*. Washington, DC: National Center for Education Statistics. Retrieved November 8, 2009, from http://nces.ed.gov/nationsreportcard/pubs/studies/2007482.asp

National Assessment of Educational Progress (NAEP). (2007b). *NAEP data explorer, 2007 Reading Test, Grade 7*. Washington, DC: National Center for Education Statistics. Retrieved October 20, 2009, from http://nationsreportcard.gov/researchers.asp

National Assessment of Educational Progress (NAEP). (2009). *NAEP trends in academic progress*. NAEP 2009–479. Washington, DC: National Center for Education Statistics. Retrieved November 2, 2009, from nces.ed.gov/nationsreportcard/pdf/main2008/2009479.pdf

National Association for Children of Alcoholics (NACA). (2005). *Children of addicted parents: Important facts*. Rockville, MD: Hope Networks, National Association for Children of Alcoholics. Retrieved September 29, 2009, from www.hopenetworks.org/addiction/Children%200f%20Addicts.htm

National Association for the Education of Homeless Children and Youth. (2008). *A critical moment: Child and youth homelessness in our nation's schools*. Retrieved September 29, 2010, from www.naehcy.org/criticalmoment.htm

National Association for the Education of Young Children (NAEYC). (2005). *Where we stand on the screening and assessment of young English-language learners*. Retrieved February 8, 2008, from www.naeyc.org/positionstatements

National Association for Gifted Children (NAGC). (2008). *The role of assessment in the identification of gifted children*. Position paper. Washington, DC: National Association for Gifted Children. Retrieved September 10, 2009, from www.nagc.org/uploadedFiles/assessment%20pos%20paper%20final.pdf

National Association for Research and Therapy of Homosexuals (NARTH). (2008). *Gay parenting does affect children differently, study finds: Authors believe gay parents have some advantages*. Retrieved June 30, 2009, from www.narth.com/docs/does.html

National Association of School Psychologists (NASP). (2006). *Position statement on corporal punishment in schools.* Retrieved June 15, 2009, from www.nasponline.org/about_nasp/pospaper_corppunish.aspx

National Career Development Association. (2007). *National career development guidelines.* Broken Arrow, OK: National Career Development Association.

National Center for Education Statistics (NCES). (2004). *Third International Mathematics and Science Study (TIMSS).* Washington, DC: U.S. Department of Education.

National Center for Education Statistics (NCES). (2007). *Public secondary schools, by grade span, average school size, and state or jurisdiction: 2005–2006.* Digest of Educational Statistics, Table 96. Retrieved July 6, 2009, from http://nces.ed.gov/programs/digest/d07/tables/dt07_096.asp

National Center for Education Statistics (NCES). (2008). *Digest of educational statistics: 200 Appendix A.5.* American College Testing Program. Retrieved November 2, 2009, from http://nces.ed.gov/programs/digest/d08/app_a5_1.asp

National Center for Education Statistics (NCES). (2009). *Numbers and types of public elementary and secondary schools from the common core of data: 2006–2007,* NCES Report No. 2009–304. Retrieved June 22, 2009, from http://nces.ed.gov/pubs2009/pesschools07/tables/table_04.asp

National Center on Family Homelessness. (2009). *America's youngest outcasts: State report card on child homelessness.* Newton, MA: National Center on Family Homelessness, Author. Retrieved May 30, 2009, from www.homelesschildrenamerica.org/

National Commission on Excellence in Education. (1983). *A nation at risk: The imperative for educational reform.* Washington, DC: U.S. Government Printing Office.

National Institute on Alcohol Abuse and Alcoholism, U.S. Department of Health and Human Services. (2001). *Alcoholism: Getting the facts.* NIH Publication No. 96–4153, Brochure. Washington, DC: U.S. Government Printing Office.

National Institute on Alcohol Abuse and Alcoholism, U.S. Department of Health and Human Services. (2003). *Alcohol alert: The genetics of alcoholism.* Retrieved September 25, 2009, from http://pubs.niaaa.nih.gov/publications/aa60.htm

National Institute on Drug Abuse (NIDA). (2005). *Selected prescription drugs with potential for abuse.* Washington, DC: U.S. Department of Health and Human Services.

National Institute of Justice. (1997). *Guns in America: National survey on ownership and use of firearms.* Washington, DC: National Institute of Justice, U.S. Department of Justice. Retrieved September 21, 2009, from www.ncjrs.gov/pdffiles/165476.pdf

National Institute of Mental Health (NIMH). (2009). *Suicide in the U.S.: Statistics and prevention.* Washington, DC: U.S. Department of Health and Human Services. Retrieved September 30, 2009, from www.nimh.nih.gov/health/publications/suicide-in-the-us-statistics-and-prevention/index.shtml

National Institutes of Health. (2009, April 17). *Research on teen dating violence.* Report 01, PA-09-169. Washington, DC: U.S. Department of Health and Human Services.

National Organization for Women. (1966). *Statement of purpose.* Paper presented at the National Organizing Conference. Washington, DC: National Organization for Women. Retrieved May 18, 2009, from http://history.hanover.edu/courses/excerpts/111now.html

National Youth Violence Prevention Resource Center, Centers for Disease Control and Prevention, U.S. Department of Health and Human Services. (2007). *Internet URL.* Retrieved September 17, 2010, from www.healthfinder.gov/docs/doc05960.htm

Nauta, M. M. (2010). The development, evolution, and status of Holland's theory of vocational personalities and future directions for counseling psychology. *Journal of Counseling Psychology, 57*(1), 11–22.

Neblett, E. W. Jr., Hammond, W. P., Seaton, E. K., & Townsend, T. G. (2010). Underlying mechanisms in the relationship between Africentric worldview and depressive symptoms. *Journal of Counseling Psychology, 57*(1), 105–113.

Neild, R. C., & Farley, E. (2004). Whatever happened to the class of 2000: The timing of dropout in Philadelphia's schools. In G. Orfield (Ed.), *Dropouts in America* (pp. 207–220). Cambridge, MA: Harvard University Press.

Ness, E., & Fraley, O. (1957). *The untouchables.* Cutchogue, NY: Buccaneer Books.

Newman, D. L., Caspi, A., Moffitt, T. E., & Silva, P. A. (1997). Antecedents of adult interpersonal functioning: Effects of individual differences in age 3 temperaments. *Developmental Psychology, 33*(2), 206–217.

Ng, I. (2006, January 13). *Family history, neighborhood affect teen behavior problems.* Paper presented at the annual meeting of the Society for Social Work and Research, San Antonio, TX. Retrieved July 3, 2009, from www.ns.umich.edu/htdocs/releases/story.php?id=31

Niles, S. G., & Trusty, J. (2004). Career development interventions in the schools. In B. T. Erford (Ed.), *Professional school counseling: A handbook of theories, programs,* and practices (pp. 311–323). Austin, TX: CAPS Press, an imprint of PRO-ED.

Noble, J. P., Roberts, W. L., & Sawyer, R. L. (2007, April). *Student achievement, behavior, perceptions, and other factors affecting ACT scores.* ACT Research Report Series, October 2006. Paper presented at the annual meeting of the American Educational Research Association, Chicago, IL.

Noguera, P. A. (2003, March/April). How racial identity affects school performance. *Harvard Education Letter.* Retrieved April 24, 2007, from www.edletter.org/past/issues/2003-ma/noguera.shtml

NORMAL. (2010) *State by state laws.* Retrieved October 5, 2010, from http://norml.org/index.cfm?Group_ID=4516

"North Korean torpedo" sank South's navy ship. (2010, May 20). British Broadcasting Corporation (BBC). Report. *BBC News, Asia-Pacific.* Retrieved October 4, 2010, from www.bbc.co.uk/news/10129703

Novotney, A. (2009a). The price of affluence. *Monitor on Psychology, 40*(1), 50–52.

Novotney, A. (2009b). Resilient kids learn better. *Monitor on Psychology, 40*(9), 32–34.

Nowinski, J. (2007). *The identity trap: Saving our teens from themselves.* New York: American Management Association.

Nunnally, J. C. (1972). *Educational measurement and evaluation.* New York: McGraw-Hill.

Nunnally, J., & Bernstein, I. H. (1994). *Psychometric theory* (3rd ed.). New York: McGraw-Hill.

Nuwer, H. (2005). *A college president makes a bad call upon leaving office: Why Iowa's ruling on a baseball initiation must be overturned.* Retrieved July 14, 2009, from www.stophazing.org/nuwer/baseball.htm

Obama, B. (2004). *Dreams from my father: A story of race and inheritance.* New York: Three Rivers Press/Random House.

Ochoa, J. (2010). Coping with ADHD's emotional distress syndrome. *Counseling Today, 52*(7), 54–56.

O'Connell, P., & Pepler, D. (1999). Peer involvement in bullying: Insights and challenges for intervention. *Journal of Adolescence, 22*(4), 437–452.

O'Connor, K. J., & Braverman, L. M. (Eds.). (1997). *Play therapy theory and practice: A comparative presentation.* New York: Wiley.

Office of Dietary Supplements. (2009). *Dietary supplementary fact sheet vitamin D.* Bethesda, MD: National Institute for Health. Retrieved October 3, 2009, from http://dietary-supplements.info.nih.gov/factsheets/VitaminD_pf.asp

Office of Juvenile Justice and Delinquency Prevention, U.S. Department of Justice. (2009). *Easy access to FBI arrest statistics.* Retrieved April 21, 2010, from http://ojjdp.ncjrs.gov/ojstatbb/ezaucr/

Office of Refugee Resettlement, U.S. Department of Health and Human Services. (2002). *The refugee act.* Retrieved October 4, 2010, from www.acf.hhs.gov/programs/orr/policy/refact1.htm

Offill, J., & Schappell, E. (2006). *The friend who got away: 20 women's true life tales of friendships that blew up, burned out or faded away.* New York: Broadway.

Ogbu, J. U. (2003). *Black American students in an affluent suburb: A study of academic disengagement.* Mahwah, NJ: Lawrence Erlbaum/Taylor & Francis.

O'Hara, M. (1995). Carl Rogers: Scientist and mystic. *Journal of Humanistic Psychology, 35*(4), 40–54.

Ohio Historical Society. (2006, August 1). *First junior high school in the United States.* Ohio History Central. Retrieved June 22, 2009, from www.ohiohistorycentral.org/entry.php?rec=2690

Olson, E. (2009, January 4). Killings prompt efforts to spot and reduce abuse of teenagers in dating. *New York Times,* p. A12.

O'Neil, D. (2009). *Evolution of modern humans: A survey of the biological and cultural evolution of archaic and modern Homo sapiens.* Online book. Retrieved October 5, 2009, from http://anthro.palomar.edu/hom02/default.htm

Onishi, N. (2008, June 8). For studies in English, Koreans learn to say goodbye to dad. *New York Times,* pp. A1, A16.

Orbe, M. P., & Harris, T. M. (2008). *Interracial communication: Theory into practice* (2nd ed.). Thousand Oaks, CA: Sage.

Orfield, G. (1998). Campus resegregation and its alternatives. In G. Orfield & C. Edley, Jr. (Eds.), *Chilling admissions.* Cambridge, MA: Harvard University Press.

Ornstein, A. C., & Levine, D. U. (1989). *Foundations of education* (4th ed.). Boston: Houghton Mifflin.

O'Rourke, J. (2009). Counseling aids teens in need: Cutters inflict own "manageable" pain. *Free Library.* Retrieved September 30, 2009, from http://pediatrics.aappublications.org/cgi/content/abstract/117/6/1939

Ortiz, A. (2001). *English language learners with special needs: Effective instructional strategies.* Washington, DC: Office of Educational Research and Improvement, U.S. Department of Education. (ERIC Digest, EDO-FL-01–08).

Osborne, L. (2002). *American normal: The hidden world of Asperger's syndrome.* New York: Copernicus Books.

Osgood, R. L. (2008). *The history of special education: A struggle for equality in American public schools.* Westport, CT: Praeger.

Otto, G. L. (2000). *A study of the perceived role of compulsory attendance laws among educational stakeholders: Their impact on schools, changes, and alternatives.* Unpublished dissertation, Widener University.

Oxford English Dictionary, 2nd ed. (2002). New York: Oxford University Press.

Page, E. B. (1975). Statistically recapturing the richness within the classroom. *Psychology in the Schools, 12*(3), 339–344.

Pakkala, T. (2006, May 31). Does it pay to reward students for success? *Gainesville Sun.* Retrieved June 5, 2006, from www.gainesville.com

Palmer, P., Hartke, D. D., Ree, M. J., Welsh, J. R., & Valentine, L. D. (1988). *Armed Services Vocational Aptitude Battery (ASVAB): Alternate forms reliability (Forms 8, 9, 10, and 11)* AFHRL.TP-87-48, AD A191 658. Brooks AFB, TX: Manpower and Personnel Division, Air Force Human Resources Laboratory.

Palosan, U., & Aro, H. (1994). The effect of timing of parental divorce on the vunerability of children to depression in young adulthood. *Adolescence, 29*(115), 681–690.

Paniagua, F. A. (2005). *Assessing and treating culturally diverse clients: A practical guide* (3rd ed.). Multicultural Aspects of Counseling and Psychotherapy Series, no. 4. Thousand Oaks, CA: Sage.

Papanek, H. (1970). Adler's psychology and group psychotherapy. *American Journal of Psychiatry, 127*(6), 783–786.

Parker-Pope, T. (2009, January 27). The myth of rampant teenage promiscuity. *New York Times,* p. D6.

Parker-Pope, T. (2010, June 15). Stupid teenage tricks, for a virtual audience. *New York Times,* p. D6.

Parsons, F. (1909/2006). *Choosing a vocation.* Alexandria, VA: National Career Development Association. (Originally published in Boston by Houghton Mifflin)

Parsons, R. D. (2009). *Thinking and acting like a solution-focused school counselor.* Thousand Oaks, CA: Corwin.

Parsons, R. D., & Kahn, W. J. (2005). *The school counselor as consultant: An integrated model for school-based consultation.* Belmont, CA: Brooks/Cole, Thomson.

Partin, R. L. (1993). School counselors' time: Where does it go? *School Counselor, 40*(4), 274–281.

Pascopella, A. (2007). The dropout crisis. *District Administration, 43*(1), 30–38.

Pascopella, A. (2009). Ninth annual salary survey. *District Administration, 45*(8), 50–52.

Paslay, C. S. (1995). *The influence of goal setting on achievement and perception of self-efficacy of inner-city high school students.* Doctoral dissertation, Widener University. (ProQuest No. 742533851).

Passel, J. S., & Cohn, D. V. (2009). *A portrait of unauthorized immigrants in the United States.* Report April 14, 2009. Washington, DC: Pew Hispanic Center. Retrieved April 16, 2009, from http://pewhispanic.org/reports/report.php?ReportID=107

Patrick, K., & Eichel, L. (2006, June 25). Education tests: Who's minding the scores? *Philadelphia Inquirer.* Retrieved June 26, 2006, from http://philly.com/mld/inquirer/living/education/14898076.htm

Patton, M. Q. (1987). *How to use qualitative methods in evaluation.* Thousand Oaks, CA: Sage.

Peck, D. (2003, November). The selectivity illusion. *Atlantic Monthly.* Retrieved July 18, 2009, from http://theatlantic.com/doc/200311/peck

Peckham, P. D., Glass, G. V., & Hopkins, K. D. (1969). The experimental unit in statistical analysis: Comparative experiments with intact groups. *Journal of Special Education, 3*(4), 337–349.

Pelley, S. (2000, March 7). Murder in the first grade. *60 Minutes II.* CBS News. Retrieved April 21, 2009, from www.cbsnews.com/stories/2000/03/07/60II/main168970.shtml

Pennington, B. (2005, December 25). One Division III conference finds that playing the slots system pays off. *New York Times.* Retrieved July 18, 2009, from www.nytimes.com/2005/12/25/sports/ncaafootball/25sidebar.html

Pennsylvania State Education Association (PSEA). (2010). *History of PSEA: A narrative.* Retrieved October 14, 2010, from www.psea.org/general.aspx?id=6619

Perkins-Gough, D. (2009). Can service learning keep students in school? *Educational Leadership, 66*(8), 91–92.

Perry, G. H., & Dominy, N. J. (2009). Evolution of the human pygmy phenotype. *Trends in Ecology and Evolution, 24*(4), 218–225.

Perry, J. C., & Vance, K. (2010). Possible selves among urban youths of color: An exploration of peer beliefs and gender differences. *Career Development Quarterly, 58*(3), 257–269.

Pescitelli, D. (1996). Rogerian therapy. *Personality & Consciousness.* Retrieved July 24, 2009, from http://pandc.ca/?cat=carl_rogers&page=rogerian_theory

Peterson, C. (2006). *A primer in positive psychology.* New York: Oxford University Press.

Peterson, J. S., & Deuschle, C. (2006). A model for supervising school counseling students without teaching experience. *Counselor Education and Supervision, 25*(4), 267–281.

Peterson, J. S., Goodman, R., Keller, T., & McCauley, A. (2004). Teachers and non-teachers as school counselors: Reflections on the internship experience. *Professional School Counseling, 7*(4), 246–255.

Peterson, L. (2009, June 10). Officials hope anonymous online reports will reduce bullying. *Tampa Tribune.* Retrieved June 11, 2009, from www2.tbo.com/content/2009/jun/10/school-officials-hope-anonymous-online-reports-wil/

Pew Center on the States. (2008). *One in 100: Behind bars in America.* Washington, DC: Pew Center on the States. Retrieved January 29, 2010, from www.pewcenteronthestates.org/uploadedFiles/One%20in%20100.pdf

Piaget, J. (1953/1936). *Origins of intelligence in the child,* London: Routledge & Kegan Paul.

Piaget, J. (1970). *Science of education and psychology of the child.* New York: Orion.

Pike, K. (1982). *Linguistic concepts: An introduction to tagmemics.* Lincoln: University of Nebraska Press.

Poehlmann, J., Dallaire, D., Loper, A. B., & Shear, L. D. (2010). Children's contact with their incarcerated parents: Research findings and recommendations. *American Psychologist, 65*(6), 575–598.

Poland, S., & Poland, D. (2007). Safe school preparations for your district. *District Administration, 43*(6), 88.

Pomerantz, E. M., Moorman, E. A., & Litwack, S. D. (2007). The how, whom, and why of parent's involvement in children's academic lives: More is not always better. *Review of Educational Research, 77*(3), 373–410.

Ponton, L. (2000). *The sex lives of teenagers: Revealing the secret world of adolescent boys and girls.* New York: Plume/Penguin Group.

Pope, J. (2005, December 19). Early decision on college is popular again, worrying some experts. Associated Press. *Naples Daily News,* A8.

Pope, M. (2008). Reclaiming our history: The NCDA journal editors (1911–2011). *Career Development Quarterly, 56,* 291–293.

Pope, M. L. (2005). Review of the Harrington-O'Shea Career Decision-Making System-Revised. *The 16th mental measurements yearbook* (Electronic version). Retrieved December 22, 2009, from www.unl.edu/buros/

Popham, W. J. (1999). *Classroom assessment: What teachers need to know* (2nd ed.). Boston: Allyn & Bacon.

Popham, W. J. (2006, April). Branded by a test. *Educational Leadership, 63*(7), 86–87.

Popielarski, J. (1998). *Characteristics, background, and teaching methodologies of advanced placement U.S. history teachers.* Unpublished doctoral dissertation, Widener University.

Portman, T. A. A. (2004). Applying outcome research to school counseling. In B. T. Erford (Ed.), *Professional school counseling: A handbook of theories, programs, and practices* (pp. 43–50). Austin, TX: CAPS Press, an imprint of PRO-ED.

Portner, J. (2000, October 4). Competing forces. *Education Week.* Retrieved June 23, 2009, from www.edweek.org/login.html?source=www.edweek.org/ew/articles/2000/10/04/05msculture.h20.html&destination=www.edweek.org/ew/articles/2000/10/04/05msculture.h20.html&levelId=2100

Preschool Curriculum Evaluation Consortium. (2008, July). *Effects of preschool programs on school readiness*. Report from the Preschool Curriculum Evaluation Research Initiative. Washington, DC: U.S. Department of Education, Institute of Education Sciences, National Center for Education Research.

Prinstein, M. J., & Cillessen, A. H. (2003). Forms and functions of adolescent peer aggression associated with high levels of peer status. *Merrill-Palmer Quarterly, 49*(3), 310–342.

Pritchard, J. (2009). Wrestling with Darwin. *Howard Hughes Medical Institute Bulletin, 22*(3), 12–19.

Project Appleseed. (2008). *Many schools in the United States are in the process of education reform*. Retrieved December 12, 2009, from www.projectappleseed.org/reform.html

Psychological Corporation. (1990). *Career interest inventory (CII)*. San Antonio, TX: Pearson Assessment.

Purvis, A. W. (2005). *The vendetta: FBI hero Melvin Purvis's war against crime, and J. Edgar Hoover's war against him*. New York: PublicAffairs/Perseus.

Pytel, B. (2007, November 28). Bully costs private school $4M: Bullying is out of control and costing millions. *Education Issues, Suite101*. Retrieved January 19, 2010, from http://educationalissues .suite101.com/article.cfm/bully_costs_private_school_4m

Quintanar, A. P., & Warren, S. R. (2008). Listening to the voices of Latino parent volunteers. *Kappa Delta Pi Record, 44*(3), 119–123.

Raber, S. M., & Frechtling, J. A. (1985). *Special education placement and longitudinal outcomes of preschool and kindergarten-identified handicapped children*. Final report. Rockville, MD: Office of Special Education and Rehabilitative Services, Montgomery County Public Schools. (ERIC Document No. ED278191).

Rado, D. (2009, May 27). School counselors face big workload in Illinois. *Chicago Tribune*. Retrieved June 19, 2009, from www.chicagotribune.com/news/local/chicago/chi-counselors-west-zone-27-may27,0,3192041.story

Radziwon, C. D. (2003, March 22). The effects of peers' beliefs on 8th-grade students' identification with school. *Free Library*. Retrieved April 27, 2010, from www.thefreelibrary.com/The effects of peers' beliefs on 8th-grade students' identification . . . -a0102695400

Rainville, G. A., & Smith, S. K. (2003). *Juvenile felony defendants in criminal courts: Survey of 40 counties, 1998*. NCJ 197961. Washington, DC: U.S. Department of Justice, Bureau of Justice Statistics.

Ramirez, E. (2009, March 20). Schools battle student stress with creative strategies. *US News & World Report*. Retrieved March 23, 2009, from www.usnews.com/articles/education/ 2009/03/20/schools-battle-student-stress-with-creative-strategies.html

Ramirez, J. (2009, June 15). Children of conflict: Since 9/11, more than a million kids have had a parent deployed. Their childhoods often go with them. *Newsweek*, pp. 54–57.

Rank, O. (1978/1936). *Will therapy: The therapeutic applications of will psychology*. New York: W. W. Norton.

Ravitch, D. (2000). *Left back: A century of battles over school reform*. New York: Touchstone Books, Simon & Schuster.

Reardon, S. F., Atteberry, A., Arshan, N., & Kurlaender, M. (2009). *Effects of the California High School Exit Examination on student persistence, achievement, and graduation*. Working paper 2009–12. Stanford, CA: Leland Stanford Jr. University, Institute for Research on Educational Policy and Practice. Retrieved April 22, 2009, from www.stanford.edu/group/irepp/cgi-bin/joomla/ index.php?option=com_content&task=view&id=27&Itemid=43

Redlener, I. (2009). *Legacy of shame: The on-going public health disaster of children struggling in post-Katrina Louisiana*. New York: Columbia University, Mailman School of Public Health, National Center for Disaster Preparedness.

Reed, W. H. (1985). *Positive listening: Learning to hear what people are really saying.* Danbury, CT: Franklin Watts.

Rees, J. (2001). Frederick Taylor in the classroom: Standardized testing and scientific management. *Radical Pedagogy.* University of Southern Colorado, Department of History. Retrieved March 25, 2009, from http://radicalpedagogy.icaap.org/content/3_2/rees.html

Reeves, D. B. (2006). *The learning leader: How to focus school improvement for better results.* Alexandria, VA: Association for Supervision and Curriculum Development.

Reinberg, S. (2008). 10% of U.S. high school seniors use Vicodin. *Medicine Net.* Retrieved September 27, 2010, from http:// health.usnews.com/health-news/managing-your-healthcare/articles/2008/12/11/10-of-us-high-school-seniors-use-vicodin.html

Renzulli, J. S., & Park, S. (2002). *Giftedness and high school dropouts: Personal, family, and school-related factors* (RM02168). Storrs, CT: University of Connecticut, National Research Center on the Gifted and Talented. Retrieved September 10, 2009, from www.gifted.uconn.edu/nrcgt/renz park.html

Report: States set low bar for achievement. (2009, October 29). Associated Press. Retrieved April 23, 2010, from www.msnbc.msn.com/id/33534379/

Reynolds, C., & Kamphaus, R. (2004). *Behavior assessment system for children* (2nd ed.). Circle Pines, MN: American Guidance Service, Pearson Education.

Rice, A. (2006). *Thanks for being my friend: A special book to celebrate friendship with someone very important . . . you.* Bel Air, CA: Blue Mountain Press.

Richards, E. (2010, April 7). New data shows similar academic results between voucher and MPS students. *Journal Sentinel.* Retrieved April 17, 2010, from www.jsonline.com/news/education/90169302.html

Rigby-Weinberg, D. N. (1986). A future direction for radical feminist therapy. *Dynamics of Feminist Therapy, 5*(2/3), 191–206.

Ripley, V. V., & Goodnough, G. E. (2001). Planning and implementing group counseling in a high school. *Professional School Counseling, 5*(1), 62–66.

Riva, M. T., & Haub, A. L. (2004). Group counseling in the schools. In J. L. DeLucia-Waack, D. A. Gerrity, C. R. Kalodner, & M. T. Riva (Eds.), *Handbook of group counseling and psychotherapy* (pp. 309–321). Thousand Oaks, CA: Sage.

Robelen, E. W. (2010). Program promoting sexual abstinence gets resurrected. *Education Week, 29*(28), 6, 7.

Roberts, W. B. (2008). *Working with parents of bullies and victims.* Thousand Oaks, CA: Corwin.

Robinson, C. H., & Betz, N. E. (2008). A psychometric evaluation of Super's Work Values Inventory-Revised. *Journal of Career Assessment, 16*(4), 456–473.

Robinson, S. L., & Ricord Griesemer, S. M. (2006). Helping individual students with problem behavior. In C. M. Evertson & C. S. Weinstein (Eds.), *Handbook of classroom management: Research, practice, and contemporary issues* (pp. 787–802). Mahwah, NJ: Lawrence Erlbaum.

Roe, A. (1956).*The psychology of occupations.* New York: Wiley.

Roediger, H. L. III, & Karpicke, J. D. (2006). The power of testing memory: Basic research and implications for educational practice. *Perspectives on Psychological Science, 1*(3), 181–208.

Rogers, C. R. (1939). *The clinical treatment of the problem child.* New York: Houghton Mifflin.

Rogers, C. R. (1942). *Counseling and psychotherapy: Newer concepts in practice.* Boston: Houghton Mifflin.

Rogers, C. R. (1951). *Client centered therapy: Its current practice, implications, and theory.* London: Constable.

Rogers, C. R. (1961). *On becoming a person: A therapist's view of psychotherapy.* Boston: Houghton Mifflin.

Rogers, C. R. (1970). *Carl Rogers on encounter groups.* New York: Harper & Row.

Rogers, C. R. (1977). *Carl Rogers on personal power: Inner strength and its revolutionary impact.* New York: Delta Books.

Rogers, C. R. (1980). *A way of being.* Boston: Houghton Mifflin.

Rogers, C. R. (1985). Toward a more human science of the person. *Journal of Humanistic Psychology, 25*(4), 7–24.

Rogers, C. R. (1992). The necessary and sufficient conditions of therapeutic personality change. *Journal of Consulting and Clinical Psychology, 60*(6), 827–832.

Rogers, C. R., & Russell, D. (2003). *Carl Rogers: The quiet revolutionary.* Roseville, CA: Penmarin Books.

Roney, J., & Wolfe, R. (2000). Making the transition to adulthood. In M. Csikszentmihalyi & B. Schneider (Eds.), *Becoming adult: How teenagers prepare for the world of work* (pp. 213–236). New York: Basic Books.

Rose, M. (2009). Standards, teaching, and learning. *Phi Delta Kappan, 91*(4), 21–27.

Roseberry-McKibbin, C., & Brice, A. (2005). *Acquiring English as a second language: What's normal, what's not.* Rockville, MD: American Speech-Language-Hearing Association. Retrieved March 30, 2006, from www.asha.org/public/speech/development/easl.htm

Rosenbaum, J. E. (2009). Patient teenagers? A comparison of the sexual behavior of virginity pledgers and matched nonpledgers. *Pediatrics, 123*(1), 110–120.

Rottinghaus, P. J., & Zytowski, D. G. (2006). Commonalities between adolescents' work values and interests. *Measurement and Evaluation in Counseling and Development, 38*(4), 211–221.

Rovet, J., Greenbaum, R., & Kodituwakku, P. W. (2009). Children with fetal alcohol spectrum disorders have more severe behavioral problems than those with AD/HD. *Medical News Today.* Retrieved September 11, 2009, from www.medicalnewstoday.com/articles/157905.php

Rowell, L. L. (2006). Action research and school counseling: Closing the gap between research and practice. *Professional School Counseling,* 376–384.

Royster, D. A. (2003). *Race and the invisible hand: How white networks exclude black men from blue-collar jobs.* Berkeley: University of California Press.

Rubin, K. H., & Stewart, S. L. (1996). Social withdrawal. In E. J. Mash & R. A. Barkley (Eds.), *Child psychopathology* (pp. 277–307). New York: Guilford.

Rumberger, R. W., Gándara, P., & Merino, B. (2006, Winter). Where California's English learners attend school and why it matters. *University of California Linguistic Minority Research Institute Newsletter, 15*(2), pp. 1–3.

Runde, C. E., & Flanagan, T. A. (2007). *Becoming a conflict competent leader: How you and your organization can manage conflict effectively.* San Francisco: Wiley.

Rundquist, J. (2009, July 13). Children in low-income cities who attend N.J. preschools perform better. *Star Ledger.* Retrieved July 15, 2009, from www.nj.com/news/index.ssf/2009/07/children_in_lowincome_cities_w.html

Russell, J., & LaCoste-Caputo, J. (2006, December 4). More kids repeating kindergarten. *San Antonio News Express.* Retrieved December 6, 2006, from www.mysanantonio.com/

Ryan, C., Huebner, D., Diaz, R. M., & Sanchez, J. (2009). Family rejection as a predictor of negative health outcomes in white and Latino lesbian, gay, and bisexual young adults. *Pediatrics, 123*(1), 346–352.

Ryser, G., & McConnell, K. (2002). *Scales for diagnosing attention-deficit-hyperactivity disorder.* Austin, TX: PRO-ED.

Sabatini, M., & Reilly-Chammat, R. (2007, June). Sexuality. *Thrive, 1*(6). Retrieved June 26, 2009, from www.thriveri.org/documents/thrive_report_0607.pdf

Saegert, S. C., Adler, N. E., Bullock, H. E., Cauce, A. M., Liu, W. M., & Wyche, K. F. (2007). *Report of the taskforce on socioeconomic status.* Washington, DC: American Psychological Association. Retrieved October 20, 2009, from www2.apa.org/pi/SES_task_force_report.pdf

Saleebey, D. (2008). Commentary on the strengths perspective and potential applications in school counseling. *Professional School Counseling, 12*(2), 68–75.

Salkind, N. J. (2004). *Statistics for people who think they hate statistics* (2nd ed.). Thousand Oaks, CA: Sage.

Samuels, C. (2008, June 11). Chicago district focusing on pathways to college. *Education Week, 27*(41), 1, 13.

Samuels, C. A. (2010, September 15). Boom in learning-disabled ends. *Education Week, 30*(3), 1 & 14.

Sanders, D., & Wills, F. (2005). *Cognitive therapy: An introduction* (2nd ed.). Thousand Oaks, CA: Sage.

Sarmah, S. (2007, February 15). Is Obama black enough? *Columbia Journalism Review.* Retrieved October 28, 2009, from www.cjr.org/politics/is_obama_black_enough.php

Save the Children. (2009). *Creating lasting change for children in need in the United States and around the world.* Retrieved December 18, 2009, from www.savethechildren.org/programs/us-literacy-and-nutrition/

Sax, C. L., & Thoma, C. A. (2002). *Transition assessment: Wise practices for quality lives.* Baltimore, MD: Paul H. Brookes.

Schab, L. M. (2008). *The divorce workbook for teens: Activities to help you move beyond the break-up* (2nd ed.). Oakland, CA: Instant Help Books.

Schachter, R. (2010). A salary recession for school administrators? *District Administration, 46*(8), 30–42.

Schafer, W. C. (1998). Review of the Career Interest Inventory®. In J. C. Impara & B. S. Plake, (Eds.), *The 13th mental measurements yearbook* (pp. 193–197). Lincoln, NE: Buros Institute of Mental Measurements.

Scheidel, W. (2007). *The Roman slavery supply.* Princeton/Stanford Working Papers in Classics. Retrieved October 5, 2009, from www.princeton.edu/~pswpc/pdfs/scheidel/050704.pdf

Schenck, P. M. (2009). Review of the Kuder Planning System. In E. A. Whitfield, R. W. Feller, & C. Wood (Eds.), *A counselor's guide to career assessment instruments* (5th ed., pp. 163–173). Broken Arrow, OK: National Career Development Association.

Schiavone, P. N. (1999). *A study of factors related to the choice of post-secondary education for physically handicapped and learning-disabled students.* Unpublished doctoral dissertation, Widener University (ProQuest No. AAT 9955362).

Schlichte, J., Yssel, N., & Merbler, J. (2005). Pathways to burnout: Case studies in teacher isolation and alienation. *Preventing School Failure, 50*(1), 35–40.

Schmidt, J. J. (2008). *Counseling in the schools: Comprehensive programs of responsive services for all students.* Boston: Pearson Education.

Schmidt, P. (2007, April 20). UCLA reverses decline in Black admissions but rejects more Asians. *Chronicle of Higher Education,* p. A42.

Schmitt, N. (1995). Review of the Differential Aptitude Test (5th ed.). In J. C. Conoley & J. C. Impara (Eds.), *The 12th mental measurements yearbook* (pp. 301–305). Lincoln, NE: Buros Institute of Mental Measurements.

School District of Philadelphia. (2009). *About Central High School.* Philadelphia: Author. Retrieved January 4, 2010, from www.centralhigh.net/?q=node/5

Schultz, K. B. (2008, August 7). Divorce during recession. *Forbes.* Retrieved July 3, 2009, from www.forbes.com/2008/07/07/divorce-recession-housing-pf-ii-in_ks_0703marriage_inl.html

Schwartz, J. (2009, March 26). Clean slates for youths sentenced fraudulently. *New York Times*. Retrieved September 21, 2009, from www.nytimes.com/2009/03/27/us/27judges.html

Schwartz, J. (2010a, October 3). Bullying, suicide, punishment. *New York Times,* pp. P-WK1, P-WK 3.

Schwartz, J. (2010b, April 18). Finding a gay-friendly campus. *New York Times Education Supplement,* p. 10.

Schwartz, K. D. (2008). Adolescent brain development: An oxymoron no longer. *Journal of Youth Ministry, 6*(2), 85–93.

Schwartzbaum, S. E., & Thomas, A. J. (2008). *Dimensions of multicultural counseling: A life story approach*. Thousand Oaks, CA: Sage.

Schweinhart, L. J. (2008, March 19). Creating the best prekindergartens: Five ingredients for long-term effects and returns on investment. *Education Week, 27*(28), 36, 27.

Schweinhart, L. J., Montie, J., Xiang, Z., Barnett, W. S., Belfield, C. R., & Nores, M. (2005). *Lifetime effects: The High/Scope Perry Preschool study through age 40*. Monographs of the High/Scope Educational Research Foundation, no. 14. Ypsilanti, MI: High/Scope Press.

Sciarra, D. T. (2004). *School counseling: Foundations and contemporary issues*. Belmont, CA: Thomson, Brooks/Cole.

Scott, L. (2009). *Children's educational outcomes: Parental school and school characteristics, Does parent-teacher race matching make a difference?* Tempe: Arizona State University, Center for Population Dynamics. Retrieved January, 29, 2009, from paa2009.princeton.edu/download.aspx?submissionId=91315

Scruggs, T. (2000). *Teaching test taking skills: Helping students show what they know*. Brookline, MA: Brookline Books/Lumen Editions.

Sears, J. (1991). *Growing up gay in the south: Race, gender, and journeys of the spirit*. New York: Harrington Park Press, Routledge.

Sears, J. (1992). Educators, homosexuality, and homosexual students: Are personal feelings related to professional beliefs? In K. M. Harbeck (Ed.), *Coming out of the classroom closet* (pp. 29–80). New York: Harrington Park Press, Routledge.

Sears, W., Sears, M., & Pantley, E. (2002). *The successful child: What parents can do to help kids turn out well*. Boston: Little, Brown.

Seipp, C. (2002). Asthma attack when "zero tolerance" collides with children's health. *Reason*. Retrieved September 29, 2009, from www.reason.com/issues/show/367.html

Self-embedding disorder: Teens putting nails, paper clips in bodies, study finds. (2008, December 3). Reuters. Retrieved September 29, 2009, from www.foxnews.com/story/0,2933,461267,00.html

Seligman, M.E.P. (2004). Can happiness be taught? *Daedalus, 133*(2), 80–87.

Sexton, E., Starr, E., & Fawcett, M. (2005). Identifying best practice principles in working with the Inupiat Eskimo: Building trust and beyond. *International Journal for the Advancement of Counseling, 27*(4), 513–522.

Shallcross, L. (2009a). Confronting addiction. *Counseling Today, 52*(2), 28–33.

Shallcross, L. (2009b). From generation to generation. *Counseling Today, 52*(5), 38–41.

Shallcross, L. (2009c). Rewriting the rules of grief. *Counseling Today Online*. Alexandria, VA: American Counseling Association. Retrieved July 13, 2009, from www.edweek.org/ew/articles/2009/06/11/34college.h28.html

Shallcross, L. (2010). A voyage of self discovery. *Counseling Today, 52*(7), 32–38.

Shapiro, L. E., & Holmes, J. (2008). *Let's be friends: A workbook to help kids learn social skills & make great friends* (2nd ed.). Oakland, CA: New Harbinger Publications.

Shaw, J. A. (2003). Children exposed to war/terrorism. *Child and Family Psychology Review, 6*(4), 237–246.

Shedd, J. (2003). *The history of the student credit hour.* Unpublished report. College Park, MD: Office of Institutional Research and Planning, University of Maryland. Retrieved March 19, 2007, from http://virtual.parkland.edu/todtreat/presentations/cet103/shedd2003%20history%200f%20credit%20hour.pdf

Shelleby, E. (2008, June 9). New Children's Defense Fund report shows children and teen firearm deaths increase for first time since 1994. *Common Dreams.org.* Retrieved September 21, 2009, from www.commondreams.org/news2008/0609–11.htm

Shulman, J. L., & Bowen, W. G. (2001). *The game of life: College sports and educational values.* Princeton, NJ: Princeton University Press.

Simpson, E. L. (1980). Occupational endeavor as life history: Anne Roe. *Psychology of Women Quarterly, 5*(1), 116–126.

Skinner, B. F. (1954). The science of learning and the art of teaching. *Harvard Educational Review, 24*(1), 86–97.

Sklare, G. B. (2005). Brief counseling that works: *A solution-focused approach for school counselors and administrators* (2nd ed.). Thousand Oaks, CA: Corwin.

Slater, L. (2009, July 27). Virtual school enrollment on upward curve. *Lawrence Journal World.* Retrieved July 29, 2009, from www.districtadministration.com/newssummary.aspx?news=yes&postid=52999

Slater, R. B. (2006). Large Black-White scoring gap persists on the SAT. *Journal of Blacks in Higher Education.* Retrieved September 8, 2009, from www.jbhe.com/features/53_SAT.html

Slowikowski, J. (2009, April). Juvenile arrests, 2007. *Juvenile Justice Bulletin.* Retrieved September 21, 2009, from www.ncjrs.gov/pdffiles1/ojjdp/225344.pdf

Smith, E. J. (2006a). The strength-based counseling model. *Counseling Psychologist, 34*(1), 13–79.

Smith, E. J. (2006b). The strength-based counseling model: A paradigm shift in psychology. *Counseling Psychologist, 34*(1), 134–144.

Smith, M., & Agus, Z. S. (2009, February 4). Brain gene linked to retardation. *Medpage Today.* Retrieved February 13, 2009, from www.medpagetoday.com/Neurology/GeneralNeurology/12751

Smith, N. B. (1999). A tribute to the visionaries, prime movers and pioneers of vocational education, 1892 to 1917. *Journal of Vocational and Technical Education, 16*(1). Retrieved March 30, 2009, from http://scholar.lib.vt.edu/wjournats/JVTE/v16n1/smith.html

Smith, S. W. (2002). *Applying cognitive-behavioral techniques to social skills instruction. ERIC/OSEP Digest.* ERIC Clearinghouse on Disabilities and Gifted Education. (Document No. ED469279).

Smrekar, C. E., & Owens, D. E. (2003). It's a way of life for defense schools. *Journal of Negro Education.* Retrieved May 27, 2008, from http://findarticles.com/p/articles/mi_qa3626/is_200301/ai_n9186199/print

Smyth, C. P. (1868). *On the antiquity of intellectual man: From a practical and astronomical point of view.* Edinburgh, UK: Edmonston and Douglas. Retrieved October 30, 2009, from http://books.google.com/books?id=zcJTxIdCsgUC&dq=Pelasgics+and+Etruscans+,+Smyth,+1868&printsec=frontcover&source=bl&ots=FP-M99HuYm&sig=LpznpLWfLhmubzsYi88503rHhFM&hl=en&ei=jvDqSve3L42_tweK7qXECg&sa=X&oi=book_result&ct=result&resnum=1&ved=0CAwQ6AEwAA#v=onepage&q=&f=false

Snyder, H. N., & Sickmund, M. (2006). *Juvenile offenders and victims: 2006 national report.* Washington, DC: Office of Justice Programs, U.S. Department of Justice.

Sohn, S. (2007). *Asian parent involvement in the home, school, and community and children's achievement in early grades.* Unpublished doctoral dissertation, State University of New York at Buffalo. (ProQuest No. AAT 3277781).

Sohn, S., & Wang, C. (2006). Immigrant parent's involvement in American schools: Perspectives from Korean mothers. *Early Childhood Education Journal, 34*(2), 125–132.

Solberg, V. S., Good, G. E., Nord, D., Holm, C., Hohner, R., Zima, N., et al. (1994). Assessing career search expectations: Development and validation of the career search efficacy scale. *Journal of Career Assessment, 2*(2), 111–123.

Solomon, B. M. (1985). *In the company of educated women.* New Haven, CT: Yale University Press.

Solomon, L. (1975). *Capital formation by expenditures on formal education, 1880 and 1890.* Doctoral dissertation, University of Chicago, 1968. New York: Arno Press.

Sousa, D. A. (2003). *How the gifted brain learns.* Thousand Oaks, CA: Corwin.

Spanierman, L. B., & Soble, J. R. (2009). Understanding Whiteness: Previous approaches and possible directions in the study of White racial attitudes and identity. In J. G. Ponterotto, J. M. Casas, L. A. Suzuki, & C. M. Alexander (Eds.), *Handbook of multicultural counseling* (3rd ed., pp. 283–299). Thousand Oaks, CA: Sage.

Sparks, E., Johnson, J. L., & Akos, P. (2010). Dropouts: Finding needles in the haystack. *Educational Leadership, 65*(5), 46–49.

Sprenger, M. B. (2009). *The developing brain.* Thousand Oaks, CA: Corwin.

Steele, C. M. (1997). A threat in the air: How stereotypes shape intellectual identity and performance. *American Psychologist, 52*(6), 613–629.

Steele, C. M. (1999, August). Thin ice: "Stereotype threat" and black college students. *Atlantic Monthly*, pp. 44–54.

Steinberg, J. (2002). *The gatekeepers: Inside the admissions process of a premier college.* New York: Penguin Books.

Steinberg, J. (2009, July 19). Add this to the high price of college: Costly advice on getting in. *New York Times*, pp. 1, 4.

Steinberg, L. (1996). *Beyond the classroom: Why school reform has failed and what parents need to do.* New York: Touchstone.

Steingraber, S. (2007). *The falling age of puberty in U.S. girls: What we know, what we need to know.* San Francisco: Breast Cancer Fund. Retrieved September 17, 2010, from www.breast cancerfund.org/assets/pdfs/publications/falling-age-of-puberty.pdf

Stephens, W. R. (1988). Birth of the National Vocational Guidance Association. *Career Development Quarterly, 36*(4), 293–306.

Sterling-Turner, H. E., Watson, T. S., & Moore, J. W. (2002). The effects of direct training and treatment integrity on treatment outcomes in school consultation. *School Psychology Quarterly, 17*(1), 47–77.

Sternberg, L., Dornbusch, S. M., & Brown, B. B. (1992). Ethnic differences in adolescent achievement: An ecological perspective. *American Psychologist, 47*(6), 723–729.

Sternberg, R. J., Grigorenko, E. L., & Kidd, K. K. (2005). Intelligence, race and genetics. *American Psychologist, 60*(1), 46–59.

Sterns, H. L., & Subich, L. M. (2002). Career development in midcareer. In D. C. Feldman (Ed.), *Work careers: A developmental perspective* (pp. 186–213). San Francisco: Jossey-Bass.

Stiggins, R. J. (2002). Assessment crisis: The absence of assessment for learning. *Phi Delta Kappan, 83*(10), 758–765.

Stinson, D. W. (2006). African American male adolescents, schooling (and mathematics): Deficiency, rejection, and achievement. *Review of Educational Research, 76*(4), 477–506.

Stolberg, S. G. (2009, July 17). Obama gives fiery address at N.A.A.C.P. *New York Times*. Retrieved August 18, 2009, from www.nytimes.com/2009/07/17/us/politics/170bama.html?_r=1& adxnnl=1&pagewanted=print&adxnnlx=1250607697-Cf61H8yhziHccjI0Sob21A

Stoltz, K. (2010). Using occupational images in career counseling: A return to yesteryear. *Counseling Today, 52*(7), 30.

Stout, H. (2010, June 17). Best friend? You must be kidding. *New York Times,* pp. E1, E8.

Strauss, V. (2006, March 21). Putting parents in their place: Outside class. *Washington Post.* Retrieved March 22, 2006, from www.washingtonpost.com

Strong, E. K. (1955). *Vocational interests 18 years after college.* Minneapolis: University of Minnesota Press.

Strong, E. K. (2005). *Strong Interest Inventory, Assessment Manual.* Palo Alto, CA: Consulting Psychologists Press.

Strong, M. (1999). *A bright red scream: Self-mutilation and the language of pain.* New York: Penguin Books.

Stufflebeam, D. L. (1981). A brief introduction to standards for evaluations of educational programs, projects, and materials. *Evaluation News, 2*(2), 141–145.

Stufflebeam, D. L. (2003, October 3). *The CIPP model for evaluation: An update.* Paper presented at the annual conference of the Oregon Program Evaluation Network (OPEN), Portland, OR. Retrieved November 9, 2009, from www.wmich.edu/evalctr/pubs/CIPP-ModelOregon 10–03.pdf

Stufflebeam, D. L. (2008). A tribute to Egon Guba. *American Journal of Evaluation, 29*(3), 325–327.

Sturgeon, J. (2009, March). The college promise. *District Administration, 45*(3), 20–23.

Substance Abuse and Mental Health Services Administration, U.S. Department of Health and Human Services. (2002). *Results from the 2001 National Household Survey on Drug Abuse: Volume I. Summary of National Findings.* Office of Applied Studies, NHSDA Series H-17 ed. Washington, DC: U.S. Government Printing Office.

Sue, D. W., & Sue, D. (2003). *Counseling the culturally diverse: Theory and practice* (4th ed.). New York: Wiley.

Super, D. E. (1970). *Occupational psychology.* Belmont, CA: Wadsworth.

Super, D. E. (1980). A life-span, life-space approach to career development. *Journal of Vocational Behavior, 13*(2), 282–298.

Super, D. E., & Haddad, W. C. (1943). The effect of familiarity with an occupational field on a recognition test of vocational interest. *Journal of Educational Psychology, 34*(2), 103–109.

Super, D. E., Sverko, B., & Super, C. M. (1995). *Life roles, values, and careers: International findings of the Work Importance Study.* San Francisco: Jossey-Bass.

Sussman, N. (2006). In session with Judith S. Beck, Ph.D.: Cognitive-behavioral therapy. *Primary Psychiatry, 13*(4), 31–34.

Suter, W. N. (2006). *Introduction to educational research: A critical thinking approach.* Thousand Oaks, CA: Sage.

Swanson, J. W. (2008). *What is the cause of demyelinating disease?* Rochester, MN: Mayo Foundation for Medical Education and Research. Retrieved June 22, 2009, from www.mayoclinic.com/health/demyelinating-disease/AN00564

Sweet, L. (2010, July 15). New consumer benefits in Obama health law available in September. *Chicago Sun-Times.* Retrieved September 8, 2010, from http://blogs.suntimes.com/sweet/2010/07/new_consumer_benefits_in_obama.html

Swisher, R. R. (2003, August 16). *Neighborhood poverty, exposure to violence, and adolescent survival expectations.* Paper presented at the annual meeting of the American Sociological Association, Atlanta, GA. Retrieved October 26, 2009, from www.allacademic.com/meta/p_mla_apa_research_citation/1/0/6/5/3/p106531_index.html

Symons, J. (Producer & Director). (2002). *Daddy & Papa*. Motion picture. U.S. distributor: ITVS, New Day Films.

Syvertsen, A. K., Flanagan, C. A., & Stout, M. D. (2009). Code of silence: Student's perceptions of school climate and willingness to intervene in a peer's dangerous plan. *Journal of Educational Psychology, 101*(1), 219–232.

Tafoya-Barraza, H. (2008). *Postmodern approaches: Solution-focused and narrative therapies.* Unpublished paper. University of New Mexico. Retrieved May 19, 2010, from www.unm.edu/~htafoya/class10.doc

Tang, M., & Erford, B. T. (2004). The history of school counseling. In B. T. Erford (Ed.), *Professional school counseling: A handbook of theories, programs, and practices* (pp. 11–21). Austin, TX: CAPS Press, an imprint of PRO-ED.

Tarshis, T. (2007). Psychometric properties of the peer interactions in primary school (PIPS) questionnaire. *Journal of Developmental & Behavioral Pediatrics, 28*(2), 125–132.

Taylor, J., & Olsen, R. K. (2010). Teacher quality moderates the genetic effects on early reading. *Science, 328*(5977), 512–514.

Teen pregnancy rates go back up. (2009, February 26). British Broadcasting Corporation (BBC). News report. Retrieved January 19, 2010, from http://news.bbc.co.uk/2/hi/health/7911684.stm

Terman, L. M. (1921). *The intelligence of school children*. London, UK: George G. Harrap.

Terman, L. M. (1947). *The measurement of intelligence*. New York: Houghton Mifflin.

Thayer, W. R., Castle, W. R., De Howe, M. A., Pier, A. S., De Voto, B. A., & Morrison, T. (1912). B. R. to play the game. Winter notes. *Harvard Graduate's Magazine, 20,* 472–475.

Thomas, J. (2009, December 9). When parent is deployed, kids struggle. Child and Adolescent Development Overview. *Health Day News*. Retrieved January 18, 2010, from www.mentalhelp .net/poc/view_doc.php?type=news&id=124214&cn=28

Thomas, S. G. (2009, May 6). *Today's tykes: Secure kids or rudest in history?* MSNBC.com. Retrieved November 17, 2009, from www.msnbc.msn.com/id/30585984/print/1/display mode/1098/

Thomas-Lester, A. (2009, July 4). Number of Black male teachers belies their influence. *Washington Post*. Retrieved July 7, 2009, from www.washingtonpost.com/wp-dyn/content/article/ 2009/07/03/AR2009070302498.html

Thompson, C. L., & Cunningham, E. K. (2000). *Retention and social promotion: Research and implications for policy.* ERIC Clearinghouse on Urban Education (ERIC Digest No. 161). Retrieved November 4, 2009, from http://ericdigenst.org/2001–3policy.htm

Thompson, C. L., & Henderson, D. A. (2007). *Counseling children* (7th ed.). Belmont, CA: Thomson.

Thompson, D. (1995a). Review of the Chronicle Career Quest®. In J. C. Conoley & J. C. Impara (Eds.), *The 12th mental measurements yearbook* (electronic version). Retrieved December 22, 2009, from www.unl.edu/buros/

Thompson, D. (1995b). Review of the Kuder General Interest Survey. In J. C. Conoley & J. C. Impara (Eds.), *The 12th mental measurements yearbook* (pp. 545–546). Lincoln, NE: Buros Institute of Mental Measurements.

Thompson, L. (2008, January 17). Recess: Time well spent or time for restructure? *Seattle Times*. Retrieved June 17, 2009, from http://seattletimes.nwsource.com/html/snohomishcountynews/ 2004126864_recess16n.html

Thompson, M. (1997, Summer). Parent support groups. *See/Hear*. Retrieved May 26, 2009, from www.tsbvi.edu/Outreach/seehear/summer97/parent.html

Thompson, W. E., & Hickey, J. V. (2008). *Society in focus* (6th ed.). Upper Saddle River, NJ: Allyn & Bacon, Pearson.

Thornberry, T. P., Huizinga, D., & Loeber, R. (2003). The causes and correlates studies: Findings and policy implications. *Juvenile Justice Journal, 9*(1), 3–19. Retrieved January 25, 2010, from www.ncjrs.gov/html/ojjdp/203555/jj2.html

Thurstone, L. L., & Jenkins, R. L. (1931). *Order of birth, parent-age, and intelligence.* Chicago: University of Chicago Press.

Tishkoff, S. A., Reed, F. A., Friedaender, F. R., Ehret, C., Ranciaro, A., Froment, A., et al. (2009). The genetic structure and history of Africans and African Americans. *Science, 324*(5,930), 1035–1044.

Toppo, G. (2006, October 9). High-tech school security is on the rise. *USA Today.* Retrieved June 9, 2007, from www.usatoday.com/news/education/2006–10–09-school-security_x.htm

Toppo, G. (2010, May 20). To fight "dropout factories," school program starts young. *USA Today.* Retrieved May 28, 2010, from www.usatoday.com/cleanprint/?1275053812703

Townsend, J. (2006). *Boundaries with teens: When to say yes, how to say no.* Grand Rapids, MI: Zondervan.

Trueit, T. S. (2007). *Surviving divorce: Teens talk about what hurts and what helps.* Bel Air, CA: Children's Press.

Tucker, J. (2009, June 9). Pressuring parents helps S. F. slash truancy 23%. *San Francisco Chronicle.* Retrieved June 11, 2009, from www.sfgate.com/cgi-bin/article.cgi?f=/c/a/2009/06/09/MN911832BT.DTL

Tugend, A. (2010, June 19). Peeking at the negative side of high school popularity. *New York Times,* p. B6.

Tyack, D. B. (1974). *The one best system: A history of American urban education.* Cambridge, MA: Harvard University Press.

Tyrrell, M. (2005). School phobia. *Journal of School Nursing, 21*(1), 147–151.

Ungar, M. (2006). *Strength-based counseling with at-risk youth.* Thousand Oaks, CA: Corwin.

Ungar, M., Lee, A. W., Callaghan, T., & Boothroyd, R. (2005). An international collaboration to study resilience in adolescents across cultures. *Journal of Social Work Research and Evaluation, 6*(1), 5–24.

University of British Columbia. (2010, January 17). Disadvantaged neighborhoods and children's reading skills on negative course. *Science Daily.* Retrieved January 29, 2010, from www .sciencedaily.com/releases/2010/01/100114143330.htm

Urban-Lurain, M. (2000, April 24–28). *Attendance and outcomes in a large collaborative learning, performance assessment course.* Paper presented at the annual meeting of the American Educational Research Association, New Orleans, LA.

Uribe, V., & Harbeck, K. M. (1992). Addressing the needs of lesbian, gay, and bisexual youth: The origins of Project 10 and school based intervention. In K. M. Harbeck (Ed.), *Coming out of the classroom closet: Gay and lesbian students, teachers, and curricula* (pp. 9–29). New York: Routledge.

U.S. Bureau of Labor Statistics. (2009). *How many jobs held in a lifetime?* Washington, DC: U.S. Department of Labor. Retrieved December 21, 2009, from www.bls.gov/NLS/nlsfaqs.htm

U.S. Bureau of Labor Statistics. (2010). *Standard Occupational Classification.* Washington, DC: U.S. Department of Labor. Retrieved April 28, 2010, from www.bls.gov/soc/home.htm

U.S. Census Bureau, Department of Commerce. (2007a, August 28). Household income rises, poverty rate declines, number of uninsured up. *U.S. Census Bureau News.* Washington, DC: U.S. Department of Commerce. Retrieved December 11, 2007, from www.census.gov/Press-Release/www/releases/archives/income_wealth/010583.html

U.S. Census Bureau, Department of Commerce. (2007b). *Custodial mothers and fathers and their child support: 2005.* Retrieved July 3, 2009, from www.census.gov/prod/2007pubs/p60–234.pdf

U.S. Census Bureau, Department of Commerce. (2009a). *Current population survey (CPS).* Retrieved October 19, 2009, from www.census.gov/hhes/www/poverty/detailedpovtabs.html

U.S. Census Bureau, Department of Commerce. (2009b). *School enrollment.* Retrieved October 21, 2009, from www.census.gov/population/www/socdemo/school.html

U.S. Department of Agriculture. (2009, March 27). Income eligibility guidelines. Authority, U. S. C. 1758(b)(1). *Congressional Record,* 13412.

U.S. Department of Defense, Military Entrance Processing Command. (2009). *Military career opportunities.* Retrieved December 21, 2009, from www.todaysmilitary.com/careers/career-fields/all

U.S. Department of Education. (2005). *Digest of education statistics, 2004.* NCES 2006–05. Washington, DC. Retrieved May 10, 2008, from http://nces.ed.gov/fastfacts/display.asp?id=64

U.S. Department of Education, Office of Elementary and Secondary Education (2006). Teacher incentive fund. *Federal Register, 71*(83), pp. 25580–25581.

U.S. Department of Education, Office of Elementary and Secondary Education. (2010, June 17). *Race to the Top Assessment program.* Retrieved September 4, 2010, from www2.ed.gov/programs/racetothetop-assessment/index.html

U.S. Department of Health and Human Services. (2005). *Child maltreatment, 2005.* Retrieved June 19, 2009, from www.acf.hhs.gov/programs/cb/stats_research/index.htm#can

U.S. Department of Health and Human Services. (2009a). *Child health USA 2008–2009.* Retrieved December 4, 2009, from http://mchb.hrsa.gov/chusa08/popchar/pages/103cp.html

U.S. Department of Health and Human Services. (2009b). *Head Start funding increase.* ACF-PI-HS-09–06. Retrieved May 19, 2009, from http://eclkc.ohs.acf.hhs.gov/hslc/Program%20Design%20and%20Management/Head%20Start%20Requirements/PIs/2009/resour_pri_006_040209.html

U.S. Department of Labor/Employment and Training Administration. (2010). *About the O*NET.* Retrieved April 28, 2010, from www.onetcenter.org/overview.html

U.S. Department of Labor and Department of Education. (2009). *Career one stop: Pathways to career success.* Retrieved December 29, 2009, from www.careerinfonet.org/videos/COS_videos_by_cluster.asp?id=,27&nodeid=28

U.S. divorce statistics. (2009). *Divorce.* Retrieved July 2, 2009, from www.divorcemag.com/statistics/statsUS.shtml

U.S. Employment Service. (1966). *General aptitude test battery.* Washington, DC: U.S. Department of Labor.

U.S. Federal Interagency Forum on Child and Family Statistics. (2008). *America's Children in Brief: Key National Indicators of Well-Being.* Washington, DC: U.S. Government Printing Office. Retrieved March 28, 2009, from www.childstats.gov

U.S. Food and Drug Administration. (2009). *Inter-agency advisory regarding claims that smoked marijuana is a medicine.* Press release 2006, updated 2009. Retrieved September 26, 2009, from www.fda.gov/NewsEvents/Newsroom/PressAnnouncements/2006/ucm108643.htm

U.S. National Center for Education Statistics (beginning in 1986, Digest of Education Statistics, National Center for Education Statistics). (2003). *1900–1985, 120 years of education, a statistical portrait: High school graduates, and college enrollment and degrees, 1900–2001.* Washington, DC: U.S. Census Bureau, Department of Commerce. Retrieved January 6, 2010, from www.census.gov/statab/hist/HS-21.pdf

U.S. Secret Service and U.S. Department of Education. (2002). *The final report and findings of the safe school initiative: Implications for the prevention of school attacks in the United States.* Retrieved May 28, 2009, from www.ed.gov/admins/lead/safety/preventingattacksreport.pdf

Vaughn, P. A. (2003). *Case studies of homeschool cooperatives in Southern New Jersey.* Unpublished dissertation, Widener University. (ProQuest No. AAT 3103755).

Vaughn, P. A., & Wright, R. J. (February, 2004). *A school for home-schoolers: A study in educational cooperatives.* Paper presented at the annual meeting of the Eastern Educational Research Association, Clearwater, FL.

Veltri, C. (2009, November 11). N.C. middle school wrongfully accepts money for grades. *Carolinian Online.* Retrieved December 4, 2009, from www.carolinianonline.com/media/storage/paper301/news/2009/11/17/Opinions/N.c-Middle.School.Wrongfully.Accepts.Money.For.Grades-3833763.shtml

Ventura, S. J., Abma, J. C., Mosher, W. D., & Henshaw, S. K. (2006). *Recent trends in teenage pregnancy in the United States, 1990–2002.* Retrieved September 17, 2010, from www.csctulsa.org/images/Teen%20Pregnancy%20Trends%201990-2002.pdf

Verdick, E., & Heinlen, M. (2003). *Teeth are not for biting.* Minneapolis: Free Spirit Publishing.

Viadero, D. (2005, February 9). Florida study shows achievement lags for racially isolated schools in the state. *Education Week, 24*(22), 9.

Viadero, D. (2006, January 11). New approach to graduation data finds falling rates in most states. *Education Week, 25*(18), 8.

Viadero, D. (2007, January 24). "What works" reviewers find no learning edge for leading math texts. *Education Week, 28*(20), 1, 21.

Viadero, D. (2008, June 11). Majority of youths found to lack a direction in life. *Education Week, 28*(41), 1, 12.

Viadero, D. (2009a, April 8). Columbine 10 years later. *Education Week, 28*(28), 1, 12, 13.

Viadero, D. (2009b, November 18). Researchers explore teens, parents, schools. *Education Week, 29*(12), 1, 14.

Walker, D. (2009, September 15). Bullying laws give scant protection. *Naples Daily News.* Retrieved September 29, 2010, from www.usatoday.com/news/education/2009-09-14-bullying-laws_N.htm

Wallace, B. D. (2009). Do economic rewards work? The jury is still out. *District Administration, 45*(3), 24–27.

Wallace, G. (1963). *Gubernatorial inauguration for the State of Alabama, January 14, 1963.* Alabama Department of Archives and History. Retrieved October 28, 2009, from www.archives.state.al.us/govs_list/inauguralspeech.html

Walsh, D., & Bennett, N. (2005). *Why do they act that way: A survival guide to the adolescent brain for you and your teen.* New York: Simon & Schuster.

Wang, L. (1993). *The Differential Aptitude Test: A review and critique.* Education Resources Information Center. (ERIC Document No. ED356257).

Warner, J. (2009, April 16). Dude you've got problems. *New York Times.* Retrieved May 28, 2009, from warner.blogs.nytimes.com/2009/04/16/who-are-you-calling-gay/

Wasley, P. (2007, February 23). College Board reports more takers, and higher scores, for advanced placement tests. *Chronicle of Higher Education, 54*(25), p. 18.

Watson, T. S., Butler, T. S., Weaver, A. D., & Foster, N. (2004). Direct behavioral consultation: An effective method for promoting school collaboration. In B. T. Erford (Ed.), *Professional school counseling: A handbook of theories, programs, and practices* (pp. 341–348). Austin, TX: CAPS Press, an imprint of PRO-ED.

Way, J. (2009, May 27). *Recession uprooting families at kid's expense.* Associated Press. Retrieved May 30, 2009, from www.msnbc.msn.com/id/30965965/

Webb, N. B. (1999). *Play therapy with children in crisis* (2nd ed.). New York: Guilford.

Webb, N. B. (2002). *Helping bereaved children: A handbook for practitioners* (2nd ed.). New York: Guilford.

Weill, S. (2005). *The real truth about teens and sex.* New York: Berkley Publishing Group.

Weisberg, J. (2010). What caused the great recession? *Newsweek, 153*(3), p. 19.

Weitzman, R. A. (1985). Review of the Armed Services Vocational Aptitude Battery (Forms 8 to 11). In R. A. Spies & B. S. Plake (Eds.), *The 16th mental measurements yearbook* (Electronic version). Retrieved December 21, 2009, from www.unl.edu/buros/

Weller, E. B., & Weller, R. A. (1991). Mood disorders. In M. Lewis (Ed.), *Child and adolescent psychiatry: A comprehensive textbook* (pp. 646–664). Baltimore: Williams & Wilkins.

West, J. D., & Dann, L. K. (1997). Children's stories for psychological self-understanding. In J. Carlson & K. S. Slavik (Eds.), *Techniques in Adlerian psychology* (pp. 312–322). London: Taylor & Francis Group.

West, J., Meek, A., & Hurst, D. (2000). *Children who enter kindergarten late or repeat kindergarten: Their characteristics and later school performance.* (Report no. 2000–039). Washington, DC: National Center for Education Statistics.

Whiston, S. C. (2002). Response to the past, present, and future of school counseling: Raising some new issues. *Professional School Counseling, 5*(3), 148–157.

White, E. (2003). *Fast girls: Teenage tribes and the myth of the slut.* New York: Berkley Books/Penguin.

White, J., & Mullis, F. (1998). A systems approach to school counselor consultation. *Education, 119*(2), 242–252.

White, J., Mullis, F., Earley, B., & Brigman, G. (1995). *Consultation in schools: The counselor's role.* Portland, ME: J. Weston Walch.

Whitfield, E. A., Feller, R. W., & Wood, C. (2009). *A counselor's guide to career assessment instruments* (5th ed.). Broken Arrow, OK: National Career Development Association.

Whiting, G. W., & Ford, D. Y. (2009). Multicultural issues: Black students and advanced placement classes: Summary, concerns, and recommendations. *Gifted Child Today, 32*(1), 23–26.

Whitlock, J., Eckenrode, J., & Silverman, D. (2006). Self-injurious behaviors in a college population. *Pediatrics, 117*(6), 1939–1948.

Whitmire, R. (2009, April 3). No jobs without college as employers treat degree as a minimum. *U.S. News & World Report.* Retrieved April 3, 2009, from www.usnews.com/articles/opinion/2009/03/27/no-jobs-without-college-as-employers-treat-degree-as-a-minimum.html

Wilcoxon, S. A., & Magnuson, S. (1999). Considerations for school counselors serving noncustodial parents: Premises and suggestions. *Professional School Counseling, 2*(4), 275–280.

Wilczynski, S. M., Mandal, R. L., & Fusilier, L. (2000). Bridges and barriers in behavioral consultation. *Psychology in the Schools, 37*(6), 495–504.

Wilens, T. E., Faraone, S. V., Biederman, J., & Gunawardene, S. (2003). Does stimulant therapy of attention-deficit/hyperactivity disorder beget later substance abuse? A meta-analytic review of the literature. *Pediatrics, 111,* 179–185.

Williams, C. H. (1998). Introduction: Respecting the citizens: Reflections on language policy in Canada and the United States. In T. Ricento & B. Burnaby (Eds.), *Language and politics in the U.S. and Canada: Myths and realities* (pp. 1–32). Mahwah, NJ: Lawrence Erlbaum.

Willing, R. (2006, February 1). DNA rewrites history for African-Americans. *USA Today.* Retrieved October 19, 2009, from www.usatoday.com/tech/science/genetics/2006–02–01-dna-african-americans_x.htm

Wilson, S. (2009, April 19). Race a dominant theme at summit. *Washington Post.* Retrieved October 19, 2009, from www.washingtonpost.com/wp-dyn/content/article/2009/04/18/AR200904180 1826.html

Wilson, W. J. (1991). Studying inner-city social dislocations: The challenge of public agenda research. *American Sociological Review, 56*(1), 1–14.

Witziers, B., Bosker, R. J., & Kruger, M. L. (2003). Educational leadership and student achievement: The elusive search for an association. *Educational Administration Quarterly, 39*(3): 398–425.

Wolak, J., Finkelhor, D., Mitchell, K. J., & Ybarra, M. L. (2008). Online "predators" and their victims: Myths, realities, and implications for prevention and treatment. *American Psychologist, 63*(2), 111–128.

Wolf, R. M. (1990). *Evaluation in education. Foundations of competency assessment and program review* (3rd ed.). New York: Praeger.

Wong, D. L., Hockenberry-Eaton, M., Wilson, D., Winkelstein, M. L., & Schwartz, P. (2001). *Wong's essentials of pediatric nursing* (6th ed.). St. Louis, MO: Mosby.

Woods, M. (2007, March 4). Hey kids, let's make an FCAT deal. *Florida Times-Union.* Retrieved March 21, 2007, from http://cgi.jacksonville.com/ [archive]

World commemorates end of slavery. (2004, August 23). *One Minute World News From the BBC.* British Broadcasting Corporation (BBC). Retrieved October 19, 2009, from news.bbc.co.uk/2/hi/africa/3589646.stm

Wrenn, R. L. (1985). The evolution of Anne Roe. Life Lines. *Journal of Counseling and Development, 63*(5), 267–275.

Wright, P.W.D., & Wright, P. D. (2007). *Wrightslaw: Special education law* (2nd ed.). Hartfield, VA: Harbor House Law Press.

Wright, R. J. (2008). *Educational assessment: Tests and measurement in the age of accountability.* Thousand Oaks, CA: Sage.

Wright, R. J. (2009). Methods for improving test scores: The good, the bad, and the ugly. *Kappa Delta Pi Record, 45*(3), 116–121.

Wright, R. J. (2010). *Multifaceted assessment for early childhood education.* Thousand Oaks, CA: Sage.

Wright, R. J. (2011). Gaposis: The use and misuse of tests. In F. W. English (Ed.), *Handbook on educational leadership* (2nd ed.). Thousand Oaks, CA: Sage.

Wright, R. J., & Lesisko, L. (2011, February 16–19). *Administrative preferences in hiring school counselors.* Paper presented during the annual meeting of the Eastern Educational Research Association Meeting, Sarasota, FL.

Yarnall, A. (2007, January 15). Test gives direction to SDSU students uncertain about career interests. *San Diego Business Journal.* Retrieved December 28, 2009, from https://www.cpp.com/Pdfs/SD_Business_Journal_Strong.pdf

Yeh, C. J. (2004). Multicultural and contextual research and practice in school counseling. *Counseling Psychologist, 32*(2), 278–285.

Yen, H. (2009, September 29). *U.S. income gap widens as poor take hit in recession.* Associated Press. Retrieved October 19, 2009, from http://finance.yahoo.com/news/US-income-gap-widens-as-poor-apf-388403228.html?x=0

Yorke, C. (1996). Anna Freud's contributions to our knowledge of child development. *Psychoanalytic Study of the Child, 51*(7), 18–24.

Young, R. A., & Valach, L. (2004). The construction of career through goal directed action. *Journal of Vocational Behavior, 64*(3), 499–514.

Zackon, J. F. (1999). *A study of the Pennsylvania System of School Assessment: The predictive value of selected characteristics of Pennsylvania school districts for student performance on the PSSA.* Unpublished doctoral dissertation, Widener University.

Zajonic, R. B. (1976, April). Family configuration and intelligence. *Science, 192*(4236), 227–236.

Zanderberg, I., Lewis, L., & Greene, B. (2008, June). *Technology-based distance education courses for public elementary and secondary school students: 2002–03 and 2004–05: Statistical analysis report.* NCES 2008–008. Washington, DC: Institute for Education Sciences, National Center for Education Statistics.

Zedeck, S. (1998). Review of the Career Interest Inventory®. In J. C. Impara & B. S. Plake (Eds.), *The 13th mental measurements yearbook* (pp. 193–197). Lincoln, NE: Buros Institute of Mental Measurements.

Zehr, M. A. (2008, May 14). NAEP scores in states that cut bilingual ed. fuel concern on ELL. *Education Week, 27*(37), 10.

Zehr, M. A. (2010, February 10). Study finds abstinence program effective. *Education Week, 29*(21), 9.

Zigler, E., & Muenchow, S. (1992). *Head Start: The inside story of America's most successful educational experiment.* New York: Basic Books.

Zill, N., & Sorongon, A. (2004, June 28–30). *Children's cognitive gains during Head Start and kindergarten.* Paper presented at the National Head Start Research Conference, Washington, DC.

Zolten, K., & Long, N. (1997). *Dealing with peer pressure and bad companions.* Little Rock: University of Arkansas for Medical Sciences, Department of Pediatrics, Center for Effective Parenting. Retrieved September 26, 2009, from www.parenting-ed.org/handout3/Specific%20Concerns%20and%20Problems/peer%20pressure.htm

Zuckerman, D., (2001). When little girls become women: Early onset of puberty in girls. *Ribbon, 6*(1), 6–8.

Zytowski, D. G. (2004). *Super's Work Values Inventory-Revised, technical manual.* Version 1.1. Adel, IA: Kuder. Retrieved December 29, 2009, from www.kuder.com/downloads/SWV-Tech-Manual.pdf

Zytowski, D. G. (2009). *Kuder® Career Search with Person Match, technical manual.* Version 1.3. Adel, IA: Kuder. Retrieved December 30, 2009, from www.kuder.com/downloads/kcs-tech-manual.pdf

Zytowski, D. G., D'Achiardi, C., & Rottinghaus, P. J. (2009). *Kuder Skills Assessment®, technical manual.* Version 2.1. Adel, IA: Kuder. Retrieved December 29, 2009, from www.kuder.com/downloads/SWV-Tech-Manual.pdf

Index

About the Author

Professor **Robert Wright** earned a bachelor's degree in chemistry and secondary education in 1966 and began teaching high school science. A few years later, in 1969, he earned a master's degree in school counseling from West Chester University and began working as a school counselor, first with high school students and later with middle school students. He completed a doctorate in educational psychology with specializations in child development and educational measurement from Temple University. As part of that degree he completed a clinical fellowship in rehabilitation counseling at Moss Hospital, part of the Albert Einstein Medical Center (Philadelphia). Following graduation he completed advanced studies in school psychology at Lehigh University.

Professor Wright has taught counseling and supervised counseling interns and has also taught educational measurement and educational statistics for graduate students in counseling. During his career as a member of a university's faculty he chaired 115 completed doctoral dissertations and assisted on many others. He is a member of the American Counseling Association, the Association for Counselor Education and Supervision, the American School Counselor Association, the American Psychological Association Division 17 (society of counseling psychologists), and the American Educational Research Association.

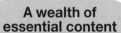

C.2. Sharing Information with Other Professionals

Professional school counselors:

a. Promote awareness and adherence to appropriate guidelines regarding confidentiality, the distinction between public and private information and staff consultation.

b. Provide professional personnel with accurate, objective, concise and meaningful data necessary to adequately evaluate, counsel and assist the student.

c. Secure parental consent and develop clear agreements with other mental health professionals when a student is receiving services from another counselor or other mental health professional in order to avoid confusion and conflict for the student and parents/guardians.

d. Understand about the "release of information" process and parental rights in sharing information and attempt to establish a cooperative and collaborative relationship with other professionals to benefit students.

e. Recognize the powerful role of ally that faculty and administration who function high in personal/social development skills can play in supporting students in stress, and carefully filter confidential information to give these allies what they "need to know" in order to advantage the student. Consultation with other members of the school counseling profession is helpful in determining need-to-know information. The primary focus and obligation is always on the student when it comes to sharing confidential information.

f. Keep appropriate records regarding individual students, and develop a plan for transferring those records to another professional school counselor should the need occur. This documentation transfer will protect the confidentiality and benefit the needs of the student for whom the records are written.

C.3. Collaborating and Educating
Around the Role of the School Counselor

The school counselor, school counseling program supervisor/director and school counselor educator:

a. Share the role of the school counseling program in ensuring datadriven academic, career/college and personal/social success competencies for every student, resulting in specific outcomes/indicators with all stakeholders.

b. Broker services internal and external to the schools to help ensure every student receives the benefits of a school counseling program and specific academic, career/college and personal/social competencies.

D. RESPONSIBILITIES TO SCHOOL, COMMUNITIES AND FAMILIES

D.1. Responsibilities to the School

Professional school counselors:

a. Support and protect students' best interest against any infringement of their educational program.

b. Inform appropriate officials, in accordance with school policy, of conditions that may be potentially disruptive or damaging to the school's mission, personnel and property while honoring the confidentiality between the student and the school counselor.

c. Are knowledgeable and supportive of their school's mission, and connect their program to the school's mission.

d. Delineate and promote the school counselor's role, and function as a student advocate in meeting the needs of those served. School counselors will notify appropriate officials of systemic conditions that may limit or curtail their effectiveness in providing programs and services.

e. Accept employment only for positions for which they are qualified by education, training, supervised experience, state and national professional credentials and appropriate professional experience.

f. Advocate that administrators hire only qualified, appropriately trained and competent individuals for professional school counseling positions.

g. Assist in developing: (1) curricular and environmental conditions appropriate for the school and community; (2) educational procedures and programs to meet students' developmental needs; (3) a systematic evaluation process for comprehensive, developmental, standards-based school counseling programs, services and personnel; and (4) a data-driven evaluation process guiding the comprehensive, developmental school counseling program and service delivery.

D.2. Responsibility to the Community

Professional school counselors:

a. Collaborate with community agencies, organizations and individuals in students' best interest and without regard to personal reward or remuneration.

b. Extend their influence and opportunity to deliver a comprehensive school counseling program to all students by collaborating with community resources for student success.

c. Promote equity for all students through community resources.

d. Are careful not to use their professional role as a school counselor to benefit any type of private therapeutic or consultative practice in which they might be involved outside of the school setting.

E. RESPONSIBILITIES TO SELF

E.1. Professional Competence

Professional school counselors:

a. Function within the boundaries of individual professional competence and accept responsibility for the consequences of their actions.

b. Monitor emotional and physical health and practice wellness to ensure optimal effectiveness. Seek physical or mental health referrals when needed to ensure competence at all times

c. Monitor personal responsibility and recognize the high standard of care a professional in this critical position of trust must maintain on and off the job and are cognizant of and refrain from activity that may lead to inadequate professional services or diminish their effectiveness with school community members Professional and personal growth are ongoing throughout the counselor's career.

d. Strive through personal initiative to stay abreast of current research and to maintain professional competence in advocacy, teaming and collaboration, culturally competent counseling and school counseling program coordination, knowledge and use of technology, leadership, and equity assessment using data.

e. Ensure a variety of regular opportunities for participating in and facilitating professional development for self and other educators and school counselors through continuing education opportunities annually including: attendance at professional school counseling conferences; reading *Professional School Counseling* journal articles; facilitating workshops for education staff on issues school counselors are uniquely positioned to provide.

f. Enhance personal self awareness, professional effectiveness and ethical practice by regularly attending presentations on ethical decision-making. Effective school counselors will seek supervision when ethical or professional questions arise in their practice.

g. Maintain current membership in professional associations to ensure ethical and best practices.

E.2. Multicultural and Social Justice Advocacy and Leadership

Professional school counselors:

a. Monitor and expand personal multicultural and social justice advocacy awareness, knowledge and skills. School counselors strive for exemplary cultural competence by ensuring personal beliefs or values are not imposed on students or other stakeholders.

b. Develop competencies in how prejudice, power and various forms of oppression, such as ableism, ageism, classism, familyism, genderism, heterosexism, immigrationism, linguicism, racism, religionism and sexism, affect self, students and all stakeholders.

c. Acquire educational, consultation and training experiences to improve awareness, knowledge, skills and effectiveness in working with diverse populations: ethnic/racial status, age, economic status, special needs, ESL or ELL, immigration status, sexual orientation, gender, gender identity/expression, family type, religious/spiritual identity and appearance.

d. Affirm the multiple cultural and linguistic identities of every student and all stakeholders. Advocate for equitable school and school counseling program policies and practices for every student and all stakeholders including use of translators and bilingual/multilingual school counseling program materials that represent all languages used by families in the school community, and advocate for appropriate accommodations and accessibility for students with disabilities.

e. Use inclusive and culturally responsible language in all forms of communication.

f. Provide regular workshops and written/digital information to families to increase understanding, collaborative two-way communication and a welcoming school climate between families and the school to promote increased student achievement.

g. Work as advocates and leaders in the school to create equity-based school counseling programs that help close any achievement, opportunity and attainment gaps that deny all students the chance to pursue their educational goals.

F. RESPONSIBILITIES TO THE PROFESSION

F.1. Professionalism

Professional school counselors:

a. Accept the policies and procedures for handling ethical violations as a result of maintaining membership in the American School Counselor Association.

b. Conduct themselves in such a manner as to advance individual ethical practice and the profession.

c. Conduct appropriate research, and report findings in a manner consistent with acceptable educational and psychological research practices. School counselors advocate for the protection of individual students' identities when using data for research or program planning.

d. Seek institutional and parent/guardian consent before administering any research, and maintain security of research records.

e. Adhere to ethical standards of the profession, other official policy statements, such as ASCA's position statements, role statement and the ASCA National Model and relevant statutes established by federal, state and local governments, and when these are in conflict work responsibly for change.

f. Clearly distinguish between statements and actions made as a private individual and those made as a representative of the school counseling profession.

g. Do not use their professional position to recruit or gain clients, consultees for their private practice or to seek and receive unjustified personal gains, unfair advantage, inappropriate relationships or unearned goods or services.

F.2. Contribution to the Profession

Professional school counselors:

a. Actively participate in professional associations and share results and best practices in assessing, implementing and annually evaluating the outcomes of data-driven school counseling programs with measurable academic, career/college and personal/social competencies for every student.

b. Provide support, consultation and mentoring to novice professionals.

c. Have a responsibility to read and abide by the ASCA Ethical Standards and adhere to the applicable laws and regulations.

F.3 Supervision of School Counselor Candidates Pursuing Practicum and Internship Experiences:

Professional school counselors:

a. Provide support for appropriate experiences in academic, career, college access and personal/social counseling for school counseling interns.

b. Ensure school counselor candidates have experience in developing, implementing and evaluating a data-driven school counseling program model, such as the ASCA National Model.

c. Ensure the school counseling practicum and internship have specific, measurable service delivery, foundation, management and accountability systems.

d. Ensure school counselor candidates maintain appropriate liability insurance for the duration of the school counseling practicum and internship experiences.

e. Ensure a site visit is completed by a school counselor education faculty member for each practicum or internship student, preferably when both the school counselor trainee and site supervisor are present.

F.4 Collaboration and Education about School Counselors and School Counseling

Programs with other Professionals

School counselors and school counseling program directors/supervisors collaborate with special educators, school nurses, school social workers, school psychologists, college counselors/admissions officers, physical therapists, occupational therapists and speech pathologists to advocate for optimal services for students and all other stakeholders.

G. MAINTENANCE OF STANDARDS

Professional school counselors are expected to maintain ethical behavior at all times.

G.1. When there exists serious doubt as to the ethical behavior of a colleague(s) the following procedure may serve as a guide:

1. The school counselor should consult confidentially with a professional colleague to discuss the nature of a complaint to see if the professional colleague views the situation as an ethical violation.

2. When feasible, the school counselor should directly approach the colleague whose behavior is in question to discuss the complaint and seek resolution.

3. The school counselor should keep documentation of all the steps taken.

4. If resolution is not forthcoming at the personal level, the school counselor shall utilize the channels established within the school, school district, the state school counseling association and ASCA's Ethics Committee.

5. If the matter still remains unresolved, referral for review and appropriate action should be made to the Ethics Committees in the following sequence:
   - State school counselor association
   - American School Counselor Association

6. The ASCA Ethics Committee is responsible for:
   - Educating and consulting with the membership regarding ethical standards
   - Periodically reviewing and recommending changes in code
   - Receiving and processing questions to clarify the application of such standards. Questions must be submitted in writing to the ASCA Ethics Committee chair.
   - Handling complaints of alleged violations of the ASCA Ethical Standards for School Counselors. At the national level, complaints should be submitted in writing to the ASCA Ethics Committee, c/o the Executive Director, American School Counselor Association, 1101 King St., Suite 625, Alexandria, VA 22314.

G.2. When school counselors are forced to work in situations or abide by policies that do not reflect the ethics of the profession, the school counselor works responsibly through the correct channels to try and remedy the condition.

G.3. When faced with any ethical dilemma school counselors, school counseling program directors/supervisors and school counselor educators use an ethical decision-making model such as Solutions to Ethical Problems in Schools (STEPS) (Stone, 2001):

1. *Define the problem emotionally and intellectually*
2. *Apply the ASCA Ethical Standards and the law*
3. *Consider the students' chronological and developmental levels*
4. *Consider the setting, parental rights and minors' rights*
5. *Apply the moral principles*
6. *Determine Your potential courses of action and their consequences*
7. *Evaluate the selected action*
8. *Consult*
9. *Implement the course of action*